Positive Psychology

Fifth Edition

For my children, who are full of strength, and who bring out strengths in those around them. And for Brian, who brings out strengths in me.

JTP

For my partner and my son, who are my world. And for my mother, Diane McDermott, who raised me to see the positive in psychology and who I miss dearly.

RCM

And as always, for those we've lost:
Shane J. Lopez

(April 4, 1970–July 23, 2016)
C. R. "Rick" Snyder

(December 26, 1944–January 17, 2006)

As a global academic publisher, Sage is driven by the belief that research and education are critical in shaping society. Our mission is building bridges to knowledge—supporting the development of ideas into scholarship that is certified, taught, and applied in the real world.

Sage's founder, Sara Miller McCune, transferred control of the company to an independent trust, which guarantees our independence indefinitely. This enables us to support an equitable academic future over the long term by building lasting relationships, championing diverse perspectives, and co-creating social and behavioral science resources that transform teaching and learning.

Positive Psychology

The Scientific and Practical Explorations of Human Strengths

Fifth Edition

Jennifer Teramoto Pedrotti

California Polytechnic State University, San Luis Obispo

Shane J. Lopez

Gallup/Clifton Strengths School

Ryon C. McDermott

University of South Alabama

C. R. Snyder

University of Kansas, Lawrence

FOR INFORMATION:

2455 Teller Road
Thousand Oaks, California 91320
E-mail: order@sagepub.com

1 Oliver's Yard
55 City Road
London, EC1Y 1SP
United Kingdom

Unit No 323-333, Third Floor, F-Block
International Trade Tower
Nehru Place New Delhi – 110 019
India

3 Church Street
#10–04 Samsung Hub
Singapore 049483

Printed in the United States of America

Library of Congress Control Number: 2024003335

ISBN: 978-1-0718-1925-8

Acquisitions Editor: Mary Dudley

Product Associate: Latoya Douse

Production Editor: Laura Barrett

Copy Editor: Michelle Ponce

Typesetter: diacriTech

Cover Designer: Candice Harman

Marketing Manager: Victoria Velasquez

This book is printed on acid-free paper.

24 25 26 27 28 10 9 8 7 6 5 4 3 2 1

BRIEF CONTENTS

DETAILED CONTENTS

PREFACE

For many of you, this is your first educational foray into the field of positive psychology. We are privileged to introduce you to this work. If your life is in some small way improved by reading the following pages, it will have made our efforts more than worthwhile.

In these pages, we introduce you to the growing field of positive psychology. We have borrowed from the therapy and research efforts of many outstanding psychologists, and we thank them for their pioneering contributions. So, too, do we thank our clients, our students, and our colleagues (Kaylene Co, Brian Cole, Lisa Edwards, Lindsey Hammond, Zachary Kasow, Molly Lowe, Jeana Magyar, Phil McKnight, Allison Newlee, Ryan Reed, Jennifer Reimer, Melinda Roberts, and Brian Werter) who have assisted in various editions of this textbook. Over the years, they have taught us as much about positive psychology as we have taught them. Much gratitude also goes to those folks who believed that college students needed a real positive psychology textbook. Our marvelous editors, Eve Oettinger, Adeline Grout, and Latoya Douse as well as Lara Parra, Reid Hester and the entire team at Sage; all thought the world would be a better place if students continued to learn about positive psychology.

We have sampled the various areas of positive psychology and have included exercises to help you to experience many of these new concepts. In Part I, titled "Looking at Psychology From a Positive Perspective," we group three chapters together. We begin with Chapter 1 ("Welcome to Positive Psychology") and introduce you to the field. In Chapter 2, we explore the Eastern and Western backgrounds of the field and ideas about blending our ME and WE styles. Next, in Chapter 3 ("Classification and Measurement in Positive Psychology"), we explain the attempts to categorize various topics in the field.

In Part II, titled "Positive Psychology in Context," we discuss the roles of emotions in a positive life. In Chapter 4 ("The Role of Culture in Developing Strengths and Living Well"), we examine the role of cultural factors in determining what is positive. In Chapter 5 ("Living Well at Every Stage of Life"), we trace the development of human strengths.

Part III, "Positive Emotional States and Processes," comprises two chapters. In Chapter 6, "The Principles of Pleasure: Understanding Positive Affect, Positive Emotions, Happiness, and Well-Being," we discuss what has been learned about emotions and happiness. And in Chapter 7, "Making the Most of Emotional Experiences: Emotion-Approach Coping, Emotional Intelligence, Socioemotional Selectivity, and Emotional Storytelling," we reveal recent findings on how emotions can contribute positively to effective coping in life.

Part IV, "Positive Cognitive States and Processes," contains three chapters. Chapter 8 ("Seeing Our Futures Through Self-Efficacy, Optimism, and Hope") covers the most powerful positive cognitive and motivational states. Then, in Chapter 9 ("Wisdom and Courage: Characteristics of the Wise and the Brave"), we introduce findings about people at their best under sometimes difficult circumstances. And in Chapter 10 ("Mindfulness, Flow, and

Spirituality: In Search of Optimal Experiences"), we detail the latest findings on the power of mental processes in relation to self and higher forces.

Part V is titled "Prosocial Behavior." In this portion of the book, we examine interpersonal matters. In Chapter 11 ("Empathy and Egotism: Portals to Altruism and Gratitude") and Chapter 12 ("Attachment, Love, Flourishing Relationships, and Forgiveness"), we show how human ties improve the quality of life.

In Part VI, "Understanding and Changing Human Behavior," we give insights into improving one's life in Chapter 13 ("Preventing the Bad and Promoting the Good").

In Part VII, "Positive Environments," we describe how school and work (Chapter 14, "Positive Schooling and Good Work: The Psychology of Gainful Employment and the Education That Gets Us There") work together to contribute to a more productive, happier life.

Finally, in Part VIII, "Finding Strengths in Others: Embodying Strengths in Everyday Life," we present you with ideas about "The Future of Positive Psychology for the Public Good" in a conversation between the authors (JTP and RMC). Finally, we have retained the stories from friends and researchers in the field of positive psychology who shared their memories of the late, great Shane J. Lopez, a man who embodied so many positive constructs and who shared his strengths and guidance with so many in the field (Appendix: "Remembering Shane: Real Strengths in a Real Person").

WHAT'S NEW IN THIS EDITION

- Addition of Learning Objectives to the beginning of each chapter to guide students throughout the chapter
- New examples and reflections on current events throughout the text make information more relevant to our current times
- Maintaining discussion of seminal research while emphasizing new and emerging areas of scholarship built on these ideas
- Personal Mini-Experiments and Life Enhancement Strategies have been updated to help students from all backgrounds broaden and enhance their inherent and learned strengths
- Streamlined chapters and overall text for a fresh new look and a more concise and linear flow to help both instructors and their students navigate the material
- New organization of some chapters to enhance flow and readability
- New content to specifically focus on neurological and biological bases of positive psychology.
- Chapter 15 has been updated to provide some new ideas about the future of positive psychology and how its tenets and constructs can be applied to problems facing today's world

Additional revisions and updates incorporated throughout the text include the following:

- Broad definition of culture used throughout the text, with increased representation of research investigating facets such as race, ethnicity, sexual orientation, generation, nation of origin, socioeconomic status, and gender, among others
- Addressing issues related to the fact that to be truly viable as a field, positive psychology and its constructs must be accessible to people from different socioeconomic groups and racial and ethnic cultures
- Continued discussion of culture, both between and within different groups, as a contextualizing factor in the manifestation of strengths
- More discussion of practical application for both research and use in everyday life.
- Redesigned complex information into digestible figures and tables to assist in better engagement with the material
- Changes made to reflect current language and terms regarding different identity groups (for example, using Black as opposed to African American in relevant spots to reflect current community preferences)
- Updated articles and references to various sociocultural issues, current political climate, and other current social and technological trends
- New focus on aspects of positive psychology related to the lifespan and resilience

This text includes an array of instructor teaching materials designed to save you time and to help you keep students engaged. To learn more, visit sagepub.com or contact your Sage representative at sagepub.com/findmyrep.

—J. T. P.
San Luis Obispo, California

–R. C. M.
Mobile, Alabama

REMEMBERING SHANE J. LOPEZ

You were the pebble. We are the ripples.

This book is dedicated to the memory of my mentor and friend, Shane J. Lopez, who died on July 23, 2016. I first met Shane at the University of Kansas, in Bailey Hall, my first week as a doctoral student in the counseling psychology program there. I didn't know until a bit later that it was his first week too–though as an assistant professor. Shane had graduated just the year before in 1998 from the same program, and his giftedness and potential had long been recognized by his professors, who readily welcomed him as a colleague. From the first lecture he gave in class, I could tell that he was someone who would teach me a multitude of ideas. I didn't yet know he would mentor me through my graduate school years, through graduation and my own job search for an academic position, through negotiating a job offer, through promotion and tenure, through book contracts, and more. I didn't know how much he would teach me about life, and how to balance many things, but to always make the most time for family.

Shane often talked about people's "signature strengths" and mentioned them to us often. That was one of his signature strengths—building others up, helping them to recognize and to use their abilities in ways they hadn't yet explored, and always encouraging us to be our best selves. When I gave one of the eulogies at his funeral, I shared a memory of him that I will always cherish that occurred the day I received notification of my tenure at Cal Poly State University, San Luis Obispo. When he answered the phone and I said, "Guess what?" he knew what I was going to say and he said, "Wait! Wait! Let me sit down, I want to really listen to this! OK—go! Start from the beginning." I told him that I had gotten my letter and that I had been tenured and he said, "OK, but start from the beginning!" and proceeded to ask me question after question: "Where were you when you knew the letter was waiting for you in your mailbox? What did you think it said? Did you *know?* What was your first thought just after you read it?" And I found myself getting so much more excited about the accomplishment as I told him the answers, building the experience into a story, savoring each moment of the success. At the end, he sighed happily and said, "I'm so proud of you, Jennifer." He was wonderful at taking time to savor the good, and he passed that on as often as he could. He was my favorite person to tell when anything good happened.

But Shane was also really good at helping when things were not so great and when positive psychology seemed far from one's mind. I remember a difficult professional situation at one time in my career, and I called him to ask for advice, hoping he might give me some magical suggestion that would solve the problem for me. He listened to me carefully, he validated my emotion over the situation, and he made it clear he thought I had handled it well up to that point. And then he asked me a question that I have asked myself over and over, in a number of different situations since: *How do you want to feel when you look back on this situation?* That question cleared the way for me, allowed me to see my own solution and to make a plan to move forward that took me in the direction I wanted to go. Shane never magically solved my problems or anyone's, but he was magic in the way he imbued you with the ability to do it yourself. That is the essence of sharing your strengths with others, and he embodied it fully.

When Shane asked me to join this book many years ago, for the second edition, it was because we had just lost C. R. "Rick" Snyder, who died just before the first edition was released. Rick was Shane's mentor and friend, and he was devastated to lose him. In that second edition, he struggled to edit the text, having a hard time being surrounded by Rick's words as he worked on the book. I found myself in the same place with the fourth edition.

Each time I revise this text, however, being surrounded by Shane's words is also a comfort in some way. It is a way to be close to his memory and to spend time thinking about the things he taught me and to reflect on how I might pass them along. The main conclusion I have come to is that though he left this earth much too soon, he leaves us with more than words but also with ideas, thoughts, inspiration, and lessons. Though I miss him daily, I hear him whispering through the pages of this book, continuing to teach anyone who opens the cover. I hope you can hear him, too.

—J. T. P.
San Luis Obispo, California

ACKNOWLEDGMENTS

The authors and Sage gratefully acknowledge the contributions of the following reviewers:

- Ray McKay Hardee, Gardner-Webb University
- John Wade, Emporia State University
- Barbara J. Walker, University of Cincinnati

ABOUT THE AUTHORS

Jennifer Teramoto Pedrotti, PhD, is associate dean for diversity and curriculum in the College of Liberal Arts and professor in the Department of Psychology and Child Development at California Polytechnic State University, San Luis Obispo, where she has been teaching positive psychology with a multicultural focus for over 10 years. She is also serving in an interim role as the associate vice president for Academic Initiatives for the Office of University Diversity and Inclusion, also at Cal Poly. She is the lead editor on a volume entitled *Perspectives on the Intersection of Multiculturalism and Positive Psychology* (with Lisa M. Edwards) and often speaks on the topic of including cultural context in positive psychological discussions, including as a keynote speaker at the Asian Pacific Conference on Applied Positive Psychology in Hong Kong, and in presentations at conferences, including those of the American Psychological Association, and the International Positive Psychology Association. Additionally, Dr. Teramoto Pedrotti is the lead author on a second textbook for undergraduate students, *Multicultural Psychology: Self, Society, and Social Change* (with Denise A. Isom). She has contributed to many different volumes throughout her career such as *The Oxford Handbook of Positive Psychology, Positive Psychological Interventions, Activities for Teaching Positive Psychology*, and the *Handbook of Multicultural Counseling*. In addition, her work has appeared in multiple journals, including the *Journal of Counseling Psychology, Journal of Positive Psychology,* and *Professional Psychology: Research and Practice.* Recently, she was part of the prestigious Emerging Leaders Program 2022 Cohort via the American Association of State Colleges and Universities. In her current role, she encourages students, staff, and faculty daily to use their strengths to make change toward a more equitable and inclusive campus.

Shane J. Lopez, PhD (deceased), was a Gallup Senior Scientist and Research Director of the Clifton Strengths Institute. Dr. Lopez published more than 100 articles and chapters and 10 books in addition to *Positive Psychology: The Scientific and Practical Explorations of Human*

Strengths. These include *Making Hope Happen*, his first trade book; *The Oxford Handbook of Positive Psychology* (with C. R. Snyder); Positive Psychological Assessment: A Handbook of Models and Measures (with C. R. Snyder); *Positive Psychology: Exploring the Best in People; The Encyclopedia of Positive Psychology*; and *The Psychology of Courage: Modern Research on an Ancient Virtue* (with Cynthia Pury). Dr. Lopez was a fellow of the American Psychological Association and of the International Positive Psychology Association. A professor at the University of Kansas in both the Schools of Education and Business for more than a decade, he passed away on July 23, 2016.

Ryon C. McDermott, PhD is a professor of clinical and counseling psychology at the University of South Alabama. He studies the measurement, applications, and intersections of culture and individual differences in emerging adulthood. Dr. McDermott has published more than 90 peer-reviewed studies in academic journals such as the *Journal of Counseling Psychology*, the *Counseling Psychologist, Health Psychology, Body Image, Psychological Assessment, Psychology of Violence, Journal of Affective Disorders, Psychology of Men and Masculinities*, and *Sex Roles*. His research has been funded by the National Science Foundation and the Centers For Disease Control and Prevention. He has been highly active in the American Psychological Association and served as the president of Division 51 (Society for the Psychological Study of Men and Masculinities). Currently, Dr. McDermott maintains an active research program and mentors doctoral students in clinical and counseling psychology research and practice.

C. R. Snyder, PhD (deceased), was the Wright Distinguished Professor of Clinical Psychology at the University of Kansas, Lawrence. Internationally known for his work at the interface of clinical, social, personality, and health psychology, his theories pertained to how people react to personal feedback, the human need for uniqueness, the ubiquitous drive to excuse transgressions, and, most recently, the hope motive. He received 31 research awards and 27 teaching awards at the university, state, and national levels. In 2005, he received an honorary doctorate from Indiana Wesleyan University. Snyder appeared many times on national American television shows, and he was a regular contributor to National Public Radio. His scholarly work on the human need for uniqueness received the rare recognition of being the subject matter of an entire Sunday cartoon sequence by Garry Trudeau. All of these accomplishments were packaged in a graying and self-effacing absent-minded professor who said of himself, "If you don't laugh at yourself, you have missed the biggest joke of all!"

PART I

LOOKING AT PSYCHOLOGY FROM A POSITIVE PERSPECTIVE

1 WELCOME TO POSITIVE PSYCHOLOGY

LEARNING OBJECTIVES

After reading this chapter you will be able to:

1.1 Understand the basic introductory tenets behind the field of positive psychology

1.2 Understand that involving strengths in positive psychology provides a more authentic view of the whole person

1.3 Understand the general organization of this textbook before moving forward

> The gross national product does not allow for the health of our children . . . their education, or the joy of their play. It does not include the beauty of our poetry or the strength of our marriages; the intelligence of our public debate or the integrity of our public officials. It measures neither wit nor courage; neither our wisdom nor our teaching; neither our compassion nor our devotion to our country; it measures everything, in short, except that which makes life worthwhile.
>
> —*Robert F. Kennedy, 1968*

The final lines in this 1968 address delivered by Robert F. Kennedy at the University of Kansas are still relevant today and point to the contents of this book: *the things in life that make it worthwhile*. In this regard, however, imagine that someone offered to help you understand human beings but in doing so would teach you only about their weaknesses and pathologies. As far-fetched as this sounds, a similar "What is wrong with people?" question guided the thinking of most applied psychologists (clinical, counseling, school, etc.) during the past 100 years. Given the many forms of human fallibility, this question produced an avalanche of insights into the human "dark side." Today, even in the face of the trauma the world has been dealing with in the post-pandemic period, another question, "What is right about people?" seems to captivate the masses. This question is at the heart of **positive psychology**, which is the scientific and applied approach to uncovering people's strengths and promoting their positive functioning. (See the seminal article "Building Human Strength," in which positive psychology pioneer Martin Seligman [1998a] gives his views about the need for positive psychology at the beginning of the century.)

Although other subareas of psychology were not focused on human weaknesses, 20th-century applied psychology and psychiatry typically were. For example, consider the statement attributed to Sigmund Freud that the goal of psychology should be "to replace neurotic misery with ordinary unhappiness" (cited in Simonton & Baumeister, 2005, p. 99). Thus, the applied psychology of yesteryear was mostly about **mental illness** and understanding and helping the people who were living such tragedies. Positive psychology, on the other hand, offers a balance to this previous weakness-oriented approach by suggesting that we also must explore people's strengths along with their weaknesses. In advocating this focus on strengths, however, in no way do we mean to lessen the importance and pain associated with human suffering.

Now we are poised to study the whole human picture by exploring psychological assets and deficits within varying cultural contexts. We present this book as a guide for this journey and to welcome those of you who are new to this approach.

In this chapter, we begin by orienting you to the potential benefits of focusing on the positive in daily life and in psychological research. In this first section, we show how a positive newspaper story can shine a light on what is right in the world and how this type of storytelling can produce very favorable reactions among readers. In the second section, we discuss the importance of a balanced perspective involving the strengths and weaknesses of people. We encourage readers not to become embroiled in the debate between the strengths and weakness camps about which one best reflects the "truth." Third, we explore the attention that psychology to date has given to human strengths within cultural contexts. In the last section, we walk you through the eight major parts of the book and give brief previews of the chapter contents.

We would like to make three final points about our approach in writing this volume. First, we believe that the greatest good can come from a positive psychology that is based on the latest and most stringent research methods. In short, an enduring positive psychology must be built on scientific principles. Therefore, in each chapter, we present what we see as the best available research bases for the various topics that we explore. In using this approach, however, we describe the theories and findings of the various researchers rather than going into depth or great detail about their methods. Our rationale for this "surface over depth" approach stems from the fact that this is an introductory-level book; however, the underlying methods used to derive the various positive psychology findings represent the finest, most sophisticated designs and statistics in the field of psychology.

Second, although we do not cover in a separate chapter the physiology and neurobiology (and, occasionally, the evolutionary) underpinnings of positive psychology, we do view these perspectives as very important. Accordingly, our approach is to discuss the physiology, neurobiology, and evolutionary factors in the context of the particular topics covered in each chapter. For example, in the chapter on self-efficacy, optimism, and hope, we discuss the underlying neurobiological forces. Likewise, in the chapter on gratitude, we explore the underlying heart and brain wave patterns. Moreover, in discussing forgiveness, we touch upon the evolutionary advantages of this response.

Third, we recognize and want to assert to the reader that nothing exists within a vacuum. We are all products of our environment to some extent, and as such, looking at cultural context before making claims about various constructs is essential. You will notice throughout the chapters that we attempt to report on studies covering a number of different cultural groups. In our studies, we use a broad definition of the term *culture* and include race, ethnicity, generation, socioeconomic status, gender, nation of origin, and sexual orientation, among other social identity facets. As you will notice, findings are not static across these different groups, and sometimes what has been put forth as a "strength" in one cultural group does not hold this label in another. In addition, some groups have been unfairly pathologized over the years as a result of investigating constructs solely in power-holding groups and then interpreting these findings as universal. We ask the reader to be cautious in interpreting any construct as universal, as findings seem to belie the existence of this. Finally, we suggest that paying attention to worldviews other than one's own can help researchers to avoid these mistakes and harms against certain groups in the future.

BUILDING HUMAN STRENGTH: PSYCHOLOGY'S FORGOTTEN MISSION

Martin E. P. Seligman

President, American Psychological Association

Before World War II, psychology had three missions: curing mental illness, making the lives of all people more fulfilling, and identifying and nurturing high talent. After the war, two events changed the face of psychology. In 1946, the Veterans Administration was created, and practicing psychologists found they could make a living treating mental illness. In 1947, the National Institute of Mental Health was created, and academic psychologists discovered they could get grants for research on mental illness.

As a result, we have made huge strides in the understanding of and therapy for mental illness. At least 10 disorders, previously intractable, have yielded up their secrets and can now be cured or considerably relieved. Even better, millions of people have had their troubles relieved by psychologists.

Our Neglected Missions

But the downside was that the other two fundamental missions of psychology—making the lives of all people better and nurturing "genius"—were all but forgotten.

We became a victimology. Human beings were seen as passive foci: Stimuli came on and elicited "responses," or external "reinforcements" weakened or strengthened "responses," or conflicts from childhood pushed the human being around. Viewing the human being as essentially passive, psychologists treated mental illness within a theoretical framework of repairing damaged habits, damaged drives, damaged childhoods, and damaged brains.

Fifty years later, I want to remind our field that it has been sidetracked. Psychology is not just the study of weakness and damage, it is also the study of strength and virtue. Treatment is not just fixing what is broken, it is nurturing what is best within ourselves.

Bringing this to the foreground is the work of the Presidential Task Force on Prevention, headed by Suzanne Bennett Johnson and Roger Weissberg. This task force will take on a number of jobs: It will attempt to identify the "Best practices in prevention," led by Karol Kumpfer, Lizette Peterson, and Peter Muehrer; it will explore "Creating a new profession: Training in prevention and health promotion" by setting up conferences on the training of the next generation of prevention psychologists, led by Irwin Sandler, Shana Millstein, Mark Greenberg, and Norman Anderson; it will work with Henry Tomes of APA's Public Interest Directorate in the ad campaign to prevent violence in children; it will sponsor a special issue on prevention in the 21st century for the *American Psychologist*, edited by Mihaly Csikszentmihalyi; and, led by Camilla Benbow, it will ask what psychology can do to nurture highly talented children.

Building Strength, Resilience, and Health in Young People

But an underlying question remains: How can we prevent problems like depression, substance abuse, schizophrenia, AIDS, or injury in young people who are genetically vulnerable or who live in worlds that nurture these problems? What we have learned is that pathologizing does not move us closer to the prevention of serious disorders. The major strides in prevention have largely come from building a science focused on systematically promoting the competence of individuals.

We have discovered that there is a set of human strengths that are the most likely buffers against mental illness: courage, optimism, interpersonal skill, work ethic, hope, honesty, and perseverance. Much of the task of prevention will be to create a science of human strength whose mission will be to foster these virtues in young people.

Fifty years of working in a medical model of personal weakness and on the damaged brain has left the mental health professions ill equipped to do effective prevention. We need massive research on human strength and virtue. We need practitioners to recognize that much of the best work they do is amplifying the strengths rather than repairing their patients' weaknesses. We need psychologists who work with families, schools, religious communities, and corporations to emphasize their primary role of fostering strength.

The major psychological theories have changed to undergird a new science of strength and resilience. Individuals—even children—are now seen as decision makers, with choices, preferences, and the possibility of becoming masterful, efficacious, or, in malignant circumstances, helpless and hopeless. Such science and practice will prevent many of the major emotional disorders. It will also have two side effects. Given all we are learning about the effects of behavior and of mental well-being on the body, it will make our clients physically healthier. It will also re-orient psychology to its two neglected missions, making normal people stronger and more productive as well as making high human potential actual.

Seligman, M. "Building human strength: psychology's forgotten mission," in *APA Monitor*, 28(1): January 1998, p. 2.

GOING FROM THE NEGATIVE TO THE POSITIVE

Imagine you are listening to a story about a group of people who are stranded one Friday evening at a large airport because of bad weather. The typical content of the news about such a situation probably would be very negative and filled with actions that portray people in a very unfavorable light. Stories of people being rude to airline attendants or debates over mask wearing might be part of the headline. Such stories emphasize the bad side of human behavior that was the focus of many 20th-century psychologists. But, as we shall see, there is usually more than one side to the story.

A Positive News Story

Juxtapose such negative news reports with the following tale reported by one of the authors of this book (Snyder, 2004c, p. D4) many years ago in a local newspaper. The scene is the Philadelphia International Airport on a Friday evening as flights arrive late or are canceled.

> People were trying to make the best of difficult situations. For example, when a young Army soldier just back from Iraq noticed that he had lost his girlfriend's ring, the people working at the airport and all of us in the waiting area immediately began to search for it. In a short period of time, the ring was located, and a cheer went out in the crowd.
>
> Around 7:40 p.m., the announcer told us that there would be yet longer delays on several of the flights. To my amazement and delight, I found that my fellow travelers (and I) just coped. Some broke out supplies of food that they had stashed away in bags, and they offered their treasures to others. Decks of playing cards came out, and various games were started. The airlines people handed out snacks. There were scattered outbreaks of laughter.
>
> As if we were soldiers waiting in the trenches during a lull between battles, someone in the distance began to play a harmonica. Small boys made a baseball diamond, and as their game progressed, no one seemed to mind when one of their home runs would sail by. Although there weren't enough seats for everyone, people creatively made chairs and couches out of their luggage. The people who had computers took them out and played video games with each other. One guy even turned his computer screen into a drive-in-movie-like setup on which several people watched *The Matrix*. I used my computer to write this column.
>
> I once heard it said that grace is doing the average thing when everyone should be going crazy. When hollering and screaming, becoming angry and upset, and generally "losing it" seem to loom just over the horizon, it is wonderful instead to see the warming grace of people—similar to the rays of the sun on a cold day.

Reactions to This Positive Story

After this story appeared, Dr. C. R. Snyder (CRS) reported that he was not prepared for readers' reactions and had these words to say:

> Never have I written anything that ignited such an outpouring of heartfelt praise and gratitude. In the first week alone after this editorial appeared, I was swamped with favorable e-mails. Some recounted how it reminded them of times they had witnessed people behaving at their very best. Others wrote about how this story made them feel better for the rest of that day and even for several days afterward. Several people said they wished there were more such news stories in the paper. Not a single person among the responses I received had anything negative to say about this column.

Why would people react so uniformly and warmly to this short story about a Friday night at the Philadelphia airport? In part, people probably want to see and hear more about the good in others. Whether it is through newspaper stories such as this one or through the scientific studies and applications we present in this book, there is a hunger to know more about the good in people. It is as if the collective sentiment were, "Enough of all this negativity about people!"

In writing this book on positive psychology, we have experienced the uplifting effects of reviewing the many research and clinical applications that are appearing on the study of strengths and positive emotions in varying groups. As you read about the assets of your fellow humans from multiple cultural perspectives and hear about the many resources that promote the best in people, see whether you, too, feel good. There are many things for which we can praise people, and we will share many examples.

POSITIVE PSYCHOLOGY SEEKS A BALANCED, MORE COMPLETE VIEW OF HUMAN FUNCTIONING

Seeing only the good in one's own actions and the bad in those of others is a common human foible. Validating only the positive or negative aspects of experience is not productive. It is very tempting to focus on just the good (or the bad) in the world, *but it is not good science*, and we must not make this mistake in advancing positive psychology. Although we do not agree with focusing solely on the negative in the ways of the previous pathology models, it would be inaccurate to describe their proponents as being poor scholars, poor scientists, poor practitioners, or bad people. Instead, this previous paradigm was advanced by well-meaning, bright people who were responding to the particular circumstances of their times. Likewise, it is not as if these people were wrong in their depictions of people. They developed diagnoses and measurement approaches for schizophrenia, depression, and alcoholism and validated many effective treatments for specific problems such as panic disorder and blood and injury phobia (see Seligman, 1994).

Thus, those operating within the pathology model were quite accurate in their descriptions of some people at some particular times in their lives. Moreover, they were able to help certain people with select problems. Nevertheless, advocates of the pathology approach were incomplete in their portrayals of humankind. Undeniably, the negative is part of humankind, but only a part, and what is viewed as negative in one group may be positive in another. In addition, a bias toward European culture is found, thus doubly pathologizing nondominant groups. Positive psychology offers a look at the other side—that which is good and strong within a cultural context, along with normative ways to nurture and sustain these assets and resources.

Although we explore the positive, we emphasize that this half is no more the entire story than is the negative side. Future psychologists must develop an inclusive approach that examines both the weaknesses *and* the strengths of people in varying cultural groups, as well as the stressors *and* the resources in the environment. That approach would be the most comprehensive and valid. When the first edition of this text was printed, the science and practice of positive psychology was still rather new. Now four editions later we see the myriad studies and theories that have been developed and validated, and still there is more to learn. Only through doing so much rigorous work on the strengths of people within their cultural contexts and the many resources of positive environments will we truly be able to understand all human beings in a more balanced fashion. Our task in these pages, therefore, is to share with you what we do know about positive psychology today.

We look forward to that future time in the field of psychology when the positive is as likely as the negative to be used in assessing people and helping them to lead more satisfying and culturally comfortable existences. That time will probably come during the lifetimes of the readers of this book; some of you may pursue careers in psychology in which you routinely will consider people's strengths along with their weaknesses. Indeed, we feel strongly that your generation will be the one to implement a culturally competent psychology that truly balances the tenets of a positive approach with those of the previous pathology orientation. We also hope that today's parents are using and will continue to use positive psychology techniques to shore up families and bring out the best in their children. Likewise, we envision a time when school-age children and youth are valued as much for their major strengths as for their scores on state tests or college entrance examinations.

You, the readers, are the stewards of the eventual culturally humble and balanced positive-negative psychology. We warn you about the debate that is already in progress as to the superiority of one approach over the other. In the next section, we attempt to inoculate you against such "us versus them" thinking.

Views of Reality That Include Both the Positive and the Negative

Reality resides in people's perceptions of events and happenings in their world (Gergen, 1985; Hibberd & Petocz, 2022), and scientific perspectives thereby depend on who defines them. Accordingly, different fields may clash over how to build meaningful systems for understanding our world. But, whether one is of a mind to believe in a more positive psychology or more pathology-based perspective, we must be clear that this debate involves **social constructions** about those facts. Likewise, because the prevailing views are social constructions that contribute to ongoing sociocultural goals and values, both the positive psychology and the pathology perspectives provide guidelines about how people should live their lives and what makes such lives worth living. It is worth noting that humans often focus more strongly on the negative for various evolutionary and other biological reasons (see Chapter 6 on this topic). And yet, we also love, and play, and enjoy. Sometimes we do these things even as we are suffering.

Thus, we believe that both the positive psychology view and the more traditional pathology view are useful. The best scientific and practical solution is to embrace both perspectives while keeping cultural context in the forefront of our minds. Therefore, although we introduce positive psychology tenets, research, and applications in this textbook, we do so in order to add the strengths approach as a complement to insights derived from being also aware of and attentive to weakness. Accordingly, we encourage the readers of this book—those who eventually will become the leaders in the field—to work toward having a balanced and contextual view of tenets within psychology.

WHERE WE ARE NOW AND WHAT WE WILL ASK

A notable accomplishment of the positive psychology initiative in its more than two decades has been its success in increasing the amount of attention given to its theories and research findings.

University of Pennsylvania psychologist Martin Seligman should be singled out for having ignited the recent explosion of interest in positive psychology, as well as for having provided the label *positive psychology*. (Abraham Maslow actually coined the term *positive psychology* when he used it as a chapter title in his 1954 book, *Motivation and Personality*.) Having grown tired of the fact that psychology was not yielding enough "knowledge of what makes life worth living" (Seligman & Csikszentmihalyi, 2000, p. 5; note the similarity in this sentiment to Robert F. Kennedy's lament about the gross national product in this chapter's opening quotation), Seligman searched for a provocative theme when he became president of the American Psychological Association in 1998. It was during his presidency that Seligman used his bully pulpit to bring attention to the topic of positive psychology. Since that time, Seligman has worked tirelessly to initiate conferences and grant programs for research and applications of positive psychological research. Throughout his leadership of the developing positive psychology movement, Seligman has reminded psychologists that the backbone of the initiative should be good science.

Martin Seligman

Courtesy of Martin Seligman.

We firmly believe that our hunt for strengths will result in some marvelous insights about people from all backgrounds. We are also aware that *humans* are incredibly diverse as a group, and so we must always look to context and identity as well. In judging the success of positive psychology, we hold that it must be subjected to the very highest standards of logic and science. Likewise, positive psychology must undergo the analyses of skeptical yet open minds. We leave this latter important role to you.

PERSONAL MINI-EXPERIMENTS

WHAT YOU WANT TO EXPERIENCE

In this chapter, we provide numerous examples of how a focus on the positive can bring more good feelings and people into your daily life. Reorienting the focus of our thinking can help to determine whether we spend our days in pursuit of meaningful experiences or remain fearful of the bad that might happen. Too often, people act as if their thoughts were out of their control when, in fact, we are the authors of daily scripts that largely determine our daily actions. With the goal of focusing your thoughts on the positive, please go through each of these steps and follow the instructions. It is important to take your time.

- Identify three good things you would like to happen tomorrow.
- Think of one thing that you do not want to happen in the upcoming days.
- Imagine what you want not to happen as a circle that is getting smaller and smaller.
- Of the three good things you want to happen tomorrow, imagine the least important one getting smaller and smaller.
- Imagine the small circle of what you want not to happen getting so small it is hard to see.
- Let go of what you want not to happen. Say goodbye to it.
- Of the two good things you want to happen tomorrow, imagine the least important one getting smaller and smaller.
- Focus your mind on the one good thing that remains as the most important for tomorrow.
- See this good thing happening in your mind's eye.
- Think of others in your social group who might support you in this endeavour.
- Practice having this good thing happen in your mind.
- When you awaken tomorrow, focus on the good thing happening.
- Repeat to yourself during the day, "I make this positive possible."
- Repeat the phrase "I choose how to focus my thoughts."

The point of this exercise is to teach people that they have more control of their mental agendas than they often realize. Furthermore, by attending to what they want to happen, people are more likely to own their daily activities rather than to be reactive. In doing this exercise, feel free to tinker with the exact words that you may say to yourself, but try to retain the empowering message in the words we have selected. In our experiences in working with people, spending mental energies on avoiding certain unwanted outcomes tends to make people reactive to other people and events. On the other hand, thinking of what we want to happen helps to keep the negative away.

A GUIDE TO THIS BOOK

This book was written with you in mind. Throughout our collaboration, we asked each other, "Will this chapter bring positive psychology to life for students?" These discussions helped us realize that the book needed to be an excellent summary of positive psychological science and practice *and* that it had to hook you into applying positive psychology principles in your daily lives. With that goal in mind, we have attempted to distill the most rigorous positive psychology studies and the most effective practice strategies, *and* we have constructed dozens of personal mini-experiments (try the first one, "What You Want to Experience," right now) and life enhancement strategies that promote your engagement with the positives in people from all backgrounds and the world. Our goal is that, by the time you have finished reading this book, you will be more knowledgeable about psychology *and* will have become more skilled at capitalizing on your own strengths and generating positive emotions.

We have divided this book into eight parts. In Part I, "Looking at Psychology From a Positive Perspective," there are three chapters. Chapter 1, which you are about to complete, is introductory. Our purpose has been to give you a sense of the excitement we feel about positive psychology and to share some of the core issues driving the development of this new field. Chapter 2 is titled "Eastern and Western Perspectives on Positive Psychology: How "ME + WE = US" Might Bridge the Gap." In the chapter, you will see that, although there are obvious positive psychology ties to Western cultures, there also are important themes from Eastern cultures, and that use of a ME-mindset (individualist) or a WE-mindset (collectivist) can both be beneficial. In addition, we encourage you here, regardless of your own mindset, to be able to view things from the different perspectives. Chapter 3, "Classification and Measurement in Positive Psychology," will give you a sense of how psychologists apply labels to the various types of human assets. For readers who are familiar with the more traditional pathology model, this will provide a counterpoint classification that is built on human strengths.

In Part II, "Positive Psychology in Context," we have dedicated two chapters to the factors associated with living well. In Chapter 4, "The Role of Culture in Developing Strengths and Living Well," we examine how the surrounding societal and environmental forces may contribute to a sense of well-being and how culture might affect understanding, function, and utility of a variety of constructs. Moreover, in Chapter 5, "Living Well at Every Stage of Life," we show how childhood activities can help shape a person to become adaptive in their later years.

Part III, "Positive Emotional States and Processes," consists of two chapters that cover topics pertaining to emotion-related processes. In Chapter 6, "The Principles of Pleasure: Understanding Positive Affect, Positive Emotions, Happiness, and Well-Being," we address the frequently asked question, "What makes people happy?" In Chapter 7, "Making the Most of Emotional Experiences: Emotion-Focused Coping, Emotional Intelligence, Socioemotional Selectivity, and Emotional Storytelling," we introduce new findings regarding emotions as extremely important assets in meeting our goals.

In Part IV, "Positive Cognitive States and Processes," we include three chapters. Chapter 8, "Seeing Our Futures Through Self-Efficacy, Optimism, and Hope," covers the three most-researched motives for facing the future: self-efficacy, optimism, and hope. In Chapter 9,

"Wisdom and Courage: Characteristics of the Wise and the Brave," we examine positive psychology topics involving the assets people bring to circumstances that stretch their skills and capacities. Likewise, in Chapter 10, "Mindfulness, Flow, and Spirituality: In Search of Optimal Experiences," we discuss how people become aware of the ongoing process of thinking and feeling, along with the human need to believe in forces that are bigger and more powerful than they.

In Part V, "Prosocial Behavior," we describe the general positive linkages that human beings have with other people. In Chapter 11, "Empathy and Egotism: Portals to Altruism and Gratitude," we show how kindness-related processes operate to the benefit of people. And in Chapter 12, "Attachment, Love, Flourishing Relationships, and Forgiveness," we review the importance of close human bonds for a variety of positive outcomes.

Part VI, "Understanding and Changing Human Behavior," describes how to prevent negative things from happening, as well as how to make positive things happen. Chapter 13, "Preventing the Bad and Promoting the Good," will help you to see how people can improve their life circumstances.

Part VII, "Positive Environments," looks at specific environments. In Chapter 14, "Positive Schooling and Good Work: The Psychology of Gainful Employment and the Education That Gets Us There," we describe recent findings related to positive learning outcomes for students, as well as the components of jobs that are both productive and satisfying.

The book closes with Part VIII, Chapter 15: "The Future of Positive Psychology for the Public Good." In this final chapter, we (JTP and RMC) have a conversation about ways in which positive psychology and strengths in general might be applied to some of today's major problems and issues. Finally, in the last edition, when we had so recently lost our friend and co-author, Dr. Shane J. Lopez, we allowed many friends to memorialize him with stories of the many strengths he embodied. We have moved these stories for you to an Appendix ("Remembering Shane: Real Strengths in a Real Person"), following the chapters, and we hope you will read and be inspired by them. Though he is gone, his life was one well-lived and provides many good examples of the way in which one can embody and share a variety of strengths, making better all the lives around him.

Personal Mini-Experiments

In most of the chapters (including this one), we encourage you to put the ideas of leading positive psychologists to the test. In Personal Mini-Experiments, we ask you to bring positive psychology into your life by conducting the kind of experiments that positive psychology researchers might conduct in a lab or the field and that positive psychology practitioners might assign to their clients for homework. Some of these experiments take less than 30 minutes to complete, whereas some will take more than a week.

Life Enhancement Strategies

Finding the positive in daily life does not necessarily require a full-fledged experiment. In fact, we believe that a mindful approach to everyday living will reveal the power of positive emotions and strengths. Therefore, for the chapters that focus specifically on positive emotions, strengths, and healthy processes, we devised Life Enhancement Strategies, which can be implemented in a matter of minutes. We decided to develop these strategies to help you attain life's three most important outcomes: connecting with others, pursuing meaning, and experiencing some degree of pleasure or satisfaction. Specifically, love, work, and play have been referred to as the three great realms of life (Seligman, 1998c). Freud defined *normalcy* as the capacity to love, work, and play, and psychological researchers have referred to this capacity as "mental health" (see Cederblad et al., 1995). Developmental researchers have described love, work, and play as normal tasks associated with human growth, and researchers have been writing about these tasks in relation to well-being for years (e.g., Van Groningen et al., 2020). Professionals interested in psychotherapy consider the ability to love, work, and play to be an aspect of the change process (e.g., Mirkin et al., 2005). Although full engagement in pursuits of love, work, and play will not guarantee a good life, we believe it is necessary for good living. With this belief in mind, we encourage you to participate in numerous Life Enhancement Strategies that will enhance your ability to love, work, and play. We have also tried to include varying cultural perspectives in these strategies. Thinking about positive psychology in your everyday life, whether work or leisure, can help to enhance your life.

This concludes our brief rundown of where we plan to go in the ensuing chapters and of our many hopes for you. If you become fully engaged with the material and the exercises in this book, you will gain knowledge and skills that may help you lead a better life.

THE BIG PICTURE

Despite the uncertainty and difficulty of our time, we must not forget to also focus on such issues as virtues, creativity, and hope. Three earlier cultures faced similar eras. In the fifth century BCE, Athens used its resources to explore human virtues—good character and actions. Democracy was formed during this period. In 15th-century Florence, riches and talents were spent to advance beauty. And Victorian England used its assets to pursue the human virtues of duty, honor, and discipline. As Martin Luther King, Jr. is quoted as saying, "Darkness cannot drive out darkness; only light can do that. Hate cannot drive out hate; only love can do that." Now is the time to focus on strengths and how they might be used to challenge us as a nation to do better and to live well. In these last few years, the world has had to bind together to fight illness and many were lost, but focusing on the strengths imbued in the survivors is one way to focus on the light.

Like the gifts emanating from these three previous eras, perhaps the contribution of the United States in the 21st century lies in adopting and exploring the tenets of positive psychology—the study and application of that which is good in people (see Seligman & Csikszentmihalyi, 2000). Certainly, never in our careers have we witnessed such a potentially important new development in the field of psychology. But we are getting ahead of ourselves because the real test will come when new students are drawn to this area. For now, we welcome you to positive psychology.

KEY TERMS

Mental illness
Positive psychology
Social constructions

2 EASTERN AND WESTERN PERSPECTIVES ON POSITIVE PSYCHOLOGY

How "ME + WE = US" Might Bridge the Gap

Contributions From Phil McKnight Included

LEARNING OBJECTIVES

After reading this chapter, you will be able to:

2.1 Describe the main differences and core emphases in individualist and collectivist mindsets

2.2 Identify major Western and Eastern influences regarding strengths perspectives in different cultural groups

2.3 Compare and contrast how value systems, orientation to time, and thought processes impact manifestation of strengths

2.4 Understand that value of different constructs represent key factors in East and West cultural norms

2.5 Critique a perspective focused solely on "Me" or "We" and cultivate an understanding of a balanced approach being most healthful

A MATTER OF PERSPECTIVE

Positive psychology scholars aim to define specific strengths and highlight the many paths that lead to better lives (Chang, Yu et al., 2016; Snyder et al., 2021). As Western civilization and European events and values shaped the vantage point of the field of psychology, it is not surprising that the origins of positive psychology have focused more on the values and experiences of Westerners. Constructs such as **hope**, optimism, and personal self-efficacy, among others, are particularly valued in these cultures and have been prominent throughout Western history. As our views in the field have broadened to understand the importance of including non-Western ideologies, populations, and ideas, however, scholars have begun to take a wider historical and cultural context into account to understand strengths and the practices associated with living well (see, e.g., Layous et al., 2017; Shin et al., 2020; Sue & Constantine, 2003). In this chapter we revisit the previously neglected wisdoms of the Eastern traditions in addition to those originating in the West, with the goal of adding different viewpoints about human strengths within a cultural context.

"A good fortune may forebode a bad luck, which may in turn disguise a good fortune." This Chinese proverb exemplifies the Eastern perspective that the world and its inhabitants are in a perpetual state of flux. Thus, just as surely as good times occur, so too will bad times visit us. This expectation of and desire for balance distinguishes many Easterners' views of optimal functioning from the more linear path taken by Westerners to resolve problems and monitor progress. Ever adaptive and mindful, Eastern populations move with the cycle of life until the change process becomes natural and **enlightenment** (i.e., being able to see things clearly for what they are) is achieved. While Western ideologies center on the search for rewards in the physical plane, Eastern mindsets seek to transcend the human plane and rise to the spiritual.

In this chapter, we discuss and contrast several Western and Eastern historical and philosophical traditions that demonstrate how these different groups characterize important strengths and life outcomes. Next, we discuss some of the inherent and fundamental differences between Eastern and Western value systems, thought processes, and life outcomes sought. We also articulate the idea of the "good life" from these two perspectives and discuss the associated strengths that assist each group in attaining positive life outcomes. We then delve into a discussion of some specific concepts that are deemed to be necessary qualities for achieving the "good life" in each group. It is important to note that what is viewed as the "good life" may be different in each cultural group. Although we will not always enclose this term in quotation marks as we

Aristotle
iStockphoto.com/PanosKarapanagiotis

do here, please note that it is always culturally bound. Also important is that in discussing these groups with broad strokes, we realize that in-group diversity is also present. In closing, we talk about the ME perspective and the WE perspective and give our thoughts on trying to see things from more than one perspective.

HISTORICAL AND PHILOSOPHICAL TRADITIONS

To summarize thousands of years of Western and Eastern ideology and traditions is obviously beyond the scope of this chapter. Therefore, we highlight the basic tenets of three influential Western traditions: (1) **Athenian**, (2) **Judeo-Christianity**, and (3) **Islam**, as well as the less well-known but important teachings from American Indian **Anishinaabe** traditions that also relate to current understandings of strengths. Next, four influential Eastern disciplines are discussed: (1) **Confucianism**, (2) **Taoism**, (3) **Buddhism**, and (4) **Hinduism**.

Western Influences: Athenian, Judeo-Christian, Islamic, and Anishinaabe Traditions

Athenian Views

Discussion of virtue and human strength is something on which both Plato and Aristotle focused heavily in their teachings in Ancient Greece. Aristotle, after expanding on Plato's ideas regarding virtue, detailed 11 moral virtues: *courage, moderation, generosity, munificence* (this relates to money spending at an appropriate level), *magnificence* (described as "greatness of soul"), *even temper, friendliness, truthfulness, wit* (describing an ability to laugh and have fun at an appropriate level), *justice*, and *friendship* (Solomon, 2006). In addition to these moral virtues, Aristotle described intellectual virtues (mainly associated with ideas regarding wisdom) and believed that "strength of character, as inculcated by the political community, would lead to enduring human excellence" (Solomon, 2006, p. 9).

Judeo-Christianity

Followers of Judaism and Christianity are instructed by The Christian Bible and Hebrew Bible (or Tanakh) and their discussions of virtues in many chapters and verses. In the Old Testament (found in both bibles, though in different orders), the virtues of *faith, hope*, and *charity* are highlighted and encouraged and were later discussed as part of the "Seven Heavenly Virtues" by Thomas Aquinas (Williams & Houck, 1982). According to historians, Aquinas lists these virtues as *fortitude* (courage), *justice, temperance, wisdom* (these four are often called the cardinal virtues; Peterson & Seligman, 2004), *faith, hope*, and *charity* (Williams & Houck, 1982). Other scholars cite the Ten Commandments given by Moses in the Old Testament as directives toward cultivating certain strengths within the Jewish tradition. Peterson and Seligman (2004) interpret the acts that the commandments prohibit as falling under the category of particular cardinal virtues: "Justice is implied in prohibitions against murder, theft, and lying; temperance in those against adultery and covetousness; and transcendence generally within the divine origin of the commands" (p. 48).

Other mentions are made of various gifts and strengths throughout the New Testament in the Christian Bible. For example, the Book of Romans describes the "gifts" that are valued by the Judeo-Christian God and includes strengths such as leadership, faith, mercy, love, joy, hope, patience, hospitality, and others (12:3–21). In addition, the Book of Proverbs has many affirmations of specific virtuous behaviors (Peterson & Seligman, 2004). In the prologue of this book of the Bible, the following words are given as the purpose and theme of Proverbs:

1. The proverbs of Solomon, son of David, king of Israel:
2. for attaining wisdom and discipline; for understanding words of insight;
3. for acquiring a disciplined and prudent life, doing what is right and just and fair;
4. for giving prudence to the simple, knowledge and discretion to the young—

(Proverbs 1:1–4)

These words caution followers to live virtuous lives, giving particular weight to the virtue of wisdom. Finally, the Beatitudes discussed in the Book of Matthew give a series of virtuous traits (e.g., meekness, being a "peacemaker," mercy, righteousness, etc.) that are said to be pleasing to God (Matthew 5:1–11).

Another book of Jewish teachings, the Talmud, also provides instructions about living a virtuous life. In the Pirke Avot, or *Ethics of the Fathers*, directives are given on how to live life as an ethical follower of Judaism with lessons on being a hospitable host, particularly to the poor; being fair in decision making and judgments; and seeking peace in everyday life (Bokser, 1989). In addition, the Talmud states, "You shall administer truth, justice and peace within your gates" (Zech 8:16), showing similar value to other religious traditions for these specific virtues.

Allah

iStockphoto.com/KittiKahotong

Islam

Although we have added Islam to the "Western" heading in this section as is commonly done in texts that discuss both Western and Eastern religions, it is important to note that scholars disagree as to whether Islam should be considered a Western or an Eastern religion (S. Lloyd-Moffet, personal communication, November 21, 2013). Islam is practiced by both Western and Eastern individuals and groups, and thus its virtues and practices may be influenced by more than one context.

Islam incorporates many virtues recognizable in other philosophical traditions and categorizes them as moral obligations. Among others, *gratitude* (e.g., to Allah for His benevolence), *love* (of Allah because of His forgiveness), *kindness* (especially toward parents), *justice* (emphasizing fraternity and equality of all), and *courage* (acts of bravery) are valued (Farah, 1968). In addition, there is a strong component of looking out for one's brother, particularly if one has more than one needs. Giving to the poor is a requirement in the Islamic faith reflected in the third pillar, *zakat* (alms), and it is something that is to be done secretly as opposed to directly if possible so that the giver maintains their humility and the recipient is not embarrassed by having to accept the gift (Ahmed, 1999). Abiding by these moral obligations and pillars assists the faithful in pleasing Allah in this tradition.

Anishinaabe Teachings

Although less well known, we would like to share one more set of Western-oriented teachings that come directly from our beginnings in North America. The Ojibwe, part of the Anishinaabe, tell a story that guides values in this cultural group, known as "The Seven Grandfathers' Teachings." In this story, the first elder of the tribe was said to have received knowledge from each of the Seven Grandfathers with the purpose of these gifts being "to help the people live a good life and to respect the Creator, the earth and each other" (Native Women's Centre, 2008, p. 5). These teachings include seven values that should be followed, and each is represented by a different animal; the teachings include *wisdom* (cherishing knowledge; represented by a beaver), *love* (absolute kindness and knowing peace; represented by an eagle), *respect* (honoring creation, other people, and ourselves among others and showing appreciation; represented by a buffalo), *bravery* (facing life with courage; represented by a bear), *honesty* (living life with integrity and being trustworthy; represented by sasquatch, the Wilderness Man), *humility* (being deferent, valuing equity; represented by a wolf), and *truth* (to apply the teachings faithfully; represented by a turtle) (American Indian Health Service of Chicago, 2021; Benton-Banai, 1988; National Museum of the American Indian, n.d.). It is obvious that there is much similarity to the other Western teachings noted in this section. This gives us another connection across groups with valuing of strength and goodness.

Eastern Influences: Confucianism, Taoism, Buddhism, and Hinduism

Confucianism

Confucius, or the Sage, as he is sometimes called, held that leadership and education are central to morality. Born during a time when his Chinese homeland was fraught with strife, Confucius emphasized morality as a potential cure for the evils of that time (Soothill, 1968), and the tenets of Confucianism are laden with quotations that encourage looking out for others. In fact, one of Confucius's most famous sayings is a precursor of the Golden Rule and can be translated as, "You would like others to do for you what you would indeed like for yourself"

(Ross, 2003; *Analects* 6:28). In some ways, these teachings are parallel to thoughts put forth by Aristotle and Plato regarding the responsibility of leaders to take *charge* of the group, although there is less emphasis in Western writings on the collectivist ideal of taking *care* of others in the group.

The attainment of virtue is at the core of Confucian teachings. The five virtues deemed central to living a moral existence are *jen* (humanity, the virtue most exalted by Confucius and said to encompass the other four virtues), *yi* (duty to treat others well), *li* (etiquette and sensitivity for others' feelings), *zhi* (wisdom), and *xin* (truthfulness). Confucian followers must strive to make wise decisions based on these five virtues; this continual striving leads the Confucian follower to enlightenment, or the good life.

Confucius
iStockphoto.com/duncan1890

Taoism

Ancient Taoist beliefs are difficult to discuss with Western audiences partly because of the untranslatable nature of some key concepts in the tradition of Taoism. Lao-Tzu (the creator of the Taoist tradition) states in his works that his followers must live according to the Tao (pronounced "dow" and roughly translated as "the Way"). The Chinese character portraying the concept of the Way is a moving head and "refers simultaneously to direction, movement, method, and thought" (Peterson & Seligman, 2004, p. 42; Ross, 2003); Tao is the energy that surrounds everyone and is a power that "envelops, surrounds, and flows through all things" (*Western Reform Taoism*, 2003, p. 1).

The Way
iStockphoto.com/cl2004lhy

According to Taoist traditions, the difficulty in understanding the Way stems from the fact that one cannot teach another about it. Instead, understanding flows from experiencing the Way for oneself by fully participating in life. In this process, both good and bad experiences can contribute to a greater understanding of the Way. Achieving naturalness and spontaneity in life is the most important goal in Taoist philosophy. Thus, the virtues of *humanity, justice, temperance*, and *propriety* must be practiced by the virtuous individual without effort (Cheng, 2000). One who has achieved transcendence within this philosophy does not have to think about optimal functioning but behaves virtuously naturally.

Lao-Tzu
E. T. C. Werner, *Myths and Legends of China*, 1922.

Buddhism

Seeking the good of others is woven throughout the teachings of "the Enlightened One" (i.e., the Buddha). In one passage, the Buddha is quoted as saying, "Wander for the gain of the many, for the happiness of the many, out of compassion for the world" (Sangharakshita, 1991, p. 17). At the same time, the Buddha teaches that suffering is a part of being and that this suffering is brought on by the human emotion of desire. In the Buddhist philosophy, **Nirvana** is a state in which the self is freed from desire for anything. It should be noted that both premortal and postmortal nirvana states are proposed as possible for the individual. More specifically, the premortal nirvana may be likened to the idea of the ultimate good life in this philosophy. Postmortal nirvana may be similar to the Christian idea of heaven.

Like the other Eastern philosophies, Buddhism gives an important place to virtue, which is described in several catalogs of personal qualities. Buddhists speak of the *Brahma Viharas*, those virtues that are above all others in importance. These virtues include love (*maitri*), **compassion** (*karuna*), joy (*mudita*), and equanimity (*upeksa*) (Sangharakshita, 1991). The paths to achieving these virtues within Buddhism require humans to divorce themselves from the human emotion of desire to put an end to suffering.

Buddha
iStockphoto.com/pixonaut

Hinduism

The Hindu tradition differs somewhat from the other three philosophies discussed previously in that it does not appear to have a specific founder, and it is not clear when this tradition began in history (Stevenson & Haberman, 1998). The main teachings of the Hindu tradition emphasize the interconnectedness of all things. The idea of a harmonious union among all individuals is woven throughout the teachings of Hinduism, which refer to a "single, unifying principle underlying all of Earth" (Stevenson & Haberman, 1998, p. 46).

One's goal within this tradition would be to live life so fully and so correctly that one would go directly to the afterlife without having to repeat life's lessons in a reincarnated form, because, "to return to this world is an indication of one's failure to achieve ultimate knowledge of one's self" (Stevenson & Haberman, 1998, p. 53). Thus, the quest of one's life is to attain ultimate self-knowledge and to strive for ultimate self-betterment. Individuals are encouraged to be good to others as well as to improve themselves. The *Upanishads* state that "good action" is also encouraged in the sense that, if one does not reach ultimate self-knowledge in one's life and thus does have to return to Earth via reincarnation after death, the previous life's good actions correlate directly with better placement in the world in the subsequent life (Stevenson & Haberman, 1998). This process is known as *karma*. The good life in the Hindu tradition, therefore, encompasses individuals who are continually achieving knowledge and continually working toward good actions (Dahlsgaard et al., 2005; Oman & Paranjpe, 2020; Peterson & Seligman, 2004).

SUMMARY OF EASTERN AND WESTERN PHILOSOPHIES

Each of the philosophies discussed here incorporates ideas about the importance of virtue, along with individual strengths, as people move toward the good life. Similarities also can be drawn among the different ideologies, especially in the types of characteristics and experiences that are valued, although there are also differences in terms of which traits are particularly prized. It is also important to mention here (although we will have more to say about this in Chapter 4 in this volume as well) that just because two virtues or values translate to the same word does not mean that they have the same meaning or function. Wisdom, in Judeo-Christian value systems, for example, is often interpreted in the Bible as understanding God's plan and thus is almost impossible for a human person to comprehend. This is somewhat different from the way Confucius talks about *zhi*, also translated as wisdom, in that Confucius focuses more on the idea of zhi as "a moral virtue that involves . . . the ability to transform and regulate the social order" (Raphals, 1992, p. 16). Different again is the Ojibwe understanding of wisdom, which instead involves cherishing knowledge (Native Women's Centre, 2008). It is interesting and thought-provoking, regardless, that so many different cultural groups have thought of what "the good life" should mean from so many different traditions. In today's world, we can make a vow to learn from these different traditions and perhaps in this way approach a truly multicultural understanding of the good life by working to understand the differences in positive psychology viewed from each perspective.

EAST MEETS WEST

Despite having some similarities, Eastern and Western ideologies stem from very different historical events and traditions. We begin this section with a brief discussion of these two different value systems (**individualism** and **collectivism**). Next, we explore ways in which differences can be seen explicitly in each cultural approach with regard to orientations toward time and their respective thought processes. These cultural differences give more information about characteristics identified as strengths in each culture and ways in which positive life outcomes are pursued and achieved within these cultural contexts.

INDIVIDUALISM: THE PSYCHOLOGY OF ME

Since the publication of Alexis de Tocqueville's (1835/2003) *Democracy in America*, the United States has been known as the land of the "rugged individualist." Since the establishment of American independence in 1776, this rugged individualism has metamorphosed into the "me generation" that held sway from the 1960s through the early 1990s (Myers, 2004). In this individualist mindset concern for the individual is greater than concern for the group. As shown in Figure 2.1, when the average person in a society is disposed toward individual independence, that society is deemed individualistic (see the bell-shaped curve drawn with the dotted line).

Core Emphases in Individualism

The three core emphases within individualism include: (a) a sense of independence, (b) a desire to stand out relative to others (**need for uniqueness**), and (c) the use of the self or the individual as the unit of analysis in thinking about life. In societies that emphasize and value individualism, such as the United States, social patterns resemble a loosely interwoven fabric, and it is the norm for each person to see themselves as independent of the surrounding group of people

FIGURE 2.1 ■ Norms and Individual Differences for Individualistic and Collectivistic Societies

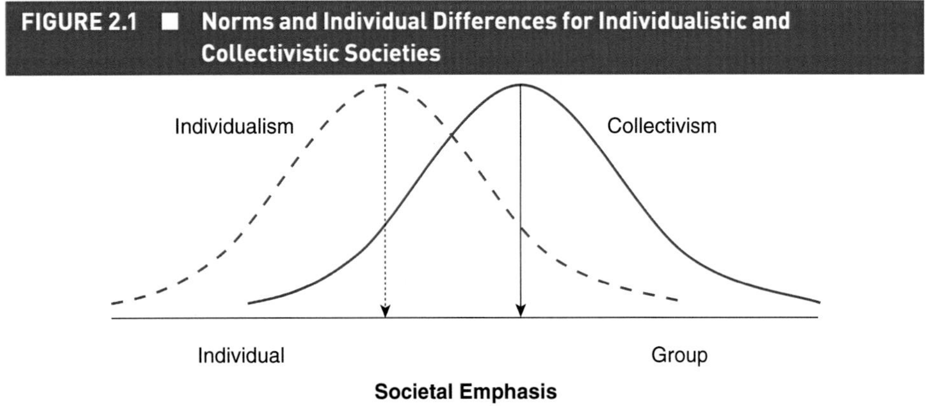

(Triandis, 1995). On this point, research involving many studies supports the conclusion that individualism in the United States reflects a sense of independence rather than dependence (see Oyserman et al., 2002).

A second core emphasis within individualism is that the person wants to stand out relative to the population as a whole. Within individualistic societies, therefore, people follow their own motives and preferences instead of adjusting their desires to accommodate those of the group. The individualistic person thus sets personal goals that may or may not match those of the groups to which they belong (Hamamura et al., 2018; Schwartz, 1994; Triandis, 1988, 1990). Because of the individualistic propensity to manifest one's specialness, coupled with societal support for actions that show such individuality, it follows that the citizens of individualistic societies such as the United States will have a high need for uniqueness. We explore this fascinating motive in greater detail later in this chapter.

A third core emphasis of individualism is that the self or person is the unit of analysis in understanding how people think and act in a society. That is, explanations of events are likely to involve the person rather than the group. Therefore, the various definitions of individualism draw upon worldviews in which personal factors are emphasized over social forces (Hamamura et al., 2018; Triandis, 1995).

These core emphases influence behavior such that secondary emphases flow from the individualistic focus upon the self rather than the group. Goals set by citizens of an individualistic society typically are for the self; moreover, success and related satisfactions also operate at the level of the self. The individualistic person pursues what is enjoyable to them, in contrast to collectivistic people, who derive their pleasures from things that promote the welfare of the group. Of course, the individualist at times may follow group norms, but this usually happens when they have deduced that it is personally advantageous to do so.

As may be obvious by now, individualists are more focused upon their own self-esteem or pleasure in interpersonal relationships and beyond. Individualists also weigh the disadvantages and advantages of relationships before deciding whether to pursue them (Hamamura et al., 2018). Individualists tend to be rather short term in their thinking and often are somewhat informal in their interactions with others.

COLLECTIVISM: THE PSYCHOLOGY OF WE

Thousands of years ago, our hunter–gatherer ancestors realized that there were survival advantages to be derived from banding together into groups with shared goals and interests (Hamamura et al., 2018; Panter-Brick et al., 2001). These groups contributed to a sense of belonging, fostered personal identities and roles for their members, and offered shared emotional bonds (Bess et al., 2002; Hamamura et al., 2018). Moreover, the resources of the people in groups helped them fend off threats from other humans and animals. Simply stated, groups offered power to their members, and as the people in such groups protected and cared for each other they formed social units that were effective contexts for the propagation and raising of offspring. Gathered into groups, humans reaped the benefits of community.

Today, more cultures across the world can be categorized as collectivist in comparison to individualist (Pedrotti & Isom, 2021), which may be in part at least because human beings always have had the shared characteristics of what social psychologist Elliot Aronson (2003) has called "social animals." In this regard, one of our strongest human motives is to belong—to feel as if we are connected in meaningful ways with other people (Baumeister & Leary, 1995). Social psychologists Roy Baumeister and Mark Leary (1995) and Donelson Forsyth (1999; Forsyth & Corazzini, 2000) and many others (see Begus et al., 2020; Oyserman & Dawson, 2021) have argued that people prosper when they join together into social units to pursue shared goals.

Core Emphases in Collectivism

Now, let's return to Figure 2.1. As shown there, when the average person in a society is disposed toward group interdependence, that society is labeled collectivist (see the bell-shaped curve drawn with the solid line). At this point, you may be curious as to which country most markedly adheres to collectivistic values. In response to this question, research suggests that China is one of the most collectivistic of the various nations around the globe (see Davis & Wu, 2019; Oyserman, 2017).

The three core emphases of collectivism are (a) dependence, (b) conformity, or the desire to fit in, and (c) perception of the group as the fundamental unit of analysis. First, the dependency within collectivism reflects a genuine tendency to draw one's very meaning and existence from being part of an important group of people. In collectivism, the person goes along with the expectations of the group, is highly concerned about the welfare of the group, and is very dependent upon the other members of the group to which they belong (Markus & Kitayama, 1991; Oyserman & Dawson, 2021). The research also corroborates the fact that collectivism rests on a core sense of dependency, as well as an obligation or duty to the ingroup and a desire to maintain **harmony** between people (Oyserman, 2017; Oyserman et al., 2002).

Regarding the desire to fit in, Oyserman et al. (2002) wrote, "The core element of collectivism is the assumption that groups bind and mutually obligate individuals" (p. 5). As such, collectivism is an inherently social approach in which the movement is toward ingroups and away from outgroups. This differs sharply from views in individualist cultures, such as the United States where a desire to fit in is often shunned.

Turning to the third core emphasis, the group as the perceived unit of analysis, the social patterns in collectivist societies reflect close linkages in which people see themselves as part of a larger, more important whole. In brief, the collectivist concern is for the group as a whole rather than its constituents (Hofstede, 1980).

Collectivists are defined in terms of the characteristics of the groups to which they belong. Thus, collectivist-oriented people pay close attention to the rules and goals of the group and often may subjugate their personal needs to those of the group. Moreover, success and satisfaction stem from the group's reaching its desired goals and from feeling that one has fulfilled the socially prescribed duties as a member of that effective, goal-directed, group effort (Oyserman & Dawson, 2021). Collectivist people obviously become very involved in the ongoing activities and goals of their group, and they think carefully about the obligations and duties of the groups to which they belong (Feinberg et al., 2019). Furthermore, the interchanges between people within the collectivist perspective are characterized by mutual generosity and equity (Toikko & Rantanen, 2020).

Because of their attention to the guidelines as defined by the group, the individual members with a collectivist perspective may be rather formal in their interactions. That is, there are carefully followed, role-defined ways of behaving.

FACTORS IMPACTING HOW STRENGTHS MANIFEST IN ME VS WE CULTURES

The Stories We Tell: Value Systems

As we have already discussed, cultural value systems (including individualist and collectivist perspectives) have significant effects on what a cultural group determines to be a strength a versus weakness (Pedrotti & Edwards, 2014, 2017; Pedrotti et al., 2021). Commonly told childhood stories in both Eastern and Western cultures teach lessons about what is "right" and can give examples of valued traits in this way, and so we would like to share some with you here. The Japanese story "*Momotaro*" ("Peach Boy," Sakade, 1958) gives an excellent example of the cultural importance of the traits of interdependence, the ability to avoid conflict, and duty to the group within Eastern traditions. The story begins with an elderly couple who have always wished for a child, although they are not able to conceive. One day, as the woman is washing her clothes in a stream, a giant peach floats to where she is standing and, upon reaching the woman, splits open to reveal a baby! The woman takes Momotaro home, and she and her husband raise him. At the age of 15, to the great pride of his parents, he decides to go to fight the ogres who have been tormenting the village and to bring back their treasure to his community. Along the way, Momotaro befriends many animals one by one. The animals want to fight each new animal they meet, but at Momotaro's urging, "The spotted dog and the monkey and the pheasant, who usually hated each other, all became good friends and followed Momotaro faithfully" (Sakade, 1958, p. 6). At the end of the story, Momotaro and his animal

Momotaro and His Animal Friends
iStockphoto.com/Mknoxgray

friends defeat the ogres by working together and bring the treasure back to the village, where all who live there share in the bounty. As the hero, Momotaro portrays the strengths valued in Japanese and other Asian cultures: (1) He sets out for the good of the group, although in doing so risks individual harm (collectivism); (2) along the way, he stops others from petty squabbling (promoting harmony); (3) he works with these others to achieve his goal (interdependence and collaboration); and (4) he brings back a treasure to share with the group (interdependence and sharing).

This story highlights important Eastern values and differs sharply from common Western stories. First, in most Western fairytales, the hero is fighting alone (which is usually viewed as valiant and brave) and takes dangers on single-handedly, as is the case with the princes in *Sleeping Beauty* and *Rapunzel* and the title character in *The Valiant Little Tailor* (Grimm & Grimm, as cited in Tatar, 2002). These types of tales show that individual independence is often valued over needing others' assistance. In instances where the hero does accept help from another, there is often a price involved where the "helper" makes sure that they also personally benefit from the transaction. Such examples can be found in the classic Western tale of *Rumpelstiltskin* (Grimm & Grimm), where the title character offers to help the maiden only if he can be promised her firstborn in return, or *The Little Mermaid* (Andersen, as cited in Tatar, 2002), where the Sea Witch will only help the Little Mermaid to gain legs to meet her love if she surrenders her beautiful voice to the witch. This more closely follows the Western value on personal gain despite potential loss to another, and to some extent is a cautionary tale in terms of what can happen when you accept help (these characters often come to bad ends). Finally, many stories emphasize the hero seeking personal fortune (or payment for service in the form of a bride or kingdom), but few discuss seeking fortune for the community (without any payment) as occurs in many Eastern stories.

"I will help you, but only if you give your first born to me!"
iStockphoto.com/ZU_09

A discussion of fairytales is not often included in a scholarly publication such as this; however, these stories tell the tale of our cultural values, and they have been used throughout the ages to promote some behaviors and to decry others. Here it is clear that cultural orientation determines which characteristics are transmitted as the valued strengths to its members.

Orientation to Time

Differences also exist between East and West in terms of their orientations to time. In Western cultures such as the United States, individuals who follow this mindset (particularly within the majority culture) often look to the future. Indeed, some of the strengths that are valued most (e.g., hope, optimism, self-efficacy; see Chapter 8) reflect future-oriented thinking. In Eastern cultures, however, there is a greater focus on and respect for the past. This past-oriented focus is revealed in the ancient Chinese proverb, "To know the road ahead, ask those coming back." Thus, Eastern cultures value the strength of "looking backward" and recognizing the wisdom of their elders, whereas Western cultures are more firmly focused on the future.

Thought Processes

When considering the unique aspects of Western and Eastern thought, we often focus on the nature of specific ideas, but we do not as commonly reflect on the process of linking and integrating ideas. Indeed, as researchers (e.g., Nisbett, 2003) have noted, stark differences exist in the very thought processes used by Westerners and Easterners, and this results in markedly divergent worldviews and approaches to meaning making. Richard Nisbett, Professor Emeritus at the University of Michigan who studied social psychology and cognition during his career illustrates how he, as a Westerner, became aware of some of these differences in thinking during a conversation he had with a student from China. Nisbett (2003) recalls,

> A few years back, a brilliant student from China began to work with me on questions of social psychology and reasoning. One day early in our acquaintance, he said, "You know, the difference between you and me is that I think the world is a circle, and you think it is a line." The Chinese believe in constant change, but with things always moving back to some prior state. They pay attention to a wide range of events; they search for relationships between things; and they think you can't understand the part without understanding the whole. Westerners live in a simpler, more deterministic world; they focus on salient objects or people instead of the larger pictures; and they think they can control events because they know the rules that govern the behavior of objects. (p. xiii)

As Nisbett's story shows, the thinking style used by the Chinese student, and not just the ideas themselves, was vastly different from Nisbett's. This more circular thinking style is best exemplified by the Taoist figure of the *yin* and the *yang.* Most people are familiar with the *yin* and *yang* symbol. This figure represents the circular, constantly changing nature of the world as viewed by Eastern thought. This more circular thinking pattern affects the way in which the Eastern thinker maps out their life and therefore may influence the decisions a person makes in the search for peace. Whereas in the United States we give high priority to the right to "life, liberty, and the pursuit of happiness," the goals of the Easterner might have a different focus. Take, for instance, the positive psychological construct of happiness (see Chapter 6). Researchers have posited that happiness (whether group or individual) is a state commonly sought by Easterners and Westerners alike (Diener et al., 1995). The difference in the philosophical approaches to life, however, may make the searches look very different. For example, a Westerner whose goal is happiness draws a straight line to that goal, looking carefully for obstacles and finding possible ways around them. Their goal is to achieve this eternal happiness, and the strength of hope is used to achieve this. For the Easterner who follows the *yin* and the *yang*, however, this goal of happiness may not make sense (Wong & Liu, 2018). If one were to seek happiness and then achieve it, in the Eastern way of thinking, this would only mean that unhappiness was close on its heels. Instead, the Easterner might have the goal of balance (perhaps based more on using the strength of endurance), trusting in the fact that, although great unhappiness or suffering may occur in one's life, it would be equally balanced by great happiness. These two different types of thinking obviously create very different ways of forming goals to achieve the good life.

Yin Yang
iStockphoto.com/Grace Maina

East and West: Is One Best?

There are substantial differences in the types of ideas and the ways in which those ideas are put together that emerge from Eastern and Western traditions, and it is important to remember that neither is inherently "better" than the other. This is especially relevant for discussions regarding strengths as we must use culture as a lens for evaluating whether a particular characteristic might be considered a strength or a weakness within a particular group. This said, there are some particular benefits and pitfalls that seem to align with one or another of the two mindsets that are perhaps particularly relevant today.

As we move out of the COVID-19 pandemic, research explaining some of the behaviors surrounding mask wearing and limiting social interaction is beginning to emerge, in addition to some of the impacts of these on well-being, and some of these relate to individualist versus collectivist cultural orientation. Several studies found that more collectivist countries (e.g., China) and regions (e.g., the South Pacific and Africa) were better able to contain the spread of COVID-19 "because of a vigilant public concerned for public safety and compliant with public safety measure" (Liu & Wang, 2021, p. 23). Further research supported that "greater collectivism is associated with more support for and uptake of COVID-19 prevention behaviors" (Card, 2022, p. 417), and this has been shown in a number of studies (e.g., Cho et al., 2022; Lu & Jin, 2021). Liu and Wang (2021) additionally suggest that adherence to individualism and preference for one's own freedom as opposed to concern for the group impacted countries like the United States greatly in terms of coordination in fighting the pandemic. Others found similar results in cross-country comparisons (Jiang et al., 2021; Webster et al., 2021). That said, additional researchers have shown that there is more nuance to predicting a particular cultural response than simply looking at collectivist or individualist tendencies. Card (2022) investigated the role of personality in the COVID-19 pandemic, specifically looking at the Big 5, and found that the personality trait of Agreeableness was the largest predictor of overall COVID-19 prevention behaviors, personal hygiene efforts, and social distancing. Second in each of these predictive relationships was Conscientiousness (Card, 2022).

A second area of research surrounding collectivism and individualism is also very relevant to today's political climate. Lin et al. (2022) found that those higher in collectivist beliefs are more likely to believe what has recently been termed "fake news" and to find it meaningful, as well as show a higher propensity to believe in pseudoscience in general. These researchers suggest that sometimes economic conditions can create a propensity toward collectivism and a dependence on this ingroup. Biddlestone and colleagues (2020) conducted research and found different results supporting the idea that those highest in "vertical individualism" (i.e., belief in a hierarchical power system in addition to individualism) were most likely to believe in conspiracy theories and less likely to engage in social distancing. Regardless, both studies seem to provide evidence for identity factors related to individualism and collectivism (i.e., "I am X, thus I belong to this group, and **we** think Y") being used to make decisions about how to act during the pandemic and in other crises (see also Kitayama et al., 2022; Oyserman & Dawson, 2021). This is something that likely all of us can relate to seeing firsthand, with the strong political party divide that has seemed to intensify in the United States in recent years. As groups see themselves as more insular to the ingroup and more dissimilar to the outgroup, belief in empty claims appears to increase (Lin et al., 2022; Oyserman & Dawson, 2021).

More research is needed in these areas and is emerging daily, but perhaps a better understanding of how collectivist and individualist ideologies might interact with personality traits and external circumstances may assist us in working toward more healthy outcomes for all in the future.

PERSONAL MINI-EXPERIMENTS

GETTING AND GIVING HELP

In this chapter, we explore how the sense of community can promote optimal human functioning. The following exercises encourage you to think about how your relationships to others and the broader community can make a positive difference in your life.

Asking for Help. A primary way in which individualists and collectivists differ is in the cultural messages they receive regarding asking for help. If you are more on the individualist side, and thus a person who finds it difficult to ask for the help of another, this exercise offers you a chance to break that habit. Select some activity for which you are especially unlikely to ask for help, and the next time you are in this situation, instead of trying to struggle through it by yourself, go ahead and ask another person for a hand. Here are some questions to ask yourself about a recent situation in which you could have asked for help:

1. Describe the circumstance, including all your thoughts and feelings. What did you imagine people would say if you asked for help? What would you have thought about yourself if you had asked for help?
2. Did you ask for help? If not, why not? If so, how did you overcome your rule of not asking for help?
3. How did the situation turn out when you did ask for help? What were the reactions of the person you asked for help? Did you get the needed help? If you did, how did you feel? Do you think you could ask for help in a future, similar situation?

Part of being in a community is being able to call upon the people in that community for assistance. Contrary to what some of you may have been taught as an individualist about not asking for help, it is not a weakness to ask for help. Indeed, it is a strength. You are human. You do need other people to get things accomplished. This is not a bad thing but a wonderful reality that is part of being a member of a community. As we have suggested in this exercise, give it a try. Once people do, they rarely turn back.

Volunteering Your Help. Remember the last time you offered your assistance to someone else? It probably took very little of your time, and you made a small improvement in your community. The other beautiful aspect of offering help is that it feels absolutely wonderful. (See the Personal Mini-Experiments in Chapter 11.) Helping thus provides two benefits: one to the recipient and one to the giver. To implement this exercise, just look around your local community and watch your neighbors. Part of this may be a simple wave or greeting. At other times, it may be obvious that someone really could use a helping hand. There are many flat tires needing to be fixed, people who need assistance carrying packages, tourists needing directions, and so on. To see how you have fared in this exercise, answer the following questions:

1. Describe the last circumstance in which you noticed that a person needed help, and include all your thoughts and feelings. What did you imagine people would say if you offered help? What did you think about yourself after offering help?
2. Did you offer help? If not, why not? If you did, how were you able to overcome any rule to the contrary (such as "Don't bother others")?
3. How did the situation turn out when you offered help? How did the person to whom you offered help react? Did you give the needed help? If you did, how did you feel? Do you think you could do this again in a future, similar situation?

EXEMPLAR CONSTRUCTS IN INDIVIDUALIST AND COLLECTIVIST CULTURES

So far, we have discussed how values, thinking styles, and orientation to time influence the development of goals in the lives of both Westerners and Easterners. Differences also exist, related to these, in the routes that each group uses to move toward its goals. Western-oriented thinking focuses on the individual's goal, whereas Eastern philosophers suggest a different focus, one in which the group is highlighted. Here, we detail constructs that may have particular value to the different groups. For Western cultures, the construct of hope is a key component mentioned throughout time. Additionally, the need for uniqueness is something that marks individualist cultures. For Eastern cultures, the constructs of compassion and harmony are highly valued.

"The Rugged Individualist" and the Construct of Hope

Hope has been a powerful underlying force in Western civilization. Indeed, looking back through the recorded history of Western civilization and religion, hope—the agentic, goal-focused thinking that gets one from here to there—has been so interwoven into the fabric of our civilization's eras and events that it can be hard to detect. In this regard, the belief in a positive future is reflected in many of our everyday ideas and words.

During the Dark Ages, intellectual and social immobility pervaded, and a paralysis of curiosity and initiative existed. From the years of the Middle Ages (500–1500), such paralysis precluded the purposeful, sustained planning and action required by a hopeful, advancing society. The fires of advancement were reduced to embers during this dark millennium and kept glowing only by a few institutions such as the monasteries and their schools. With the advent of the Renaissance, hope was seen as more relevant to present life on Earth than to the afterlife, and these active and hopeful thoughts began to be coupled with goal-directed actions. The period following the Renaissance, the Age of Enlightenment, created an atmosphere conducive to exploration and change and reflected the nature of hope because of its emphases on rational agencies and rational abilities. These qualities were interwoven in the dominant belief of the age: that reason brought to life with the scientific method led to the achievements in science and philosophy. Education, free speech, and the acceptance of new ideas burgeoned during the Enlightenment. Indeed, the consequences of such enlightened thinking were long lasting and reflective of the power of hope. Next, the period known as the Industrial Revolution (or the Age of Industrialization) drove movement of production from homes and small workshops to large factories and vastly increased material benefits for individual citizens making hope for the future seem more attainable.

Western civilization has been defined by its critical mass of hopeful events and beliefs. Throughout the Renaissance, the Enlightenment, and the Industrial Revolution, hopeful thinking was a critical part of the Western belief system, and the idea of hope has long served as an underpinning for thinking in Western civilization. Personal and individual goals, as exemplified by the construct of hope, seem to be the primary tool of the Western "rugged individualist" in moving toward their depiction of the good life.

The Need for Uniqueness

Let's take another look at Figure 2.1. You will notice that the two curves overlap with some people toward the group end of the continuum and others toward the individual end. In this latter regard, we now explore the desire to manifest specialness relative to other people.

The pursuit of individualistic goals to produce a sense of specialness has been termed the need for uniqueness (see Lynn & Snyder, 2002; Ruvio et al., 2008; Vignoles, 2009). This need is posited to have a strong appeal to many, as people often seek to maintain some degree of difference from others (as well as to maintain a bond to other people). In the 1970s, researchers Howard Fromkin and C. R. Snyder (see Snyder & Fromkin, 1977) embarked on a program of research based on the premise that most people in Western groups have some desire to be special relative to others. They called this motive

iStockphoto.com/Ivan-balvan

the *need for uniqueness;* others have termed it the *motive for distinctiveness* (Vignoles, 2009). Beyond establishing that some specialness was desirable for most of the people in their samples from the United States, these researchers also reasoned that some people have a very high need for uniqueness, or distinctiveness, whereas others have a very low need for uniqueness.

Encoding and Emotional/Behavioral Reactions to Similarity Information

As noted previously, people evaluate the acceptability of their having varying degrees of similarity to other people. These hypothetical encodings on the uniqueness identity dimension are shown in Figure 2.2. As can be seen, the similarity information is encoded as increasingly higher in acceptability, until one gets to a very high level of similarity in which it becomes clear that people desire some specialness. It should be noted that people in Western cultural groups seem least comfortable with either of the extremes of low similarity (point A in Figure 2.2) or high similarity (point E in Figure 2.2).

When confronted with the varying degrees of perceived similarity that produce the acceptability encodings of Figure 2.2, people then should have the most positive emotional reactions when they perceive that they are highly similar to others (point D in Figure 2.2). Consistent with this hypothesis, people's emotional reactions become more positive as levels of similarity increase from the very slight, to slight, to moderate, to high, becoming negative as the level of similarity enters the very high range (Figure 2.3). Note that the very highest positive emotional reactions occur when people perceive that they have a relatively moderate to high degree of similarity, thereby showing the maximal pleasure derived from human bonds.

FIGURE 2.2 ■ Acceptability Encoding as a Function of Perceived Similarity to Other People

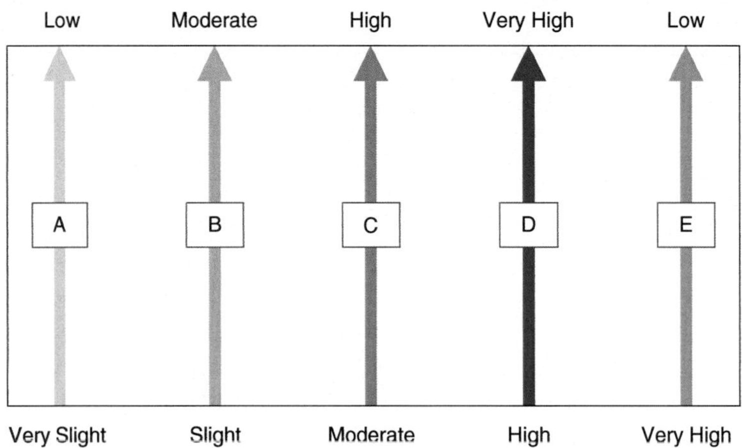

FIGURE 2.3 ■ Emotional Reactions as a Function of Perceived Similarity to Other People

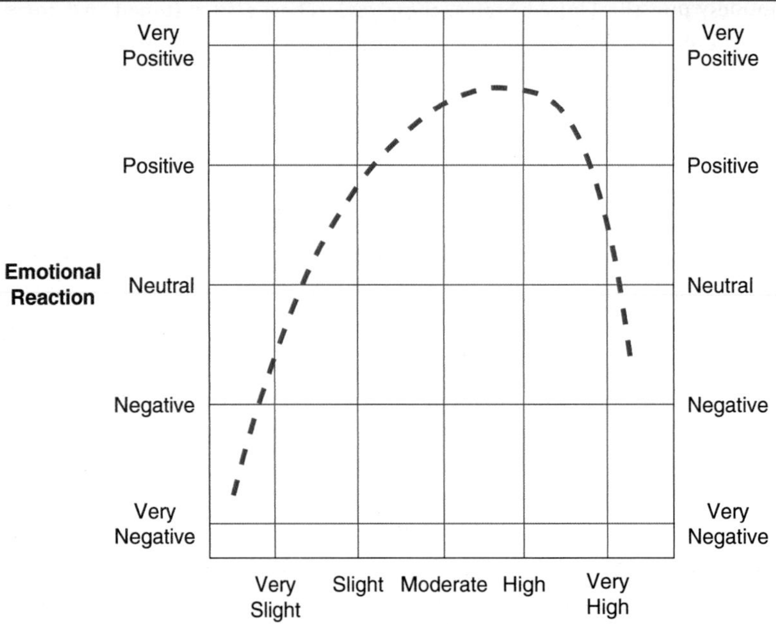

It may help here to give an example of how moderate similarity to another person is emotionally satisfying. I (JTP) reflect upon my initial reaction at moving from California to the Midwest for graduate school as a good example of the desire for moderate similarity. At first, I was a bit taken aback at being one of very few individuals of racial minority background on my new campus. Feeling very different was a challenge at first, and looking for some similarity in fellow students became a goal of mine. It was a stroke of good luck that another student in my cohort shared this circumstance and was having a similar experience. We soon discovered that we were also both of biracial descent, although of different racial groups. This moderate similarity provided us with some shared experiences and understandings, while still allowing for our own individual differences. From time to time, however, and especially when we were in graduate school, others confused us for one another from time to time. Although neither of us believe that we look much alike, we both have dark hair that was approximately the same length at the time, and both of our skin tones are a bit darker than the average majority culture person in the Midwest. We have discussed our negative reaction to others thinking we "looked exactly alike" or confusing our names at times. Here, similarity was presented as too great—we desired some uniqueness, even though a moderate level of similarity was fine. Our friendship has now lasted more than 20 years, and as we have moved through other experiences in life (parenthood, professional development, etc.), we continue to enjoy the emotional satisfaction that comes from having these moderate similarities.

The acceptability reactions that result from a degree of perceived similarity to others (see Figure 2.2) also can cause people to change their actual behaviors to become more or less similar to another person. More specifically, the most positive acceptability (i.e., high similarity) not only produces the highest positive emotional reactions but also should result in no need to make any behavioral changes relative to other people. On the other hand, a very slight level of similarity to others yields low acceptability; therefore, people should change to become more similar to others. Moreover, a very high level of similarity to other people is low in acceptability, and therefore people should change to become less similar to others. In this latter sense, because people's need for uniqueness is not being satisfied, they should strive to reestablish their differences. Consistent with these predicted behavioral reactions, the results of several studies (see Figure 2.4) have supported this proposed pattern (Snyder & Fromkin, 1980).

Taken together, these findings suggest that people in Western cultures such as those studied in the research elucidated here are drawn to moderate-to-high levels of perceived similarity to their fellow humans but that there are upper limits to this desire for the human bond. Furthermore, there appears to be a desire for balance in this area, such that people are motivated by a need for uniqueness when they feel too much similarity and that they will strive for similarity when they feel too different. Based on the previously discussed theoretical predictions and findings on uniqueness-related behaviors, Snyder and Fromkin (1977) developed and validated the Need for Uniqueness Scale. If you would like to get a sense of your own desire for specialness by completing the scale, refer to the Appendix.

Having explored the personal need for uniqueness, at this point we describe the acceptable societal processes by which our uniqueness needs are met. People are punished when they

FIGURE 2.4 ■ Direction and Amount of Change as a Function of Perceived Similarity to Other People

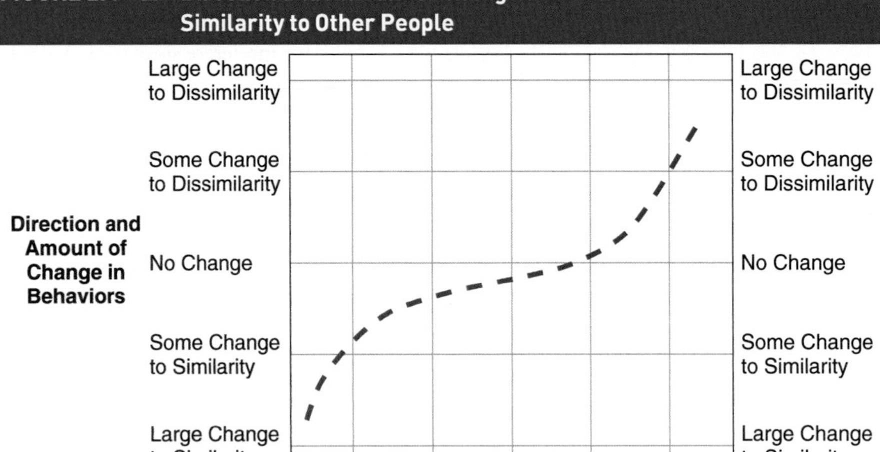

deviate sharply from normal or expected behaviors in a society (Goffman, 1963; Schachter, 1951). Thus, unusual behaviors quickly may elicit societal disapprovals and rejections (see Kaufman et al., 2022; Schur, 1969). On the other hand, the following of rules (normal behaviors) typically does not elicit much reaction from other people. How, then, are people to show their specialness? Fortunately, each society has some acceptable attributes whereby its citizens can show their differences without being labeled as deviant, and these are called *uniqueness attributes*. One example may be found in the attractiveness to "scarce commodities" in our society. Salespeople know this is a desire and often use a "Hurry on down while the supply lasts" pitch to draw in potential buyers. In what has been called a "catch-22 carousel" (Snyder, 1992), advertisers use uniqueness appeals to persuade people to buy products and then, by making yearly changes in their products (styles of clothes, cars, etc.), motivate customers to purchase the latest version. The irony is that, after the latest uniqueness-based advertisement has persuaded people to buy, they notice that what they have bought is now quite common—many other people also have it. Of course, the yearly change of styles keeps people on the consumer "catch-22 carousel." Other studies have noted that when leaders attend to individuals' needs for uniqueness, they may be seen as more inclusive (Randel et al., 2017), and that more valuing of differentness in general (termed "embracing weirdness" by these authors) may create more inclusive leaders (Davidson, 2021, p. 125; see the whole chapter for more on this interesting topic).

We have reviewed the theory and measurement of hope and the need for uniqueness, which are perhaps two of the quintessential Western constructs. We now turn to the Eastern side, for a closer look at two more collectivist constructs: compassion and harmony.

Eastern Values: Compassion and Harmony

In the main Eastern philosophical branches of learning (Confucianism, Taoism, Buddhism, and Hinduism), repeated mention is made of two constructs: compassion for others and the search for harmony or life balance. Thus, each has a clear place in the study of positive psychology from an Eastern perspective.

Though the idea of compassion is discussed in both Western and Eastern philosophies, it is more frequently written about in Eastern traditions. In Confucian teachings, compassion is discussed within the concept of *humanity* and is said to encapsulate all other virtues, while within the Hindu tradition, compassion is called for in good actions toward others as it will direct followers upon the path that will not require them to return to Earth after death. Compassion is most thoroughly discussed however in Buddhist writings, with the Buddha often described as "perfectly enlightened, and boundlessly compassionate" (Sangharakshita, 1991, p. 3).

Buddhist teachings describe the attainment of compassion as the ability to "transcend preoccupation with the centrality of self" (Cassell, 2009, p. 397). As such, the idea of compassion, or *karuna*, also is woven throughout Buddhism as a virtue on the path toward transcendence. The ability to possess feelings for something completely separate from our own suffering allows us to transcend the self and, in this way, to be closer to the achievement of the "good life." In fact, transcendental compassion is said to be the most significant of the four universal virtues and it often is called Great Compassion (*mahakaruna*) to distinguish it from the more applied *karuna* (Sangharakshita, 1991).

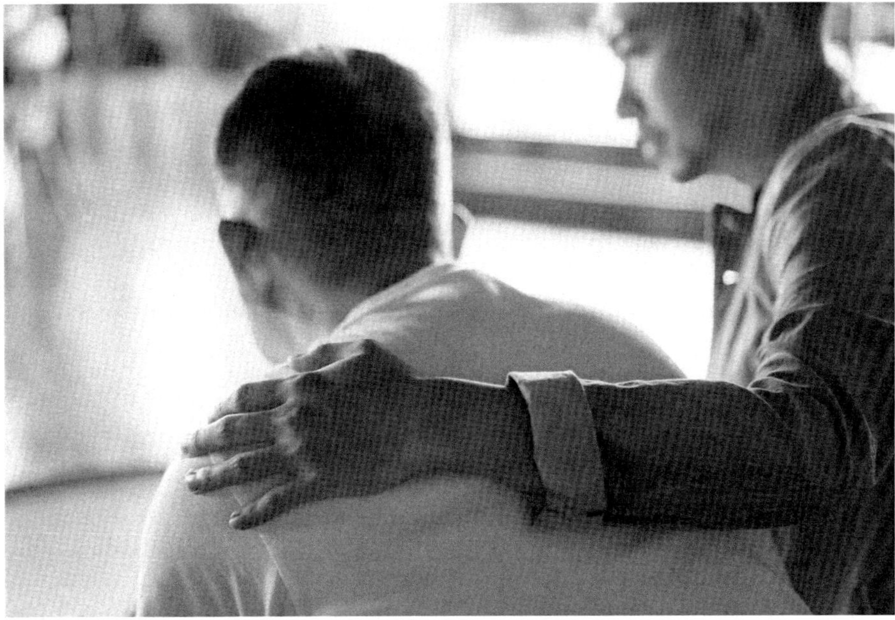

iStockphoto.com/AsiaVision

In more recent writings in positive psychology, physician Eric Cassell (2021) proposes the three following requirements for compassion to occur: (1) the difficulties of the recipient must be serious, (2) the recipient's difficulties cannot be self-inflicted, and (3) we, as observers, must be able to identify with the recipient's suffering. Compassion is described as a "unilateral emotion" (Cassell, 2009, p. 394) that is directed outward from oneself. Similarly, although discussed in somewhat different ways as Confucian, Taoist, and Hindu principles, the capacities to feel and to do for others are central to achieving the "good life" for each of these traditions as well. Furthermore, acting compassionately fosters group, rather than personal, happiness and can be used to ease suffering overall (Cassell, 2016, 2021). Compassion also may come more naturally to a person from a collectivist culture than to someone from an individualist culture. On this point, researchers have argued that a collectivist culture may breed a sense of compassion in the form of its members' prosocial behaviors (Batson, 1991; Batson et al., 2009; Calder et al, 2022). When a group identity has been formed, therefore, the natural choice may be group benefits over individual ones. More information from qualitative and quantitative studies in this area would be helpful in defining the mechanisms used to foster such compassion.

In addition to compassion, though related, happiness is described in Eastern philosophies as having the "satisfactions of a plain country life, shared within a *harmonious* social network" (Nisbett, 2003, pp. 5–6, emphasis added). In this tradition, harmony is viewed as central to achieving happiness. In Western history, the Greeks are said to have viewed happiness as the ability "to exercise powers in pursuit of excellence in a life free from constraints" (Nisbett, 2003, pp. 2–3). Thus, the good life was viewed as a life with no ties to duty and the freedom to pursue individual goals. There are clear distinctions in comparing this idea of happiness to Confucian teachings, for example, in which duty (*yi*) is a primary virtue.

In Buddhist teachings, when people reach a state of nirvana, they have reached a peacefulness entailing "complete harmony, balance, and equilibrium" (Sangharakshita, 1991, p. 135). Similarly, in Confucian teachings, harmony is viewed as crucial for happiness, and getting along with others allows the person to be freed from individual pursuits and, in so doing, to gain "collective agency" (Nisbett, 2003, p. 6) in working out what is good for the group. Thus, the harmonizing principle is a central tenet of the Eastern way of life. The balance and harmony that one achieves as part of an enlightened life often are thought to represent the ultimate end of the good life.

The concept of harmony has received minimal attention in the field of positive psychology to date, although some attention has been given to the idea of appreciating balance in one's life in reference to certain other constructs (e.g., wisdom; see Baltes & Staudinger, 2000, and Chapter 9). Moreover, Clifton and colleagues (Buckingham & Clifton, 2001; Lopez, Hodges, & Harter, 2005) include a harmony theme in the Clifton StrengthsFinder (see Chapter 3); they describe this construct as a desire to find consensus among the group, as opposed to putting forth conflicting ideas. Some research appears to find in inverse relationship between harmony and depression but only in individuals who define themselves by cultural models that emphasize reliance on others (Smith & Bryant, 2016; Yang, 2016), that is, those that are collectivist in nature. This shows the importance of taking context into account when describing a strength. Given the central role of harmony as a strength in Eastern cultures, more research may be warranted on this topic in the future. Finally, after more conceptual work is completed, positive psychology scholars interested in harmony would benefit greatly from the development of reliable and valid measuring devices. Such tools would help researchers to uncover the primary contributors and correlates of harmony.

ME/WE BALANCE: THE POSITIVE PSYCHOLOGY OF US

Both the Individualistic and the Collectivistic Perspectives Are Viable

Social scientists often have conceptualized individualism and collectivism as opposites (Hui, 1988; Oyserman et al., 2002), and this polarity typically has been applied when contrasting the individualism of European Americans with the collectivism of East Asians (Chan, 1994; Kitayama et al., 1997). This polarity approach strikes us as being neither good science nor necessarily a productive strategy for fostering healthy interactions among people from varying ethnicities within and across societies, and some research has shown that investigations of individualism and collectivism must be much more nuanced in order to fully understand how members of these groups function in the world (Card, 2022).

Viewing individualism and collectivism as opposites also has the potential to provoke disputes in which the members of each camp attempt to demonstrate the superiority of their approach. Such acrimony between these two perspectives seems especially problematic given that the distinctions between individualism and collectivism have not been found to be clear-cut. For example, Vandello and Cohen (1999) found that, even within individualistic societies such as the United States, the form of the individualism differs in the Northeast, the Midwest, the Deep South, and the West. Moreover, cultures are extremely diverse; each has dynamic and changing social systems that are far from the monolithic simplicities suggested by the labels "individualist" and "collectivist" (Bandura, 2000; Vargas & Kemmelmeier, 2013). Likewise, there may be generational differences in the degree to which individualism and collectivism are manifested (e.g., Matsumoto et al., 1996). And when different reference groups become more salient, propensities toward individualism and collectivism vary (Freeman & Bordia, 2001). Finally, we've seen in research described here that individualism and collectivism may interact with specific personality traits that may elicit different types of behavior within a single tradition (Card, 2022).

The United States has always been thought of as a very individualistic nation. Current reports, however, suggest that this may have had more to do with the fact that the majority of individuals living in the United States were originally of European (Western) origin. Interestingly, today, as racial and ethnic diversity increases in the United States, changes are beginning to emerge with regard to the individualist orientation of the country as a whole. Today, there is preliminary "evidence of convergence of cultural orientations" (Vargas & Kemmelmeier, 2013, p. 195). In this way, perhaps due to its unique diversity of cultural influences, the United States is becoming more of an "US" nation. That said, there are still verifiable differences between cultural groups (e.g., Black American, Latina/o/x, Asian American, and White) that appear to be related to systematic socioeconomic differences between these groups

(Vargas & Kemmelmeier, 2013). These distinct economic differences are most marked between White Americans/Asian Americans versus their Black/Latina/o/x counterparts. The fact that the economically disadvantaged groups are lower in competitiveness is a finding that might suggest a sense of hopelessness at being able to compete in the first place due to their disadvantages. It is also a possibility that cooperation is more necessary in lower socioeconomic status groups. If our goal is to see more of an understanding of both individualistic and collectivistic mindsets, and a potential convergence toward each other to some extent, we may need to work harder to extend economic equality across cultural groups.

Based on findings such as these and others, researchers in the field have suggested that we should move beyond the rather static view of individualism and collectivism as separate categories and instead take more dynamic approaches to culture to find when, where, and why these mental sets operate (Card, 2022). They argue for an understanding of how individualism and collectivism can operate together to benefit people. We, too, believe that both the individualist and collectivistic perspectives have advantages for people and that the best resolution is to learn to embrace aspects of each.

One characteristic of a happy and productive life is a sense of balance in one's views and actions. We believe that a positive psychology approach to this issue would equate the ME and the WE emphases. The ME/WE perspective allows a person to attend to both the person and the group. Indeed, this is what has been found to characterize the perspectives of high-hope people about their lives and their interactions with others (Snyder, 1994/2000c, 2000b). That is to say, in their upbringings, the high-hope children learned about the importance of other people and their perspectives and the role that consideration for others plays in the effective pursuit of personal goals. Just as the high-hopers think of ME goals, then, they simultaneously can envision the WE goals of other people. In addition, being able to see things from a ME perspective and a WE perspective allows us all to interact with a larger group of individuals, even those who come from different perspectives than our own: "As the heterogeneity of American culture continues to expand, more opportunities for meaningful interaction between differing ethnic/racial groups have emerged than ever before" (Vargas & Kemmelmeier, 2013, p. 198). Being rigidly ME or WE may be problematic for these types of interactions.

Suggestions for ME People (Individualists)

You now should have better ideas about your individualist and collectivist tendencies (see the Personal Mini-Experiments in this chapter for more self-assessment). In this section and the next, therefore, we offer some suggestions to help you navigate more effectively in environments in which people hold perspectives that differ from the individualistic or collectivistic ones that you typically hold.

To begin, individualists often perceive collectivists as being far too conforming and lacking in competitiveness. In this regard, it helps to realize that collectivists derive their sense of status from their group memberships and not from their personal accomplishments. Individualists should understand that collectivists want interpersonal harmony and therefore try very hard to avoid situations involving conflict (Ting-Toomey, 1994). In such circumstances, the individualists may view conflicts as a useful means of clearing the air so that people can move on to other matters, but they should realize that collectivists are quite concerned with saving face after such conflicts. Thus, individualists can help by solving problems before they escalate into huge confrontations. Similarly, the individualist should not push the collectivist into a corner by repeatedly asking confrontational "Why?" questions in response to which the collectivist must defend their position. Moreover, if conflict is necessary, the individualist should try, whenever possible, to help the collectivist maintain their pride (what sociologists call *face* or *honor;* Oyserman, 2017).

Suggestions for WE People (Collectivists)

Collectivists, on the other hand, often see individualists as too competitive. Similarly to what is stated above, a useful lesson here is to understand that individualists see their status as based on their personal accomplishments rather than on their memberships in groups. Moreover, the more recent the accomplishments, the more power they wield in terms of status. Thus, collectivists should not be shocked when individualists do not seem impressed with group successes that are based in large part on lineage, family name, age, or gender (males may have more status in some collectivistic societies). It may help collectivists to use recent accomplishments to attain status in the eyes of individualists with whom they interact.

Collectivists' dependence on cooperative solutions to dilemmas may not work when they are dealing with individualists. Instead, the collectivist must be able to take into account the "What's in it for me" perspective of the individualist in order to understand the latter's reactions during negotiations. Likewise, the normal arguing of individualists should not be interpreted by collectivists as intentionally hurtful behavior; this is just how the individualist conducts business. Thus, whereas a collectivist interacting with another collectivist may interpret "Let's have lunch" as a genuine invitation, it is often merely social talk when uttered by the individualist. Recognizing these cultural differences may help to diminish hurt feelings and misunderstandings, both of which can be detrimental to meaningful interactions between groups.

FINAL THOUGHTS

It is important to recognize that, in discussing Western and Eastern thoughts in this chapter, a central tenet of Eastern ways of life is broken in the decidedly Western, didactic teaching method used to bring this information to students of positive psychology. The traditional Easterner would object to the notion that the concepts here could be learned from mere words and would argue that only life experience would suffice. As part of Eastern teachings, self-exploration and actual hands-on experience are essential for true understanding of the concepts that are presented in only an introductory fashion in this chapter. Thus, we encourage students to seek out more experience of these ideas in everyday life and to attempt to discover the relevance of strengths such as hope, compassion, and harmony in your own lives, regardless of your cultural background. Ideas that stem from Eastern ideology can be relevant for Westerners who want to discover new ways of thinking about human functioning and vice versa. Challenge yourself to be open-minded about the types of characteristics to which you assign the label "strength" and about different perspectives, and remember that different traditions bring with them different values.

Additionally, those with individualist perspectives must realize that their views are not widely shared around the world. It has been estimated that 70% of the present 6.5 billion or so people on Earth take a collectivist view of people and their interactions (Triandis, 1995). Let's do the math here: *That is about 4.5 billion collectivists and 2 billion individualists.* As cherished as the individualist perspective held by many who reside in the United States may be, *individualists are the minority in a world populated by collectivists.* In thinking about our relationships with each other, our futures will rest upon a willingness to cooperate and come together. Although the pursuit of specialness certainly can and has produced benefits for humankind, if too many people act in pursuit of their own individuality especially at the expense of harmony, we will miss our chance to work together to build shared cultures.

WHERE WE ARE GOING: FROM ME TO WE TO US

In this chapter, we have discussed two important human frameworks—individualist and collectivist—and the historical traditions derived from them that are relevant to positive psychology. In closing this chapter, we propose that being able to use a blend of the one and the many—the ME/WE or, more simply, US—may enhance our ability to interact with a variety of others and spur our multicultural competence. This approach represents an intermingling in which both the individual and the group are able to be considered for satisfying and productive lives. Diversity can assist in productivity overall due to the increase of ideas and thinking strategies (Cunningham, 2009), but if leaders are not cognizant of the differences in how collectivists and individualists interact, this gain could be lost.

As we see it, the US perspective reflects a viable positive psychology resolution for a more multiculturally competent world. Some communications and psychology programs offer courses in intergroup dialogues or intergroup relations (see the University of Michigan's program at https://igr.umich.edu). The idea behind this type of program is to teach individuals to be able to listen to a perspective that differs from their own, particularly when coming from someone who is different culturally from them in some way. Understanding another perspective does not mean that we have to adopt that other perspective, but listening without anger and trying to see where others are coming from can help us to understand a bit more. The US perspective follows with this ideology in that in using it, we seek to move a bit more toward the middle ground so as to hear one another's diverse views.

Considering the increased global access we have to one another as technology shrinks the distance between us, and the ever-increasing diversity occurring in the United States in particular, we are poised on the cusp of a major change in the balancing of individualism and collectivism—the needs of the "one" and the "many" (Newbrough, 1995; Snyder, Feldman et al., 2000). As such, the positive psychology of US may be just around the corner.

APPENDIX: THE NEED FOR UNIQUENESS SCALE

Directions: The following statements concern your perceptions about yourself in several situations. Rate your agreement with each statement by using a scale in which 1 denotes strong disagreement, 5 denotes strong agreement, and 2, 3, and 4 represent intermediate judgments. In the blanks before each statement, place a number from 1 to 5 from the following scale:

1	2	3	4	5

Strongest Disagreement Strongest Agreement

There are no right or wrong answers, so select the number that most closely reflects you on each statement. Take your time, and consider each statement carefully.

_____ 1. When I am in a group of strangers, I am not reluctant to express my opinion publicly.

_____ 2. I find that criticism affects my self-esteem.

_____ 3. I sometimes hesitate to use my own ideas for fear that they might be impractical.

_____ 4. I think society should let reason lead it to new customs and throw aside old habits or mere traditions.

_____ 5. People frequently succeed in changing my mind.

_____ 6. I find it sometimes amusing to upset the dignity of teachers, judges, and "cultured" people.

_____ 7. I like wearing a uniform because it makes me proud to be a member of the organization it represents.

_____ 8. People have sometimes called me "stuck-up."

_____ 9. Others' disagreements make me uncomfortable.

_____10. I do not always need to live by the rules and standards of society.

_____11. I am unable to express my feelings if they result in undesirable consequences.

_____12. Being a success in one's career means making a contribution that no one else has made.

_____13. It bothers me if people think I am being too unconventional.

_____14. I always try to follow rules.

_____15. If I disagree with a superior on his or her views, I usually do not keep it to myself.

_____16. I speak up in meetings in order to oppose those whom I feel are wrong.

_____17. Feeling "different" in a crowd of people makes me feel uncomfortable.

_____18. If I must die, let it be an unusual death rather than an ordinary death in bed.

_____19. I would rather be just like everyone else than be called a "freak."

_____20. I must admit I find it hard to work under strict rules and regulations.

_____21. I would rather be known for always trying new ideas than for employing well-trusted methods.

_____22. It is better to agree with the opinions of others than to be considered a disagreeable person.

_____23. I do not like to say unusual things to people.

_____24. I tend to express my opinions publicly, regardless of what others say.

_____25. As a rule, I strongly defend my own opinions.

_____26. I do not like to go my own way.

_____27. When I am with a group of people, I agree with their ideas so that no arguments will arise.

_____28. I tend to keep quiet in the presence of persons of higher ranks, experience, etc.

_____29. I have been quite independent and free from family rule.

_____30. Whenever I take part in group activities, I am somewhat of a nonconformist.

_____31. In most things in life, I believe in playing it safe rather than taking a gamble.

_____32. It is better to break rules than always to conform with an impersonal society.

To calculate your total score, first reverse each of the scores on Items 2, 3, 5, 7, 9, 11, 13, 14, 17, 19, 22, 23, 26, 27, 28, and 31. That is, on these items only, perform the following reversals: 1 → 5; 2 → 4; 3 → 3; 4 → 2; 5 → 1. Then, add the scores on all 32 items, using the reversed scores for the aforementioned items. Higher scores reflect a higher need for uniqueness.

KEY TERMS

Anishinaabe Teachings
Athenian tradition
Buddhism
Collectivism
Compassion
Confucianism
Enlightenment
Harmony
Hinduism
Hope
Individualism
Islam
Judeo-Christian tradition
Need for uniqueness
Nirvana
Taoism

3 CLASSIFICATION AND MEASUREMENT IN POSITIVE PSYCHOLOGY

LEARNING OBJECTIVES

After reading this chapter, you will be able to:

3.1 Identify ways in which psychology has traditionally focused more on classifying and measuring human weaknesses than human strengths

3.2 Describe the development and underlying theories of two widely used classification systems of human strengths

3.3 Identify strengths and limitations of the assessment measures associated with two widely used classification systems of human strengths

3.4 Recognize how to use the information from a strengths-based assessment intentionally for self-improvement

3.5 Explain the importance of between-group and within-group cultural differences in the measurement of psychological strengths

3.6 Describe how to navigate and evaluate the vast array of measurement tools available in the positive psychology literature

> Let us imagine that one could set up a kind of scale or yardstick to measure the success of life—the satisfactoriness to the individual and the environment in their mutual attempts to adapt themselves to each other. Toward the end of such a yardstick, positive adjectives like "peaceful," "constructive," "productive," might appear, and at the other end such words as "confused," "destructive," "chaotic." These would describe the situation in general. For the individual . . . there might be at one end of the yardstick such terms as "healthy," "happy," "creative," and at the other end "miserable," "criminal," "delirious."
>
> —*Menninger et al. (1963, p. 2)*

Karl Menninger, one of the individuals who helped build the world-renowned Menninger Clinic, attempted to change how health care professionals viewed the diagnosis, prevention, and treatment of mental illness. As part of this mission, Menninger encouraged clinicians and researchers to dispense with the old, confusing labels of sickness. Then, he called for the development of a simple diagnostic system that described the life *process* rather than *states* or *conditions*. Finally, he reminded us of the power of the "sublime expressions of the life instinct" (Menninger et al., 1963, p. 357), specifically hope, faith, and love. Although the missions of many positive psychologists bear similarities to Menninger's ideas, there is still a long way to go in measuring human strengths (note: we subscribe to Linley and Harrington's [2006] definition of **strength** as a capacity for feeling, thinking, and behaving in a way that allows optimal functioning in the pursuit of valued outcomes).

One could easily argue that psychology in general has a better understanding of human weaknesses than strengths. In the 21st century, for example, two classifications of illness have attained worldwide acceptance. First, the World Health Organization's (2019) *International Classifications of Diseases* (*ICD*) is in its 11th edition and continues to evolve. Second, the American Psychiatric Association's (2022) *Diagnostic and Statistical Manual of Mental Disorders* (*DSM*) now is in its seventh iteration as the *DSM-5 TR*. The *ICD* is broader in scope than the *DSM* in that it classifies all diseases, whereas the *DSM* describes only mental disorders.

Currently, no classification of strengths or positive outcomes has achieved worldwide use or acceptance at the same level as either the DSM or the ICD. Nevertheless, some classifications have been created, refined, and broadly disseminated. While we recognize that it would be beyond the scope of this text to offer a thorough review of *all* positive psychology classification systems, we provide an in-depth overview of two such systems and their accompanying **assessments**: (1) The Gallup Themes of Talent (Buckingham & Clifton, 2001; Rath, 2007), as measured by the Clifton StrengthsFinder 2.0 and the Clifton Youth Strengths Explorer, and (2) The Values in Action (VIA) Classification of Strengths (Peterson & Seligman, 2004), as measured by the adult and youth versions of the VIA Inventory of Strengths. Specifically, in the first sections of this chapter, we discuss the conceptual definitions underlying these classification systems, along with their accompanying questionnaire measures and their **psychometric properties** (i.e., the measurement characteristics of each assessment). We comment on the **reliability** (i.e., the extent to which a measure is consistent internally and over time) and the **validity** (i.e., the extent to which a scale measures what it purports to measure) of these tools, as well as the cross-cultural applicability of each measure. Then, in the remaining sections, we provide a broad overview and guide to understanding other measures in positive psychology, and we emphasize the need for comprehensive and culturally sensitive assessments.

GALLUP'S CLIFTON STRENGTHS FINDER

Over his 50-year career at the University of Nebraska, Selection Research Incorporated, and Gallup, Donald Clifton[1] studied success across a wide variety of business and education domains (Clifton & Anderson, 2002; Prisant & Lesko, 2016; Rath, 2007). Clifton and colleagues based their analysis of success on a simple question: "What would happen if we studied what is right with people?" Clifton believed that talents could be operationalized, studied, and accentuated in work and academic settings. Specifically, he defined **talent** as "naturally recurring patterns of thought, feeling, or behavior that can be productively applied" (Hodges & Clifton, 2004, p. 257) and manifested in life experiences characterized by yearnings, rapid learning, satisfaction, and timelessness. Clifton considered these trait-like "raw materials" to be the products of normal, healthy development. Likewise, Clifton viewed strengths as extensions of talent. More precisely, the strength construct combines talent with associated knowledge and skills and is defined as the ability to provide consistent, near-perfect performance in a specific task.

Clifton constructed **empirically based** (i.e., grounded in theory and research findings), semistructured interviews for identifying talents. When developing these interviews, Clifton and colleagues examined the prescribed roles of a person (e.g., student, salesperson, administrator) and identified outstanding performers in these roles and settings. Moreover, the study team determined the longstanding thoughts, feelings, and behaviors relevant to success among these participants. These interviews also were useful in predicting positive outcomes (Schmidt & Rader, 1999) and subsequently were administered to more than 2 million people for the purposes of personal enrichment and employee selection. When considering the creation of a self-report questionnaire measure of talent in the mid-1990s, Clifton and colleagues systematically reviewed data from these interviews and identified about three dozen themes of talent involving enduring positive characteristics. These qualities eventually became the 34 themes used in a self-report questionnaire, the Clifton Strengths Finder (CSF; see Table 3.1 for a listing and description of the 34 themes assessed by the CSF; see also www.strengthsfinder.com for more information).

iStockphoto.com/aydinynr

TABLE 3.1 ■ The 34 Clifton Strengths Finder Themes

Achiever: People strong in the Achiever theme have a great deal of stamina and work hard. They take great satisfaction from being busy and productive.
Activator: People strong in the Activator theme can make things happen by turning thoughts into action. They are often impatient.
Adaptability: People strong in the Adaptability theme prefer to "go with the flow." They tend to be "now" people who take things as they come and discover the future one day at a time.
Analytical: People strong in the Analytical theme search for reasons and causes. They have the ability to think about all the factors that might affect a situation.
Arranger: People strong in the Arranger theme can organize, but they also have a flexibility that complements that ability. They like to figure out how all of the pieces and resources can be arranged for maximum productivity.
Belief: People strong in the Belief theme have certain core values that are unchanging. Out of those values emerges a defined purpose for their life.
Command: People strong in the Command theme have presence. They can take control of a situation and make decisions.
Communication: People strong in the Communication theme generally find it easy to put their thoughts into words. They are good conversationalists and presenters.
Competition: People strong in the Competition theme measure their progress against the performance of others. They strive to win first place and revel in contests.
Connectedness: People strong in the Connectedness theme have faith in links between all things. They believe there are few coincidences and that almost every event has a reason.
Consistency: People strong in the Consistency theme are keenly aware of the need to treat people the same. They try to treat everyone in the world with consistency by setting up clear rules and adhering to them.
Context: People strong in the Context theme enjoy thinking about the past. They understand the present by researching its history.
Deliberative: People strong in the Deliberative theme are best characterized by the serious care they take in making decisions or choices. They anticipate the obstacles.
Developer: People strong in the Developer theme recognize and cultivate the potential in others. They spot the signs of each small improvement and derive satisfaction from those improvements.
Discipline: People strong in the Discipline theme enjoy routine and structure. Their world is best described by the order they create.
Empathy: People strong in the Empathy theme can sense the feelings of other people by imagining themselves in others' lives and in others' situations.
Focus: People strong in the Focus theme can take a direction, follow through, and make the corrections necessary to stay on track.

Futuristic: People strong in the Futuristic theme are inspired by the future and what could be. They inspire others with their vision of the future.

Harmony: People strong in the Harmony theme look for consensus. They don't enjoy conflict; rather, they seek areas of agreement.

Ideation: People strong in the Ideation theme are fascinated by ideas. They are able to find connections between seemingly disparate phenomena.

Includer: People strong in the Includer theme are accepting of others. They show awareness of those who feel left out and make efforts to include them.

Individualization: People strong in the Individualization theme are intrigued with the unique qualities of each person. They have a gift for figuring out how people who are different can work together productively.

Input: People strong in the Input theme have a craving to know more. Often they like to collect and archive all kinds of information.

Intellection: People strong in the Intellection theme are characterized by their intellectual activity. They are introspective and appreciate intellectual discussions.

Learner: People strong in the Learner theme have a great desire to learn and want to improve continuously.

Maximizer: People strong in the Maximizer theme focus on strengths as a way to stimulate professional and group excellence. They seek to transform strengths into something superb.

Positivity: People strong in the Positivity theme have an enthusiasm that is contagious. They are upbeat and can get others excited about what they are going to do.

Relator: People who are strong in the Relator theme enjoy close relationships with others. They find deep satisfaction in working hard with friends to achieve a goal.

Responsibility: People strong in the Responsibility theme take psychological ownership of what they say they will do. They are committed to stable values such as honesty and loyalty.

Restorative: People strong in the Restorative theme are adept at dealing with problems. They are good at figuring out what is wrong and resolving it.

Self-Assurance: People strong in the Self-Assurance theme feel confident in their ability to manage their own lives. They possess an inner compass that gives them confidence that their decisions are right.

Significance: People strong in the Significance theme want to be very important in the eyes of others. They are independent and want to be recognized.

Strategic: People strong in the Strategic theme create alternative ways to proceed. Faced with any given scenario, they can quickly spot the relevant patterns and issues.

WOO: WOO stands for "winning others over." People strong in the WOO theme love the challenge of meeting new people and winning them over. They derive satisfaction from breaking the ice and making a connection with another person.

In the past two decades, extensive psychometric research on the CSF was conducted by Gallup researchers (and summarized in a technical report by Lopez, Hodges, & Harter, 2005), which resulted in the revised 177-item CSF 2.0 (Rath, 2007). The CSF 2.0 measures strengths by asking respondents to choose the option that "strongly describes me" between two trait descriptors (e.g., sensitive vs. logical) using a five-point scale. Responses to these items are used to calculate 34 talent themes, the top five of which are considered signature themes and are provided in a report to the respondent (see Figure 3.1 for a report of one of the original authors of this textbook, Dr. Shane Lopez).

Psychometric Properties of the CSF 2.0

With respect to reliability, CSF 2.0 scores have been found to be internally consistent (Asplund et al,. 2014; Asplund et al., 2016). In other words, if you score high on one item, you are likely to score high on other items in the measure with similar content. Specifically, the coefficient alphas have ranged from .52 to.79 (.70 or above is considered acceptable). Winning Others Over (WOO) scores had the highest **internal consistency** coefficients (.79), and Individualization, Input, and Relator scores evidenced the lowest (all below .60). The CSF has evidenced acceptable test-retest reliability over periods ranging from 1 week to 6 months. Specifically, test-retest reliability correlations were above .70, suggesting that CSF scores reflect stable characteristics. Regarding validity, Harter and Hodges (2003) correlated CSF themes with Big 5 personality constructs (openness, conscientiousness, extroversion, agreeableness, and neuroticism; McCrae & Costa, 1987). Their results provided initial evidence for the measures' convergent validity (i.e., they were correlated, but not at such a high level as to suggest redundancy between the CSF and the Big 5).

Today, the CSF is available in numerous languages, and it is modifiable for individuals with disabilities. It is appropriate for administration to adolescents and adults with reading levels at 10th grade level or higher. Although it is used to identify personal talents, the related supporting materials can help individuals discover how to build on their talents to develop strengths within their particular life roles. It should be noted, however, that this instrument is not designed or validated for use in employee selection or mental health screening. Another caveat also is warranted. Namely, given that CSF feedback (presented as your "Five Signature Themes") is provided to foster personal development, using it for comparisons of individual profiles is discouraged. Furthermore, the CSF is not sensitive to change, and as such, it should not be used as a pre–post measure of growth. Finally, it is important to note that, although the CSF 2.0 is a popular and widely used measure, it has received criticism for the way in which it assesses strengths. Specifically, researchers have documented how strengths can be overemphasized due to the unique question format of the CSF (Chara & Eppright, 2012). Such biases could impact the results of the instrument by influencing which signature strengths emerge for a particular person.

The CSF 2.0 has been used in several different populations, including business circles and college campuses. Asplund and colleagues (2016) noted, "The relationship between strengths-based employee development and performance at the business/work unit level is substantial and generalizable across organizations" (p. 2). Among college students, the CSF has been used in the broader framework of a strengths-based education (Lopez & Louis, 2009) in which students assess their strengths, and faculty provide tailored educational experiences based on signature strengths (Soria & Stubblefield, 2015). Use of the CSF 2.0 in college in this way (advising and

FIGURE 3.1 ■ Clifton StrengthsFinder Signature Themes for Shane Lopez

Your Signature Themes

Many years of research conducted by the Gallup Organization suggest that the most effective people are those who understand their strengths and behaviors. These people are best able to develop strategies to meet and exceed the demands of their daily lives, their careers, and their families.

A review of the knowledge and skills you have acquired can provide a basic sense of your abilities, but an awareness and understanding of your natural talents will provide true insight into the core reasons behind your consistent successes.

Your Signature Themes report presents your five most dominant themes of talent, in the rank order revealed by your responses to StrengthsFinder. Of the 34 themes measured, these are your "top five."

Your Signature Themes are very important in maximizing the talents that lead to your successes. By focusing on your Signature Themes, separately and in combination, you can identify your talents, build them into strengths, and enjoy personal and career success through consistent, near-perfect performance.

Futuristic

"Wouldn't it be great if. . . ." You are the kind of person who loves to peer over the horizon. The future fascinates you. As if it were projected on the wall, you see in detail what the future might hold, and this detailed picture keeps pulling you forward, into tomorrow. While the exact content of the picture will depend on your other strengths and interests—a better product, a better team, a better life, or a better world—it will always be inspirational to you. You are a dreamer who sees visions of what could be and who cherishes those visions. When the present proves too frustrating and the people around you too pragmatic, you conjure up your visions of the future, and they energize you. They can energize others, too. In fact, very often people look to you to describe your visions of the future. They want a picture that can raise their sights and thereby their spirits. You can paint it for them. Practice. Choose your words carefully. Make the picture as vivid as possible. People will want to latch on to the hope you bring.

Maximizer

Excellence, not average, is your measure. Taking something from below average to slightly above average takes a great deal of effort and in your opinion is not very rewarding. Transforming something strong into something superb takes just as much effort but is much more thrilling. Strengths, whether yours or someone else's, fascinate you. Like a diver after pearls, you search them out, watching for the telltale signs of a strength. A glimpse of untutored excellence, rapid learning, a skill mastered without recourse to steps—all these are clues that a strength may be in play. And having found a strength, you feel compelled to nurture it, refine it, and stretch it toward excellence. You polish the pearl until it shines. This natural sorting of strengths means that others see you as discriminating. You choose to spend time with people who appreciate your particular strengths. Likewise, you are attracted to others who seem to have found and cultivated their own strengths. You tend to avoid those who want to fix you and make you well rounded. You don't want to spend your life bemoaning what you lack. Rather, you want to capitalize on the gifts with which you are blessed. It's more fun. It's more productive. And, counterintuitively, it is more demanding.

(Continued)

FIGURE 3.1 ■ Clifton StrengthsFinder Signature Themes for Shane Lopez (Continued)

Arranger

You are a conductor. When faced with a complex situation involving many factors, you enjoy managing all the variables, aligning and realigning them until you are sure you have arranged them in the most productive conf guration possible. In your mind, there is nothing special about what you are doing. You are simply trying to figure out the best way to get things done. But others, lacking this theme, will be in awe of your ability. "How can you keep so many things in your head at once?" they will ask. "How can you stay so flexible, so willing to shelve well-laid plans in favor of some brand-new conf guration that has just occurred to you?" But you cannot imagine behaving in any other way. You are a shining example of effective flexibility, whether you are changing travel schedules at the last minute because a better fare has popped up or mulling over just the right combination of people and resources to accomplish a new project. From the mundane to the complex, you are always looking for the perfect conf guration. Of course, you are at your best in dynamic situations. Confronted with the unexpected, some complain that plans devised with such care cannot be changed, while others take refuge in the existing rules or procedures. You don't do either. Instead, you jump into the confusion, devising new options, hunting for new paths of least resistance, and figuring out new partnerships—because, after all, there might just be a better way.

Ideation

You are fascinated by ideas. What is an idea? An idea is a concept, the best explanation of the most events. You are delighted when you discover beneath the complex surface an elegantly simple concept to explain why things are the way they are. An idea is a connection. Yours is the kind of mind that is always looking for connections, and so you are intrigued when seemingly disparate phenomena can be linked by an obscure connection. An idea is a new perspective on familiar challenges. You revel in taking the world we all know and turning it around so we can view it from a strange but strangely enlightening angle. You love all these ideas because they are profound, because they are novel, because they are clarifying, because they are contrary, because they are bizarre. For all these reasons, you derive a jolt of energy whenever a new idea occurs to you. Others may label you creative or original or conceptual or even smart. Perhaps you are all of these. Who can be sure? What you are sure of is that ideas are thrilling. And on most days this is enough.

Strategic

The Strategic theme enables you to sort through the clutter and find the best route. It is not a skill that can be taught. It is a distinct way of thinking, a special perspective on the world at large. This perspective allows you to see patterns where others simply see complexity. Mindful of these patterns, you play out alternative scenarios, always asking, "What if this happened? Okay, well what if this happened?" This recurring question helps you see around the next corner. There you can evaluate accurately the potential obstacles. Guided by where you see each path leading, you start to make selections. You discard the paths that lead nowhere. You discard the paths that lead straight into resistance. You discard the paths that lead into a fog of confusion. You cull and make selections until you arrive at the chosen path—your strategy. Armed with your strategy, you strike forward. This is your Strategic theme at work: "What if?" Select. Strike.

education) has been associated with greater student retention (Soria & Stubblefield, 2015; Soria et al., 2017). Drawing on longitudinal research findings, one possibility for the positive relationship between use of the CSF 2.0 and academic retention is that knowledge of one's strengths leads to greater use of those strengths over time, which, in turn, predicts greater academic satisfaction and achievement (Allan et al., 2021).

Youth Strengths Explorer

Gallup also developed a talent classification system and a measure that is appropriate for children and youth (ages 10 to 14). This is called the Clifton Youth Strengths Explorer (CYSE) and was released in 2006. CYSE developers believe that knowledge about young people's strengths will help in directing their energies to maximize their potentials. The CYSE has 10 themes (Achieving, Caring, Competing, Confidence, Dependability, Discoverer, Future Thinker, Organizer, Presence, and Relating) (see https://www.strengths-explorer.com/home.aspx for more details). When respondents complete the measure, they receive the Youth Workbook summarizing their top three themes. These materials also include action items and exercises that, if completed, could help youth capitalize on their strengths. Parent and educator guidebooks also are available so that caregivers can help youth in developing their positive characteristics.

A psychometric report detailed the reliability and validity of the measure (Lopez et al., 2007). Specifically, the internal consistency of the CYSE was reported to range from .72 to .87, and the test-retest reliability has ranged from .44 to .88 over an interval of five to seven weeks. Validity evidence is somewhat scarce on the CYSE, but Lopez and colleagues (2007) provided evidence that the instrument measured 10 distinct themes for children. Nevertheless, additional research is needed on the CYSE to continue to understand how strengths operate in children and to explore the validity and reliability of the instrument in different populations and contexts.

THE VIA CLASSIFICATION OF STRENGTHS

The VIA classification system, originally commissioned by the Mayerson Foundation, was generated in response to two basic questions: "(1) How can one define the concepts of 'strength' and 'highest potential,' and (2) how can one tell that a positive youth development program has succeeded in meeting its goals?" (Peterson & Seligman, 2004, p. v). These questions led to more philosophical and practical questions about character. Ultimately, Peterson and Seligman (2004) and many colleagues decided that components of character included virtues, character strengths, and situational themes. They defined virtues as social ideals prevalent in seminal texts reflecting the overlap of moral teaching from Taoism, Confucianism, Hinduism, Islam, and Judeo-Christianity. Virtues reflected different character strengths (psychological processes and mechanisms that define virtues), and situational themes (specific habits that lead people to manifest strengths in particular situations). After reviewing numerous measures of strengths and virtues, a list of 24 potential strengths were identified and then conceptually organized under six overarching virtues (wisdom and knowledge, courage, humanity, justice, temperance, and transcendence) thought to "emerge consensually across cultures and throughout time" (Peterson & Seligman, 2004, p. 29). Table 3.2 lists and describes the sox virtues and 24 strengths as they were originally conceptualized.

The measure of this system of virtues and strengths, the Values in Action Inventory of Strengths (VIA-IS) is available free of charge at the VIA Institute on Character (https://www.viacharacter.org/). The VIA-IS originally consisted of 240 items but has been refined several times to address psychometric concerns. Specifically, one of the most significant criticisms of the instrument is the fact that the six virtues have only limited empirical support, while the 24 strengths are well supported. To resolve this issue, the most current version (at the time of this volume), the VIA-IS-R (McGrath, 2019), consists of 196 items (about eight items per strength) empirically and conceptually grouped under three virtues: caring, inquisitiveness, and self-control

TABLE 3.2 ■ The VIA Classification of Virtues and Strengths
Wisdom—Cognitive strengths that entail the acquisition and use of knowledge
Creativity: Thinking of novel and productive ways to conceptualize and do things
Curiosity: Taking an interest in ongoing experience for its own sake
Judgment/Open-mindedness: Thinking things through and examining them from all sides
Love of learning: Mastering new skills, topics, and bodies of knowledge
Perspective: Being able to provide wise counsel to others
Courage—Emotional strengths that involve the exercise of will to accomplish goals in the face of opposition, external and internal
Bravery: Not shrinking from threat, challenge, difficulty, or pain
Perseverance: Finishing what one starts; persisting in a course of action in spite of obstacles
Honesty/Integrity: Speaking the truth but more broadly presenting oneself in a genuine way
Zest/Vitality: Approaching life with excitement and energy; not doing anything halfheartedly
Humanity—Interpersonal strengths that involve tending and befriending others
Love: Valuing close relations with others, in particular those in which caring is reciprocated
Kindness: Doing favors and good deeds for others; helping them; taking care of them
Social intelligence: Being aware of the motives and feelings of other people and oneself
Justice—Civic strengths that underlie healthy community life
Teamwork: Working well as a member of a group or team; being loyal to a group
Fairness: Treating all people the same according to the notions of fairness and justice
Leadership: Encouraging a group of which one is a member to get things done
Temperance—Strengths that protect against excess
Forgiveness: Forgiving those who have done wrong; accepting others' faults

(*Continued*)

TABLE 3.2 ■ The VIA Classification of Virtues and Strengths (*Continued*)

Humility: Letting one's accomplishments speak for themselves
Prudence: Being careful about one's choices; not taking undue risks
Self-regulation: Regulating what one feels and does; being disciplined
Transcendence—Strengths that forge connections to the larger universe and provide meaning
Appreciation of beauty and excellence: Noticing and appreciating beauty, excellence, and/or skilled performance in various domains of life
Gratitude: Being aware of and thankful for the good things that happen
Hope: Expecting the best in the future and working to achieve it
Humor: Liking to laugh and tease; bringing smiles to other people
Spirituality: Having coherent beliefs about the higher purpose and meaning of the universe

Source: From Peterson, C., & Seligman, M. E. P. (2004). *Character strengths and virtues: A handbook and classification,* Table 1.1: Classification of character strengths. Copyright © 2004 by Values in Action Institute. Used by permission of Oxford University Press, Inc.

(McGrath & Wallace, 2021). Two shorter versions are available consisting of 96 items each created by taking only the items that were selected based on how they maximized internal consistency reliability: the VIA-IS-P and the VIA-IS-M. The VIA-IS-P uses only items that are positively worded (i.e., higher scores indicate more of a particular strength). The VIA-IS-M uses both positively and negatively worded items to help flag individuals responding randomly or haphazardly. Each of these versions provides information on the six virtues originally specified by theory, as well as the three virtues that have both conceptual and empirical support.

Researchers have also developed versions to measure the specific virtues that can be given separately from the main VIA-IS-R if one wants to assess virtues directly in an even shorter format. When completing any version of the VIA-IS, participants read a trait-like descriptor (e.g., "I find the world a very interesting place") and indicate how well that description fits personally using a 1 (*very unlike me*) to 5 (*very much like me*) rating scale. The feedback report consists of the top five strengths, which are called signature strengths. An adolescent version of the VIA-IS, referred to as the Values in Action Inventory of Strengths for Youth (VIA-Y; for ages 10 to 17), has also been developed (Park et al., 2006). The VIA-Y was developed by using statistical criteria to select certain items from the VIA-IS, and the most recent version consists of 96 self-report items using the same 1-5 Likert scale as the VIA-IS and the VIA-IR.

Psychometric Properties of the VIA-IS, VIA-R, and VIA-Y

The reliability and validity of the original 24 strengths on the VIA-IS has been studied extensively (Peterson & Seligman, 2004), and the measure has been used in hundreds of studies. Internal consistency coefficients have generally been excellent, ranging from

.75 (Self-Regulation) to .90 (Spirituality), and with a mean coefficient across all 24 strengths of .85 (VIA Institute of Character, 2022). Indeed, the validity and reliability of the 24 strengths assessed in the VIA have received considerable empirical support. For example, nominations of strengths by friends and family correlate strongly with matching scales' scores for most of the 24 strengths. Additionally, the majority of the strengths correlate positively with scores on measures of life satisfaction (VIA Institute of Character, 2022).

While the 24 strengths of the VIA-IS are consistently supported in the literature, the six-virtues believed to underly the VIA-IS failed to replicate in some studies. The instrument may actually be measuring between four and five distinct virtues (see McGrath & Wallace, 2021 for a review). The VIA-IS-R is newer and thus has a smaller literature base than the original VIA-IS. Nevertheless, recent research suggests VIA-IS-R scores can be considered reliable and valid, possibly even more so than the original VIA-IS with respect to virtues. McGrath and Wallace (2021) found support for a three-factor structure of the VIA-IS-R consistent with the three overarching virtues underlying its 24 strengths. The authors also reported excellent internal consistency reliability coefficients, strong test-retest reliability, and consistent positive correlations between participants' VIA-IS-R scores and their behavioral enaction of each strength. In subsequent research, investigators found that the three-virtue structure was replicable in a large and diverse sample (McGrath et al., 2022). Interestingly, despite ample evidence to now support a three-virtue classification of the VIA-IS-R, the six-virtue structure continues to be used for interpretative purposes (at the time of this writing).

The VIA classification system has also been extended to youth via the VIA-Y (VIA Institute of Character, 2022). Preliminary validation of the VIA-Y also suggested that internal consistency of the scales was excellent (i.e., mean coefficient alpha = .84), and that scores were stable over a 6-month testing period. Regarding validity of the VIA-Y, Park and colleagues (2006) found that teachers' ratings of youth strengths generally correlated positively with youths' self-reported strengths. Additionally, they reported that most strengths were positively and significantly associated with life satisfaction. Positive associations between some (but not all) youth strengths and measures of positive well-being have been reported by subsequent researchers (e.g., Toner et al., 2012). The VIA-Y is a widely used instrument for research and practice that continues to be used in a variety of research studies across the world. For instance, investigators recently found that character strengths served as a protective factor for adolescents' psychological well-being during the COVID-19 pandemic in China (Liu & Wang, 2021). However, like the original VIA-IS, the basic structure of the measure may not truly reflect six distinct virtues (Toner et al., 2012). Moreover, although the VIA-Y was developed using the same items as the original VIA-IS, emerging evidence suggests that the VIA-Y is not measuring the same constructs as the VIA-IS (Kretzschmar et al., 2022). Therefore, it appears that the VIA-Youth and the VIA-IS have very similar pros and cons as tools for research and practice, but they are distinct instruments. Our suggestion based on the current literature is that you can feel confident interpreting the 24 strengths on all versions of the VIA-IS and VIA-Y. Still, caution may be warranted when interpreting the distinct virtues believed to underlie those strengths. The lack of support for the overarching virtues assessed by different versions of the VIA-IS also raises some intriguing questions. Do character strengths exist independent of one's broader virtues, or is the VIA-IS simply not capable of capturing the nuanced differences between virtues? Indeed, the true factor structure of this instrument will remain an important area of inquiry for years to come.

ISSUES OF CULTURAL EQUIVALENCE

Both the CSF and VIAS-IS were created within the United States. As such, different cultural groups may not define these concepts similarly and may not respond to questions about the various constructs using the same signifiers. More research in the areas of *cultural equivalence* must be conducted (Pedrotti & Edwards, 2009, 2017; Singh et al., 2016). Indeed, in attempting to measure various strengths, researchers develop questionnaire items that inherently reflect their culturally normative understanding of a particular construct. This can be problematic, because there may be cultural differences in the way that this trait is defined (i.e., the two cultures do not have **conceptual equivalence**). In addition, other types of measurement nonequivalence can mask our true understanding of cultural similarities and differences (Ho et al., 2014). While some cultures may share the same conceptual understanding of a strength, idioms or common phrases may not translate well depending on the phraseology used in the scale. Thus, **linguistic equivalence,** must also be established when measures for these positive traits are translated into languages other than the one in which they were originally developed (Mio et al., 2015).

Appropriate procedures of translation and back-translation can help ensure linguistic equivalence, but they are not a panacea for this issue. For example, researchers have still found significant and troubling differences between translated versions of the VIA-IS. In one study, Choubisa and Singh (2011) analyzed the factor structure of the VIA-IS in past studies in different cultural groups and languages (i.e., the English version with an Indian sample, the Hindi version with an Indian sample, the English version with an Australian sample, the Croatian version with a Croatian sample, and another English version in a mixed sample). Researchers found that in comparing the use of the various versions of the VIA-IS in these studies, there was not a single consistent factor structure. Instead, different factor solutions were found for the different populations. The main finding we might take from this research "suggests that culture may play a substantial role in the preferential treatment, expression and usage of the character strengths" (Choubisa & Singh, 2011, p. 328). As such, it is important not to interpret linguistic equivalence as actual conceptual equivalence. Said another way, just because an assessment is offered in another language does not mean it is measuring the same construct in both cultures.

Cultural Differences and Test Bias

When a measure is shown to perform differently in one group vs. another, either due to conceptual or linguistic nonequivalence, this is an example of **test bias** (i.e., a tendency for a measure to consistently underestimate or overestimate scores for people from certain groups). In other words, the VIA-IS may *systematically* distort peoples' strengths based on their cultural heritage and differences in how certain strengths are defined in their culture. One of the most rigorous ways to identify test bias is through measurement invariance/equivalence (MI/E) testing

(Boer et al., 2018). MI/E involves sophisticated statistical procedures (e.g., structural equation modeling) to determine if the same number of factors exist across cultural groups and whether individuals in different groups respond to an instrument's items in systematically different ways.

We were unable to locate any cross-cultural or MI/E research on the CSF. However, the VIA-IS has been examined extensively in a variety of contexts with mixed results. On the one hand, as mentioned previously, some researchers have found significant areas of concern regarding the equivalence of translations of the VIAS-IS between specific groups (e.g., Choubisa & Singh, 2011). On the other hand, Park and colleagues (2006) explored VIA-IS scores across 54 nations and the 50 U.S. states. After analyzing the strengths profiles in these different cultural contexts, they concluded that there was substantial convergence between the profiles regardless of the cultural context. Nine years later, McGrath (2015) extended Park and colleagues' (2006) study by studying VIA-IS profiles across 75 nations with a much larger sample. They concluded that, in general, strength profiles were similar across all countries and regions of the United States. In a smaller sample of 16 nations, McGrath (2016) examined the VIA-IS for MI/E and found evidence that the VIA-IS measures the same constructs in the United States and abroad. However, these findings should be considered with respect to some critical caveats. Mainly, most participants across all countries were college educated, economically stable, and were interested in the topic of virtues and character strengths. These demographic characteristics may have homogenized the sample, thus raising questions about the generalizability of MI/E results to other populations. Additionally, while participants across each country tended to evidence similar strengths profiles, they were all using the same VIA-IS items created in a Western and U.S. context. A strengths measure created in a different cultural context may reveal culturally defined strengths and virtues not captured by the original U.S. version. Nevertheless, these initial cross-cultural findings suggest that there may be some universality to certain strengths, particularly honesty, fairness, kindness, judgment, and curiosity (McGrath, 2015).

In addition to cross-cultural research, several investigators have examined the VIA-IS within different cultures, particularly with respect to specific identities (e.g., race, gender, sexual orientation). It is important to remember that the VIA-IS and the CSF were both spearheaded by white men. Given that all measures are inherently influenced by the cultural context in which they were developed and by the cultural background of the people who create them, it is possible that scores on the VIA-IS or the CSF differ between individuals that identify as racial, gender, sexual, or ethnic minorities in the same country or region. Unfortunately, very little research is available examining these identity factors in relation to performance on the CSF. Likewise, researchers have yet to examine the VIA-IS for invariance between cisgender men and women or between different racial or sexual minority groups using traditional MI/E testing procedures. Instead, most researchers have relied on less sophisticated methods to determine whether the average scores in one group are different from the average scores in another group. Results from these studies suggest that the VIA-IS may not differ much between cisgender men and women. Specifically, Heintz et al., 2019 conducted a meta-analysis on 65 studies covering over 1 million individuals in Switzerland who completed the VIA-IS. They concluded that, although there were some differences between cisgender men and women on the prevalence of certain strengths, these differences were statistically small. Likewise, although researchers have paid little attention to exploring differences between races on the VIA-IS, some researchers suggest that there may be more similarities than differences between racial majority and racial minority groups on the instrument (Karris & Craighead, 2012). Recently, Taube and Mussap (2020) found evidence that the VIA-IS measured the same character strengths between trans men, trans women, and gender nonbinary participants using MI/E procedures. However, these authors did not examine differences between transgender and cisgender individuals. Thus, the lack of foundational MI/E testing of the VIA-IS means that there are still questions to be answered regarding the true equivalence of character strengths and virtues between racial, gender, and sexual minority and majority identities. Indeed, only MI/E testing can reveal if the differences between these groups are the result of test bias.

In summary, we must consider the CSF and VIA-IS classification systems as useful but imperfect tools. This is the case with all psychological instruments, so they are in good company. Still, the mixed findings of the VIA-IS and the general lack of investigation regarding the CSF highlight a need for additional cross-cultural (i.e., different nationalities and instrument translations) and within-culture (i.e., race, gender, sexual orientation, and other identities) measurement equivalence research. Addressing these gaps in the literature will help inform the development of a culturally sensitive classification system of human strengths for specific populations.

Identifying Your Personal Strengths

Over the years, we have asked hundreds of clients and students about their weaknesses and strengths. Almost without exception, people are much quicker to respond about weaknesses than strengths. (See the Personal Mini-Experiments to examine this issue and to explore your strengths by taking the measures discussed in this chapter.) We also have observed that people struggle for words when describing strengths, whereas they have no shortage of words or stories that bring their weaknesses to life.

PERSONAL MINI-EXPERIMENTS

DISCOVERING AND CAPITALIZING ON YOUR STRENGTHS

In this chapter, we have discussed classifications and measures of strengths. We encourage you to learn more about your personal strengths as they exist within your own cultural framework and to share them with friends, family, teachers, and coworkers.

Getting to Know Your Friend's Weaknesses and Strengths: Ask a friend (or several friends), "What are your weaknesses?" and note how quickly they respond to the question, how many weaknesses they identify, and how descriptive they are when telling the story of weaknesses. Then, ask that friend (or friends), "What are your strengths?" Make similar mental notes about reaction time, number of strengths, and descriptiveness. If you are asking these questions of more than one friend, alternate between asking the weaknesses question first and the strengths question first. In turn, share your thoughts about your strengths (before or after you complete the measures presented in this chapter), and ask for your friend's feedback on your self-assessment.

Discovering Your Strengths: In just over an hour, you can identify 10 of your personal strengths by completing the Clifton StrengthsFinder (www.gallupstrengthscenter.com) for a small fee and the Values in Action Inventory of Strengths (www.authentichappiness.sas.upenn.edu/) for free. We encourage you to take both inventories and share the results with people close to you.

Capitalizing on Your Strengths: There are numerous strategies for capitalizing on your strengths (see www.strengthsquest.com and/or www.happier.com). For now, we would like you to capitalize on one strength. Pick one of your top strengths and try to use that strength five times a day for 5 days. Your 25 attempts to capitalize on that strength have the potential to bolster it and create a habit of using that strength more each day.

Viewing Your Strengths Within Your Personal Context: As stated above and in subsequent chapters in this text, strengths must be viewed within a cultural context. They can also be derived from your personal cultural facets (e.g., gender, race, nation of origin). For example, a Latinx individual's heritage of collectivism might imbue her with natural strength in caring for others, and individuals born in the United States might find that the nation's ideal of possessing a "can-do" attitude has helped them to develop the strengths of perseverance and determination. What strengths might your cultural facets provide for you?

We hope that readers take advantage of the opportunity to discover their strengths and that, in several decades, people will have as much to say about their strengths as they do about their weaknesses. Our observations of people upon the completion of a strengths measure suggest that the new or validated information about your personal strengths will give you a slight, temporary boost in positive emotions and confidence. Also, you will want to share the results with people around you. In addition, research points to the idea that using one's strengths is a source of, and sometimes a precursor to, increases in well-being. Researchers have found that use of strengths can predict changes and variance in subjective well-being within the individual (Duan & Ho, 2017; Govindji & Linley, 2007; Proctor et al., 2011). It follows logically that in knowing about our strengths, we might more readily think of using them in our daily lives, and this can have an overall positive effect upon our personal well-being.

The Case of Shane

As positive psychologists, we have committed ourselves to the development of the positive in others, and of course, we try to practice what we preach. We have identified our strengths through formal and informal assessment, and we try to capitalize on our strengths every day. Here is a brief account of how Dr. Shane J. Lopez (one of the original authors of this text) used his strengths in daily life.

> When I received the results of the Clifton StrengthsFinder (see Figure 3.1) and the VIA-IS, I reflected on the findings and tried to figure out how I could put them to immediate use. Then, I realized that I have been using these strengths every day. . . . that is why they are my strengths! Nevertheless, I decided to be more intentional in my

efforts to make my strengths come alive. That goal of intentionality addressed *how* I would capitalize on my strengths, but I hadn't addressed *why*. It turns out, however, that it was pretty simple—I wanted to make my good life even better. That was the outcome I desired, and I thought that these "new" strengths would provide pathways to that goal.

Admittedly, my initial efforts to intentionally use my strengths every day were not that successful. Although I thought the findings were accurate, and I was excited to receive the strengths feedback, I was overwhelmed by the idea of refining my use of 5 or 10 strengths at the same time. For that reason, I decided to capitalize on the strengths that I thought would help me the most in making my life better. I chose the top two themes (Futuristic and Maximizer) from the Gallup feedback and the top strength (Gratitude) from the VIA results. Right away, focusing on three strengths seemed doable.

With those "three strengths that matter most" (as I began to refer to them) in hand, I consulted the action items (shared in a printable form as a supplement to the Signature Themes presented in Figure 3.1) associated with my Futuristic and Maximizer themes. For Futuristic, I settled on one daily activity that might spark my tendency to project into the future: Take time to think about the future. Pretty straightforward, but reading this action item made me realize that I would go for a considerable time without thinking about the future, and this led to dissatisfaction with how my life was going. Putting this guidance into action has involved taking daily walks dedicated to thinking about the future. Often, I walk in the evening, and I chat with my partner about the future of our work and our family. At other times, I leave the office around midday and walk through the campus reflecting on some of my aspirations. These walks have turned into a cherished time that yields exciting ideas and considerable satisfaction.

Regarding my Maximizer theme, I believe this talent of making good ideas, projects, and relationships better contributes greatly to my success at work. Through examining my habits at home and work, I realized I was doing a fairly good job of systematically using this strength. This left me feeling unsure about how to proceed in my efforts to capitalize on this strength. Then, one day I encountered a person who prided herself on playing "the devil's advocate" every time an idea was presented during a meeting. I thought about the many devil's advocates whom I have encountered over the years, and I concluded that these people were not necessarily providing constructive feedback that made a good idea better. They also were not offering alternative ideas that would work better. In my opinion, all they were doing was undercutting my creativity and enthusiasm (or that of other people). To maximize, I realized that I had to surround myself with people who knew how to make good ideas better. That criterion has become a critical one when I select friends, colleagues, and students, and I believe it has boosted my creativity and the quality of my work.

I have used Futuristic and Maximizing themes both at work and at home, and I think my efforts have helped me in both domains. I believe that capitalizing on these strengths has led to more creativity and productivity at work and greater sense of purpose for

my family and me. Using gratitude (my third "strength that matters most") with more intentionality has not generated more productivity or greater clarity in my personal mission, but it has been rewarding in that it brings joy and a sense of closeness to people. To make the most of my gratitude, I decided to spend part of most Friday afternoons writing thank-you notes (handwritten and mailed the old-fashioned way) to people who have touched my life that week, and at other times I thank people who have done something nice for me that week. Occasionally, I write to a person who did a good deed for me years ago (and whom I had never thanked or whom I wanted to thank again). Finally, I also write to people who have done good works (I may or may not know them personally) to express my gratitude for their efforts. This practice has enriched my emotional life, and it has strengthened many of my relationships.

MEASUREMENT IN POSITIVE PSYCHOLOGY: A GUIDE

In the previous sections, we discussed two broad classification systems of human strengths, the CSF 2.0 and VIA-IS. Although these instruments were designed to classify strengths at a broad level, most research in positive psychology relies on stand-alone, self-report questionnaires of specific positive characteristics, experiences, behaviors, or outcomes. Throughout this text, you will be exposed to various psychological constructs, and it is important to note that nearly all of them have an accompanying stand-alone measure that has undergone some degree of psychometric evaluation. There are also some important differences between stand-alone measures and broad classification instruments. First, whereas the CSF 2.0 and VIA-IS come with an interpretive report that, in some cases, is locked behind a paywall, most stand-alone instrumentation in positive psychology is available at no cost if you get permission from the researcher who owns the scale. Second, most stand-alone measures do not come with an interpretative report or a profile report. Instead, you simply sum or average your scores on each questionnaire item to receive a total or subscale score indicating your level of a particular construct. Third, stand-alone measures often rely on smaller samples to inform their development than the broader classification systems. That is, they are often created with limited resources, and, if they become widely used, then the evidence for reliability and validity grows as researchers use those instruments in different or larger samples.

Deciding on a Measure

It is beyond the scope of this book (and certainly this chapter) to discuss all self-report, stand-alone measures widely used in positive psychology. Indeed, identifying which measure to use for research or clinical practice can be a daunting task. Fortunately, there are a few guidelines to consider. For example, are you looking for an instrument to measure a state or a trait? A **state measure** captures what someone is feeling or experiencing during the assessment, whereas a **trait measure** captures more enduring, stable characteristics. State measures are often malleable, and thus they can be useful when one wants to measure the outcome of a manipulation (i.e., priming effects or an intervention) or when trying to capture fluctuations during a brief amount of time (i.e., daily diary studies or other **momentary ecological assessment** procedures). Trait measures are generally less malleable and are better for understanding the correlates of certain positive psychological characteristics (e.g., examining the association between a particular strength and a specific positive outcome or experience). The CSF 2.0 and the VIA-IS are both considered trait measures.

After you have decided whether you need a state or trait instrument, it is important to consider its psychometric properties. As discussed previously, the psychometric properties of the CSF 2.0 and the VIA-IS have been extensively studied, but clearly, neither instrument is perfect. Indeed, all psychological instruments will have limitations. However, researchers have developed best-practice guidelines to inform scale development (see DeVellis, 2017 for a review). Generally, a scale that follows best practices will be developed based on a thorough review of theory, literature, and other related instruments. Sometimes researchers will take a recommended extra step and interview individuals to get a better perspective of the construct they wish to measure (Boateng et al., 2018). Then, a series of test items are written to capture the construct from a variety of different angles. Next, researchers have a sample of individuals respond to those test items and then subject data from those responses to an **exploratory factor analysis** (EFA) to identify how many factors (i.e., subscales) explain the shared/common variation among test items. Additionally, they will use the information from the EFA to trim items based on a variety of statistical criteria (DeVellis, 2017). This process produces a set of items that empirically and conceptually best represent the construct being measured. Next, researchers confirm the factor structure from the EFA on a separate sample via **confirmatory factor analysis** (CFA). This process ensures that the factor structure from the EFA was not a spurious result and can be replicated. Finally, researchers must subject their scale to a variety of validity and reliability analyses. Look for terms such as **construct validity** and **criterion validity**, as this will help you understand if the instrument actually measures what it is supposed to measure (construct validity) and how well it can predict relevant outcomes (criterion validity). In short, instruments need to have undergone a set of rigorous and systematic development processes. You can learn about the development of any instrument by tracking down the original validation paper. If you are unable to find any exploration of factor structure, reliability, or validity of a particular instrument, that may be grounds to skip that instrument in favor of one with more scientific rigor.

Our final recommendation in selecting an instrument is to interpret its psychometric properties with respect to the demographic characteristics of its validation sample. As we discussed with the CSF 2.0 and the VIA-IS, an instrument may have evidence supporting its reliability and validity, but it is inherently a product of the worldview of the researchers who created it. Most foundational research in positive psychology was created by individuals from gender, racial, and sexual majority groups and reflects a Western perspective. As positive psychology continues to grow, we need instruments reflecting the perspectives of individuals from a variety of identities. This is one reason that interviews informing the initial test items are critical to developing culturally sensitive instruments. Talking to people from different groups allows researchers to take a deeper dive into perspectives they may not have otherwise considered, possibly because those perspectives do not reflect the researchers' lived experiences. If such perspectives are critical to the lived experiences of a particular group, overlooking them could lead to an incomplete picture of individuals in that group. Accordingly, studies of gender, race, and sexual orientation equivalence of positive psychology instruments are essential. Likewise, studies of cross-cultural or country-level differences in positive psychological instrumentation help us understand the similarities and differences among diverse groups worldwide. For example, Bieda and colleagues (2017) examined a variety of widely used stand-alone instruments of positive psychology constructs (i.e., social support, happiness, life satisfaction, positive mental health, optimism, and resilience) for measurement invariance using structural equation modeling. Across a large sample of German (n = 4,453), Russian (n = 3,806), and Chinese (n = 12,524) university students. These researchers found that most of these instruments demonstrated some degree of measurement equivalence, suggesting that the same constructs were being assessed in Western and Eastern cultural groups. However, they found some differences, particularly in optimism, indicating that this construct may have a different meaning for different groups. They also noted differences in the way individuals from each sample responded to these instruments. Therefore, when selecting an instrument, it is important to consider whether the population you want to study is consistent with the validation sample, as well as whether researchers have examined the instrument for measurement invariance between different groups.

Putting It All Into Practice

We hope that the information in this chapter helps you both personally and professionally. Personally, it is important to know your strengths. We encourage you to learn about yours and to find ways to use them intentionally in your daily life. Understanding your strengths can also help you professionally. For one thing, you will have a great answer to any job interview questions about your strengths! At the same time, we have highlighted the fact that all instruments in positive psychology have limitations, particularly with respect to cultural equivalence, and we encourage you to consider those limitations in your own work.

Such limitations notwithstanding, positive psychology has clearly progressed significantly over the years, as is reflected by the number and diversity of positive psychological constructs, classification systems, and stand-alone assessments. In this way, the field has answered some of the challenges proposed by people like Karl Menninger (1963) to provide a more balanced perspective of the human condition. Today, positive psychologists highlight a new type of balance—a view of people that gives attention both to weaknesses and to strengths but that is presented with consideration of cultural context. Although there is no question that we presently know much more about human fallibilities than about assets, a strong culturally competent science and robust applications aimed at strengths will continue to yield a more thorough and more accurate view of the world and its inhabitants.

KEY TERMS

Assessment
Conceptual equivalence
Confirmatory Factor Analysis
Construct validity
Criterion validity
Empirically based
Exploratory Factor Analysis
Internal Consistency
Linguistic equivalence
Momentary Ecological Assessment
Psychometric properties
Reliability
State Measure
Strength
Talent
Test Bias
Trait Measure
Validity

NOTE

1. In January 2003, Dr. Clifton was awarded an American Psychological Association presidential commendation in recognition of his pioneering role in strengths-based psychology. The commendation states, "Whereas, living out the vision that life and work could be about building what is best and highest, not just about correcting weaknesses, [Clifton] became the father of Strengths-Based Psychology and the grandfather of Positive Psychology."

PART II

POSITIVE PSYCHOLOGY IN CONTEXT

4 THE ROLE OF CULTURE IN DEVELOPING STRENGTHS AND LIVING WELL

LEARNING OBJECTIVES

After reading this chapter, you will be able to:

4.1 Recognize the influence culture has on recognition, relevance, and development of strengths

4.2 Understand culture as multifaceted

4.3 Critique historical treatment of culture in discussions of psychology and strengths

4.4 Apply a culturally embedded perspective to positive psychology

4.5 Critique representations of strengths that do not take culture into account

4.6 Describe the Cultural Wealth Model

CULTURE AND PSYCHOLOGY

David Satcher, the 16th surgeon general of the United States, who served from 1998 to 2002, sat on a dimly lit stage in the overflowing convention hall. He clutched a copy of a thick document, the report titled *Mental Health: Culture, Race, Ethnicity* (U.S. Department of Health and Human Services [DHHS], 2001), which was being officially released that same day. Psychologists poured into the meeting room to hear Dr. Satcher's summary of this report, which had been years in the making. To a packed house, Satcher spoke on the crucial influences of **culture** on mental health. This excerpt from the report summarizes some of the surgeon general's comments:

> Culture is broadly defined as a common heritage or set of beliefs, norms, and values (U.S. DHHS, 1999). It refers to the shared attributes of one group. . . . Culture bears upon whether people even seek help in the first place, what types of help they seek, what coping styles and social supports they have, and how much stigma they attach to mental illness. All cultures also feature strengths, such as resilience and adaptive ways of coping, which may buffer some people from developing certain disorders.

> Consumers of mental health services naturally carry this cultural diversity directly into the treatment setting. . . . The culture of the clinician and the larger health care system govern the societal response to a patient with mental illness. They influence many aspects of the delivery of care, including diagnosis, treatment, and the organization and reimbursement of services. Clinicians and service systems have been ill equipped to meet the needs of patients from different backgrounds and, in some cases, have displayed bias in the delivery of care. (U.S. DHHS, 2001)

There were two take-home messages from Dr. Satcher's summary. First, "culture counts" in the consideration of the **etiology** (the cause of something, such as an illness), effects, and treatment of educational and psychological problems. Second, psychologists need to incorporate cultural issues into their conceptualizations of psychological problems and treatments.

The need to acknowledge cultural influences also applies to our efforts to understand educational successes, psychological strengths, and the very nature of the good life. When Martin Seligman reintroduced the concepts of positive psychology upon beginning his role as president of the American Psychological Association at the beginning of the millennium, it was noted that although positive psychology purported to be a "balanced" view of people, there were still very few discussions of the importance of culture in making distinctions about strengths and weaknesses (Pedrotti & Edwards, 2017). Critics at the time observed that most strength-focused scholarship failed to address cultural influences in its research plans, service delivery, and program evaluations (see Sue & Constantine, 2003 for a seminal overview). Noting that the field of psychology, as a whole, had often pathologized people of color, women, and other groups, many critics saw positive psychology as a way to undo such past harms. Elsewhere, I (JTP) and colleagues have written, "A multiculturally competent positive psychology, one that effectively embraces, values, and works to understand these differences and values, has the potential to provide a salve for the wounds [people of color and other minorities] have suffered" (Pedrotti & Edwards, 2014, p. xvi). Today, we have started to build a better discussion about how "culture counts" into positive psychology research and practice activities. Finally, as Satcher mentions and as others have written, culture must be viewed in a broad sense as including facets such as race, ethnicity, gender, sexual orientation, socioeconomic status, religion, disability, and nation of origin (Hays, 2016). Each of these facets may have different meaning, relevance, and salience in the lives of unique individuals, and all may affect what is decided to be a "positive" behavior or trait within a particular cultural context. Christopher and Howe (2014) have noted, "Evaluating current positive psychological theory and its implicit assumptions (e.g., how these assumptions are Western assumptions), will reward us deeper and more nuanced theory, research, and practice" (p. 253). Although we have made some progress, we are not yet at a point where this has been accomplished in the field of positive psychology (Chang et al. 2020; Chang, Downey et al., 2016; Pedrotti & Edwards, 2017).

Today, culture and social identities are often a commonplace part of everyday conversation. Thus it makes sense that any future positive psychologists who are reading this chapter make efforts to count culture as a major influence on the development and manifestation of human strengths and good living. This goal is challenging because, as noted previously, psychology as a discipline has been ineffective in including cultural variables in the study of mental health and illness. This is doubly problematic when considering the impact on groups lacking in power either historically or currently in a number of different settings. As psychology as a whole has focused almost singularly on weakness, without attention to strength (Seligman & Csikszentmihalyi, 2000), and within this framework has often pathologized those who do not adhere to Western norms via deficit models, people of color, women, sexual minorities, and other underrepresented groups have been subjected to a sort of "double jeopardy" (Pedrotti et al., 2009). In this way, they are "branded as pathological in comparison to the majority group, and within a system that only acknowledges weakness and leaves no room for a balanced description of behavior" (Pedrotti & Edwards, 2010, p. 166). For positive psychology to remain viable, we must open our minds in terms of understanding that "healthy functioning" and "positive trait" are subjective phrases influenced heavily by cultural worldview (Pedrotti, 2014; Pedrotti & Edwards, 2014, 2017).

In this chapter, we first address the field's historical (and often flawed) attempts to understand the roles of cultural forces in determining our psychological makeups. Second, we examine the assertions that positive psychology is culture free or culturally embedded. Third and finally, we discuss the steps that need to be taken to position positive psychology within cultural context. At the end of this chapter, we offer some examples for future research that approaches research from within specific cultural contexts, guided by some of Chang, Downey, and colleagues' (2016) directions for future research as well as others (Pedrotti et al., 2021). Obviously, we view these questions as central to the future of positive psychology, and most of the readers of this text will likely be called upon to address these issues in their careers.

HISTORICAL TREATMENT OF STRENGTHS AND CULTURE

Psychology in the 20th century grappled with the topic of individual differences. Many of these discussions of individual differences pertained to culture. Over the past 100 years, for example, psychology has moved from identifying differences associated with culture as the basis of strengths and deficits, to the recognition that while cultural groups share certain features, the individuals within them should be treated as individuals. Additionally, the idea of what is a strength and what is not must be judged within the cultural context in which the person is from (Pedrotti & Isom, 2021).

In the late 1800s and early 1900s, anthropologists and psychologists often referred to race and culture as determinants of positive and negative personal characteristics and behaviors. Research paradigms, influenced by the sociopolitical forces of the times, produced findings that were generally consistent with the belief that the dominant race or culture (i.e., of European ancestry) was superior to all other racial or ethnic minority groups within the United States. These approaches to highlighting the inferiority of certain racial and cultural groups have been referred to as the **genetically deficient perspective** and the **culturally deficient perspective** on human diversity (Sue & Constantine, 2003). Psychologists who subscribed to the genetically deficient model hypothesized that biological differences explained perceived gaps in intellectual capabilities between racial groups. Moreover, the proponents of the genetically deficient model argued that people who possessed "inferior intelligence" could not benefit from growth opportunities and, as such, did not contribute to the advancement of society.

Pseudoscience was used to demonstrate the presumed genetic basis of intelligence and to emphasize the "finding" of intellectual superiority of Europeans and European Americans. Racist comparisons of skulls of White versus African or Asian skulls to monkeys and the like, were often used as "science" that supported deficits in non-White populations. These notions of genetic inferiority were a prominent focus of **eugenics** (the study of methods of reducing "genetic inferiority" by selective breeding) research led by U.S.-based psychologists such as G. Stanley Hall and Henry Goddard. Hall "was a firm believer in 'higher' and 'lower' human races" (Hothersall, 1995, p. 360). Goddard held similar views about race and intelligence, and in the early 1900s, he established screening procedures (using formal intelligence tests similar to those used today) at Ellis Island to increase the deportation rates of the "feeble-minded" (Hothersall, 1995). In this regard, people from around the world were given complex intelligence tests—typically in a language other than their native tongue—the same day that they completed a long, overseas voyage. Not surprisingly, these test results generally were a poor estimate of the immigrants' intellectual functioning. Goddard eventually abandoned use of such formal tests and purported to be able to tell who was intelligent and who was not, just by looking at the faces of people (Gould, 1996). Facial features such as a "high brow" (deemed more intelligent) versus a "low brow" (deemed less intelligent) were said to be due to genetic deficiencies that linked to lower potential intelligence overall, and Goddard often used photos paired with descriptions of a "good" or "bad" life to emphasize his points (Gould, 1996). Clearly, this is pseudoscience, and it cannot be validated that anything to do with the height of a brow is related to a person's intellectual potential. In fact, Goddard himself must have eventually realized this as it was later found that he had retouched with ink faces of those deemed "feebleminded" in his photos, to give them a stronger connection to the facial features he determined to be more prominent in this group (Gould, 1996). Even someone who believed in this fallacious connection could not find actual data to support it.

By the middle of the 20th century, most psychologists had abandoned the belief that race predetermined cognitive capacities and life outcomes. Indeed, the focus shifted from race to culture or, more specifically, the cultural deficiencies evidenced in the daily lives of some people. In the culturally deficient approach to understanding differences among people, psychologists (e.g., Kardiner & Ovesey, 1951) identified a host of environmental, nutritional, linguistic, and interpersonal factors that supposedly explained the stunted physical and psychological growth of members of selected groups. It was hypothesized that people were lacking in certain psychological resources because they had limited exposure to the prevailing values and customs of the day, namely, those of White Americans (see the discussion of cultural deprivation in Parham et al., 1999). Many researchers and practitioners attempted to explain problems and struggles of people by carefully examining the juxtaposition of cultures, specifically those cultures that were viewed as somewhat marginal compared to those considered mainstream (middle-class, suburban, socially conservative). Deviations from the normative culture were considered "deficient" and cause for concern. Although this model focused greater attention on the effects of external variables than the earlier genetically deficient model, it nevertheless continued to apply a biased, negative, and oversimplified framework for appraising the cognitive capacities of racial or ethnic minority group members (Kaplan & Sue, 1997). In addition, confounding of race with other facets was also common. For example, assuming that any person of color was brought up in a poor environment or one with limited education.

After decades in which some psychologists argued that specified races and cultures were better than others (i.e., that Whites were superior to non-Whites), many professionals began to subscribe to the culturally different perspective, in which the uniqueness and strengths of all cultures were recognized. All too recently, researchers and practitioners have begun to consider **culturally pluralistic** (i.e., recognizing distinct cultural entities and adopting some values of the majority group) and **culturally relativistic** (i.e., interpreting behaviors within the context of the culture) explanations of the diversities inherent in positive and negative human behavior (Chang, Downey et al., 2016; Pedrotti et al., 2021; Sue & Constantine, 2003). We share this fraught history with you as students of positive psychology in order to set the stage for where we are today in the field. It is important to recognize the stark influence of the racist, pseudo-scientific, and unethical research and writing noted above. Even today, some may believe that potential is limited by race and use examples of environmental deficit (e.g., poverty) to suggest personal deficit (e.g., lack of ability to succeed). We trust you to look carefully at statements such as this and to use the historical foundations here as a lens for other work done at this time.

POSITIVE PSYCHOLOGY: CULTURE IS EVERYWHERE

Positive psychology scientists and practitioners are committed to studying and promoting optimal functioning. Although we share this common goal, we pursue it along many different routes. Outside observers might conclude that all positive psychology researchers ask similar questions and use similar methods. Such observers also may note that all positive psychology practitioners focus on clients' strengths and help move people toward positive life outcomes. Our educational specialties (e.g., social, health, personality, developmental, counseling, and clinical psychology), however, may determine particular aspects of the questions examined and research tools used. Likewise, our theoretical orientations to counseling (e.g., humanistic, cognitive–behavioral, solution focused) may influence our efforts to help people to function more optimally. Along these same lines, and as exemplified above, our cultural facets, including race, socioeconomic status, nation or origin, gender, and others, may shape our foci, our hypotheses, and our methods.

Most professionals probably have confidence in the objectivity of their methods. They also are likely to acknowledge the need to make sense of the amazing diversity in human existence. Three recurring issues appear to involve (1) the effects of professionals' cultural values on their research and practices, (2) the universality of human strengths, and (3) the need for research that addresses specific populations from within their own contexts.

Can Science Be Culture Free?

Researchers in the past have at times made the claim that science is objective and as such might be able to "transcend culture" (Seligman & Csikszentmihalyi, 2000, p. 5). However much some may hope this to be the case, we entreat you to see this as the fallacy it is. Hypotheses and

iStockphoto.com/Feverpitched

research designs are not called out of thin air, but instead formed in the minds of humans . . . with cultural perspectives. Caroline Clauss-Ehlers (2008), a researcher in the field of resilience, notes that our own perceptions of what a population is like may color the tone of our hypothesis such that deficits are found, while strengths are ignored. As an example, Clauss-Ehlers posits the difference between two studies which both have the goal of finding out how to help increase success in Latinx students. In Study A, the researchers go into schools and find the poorest achieving Latinx students to discover what similarities exist amongst them such that these barriers can be eliminated in the future. In Study B, the researchers instead study high achieving Latinx students to determine what similarities exist amongst this group such that these protective factors can be put into place for the future benefit of Latinx students (Cabrera & Padilla, 2004). Both studies may be useful to the field, but while Study A paints the Latinx population as being at a deficit, needing help, and low-achieving, Study B does the exact opposite and presents the Latinx population as being capable, having potential, and possessing high-achieving members. Clauss-Ehlers (2008) argues that these studies vary as a function of the viewpoint of the researcher. Though both Study A and Study B researchers may want to help the Latinx population, the first study highlights negative stereotypes of the Latinx population while the second strives to show their strengths. This is just one example of the way in which personal mindset and cultural values of the researcher may impact the way science is conducted.

Culturally Embedded Positive Psychology Research and Practice

Today, most psychologists take a culturally embedded approach to their research at least in part in recognition of the fact that worldview determines what is seen as a strength, what is seen as a weakness, and what is able to be seen (or measured) at all. Many researchers in times past have asserted that certain characteristics or virtues are present as positive facets across many cultures, and for this reason, we should assume some strengths to be *universal.* Although professionals who study the culturally embedded nature of strengths concede that a core group of positive traits and processes might exist across cultures, they may not (a) be defined or manifest the same way in different cultures, (b) show the same relationships to other constructs within different cultural constructs, and (c) be differently relevant to different cultural groups (Pedrotti, 2014a). In this section, we will give some brief examples of ways in which strengths are culturally embedded, but you will also see exemplars throughout the other chapters of this book.

Happiness as a construct is a good place to start our discussion. Some research has found that distinct differences exist in how happiness is defined across cultures. For example, when asked questions about their own happiness, Western individuals, such as those from majority culture in the United States, usually mention personal achievement and other individual-related contributing factors. In contrast, Eastern individuals, such as those from China or Japan, more commonly reference harmony and aspects related to their social spheres as contributing heavily to their happiness (Uchida et al., 2004). As another example, people from different cultural groups also define wisdom differently. While individuals from the majority culture in the United States define wisdom as more of a cognitive construct, other groups define it as both affective and cognitive (Benedikovicová & Ardelt, 2008; Yang, 2008). One might note that the way a construct is defined might also impact its measurement. If a researcher from the United States holds a view of wisdom as cognitive and designs an instrument to measure wisdom that includes not affective components, they may "miss" the wisdom most relevant to the Slovak culture (Benedikovicová & Ardelt, 2008). In all of these cases, the bottom line is the perspective of the researcher matters. Measuring a construct from your own cultural context, does not mean you can use that same definition to measure it in others.

It is also the case that happiness may not look the same in different cultural groups. In a study by Lu and Gilmour (2004), participants from Asia and from the United States were asked to think of an experience that had brought them profound happiness and to make their face show this emotion while being photographed. When these photographs were later shown to United States college students, they rated the photos of the non-Asian participants as more happy than those of the Asian participants (Lu & Gilmour, 2004) despite the attestation of the photo subjects that they were equally happy. This study provides evidence that the way in which the Asian participants manifested their happiness looked different than the way those from the United States manifested theirs.

As a second example, Sandage and colleagues (2003) provide a good example of how forgiveness is valued cross-culturally and yet operates very differently within cultures. In their examination of the forgiveness process of Hmong Americans, Sandage and colleagues discovered that forgiveness focuses on the restoration of respect and relational repair, emphasizes a spiritual component, and is facilitated by a third party. Although other conceptualizations of forgiveness also emphasize relationship repair, the spiritual components and the need for third-party facilitation appear to be rare. Thus, in this example, the manifestation of forgiveness is different due to cultural values.

PERSONAL MINI-EXPERIMENTS

CULTURALLY EMBEDDED DAILY PRACTICE

In this chapter, we have discussed the extent to which you "count culture" in your daily work as a positive psychologist or student. These examples of culture's role in positive psychology come to life when applied to a real professional situation.

Imagine that you join a professor's lab that is committed to the study of positive functioning of first-generation college students. During your initial discussion with the faculty member, you learn that the project you will be working on involves developing and evaluating a mentoring program for a culturally diverse group of students, some of whom first moved to the United States only years ago when their families were providing seasonal labor to regional farmers. At the first meeting of the research group, you, fellow students, and the faculty member brainstorm ideas about the content and process of the mentoring sessions and about the salient outcome measures. As these topics are discussed, the professor interjects the following questions:

- Which of the students' strengths are most likely to aid them in school and in life?
- Should we measure happiness as a desired outcome in addition to academic self-efficacy, performance, and retention?
- What cautions should we take with regard to the measures we choose?
- What about family-of-origin influence on a student's academic behaviors? Should we account for that?
- How might our own values affect the mentoring process or research (e.g., hypothesis formation)?

Please share your response with fellow students, and attempt to determine the extent to which you account for the role of culture in your responses. Remember to use a broad definition of culture in your considerations (e.g., does your gender influence what you value? Your race or ethnicity? Your religion?). Please also ask yourself questions: Are you unintentionally confounding race and socioeconomic status (i.e., assuming that all people of color might also be poor); are you assigning a deficit model to these students before you meet them (i.e., assuming that English will not be spoken, that family support may not be there, etc.)?

Finally, links between constructs may not follow the same. Researchers have often found differences in how various constructs relate to others in different cultural groups. Hope, for example, correlates strongly with life satisfaction, optimism, and other traits and states that those in the United States find to be beneficial (Snyder et al., 1991). These links, however, are not found in the same strength, direction, or significance in other groups. Hope, as an example, has different significant predictors depending on which cultural group one is studying (Chang & Banks, 2007; see Chapter 8 for a more thorough description of this work). Gratitude and interventions related to this construct, such as gratitude journaling, have also been found to have different impacts on well-being in different cultural groups (Layous et al., 2013; see Chapter 6 for more information on this difference). And while optimism and pessimism are respectively inversely and positively related to depression in White American college students, results from Chinese American college students showed positive links between pessimism and problem solving, with no greater incidence of depression (Chang, 1996). Thus, relationships between constructs may be different as a function of culture. See Pedrotti and Edwards's (2017) chapter entitled, "Cultural Context in Positive Psychology: History, Research, and Opportunities for Growth," for a detailed overview of research that has been conducted to date on positive psychology and a variety of specific cultural facets (e.g., race and ethnicity, gender, disability, sexual orientation, and social class). John Chambers Christopher (2005), an American Psychological Association (APA) fellow and Fulbright grant recipient who studies culture and various aspects of positive psychology, contends that "positive psychology requires a philosophy of social science that is robust enough to handle ontological, epistemological, and ethical/moral issues and move beyond both objectivism and relativism" (pp. 3–4). The full text of Christopher's article, reprinted here, details his suggestions for undergirding positive psychology with a stronger conceptual framework.

SITUATING POSITIVE PSYCHOLOGY

John Chambers Christopher

To post-modern thinkers of a variety of stripes, ontological and moral commitments are increasingly recognized to be inescapable in the social sciences. This poses problems for positive psychology if it is pursued as if it were a "descriptive" or objective science that can "transcend particular cultures and politics and approach universality" (Seligman & Csikszentmihalyi, 2000, p. 5). Prior initiatives in the field of psychology that claimed to be objective, value free, culture free, ahistorical, and universal were shown by critical psychologists to presuppose individualistic cultural values and assumptions. Preliminary inquiry suggests that theory and research in positive psychology is likewise influenced by Western cultural outlooks (Christopher, 1999, 2003; Guignon, 2002; Woolfolk, 2002). One implication is that positive psychology requires a philosophy of social science that is robust enough to handle ontological, epistemological, and ethical/moral issues and move beyond both objectivism and relativism.

I believe conceptual resources for positive psychology can be found in the philosophical hermeneutics of Charles Taylor and Martin Heidegger and in Mark Bickhard's interactivism. These metatheories provide (a) conceptual tools for critiquing how cultural values and assumptions shape psychological theory, research, and practice; (b) an alternative non-individualistic and non-dualistic metatheory regarding the nature of the self and how the self is related to culture; and (c) ways of thinking interpretively about cultural meanings and discerning their specific manifestations (Campbell et al., 2002; Christopher, 2001, 2004). A useful way of thinking about culture comes from considering how human beings always and necessarily exist within *moral visions.* Moral visions entail a set of ontological presuppositions about the nature of the person or self and a set of moral or ethical assumptions about what the person should be or become. I believe that any positive psychology, whether in the current movement or in the indigenous psychologies of other cultures, is based on moral visions.

From this moral visions framework, positive psychology will need to be able to address how the self varies across culture. To promote subjective well-being, psychological well-being, or character, we need to have a clear understanding of the self that is at stake. Failing to do this can potentially pathologize individuals whose sense of self is not the "bounded, masterful self" of Western psychology (Cushman, 1990). In addition, positive psychology will need to address what role the various configurations of the self have for positive psychology. For example, positive psychology encourages the development and enhancement of the self. Yet, for many non-Western indigenous psychologies such as Buddhism and classical yoga, identification with this notion of the self is the source of suffering and the true stumbling block to growth. Or as Alfred Adler suggested, mental health and well-being may in part require a sense of identification with the larger communities of which one is a part. Dialogue and debate regarding these types of underlying assumptions will be essential to help positive psychology not become culture-bound.

The second aspect of moral visions that positive psychology will need to contend with are those assumptions regarding how we should be or become (or what the good person and the good life are). Psychology tends to define its virtues, like autonomy, relatedness, and personal growth, in abstract and decontextualized ways that tend to obscure the local and specific interpretations with which these virtues are actually lived out (Campbell & Christopher, 1996b; Christopher, 1999; Christopher et al., 2004). This is a point that applies to various aspects of positive psychology, including Peterson and Seligman's (2004) VIA project, character education, and well-being (Christopher et al., 2004). I contend that positive psychology will need to more fully consider how interpretation plays a central role in understanding those characteristics and qualities that define the good person and the good life. To the extent that certain virtues can be found to be present across most cultures, there are huge and generally unexplored ways that the meaning of these virtues can be radically different for those who hold them. The virtue of caring, for instance, is generally interpreted within Western cultures to mean caring about other people—yet there are traditions for whom caring about the environment and about the self are also moral imperatives (Campbell & Christopher, 1996b). Moreover, even when there is consensus about the object or domain of caring, there are frequently considerable differences across and within cultures around what it means to care in a particular situation, such as with the elderly. A hasty attempt to declare that certain virtues are universally endorsed can obscure how these common virtues are often prioritized in very different ways. Respect, for example, is an important virtue in most cultures. Yet, while Turkish and Micronesian college students consider respect the most important attribute of the good person, American students ranked it 35th (Smith et al., 1998).

Comprehending how culture shapes peoples' understanding of virtues, values, and well-being will indeed complicate research endeavors. Our commitment to cultural pluralism demands more of us than the inclusion of other countries in standard research relying on self-report measures. One implication of the moral visions perspective is that people already live out positive folk psychologies: The structure of their lives provides an answer to the question of the good person and good life. These implicit and embodied outlooks need to be juxtaposed with notions of the good that are consciously accessible and espoused by lay persons, as well as with indigenous professional theories of well-being. To fully address how positive psychologies exist at a variety of levels of awareness requires the addition of interpretive methods. This will initially result in a kind of messiness, as some moral development theorists now acknowledge is necessary (Campbell & Christopher, 1996a; Walker & Hennig, 2004; Walker & Pitts, 1998), but this is offset by the potential to capture more of the richness and diversity of human experience.

Positive psychology is critical to the well-being of 21st-century psychology. It will require vigilance to ensure that positive psychology does not become yet another form of a disguised individualistic ideology that perpetuates the sociopolitical status quo and fails to do justice to the moral visions of those outside the reigning outlook. I believe that by paying attention to our underlying moral visions, learning about the moral visions of those across cultures and across time, and learning to think culturally, we can avoid prematurely rushing to ethnocentric conclusions that fail to take full measure of the wisdom of non-Western cultural traditions.

Source: Christopher (2005). Reprinted with permission of the author.

Note: Citations for Dr. Christopher's article are presented in the References section at the back of this book.

PUTTING POSITIVE PSYCHOLOGY IN A CULTURAL CONTEXT

Psychology's past perspectives on culture tell of the pitfalls and progress associated with professional attempts to understand the influence of culture on positive psychology research and practice. Here we provide recommendations to help make sense of culture's role in positive psychology.

Examining the Equivalence of the "Positives" to Determine What Works

Establishing cross-cultural or multicultural applicability of positive constructs and processes goes beyond determining whether strengths and coping mechanisms exist and are valued by members of different cultural groups. It requires an understanding of the indigenous psychology of the group (Sandage et al., 2003) that tells the story of how and when the strength or process became valued within the culture and how it currently functions positively. Studies may be conducted *across* nations (cross-culturally) but must also investigate potential differences between cultural groups *within* diverse nations (multiculturally), such as the United States, to fully appreciate within-group heterogeneity. Qualitative study of a people's development of particular strengths, or use of them in their daily lives, could enhance our understanding of how culture counts in the development and manifestation of that strength (Rich, 2017). At the same time, rigorous, quantitative, cross-cultural, and multicultural studies could reveal additional information about how a strength leads to or is associated with a particular outcome in one culture but a different outcome in another. As a part of this process, a broad cultural definition is wise. Pamela Hays (2016), a practitioner and counseling psychologist, has developed a framework called the ADDRESSING Framework that assists us with this breadth. In the ADDRESSING Framework, each letter stands for a different cultural facet (see Table 4.1), and status on each of these (and their combined effect) can influence the worldview and experience one has in their lives.

Part of the utility of this framework is its ability to be used in talking with clients or research participants. Hays (2016) suggests that creating a "cultural sketch," that is, a review of a person's status or identity along the different facets, can assist a client in noting what areas of their

TABLE 4.1. ■ Pamela Hays's ADDRESSING Framework

A	Age, generational influences
D	Disability (developmental); i.e., a disability that you were born with
D	Disability (acquired); i.e., a disability that occurred later in life
R	Religion (the absence of religion may also be relevant here)
E	Ethnic and racial identity
S	Socioeconomic status or social class
S	Sexual orientation
I	Indigenous heritage
N	Nation of origin
G	Gender; viewed as a continuum, not as a binary

identity are important to them or play a large role in their daily life. In therapy, one might use this process to assess where a client is coming from the beginning, allowing a therapist to take culture into account while assessing strengths and weaknesses and asking good questions of their client to determine the utility of different characteristics in their own lives. In qualitative research, it might serve to make sure that assumptions are not made about the origin of certain characteristics or their value in the life of the participant.

Similarly, one may gain insight as to how a strength plays out in one's life by asking about how the salience of various cultural identities may provide sources of strength for different individuals. This exercise was developed as a class activity by one of this textbook's authors (JTP) and is introduced by asking people to identify three cultural facets (such as race, gender, religion) and to then think about which personal strengths might be derived from membership in these various groups. In the ensuing discussion, it is easy to see that cultural facets can provide many sources of strength for individuals (Pedrotti, 2013b). For example, one may say that coming from a low socioeconomic status has forced them to come up with creative solutions to various problems. Others may feel that being a member of a collectivist group (such as Asian or Latino cultures) may have helped them to develop strong networking skills in their lives. Individuals who hold religion to be a salient factor in their lives may feel that they have more opportunities to cultivate strengths such as altruism or gratitude. In exercises such as these, it seems that identification with various cultural facets can influence the recognition, development, and enhancement of personal strengths.

Discussions with clients, along with well-designed quantitative and qualitative studies with research participants, can provide good data on the equivalence of positive constructs and processes across cultures. With these data in hand, we will be better able to assess what strengths benefit whom (in what situations) and what positive interventions might help people create better lives for themselves (Pedrotti, 2014b; Pedrotti et al., 2021). As professionals attempt to enhance strengths in culturally diverse groups of people, we must ask and answer the question, "What works for whom?"

Cultural Wealth and Culturally Relevant Strengths

Dr. Tara Yosso's (2005) seminal work in her Cultural Wealth Model (see Figure 4.1) is a good example from the field of higher education that centers culture in discussions of strength, challenging the deficit view of communities of culture. In her framework, Dr. Yosso (2005) presents six different types of capital (or strength) that can be used to think about and empower students of color. **Aspirational capital** is defined by Yosso as the "hopes and dreams" (p. 77) held by students and their families as they think about their educational goals, despite the fact that educational inequities still exist as barriers for these students. Those high in this area are able to call upon this strength when facing these inequities in their college experience. **Linguistic capital** is a second part of the Cultural Wealth Model and refers to the strengths around communication including the strong role of storytelling that exists in many communities of color. In addition, some students might have exposure or fluency in languages other than English as given to them by their home cultures, furthering their skills in communication with a larger audience (Yosso, 2005). **Familial capital** refers to the benefit of the often present extended family in the lives of students of color and the benefit they can derive from having many sources of support to turn to in times of need. Interestingly, in other models, family is sometimes shown as a weakness in terms of being the source of less information about college or as a pull on the student that may affect their daily work as a college student. Yosso (2005) recognizes that home communities are not just full of deficits but also possess a source of strengths for students in this part of her theory.

FIGURE 4.1 ■ Yosso's Cultural Wealth Model

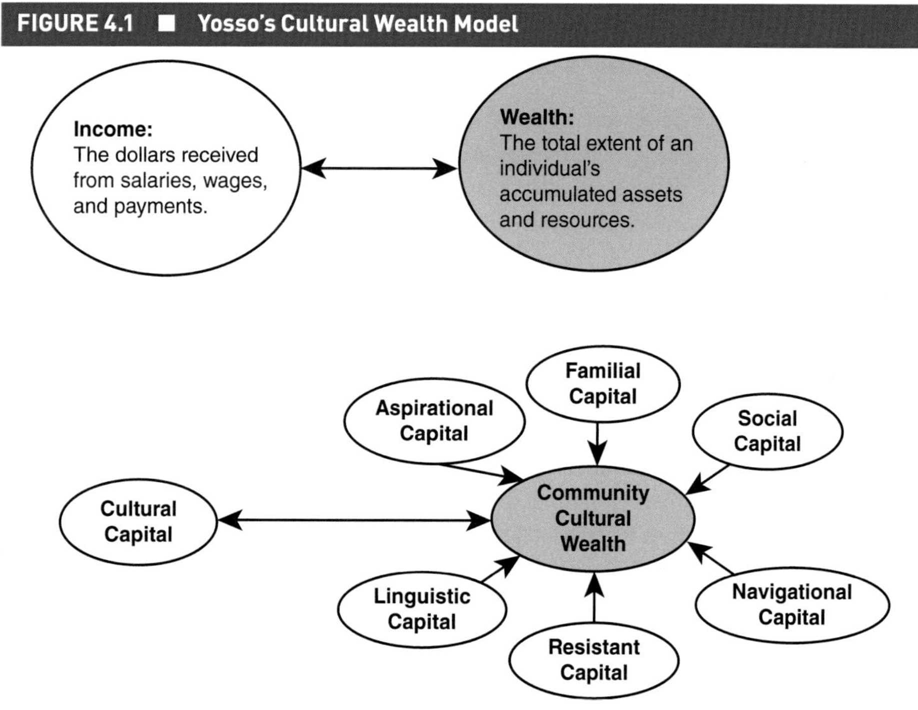

Source: Reprinted with permission from Yosso, T. J. (2005). Whose culture has capital? *Race, Ethnicity, and Education, 8*, 69–91.

Next, social capital, is something that Yosso lists as referring to the connections students of color may have with their home community. Beyond the familial capital noted above, this community may also provide a source of information and may be more readily passed from family to family in communities of color (Yosso, 2005). For example, when one neighbor's child goes to college, they may pass information about the process to another neighbor, effectively sharing this capital through social means. This "networking" also occurs between White families, but is not always recognized as a similar strength in families of color. **Navigational capital** is the fifth form discussed by Yosso (2005) and is meant to describe a student of color's ability to navigate different institutions that are not necessarily set up for them. Higher education has only recently become more racially diverse and as such those who set it up and who work within it may be culturally dissimilar to students of color. Navigational capital refers to students' ability to traverse the system despite these potentially less than supportive environments. Finally, **resistance capital**, is an important capstone piece in Yosso's (2005) model and refers to the fact that communities of color have their very foundations in their fight for equal rights. A student of color's knowledge that they come from stock that has had to fight before, and has won certain rights, may assist them in continuing to engage in social justice, and resisting falling into despair.

Though Yosso's model is almost 20 years old, we wanted to present it to you here as it holds much wisdom for thinking about how strength can be derived from the wealth of being a part of a cultural community. It is a seminal model in its framing of communities of color as sources of strength and positivity.

Determining the Foundations of "the Good Life"

As suggested in the previous section, people's cultural beliefs about forgiveness, hope, optimism, coping, independence, collectivism, spirituality, religion, and many other topics may bear on how particular strengths work in their lives, how they respond to efforts to enhance personal strengths, and which life outcomes they value. Views of the good life are personally constructed over our lifetimes. At the beginning of life, we have natural urges that persist, such as eating and sleeping, and, as we become more cognizant of our surroundings, we link our natural urges to cultural ones, such as eating certain foods and adopting sleep rituals. From the experiences of our daily lives, we construe personal views of what life is all about, and we form **worldviews** (Koltko-Rivera, 2004), or "way[s] of describing the universe and life within it, both in terms of what is and what ought to be" (p. 4). Given that our cultural experiences may be inextricably linked to what we consider to be the foundations of the good life, is it reasonable to believe that all people (in the world) desire happiness as positive psychologists from majority cultures in the West define it (see Chapter 6)? Or are there life outcomes that are just as valued and as valuable as happiness? These are questions that can be explored in a casual debate among friends (and we encourage you to do this), but they also must be examined empirically. Other cultural facets, such as socioeconomic status, may determine what the good life looks like. To an individual who can barely make ends meet, the good life may include having consistent shelter in the winter or having enough food to feed one's entire family. To an individual at a higher end of the socioeconomic spectrum, the good life may include the feeling of accomplishment at being able to afford to travel or to send one's children to a good college. The value of these material objects and events is influenced by what we consider to mean that we are actually flourishing as opposed to just surviving. Future positive psychology clinical work and research also must consider the possibility that cultural forces influence what individuals consider to be the basic foundations of the good life.

To this end, it is important to consider our own positionality in relation to a particular community before we begin to investigate within a group (Williams & Wilson, 2016). Some of us might be members of these cultural communities and will thus have insider knowledge of the best way to investigate our cultures' strengths. If we are not members, we must first turn toward the communities we intend to study to ask the questions "What is important to measure?" and "How can we best describe the good life in that specific context?" Edward Chang and colleagues have recently edited a new resource text entitled *Positive Psychology in Racial and Ethnic Groups* (Chang, Downey et al., 2016). In this book, multiple authors describe what they would like to see in the way of research within Asian American, African American, American Indian/Alaskan Native, and Latinx groups. We have summarized some of these future directions for thoughtful research in culturally specific positive psychology in Table 4.2.

TABLE 4.2 ■ Future Directions for Research With Racial and Ethnic Minority Groups

Population	Guidelines and Suggestions
Asian American (Yu, Chang, Yang & Yu)	Incorporate the role of culture in psychological research and the function that culture plays in Asian American positive psychology.
	Balance research regarding positive and negative emotions. It is recommended that future research on Asian American positive psychology examines the effect of positive and negative emotions on optimal well-being.
	More research is needed that focuses on diverse emotions experienced by different cultural groups. [Do] qualitative or quantitative differences exist between, for example, ethnic groups or members of different acculturative generations?
	Positive psychology research emphasizes increasing optimism and positive emotions and thinking, but it might not be useful to focus solely on examining optimism in Asian American culture. It is important for researchers to include suffering as part of the road to happiness because for Asian Americans, happiness may encompass the balance of both suffering and happiness.
African Americans (Mattis et al.)	Examine the diversity of African Americans and the historical and contemporary context within which African Americans reside.
	Seek to understand how African American people develop character strengths and virtues within contexts that might otherwise yield less positive outcomes.
	[Study] (a) the extent to which African Americans are able to identify and use personal and ecological assets to mitigate negative forces (e.g., racial discrimination), (b) the processes by which these outcomes are achieved; and (c) the virtues, character strengths, and areas of positive functioning that may be absent from the existing taxonomy of positives represented in the field but that may be especially relevant to the lives of African Americans.

(Continued)

TABLE 4.2 ■ Future Directions for Research With Racial and Ethnic Minority Groups (*Continued*)

Population	Guidelines and Suggestions
American Indians (Morse, McIntyre, & King)	[Conduct research on] defining strengths of AI/AN traditional health practices, which may lead to better health outcomes. These health practices include cultural values, elders, spiritual practices, and community support (J. T. Garrett & Garrett, 1994).
	Identification of associated cultural factors [with resilience] which can include research on AI/ANs. Future research must examine the multidimensional nature of cultural identity to better understand how various domains of ethnic self-identification are correlated with well=-being.
	Creation of AI/AN norms for positive psychology measures, for example the Coping Humor Scale (Martin, 1996), Connectedness to Nature Scale (Perrin & Bebassum, 2009) and others. It may be useful to implement these measures in AI/AN communities in which humor and man's connection to nature are considered important coping mechanisms. Mohatt et al.'s (2011) assessment of awareness of connectedness as a culturally based protective factor could serve as a prototype for other tribal communities to assess culture-specific sources for resilience and positive coping.
Latinx (Castellanos & Gloria)	[Direct scholarly inquiry] by connecting theory and practice while underscoring social advocacy for Latina/os. For example, implementing a mixed-methods design of interacting with the community and learning community challenges, social issues, and unique ethnic specific resilience beliefs and practices will help researchers better understand the process, value, and meaning of well-being for Latina/o communities.
	[Consider] emic theories or frameworks that will generate a culturally inclusive examination of Latina/os and psychology. How are the phenomenological processes accounted for in the design and do the measures encompass Latina/o group values, beliefs, and practices that allow transformation (i.e., the removal of filters through which life experiences or processes are understood)? Scholars and trainers must capture the scope of Latina/o realities (e.g., life challenges and social struggles), coping processes (e.g., aguantarse), and values (e.g., familismo/family, comunidad/community) in the context of re-storying and un-filtering the notions of individual and collective well-being.
	Recognize [researchers'] intent and social responsibility to assess properly all groups in the xprocess of studying a phenomenon. To fully examine the multidimensionality of Latina/os (e.g., identity, gender, sex), research questions must be dimensionalized to include psychological (e.g., self-power), social (e.g., community), and cultural (e.g., spirituality) processes within the context or setting of the individual to engage wellness.

FINAL THOUGHTS ON THE COMPLEXITY OF CULTURAL INFLUENCES

John Chambers Christopher and Katie Howe (2014) state,

> A multiculturally inclusive positive psychology requires not only extending positive psychology to groups that have been ignored or marginalized. It also requires critically examining the values and assumptions that underlie the field of positive psychology to prevent perpetuating the socioeconomic and political status quo. (para. 1)

This is our charge as positive psychologists. Psychology and future positive psychologists must continue to work to understand the complexity of cultural influences on the development and manifestation of positive personal characteristics and desirable life outcomes. The increasing cultural diversity in the United States, along with rapid technological advances that facilitate our interaction with people from around the world (Friedman, 2005), will outpace our discoveries of the specific roles that cultural backgrounds play in psychology. Given that we cannot be certain about issues such as the universality of particular strengths or the extent to which culture modifies how a strength is manifested, we must do our best to determine if and how "culture counts" in each interaction with a client or research participant. A culturally embedded perspective on positive psychology must work to contextualize all research and practice efforts. Specifically, culture-sensitive recommendations for research, practice, and policy making (American Psychological Association, 2003) encourage professionals to develop specific competencies to help account for cultural influences on psychology. Accordingly, culturally responsible research and practice are conducted at the intersections of the professionals' cultures and the research participants' or clients' cultures with researchers and practitioners acknowledging that their own cultural values influence their work.

It has been suggested that discussions of strengths may be particularly necessary when investigating underrepresented individuals in the United States and their experiences due to the damage done by the early pseudoscience discussed earlier in this chapter (Constantine & Sue, 2006; Pedrotti & Edwards, 2009; Pedrotti & Isom, 2021). In fact, people in nondominant cultural groups across the world have often been pathologized for failing to assimilate fully into dominant cultural groups and may experience negative phenomena as a result (e.g., stereotype threat; Aronson & Rogers, 2008; Steele, 1994). As such, it becomes particularly important to broaden our efforts toward investigation of strengths in traditionally marginalized groups such as women and nonbinary genders, racial and ethnic minorities, sexual minorities, and other similarly historically disenfranchised groups. It is also important to recognize that these groups may have specific wisdom and experience to share in the form of coping strategies and resilience as they have, as groups, persevered despite hardships such as stigma, prejudice, racism, heterosexism, sexism, and other types of discrimination (Yosso, 2005). These strengths may have been developed out of need but can be investigated for replication in other groups wanting to hone these powerful traits (Duan & Sager, 2021; Morse et al., 2016).

In addition, research must be expanded beyond the constructs most often studied today. In a quick PsycINFO search completed at press time of articles published in the *Journal of Positive Psychology* (2006–2023) and the *Journal of Happiness Studies* (2000–2023), the keyword of *happiness* yields 223 and 1,715 hits, respectively, in the two journals; *hope* is listed 120 and 73 times, respectively; and *optimism* 60 and 65 times, respectively. These are all very Western-oriented constructs, as discussed in Chapter 2 in this volume. In contrast, we find only 31 total articles on *altruism* in the two journals combined, 79 on *compassion* (though 40 of which are focused on the more Western construct of *self-compassion* and 1 of which is one of the articles above on the topic of altruism), and 25 on *harmony* (most of which are from researchers outside the United States); all of these are constructs that may be more relevant to Eastern groups. In our last edition of this textbook, we performed the same searches up to press time (2018), and although numbers of all articles have obviously gone up, we find that increases across all are constant, meaning that we are no more focused on these non-Western constructs than 7 years ago. We believe broadening our areas of study as a field and publishing results about a diverse array of individuals both within and outside the United States would be beneficial to all groups in that it may lead to greater understanding of strengths in a wider range of people.

Progress toward the goal of counting culture as a primary influence on the development and manifestation of strengths and good living in your research and practice may be best facilitated when you become aware of what you believe about the interplay between cultural and psychological phenomena. Through our personal and professional experiences, we have made some progress toward putting the positive in a cultural context. The authors of this text have different levels of power and privilege based on our various cultural facets as well, and this makes our understandings of how and when culture plays a role in our lives different from one another, even in talking among ourselves. We have come to some general agreement, however, on the following issues. First, psychological strength is universal. Across time, place, and culture, most people have developed and refined extraordinary qualities that promote adaptation and the pursuit of a better life. Second, there are no universal strengths. Although most people manifest strengths, the nature of the manifestation differs subtly and not so subtly across time, place, and culture. Third, life's contexts affect how strengths are developed, defined, manifested, and enhanced, and our understanding of these contexts contributes to diverse presentation of human capacity. History, passage of time, culture, situations and settings, professional perspectives, and human potentialities are reciprocally determined. Fourth, culture is a reflection of, as well as a determinant of, the life goals that we value and pursue. More research must be conducted on constructs that are central to non-Western groups as well. Finally, we must be willing to look beyond our own worldview to truly be able to see strengths in all individuals. The good life is in the mind of the beholder, and the vision of what is meaningful will drive our life pursuits.

In honor of this last statement, we encourage you to look at the field of positive psychology from both your cultural perspective and from the perspective of others. Some of you may find that you are drawn to constructs such as happiness, hope, and optimism. Others of you may find that constructs such as compassion, altruism, and harmony make more sense in your lives. All of these constructs are viable and cannot be ranked except for in our own minds and from our own perspectives. Be cautious of statements regarding "the most important" strength or "universal strengths" and instead learn to view all constructs through the lens of culture. In doing this, *you* become the viable future of the field! We leave you with words from the end of another chapter on culture and positive psychology:

> In closing, Csikszentmihalyi (2014) has discussed the idea that positive psychology has for too long been treated as a "niche field" or "sub-field" such that we have separated it from the field of psychology at large. He argues that all psychology research should attend to a more balanced approach between strength and weakness, regardless of our own specific areas of study. Csikszentmihalyi states that we should think about ways that we can now "fold" positive psychology back into the field at large. We offer that this same "folding" must occur with attention to cultural context. For too long, multicultural and cross-cultural psychology have been treated as "special" topics within the field

at large, as well as within the study of positive psychology (Sue & Constantine, 2014). This is a false separation, as culture must always be a backdrop to the study of people, and therefore lies at the heart of understanding any cognitive, affective, and behavioral process or state, whether the focus is on strength, weakness, or both. Therefore, it is important to the future of positive psychology to think about how we can blend it with cultural context in a more seamless way in order for this field to remain viable. This may be the greatest accomplishment of positive psychology if it can occur, and as our society becomes more and more diverse, perhaps its greatest salvation. If positive psychology can be used as a vehicle to show that strengths and weakness exist in any context and in any person, disenfranchised or not, we may truly be able to move toward equity across different groups in society. (Pedrotti & Edwards, 2017, p. 278)

KEY TERMS

Aspirational capital
Culturally deficient perspective
Culturally pluralistic
Culturally relativistic
Culture
Etiology
Eugenics
Familial capital
Genetically deficient perspective
Linguistic capital
Navigational capital
Resistance capital
Worldview

5 LIVING WELL AT EVERY STAGE OF LIFE

LEARNING OBJECTIVES

After reading this chapter, you will be able to:

5.1 Describe the concept of resilience and the characteristics of resilient children and adults

5.2 Identify emerging trends in resilience research

5.3 Discuss limitations of resilience research across the life span

5.4 Define Positive Youth Development (PYD), and describe how researchers and clinicians facilitate this concept through PYD-oriented programming and intervention.

5.5 Describe the life tasks of adulthood and how they can lead to successful aging

5.6 Identify the components of successful aging and emerging trends in successful aging research

As a discipline, positive psychology grew from a reaction to historically focusing on what is wrong with people. However, some disciplines in psychology have never wavered from a commitment to understanding what is *right* with people. Developmental psychologists, for example, have studied factors contributing to healthy and adaptive functioning for decades. Rather than taking snapshots of life, developmentalists use a methodology akin to time-lapse photography—thousands of still pictures of life (or interviews of people) are linked together to tell a compelling story of individual development. Such in-depth knowledge of the past and the present helps them predict how individuals will function and behave in the future.

In this chapter, we review developmental researchers' discoveries about "what works" across the life span via three interrelated sections. First, we highlight what developmental researchers have discovered about resilience (i.e., the ability to overcome adversity). Second, we address the research and theory on positive youth development. Third, we explore the life tasks associated with adulthood and the ways psychologists are helping individuals meet those challenges. Throughout this chapter, we encourage you to consider the developmental factors associated with adaptation and good living through all the seasons of one's life.

RESILIENCE AT EVERY AGE

Gun violence has become the leading cause of death for children in the United States.
iStockphoto.com/gguy44

On May 24th, 2022, an armed gunman forced his way into Robb Elementary school in Uvalde Texas. He was equipped with two assault-style weapons and several high-capacity magazines. On that tragic day, he murdered 19 young children and two teachers. In the immediate aftermath, mental health professionals rushed to the small town to offer their services to survivors and their parents. Just a few years earlier, a gunman armed with a similar weapon killed 17 students at Parkland High School in Parkland Florida. Only a few years before that, a gunman (again armed with a semi-automatic rifle), murdered 20 first graders and six adults at Sandy Hook Elementary in Newtown Connecticut.

Most children, adolescents, and adults in the United States will likely (and hopefully) *not* encounter such extreme trauma. Nevertheless, traumatic, and other adverse experiences (e.g., abuse, divorce, death of loved one) are increasingly common in childhood and across the life span. For example, the Department of Health and Human Services (2022) reported that more than 3.15 million child protective services investigations were conducted in 2020. Of the identified child victims, three-quarters (76.1%) were neglected, 16.5% were physically abused, 9.4% were sexually abused, and 0.2% were sex trafficked. Likewise, most adults will experience trauma or a stressful life event in their lifetimes (Anders et al., 2012; Roberts et al., 2011; U.S. Department of Veterans Affairs, 2023). Fortunately, as we discuss in more detail in the sections to follow, the science of resilience tells us that many (perhaps most) individuals experiencing adversity will overcome those struggles over time.

The Roots of Resilience Research

The science of **resilience** grew out of research on children and adolescents. In the 1970s, a core group of developmental scientists began to study children who succeeded in life despite having lived through significant adverse experiences. These children were referred to as "resilient," and their stories captivated the interests of clinicians, researchers, and laypeople for decades. Over time, research on resilience spread beyond focusing solely on children to include resilience at other stages of life.

How does one define resilience? This question has sparked much debate over several decades (Southwick et al., 2014). For this text, we assert that the most parsimonious definition of resilience is "bouncing back" after experiencing adversity. In general, observers are looking for a return to normal functioning (e.g., attainment of developmental milestones in children or a return to normal functioning in adults). The following comment on resilience from Cutuli and colleagues (2021) illustrates this definition (p. 172):

> "Resilience" generally refers to the capacity of a dynamic system to adapt successfully to disturbances that threaten its ability to function and continue developing. . . . In developmental science, resilience is usually viewed as an inferential concept that requires two important determinations. . . . First, there is a judgment that individuals are demonstrating competence ("doing okay" at a minimum) with respect to a set of expectations for behavior. Second, there must be significant exposure to risk or adversity that has posed a serious threat to good outcomes.

Cutuli and colleagues' (2021) definition of resilience builds on a rich history of scholarship generally following one of two paths: **variable-focused research** (i.e., looking at how certain *variables* serve as protective or risk factors for individuals facing adversity) or **person-centered research** (i.e., identifying *people* considered to be resilient and studying how they are different from individuals deemed not to be resilient—people struggling after adversity or not currently experiencing adversity).

One scholar, Emmy Werner (1929–2017), is sometimes called the "mother of resiliency." She was a person-centered researcher. That is, she identified resilient people and then got to know them extremely well over time. Given her prominence in this area of positive psychology, we discuss her work as an exemplar of informative resilience research. Werner collaborated with her colleague, Ruth Smith (Werner & Smith, 1982, 1992), in a study involving a cohort of 700 children born on the Hawaiian island of Kauai from 1955 to 1995. From birth on, psychological data were collected from children and adult caregivers, many of whom worked in jobs associated with the sugarcane plantations that used to dominate the island. At birth, one third of these children were considered as "high-risk" for academic and social problems because of their deficits in family support and home environments (e.g., poverty, parental alcoholism, and domestic violence).

Of the at-risk students in the Kauai study, one third also appeared to be invulnerable to risk factors. Two primary characteristics accounted for the resiliency of these children. First, they were born with outgoing dispositions. Second, they were able to engage several sources of support. Better care during infancy, greater intelligence, and positive perceptions of self-worth also contributed to adaptive outcomes for these children. The other two-thirds of the children in the high-risk group developed significant life problems in childhood or adolescence. By their mid-30s, however, most research participants in the Kauai study reported (and psychological tests and community reports corroborated) they had "bounced back" from the challenges faced earlier in their lives. Over time, more than 80% of the original high-risk group had bounced back. In retrospect, many of those who were resilient attributed their buoyancy to the support of one caring adult (e.g., a family member, neighbor, teacher, mentor).

Building off the historic Kauai study findings, resilience researchers over the past four decades have examined the dispositions of a variety of at-risk children, along with the physical and social resources of the youngsters who faced these disadvantages successfully. According to Cutuli et al. (2021), findings from case studies, qualitative research, and large-scale quantitative projects "converge with compelling regularity on a set of individual, relationship, and environmental attributes associated with good adjustment and development under a variety of life-course threatening conditions across cultural contexts" (p. 182). These potent protective factors in development were identified in research and reviews in the 1980s (e.g., Garmezy, 1985; Werner & Smith, 1982), and some continue to be borne out in recent meta-analyses where researchers aggregate the findings from a variety of studies (Yule et al., 2019). Indeed, this broad list has held up reasonably well over time and across groups (see Figure 5.1 for examples). Some of these factors are addressed elsewhere in this volume. For example, self-efficacy and a positive outlook on life are discussed in Chapter 8.

A number of researchers have also attempted to operationalize (i.e., measure) resilience in childhood and adolescence via self-report, parent-report, or teacher-report questionnaires. These instruments include the Child and Youth Resilience Measure (Ungar & Liebenberg, 2011), the Connor-Davidson Resilience Scale (Connor & Davidson, 2003), the Resiliency Scales for Children and Adolescents (RSCA; Prince- Embury, 2006), the Social Emotional Assets and Resilience Scales (SEARS; Merrell, 2011; Nese et al., 2012), and the Resiliency Skills and Abilities Scales (RSAS; Jew et al., 1999). Most of these instruments capture sources of resilience internal to the child; however, some instruments, such as the RYDM and the CYRM, address internal and external sources of resilience. In a recent systematic review of child and youth resilience measures, Vannest and colleagues (2021) found evidence to support the use of these scales but noted that researchers have stopped developing new measures of resilience. Thus, some of these instruments may need to be updated to reflect new scientific findings and changing environmental contexts.

Studying Resilience Throughout the Life Span

The bedrock research on resilience in children and adolescents has expanded over the years to encompass the entire life span. Nevertheless, there are few universal truths in the resilience

FIGURE 5.1 ■ Protective Factors for Psychosocial Resilience in Children and Youth

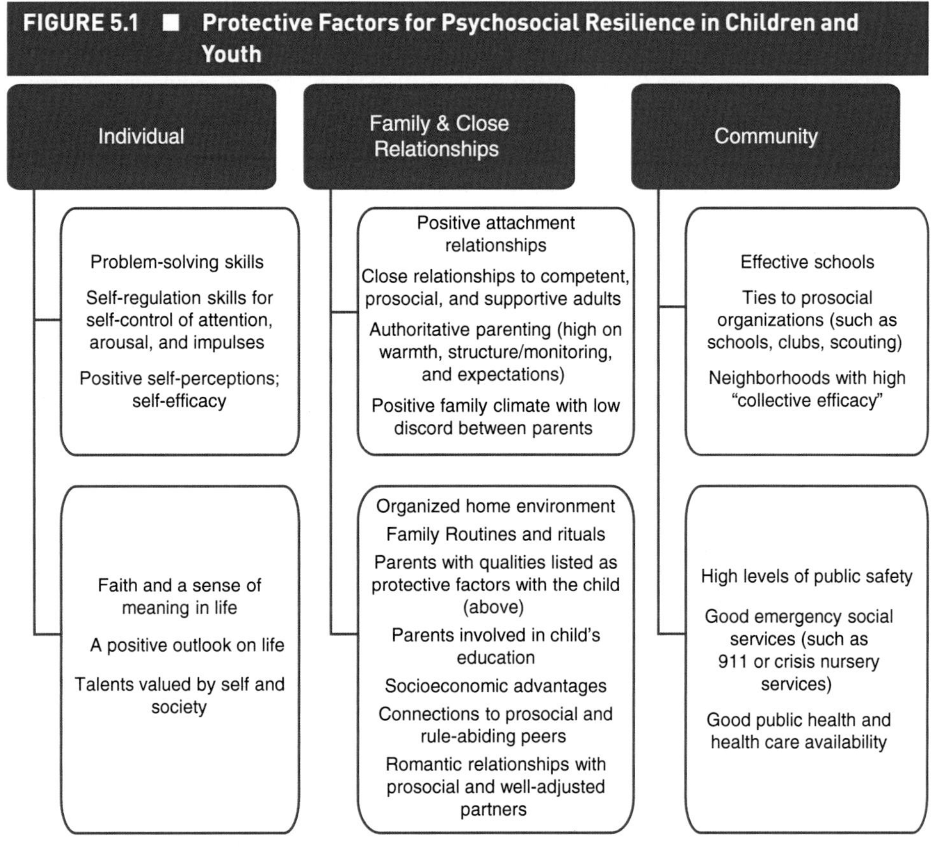

Adapted from Cutuli et al. (2021). In Lopez & Snyder (Eds.), *Oxford handbook of positive psychology* (3rd ed., pp. 170–188). New York: Oxford University Press.

literature for any age group. Indeed, resilience is a complicated and multifaceted construct with biological, psychological, interpersonal, and sociological roots that changes over time (Cutuli et al., 2021). Additionally, there is no agreed upon universal definition for resilience, and there are likely as many definitions of the construct as there are prominent researchers who study it (Southwick et al., 2014). For example, a recent content analysis of the adult resilience literature—including book chapters and reviews published from 2000 to 2016—found that scholars generally fell into different camps regarding the *processes* and *characteristics* of resilience (Ayed et al., 2019). Regarding the former, Ayed and colleagues noted that different perspectives of resilience as a process were evident in how scholars discussed the proposed trajectories of the construct over time. Specifically, some scholars focus on resilience as representing an invulnerability to the deleterious effects of an adverse experience, whereas others describe it as when a person bounces back after an event. Still, other researchers portray resilience as a form of growth after an adverse experience (i.e., a person not only bounces back but comes back even stronger). Of course, some individuals may not display resilience and thus never bounce back from an adverse event at all.

Regarding the characteristics of resilience, most researchers seem to focus on internal psychological assets and strengths (Ayed et al., 2019). This perspective is evident in the way many researchers have operationalized (i.e., measured) resilience in children and adults via self-report questionnaires (Vannest et al., 2021). Specifically, researchers have identified the characteristics and resources of resilient individuals and then developed test questions tapping the degree to which one personally identifies those qualities or resources in their lives. One widely used measure of resilience in adults, The Connor-Davidson Resilience scale (CD-RISC; Connor & Davidson, 2003) is an exemplar of this approach with items such as, "I am able to adapt when change occurs" and "I have one close and secure relationship." As may be evident from the content of these items, the CD-RISC positions resilience as an overall character strength or personal asset allowing individuals to bounce back from difficult events by promoting psychological resilience and providing access to a variety of external resiliency resources. In short, resilience is positioned as a psychological trait (i.e., an enduring characteristic) that helps individuals make the most of their internal and external resources. In a meta-analysis, Oshio et al. (2018) put this assumption to the test by aggregating research on character measures of resilience with Big 5 personality traits (Costa & McCrae, 1992). In support of a trait perspective of resilience, the authors noted a variety of statistically significant aggregate correlations (r)s between self-reported resilience and personality across 30 studies: $r = -0.46$ with Neuroticism, $r = .42$ for Extraversion, $r = .34$ for Openness, $r = .31$ for Agreeableness, and $r = .42$ for Conscientiousness. In other words, there appears to be some nontrivial overlap between resilience and personality traits.

While trait perspectives of resilience have received a great deal of scientific support (e.g., there have been hundreds of studies using the CD-RISC), even the most naturally resilient

Parents have a profound effect on child resilience.
iStockphoto.com/VasylDolmatov

person may falter in the face of extreme adversity (see Ungar & Theron, 2020 for a review). For example, imagine a child or an adult who has a variety of personality characteristics allowing them to make the most of their environmental resources (e.g., teachers, friends, family) in the face of adversity. What happens to that child or adult when they lack a supportive family, teacher, friends, or otherwise do not have the external resources that they need? Clearly, resilience is also conditional on the environment in which a person is embedded (Cutuli et al., 2021; Ungar & Theron, 2020). Thus, models focusing primarily on resilience as a trait may not capture important environment contributions. Fortunately, researchers have also developed holistic models of resilience in childhood and beyond that account for both trait and environmental factors. Next, we briefly touch on two of these models, both of which incorporate a nested ecological system perspective of resilience.

Conceptualizing resilience as more than just an internal trait draws heavily from Bronfenbrenner's ecological systems theory (Bronfrenbrenner, 2005). Specifically, as illustrated in Figure 5.2, all individuals exist in an interrelated set of systems. This holds true for everyone across their entire life span, and we encourage you to consider how you fit into this framework. At the center of the system is you (e.g., your personality characteristics, biological qualities, innate and learned strengths and weaknesses). Your experiences are shaped (and have been shaped) by various systems in your immediate orbit. These proximal systems are referred to as microsystems (e.g., your parents, siblings, peers, teachers). The way these systems interact can also influence you via a broader mesosystem. For example, problems in the home (e.g., abuse, divorce) can influence how one performs at school and vice versa. At an even broader level, your experiences are influenced by an exosystem (e.g., neighbors, where you live, where your parents' work or worked, the media you consume or have consumed). All of these systems are, in turn, influenced by an even broader cultural sphere, the Macrosystem (e.g., cultural norms, laws, historical power inequities in society such as racism, sexism, or other "isms"). Finally, all these systems can change over time, which is referred to as the chronosystem. In summary, development and functioning at all stages of life are likely impacted by a variety of intersecting and interacting factors at the individual, family, community, and broader societal levels.

An ecological systems model of resilience holds that it occurs because of a combination of individual and systemic factors that *protect* against the harmful impacts of adverse experiences or *promote* the development of resilient qualities (Racine et al., 2022). Moreover, this model of resilience has been around long enough to amass a sizeable amount of empirical support across a variety of research studies for children and adolescents (Yule et al., 2019). While the ecological systems model has generally been applied to children and youth, some researchers incorporate a systems perspective into models of resilience across the life span. The Resilience Portfolio model (RPM; Grych et al., 2015), for instance, integrates Bronfenbrenner's ecological systems perspectives, positive psychology, traumatology, and the psychology of stress and coping to provide a holistic view of how adults thrive in the face of adversity, particularly when experiencing violent trauma. Similar to how people are better equipped to handle the volatility of the market if they have a diverse stock portfolio, the RPM suggests that individuals are best prepared to weather significant adversity if they have a variety of psychological assets and a wide array of community and cultural resources (Hamby et al., 2018).

FIGURE 5.2 ■ Bronfenbrenner's Ecological Theory Model (2005).

A key component of this model is that different systems interact and influence each other, with some (such as the Macrosystem) having a more indirect effect on the individual, and others (e.g., the Microsystem) having a much more proximal and direct effect on the individual.

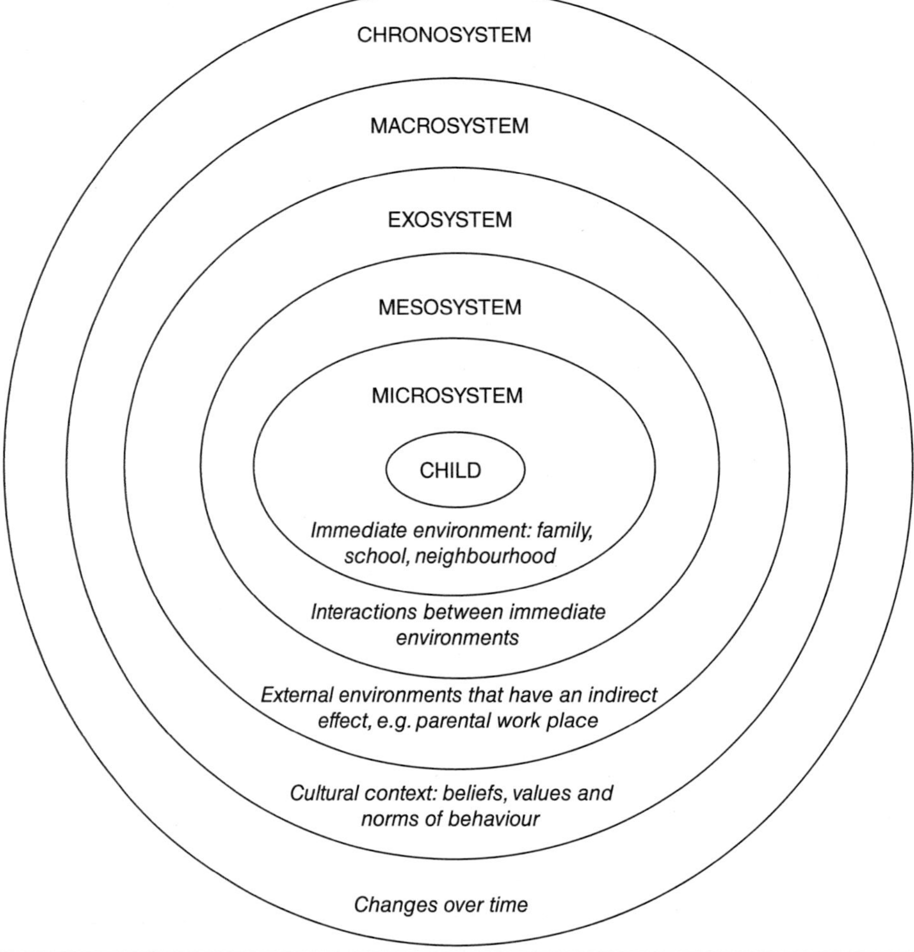

Source: Upton, P. (2011) *Developmental Psychology*. SAGE Publications Ltd.

As illustrated in Figure 5.3, a strong resilience portfolio consists of three interrelated domains. First, a good portfolio should include a variety of self-regulatory strengths. These are personal assets that help people regulate their emotional, cognitive, behavioral, and physiological experience in times of distress (Gyrch et al., 2015). Self-regulation assets help individuals sustain and support their progress toward short- and long-term goals (Hennessy et al., 2020). The RPM emphasizes several self-regulatory constructs from the positive psychology literature such

FIGURE 5.3 ■ The Resilience Portfolio (Gyrch et al. 2015).

The top panels provide the conceptual definitions of the three domains of strengths needed for a strong resilience portfolio. The bottom panels provide specific constructs that represent each strengths domain in the portfolio.

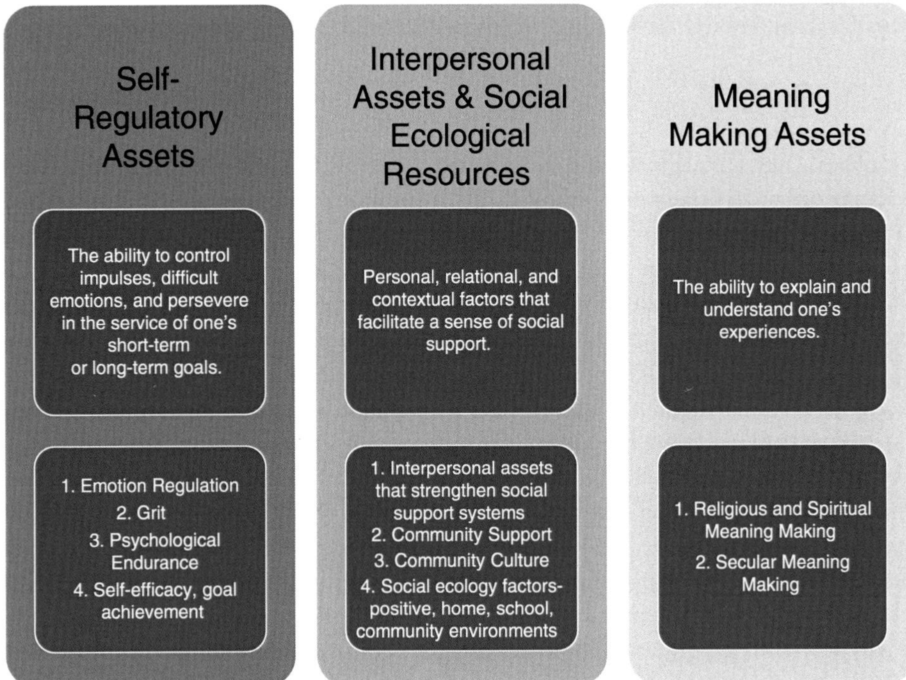

as perseverance and grit (Duckworth, 2016; Duckworth et al., 2019), self-efficacy (Bandura, 2005; Bandura & Adams, 1977), and optimism and future mindedness (Alarcon et al., 2013).

Second, in addition to self-regulatory strengths, a strong resilience portfolio contains a variety of interpersonal assets and external resources. This domain of the RPM consists of internal qualities that help individuals connect with others, as well as the different social and community systems in which a person is embedded. The key to this domain is perceived social support, a variable that has been linked to resilience across multiple studies over the years (Yule et al. 2019). Personal assets such as gratitude, compassion, generosity, or forgiveness may enhance and strengthen social networks for an individual when they express these qualities outwardly, thus leading to a stronger social support network (Deichert et al., 2021). Additionally, interpersonal resources, such as a positive home, school, neighborhood climate, and a sense of community or cultural belonging are an important part of the RPM (Gyrch et al., 2015).

The third domain of the RPM addresses the concept of meaning-making (i.e., the ability to find a sense of meaning in difficult or traumatic life events). Drawing on research in traumatology, particularly the concept of posttraumatic growth (Tedeschi & Calhoun, 1996), the RPM asserts that, "making meaning of difficult experiences is facilitated when individuals have a clear set of beliefs, values, and goals and the sense that life has meaning or purpose" (Gyrch et al. 2015, p. 347). Factors such as religious and spiritual beliefs, as well as secular meaning-making, may be a profound source of resilience for many individuals (Aten et al., 2019) and may be particularly salient for Black (Robinson & Golphin, 2021) and Latinx populations (Ceballo et al., 2020).

While the RPM is a relatively new concept within a vast array of resilience research, its development was informed by a large body of scientific evidence from a variety of different disciplines. Thus, it is not surprising that research guided by the RPM largely supports the key tenants of the model at the time of this writing. For example, Hamby et al. (2018) examined the RPM in a large sample of participants from the rural Appalachia region of the Southern United States (N = 2,565; mean age = 30; standard deviation = 13.2). Consistent with the expected characteristics of the population, 98% of their sample reported having experienced significant adversity. The authors invited community members to complete self-report assessments capturing each component of the RPM, and they also created an index of "poly-strengths" by calculating the number of strengths with scores above the sample average for each individual. Hamby and colleagues found that a portfolio of self-regulatory, interpersonal, and meaning-making assets and resources explained significant variation in greater well-being, posttraumatic growth, and mental health even when statistically accounting for experiences of adversity, age, and gender. Moreover, they identified that having more poly-strengths explained unique variation in each outcome variable, suggesting that the number and density of strengths may be more critical to thriving in the face of adversity than any single asset or resource alone. These findings are consistent with those reported by other researchers. For instance, in a sample of 407 Spanish speaking adolescents, Gonzalez-Mendez et al. (2021) found that density (i.e., more intensity of strengths) and diversity (i.e., more variety of strengths) in one's resilience portfolio discriminated between those who scored high or low in posttraumatic growth.

Limitations of Resilience Research: Cultural Considerations

Resilience research, like all areas of inquiry in psychology, is not without limitations. For example, although researchers are now placing greater emphasis on how different ecological systems impact resilience in children (Racine et al., 2022) or adults (Gyrch et al. 2015), most studies focus on the family or the individual. This means that other cultural systems, particularly macro systems, are neglected in the literature (Yule et al., 2019). Additionally, when macrolevel factors are included, researchers tend to focus on risk factors such as racism, prejudice, or other experiences of discrimination linked to historical power inequities rather than cultural assets and strengths in minority samples. However, it is possible that macrolevel factors may be a source of resilient strength in certain contexts. For example, some investigators have argued that more, "positive feelings about the self, one's culture, and one's ethnic group promotes resiliency and are linked to positive behaviors" (Belgrave et al., 2000, p. 143). Research has generally supported this assertion. In a study with Black girls, for instance, a strong racial identity was associated with greater resilience in an academic context (Butler-Barnes et al., 2018). Additionally, some evidence suggests Blacks may be resilient as a result of the racial hardships unique to their experiences in a racist and classist culture (Cavalhieri & Wilcox, 2022). Thus, encouraging children and adults to develop positive connections with cultural communities may increase resiliency toward negative factors in life, which may include adaptive reactions to discrimination, racism, and prejudice.

In addition to a lack of research incorporating *all* levels of the ecological system, it is possible that researcher bias may be coloring the way we think about resilience in general. For example, Waller (2001) pointed out that the notion of resilience as being an internal characteristic likely reflects broader, Western, and Eurocentric values and beliefs. Additionally, most resilience research is conducted by a team of investigators with little or no input in the design, assessment, or interpretation from members of the community being studied. Researchers must account for culture and the expectations of a community when determining what might constitute a positive outcome from an adverse experience for specific groups. Cultural forces dictate whether researchers examine positive educational outcomes, healthy within-family functioning, or psychological well-being—or perhaps all three. Due to unexamined bias, sometimes researchers may not be asking the types of questions that help to obtain an accurate picture of some groups, particularly when dealing with participants from racial and ethnic backgrounds who have been historically pathologized. Clauss-Ehlers (2008) suggested that researchers can be unintentionally biased in the types of topics they examine (e.g., looking at reasons for *poor* school achievement in Latino youth rather than looking for reasons for *exceptional* school achievement in the same sample). Unconscious or conscious stereotypes about certain groups can lead us away from asking questions that allow for members of traditionally marginalized groups to show their true strengths. Research designs involving participant interviews (i.e., mixed methods or qualitative research), as well as designs that include community members in the conceptualization, implementation, and interpretation stages of a project (i.e., community-based participatory action research) may hold promise for overcoming these limitations.

FOSTERING POSITIVE YOUTH DEVELOPMENT

How might psychological science be leveraged to help develop resilient children and youth? This is a question that many psychologists have addressed via the concept of **positive youth development (PYD)**. These researchers (i.e., **positive youth developmentalists**) focus on ways of fostering positive development that provide a solid psychological, relational, and environmental foundation for children and better prepare them for the eventual challenges of adulthood. In the following sections, we first define and describe PYD and the socially valued positive outcomes that have been identified by youth advocates and researchers. Then, we discuss and critique some examples of different types of PYD programs.

What Is Positive Youth Development?

Historically, problems in youth or adolescence have been addressed via a deficit model (i.e., the goal has been to reduce risk factors that lead to problematic behaviors). However, a deficit model only yields information about what factors need to be removed. A PYD framework provides a way for researchers and practitioners to reduce problematic behaviors by building on and enhancing strengths or assets. These assets can be targeted in youth, family, and the community, often through a combination of group and individual interventions ranging from specialized classes/workshops to ongoing extracurricular activities (García-Poole et al., 2019). Through the benefits provided to youth via the intentional combination of these environmental resources and caring supporters in the context of PYD programs, youth can thrive.

Researchers Peter Benson and Peter Scales (2009) define thriving as "a specific expression of positive youth development" (p. 90) and discuss it as a process between self and environment that develops over time. Thriving youth are doing more than just "surviving" or "getting by." They are achieving their potential and living a rich life that involves giving back to their communities, and that brings them high levels of personal well-being. Such healthy development is marked by the attainment of some of the following nine positive outcomes (Catalano et al., 2004; Ciocanel et al., 2017; Koller & Verma, 2017; Roos & Haanpää, 2017; Williams & Deutsch, 2016) (Many of these positive outcomes are addressed elsewhere in this volume).

1. Rewarding bonding
2. Promoting social, emotional, cognitive, behavioral, and moral competencies
3. Encouraging self-determination
4. Fostering spirituality
5. Nurturing a clear and positive identity
6. Building beliefs in the future
7. Recognizing positive behavior
8. Providing opportunities for prosocial development
9. Establishing prosocial norms

Several scholars have attempted to define the components of PYD. Like the construct of resilience, there is no universal definition. For example, Benson and colleagues (1998) proposed a list of 40 developmental assets that help children thrive. These assets can be organized into four broad categories of external and internal assets; you can purchase an assessment of all 40 via the Search Institute (https://searchinstitute.org/). Specifically, external assets include *support* (i.e., a supportive community and a positive and safe school, family, and neighborhood climate), *empowerment* (i.e., feeling valued by one's community, having the opportunity to contribute positively to community development), *boundaries and expectations* (i.e., having clear rules and boundaries in one's family and community), and *constructive use of time* (i.e., having opportunities—outside of school—to learn and develop new skills). Internal assets consist of a *commitment to learning* (i.e., a sense of mastery and appreciation for learning), *positive values* (i.e., developing strong guiding values and principles to help make healthy choices), *social competencies* (i.e., the ability to effectively interact with others and cope with new situations), and a *positive identity* (i.e., having self-worth and a sense of control over how one experiences life).

Subsequent researchers, such as Richard Lerner, developed similar models of PYD. Lerner et al.'s (2009) "5c" model focuses on five essential competencies necessary for PYD: competence, confidence, connection, character, and caring. Likewise, Catalano and colleagues (2004) identified 15 components of PYD: bonding, resilience, social competence, emotional competence, cognitive competence, behavioral competence, moral competence, self-determination, spirituality, self-efficacy, clear and positive identity, belief in the future, recognition for positive behavior, opportunities for prosocial involvement, and fostering prosocial norms. Whether the components of PYD consist of 40, 5, or 15 internal or external attributes remains to be settled in the literature. Nevertheless, scholars seem to agree that a conceptual definition of PYD should emphasize (a) strengths, (b) developmental plasticity, (c) internal developmental assets (such as self-competence), and (d) external developmental assets (such as a supportive family and community) (Shek et al., 2019).

Positive Youth Development in a Cultural Context

Many authors call for a complex understanding of what it means to study PYD, with the conclusion that positive behaviors can only be promoted once one understands the types of pitfalls and difficulties that exist for youth today (Ciocanel et al., 2017; Lewis, 2011). Others counter by saying that focusing on decreasing problems has overshadowed efforts to bolster positive growth (Lerner et al., 2010). This places researchers of positive psychology, with their commitment to balance both positive and negative sides, in an excellent position to study more about this important area. Regardless of which direction we go, we must also evaluate PYD programs in a number of different ways. Importantly, we must be sure that such programs are in fact positive (Ciocanel et al., 2017; Lerner et al., 2016; Tolan, 2016).

In addition, exploring both positive and stressful situations for youth in many different social identity circles is very important. It may be that different developmental assets exist for different populations and cultures (Holtz & Martinez, 2014). In some groups, such as Black youth, strong ethnic identity is related to positive characteristics like higher self-esteem (Negy et al., 2003; Sellers et al., 2006). In addition, Mexican immigrant children with a strong, positive ethnic identity demonstrated greater academic performance, particularly at schools that were predominantly White (Spears-Brown & Chu, 2012). Furthermore, particular elements of PYD may be especially important for racial and ethnic minority youth. In a study involving a group of Black and Latinx youth, researchers found that including a component on self-transformation emphasizing self-discovery and self-definition appeared to be particularly effective (Eichas et al., 2017). In thinking about ways in which racial and ethnic minority youth may be defined by others in more negative ways (e.g., stereotypes), this type of program seems especially beneficial. Benefits have been found cross-culturally as well, especially when assets were considered within a cultural context (Koller & Verma, 2017). Thus, continuing to explore diverse youth will add information about how to enrich the development of children and adolescents in different racial, ethnic, and national groups.

Some of this work might look individually at different social identity groups (e.g., racial or gender minorities) without making comparisons with a majority group. Kenyon and Hanson (2012) investigated programs that were particularly helpful for American Indian and Alaska

Native (AI/AN) youth. These researchers highlight the PYD program Project Venture, which is specifically designed for AI/AN youth and uses traditional American Indian approaches and values to help youth to develop many positive qualities. Other programs have specifically targeted girls by bringing gender into a positive youth development program using sports, instead of using a previously gender-neutral or boy-focused defined program for girls (Rauscher & Cooky, 2016). In particular, Rauscher and Cooky (2016) noted how programs that center on sports but do not address gender in working with girls often "risk unwittingly maintaining the gender status quo" (p. 288). Rauscher and Cooky, as well as others, recommend that programs should specifically address gender when working with a particular population.

Some researchers also have noted that programs aimed at positive youth development may not be equally accessible to all youth for various reasons. For example, Fredricks and Simpkins (2012) note that Black and Latinx youth disproportionately do not participate in after-school activities (which can fulfill the function of positive youth development) as often as White youth. There may be many reasons for this finding, such as differences in cultural orientation, variations in feelings of belongingness, or combined effects of race and other social facets (e.g., socioeconomic status). In impoverished communities of color, positive youth development programs can work to offset some of the possible risks inherent in a lower-income neighborhood while also providing more opportunities for children in these communities to flourish (Smith et al., 2017).

As mentioned in the section on resilience, studying positive development in more than just White communities is an important step toward reducing stereotypes against youth of color (Clauss-Ehlers, 2008). At the same time, the way such research is conducted may further harmful stereotypes. For example, Evans and colleagues (2012) talk about the fact that studies on Black youth more often investigate deficits and negative outcomes, whereas articles on Asian American and European youth in these same journals tend to focus on positive development or standard outcomes. Although researchers often have good intentions, including attempting to help populations that are struggling, they run the risk of stigmatizing or creating deficit models from which it is difficult for these groups to recover (Reyes & Elias, 2011). Thus, Researchers must be purposeful in not only studying negative outcomes for racial and ethnic minority groups but also making sure to include underrepresented groups in positive youth development research (Smith et al. 2017). Focusing on positive development may balance some of the more negatively focused research about these groups (Pedrotti & Edwards, 2014).

Positive Youth Development Programs

PYD programs come in many forms (Benson & Saito, 2000), including structured or semistructured mentoring programs; organizations providing activities and positive relationships; socializing systems promoting growth (e.g., daycare centers, school, libraries, museums); and communities facilitating the coexistence of programs, organizations, and communities. Here, we discuss the efficacy of some well-known PYD programs reflecting some common approaches. Specifically, some programs focus their energy toward developing positive mentoring relationships (e.g., Big Brothers Big Sisters of America), whereas other programs provide life skills to promote resilience and positive coping (e.g., the Penn Resilience Program). Others focus on youth empowerment and fostering a positive identity (the Changing Lives Program). The soundness of these interventions is determined by the extent to which they promote the "good" and prevent the "bad" in today's youth.

PYD Programs Focused on Mentoring. Social support, especially via a caring adult, is critical to resilience in childhood (Yule et al., 2019). Thus, it is not surprising that PYD programs focused on positive mentoring have a great deal of scientific evidence supporting their effectiveness. For instance, Raposa and colleagues (2019) conducted an extensive meta-analysis of the literature published on youth mentoring programs from 1975 to 2017. They found that when aggregated together, programs evidenced a statistically significant, medium-sized beneficial effect on five main outcomes: school functioning, social relationships, health, cognition, and psychological symptoms. Moreover, Raposa and colleagues noted that there was little variation in the effectiveness of youth mentoring programs across these five outcome domains.

Big Brothers and Big Sisters (BBBS) of America is one of the oldest (initiated in 1905) and best known mentoring programs in the United States designed specifically to help youth find a caring adult mentor. For no fee, the program matches low-income children and adolescents with adult volunteers who are committed to providing caring and supportive relationships. BBBS has over 230 agencies in over 5,000 communities in all 50 states and served 109,254 children in 2020 (Porzig, 2021). Mentors are screened carefully and then provided with some training and guidelines for positively influencing youth. Mentoring activities are unstructured or semistructured, and they typically take place in the community, though some BBBS activities are school sponsored. Regarding the effectiveness of the program, randomized control trials over the years suggest that youth assigned to be in the BBBS program generally fare better than youth not in the program. For example, Tierney and Grossman (2000) found that, compared to youth not matched through BBBS, the program did promote the good (academic achievement, parental trust) and prevent the bad (violence, alcohol and drug use, truancy). Likewise, Herrera and colleagues (2011) found that, relative to the control group, mentored youth performed better academically, had more positive perceptions of their own academic abilities, and were more likely to report having a "special adult" in their lives after 1.5 years of mentorship. These findings are consistent with the yearly impact report published by BBBS, which highlights that more than 90% of youth in the program tend to report that their mentor is a "special adult" in their life after one year of mentoring (Porzig, 2021).

While the BBBS program has been deemed effective, many researchers have noted areas for improvement. For instance, some mentoring relationships end prematurely, and this has been associated with greater problematic outcomes (DeWit et al., 2016). Additionally, approaches to mentoring among BBBS volunteers differ widely, and some approaches may be more effective than others. Mentors who involved their youth in the decision-making process, for example, were more effective than mentors who made unilateral decisions with their mentees (Lyons et al., 2021). Additionally, while BBBS clearly has noted academic benefits in the short term, many of those benefits did not carry forward over time in the most recent randomized control study (Herrera et al., 2011). Given the wide use of the BBBS program, therefore, more research is needed to understand how and for whom mentoring has the best impact over time.

iStockphoto.com/JHVEPhoto

PYD Programs Focused on Life Skills. Some PYD programs teach children and adolescents to self-regulate their thoughts, feelings, and behaviors. One well-known example of this approach is the Penn Resiliency Program (PRP; Gillham & Reivich, 2004). The PRP consists of highly structured life-skills development workshops and classes offered mainly to schoolchildren based on cognitive-behavioral therapy (CBT). A highly trained facilitator conducts scripted sessions. The 12 sessions focus on awareness of thought patterns and on modifying the explanatory style of students to change the attributions for events so that they can engage in more adaptive behaviors. Extensive evaluation of the program demonstrated its effectiveness at reducing internalizing problems (e.g., depression and anxiety symptomology) and externalizing problems (e.g., conduct problems) in 697 middle school children compared to a control condition over three years of observation (Cutuli et al., 2013). However, Cutuli and colleagues (2013) noted that the PRP was no more effective than an alternative intervention. Additionally, researchers synthesizing the results from several PRP intervention studies found evidence that a variety of contextual factors (e.g., intervention site, marital status of parents, and child age/grade level) may influence program efficacy (Brunwasser & Gillham, 2018).

PYD Programs Focused on Youth Empowerment. Although not as common as PYD programs focused on positive mentoring or promoting positive coping skills, some interventions address youth empowerment. For example, the Changing Lives Program (CLP; Eichas et al., 2010) is a community-based program that aims to be inclusive of both gender and ethnicity. In this program, facilitators work with a two-pronged approach, attempting to decrease problem behaviors while at the same time promoting positive development. This program works to enhance positive **identity** development while "facilitating mastery experiences" (Eichas et al., 2010, p. 213). Research has shown that this program achieves both of these goals in a diverse sample, although these researchers allowed that some of the findings may be differential at times as a result of race or gender. More research is needed with minority groups to understand the impact of race, ethnicity, and gender more fully on the applicability and design for future youth empowerment programs (Eichas et al., 2010).

Other Avenues to Positive Development. Specific programs designed by psychologists, such as those just discussed, are valuable options for fostering PYD, but they may not be available to all youth. Bundick (2011) asserted that other more general extracurricular activities may also promote PYD. In his comprehensive analysis of different types of clubs and activities, Bundick found that leadership activities and volunteering in a prosocial way predicted positive outcomes. Participation in leadership activities seemed to promote a development of purpose in life and a sense of a hopeful future. Even if one was not in a leadership role, participation or volunteering appeared to also contribute to overall positive development, particularly greater life satisfaction (Bundick, 2011). Additionally, several researchers have noted the effectiveness of sports-based PYD programs (SPYD). Bruner and colleagues (2021) conducted a meta-analysis of research on SPYD and found that participation in organized sports can lead to a variety of positive outcomes such as self-regulatory life skills, a sense of competence, and feelings of confidence. These findings show that some potentially more accessible activities can also make a difference in developing positive attributes.

THE LIFE TASKS OF ADULTHOOD

Thus far, we have focused primarily on resilience in childhood and adulthood. Developmental psychologists have also highlighted the basic tasks associated with successfully navigating adulthood. From a positive psychology perspective, therefore, good living would be associated with a successful resolution of each of these tasks. Specifically, guided by Erik Erikson's (1950) stage theory of development and informed by extensive longitudinal data of men and women's psychology across the life span, George Vaillant mapped out (1977) and refined (2002) six tasks of adult development: identity, **intimacy**, **career consolidation**, **generativity**, **keeper of meaning**, and **integrity**. Identity is typically developed during adolescence or early adulthood, when people's views, values, and interests begin to become their own rather than a reflection of their caregivers' beliefs. (Failure to develop a personal identity can preclude meaningful engagement with people and work.) With the development of identity, a person is more likely to seek an interdependent, committed relationship with another person and thereby achieve intimacy.

Career consolidation is a life task that requires the development of a social identity. Engagement with a career is characterized by contentment, compensation, competence, and commitment. For many people, career consolidation, like the other tasks, is "worked on" rather than achieved. That is, people may consolidate their career for decades, even as they move toward and into retirement. In today's workforce, consolidation often is compromised by the need to transition into a new job. As a result, career adaptability (Ebberwein et al., 2004) has emerged as a prerequisite of career consolidation. The level of adaptability required may be more marked in today's difficult economic times. Ability to adjust to layoffs, loss of income, and lack of new job opportunities may be new markers of this type of resilience.

Regarding tasks associated with generativity, people become involved in the building of a broader social circle through a "giving away" of self. As mastery of the first three tasks is achieved, adults may possess the competence and altruism needed to directly mentor the next generation of adults. Indeed, as people age, social goals become more meaningful than achievement-oriented goals (Carstensen et al., 2000). Generativity has been shown to contribute to longer life and less impairment in daily living activities (Gruenewald et al., 2012) as well as better adjustment to retirement years (Serrat et al., 2017). The way in which this works may differ depending on racial group, however (Fabius, 2016; Languirand, 2016; Versey & Newton, 2013).

In the context of a larger social circle, some people take on the task of becoming keepers of meaning. The keeper of meaning has perspective on the workings of the world and of people, and this person is willing to share that wisdom with others. The keeper protects traditions and rituals that may facilitate the development of younger people. In essence, the keeper links the past to the future. Sometimes these meanings are passed through narratives and storytelling, particularly in Black and other collectivist cultural groups (Fabius, 2016). Finally, achieving the task of developing integrity brings peace to a person's life. In this stage, increased spirituality often accompanies a greater sense of contentment with life.

According to many developmental psychologists, mastery of the aforementioned tasks is the object of adulthood. Intentional work on each of these tasks leads sequentially to work on the next task, and the mastery of all tasks is the essence of successful aging. At the same time, it is important to note that much of this research and related theory has been filtered primarily through the identity lens of racial, gender, and sexual majority groups in the United States. Indeed, many of the formative research that serves as the bedrock of adult developmental theory was conducted entirely on White, affluent men. As we continue to learn more about adult development, it will be important to conduct similar longitudinal research with racial, gender, and sexual minorities, as well as individuals from a variety of socioeconomic backgrounds.

Successful Aging

The study of the positive aspects of aging is already several decades old. However, it will become a primary focus of psychological science given the trends in United States demography that will demand the attention of scientists and the general public. It is expected, for example, that the number of individuals in the United States over the age of 65 will double by 2060 (Vespa et al., 2020).

The term ***successful aging*** was popularized by Robert Havighurst (1961) when he wrote about "adding life to years" (p. 8) in the first issue of *The Gerontologist.* Havighurst also primed scholarly interest in healthy aspects of getting older. Rowe and Kahn (1998), summarizing the findings from a well-known longitudinal study of physical, social, and psychological factors related to abilities, health, and well-being in a random sample of 1,189 healthy adult volunteers between the ages of 70 and 79 (i.e., the MacArthur Study of Successful Aging), proposed three components of successful aging: (1) avoiding disease, (2) engagement with life, and (3) maintaining high cognitive and physical functioning. These three components are aspects of "maintaining a lifestyle that involves normal, valued, and beneficial activities" (Williamson & Christie, 2009, p. 168). Vaillant (2002) simplified the definition further by characterizing successful aging as joy, love, and learning. In addition, Carr and Weir (2017) surveyed a large group of older adults and found three distinct themes related to successful aging across several different age groups (e.g., 65–74, 75–84, etc.): (1) staying healthy, (2) maintaining an active engagement with life, and (3) keeping a positive outlook on life. Secondary themes among these age groups differed a bit, meaning that some of what it means to "age successfully" might differ for a 65-year-old versus an 85- or 90-year-old. These descriptions, although not detailed, provide an adequate image of successful aging. Notice that this description leaves much room for cultural interpretation as well, which strengthens its continued utility with multiple groups. While for one person, some of these components may be fulfilled in the home and with family, others may find them in the workplace (particularly since retirement does not always occur at age 65 these days). Different genders, racial and ethnic groups, and other social identity groups may also achieve successful aging in different ways. For example, some research shows that factors such as being male and having a higher income lead to more successful aging (Araújo et al., 2016), while others show links between successful aging and higher levels of education (Cosco et al., 2017).

Two kinds of support are also important for successful aging: **socioemotional support** (liking and loving) and **instrumental support** (assistance when someone is in need). Further examination of the MacArthur data, for example, revealed that support increased over time (Gurung et al., 2003). Moreover, the respondents with more social ties showed less decline in functioning over time (Unger et al., 1999). The positive effects of social ties were shown to vary according to the individual's gender and baseline physical capabilities (Unger et al., 1999). Gender also influenced how married participants (a 439-person subset of the total sample) received social support: "Men received emotional support primarily from their spouses, whereas women drew more heavily on their friends and relatives and children for emotional support" (Gurung et al., 2003, p. 487). Other more recent studies provide additional evidence for the fact that social support and engagement seem to provide a more successful aging experience (e.g., Lee et al., 2017). Relatedly, an emerging area of research highlights the positive benefits of companion animals as a source of social support for elderly populations (Pruchno et al., 2018; Hui-Guan et al., 2020).

A sense of productivity may also be an important ingredient of successful aging. For example, Glass and colleagues (1995) examined patterns of change in the activities of a highly functioning sample of 70- to 79-year-olds and in a group of 162 moderate- to low-functioning 70- to 79-year-olds over a 3-year period. The highest-functioning cohort was found to be significantly more productive than the comparison group. Decreases in productivity over time were associated with more hospital admissions and strokes, whereas age, marriage, and increased mastery of certain skills were related to greater protection against declines. These findings are consistent with the work of Williamson and Christie (2009), who suggest that sustained physical activity (an aspect of productive activity) helps to maintain healthy functioning. Accordingly, interruptions of physical activity regimens often precipitate declines in overall well-being, and thus physical activity in older age is an important intervention target. Advancements in technology have created new avenues for meeting this goal such as eHealth (i.e., video communication, exergames, or other electronic games that help individuals engage in physical activity and mobile apps that track, monitor, and encourage various activities). In a review of 40 eHealth intervention studies worldwide published between 2007 to 2018 and with populations over 70 years of age, Kraaijkamp and colleagues (2021) reported that eHealth may be a promising new frontier to support successful aging, especially in combination with more traditional (non-eHealth) methods.

While many researchers have focused on the experiences (e.g., social support, productivity) of older adulthood, some investigators have suggested that our earlier life experience may be equally (if not more) important. For instance, Danner et al. (2001), in their study of the autobiographies of 180 Catholic nuns written in the early 20th century, demonstrated that positive emotional content in the writings was inversely correlated with risk of mortality 60 years later. These nuns, who had seemingly had a lifestyle conducive to successful aging, were more likely to live past their 70th and 80th birthdays if they had told stories of their lives that were laden with positive emotions many decades before. Perhaps these nuns had certain learned or innate strengths that helped them focus on the positive in their lives? Supporting this possibility, numerous researchers have found links between certain personality characteristics and successful aging. In a recent review, Pocnet and colleagues (2021) concluded the following:

> The lifelong contributions of behavioral styles (e.g. health behaviors, social interaction styles), emotions (e.g. emotional stability, optimism, motivations), and cognitive tendencies (e.g. perception and interpretation, selection of environments and comparison frames) may influence how individuals develop over their lifespan and how they age. (p. 281).

Therefore, as we have described throughout this chapter, our understanding of successful aging and other constructs (i.e., resilience and positive youth development) clearly continues to grow.

iStockphoto.com/JuanAlbertoCasado

The body of research on successful aging is growing quickly, and the findings suggest that people have more control over the quality of their lives during the aging process than we once believed. Furthermore, across studies, social support is one of the psychological factors that promotes successful aging. Despite this commonality, as more cross-cultural and multicultural research is conducted and published, it appears that aging and successful aging may vary depending on the particular groups studied. Therefore, successful aging should not be measured against a universal standard (Cosco et al., 2017; Lewis & Allen, 2017). This suggests that future work should consider the cultural aspects of adaptive aging in pursuing clues to the good life in the later years.

RESEARCH SPOTLIGHT: DR. VIRGINIA STURM AND THE POWER OF "AWE WALKS" FOR OLDER ADULTS.

There are many emerging areas or research on successful aging. While we do not have the space to focus on each new area of investigation, we sat down with Dr. Virginia Sturm from the University of California Memory and Aging Center to talk about her recent paper, "Big Smile, Small Self: Awe Walks Promote Prosocial Positive Emotions in Older Adults." The following is the citation:

Sturm, V. E., Datta, S., Roy, A. R. K., Sible, I. J., Kosik, E. L., Veziris, C. R., Chow, T. E., Morris, N. A., Neuhaus, J., Kramer, J. H., Miller, B. L., Holley, S. R., & Keltner, D. (2022). Big smile, small self: Awe walks promote prosocial positive emotions in older adults. *Emotion (Washington, D.C.)*, *22*(5), 1044–1058. https://doi.org/10.1037/emo0000876

What were the key questions you were addressing with this study?

Dr. Sturm: In this study, we investigated whether we could increase experiences of awe with a simple behavioral intervention. All participants were asked to take a weekly, 15-minute outdoor walk. Participants were randomly assigned to either a "control walk" condition, where they received no additional instructions, or to an "awe walk" condition. Those in the awe walk condition were instructed how to experience awe. They were encouraged to approach their walks with fresh eyes, to tap into their child-like sense of wonder, and to focus outward on the details of the world around them. The first key question we examined was whether people who took awe walks would indeed experience more awe. We also wondered whether participants who took awe walks would report greater gains in prosocial positive emotions (e.g., compassion and admiration), which awe are thought to foster, than those who took control walks. We also examined whether they would report greater feelings of a "small self" and being in the presence of vast things. We used photographs that participants took of themselves during their walks to investigate whether there were convergent behavioral results.

What do you feel is the most important finding from this study?

The most important finding from this study was that you could encourage experiences of awe with just a very brief conversation that oriented people to focus outward on the world around them! We found awe walks improved emotional experience both during the walks and on a day-to-day basis. Not only did participants who took awe walks report greater experiences of awe, but they also reported greater experiences of daily prosocial positive emotions over time than those who took control walks—even on days that they did not take awe walks. We used participants' photographs to examine whether awe walks also had effects on their behavior. Over time, the participants in the awe walk group displayed bigger smiles than those in the control walk group and exhibited a smaller self (they filled less of the photographs with their own image and more with the background). These results are consistent with theories that awe promotes feelings of a smaller, yet more connected, self.

How did you become interested in this line of research?

Most of my research focuses on emotional alterations in older adults with dementia. There is increasing interest, however, in simple things that we all can do to promote healthy brain aging across our lives. Behavioral practices that promote positive emotions not only improve well-being but also can help to reduce risk of dementia in later life. I became interested in awe because it has so many important social functions. When we feel awe, we attend to the needs of the collective and are more humble, generous, and kind. Awe is also a relatively easy positive emotion to experience in everyday life without much effort—it just takes an outward focus away from the self and onto the wonders of the world around us. They are easy to find when you look with an open mind.

Courtesy of Dr. Virginia Sturm.

PERSONAL MINI-EXPERIMENTS

FINDING AMAZING PEOPLE OF ALL AGES

In this chapter, we discuss many of the factors that promote healthy development over the life span. Here are a few ideas that might help you discover the positive in people of all ages.

Testing the Effectiveness of Your Mentorship. According to resilience research, a warm relationship with one caring adult can bring out the positive in children and youth. The effectiveness of your own mentorship can be tested through your ongoing work with Big Brothers and Big Sisters or another community-based mentoring program.

Building a Stronger Social Circle. Several of the life tasks of adults are related to developing a stronger social network. Consider the state of your own social network. Draw four concentric circles. In the middle circle, write "Me," and then fill in the remaining circles with the names of the people to whom you give your time and talents on a regular basis; the closer the names are to the center circle, the closer these people are to you. Consider how you can maintain the people in the circles closest to you and bring the other folks closer to you. In particular, look to make new connections to those who may be from a different background than yourself. When you have identified a few strategies, end the exercise by acting on one of your thoughts and giving your time or talent to someone close to you.

Collecting Stories of Aging Well. Every day you encounter people 60 and older. Some of these folks are exuberant; they could be members of Vaillant's happy–well group. Approach five of these people, and ask them if they would be willing to participate in a brief interview. (Tell them that you have just learned about successful aging and you would like to develop a better understanding of how people live well as they age.) Here are some questions you can ask (some derived from Dr. Vaillant's Scale of Objective Mental Health, 2002, p. 342):

- How well are you enjoying your career/retirement?
- How would you describe your last vacation?
- What personal relationships have been important to you since you turned 50? Please describe the most important one.
- In what way does culture impact your aging process? Think about your gender, race, socioeconomic status, or religion when answering this question.

Log your responses to these questions, and attempt to draw conclusions about successful aging in your community from these five interviews.

TOWARD A MORE DEVELOPMENTAL FOCUS IN POSITIVE PSYCHOLOGY

We all face daily hassles and adversities. This is true during childhood, adolescence, adulthood, and older adulthood. Hopefully, as we age, we become more resourceful and adaptable. This appears to be the case because, as we have outlined in this chapter, numerous positive developmental factors help children and adults to bounce back. The findings discussed in this chapter also suggest that positive psychology is well on its way to identifying and sharing meaningful information about how to live a better life. At the same time, we highlighted some significant areas for growth, particularly with respect to cultural factors such as racial, gender, and sexual identities. As the field evolves, we hope to see more inclusive research. Nevertheless, we hope the information provided here resonates with you and provides some insight into the factors that have led to your own development. Additionally, we hope you will try the Personal Mini-Experiments to bring some of these findings to life.

KEY TERMS

Career consolidation
Generativity
Identity
Instrumental support
Integrity
Intimacy
Keeper of meaning
Person-centered research
Positive youth development (PYD)
Positive youth developmentalists
Resilience
Socioemotional support
Successful aging
Variable-focused research

POSITIVE EMOTIONAL STATES AND PROCESSES

6 THE PRINCIPLES OF PLEASURE

Understanding Positive Affect, Positive Emotions, Happiness, and Well-Being

LEARNING OBJECTIVES

After reading this chapter, you will be able to:

6.1 Define and distinguish terms used to talk about happiness and positive affect

6.2 Describe key features of seminal and current research on positive affect (e.g., The Broaden and Build Model)

6.3 Describe key features of scientific research conducted on happiness and satisfaction with life

6.4 Apply research on positive affect and subjective well-being to understanding current issues (e.g., social media use, COVID-19 pandemic, etc.)

6.5 Examine and explain cultural differences that exist in definitions, manifestations, and correlations of positive emotional experiences

6.6 Argue benefits of increasing happiness in the lives of all individuals in an equitable way

Standing at the front of a small lecture hall, Ed Diener, the late University of Illinois psychologist and world-renowned happiness researcher, held up a real brain in a jar with a blue liquid, which he called "joy juice," trickling into it from a small plastic pouch held above. He asked the audience to pretend that their brains could be treated with a hormone (i.e., joy juice) that would make them ecstatically happy and that they could be happy *all the time.* Then he asked the crucial question, "How many people in this room would want to do this?" Of the 60 audience members, only two raised their hands to signify their desires for perpetual happiness.

Shane Lopez told this story:

> Given that I had little exposure to philosophy coursework and that my undergraduate and graduate training in psychology had not exposed me to the science of happiness, I hadn't thought much about happiness in its many forms. Dr. Diener's question intrigued me, and since attending his lecture in 1999, I have attempted to develop a better understanding of the positive side of the emotional experience.

It was in part Dr. Lopez's curiosity about this topic that lead to the first edition of this textbook and the solid research summarized here.

In this chapter, we attempt to add to what you know about pleasure by going far beyond Freud's (1936) **pleasure principle** (the demand that an instinctive need be gratified regardless of the consequences) and by fostering an understanding of the many principles of pleasure that have been linked to good living. In this process, we present what we know about that which makes modern life pleasurable. We also summarize research that examines the distinctions between positive and negative affect. Likewise, we highlight positive emotions and their pleasure-expanding benefits, and we explore the many definitions of happiness and well-being, qualities of pleasurable living. To begin, we clarify the numerous terms and concepts used in this chapter.

DEFINING EMOTIONAL TERMS

The terms ***affect*** and ***emotion*** often are used interchangeably in scholarly and popular literatures. Furthermore, *well-being* and *happiness* appear to be synonymous in psychology articles. Unfortunately, however, the interchangeable use of these terms is sometimes confusing. Although we try to clarify the distinctions among these closely related ideas, we acknowledge the overlap that exists. We begin by suggesting that affect is a component of emotion, and emotion is a more specific version of **mood**.

Ed Diener (1946-2021)
Reprinted with permission of Ed Diener.

Affect

Affect is a person's immediate, physiological response to a stimulus, and it is typically based on an underlying sense of arousal. Specifically, Professor Nico Frijda (1999) reasoned that affect involves the appraisal of an event as painful or pleasurable—that is, its **valence**—and the experience of autonomic arousal.

Emotion

Parsimonious definitions of emotion are hard to find, but this one seems to describe the phenomenon succinctly: "Emotions, I shall argue, involve judgments about important things, judgments in which, appraising an external object as salient for our own well-being, we acknowledge our own neediness and incompleteness before parts of the world that we do not fully control" (Nussbaum, 2001, p. 19). These emotional responses occur as we become aware of painful or pleasurable experiences and associated autonomic arousal (i.e., affect; Frijda, 1999) and evaluate the situation. An emotion has a specific and "sharpened" quality, as it always has an object (Tugade et al., 2021), and it is associated with progress in goal pursuit (Snyder, 2000c; Snyder et al., 1991). In contrast, a mood is objectless, free floating, and long lasting.

Happiness

Happiness is a positive emotional state that is subjectively defined by each person. The term is rarely used in scientific studies because there is little consensus on its meaning. In this chapter, we use this term only when it is clarified by additional information.

Subjective Well-Being

Subjective well-being involves the subjective evaluation of one's current status in the world. More specifically, in his seminal work in this area Diener (1984, 2000, 2013; Diener et al., 2009) defined subjective well-being as a combination of positive affect (in the absence of negative affect) and general life satisfaction (i.e., subjective appreciation of life's rewards). The term *subjective well-being* often is used as a synonym for *happiness* in the psychology literature. Almost without exception, the more accessible word *happiness* is used in the popular press in lieu of the term *subjective well-being*.

DISTINGUISHING THE POSITIVE AND THE NEGATIVE

Hans Selye (1936) is known for his research on the effects of prolonged exposure to fear and anger. Consistently, he found that physiological stress harmed the body yet had survival value for humans. Indeed, the evolutionary functions of fear and anger have intrigued both researchers and laypeople. Given the historical tradition and scientific findings pertaining to more negative emotions and affect, their importance in our lives has not been questioned over the past century.

Historically, positive affect has received less attention over the past century because few scholars hypothesized that the rewards of joy and contentment went beyond hedonic (pleasure-based) values or had any possible evolutionary significance. More recently, however, the potentialities of positive affect have become more obvious (Tugade et al., 2021; Doty et al., 2017; Fredrickson, 2016) and research has drawn more clear distinctions between the positive and negative affects.

David Watson (1988, 2000; Stanton & Watson, 2014) of the University of Notre Dame conducted important research on the approach-oriented motivations of pleasurable affects—including rigorous studies of *both* negative and positive affects. To facilitate their research on the two dimensions of emotional experience, Watson and his collaborator Lee Anna Clark (1994) developed and validated the Expanded Form of the Positive and Negative Affect Schedule (PANAS-X), which is even today one of the most commonly used measures in this area of research. This 60-item scale has been used in hundreds of studies to quantify two dimensions of affect: valence and content. More specifically, the PANAS-X taps both "negative" (unpleasant) and "positive" (pleasant) valence. The content of negative affective states can be described best as general distress, whereas positive affect includes joviality, self-assurance, and attentiveness. (See the PANAS, a predecessor of the PANAS-X, which is brief and valid for most clinical and research purposes. There is also a schedule for children, the PANAS-C; see Laurent et al., 1999.)

Using the PANAS and other measures of affect, many researchers have addressed a basic question: "Can we experience negative affect and positive affect at the same time?" (See Green et al., 1999; Larsen & McGraw, 2011.) Although negative and positive affects once were thought to be polar opposites, much research today shows that unpleasant and pleasant affects are independent and have different correlates (see Bradburn, 1969 for an initial discovery). In more recent research, correlations between positive emotions like joviality, self-assurance, and attentiveness and negative affect were negative (meaning that they were inversely related), but very small (Naragon-Gainey & Watson, 2019; Watson, 2002; Watson & Naragon-Gainey, 2014). You may be able to relate to these findings having perhaps felt both excitement and fear following a scary movie or gratefulness and sadness at a funeral as you remember a loved one. The size of these relationships, however, may increase when some people are taxed by daily stressors and may also increase as a function of age, particularly when combined with higher stress (Blaxton et al., 2021; Keyes & Ryff, 2000). Events that are more relevant to an individual may also elicit more clear positive or negative affect, as shown by a greater negative relationship between the two in these conditions (Dejonckheere et al., 2021).

A more consistent positive relationship between positive and negative affect, however, is found in many Eastern cultural groups, namely in Asian samples (Spencer-Rodgers & Peng, 2018; Spencer-Rodgers et al., 2010). This ability to feel and think dialectically (i.e., in more than one direction or from more than one point of view) about events in one's life is labeled a strength in Asian cultures. It may be that this emotional complexity allows Asians to have a greater level of social intelligence, which is of course beneficial in a collectivist society (Spencer-Rodgers & Peng, 2018).

THE POSITIVE AND NEGATIVE AFFECT SCHEDULE

This scale consists of a number of words that describe different feelings and emotions. Read each item and then mark the appropriate answer on the line provided. **Indicate to what extent you feel this emotion right now.** Use the following scale as you record your answers.

Feeling or Emotion	*Very Slightly or Not at All*	*A Little*	*Moderately*	*Quite a Bit*	*Extremely*
1. interested	1	2	3	4	5
2. distressed	1	2	3	4	5
3. excited	1	2	3	4	5

Feeling or Emotion	Very Slightly or Not at All	A Little	Moderately	Quite a Bit	Extremely
4. upset	1	2	3	4	5
5. strong	1	2	3	4	5
6. guilty	1	2	3	4	5
7. scared	1	2	3	4	5
8. hostile	1	2	3	4	5
9. enthusiastic	1	2	3	4	5
10. proud	1	2	3	4	5
11. irritable	1	2	3	4	5
12. alert	1	2	3	4	5
13. ashamed	1	2	3	4	5
14. inspired	1	2	3	4	5
15. nervous	1	2	3	4	5
16. determined	1	2	3	4	5
17. attentive	1	2	3	4	5
18. jittery	1	2	3	4	5
19. active	1	2	3	4	5
20. afraid	1	2	3	4	5

POSITIVE EMOTIONS: EXPANDING THE REPERTOIRE OF PLEASURE

As some psychologists refined the distinction between the positive and negative sides of the emotional experience through basic research and measurement, other scholars in this area began to explore questions about the potency and potentialities of positive emotions. (In the following sections we use the term *emotion* rather than *affect* because we are addressing the specific response tendencies that flow from affective experience.)

The Seminal Work of Dr. Alice Isen

The late Cornell University psychologist Dr. Alice Isen was a pioneer in the examination of positive emotions. Throughout her life's work, Dr. Isen found that people experiencing mild positive emotions are more likely (1) to help other people (Isen, 1987), (2) to be flexible in our thinking (Ashby et al., 1999), (3) to come up with solutions to our problems (Isen et al., 1987), and (4) to be more willing to exhibit self-control (Pyone & Isen, 2011). In classic research related to these points, Isen (1970; Isen & Levin, 1972) performed an experimental manipulation in which the research participants either did or did not find coins (placed there by the researcher) in the change slot of a public pay phone. Compared to those who did not find a coin, those who did were more likely to help another person carry a load of books or to help pick up another's dropped papers. Therefore, the finding of a coin and the associated positive emotion made people behave more altruistically.

Isen and colleagues also found that eliciting positive emotion helped in better problem solving and finding clues for good decision making (Estrada et al., 1997). In this study, researchers randomly assigned physicians to one of the following experimental conditions: in one condition doctors were given a small bag that contained six hard candies and four miniature chocolates, and in another they were not given this treat (the doctors were not allowed to eat the candy during the experiment). Those physicians who received the gift of candy at the beginning of the experiment displayed superior reasoning and decision making relative to the physicians who did not receive the candy. Specifically, the doctors in the positive emotion condition did not jump to conclusions; they were cautious even though they arrived at the diagnosis sooner than the doctors in the other condition (A. Isen, personal communication, December 13, 2005). Perhaps, therefore, we should give our doctor some candy next time we see them!

In more recent research following Isen's lead, positive emotion has been found to lead people to make less emotional and more utilitarian decisions (Guzak, 2015) and can influence risk taking when the return on the risk is anticipated to be high (Xing & Sun, 2013). Regarding this last finding, research has shown that happier participants showed greater willingness to make decisions to take greater financial risks for high returns. Risk taking could, of course, lead to either a positive or negative outcome (e.g., one could lose money or gain money with a risky financial investment). That said, taking opportunities as they come could provide more benefits in the long term (Xing & Sun, 2013). Finally, experiencing positive affect has been linked to career self-efficacy and less career making indecision, showing another facet of the decision-making properties of positive emotion (Park et al., 2020).

The Broaden and Build Model

Building on Isen's work, Dr. Barbara Fredrickson developed a new theoretical framework in 2000: the **Broaden-and-Build Model of Positive Emotions**. This model provides some explanations for the robust social and cognitive effects of positive emotional experiences. In Fredrickson's review of models of emotions, she found that in addition to responses to positive emotions not having been extensively studied, when researched they were usually examined in a vague and underspecified manner. Furthermore, action tendencies related to negative emotions generally have been associated with physical reactions (for example "fight or flight"), reactions to positive emotions are more often cognitive in nature (for example, the above research regarding better decision making). For these reasons, she proposed discarding the **specific action**

tendency concept (which suggests a restricted range of possible *behavioral* options) in favor of a newer, more inclusive term, **momentary thought–action repertoires** (which suggest a possibility of a broad range of behavioral *and cognitive* options; for example "taking off blinders" and seeing available opportunities).

To illustrate the difference in that which follows positive and negative emotions, consider the childhood experience of one of the authors (SJL). Notice how positive emotions (e.g., excitement and glee) lead to cognitive flexibility and creativity, whereas negative emotions (e.g., fear and anxiety) are linked to a fleeing response and termination of activities.

> During a Saturday visit to my grandmother's home, I had the time of my life playing a marathon game of hide-and-seek with my brother and four cousins. The hours of play led to excitement and giggling . . . and the creation of new game rules and obstacles. The unbridled joy we experienced that afternoon made us feel free; we felt like that day would go on forever. Unfortunately, the fun was interrupted. The abrupt end to the game came when my cousin Bubby spotted me hiding behind the tall grasses on the back of my grandmother's property. I darted out of my hiding place to escape from him. As I ran around the house, I veered off into the vacant lot next door. Laughing with glee, I ran as hard as I could. Suddenly, there was an obstacle in my path. I leaped over it as Bub screamed uncontrollably. As I turned around, I realized I had jumped over a four-foot water moccasin, a highly poisonous snake. As my cousin's screaming continued, I grew increasingly jittery. Without thinking, we backed away from the snake . . . and then ran for our lives. When we finally stopped running, we could not catch our breaths. No one was hurt, but our fear and anxiety had taken the fun out of our day.

In testing her model of positive emotions, Fredrickson (2000) demonstrated that the experience of joy expands the realm of what a person feels like doing at the time; this is referred to as the *broadening* of an individual's momentary thought–action repertoire. To do this, she asked research participants to watch an emotion-eliciting film clip (the clips induced one of five emotions: joy, contentment, anger, fear, or a neutral condition). Following this, she asked them to list everything they would like to do at that moment (see the results in Figure 6.1). Those participants who experienced joy or contentment listed significantly more desired possibilities than did the people in the neutral or negative conditions. In turn, those expanded possibilities for future activities should lead the joyful individuals to initiate subsequent actions. Those who expressed more negative emotions, on the other hand, tended to shut down their thinking about subsequent possible activities. Simply put, joy appears to open us up to many new thoughts and behaviors, whereas negative emotions dampen our ideas and actions.

Dr. Fredrickson's work has been built upon by many others who have studied broadening and building impacts positive affect can have in the lives of everyday people. For example positive affect can (1) assist in our relationships, (2) help us to make changes in our life, (3) enhance our memories and visual attentiveness, and (4) increase our social cognition. We'll summarize a few here.

Joy has been found to increase our likelihood of behaving positively toward other people, along with aiding in developing more positive relationships. Furthermore, joy induces

FIGURE 6.1 ■ The Broadening Effects of Positive Emotions

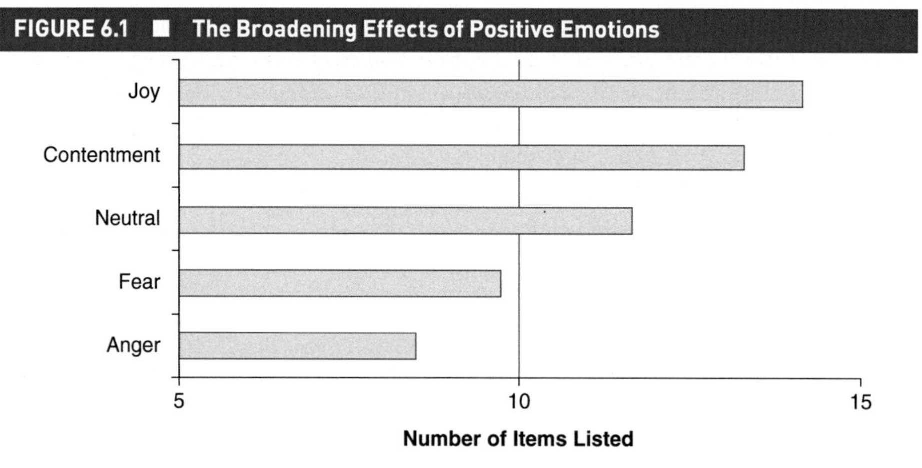

Fredrickson (2002). By permission of Oxford University Press, Inc.

playfulness (Frijda, 1999), which is quite important because such behaviors are evolutionarily adaptive in acquisition of necessary resources. Juvenile play builds (1) enduring social and intellectual resources by encouraging attachment, (2) higher levels of creativity, and (3) brain development (Fredrickson, 2002; Tugade et al., 2021). Playfulness has been studied in children and adolescents, but also more recently in adults as well, and with more positive results. It may also be linked to more happiness and subjective well-being in children overall even when accounting for personality (Demir, 2021). Adolescents who researchers found to be high in lighthearted playfulness (which can be defined as impulsive and easygoing playfulness without much attention to consequences) also had a higher satisfaction with self (Proyer & Tandler, 2020). Additionally, in the United States, young adults who are more playful have less perceived stress and are found to cope better with various stressors in their lives (Magnuson & Barnett, 2013) and induction of playfulness may assist in the treatment of trauma (Rubinstein & Lahad, 2023). Playful adults also may be more likely to be engaged when interacting with others, to have increased positive emotion, and more general well-being overall (Farley et al., 2021). Other research has found that playfulness can be linked to greater life satisfaction (Proyer, 2012, Proyer & Tandler, 2020), positive relationship satisfaction (Proyer et al., 2019) and other positive attributes (Brauer et al., 2021; Proyer & Ruch, 2011). Similar results have been found in studies with Chinese participants as well, meaning that the positive impact of playfulness may be present in more cultures as well (Yue et al., 2016).

Positive affect may also affect the process of making change. This is probably something that you have experienced in your life already. Making changes in our lives, such as starting a new workout program or ending a bad habit, can often seem impossible when we are stressed, angry, or upset. Often, however, they seem much more doable and we are more likely to take steps toward these kinds of positive change when we are in a good mood. Studies have found evidence for this idea as well. Positive affect can take many forms, and Armenta and colleagues (2017) found that in United States research samples, expressing gratitude appeared to increase engagement in activities that lead to self-betterment in multiple domains, including personal life, work, and physical health (it should be noted that other studies by Lyubomirsky and colleagues have not replicated this in East Asian samples; we discuss these studies and others later on in this chapter). Others have found similar results, with some showing that positive affect appears to help individuals to make changes toward developing positive leadership abilities and in being more creative toward making organizational change (Lin et al., 2016). As discussed more fully in Chapter 14 of this text, positive affect can be induced in different ways at work as well via positive activities at work, stress reduction, and other methods.

It appears that, through the effects of broadening processes, positive emotions also can help *build* resources. In 2002, Fredrickson and her colleague, Thomas Joiner, demonstrated this building phenomenon by assessing people's positive and negative emotions and broad-minded coping (solving problems with creative means) on two occasions, five weeks apart. The researchers found that initial levels of positive emotions predicted overall increases in creative problem solving. These changes in coping also predicted further increases in positive emotions (see Figure 6.2). Similarly, controlling for initial levels of positive emotion, beginning levels of coping predicted increases in positive emotions, which in turn predicted further increases in coping. These results held true only for positive emotions, *not* for negative emotions. Therefore, positive emotions such as joy may help generate resources, maintain a sense of vital energy (i.e., more positive emotions), and create even more resources. These findings have been upheld by a number of studies since (e.g., Don et al., 2022; Doty et al., 2017; Gloria & Steinhardt, 2016). Tugade and colleagues (2021) referred to this positive sequence as the "upward spiral" of positive emotions (p. 20; see Figure 6.3). As always, however, paying attention to cultural equivalence is

FIGURE 6.2 ■ The Building Effects of Positive Emotions

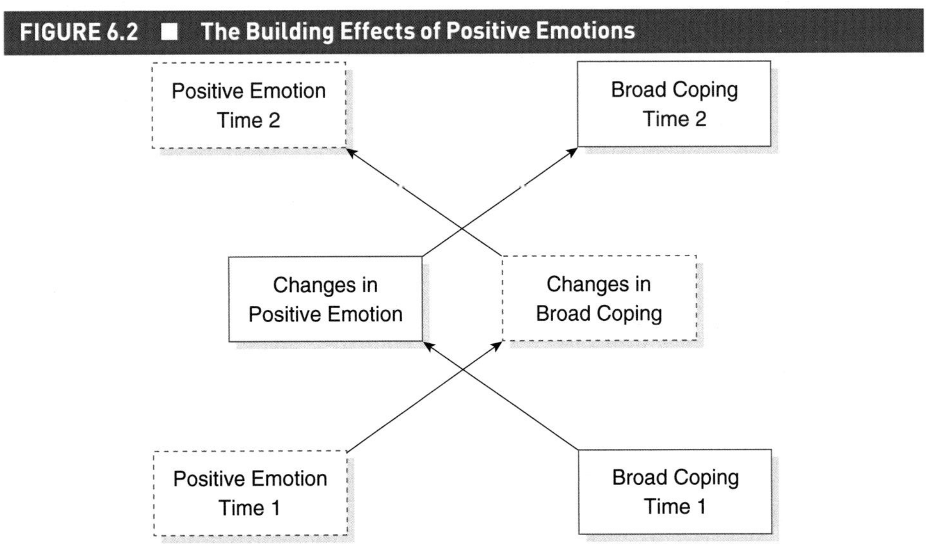

From Mayne, T., & Bonanno, G., *Emotions: Current issues and future directions*. Copyright © 2001. Reprinted with permission of Guildford Publications, Inc.

FIGURE 6.3 ■ The Upward Spiral of Positive Emotions

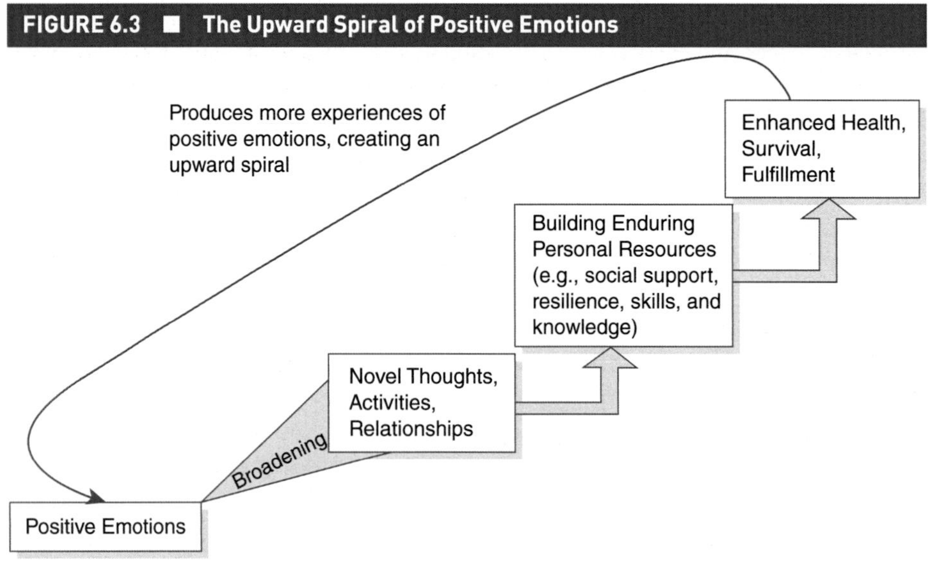

From Cohn, M. A., & Fredrickson, B. L., "Positive emotions" in S. J. Lopez & C. R. Snyder (Eds.), *Oxford handbook of positive psychology* (pp. 13–24). © 2009. Reprinted with permission of Oxford University Press.

important, and researchers who have tested the Broaden and Build theory in Asian American populations have found that increasing positive affect was not enough to start the process in the same way it has been found to do in non-Asian American samples (Wu & Chang, 2019). Instead, these researchers noted that increase of positive affect *and* decrease of negative affect is recommended to start the broaden and build process. Studies like this continue to refine our understandings of how positive and negative affect can be elicited and helpful in myriad populations.

If you are a college student reading this text, you may be interested to find out that positive affect may also have a way toward helping you remember things more clearly and accurately as well (Storbeck & Maswood, 2016; Xie & Zhang, 2016). Increases in both spatial and verbal memory have been found in participants experiencing positive mood in a variety of studies, with results showing that working memory is increased in both cases with the induction of positive affect (Storbeck & Masswood, 2016). Additionally, cognitive functioning appears to be enhanced in participants who, while experiencing a positive mood, were given a list of three words and were able to find a word that linked all three more quickly and accurately than those who were not experiencing increased positive affect (Tugade et al., 2021). There may also be links between positive affect and increased visual attention. In a study by Johnson and Fredrickson (2005), White Americans who were asked to identify the faces of Black Americans were able to correctly identify them from memory as well as they could identify other White American faces when experiencing greater positive affect. Past research has shown that accurate cross-racial face identification is particularly difficult for White Americans (Meissner & Brigham, 2001), which may lead to a host of other problems, from harmful mistakes involving misidentification in line-up procedures in criminal proceedings and unfair prosecution of Black Americans, to other more benign social mistakes that can cause negative relationships between races. Inducing positive affect might increase accuracy and fairness in these cross-race circumstances, as well as toward other positive change. Findings such as this provide support for the Broaden-and-Build theory as a whole, as it makes sense that one would be able to better find a solution to a situation if they were experiencing these other cognitive benefits at the time (i.e., increased visual attention, better recall, more accuracy in making correct guesses, and increased social cognition). Secondly, some research has linked the Broaden and Build model structure to the way in which other psychological assets might be increased. Mikulincer and colleagues (2020) have proposed that attachment and the positive benefits a secure attachment brings may be similarly impacted in a broaden and build framework. Very recently, Mikulincer and Shaver (2022) proposed that using this broaden and build cycle of attachment security might have the power to decrease the likelihood of prejudice, discrimination, and racism in individuals who have developed this strong secure attachment. This is an interesting finding that deserves more research but points to the strength of expanding on positive benefits toward greater psychological strength.

We'd like to note one other final area of research that Fredrickson addresses in her work. Extending her model of positive emotions, she and colleagues examined the "undoing" potential of positive emotions (Fredrickson et al., 2000) and the ratio of positive to negative emotional experiences that is associated with human flourishing (Fredrickson & Losada, 2005). Fredrickson et al. (2000) hypothesized that, given the broadening and building effects of positive emotions, joy and contentment might function as antidotes to negative emotions. To test this hypothesis, the researchers exposed all participants in their study to a situation that aroused negative emotion and immediately randomly assigned people to emotion conditions (sparked by evocative video clips) ranging from mild joy to sadness. Cardiovascular recovery represented the undoing process and was operationalized as the time that elapsed from the start of the randomly assigned video until the physiological reactions induced by the initial negative emotion returned to baseline. The undoing hypothesis was supported, as participants in the joy and contentment conditions were able to undo the effects of the negative emotions more quickly than the people in the other conditions. These findings suggest that there is an incompatibility between positive and negative emotions and that the potential effects of negative experiences can be offset by positive emotions such as joy and contentment.

Given that positive emotions help people broaden many positive abilities, build enduring resources, and recover from negative experiences, Fredrickson and Losada (2005) hypothesized that positive emotions might be associated with optimal mental health or flourishing (i.e., positive psychological and social well-being; see the complete mental health model in the next section in Figure 6.7). Additionally, some researchers have shown that positive affect and happiness with one's life may be the cause of success and other beneficial outcomes in general (Lyubomirsky et al., 2005).

In daily life, looking for the positive more often than the negative seems to be a worthwhile pursuit.

PERSONAL MINI-EXPERIMENTS

IN SEARCH OF JOY AND LASTING HAPPINESS

In this chapter, we discuss positive emotion and happiness. Our review suggests that pleasant emotional experiences can be induced via brief mini-experiments. Here are a few ideas for experiments aimed at boosts in joy and happiness.

The Cartoon/Comedy Pretest–Posttest. Respond to the PANAS based on how you feel at the moment, then watch an episode (5 to 20 minutes without commercials, if possible) of your favorite cartoon, TV show, or YouTube channel that showcases good-natured humor (not sarcastic or sardonic humor). Complete a second PANAS immediately after viewing the content. Then, note the changes that have occurred in your positive and negative affect.

The "Movie, Then What?" Experiment. This experiment requires careful selection of two movies: one that has sad themes and a sanguine ending (a "feel-bad" film) and one that emphasizes joy and triumph (a "feel-good" film). Across two occasions, invite the same group of friends for movie watching at home or in the theater. After the movies, ask your friends, "Hey, if you could do anything at all right now, what would you do? What else?" Make mental notes of how many future activities are mentioned and the exuberance with which your friends discuss these activities. Identify the differences in the expansiveness (or not) of thought–action repertoires across the conditions of the "feel-bad" movie and the "feel-good" movie.

Commonsense Definitions of Happiness. Have you ever asked someone about their views on happiness? We encourage you to ask friends and acquaintances of various ages and backgrounds, "How do you define happiness in your life? What are some benchmarks or signs of your happiness?" You will be surprised by the diversity of answers and refreshed and entertained by the many stories accompanying people's responses. In listening, pay attention to the cultural contexts that often shape these definitions. You may find that not everyone thinks of "happiness" the way you do.

POSITIVE AFFECT IN ADOLESCENTS DURING COVID-19

During the pandemic, parents across the globe worried about the impact of school closures and decreased social opportunities for their children. In each developmental stage, different worries emerged, but adolescents were a particular age group many focused on during this time. Deng and colleagues (2021) were already in the midst of completing a study on adolescent emotional regulation when the pandemic took hold of the world, and as a result, they were able to make use of data on emotional regulation styles captured pre-pandemic, to see if similarities or impacts existed on the type of emotional regulation used and experience of both positive and negative affect during the early days of the pandemic.

Adolescents were asked to keep a daily diary of the emotions they were experiencing for 28 days, in addition to taking other measures designed to measure emotional regulation. Unsurprisingly, a significant increase in negative affect occurred in this sample during the pandemic, but positive affect did not dip in any significant way. Even more interesting, though, the variability in negative affect increased (meaning it fluctuated from time to time), the variability in positive affect also decreased significantly, signalling a more stable state.

With regard to emotional regulation, frequent use prior to COVID of *savoring* (i.e., thinking more and in greater detail about a positive event prior to, during, and after it occurred), helped positive affect to stay high and stable in these adolescents. The opposite was found for adolescents who had more frequently used *dampening* (i.e., spending time ruminating about a negative event). Thus, it seems using tactics to induce positive affect was a protective factor in these adolescents and shows the importance of something like savoring as a coping strategy for adolescents.

One important note: These impacts were only found to be significant in adolescents who were not experiencing severe levels of isolation or other impacts due to COVID. When isolation conditions were high, previous emotional regulation did not buffer in the same way. Thus, this research highlights the importance of decreasing stress as much as possible in crisis situations such that previous positive strategies like savoring can be utilized.

HAPPINESS AND SUBJECTIVE WELL-BEING: LIVING A PLEASURABLE LIFE

Scientific Theories of Happiness

Buddha left home in search of a more meaningful existence and ultimately found enlightenment, a sense of peace, and happiness. Aristotle believed that **eudaimonia** (human flourishing associated with living a life of virtue), or happiness based on a lifelong pursuit of meaningful, developmental goals (i.e., "doing what is worth doing"), was the key to the good life (Waterman, 1993). The authors of the United States constitution reasoned that the pursuit of happiness was just as important as our inalienable rights of life and liberty. These age-old definitions of happiness, along with many other conceptualizations of emotional well-being, have had clear influences on the views of 20th- and 21st-century scholars, but more recent psychological theory and genetic research have helped us to clarify happiness and its correlates.

Theories of happiness in the field of psychology have been divided into three types: (1) **need/goal satisfaction theories,** (2) **process/activity theories,** and (3) **genetic/personality predisposition theories** (Diener et al., 2009). (To do your own research, explore folk definitions of happiness by completing the third exercise in the Personal Mini-Experiments earlier in this chapter.)

In regard to need/goal satisfaction theories, the leaders of particular schools of psychotherapy proffered various ideas about happiness. For example, psychoanalytic and humanistic theorists (Sigmund Freud and Abraham Maslow, respectively) suggested that the reduction of tension or the satisfaction of needs leads to happiness. In short, it was theorized that we are happy because we have reached our goals. Such "happiness as satisfaction" makes happiness a target of our psychological pursuits.

In the process/activity camp, theorists posit that engaging in particular life activities generates happiness. For example, Mike Csikszentmihalyi, who was one of the first 20th-century theorists to examine process/activity conceptualizations of happiness, proposed that people who experience **flow** (engagement in interesting activities that match or challenge task-related skills) in daily life tend to be very happy. Indeed, Csikszentmihalyi's (1975/2000, 1990) work suggests that engagement in activity *produces* happiness. Other process/activity theorists (e.g., Kumar, 2022; Snyder, 2000c) have emphasized how the *process* of pursuing goals generates energy and happiness. Activities such as the practice of gratitude and kindness may also provide boosts in well-being for some cultural groups, though not in all. Empirical evidence exists for the fact that regular engagement in these types of positive acts can help individuals to improve their happiness over time by prescriptive use of tasks such as the writing of gratitude letters and purposeful acts of kindness in United States populations (Curry et al., 2018; Sin & Lyubomirsky, 2009) or strategic use of optimism (Lyubomirsky et al., 2011). In fact newer research has found that stepping outside of one's comfort zone for "stretch" behaviors within the realm of positive psychology can increase happiness in participants, especially for those who are least happy in their lives (Russo-Netzer & Cohen, 2022).

Those who emphasize the genetic and personality predisposition theories of happiness (Diener & Larsen, 1984; Watson, 2000) tend to see happiness as stable, whereas theorists in the happiness-as-satisfaction and process/activity camps view it as changing with life conditions. On this latter point, seminal research conducted by Costa and McCrae (1988) found that happiness changed little over a 6-year period, thereby lending credence to theories of personality-based or biologically determined happiness. Other research, found evidence that the links between personality and happiness may be more idiographic than previously thought (e.g., personal set points for happiness may not be neutral and may be more dependent on temperament, or individuals may vary in the type of adaptation to positive or negative external experiences; Diener et al., 2006). Shiota and colleagues (2006) found similar results with regard to these Big 5 personality factors and also linked positive affect to adult attachment styles. The link between personality and life satisfaction has been found to occur in many cultures; however, the strength of influence of personality on well-being has been shown to be moderated by culture (Pavot & Diener, 2008). Finally, some studies have found links between some genetic markers and certain domains of life satisfaction (e.g., family life satisfaction, leisure, etc.; Lachmann et al., 2021). More work is needed in this area to determine the nuances of these complex relationships between happiness and personality and happiness and genetics in general.

Subjective Well-Being From Hedonic and Eudaimonic Perspectives

Psychologists who support the hedonic perspective view subjective well-being and happiness as synonymous. Alternatively, the scholars whose ideas about well-being are more consistent with Aristotle's views on *eudaimonia* believe that happiness and well-being are not synonymous. In this latter perspective, *eudaimonia* comprises happiness and meaning. Stated in a simple formula: well-being = happiness + meaning. To subscribe to this view of well-being, one must understand virtue and the social implications of daily behavior. Authenticity according to their real needs and desired goals is also valued from this viewpoint. Thus, living a eudaimonic life goes beyond experiencing pleasure and embraces flourishing as the goal in all our actions. Both hedonistic and eudaimonic versions of happiness have influenced the 21st-century definitions, and we take the time to discuss some here.

Building on a utilitarian tradition and the tenets of hedonic psychology (which emphasizes the study of pleasure and life satisfaction), Diener (1984, 2000; Diener et al., 2009) considers well-being to be the subjective evaluation of one's current status in the world in his seminal work. More specifically, this view of well-being involves our experience of pleasure and our appreciation of life's rewards. Given this view, Diener defines subjective well-being as a combination of positive affect (in the absence of negative affect) and general life satisfaction. Furthermore, he uses the term *subjective well-being* as a synonym for *happiness*. (The satisfaction component often is measured with the Satisfaction With Life Scale; Diener et al., 1985.)

Subjective well-being emphasizes people's reports of their life experiences. Accordingly, the subjective report is taken at face value. This subjective approach to happiness assumes that people from many cultures are comfortable focusing on individualistic assessments of their affects and satisfaction and that people will be forthright in such personal analyses (Diener et al., 2009). These assumptions guide the researchers' attempts to understand a person's subjective experiences in light of their objective circumstances.

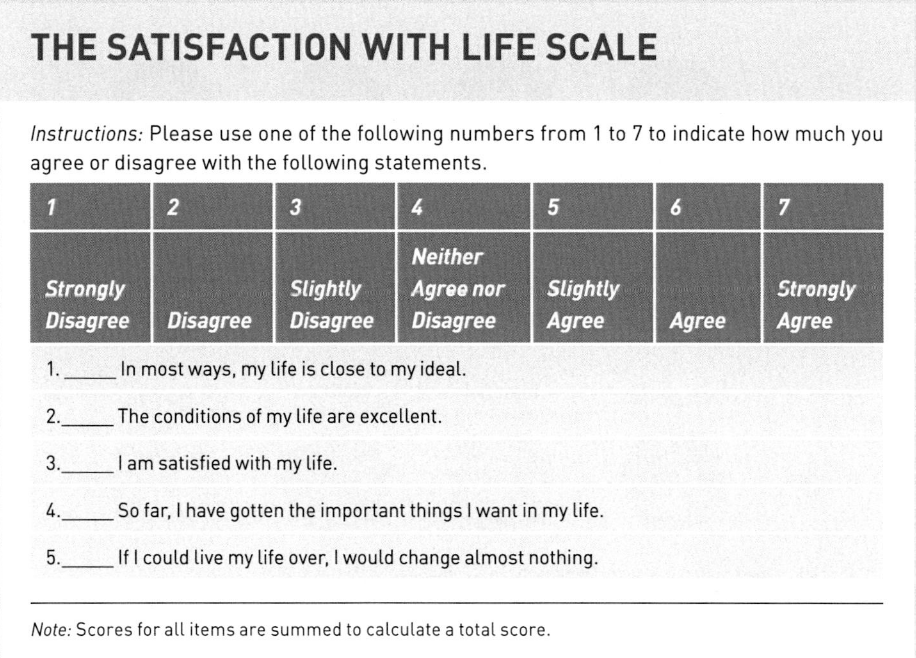

THE SATISFACTION WITH LIFE SCALE

Instructions: Please use one of the following numbers from 1 to 7 to indicate how much you agree or disagree with the following statements.

1	2	3	4	5	6	7
Strongly Disagree	Disagree	Slightly Disagree	Neither Agree nor Disagree	Slightly Agree	Agree	Strongly Agree

1._____ In most ways, my life is close to my ideal.

2._____ The conditions of my life are excellent.

3._____ I am satisfied with my life.

4._____ So far, I have gotten the important things I want in my life.

5._____ If I could live my life over, I would change almost nothing.

Note: Scores for all items are summed to calculate a total score.

Modern Western psychology has focused primarily on a postmaterialistic view of happiness that emphasizes pleasure, satisfaction, *and* life meaning. Indeed, the type of happiness addressed in much of today's popular literature emphasizes hedonics, meaning, and authenticity. For example, Seligman (2002) suggests that a pleasant and meaningful life can be built on the happiness that results from using our psychological strengths.

The areas from which we derive our source of meaning may vary in important ways in different age groups. In a recent global study of attitudes across the world, differences and similarities were found in looking at groups in different developmental stages of life (Clancy & Gubbala, 2021). While all age groups surveyed noted that family was the most important source of meaning in their lives, friends were the second most important source to 18- to 29-year-olds. Those whose age fell between 30 and 64 noted that occupation held the second rank in terms of sources of meaning in life. Finally older adults, ages 65 and beyond, noted that material well-being was just below family. In terms of third ranks, as can be seen in Figure 6.4, health takes the third spot for this same age group, while material well-being and occupation are sources

FIGURE 6.4 ■ Meaning in Life Varies by Age Group

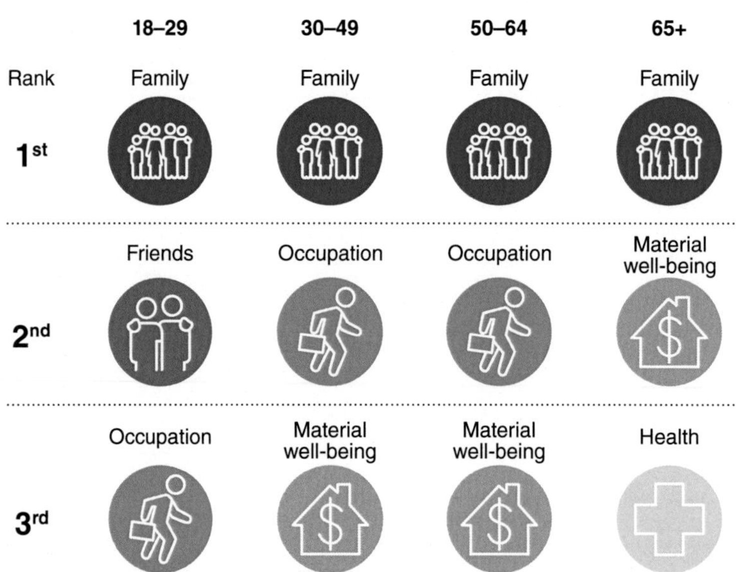

Clancy, L., & Gubbala, S.(2021, November 23). *What makes life meaningful? Globally, answers sometimes vary by age.* Pew Research Center, Washington, D.C. https://www.pewresearch.org/fact-tank/2021/11/23/what-makes-life-meaningful-globally-answers-sometimes-vary-by-age/

of meaning for the middle and younger groups respectively (Clancy & Gubbala, 2021). This may make for some interesting interactions between these different groups, for example parents trying to explain the value of material well-being or occupational well-being to children who are in stages that more value friends. It may also help us to better understand what might make someone who is a different age than us happy. Instead of parents being frustrated with their young adult children spending so much time with friends, they may remind themselves that this is an important piece of well-being for this age group. Helping all people earlier in life (not just those who come from generations of property ownership and wealth) to gain financial literacy enough to ensure a more comfortable lifestyle as a middle or older adult may be another way we can assist with increasing well-being in a population overall. This type of information may be especially important for groups who have only recently been treated more fairly in terms of things like the ability to own property (e.g., Black Americans who have faced centuries of discrimination regarding property ownership).

Describing a newer model of happiness combining some of the above areas discussed, Lyubomirsky et al. (2005) propose that "[a] person's chronic happiness level is governed by three major factors: a genetically determined set point for happiness, happiness-relevant circumstantial factors, and happiness-relevant activities and practices" (p. 111). Lyubomirsky and colleagues' "architecture of sustainable happiness" (p. 114) incorporates what is known about the genetic components of happiness, the circumstantial/demographic determinants of happiness, and the complex process of intentional human change. Based on past research, which they summarize, Lyubomirsky et al. propose that genetics accounts for 50% of population variance for happiness, whereas life circumstances (both good and bad) and intentional activity (attempts at healthy living and positive change) account for 10% and 40% of the population variance for happiness, respectively. This model of happiness acknowledges the components of happiness that can't be changed, but it also leaves room for volition and the self-generated goals that lead to the attainment of pleasure, meaning, and good health.

Interestingly, this theory seems to explain some findings regarding happiness levels and the COVID pandemic. If you think back to your journey through the pandemic, you may recall experiencing different emotions at different times, and some of these were inherently negative as the world coped with fear, anxiety, and perceived restrictions to freedom. Gallup, in their annual "World Happiness Report" (Helliwell et al., 2022) found that despite what one might guess, positive emotions *even during the worst parts of the pandemic* are generally two times as prevalent as negative emotions across the world. This is a finding that has held stable across the past 10 years, though some evidence suggests this gap may be narrowing slightly. As one reporter noted in an article summarizing these findings, "the world was about as happy in the teeth of an awful pandemic as it was before the coronavirus struck" (Anon., 2021, para. 3). This may be due to the lower impact of life circumstances on overall happiness as hypothesized by Lyubomirsky and colleagues (2005).

One other very interesting and beneficial finding in the "World Happiness Report" (Helliwell et al., 2022) was the impact the pandemic has seemed to have on happiness in different age groups. In the past, many researchers have described happiness as "U-shaped" with younger age groups showing more happiness, middle-age groups showing low (the bottom of the U), and then gradually moving up with older-age groups showing higher happiness again; these findings are from a global sample. Following the pandemic, however, "the shape of global happiness" appears to have changed from a U, to more of a straight increase over time. As shown in Figure 6.5, older adults became more happy post-COVID-19 (Helliwell et al., 2022). While this seems counterintuitive as older adults were also at more risk during the pandemic, some other findings seem to point to possible reasons. For example, numbers of older people who said they have a health problem have fallen rather substantially in both men and women (this study looked at gender in a binary fashion, so no other genders' information is available; Helliwell et al., 2022). Some posit that the reason for this could be that "COVID-19 changed the yardstick [on healthiness]. They feel healthier because they have dodged a disease that could kill them" (Anon., 2021, para. 7).

Determinants of Subjective Well-Being

When examining satisfaction in various life domains of college students from 31 nations, financial status was more highly correlated with satisfaction for students in poor nations than for those in wealthy nations (Diener et al., 1995). Moreover, the students in wealthy nations generally were happier than those in impoverished nations. This research is still supported more than 25 years later, as noted previously with wealthier nations continuing to have happier populations (Helliwell et al., 2022). Within-nation examination of this link between income and

FIGURE 6.5 ■ Changes in Age-Related Patterns of Happiness Due to the Pandemic

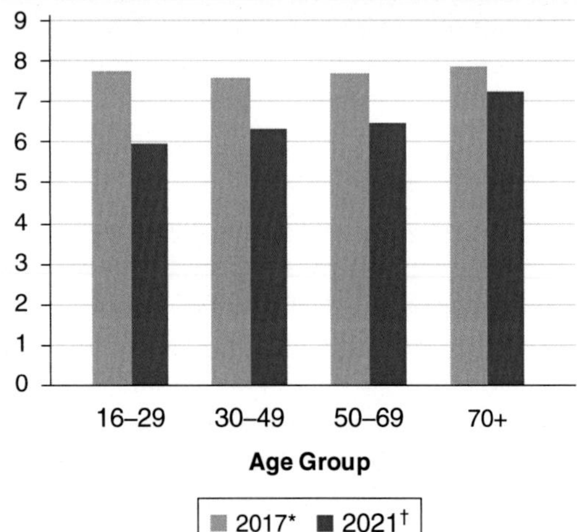

Adapted from figure in Anonymous (2021, March 22). "The pandemic has changed the shape of global happines s." The Economist. https://www.economist.com/international/2021/03/20/the-pandemic-has-changed-the-sh ape-of-global-happiness.

well-being reveals that, once household income rises above the poverty line, additional bumps in income are not necessarily associated with increases in well-being. When well-being data are divided further by categories of economic status (very poor versus very wealthy), it appears that there is a strong relationship between income and well-being among the impoverished but an insignificant relationship between the two variables among the affluent (Diener et al., 1995). It is important to note (as Diener et al., 1995, and others have) that basic needs may have to be met before a higher level of well-being is established and able to be maintained, and this may be the reason for the stronger relationship between income and well-being at the lower end of the financial spectrum. In a study of people living in extreme poverty in Mozambique, researchers found that only 16% of the respondents reported being happy and that many participants stated that "when basic needs are not satisfied happiness is impossible" (Galinha et al., 2016, p. 67). One more interesting finding is that in addition to those with more income having higher well-being than those who are financially struggling, it appears also to be the case "that happy people are more likely to ultimately earn more money, even after controlling for possible confounds such as occupation and family income" (Kansky & Diener, 2020, p. 18). This relationship, however, was strongest in families that were already high income.

Other findings have shown that more interpersonal, social, and spiritual sources appeared to lead individuals toward higher well-being once these more basic needs were met (Galinha et al., 2016). Other analyses have shown that the link between wealth and happiness may be strongest when "wealth" is defined as economic status (as opposed to flow of income) and when measures of life satisfaction are used (as opposed to measures of happiness) to determine subjective well-being (Howell & Howell, 2008). While some may feel that their road to happiness is by spending some of this wealth, studies show that thrift is actually much more closely related to *hedonic* happiness. Although the idea that thrift could be a hedonic pleasure sounds like an oxymoron, Chancellor and Lyubomirsky (2011) found that hedonic happiness can be derived from refraining from spending with the goal of eliminating debt and savoring what one has as opposed to replacing those materials. As overconsumption, materialism, and greed are all detractors from a healthy society, these data bode well for our future. In summary, it is important not to diminish the impact of meeting basic needs (shelter, food, safety, etc.) with regard to the development and experience of well-being. If looking at findings between wealth and happiness in general, it may be tempting to state that "money can't buy happiness." It is true that money may not increase happiness as wealth grows, but a base amount of money may be imperative at very low levels of income and buy a certain amount of "freedom" for the individual (Jackson, 2017).

Data specific to Western samples indicate that married people report more happiness than those who are not married (never married, divorced, or separated; DeMaris, 2018; Huntington et al., 2022; Lee et al., 1991). The link between subjective well-being and being married is different for people of all ages, incomes, and educational levels, and it also varies across racial and ethnic backgrounds (Argyle, 1987), though some differences may occur in the determinants of happy marriage in Black versus White and Hispanic samples (Riley et al., 2015). Same-sex couples who have legalized unions (i.e., marriages and/or civil unions) also report greater levels of well-being, though some of this depends a bit on the social interpretation of the legitimacy of same-sex marriage in their environment (Kennedy & Dalla, 2020). Not surprisingly, marital quality also is positively associated with personal well-being

(Huntington et al., 2022; Sternberg & Hojjat, 1997). Although some believe that a dimming of passion and happiness is a natural by-product of being in a long-term relationship, this is not always (or even often) the case. Couples who practice certain behaviors in their relationships may have an even better chance at avoiding this decrease. Bao and Lyubomirsky (2013) created a list of ways to combat this "hedonic adaptation"—that is, the tendency for people to adjust back to their baseline happiness after a positive event such as the start of a relationship. Their specific strategies are presented in Table 6.1 (see also Chapter 12 in this volume on love and relationships). One interesting finding is that men who subscribe to a traditional hypermasculine gender identity with regard to positive affect (e.g., endorse items such as "Caring is a weakness for me" or "Only girly men care") may have an aversion to experiencing these types of emotions. In a study by Burris and colleagues (2016), this aversion to positive empathic emotion was counteracted with statements like "Real men care" and "Caring is strength." When paired with statements that better fit with these men's gender identity, they were more empathic and able to experience the benefits that go along with these positive affective states (Burris et al., 2016). Making sure that we help young men and boys in particular to develop positive ideas about constructs like empathy and caring may help them in myriad ways (Borgogna & McDermott, 2022; McDermott et al., 2021). Other studies of heterosexual couples show that though marriage is linked to more well-being overall, women experience a decrease in life satisfaction just following wedding their partner, as well as increases in psychological distress, while men experience the exact opposite (Huntington et al., 2022). The authors of this study posit these findings could be related to new roles that women in these relationships find themselves taking on as "wife" that are not necessarily positive, and that this is likely mediated by the characteristics of the relationship (e.g., chore

TABLE 6.1 ■ Strategies to Combat Hedonic Adaptation in Long-Term Relationships

Strategy	*Explanation*
Experience more positive events and feel more positive emotions	The more positive events and emotions one experiences, the more slowly one adapts.
Variety is the spice of relationships	Increasing variety in a relationship may help increase well-being and decelerate adaptation.
Maintain reasonable aspirations	Couples might benefit from remaining mindful of their aspirations about the relationship and their partner and trying to avoid ever-increasing aspirations.
Cultivate appreciation	Appreciation draws an individual's attention back to the positive change in their life (e.g., getting married or promoted), allowing them to continue to experience that positive change and the events and emotions that accompany it.

Source: Data from Bao, K. J., & Lyubomirsky, S. (2013). Making it last: Combating hedonic adaptation in romantic relationships. *The Journal of Positive Psychology, 8*, 196–206.

equity or other similar items). Thus, taking care to create and sustain roles that bring both partners well-being is another important suggestion.

In a study of the happiest 10% of U.S. college students, Diener and Seligman (2002) found that the qualities of good mental health and good social relationships consistently emerged in the lives in the sample of the happiest young adults. This has been replicated in many studies since (Bowjanowska & Zalewska, 2016; Fu & Vong, 2016; Yamaguchi et al., 2016). Upon closer inspection of their data, analyses revealed that good social functioning among the happiest subset of students was a necessary but not sufficient cause of happiness. In today's world, "social" has a different meaning than in past generations. Whereas before, "social" may only have described relationships that involved face-to-face contact, social media has become a common way of interacting with others in ways that are not limited by location or time. Smith (2018) discusses a Pew Research study that found that users experience different types of emotions related to content they see on social media. An important point to note is that this content is often filtered or mechanized in some way due to the algorithms used by many social media platforms. In some ways, one might think that this customized content would lead toward more positive emotions, and it was found that amusement was the most common positive emotion experienced frequently. Interestingly, however, the negative emotion of anger was the second most frequently experienced emotion, in addition to other positive and negative affective responses also found (see Figure 6.6). The research noted first in this section had to do with "good social relationships" being linked to positive emotions, and so it may be that some of the

FIGURE 6.6 ■ Positive and Negative Emotions While Using Social Media

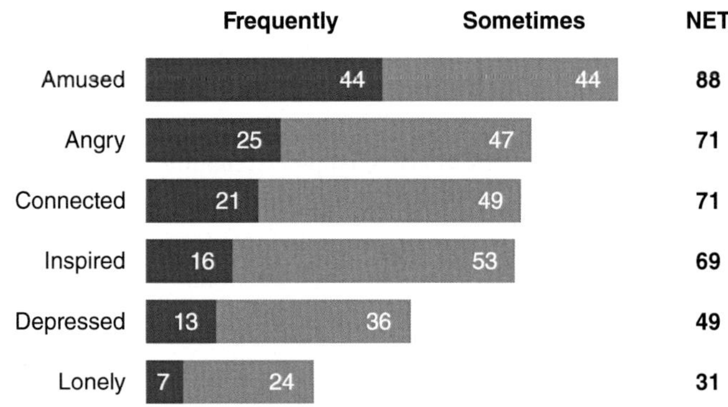

Source: "2. Algorithms in action: The content people see on social media." Pew Research Center, Washington, D.C. (NOVEMBER 16, 2018) https://www.pewresearch.org/internet/2018/11/16/algorithms-in-action-the-content-people-see-on-social-media/.

relationships experienced via social media platforms aren't necessarily "good," but more investigation into impacts of social media are important on both sides. That said, a positive emotional state (amusement) was still the most frequently experienced, and so social media may in some ways be a viable vehicle for bringing positive emotion to some individuals.

EXCERPTS FROM *AUTHENTIC HAPPINESS*

When well-being comes from engaging our strengths and virtues, our lives are imbued with authenticity. Feelings are states, momentary occurrences that need not be recurring features of personality. Traits, in contrast to states, are either negative or positive characteristics that bring about good feeling and gratification. Traits are abiding dispositions whose exercise makes momentary feelings more likely. The negative trait of paranoia makes the momentary state of jealousy more likely, just as the positive trait of being humorous makes the state of laughing more likely. (p. 9)

The well-being that using your signature strengths engenders is anchored in authenticity. But just as well-being needs to be anchored in strengths and virtues, these in turn must be anchored in something larger. Just as the good life is something beyond the pleasant life, the meaningful life is beyond the good life. (p. 14)

Source: Seligman (2002).

Cultural Differences in Happiness

You may have noticed that several times throughout this chapter we have used caveats regarding results of studies, for example "in some populations" or "in some cultural groups." Though ordinarily, we would follow the best practices of incorporating research from all cultures by topic (and do in many of the chapters in this book), there are some nuances in looking at happiness in different cultural groups that warrant a separate section in this chapter. Publications on the topic of cultural differences and well-being have grown substantially in the field, and differences have been noted in definitions of happiness, manifestations of positive affect, and in the value that different cultures have for happiness in general (Pedrotti, 2014a). The fact that "culture counts" in these studies is becoming more and more apparent (Pedrotti et al., 2021).

Past research has found that the extent to which a nation is more collectivist (i.e., cooperative and group oriented) in orientation versus individualistic (i.e., competitive and individual focused) is one of the strongest predictors of differences in subjective well-being across nations, even when national income level was held constant (Diener et al., 1995; Myers & Diener, 2018). Something that must be considered in analyzing the results from the above studies is the fact that Western measures of well-being were used in these cases. Although translated appropriately, and thus these scales can be called linguistically equivalent measures, this does not account for the differences in *conceptual* equivalence with regard to definitions and culturally normative manifestations of happiness that are found in other studies. Myers and Diener (2018) commented later on these findings, noting that emotional support and relationship harmony matter more to well-being levels of those in collectivist nations, while pride and satisfaction with self are the best predictors in individualist countries.

In another study, Lu and Gilmour (2004) analyzed essays entitled "What Is Happiness?" from Chinese students and compared them with those of students in the United States, and differences were found in the way in which these two groups described the construct. The Chinese students "emphasized spiritual cultivation and transcendence of the present," whereas their U.S. counterparts "emphasized the enjoyment of present life" (Suh & Koo, 2008, p. 416). Other researchers have found similar differences between Western and Eastern individuals with predictors of happiness varying from independence, autonomy, and agency (West) to interconnectedness of self and closeness to others (East) (Choi & Chentsova-Dutton, 2017; Kitayama & Markus, 2000; Uchida et al., 2004). Some research seems to suggest that acculturation may affect these findings. Asian Americans and White Americans were found in a study to have similar types of inverse relationships between well-being and depression, although correlations were slightly less strong in Asian American groups ($r = -0.46$ in White Americans; $r = -0.26$ in Asian Americans, although both were significant findings; Leu et al., 2011). No statistically significant relationship was found between depression and positive affect in Asian immigrants, however ($r = -.03$). This suggests that acculturation to more Western values may affect the types of relationships found. Interestingly, other research showed that external raters from the United States evaluated Asian research participants as less happy than White American research participants when viewing videos of them thinking about a very happy event (Lu & Gilmour, 2004). This was despite the fact that both sets of participants had reported the same level of happiness on a scale as they thought about the story. In this case, manifestations of happiness looked different to an evaluator outside the cultural context.

Other findings point to the fact that different racial and ethnic groups may also obtain happiness by different methods (Le et al., 2009). Although the majority of research has looked at differences *between* Eastern and Western cultures, there also may be differences *within* these groups. African American individuals, for example, may gain more satisfaction in life when they are stronger in their racial and ethnic identity, and this relationship may be increased by a stronger religious commitment (i.e., those with a strong ethnic identity and a strong religious commitment may report higher life satisfaction (Ajibade et al., 2016). Interventions aimed at increasing positive mental health in these groups might need to be framed in terms of Black identity to be effective (Williams & Wilson, 2016). Some research with Spanish-speaking Latinx populations within the United States also follows this trend, with faith and religiosity appearing to correlate with well-being in a different way than it may in White American populations (Hernandez et al., 2016), and higher ethnic and gender identity has been found to be linked with positive affect in Mexican and Mexican American women (Diaz & Bui, 2017). Physical health, strong interpersonal communication, perceived social support, and financial security were correlated with well-being, which is similar to what is found in White American populations (Diaz & Bui, 2017; Hernandez et al., 2016). And as we've already discussed previously, age seems to play a role in what is correlated with well-being in older and younger populations, including what is meaningful to life (Clancy & Gubbala, 2021; Helliwell et al., 2021).

Finally, it is also the case that different cultural groups may *value* happiness in different ways. Joshanloo and Weijers (2014) found that many non-Western cultural groups have more of an aversion to happiness than an affection for it. Reasons may span from a sort of "fear of happiness" (e.g., "If things become too good, it means something bad will happen next") or from a belief that happiness is not as important as other factors (see Chapters 2 and 4 for more complete discussions of happiness in Eastern cultural groups).

More research must be done in these areas; however, these findings remind us that we must view constructs through the appropriate cultural lens to have a fuller understanding of them. Some findings may show that similarities exist across cultural groups, while differences appear between others. In addition, we must be careful to be culturally competent in interpreting studies that are conducted from Western perspectives on non-Western samples or vice versa. Careful consideration of cultural, linguistic, functional, and metric equivalence is necessary in any cross-cultural or multicultural research (see Chapter 3 for a more thorough description of equivalence).

Today's scholars will undoubtedly produce many more refined views of happiness and its value depending on cultural differences and beliefs. Our prediction is that the pursuit of happiness through positive psychological science and practice ultimately will develop a better sense of the genetic (summarized in Lyubomirsky et al., 2005), neural (Urry et al., 2004), and neurobiological correlates and underpinnings of happiness and will embrace the contentment, peace, and happiness of Eastern philosophy along with the folk wisdom of the Western world. So imagine a science of happiness that is grounded in what is known about the genetic and biological bases of happiness, that examines the rigor and relevance of Buddha's teachings alongside Benjamin Franklin's recommendations for virtuous living, and pays attention to the context of the sample studied. Through good biological and psychological science and an appreciation of philosophical and cultural stances on happiness, we can increase the cultural and international relevance of our scholarship in positive psychology and have a better understanding of how well-being and life satisfaction are experienced.

Complete Mental Health: Emotional, Social, and Psychological Well-Being

Ryff and Keyes (1995; Keyes et al., 2020; Keyes & Lopez, 2002; Keyes & Magyar-Moe, 2003) combine many principles of pleasure to define complete mental health. Specifically, they view optimal functioning as the combination of emotional well-being (as they refer to subjective well-being; defined as the presence of positive affect and satisfaction with life and the absence of negative affect), social well-being (incorporating acceptance, actualization, contribution, coherence, and integration), and psychological well-being (combining self-acceptance, personal growth, purpose in life, environmental mastery, autonomy, positive relations with others). Taking the symptoms of mental illness into consideration, they define "complete mental health" as the combination of "high levels of symptoms of emotional well-being, psychological well-being, and social well-being, as well as the absence of recent mental illness" (Keyes & Lopez, 2002, p. 49). This view of mental health combines all facets of well-being into a model that is both dimensional (because extremes of mental health and illness symptomatology are reflected) and categorical (because assignment to distinct diagnostic categories is possible). This **complete state model** (Keyes & Lopez, 2002, p. 49; see Figure 6.7) suggests that combined

FIGURE 6.7 ■ A Model of Complete Mental Health

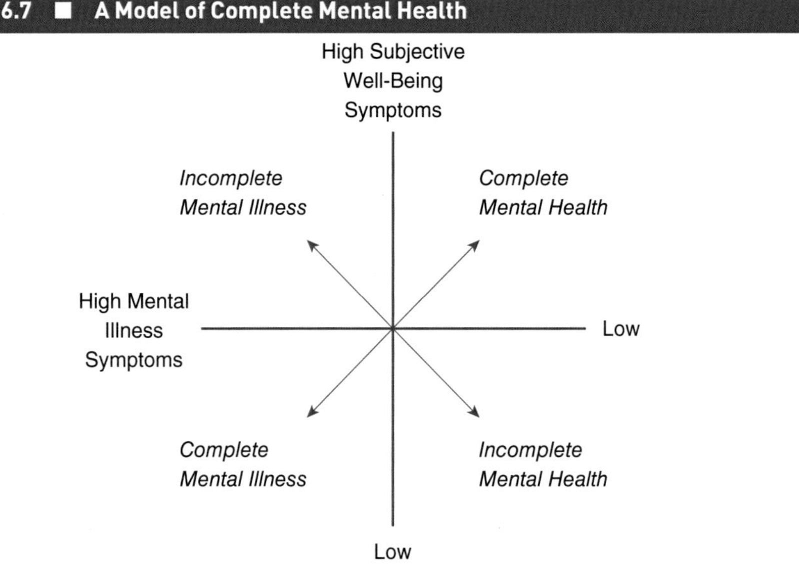

C. R. Snyder & S. J. Lopez. *The handbook of positive psychology* – 2002. By permission of Oxford University Press, Inc.

mental health and mental illness symptoms may be always changing and may be evaluated differently in different cultural contexts, resulting in fluctuations in states of overall well-being ranging from complete mental illness to complete mental health.

Increasing Happiness in Your Life

Although there are numerous theories of happiness and countless definitions of it, researchers (e.g., Sheldon & Lyubomirsky, 2004) have begun to build on past work (Fordyce, 1977, 1983) in their attempts to answer the question many of our clients ask: "Can I learn how to be happier?" David Myers, the author of *The Pursuit of Happiness*, provided several general strategies for increasing the happiness in daily life in his 1993 work, and we have left a few of these here for you (see Figure 6.8). Though Myers wrote these words almost 30 years ago, they still ring true. We provide additional Life Enhancement Strategies for boosting happiness in specific domains of your life. When looking at the following suggestions, we would ask the reader to consider that not all suggestions necessarily work for all cultural groups. Use a discerning eye while reading, and this may help you determine what seems plausible and culturally valid in your own life.

Well-being and happiness are also not always improved by the same activities in different cultural groups. In a comparison of a diverse group of participants from the United States and a second sample from South Korea, it was found that while expressing gratitude benefited the U.S. participants with spikes in well-being, this activity was unhelpful for South Korean participants, actually resulting in *de*creases in well-being (Layous et al., 2013). The authors of this study suggest that because a construct such as gratitude has different cultural meanings for the two groups, the impact was also different. In South Korea, feelings of gratitude may be

FIGURE 6.8 ■ David Myers's Suggestions for a Happier Life

1. **Realize that enduring happiness doesn't come from success.** People adapt to changing circumstances—even to wealth or a disability. Thus wealth is like health: its utter absence breeds misery, but having it (or any circumstance we long for) doesn't guarantee happiness.
2. **Take control of your time.** Happy people feel in control of their lives, often aided by mastering their use of time. It helps to set goals and break them into daily aims. Although we often overestimate how much we will accomplish in any given day (leaving us frustrated), we generally underestimate how much we can accomplish in a year, given just a little progress every day.
5. **Join the "movement" and give your body the sleep it wants.** Exercise not only promotes health and energy, it also is an antidote for mild depression and anxiety. Sound minds reside in sound bodies. This includes reserving time for renewing sleep and solitude. Many people suffer from a sleep debt, with resulting fatigue, diminished alertness, and gloomy moods.
7. **Give priority to close relationships.** Intimate friendships with those who care deeply about you can help you weather difficult times. Confiding is good for soul and body. Resolve to nurture your closest relationships, to not take those closest to you for granted, and to affirm them.
8. **Focus beyond the self. Reach out to those in need.** Happiness increases helpfulness (those who feel good do good). But doing good also makes one feel good.

Adapted from Myers, D., *The pursuit of happiness.* Copyright © 1993. Reprinted with permission of the author.

more closely linked with feelings of indebtedness, showing the dialectical pattern that is often found between positive and negative affect in Asian groups. In U.S. samples, gratitude may not be linked to negative feelings in quite the same way. Other research has shown that even when the same construct boosts well-being in multiple cultures, there may be significant differences in the amounts of increases seen in different groups (Boehm et al., 2011). These differences may be decreased, however, by attending to specific definitions of these constructs in the home culture. When Muslim students practiced gratitude that was based in Islamic principles (e.g., linking good fortune to Allah), they showed higher happiness levels overall in comparison to Muslim participants who used secular definitions of gratitude (Al-Seheel & Noor, 2016). Another study involving members of the Yup'ik tribe in Western Alaska showed that when cultural context was taken into account in measuring and increasing wellness in this population, more positive gains were made (Lardon et al., 2016). In addition, differences have been found between cultural groups in the administration of various interventions aimed to increase positive affect (Shin & Lyubomirksy, 2017). For example, self-administered interventions may be more beneficial and functional for Asian and Asian American individuals, perhaps because they are less stigmatizing. Finally, providing increases in social connectedness appears to influence well-being in Asian American groups as well (Fu & Vong, 2016). Thus, we must consider which types of processes and activities are valued and deemed positive by a particular cultural group and take care to devise interventions and activities that have cultural relevance for the group one is studying.

Though the title of this section is "Increasing Happiness in *Your* Life," it may be equally important to think about how we can help all people have increased happiness in *their* lives; this includes those that may have a smaller amount of privilege in their lives due to level of income, race, gender, ability, sexual orientation, and other social identities (Sullivan, et al., 2021). Many researchers have found that inequity, racism, sexism and other forms of discrimination decrease the well-being of those at whom these behaviors are directed (Cavalhieri & Wilcox, 2022; Choi et al., 2022; Thomas-Hawkins et al., 2022). This has lead some authors to call for "A human rights approach to well-being for all," (Lomax et al., 2022, p. 364). Using this lens, the authors argue, we must provide a better framework in our country such that all individuals have equitable access to some kind of opportunity to build strengths, to prioritize their health, and to receive culturally competent mental health services when needed, among other mental health benefits. We would add that all individuals also should have the right to live without oppression and its negative impacts. One thing you can do right now is to learn more about the history in our country that has gotten us to this state of inequality and to join the fight to try to dismantle barriers that have created the structural inequities many minoritized populations still live with today. With more education, we can then take next steps to create systems in which all individuals can not only survive but *thrive.*

MOVING TOWARD THE POSITIVE

It is very easy to find the unpleasant, negative aspects of emotions and dysfunctions in life. All you have to do is read your regular online source or watch the nightly news. Our human need to understand the negative is great, given the suffering and loss associated with anger and fear, as well as the evolutionary functions of avoidance strategies. Although the positive aspects of emotional experiences rarely capture the attention of media or science, things are beginning to change. It was only three decades ago, for example, that a few brave social scientists (e.g., Bradburn, 1969; Meehl, 1975) shared their thoughts about the lighter side of life. Today, we know that the flow of "joy-juice" and biological factors are important, but they do not define our entire emotional experience. In addition, we must shift our lens to look at things from perspectives other than our own or risk missing the emotional experiences of those who are different from us. By doing this, we can also contribute to the happiness of others in ways that feel culturally relevant for them; this might also open our minds to new perspectives that can lead to more happiness experiences of our own. In the words of Diener et al. (2002), "It appears that the way people perceive the world is much more important to happiness than objective circumstances" (p. 68).

It seems evident that cultural differences exist between the origins, determinants, and moderators of well-being (Ajibade et al., 2016; Cavalhieri & Wilcox, 2022; Choi et al., 2022; Diaz & Bui, 2017; Hernandez et al., 2016; Layous et al., 2013; Thomas-Hawkins et al., 2022; Uchida et al., 2004; and others), and different rankings may be applied by different cultures as to how important personal happiness is for the individual (Joshanloo & Weijers, 2014; Lu & Gilmour, 2004).

This said, it must be made clear that well-being is still a desired goal across cultural groups, *especially when it is experienced in culturally normative ways* (Diener, 2013; Myers & Diener, 2018). Ed Diener spearheaded talk about the need for our nations to develop "National Accounts" of subjective well-being alongside the economic accounts they regularly determine, and as of 2018 at least 40 nations heeded this call. These accounts of how our various nations are doing with regard to well-being overall could influence policies on funding for initiatives that would benefit large portions of a nation (Kansky & Diener, 2020). As we've noted, inequity is known to have the potential undermine well-being (Choi et al., 2022; Thomas-Hawkins et al., 2022) and so increasing efforts toward greater racial and gender equity in the United States could go a long way toward increasing well-being. Knowing more about well-being on a more global scale can only be beneficial for our continued health across the world. As Flores and colleagues (2020) so eloquently put it, "In a world without equity, well-being is impossible" (p. 3).

LIFE ENHANCEMENT STRATEGIES

Following is a list of additional tips for increasing pleasant emotional experiences, happiness, and well-being in your life. Although we categorize these suggestions within life's important domains, as we do in most chapters, we do not mean to suggest that all aspects of positive affect, emotions, and happiness are domain specific. We do believe, however, that some aspects of both the pleasant life and the meaningful life can be found in each of life's domains.

Love

- Be kind to those you love and those you have just met! Research shows that engaging in kind acts on a regular basis increases well-being in many different types of people.
- Tell those close to you that you love them while you can; so many have lost loved ones in these past few years. Your sincere expression of love will bolster your relationship and induce positive affect in others.

Work

- Start a meeting with positive comments about peers' contributions. This may raise positive affect that generates creativity and good decision making.
- Make efforts toward developing an equitable workplace. Be clear about valuing diversity overall and specific strengths that may be rooted in different cultural contexts.

Play

- Help others to find time to play! Take a moment to think of someone in your life who may need some play time but whose responsibilities make it difficult to take that time. Offer to babysit for new parents, take a larger share of a project for someone who is overloaded at work, or bring dinner and a board game to a single parent and stay to play yourself!
- Participate in brief relaxation activities to break up your day. Relaxation can make your mind and body more sensitive to the pleasurable daily moments.

KEY TERMS

Affect
Broaden-and-build model of positive emotions
Complete state model
Emotion
Eudaimonia
Flow
Genetic/personality predisposition theories
Momentary thought–action repertoire
Mood
Need/goal satisfaction theories
Pleasure principle
Process/activity theories
Specific action tendency
Subjective well-being
Valence

7 MAKING THE MOST OF EMOTIONAL EXPERIENCES

Emotional Approach Coping, Emotional Intelligence, Socioemotional Selectivity, and Emotional Storytelling

LEARNING OBJECTIVES

After reading this chapter, you will be able to:

7.1 Describe the emotional approach coping processes and identify how their psychological impact may be conditional on a variety of mediating and moderating variables

7.2 Discuss different definitions of emotional intelligence and describe key findings in the emotional intelligence literature

7.3 Describe key findings from research examining socioemotional selectivity theory

7.4 Discuss the benefits of expressive writing

7.5 Identify the biological/neural mechanisms related to emotional approach coping and emotional intelligence

7.6 Understand the cultural differences and similarities identified in the research regarding emotional approach coping, emotional intelligence, socioemotional selectivity, and expressive writing

At times during the 20th century, psychology research and practice sullied the reputation of emotions. At worst, helping professionals and the public at large characterized emotions as toxic to our lives or detrimental to rational decision making. At best, emotions were portrayed as reflections of life satisfaction or signals of specific daily actions that needed to be taken. Research popularized in the 21st century (reviewed in Chapter 6) demonstrates that both positive and negative emotions may determine how adaptive we are in our daily lives and contexts (see Chapter 6 to review Nussbaum's [2001] definition of *emotion*).

The purpose of this chapter is to introduce you to how people make the most of their emotional experiences—that is, how they generally handle positive and negative emotions in a manner that leads to a positive outcome—by discussing theory and research associated with emotion approach coping, **emotional intelligence**, socioemotional selectivity, and **emotional storytelling**. We discuss how we *benefit* from engaging our emotions, how we can *learn* to process and use emotion-laden material competently, and how we more efficiently *sort* the good from the bad emotional content of life as we age. Finally, we describe how sharing stories of emotional upheaval helps us *overcome* traumatic stress and pain.

EMOTION-FOCUSED COPING: DISCOVERING THE ADAPTIVE POTENTIAL OF EMOTIONAL APPROACH

The power of emotions traditionally was described in such negative terms as "the beast within" (Averill, 1990). Intense emotions were seen as dysfunctional and opposed to rationality. Research in the 20th century often supported this view of emotional experiences by linking them with maladaptive outcomes in life. However, Annette Stanton, a positive psychologist at the University of California at Los Angeles, considered the adaptive potential of emotion-focused coping (i.e., regulating the emotions surrounding a stressful encounter), and found there was a problem in how emotions were defined and measured at the time. Indeed, wide disparity was apparent in the items used to measure the emotion-focused coping phenomenon, and this led to unclear associations between what was referred to as "emotion-focused coping" and psychological adjustment. Stanton et al. (1994) noted that items such as "I blame myself for becoming too emotional" (Scheier et al., 1986) and "I get upset and let my emotions out" (Carver et al.,1989) seemed to be capturing a negative view of self or an underlying psychological problem. Moreover, when such items were removed, the frequently cited relationship between greater emotion-focused coping and poorer life outcomes disappeared.

Stanton and colleagues have spent many years working to clarify what "emotion-focused coping" means. Specifically, Stanton, Parsa, and Austenfeld (2002) stated that "coping through emotional approach might be said to carry adaptive potential, the realization of which may depend on . . . the situational context, the interpersonal milieu, and attributes of the individual" (p. 150). What they call **emotional approach** involves active movement *toward, rather than away from*, a stressful encounter. This distinction between emotional approach and **emotional avoidance** is supported by the existence of two neurobiological systems. The *behavioral activation system* regulates our approach motivation, which helps us realize emotional or behavioral rewards, whereas the *behavioral inhibition system* functions to help us avoid negative events and punishment (Depue, 1996; Van de Vyver & Abrams, 2017).

In a series of landmark studies, Stanton, Kirk et al. (2000) identified two related but distinct processes involved in approach-oriented emotion-focused coping. One involves **emotional processing (EP)**, or attempts to understand emotions, and a second reflects **emotional expression (EE)**, or free and intentional displays of feeling. The researchers then created scales to tap these two approaches (see Figure 7.1 for a list of components of EP and EE). Stanton, Kirk et al.'s (2000) emotional approach coping scales have been used extensively since they became available. Over the past 20 years, researchers have generally found that higher emotional approach coping is associated with better psychological outcomes, and a small number of studies have also linked this form of coping to indicators of physical health (Moreno et al., 2021). For example, in

FIGURE 7.1 ■ Questionnaire Items Measuring Emotion-Focused Coping

Emotional Processing (EP)	Emotional Expresssion (EE)
☐ I realize that my feelings are valid and important	☐ I feel free to express my emotions.
☐ I take time to figure out what I am really feeling.	☐ I take time to express my emotions.
☐ I delve into my feelings to get a thorough understanding of them.	☐ I allow myself to express my emotions.
☐ I acknowledge my emotions.	☐ I let my feelings come out freely.

Adapted from Stanton, A. L., Kirk, S. B., Cameron, C. L., & Danoff-Burg, S. (2000). Coping through emotional approach: Scale construction and validation. *Journal of Personality and Social Psychology, 78*(6), pp. 1150–1169.

the initial validation study of the construct, Stanton, Danoff-Burg et al. (2000) examined the impact of emotional approach coping on women's adjustment to breast cancer. Over a 3-month period, women who used emotional approach coping perceived their health status as better, had lower psychological distress, and had fewer medical appointments for cancer-related pain and ailments, as compared to those who did not use emotional approach coping. This result has generally been replicated with many types of cancer and illness (Gilbertson-White et al., 2017; Hoyt et al., 2017; Marroquín et al., 2016; Reese et al., 2017), in different cultural groups (e.g., Chang, Yu et al., 2016; Moreno et al., 2021), and in different age groups (Hoyt et al., 2020; Moreno et al., 2021).

Mediating and Moderating Factors

Although research generally supports the benefits of emotional approach aspects of emotion-focused coping, there have been a fair number of null (i.e., nonsignificant findings), as well as a few instances where emotional approach coping may have contributed to poorer outcomes. Such results indicate that the associations between emotional approach coping and positive outcomes are complex and nuanced. To address this issue, Stanton and Low (2012) developed a theory-based model of the mechanisms (i.e., mediating factors) and contexts (i.e., moderating factors) that explain how and why emotional approach coping is associated with better physical and mental health outcomes (see Figure 7.2).

As summarized and updated by Moreno and colleagues (2021), mediating factors include the ability to put feelings into words (i.e., affect labeling) and the ability to cognitively reframe or reappraise a particular stressor. Said another way, successful emotional approach coping may facilitate greater use of affective and cognitive strategies that allow one to identify a feeling and clarify whether the way they view a stressor is ultimately adaptive or maladaptive. If it is the latter, then being in touch with one's emotions may help an individual to think about the situation in a more adaptive fashion. Another mediator of successful emotional approach coping

FIGURE 7.2 ■ Mediating and Moderating Factors that Drive (Mediate) and Condition (Moderate) the Associations Between Greater Emotional Approach Coping Processes and Positive Physical and Mental Health Outcomes

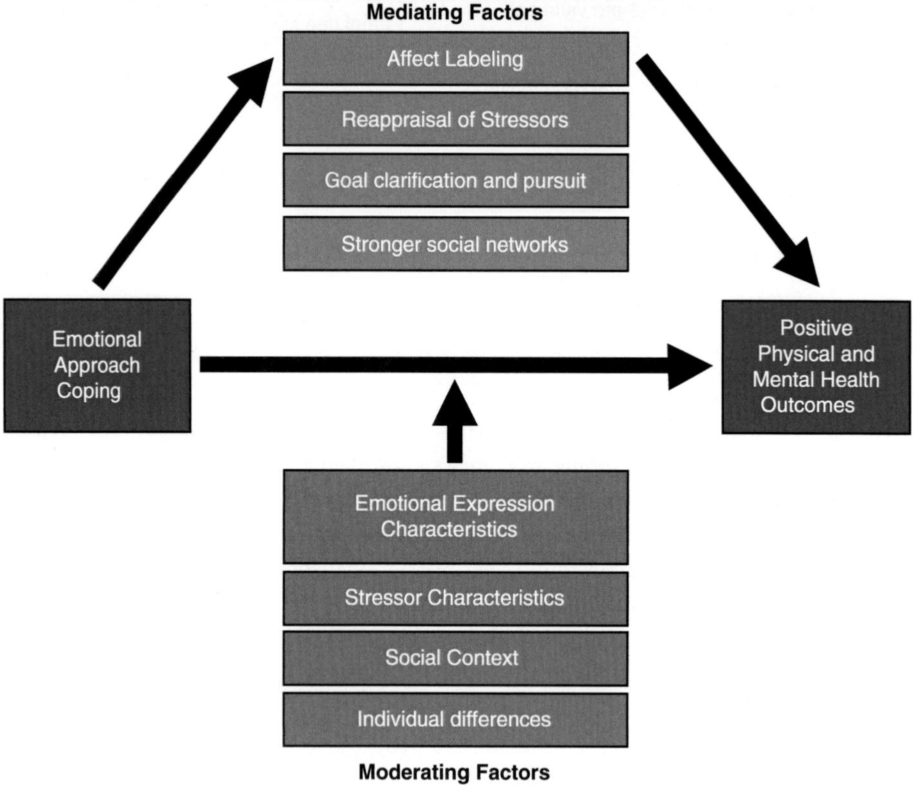

Adapted from Stanton and Low (2012) and Moreno et al. (2021).

is dispositional hope (see Snyder et al., 1991 and Chapter 8 of this text for more information). Successful emotional approach coping helps focus attention toward one's goals and allows for the identification of pathways around possible goal-blocking obstacles. Additionally, emotional approach coping may help us strengthen our social networks. That is, it may help people to effectively communicate their needs in times of distress, thus strengthening our social bonds.

Moderating factors include those variables that strengthen or weaken the relationship between emotional approach coping and good outcomes. Stanton and Low (2012) and Moreno and colleagues (2021) noted four such factors based on the extant literature (see Figure 7.2). First, the characteristics of the emotional expression and the stressor may help or hinder the effectiveness of emotional approach coping. For example, emotional expression may be especially helpful in situations where one perceives the stressor to be out of one's control and if one expresses emotions to gain social support. Relatedly, the context in which one engages in emotional expression can impact the outcome. A supportive environment or social context is helpful for any form of coping, but given the inherent vulnerability associated with expressing one's emotions, an environment or social context that validates those feelings may be especially helpful. One of the more consistent findings in the emotional approach coping literature, for example, is that men tend to engage in emotional processing or emotional expression far less than women. It is well documented that expression of vulnerable emotions (e.g., sadness, fear, loneliness) is socially prohibited for men (American Psychological Association, 2018). It is possible that the social prohibitions on emotional expression for men may impact the feasibility and effectiveness of emotional approach coping in this population. Finally, Moreno et al. (2021) noted that individuals can be naturally disposed toward emotional expression or adaptive coping overall. Thus, the effectiveness of emotional approach coping appears to be conditional on both interpersonal (social and environmental contexts) and intrapersonal (individual difference) factors.

Cultural Factors

Emotional Approach coping was originally studied in homogenous, primarily White Western samples (Moreno et al. 2021). However, some evidence suggests it may be equally important for racial minorities. Across the life span, racial minorities, particularly people of color, experience racial stressors in the form of racism, discrimination, and prejudice. Moreover, recent research suggests that many Black Americans feel social and racism-related pressures to suppress their emotions at every stage of life (Wilson & Gentzler, 2021). Nevertheless, in one of the first studies to examine emotional approach coping in a Black sample, Peters (2006) found that it was negatively correlated with the experience of chronic stress emotions as brought on by exposure to racism. Subsequent researchers found that when dealing with the stress of chronic racism, racial and ethnic minority individuals' positive appraisal of emotion-focused coping options may intervene in the relationship between self-esteem, life satisfaction, and racial identity development (Outten et al., 2009). Specifically, when individuals of racial and ethnic minority groups feel that they have ways of coping emotionally with experiences of discrimination, greater self-esteem and greater life satisfaction were more closely linked with a strong identification with their racial group (Outten et al., 2009). These results point to the conclusion that use of emotion-focused styles of coping to deal with stressors related to personal racism, or as part of a racial group, may increase well-being and decrease stress for individuals experiencing these types of stressors in their environments. Additionally, a study looking at perceived discrimination in Black and Latinx populations found that individuals who felt they were being discriminated against used more emotion-focused coping as compared with other types and used it more frequently than White populations (Vassillière et al., 2016). Results in this study highlighted the fact that using emotion-focused approaches appears to be a function of regular exposure to racial discrimination (Vassillère et al., 2016). Finally, studies looking at other types of harassment found that women who were dealing with situations of sexual harassment often used emotion-focused strategies (e.g., seeking support, expressing emotion) and styles (Scarduzio et al., 2018). Thus, emotion-focused styles, especially those that are more active, might be used beneficially in a variety of ways to deal with discrimination or other negative circumstances among racial minorities and women.

This may not always be the case for all racial minorities or outside of the United States, however. Specifically, many Asian cultures encourage suppression of emotions, as opposed to expression, with the goal of preserving harmony in the group (Chiang, 2012; Lee, 2013; Murata et al., 2013). This said, there may be some circumstances, such as within close personal relationships, where emotional expression is considered by Asians to be appropriate and healthy. Contemporary Asian individuals may use a mixture of emotion suppression (culturally normative in traditional Asian culture) and emotional expression (culturally normative in more contemporary Asian culture, which is influenced by Western values). In situations where Asians are expected to emote expressively, they may feel stress. On the other hand, they may also feel stress in contexts where they are expected to suppress their emotions but have a desire to emote. In this way, "this cultural complexity may result in value conflict whereby some Asians may become emotionally ambivalent when their expressive styles clash with different sociocultural norms" (Lee, 2013, p. 171). Many of these findings may depend on one's level of acculturation and one's adherence to traditional Asian values. Different coping strategies may be used in these cultural groups to combat this stress.

Regardless of an individual's race or ethnicity, it is clear that culture does play a role in which types of coping are beneficial, likely based partially on the role emotion plays in the culture at hand (Chang, Yu et al., 2016). It is also true that some cultural groups may have more things to cope with on a daily or weekly basis (e.g., racism, sexism, heterosexism, classism). As always, attending to cultural context before employing strategies that have been found to work in White, Western populations for use with non-White or Eastern populations is advised.

Neurological Factors

Given the robust findings linking emotion-focused coping and adaptive outcomes under particular circumstances, it is important to understand how emotional approach works to our benefit at a physiological level. In early research, Depue (1996) pointed to the involvement of the behavioral activation system, and LeDoux (1996) revealed that a particular brain structure, the amygdala, plays a significant role in processing matters of emotional significance. Specifically, LeDoux suggested that, under stress-free life circumstances, our thinking is governed by the hippocampus, but during more stressful times, our thought processes—and hence aspects of our coping—are ruled by the amygdala. More recently, Brooks and colleagues (2017) looked at brain activity while participants processed emotional words (e.g., *anger, disgust*) and found that regions related to semantic process (such as the prefrontal cortex) were more activated. When nonemotional words were stated, the amygdala and the parahippocampal gyrus were the active regions. In functional magnetic resonance imaging (fMRI) studies, labeling one's affect—one mechanism believed to underlie successful emotional approach coping (see Figure 7.2)—increased activation in the prefrontal cortex and reduced amygdala activity (e.g., Burklund et al., 2014). Thus, emotional approach coping may help individuals return from a state of emotional distress governed by the amygdala to a state where they can better analyze the situation (i.e., governed by the prefrontal cortex). Such brain activity changes may also coincide with hormonal changes. Although findings are somewhat mixed, the extent to which emotional approach coping positively impacts our physical health may be conditional on how it reduces various inflammatory hormones (e.g., cortisol, Moreno et al., 2021).

Interestingly, culture may even affect individuals at the neurological level to some extent. In comparing Asian individuals to White American individuals, a study found that Asians seem to be "culturally trained to down-regulate emotional processing when required to suppress emotion" (Murata et al., 2013, p. 595). Researchers in this study measured emotional processing at a neurological level and found that when asked to suppress their reactions to negative pictures, Asians were able to decrease their neurological reaction to such a picture. European Americans in comparison did not seem to be able to control this in the same way. This provides intriguing information for potential environmental control on neurological response. Future examination of the neurobiology of emotion-focused coping and emotional processing may further demystify the potential benefits of approaching emotions in certain contexts and the related workings of brain structures such as the amygdala, the parahippocampal gyrus, and others related to these processes.

EMOTIONAL INTELLIGENCE: LEARNING THE SKILLS THAT MAKE A DIFFERENCE

For more than a century, psychologists and other researchers have been interested in the concept of intelligence. For example, the British psychologist, Charles Spearman (1863-1945), noted that individuals who performed well on one mental ability test tended to perform well on other tests, and thus proposed the concept of "G" or a "general" intelligence factor. Such tests of ability almost always focused on mental or physical skills and not emotions. However, Mowrer (1960) suggested that emotion was, in fact, "a high order of intelligence" (p. 308). Peter Salovey of Yale University and John Mayer of the University of New Hampshire (Mayer et al., 1990; Salovey & Mayer, 1990) were influenced by Mowrer's sentiment and theorized that adapting to life circumstances required cognitive abilities and emotional skills that guide our behavior. In their original 1990 papers, Salovey and Mayer constructed a theoretical framework for an emotional intelligence (EI). The framework comprised three core components: appraisal and expression, regulation, and utilization. These fledging ideas about a set of emotional abilities that might provide people with a reservoir of intellectual resources were well received by the public and the profession. Over the years, they have become particularly important within business leadership and management research and practice (Lopes, 2021).

The Ability Model of EI

The Salovey and Mayer four-branch ability model of EI (see Figure 7.3 and see Mayer et al., 2016 for a thorough review) suggests that the skills needed to reason about emotions and to use emotional material to assist reasoning can be learned. The model is organized from the simplest abilities to the most complex. Branch 1 (i.e., the simplest abilities) of the model involves basic skills needed to perceive and express feelings. More specifically, perception of emotions requires

FIGURE 7.3 ■ The Ability Model of Emotional Intelligence

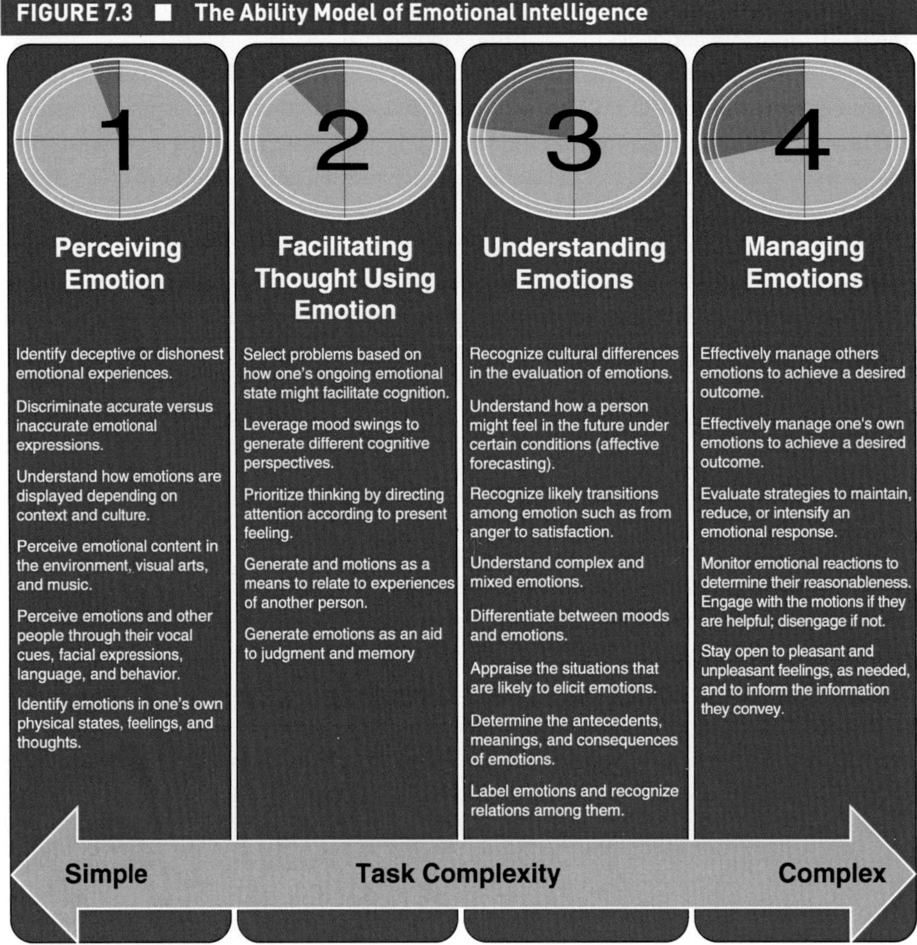

Adapted from Mayer et al. (2016).

picking up on subtle emotional cues that might be expressed in a person's face or voice. For example, when chatting with a friend about an emotionally charged political topic, a person skilled in perceiving emotions can determine what aspects of the discussion are safe or unsafe territory based on the friend's nonverbal behavior. Mayer et al. (2016) updated this branch to include an understanding of how emotions are displayed depending on context and culture. Such basic skills in perceiving and understanding emotions can be considered a threshold competency that needs to be acquired so that the other three emotional intelligence competencies can be developed.

Branch 2 of this ability model concerns using emotions and emotional understanding to facilitate thinking. Simply stated, people who are emotionally intelligent harness emotions and work with them to improve problem solving and to boost creativity. Physiological feedback from emotional experience is used to prioritize the demands on our cognitive systems and to direct attention to what is most important (Easterbrook, 1959; Mandler, 1975). In this regard, imagine that a person has to make an important decision about a relationship. Should they invest more energy in a friendship that has been on the rocks, or should they cut their losses and end the friendship in a civil manner? How this person feels physically and emotionally when they think about continuing or ending the friendship can provide some clues about how to proceed. Indeed, this is one of the theorized benefits of emotional approach coping discussed earlier (Stanton & Low, 2012). In other words, emotional information turns attention to alternatives about how to handle the friendship. Also, the more the emotions are used in efforts to make good decisions, the greater the increase in EI ability (Mayer et al., 2016).

Branch 3 of the ability EI model highlights the skills needed to foster an understanding of complex emotions, relationships among emotions, and relationships between emotions and behavioral consequences. Mayer and colleagues (2016) updated this branch to focus more on cultural competencies (i.e., the ability to recognize cultural differences in the evaluation of emotion). This is clearly a higher-level skillset. For example, someone displaying a heightened level of emotional understanding would know that hope is an antidote to fear (see Chapter 8) and that sadness and apathy are more appropriate responses to lost love than hate. At the same time, this person would be able to understand the context of these emotions and detect the cultural norms that impact the way they are evaluated and translate to various behaviors. Appreciating the dynamic relationships among emotions and behaviors gives an emotionally intelligent person the sense that they can better "read" a person or a situation and act appropriately, given contextual demands. For example, imagine the emotional struggle of a person who is placed in the awkward situation of being asked by a close friend to betray the confidence of a classmate or work colleague. They might feel disappointment or disgust that the friend asked them to behave in an inappropriate manner. If they were tempted to break the trust, they might experience a wave of shame or guilt. Understanding these complex emotions might help them choose the right course of action at that time (i.e., behaviors that are consistent with their moral principles and values).

The more we practice skills that are associated with Branches 1 through 3, the more emotional content there is to manage. Managing emotions, Branch 4, involves numerous mood regulation skills. These skills are the most complex (Mayer et al., 2016) and are difficult to master, because regulation is a balancing act. With too much regulation, a person may become emotionally repressed. With too little, one's emotional life becomes overwhelming.

Each of the four dimensions of the ability model is assessed with two sets of tasks in a measure called the Mayer-Salovey-Caruso Emotional Intelligence Test (the most recent version is the MSCEIT 2.0; Mayer et al., 2001). Although Mayer et al. (2016) admitted that the factor structure of the MSCEIT does not match the four branches of the ability model directly, they still maintain the four branches have utility from a conceptual framework, and the MSCEIT continues to be used widely (Lopes, 2021). The tasks concerned with perceiving emotions ask respondents to identify the emotions expressed in photographs of faces and the feelings suggested by artistic designs and landscapes. For the measurement of using emotions to facilitate thought, respondents are asked to describe feelings using nonfeeling words and to indicate the feelings that might facilitate or interfere with the successful performance of various tasks. The understanding–emotions dimension is assessed with questions concerning the manner in which emotions evolve and how some feelings are produced by blends of emotions. To tap the ability of managing emotions, the MSCEIT 2.0 presents a series of scenarios eliciting the most adaptive ways to regulate one's own feelings, as well as feelings that arise in social situations and in other people.

Abilities linked to the four branches of EI are associated with a variety of positive outcomes including greater psychological adaptation and mental health, positive interpersonal interactions, better work performance, and subordinates' reports of job satisfaction (Lopes, 2021). Ability EI has also been positively associated with greater adaptive emotion regulation and coping strategies (e.g., problem solving and positive reinterpretations; Peña-Sarrionandia et al., 2015), confirming that it is likely a critical component of emotional approach coping. Moreover, ability EI emerged as the third most important predictor of academic performance in secondary (K-12) and postsecondary (college) students across the world in a recent meta-analysis aggregating the results of 162 different studies. Specifically, MacCann et al. (2020) found that ability EI explained an additional 1.7% of the variance in academic performance after controlling for intelligence and Big 5 personality factors. The Understanding and Management branches of ability EI explained an additional 3.9% and 3.6%, respectively, suggesting that these more complex facets of EI are especially relevant to academic performance in children and adults. Perhaps the ability to manage one's emotions can help children and adults regulate negative feelings such as anxiety, boredom, or even disappointment in relation to academic performance (MacCann et al., 2020). Indeed, as you read this text, what emotions are you experiencing? Although we hope it is not boredom or disappointment (we hope you are feeling excited and enthralled), we were once college students ourselves. We remember those long nights of reading dense material and the feelings associated with those tasks. Recognizing that one is feeling bored or disappointed may be the first step toward reframing that experience to elicit a more pleasurable emotion to help meet your educational goals.

Greater ability EI may also inform social intelligence (Lopes, 2021; Mayer et al., 2016). That is, EI tells us something about social functioning that personality traits and analytical intelligence do not fully explain. The reason, according to Mayer and colleagues (2016), is that ability EI is a form of **hot intelligence**. Whereas **cool intelligence** characterizes relatively impersonal knowledge (e.g., math and verbal abilities, visuospatial processing), hot intelligence involves reasoning with information that is significant to one's person (e.g., sense of social acceptance, identity coherence, and well-being). Ability EI is believed to work in concert with other hot intelligence, such as the ability to reason about people's motivations (personal intelligence) and the ability to understand social rules (social intelligence), to help individuals deal with others in a skilled and effective manner. Several researchers have confirmed the links between ability EI and interpersonal effectiveness (Lopes, 2021). Recently, for example, researchers found that college students trained briefly to recognize emotions were more rated as more interpersonally effective in a dyadic interaction than those who did not receive EI training (Schlegel, 2021).

Mixed Models of EI

Although the ability model has received the most attention in the literature, other perspectives have gained traction over the years in terms of measuring and conceptualizing EI such as Goleman's concept of emotional competence (Goleman, 1998), Bar-On's emotional and social competence (Bar-On, 2006), and Petrides and Furnham's Trait EI (Petrides, Perez-Gonzalez et al., 2007; Petrides, Pita et al., 2007) (see also the Consortium for Research on Emotional Intelligence in Organizations, 2022 for a complete list of widely used ability, self-report, and mixed EI instrumentation). Whereas the ability model focuses solely on EI as a set of skills, these models blend self-perceived emotional competencies, personality traits, and a variety of adaptive functioning characteristics together and are thus referred to as "mixed models" of EI (Lopes, 2021). For example, a mixed model perspective conceptualizes EI as a combination of both ability and nonability facets. The four self-reported ability facets are (a) accurately perceiving emotions in oneself and others, (b) expressing and communicating emotions clearly, (c) managing others' emotions, and (d) regulating one's own emotions. Self-reported non-ability facets include adaptability, assertiveness, low impulsivity, fulfilling personal relationships, self-esteem, self-motivation, social awareness, stress management, trait empathy, trait happiness, and trait optimism. One of the most widely used measures drawing on a mixed model of EI, the Trait Emotional Intelligence Questionnaire (TEIQue; Petrides, 2009) is a 153-item self-report measure assessing 15 interrelated dimensions of ability and nonability related EI factors. A shorter version of the TEIQue, the TEIQue-SF, (Petrides, 2009) consists of 30 items derived statistically from the original instrument.

Data drawn from mixed models of EI are generally associated with the same positive personal and relational outcomes as data drawn from the ability EI model. However, mixed EI is often more strongly associated with personality factors and other positive psychological characteristics than ability EI. Some of this discrepancy may be because mixed EI models include a variety of characteristics considered adaptive and healthy in any context (e.g., trait optimism) and may mostly reflect one's personality rather than true EI ability (Lopes, 2021). Despite sharing some common variance with personality, however, Trait EI predicts unique variation in some outcomes when controlling for personality. For example, MacCann and colleagues (2020) found that Trait EI explained significant unique variation in academic success when controlling for measures of personality and intelligence. In a large meta-analysis of the TEIQue, Andrei and colleagues (2016) found evidence that the Trait EI explained additional variance when controlling for personality factors and general adaptive coping across a wide range of positive outcomes such as lower stress, less anxiety, and greater motivation. Therefore, Trait EI and other mixed models may account for aspects of EI not captured by ability but also not entirely overlapping with personality or general adaptive functioning.

Culture and EI

As we discussed in the previous section's review of research on emotion-focused coping, engaging more deeply in your emotional experiences (or perceiving, using, understanding, and managing emotions, to use the parlance of EI researchers) has benefits in some cultural contexts. Additionally, for people who demonstrate emotional intelligence, positive social functioning may be realized. Still, it is important to note that EI may not look the same or hold the same positive outcomes for all cultures. For example, differences have been found between German and Indian samples (Koydemir et al., 2013; Sharma et al., 2009) and Eastern (Thai) versus Western (United States) samples (Young et al., 2014). Such differences are not relegated solely to West vs East. In a recent study of trait EI across three Spanish speaking countries (i.e., Chile, Peru, and Spain), researchers found significant between-country differences, particularly when they considered sociodemographic factors such as age, gender, and civil status (Pérez-Díaz et al., 2022). Researchers have also found a number of cultural similarities in EI and its correlates. Recent meta-analytic research, for instance, suggests that EI may be especially relevant to job performance for workers in the hospitality industry regardless of cultural background (Miao et al., 2021). Likewise, extensive research on the psychometric properties of the MSCEIT over the past 20 years suggests that EI ability scores generalize across translated versions of instruments in different cultures (Iliescu et al., 2013; Karim & Weisz, 2010; Sanchez-Garcia et al., 2016). Investigations of Trait EI using different versions of the TEIQue have returned similar results (Chiesi et al., 2020; Feher et al., 2019; Perazzo et al., 2021). Taken together, these findings suggest that ability EI and Trait EI may capture some ability and experiences that are universal, but the expression of these universal qualities is likely conditional on cultural context.

In addition to between-culture differences and similarities in EI, numerous researchers have examined differences within cultures. The majority of this work has been conducted with Trait EI using the TEIQue and the TEIQue-SF. For example, researchers found that, even though gender differences have been noted in EI (Pardeller et al., 2017), measures of Trait EI appear to be capturing the same constructs among men and women (Perazzo et al., 2021; Tsaousis & Kazi, 2013). The correlates of EI, such as personality factors (MacCann et al., 2020; Siegling et al., 2015) and academic performance (MacCann et al., 2020), also appear to demonstrate very little variability across men and women. Thus, across the traditional gender binary, EI appears to have more similarities than differences. However, additional research is needed with gender minority groups such as transgender and nonbinary individuals for a more complete view of EI across different gender identities.

Compared to studies of gender and EI, comparatively little attention has been given to racial differences or similarities. Nevertheless, some evidence suggests that racial majority and racial minority groups may also share more similarities than differences on EI. For example, MacCann and colleagues (2020) found that the proportion of racial/ethnic minority groups vs majority groups in a sample had no effect on the strength of the meta-relationships between ability EI and Trait EI with academic success worldwide. Recent evidence also suggests that EI may be important to how individuals from marginalized groups cope with systemic discrimination stressors. In a study of 456 U.S. Black and immigrant college students, Espinosa and colleagues (2022) found that the links between racial discrimination and symptoms of severe mental illness were moderated by Trait EI and ethnic identity. Individuals were most at risk of severe mental illness if they reported low EI and less of an ethnic identity. However, among individuals with high EI, having a more of an ethnic identity appeared to be less important for coping with discrimination. Consistent with research on emotional approach coping among racial minorities, these emergent findings highlight the potential importance of being able to understand and manage emotions in situations where racial discrimination is likely.

Biological Bases of EI

A growing body of researchers have sought to determine the neurological substrates of EI. Similar to work on emotional approach coping, there is some evidence that efficient operation of the amygdala and the ventromedial prefrontal cortex may be implicated in EI, but the interplay between brain structures in people with high emotional intelligence continues to be debated. One interesting finding involved a study measuring emotional intelligence in individuals with agenesis of the corpus callosum (AgCC). AgCC is a condition in which, during the fetal period, the corpus callosum (the connective tissue that transmits messages between the left and the right hemispheres in the brain) does not develop normally. While AgCC does not appear to affect the experience of emotions themselves, distinct differences were found in the emotional intelligence of individuals with and without an AgCC diagnosis (Anderson et al., 2017). This points to some of the more complex processing involved in EI.

Another way that researchers can identify the neurological bases of EI is by examining individuals with brain lesions (e.g., damage to different parts of the brain). In a comprehensive review of brain lesion studies, Hogeveen et al. (2016) noted that EI abilities are fundamentally impaired in individuals with damage to specific areas of the brain including the amygdala, ventromedial prefrontal cortex (vmPFC; a highly interconnected area of the brain that links a number of large scale networks involved in emotional process, decision making, memory, self-perception, and social cognition), insula (an area related to emotional processing), and anterior cingulate cortex (ACC; an area implicated in complex cognitive functioning, such as empathy and impulse control). Thus, EI may be intricately linked to other higher-order executive functions. That is, EI may represent individual differences in the degree to which people incorporate or attend to emotional content in their decision-making processes (Hogeveen et al., 2016). In a more recent review of the EI literature, Kerr et al. (2019) proposed that EI, as an individual difference characteristic, may be imprinted in the brain due to the ways in which early childhood environment (e.g., parents, family, and environmental influences) impact the development of EI-related neurocircuitry. Thus, the areas of the brain most linked to EI are present in all of us, but the degree to which they are used and strengthened likely depends on a variety of contextual and environmental factors.

Training for EI

Given that these two lines of research (Stanton's work on emotional approach coping and Salovey and Mayer's examination of EI) establish the potential of working with your emotions, one wonders whether emotional skills can be learned. Entrepreneurs certainly are banking on it (no pun intended). Indeed, EI training has turned into a business onto itself, with a Google search for "emotional intelligence training" returning about 157,000,000 results—the first few pages consisting mostly of advertisements. Most of these programs are targeted toward business leaders, which is not surprising given the links between EI and leadership (Lopes, 2021). However, it is not uncommon for business to get ahead of the research, so we now take a few moments to digest the findings on the efficacy of EI training programs.

One of the most common ways researchers study EI training programs is via a pre-test, post-test design. Thus, participants who enter a program take an EI assessment at baseline and then another at the completion of the program. This form of evaluation has been used in EI training studies across many different populations and contexts. Less common are treatment vs control studies where participants are randomly assigned to either a treatment condition or a control condition and evaluated for changes in EI. In a meta-analysis of 50 pre-test post-test studies and 28 treatment vs. control studies published between 2000 and 2016 addressing a range of participants and EI training contexts, Mattingly and Kraiger (2019) found evidence for a moderate positive effect of training on increasing EI. The size of this effect was consistent with other studies of learning new information through training. However, they also noted that the effect was much stronger for pre-test post-test designed studies than those with a control group. Thus, these findings suggest that EI may naturally increase over time, regardless of training, but that training can help increase one's emotional abilities. This is consistent with my (McDermott) anecdotal evidence as well. Specifically, I am a counseling psychologist, and I train doctoral students in the science and provision of psychotherapy. EI abilities are critical for effective therapy, and some students appear more naturally gifted in working with emotions than others. Still, with support and proper guidance, I have seen tremendous growth in students' abilities to work effectively with emotions in the therapy room. Indeed, if EI skills were not trainable, I might find myself out of a job!

SOCIOEMOTIONAL SELECTIVITY: FOCUSING IN LATER LIFE ON POSITIVE EMOTIONS AND EMOTION-RELATED GOALS

The extent to which we are able to make the most of our emotional experiences is determined in part by personal and environmental demands such as our health status, social surroundings, and cultural norms. Humans' unique ability to monitor time across their entire span of life may also determine how much energy is dedicated to emotional goals. Laura Carstensen's (Carstensen & Charles, 1998; Carstensen, 2021) **socioemotional selectivity theory (SST)** posits that our later years (the "golden years") may be valuable as we focus less on negative emotions, engage more deeply with the emotional content of our days, and savor the "good stuff" in life (e.g., establishing and enhancing relationships). Carstensen reasons that we are able to appreciate these benefits in our advanced years because we come to realize that we have a shorter amount of time left.

In her laboratory, Carstensen has demonstrated that young people and their older counterparts manage emotion-laden material quite differently (Carstensen, 2021). In tests of attention to novel stimuli, for example, the younger participants attended to negative images more quickly, whereas the older participants oriented faster to images laden with positive emotions (smiling face, happy baby, puppy) (Charles et al., 2003). Regarding recall of emotional events, it appears that young people (college age and a bit older) remembered the positive and negative material to the same degree, but the older people had a positivity bias in which they recalled the positive material more quickly than the negative material (Charles et al., 2003; Reed & Carstensen, 2012). The "positivity effect" shown in these studies suggests that the process of interacting with emotions is different for young adults and older adults.

Irrespective of our tendencies to attend to and remember certain types of events, life provides all of us with blessings and burdens. Related to this point, Carstensen and her colleagues have found that there are age cohort effects for how we handle positive and negative daily life experiences. After monitoring the moods of 184 people (age 18 and up) for a week, Carstensen and colleagues (2000) discovered that their older research participants not only did not "sweat the small stuff" (which is how they viewed negative events) but also savored the positive events (experienced the good residuals of positive events for longer periods than their younger counterparts did). Older adults may also be able to continue to perform at high levels on tasks involving emotions well beyond their abilities to do this on cognitive tasks (Samanez-Larkin et al., 2014), showing differential processing of these tasks. Given these findings, it appears that positive experiences and positive emotions become our priority as we age and consider our mortality.

In addition, contrary to young people's fascination with future-oriented goals pertaining to acquiring information and expanding horizons, older people seem to orient to here-and-now goals that foster emotional meaning (Kennedy et al., 2001; Reed & Carstensen, 2012). This selectivity toward positive stimuli might be able to be used in promoting other positive behaviors in older adults. Notthoff and Carstensen (2014, 2017) have showed that using positive messaging (e.g., "Walking can have important cardiovascular health benefits," p. 331) to motivate older adults to get more exercise is more successful than using negative messaging ("Not walking enough can lead to increased risk for cardiovascular disease," p. 331). This study was conducted in a racially diverse sample and similar results were not found to be significant in younger adults. This type of messaging might have implications for encouraging older adults to engage in other helpful behaviors. In addition, paying attention to strengths (as opposed to weaknesses) in older adults might help to allow them to remain a part of the workforce (Carstensen et al., 2015). Thinking about ways to develop work teams that include different ages or generations and to establish older workers as mentors for younger workers might assist in helping older workers to feel useful and positive about their work for longer.

In general, the differences noted here between older adults and younger adults, according to SST, may be explained due to age differences in perceptions of time. That is, when an experimenter manipulates participants' perception of time, age differences tend to disappear. As one example, Ersner-Hershfield et al., (2008) compared experiences of **poignancy** (mixed emotions related to an ending or to losing something meaningful) in younger and older adults. Both younger and older adults in the experimental condition in this study were taken through a series of guided imagery scenarios of being in a personally meaningful location, ending with a final scenario that asked them to imagine that they were at this meaningful location for the very last time. Results showed that age was not a significant factor in the experience of poignancy, suggesting that "a meaningful limited-time situation such as an ending can produce poignancy regardless of age" (Ersner-Hershfield et al., 2008, p. 163). The researchers posited that the higher incidence of these feelings in older adults that have been reported previously may be more related to the feeling that time is limited (in life) as opposed to something organic to the aging process.

In summary, SST indicates that recall of positive experience, savoring the good times, and setting and investing in personal emotion-focused goals systematically influence social preferences, emotion regulation, and cognitive processing, and all of this is likely conditioned on our perceptions of time (particularly how much time we have left). Overall, therefore, looking at the aging process from a positive psychology perspective may be able to provide us with valuable information about how best to strive for a deeper emotional life, especially later in life. Not surprisingly, SST is particularly prevalent in the field of gerontology (i.e., the scientific study of old age and the process of aging). For instance, SST may inform how to best reach older adults through advertising or other media to improve their health and well-being (Carstensen & Hershfield, 2021). Likewise, emerging research is starting to examine SST in relation to the size and quality of social media networking relationships (Chiarelli & Batistoni, 2021) in older adults, as well as how older adults share information that could be beneficial to their overall health via social media (Rui, 2022). As social networking technology continues to evolve, using SST to inform the health and well-being of older adults will likely be an active area of research.

Cultural and Biological Perspectives of SST

SST has received little empirical scrutiny regarding its ability to generalize to other cultures. Still, there is some evidence that SST may be applicable to emotional processes in other cultures (Carstensen, 2021). Specifically, the tendency to remember more positive than negative information has been found in both Western and Eastern contexts. Studies demonstrate that Chinese older adults have the same pattern of memory of positive and negative pictures (Chung & Lin, 2012), although they may not have the same pattern with regard to visual attention to positive images (Fung et al., 2008). In a study by Chung and Lin (2012), Chinese older adults remembered fewer negative pictures in comparison to positive pictures, and they remembered fewer negative pictures in comparison to their U.S. counterparts. Researchers hypothesized that this may be partially due to the more negative view of aging held by older adults in the United States as compared to views of aging in China. With regard to attention, Fung and colleagues (2008) found that it was more common for older Chinese (but not younger) to look away from positive images, showing no attentional preference toward positivity. These interesting findings must be explored in greater detail to truly understand the process at hand. As with most situations, cultural context appears to play some role in the equation. Additionally, considering that SST revolves around perceptions of time, and that researchers have documented cultural differences in time perception (Arman & Adair, 2012), a detailed examination of cultural differences is needed.

Whereas cultural differences have received less attention in SST research, the clear implications for aging and older adults have led to a thriving body of literature on SST concepts in neuroscience and neuropsychology (Kaszniak & Menchola, 2012; Kehoe et al., 2013; Samanez-Larkin et al., 2014). Using fMRI studies and similar methodologies, researchers have identified that, although experimenters can manipulate age differences in SST by changing the perception of time, there appear to be functional differences in the older vs younger adult brain in the way we selectively attend to positive emotional stimuli (Samanez-Larkin et al., 2014). For example, Ku and colleagues (2022) recorded older and younger participants' brainwaves (EEG) while they read positive/negative and high/low-arousing words and pseudowords and made word/non-word judgments. In addition to detecting the expected differences between older and younger adults, the authors noted that the positivity bias was highly evident among older adults in their sample, despite their various life experiences and possible exposures. While the exact neural substrates that create this positivity bias have yet to be discovered, brain and behavior research may be the next frontier for investigators studying SST.

EMOTIONAL STORYTELLING: THE PENNEBAKER PARADIGM AS A MEANS OF PROCESSING INTENSE NEGATIVE EMOTIONS

Every now and again, we experience life events that shake us to our core. Traumatic events that cause emotional upheaval may outstrip the resources of good emotion-focused copers, the emotionally intelligent, and the young and old alike. It is quite likely (with a 95% probability) that, when we experience an overwhelming emotional event, we will share the experience with a friend or family member within the same day of its occurrence, typically in the first few hours (Rime, 1995). It is almost as if we are compelled to tell the story of our emotional suffering. Is it possible that we have learned that not talking about our intense emotions has dire consequences? This question and many related research hypotheses have served as the impetus for the work of psychologist James Pennebaker. In 1989, Pennebaker broke ground on this research area by making the following request of undergraduate research participants in an experimental group of a study:

> For the next four days, I would like . . . you to write about your deepest thoughts and feelings about your most traumatic experience in your life. In your writing, I'd like you to really let go and explore your very deepest emotions and thoughts. You might tie your topic to your relationships, including parents, lovers, friends, or relatives. You may also want to link your experience to your past, your present, or your future, or to who you have been, who you would like to be, or who you are now. You may write about the same general issues or experiences on all days of writing, or on different traumas each day. All of your writing will be completely confidential. (p. 215)

The control group participants were asked to write for 15 minutes a day for 4 days but about a non-emotional topic (e.g., a description of the room they were seated in). All participants were asked to write continuously, without regard to spelling, grammar, and sentence structure. The immediate effects of the two interventions were such that the experimental group was more distressed. Then, over time (beginning 2 weeks after the study), the members of the emotional storytelling group experienced numerous health benefits, including fewer physician visits over the next year, compared with the members of the control group.

Emotional Storytelling Through Writing: The Pennebaker Paradigm

The research procedure involving the mere act of written disclosure of emotional upheaval—what we generally call emotional storytelling or expressive writing—is referred to as the **Pennebaker paradigm** (systematic written disclosure across brief sessions). This technique has been used to address the emotions associated with job loss (discussed in Chapter 15), diagnosis of illness, and relationship breakup (reviewed in Pennebaker, 1997). It has also been used with a number of different populations, including helping those who want to forgive a transgressor (Barclay & Saldanha, 2016), youth involved in the juvenile justice system (Greenbaum & Javdani, 2017), and people with depression and other mental health issues (Lee et al., 2016; Reinhold et al., 2018). Some of the most common outcomes investigated in relation to expressive writing are *physical functioning* (e.g., respiratory problems, immune response, cardiovascular functioning, fatigue, wound healing, and chronic pain), performance (e.g., academic achievement and grades), and *mental health* (e.g., changes in distress, bereavement or grief, suicidal ideation, and anxiety/depression). Expressive writing and other emotional journaling activities are also included in some evidence-based treatments for Posttraumatic Stress Disorder (PTSD).

Researchers have studied the benefits of expressive writing across a wide range of studies to date. While many individual investigations have found positive short and long-term effects, meta-analyses have, at times, revealed mixed results (Kállay, 2015; Reinhold et al., 2018). Moreover, at least one study has found that expressive writing may actually exacerbate problems in the short term in some situations, such as processing trauma from a recent natural disaster (Paquin et al., 2021). These findings suggest that there are many different moderating factors that increase (or decrease) the positive benefits of expressive writing. For example, writing about emotions and emotional experiences may be particularly beneficial to individuals who prefer to use an emotion approach style of coping in dealing with problems in their lives (Austenfeld & Stanton, 2008). Likewise, those who prefer emotion-approach coping with stress and trauma showed more benefit from emotional writing following a stress test than those who did not use emotion-approach coping (Seeley et al., 2017). Relatedly, in a large randomized control study of breast cancer patients in Denmark, researchers noted that women who were already comfortable with emotional expression (i.e., low levels of alexithymia) benefited the most from an expressive writing intervention when they wrote about their own experiences with cancer (Jensen-Johansen et al., 2018). These results direct us to remember to attend to the vast array of individual differences that can affect the effectiveness of various strategies (Stickney, 2010).

Theories of Expressive Writing

Several theories have been advanced to explain the physical, relational, and psychological benefits of expressive writing (Kállay, 2015). One of the first was *Inhibition Theory* (Pennebaker et al., 1987). Inhibition theory posited that not expressing one's emotions about a past traumatic event contributed to physiological indicators of stress over time. Thus, expressive writing allowed individuals to reduce that stress. However, critics have noted that this theory cannot adequately explain why expressive writing produced beneficial effects when writing about an imaginary trauma (Kállay, 2015). A related theory that has gained more traction in the literature, ***Cognitive Processing Theory***, suggests that the active conversion of traumatic or stressful memories into language allows a person to develop distance from those distressing memories and reinterpret them from different perspectives (Harber & Pennebaker, 1992; Smyth et al., 2008). In other words, expressive writing may help a person make new meaning from their trauma (Kállay, 2015). Supporting this perspective, expressive writing is included in a variety of PTSD treatments. Like the Inhibition Theory, however, cognitive processing cannot fully account for the benefits reported from expressive writing for imaginary traumas or nontraumatic events (Kállay, 2015). To address these issues, some researchers have proposed that expressive writing may help with self-regulation and cognitive control during the writing process, which, in turn, may facilitate self-efficacy in one's ability to regulate emotions (Lepore & Greenberg, 2002). Kállay (2015) described this perspective as a *Self-Regulation Theory* of expressive writing. Additionally, Pennebaker and Graybeal (2001) proposed the *Social Integration Model* of expressive writing. This model suggested that expressive writing changes the way individuals interact with their social environment (e.g., they may be more likely to ask their social support networks for help or to share their stories with other people). However, each of these theories and models only provide partial explanations of the benefits of expressive writing, and the most likely explanation is a combination of all these perspectives, as well as several mechanisms yet to be discovered (Kállay, 2015).

Despite several competing theories, it does appear that disinhibition (letting go of emotion-related stress), cognitive processing, and social dynamics (when disclosure occurs outside the laboratory) are at work (Niederhoffer & Pennebaker, 2002) when someone experiencing emotional upheaval shares their story. Others have stated, "Emotional writing . . . reveals the natural abilities people have to construct stories" (Ramírez-Esparza & Pennebaker, 2006, p. 212). Plainly stated, "Putting upsetting experiences into words allows people to stop inhibiting their thoughts and feelings, to begin to organize their thoughts and perhaps find meaning in their traumas, and to reintegrate their social networks" (Niederhoffer & Pennebaker, 2002, p. 581). This is supported by neurological studies that seem to suggest that "affect labelling (putting feelings into words) is a form of incidental emotional regulation" (Memarian et al., 2017, p. 1437).

Expressive Writing: Cultural Factors

Research on expressive writing in different cultural groups has returned mixed results. For example, expressive writing about trauma evidenced benefits for European Americans but not Asian American undergraduate students (Knowles et al., 2011). In a study aimed at using expressive writing techniques as an attempt to decrease alcohol use, researchers found that when Asian participants wrote expressively about their alcohol use and future intentions to drink, they experienced more shame about these behaviors than their White counterparts (Rodriguez et al., 2016). These results were even found in light drinkers within the Asian sample, although this shame did not lead to more drinking in this group. Shame was not a common reaction in White participants who wrote about their alcohol use in this study, and in many cases, this intervention was found to be beneficial to this group. More recently, researchers in China found that expressive writing slightly *increased* posttraumatic stress symptoms and *decreased* posttraumatic growth in a large study of breast cancer survivors (Gallagher et al., 2018).

At face value, such findings may call into question the universality of expressive writing interventions; however, other researchers have found that emotional expression through writing may be especially beneficial to Asian Americans who (as culturally mandated) tend to suppress their emotions. For example, Lu and Stanton (2010) found that expressive writing about challenges, consequences, and opportunities was more beneficial for Asian Americans than European Americans. Tsai and colleagues (2015) coded the content of expressive writing and found that different themes were beneficial to both Asian and European Americans in unique ways. Specifically, writing reflecting downward social comparisons (i.e., comparing oneself to someone who is believed to be worse off) were associated with positive mental health outcomes at a 3-month follow-up among European Americans. Writing reflecting persistence themes was associated with poorer mental health outcomes for European Americans. However, the oppositive pattern emerged for Asian Americans. That is, writing reflecting downward social comparisons was associated with poorer outcomes, and themes reflecting persistence were associated with more positive outcomes. In a later critical review paper of cultural differences in emotional expression and expressive writing, Tsai and Lu (2018) suggested, "expressive writing is a culturally sensitive and effective intervention when writing instructions are culturally congruent" (p. 8). This makes the point, yet again, that cultural context must be considered with interventions of all types.

Expressive Writing: Biological Factors

Researchers are only now beginning to explore the biological mechanisms involved in expressive writing. Most of this research, to date, has been spearheaded by Dr. Brynne Catherine DiMenichi. DiMenichi and colleagues (2018) concluded that expressive writing about a past failure may inoculate individuals to stressful events by reducing their cortisol reactivity and increasing their cognitive performance (DiMenichi et al., 2018). In a second study, participants who wrote about a past failure appeared to have altered neural processing during an attentional task (word-pairing/matching) in the mid cingulate cortex (MCC), an area associated with negative emotion and cognitive control (DiMenichi et al., 2019). Across both of these studies, it is important to note that participants did not write about emotionally traumatic events. Thus, while DiMenichi and colleagues speculated that writing about a past failure may have the same neural impact as writing about a past trauma, much is still yet to be discovered regarding the chemical and neural mechanisms behind expressive writing for trauma or other more emotionally-heavy content.

EMOTIONAL STORYTELLING THROUGH THERAPY

Emotions and Evidence Based Psychotherapies: A Personal Account

I (McDermott) sat down with Hannah Hinkle, an advanced graduate student in the combined-integrated Clinical and Counseling Psychology PhD program at the University of South Alabama. Hannah was recently recognized by her doctoral program for her excellence in psychotherapy, and I thought it would be interesting to let her share a bit about how she uses emotions in psychotherapy.

How I use emotions in psychotherapy largely depends upon the theoretical orientation I am implementing and how the orientation conceptualizes emotions. For instance, within Cognitive Behavioral Therapy (CBT), emotions are conceptualized as a result of what we think and how we behave. Thus, in order to improve emotional states from a CBT framework, I modify unhelpful thinking styles and behaviors linked to negative emotional states. To address unhelpful ways of thinking, I implement guided discovery, Socratic questioning, thought records, cognitive restructuring, and problem-solving skills to cope with difficult situations. I implement behavioral activation, exposures, relaxation skills training, and role-playing to address learned patterns of unhelpful behavior. Successful implementation of these cognitive and behavioral strategies frequently yields decreased emotional intensity.

Within Acceptance and Commitment Therapy (ACT), psychopathology and problems are conceptualized to arise when an individual attempts to control or avoid their internal experiences (i.e., emotions, thoughts, images, urges, memories, sensations), which leads an individual to engage in values-incongruent behavior. Thus, contrary to CBT, ACT does not aim to reduce the frequency of unpleasant or unwanted emotions. Rather, ACT teaches clients new skills to reduce the impact of their emotions over their actions in order to facilitate values-based living. I target core processes such as acceptance, mindfulness, defusion, and self-as-context to promote psychological and emotional flexibility. Thus, within ACT, I teach clients acceptance skills to be willing to experience all emotions, with a stance of curiosity and nonjudgment. For instance, I frequently implement the following acceptance and mindfulness-based exercises: dropping anchor, non-judgmentally noticing and naming relevant aspects of their emotional reaction, and emotion surfing. Further, I frequently utilize physicalizing and labeling feelings to promote defusion from emotion or the ability to detach and promote distance from emotions. To promote self-as-context or the idea that clients are not the content of their feelings, I frequently implement the sky and the weather metaphor (i.e., thoughts and feelings are like the weather: the weather naturally and constantly changes, but it can never harm or fundamentally change the sky), or the chessboard metaphor. Regarding the latter, this metaphor encourages individuals to think of their thoughts as chess pieces—the chessboard carries the pieces, but it is not equal to the pieces. Similarly, you carry your difficult thoughts, and you observe them, but you are not equivalent to those thoughts. Across the core processes in ACT, I use metaphors like these as a teaching and therapeutic tool to see challenging emotions in a new way.

I also routinely integrate an interpersonal process approach in therapy as an adjunct to the aforementioned cognitive approaches. Within interpersonal process, I attend to the content of what clients are saying and the process dimension, or how clients say it. Interpersonal process can promote a corrective emotional experience for clients when the therapist highlights maladaptive relational patterns or themes that occur for the client and works with the client to modify the maladaptive pattern, disconfirm faulty expectations or schemas, or change this problematic interpersonal pattern in the client's real-life relationships. To provide a corrective emotional experience, I implement process comments, meta-communicate with clients regarding how we interact (as client and therapist), and engage the client in role-plays to try out new behaviors with myself and then generalize these behaviors to others outside of the therapy room.

Lastly, how I approach emotions within psychotherapy also depends upon the setting that I am working in. For instance, I specialize in brief, evidence-based interventions within integrated medical settings. Thus, I am not routinely employing full, manualized treatments. Instead, I may be pulling evidence-based interventions to help reduce symptoms and ameliorate suffering for clients. For instance, within integrated primary care, I routinely implement Dialectical Behavior Therapy (DBT) interventions (e.g., emotion regulation skills, distress tolerance skills) and CBT interventions (e.g., activity scheduling, worry postponement, relaxation training, mindfulness).

WORKING WITH EMOTIONS TO BRING ABOUT POSITIVE CHANGE

Practicing psychologists have long discussed the role of emotions in the psychological change process. During our training as psychologists, we were encouraged to identify clients' emotions and reflect the emotional content of clients' stories. Emotions, as understood within the cultural context of our clients, are considered the indicators of quality of functioning; they helped us track how well a client was doing. They are also an emotional compass—they tell us what needs to be processed at a deeper level. Given the research discussed in this chapter, we now train our graduate students to view emotions as determinants of positive change, not just markers of growth, and we caution them to look for varying ways of expressing emotions in different cultural groups. Indeed, how well we and our clients handle emotional events sets, in part, the outer limits of personal well-being.

Now, with what we have learned in our roles as teachers and clinicians in mind, we share ideas that will reveal the potential benefits of strategically working with your emotions. First, we want you to approach the Personal Mini-Experiments as a psychologist gathering data about the phenomena discussed in this chapter. Be as objective as possible when you conduct each experiment, and determine whether your personal results line up with the research findings in this text. Then, make some attempts to hone your personal skills for dealing with the emotion-laden information you encounter every day by implementing the Life Enhancement Strategies for love, work, and play. Consistent with the research and theory reviewed in this chapter, we hope that you find making the most of emotional experiences helps create a balanced means of dealing with the information gained from all emotional experiences and contributes to a happier and healthier life.

PERSONAL MINI-EXPERIMENTS

MAKING THE MOST OF EMOTIONS IN EVERYDAY LIFE

In this chapter, we discuss the "how-tos" and benefits of engaging our emotions. Our review suggests that engaging our emotional selves leads to better and deeper living. Here are a few ideas (and don't forget about the Pennebaker writing exercise described previously) for experimenting with making the most of emotions in your everyday life.

The Emotions Daily Journal. Based on your physiological reactions or the duration of the emotional experience, carefully identify the intense emotions (see Chapter 6 for listings of positive and negative feelings) that you feel every 4 waking hours for 2 days. Note these feelings in your paper or electronic calendar. At the end of each 4-hour segment, spend 5 minutes reflecting on these experiences to determine if you tend to *approach* or *avoid* provocative emotions. (If necessary, create a 5-point Likert-type rating system to gauge your responses.) After 2 days' time, identify the benefits and pitfalls of moving toward and moving away from emotion-laden information.

"Acting as If" You Were Emotionally Intelligent for a Day. Think about the people in your life who manage their emotions very well. Make a list of these people and informally rank them from good to best in terms of their emotional intelligence. Then, pick a day of the week when you are sure to have a great deal of social interaction. Spend the day emulating one of your emotionally intelligent role models and act as if you were highly skilled in working with your emotions. When faced with problems or opportunities to excel, ask yourself, "What would my EI role model do in this situation?" and then do it! At the end of the day, identify the top three emotional skills you acted as if you had (see Figure 7.3) for the list of the 16 skills of emotional intelligence. In the days that follow, use the three skills again and again until you feel like you have mastered them.

The Buoyant Grandparent Visit. Have you ever asked your grandmother or grandfather (or another family elder or non-relative) how she or he stays optimistic, happy, compassionate, or working to create harmony despite all the life challenges that she or he has endured? Identify your most resilient or most buoyant family or non-family elder you know and ask this person, "What's important to you these days? What helps you to be in the moment? How do your friends figure into your daily life?" Emotional strategies and plans for spending time with family and friends are sure to be mentioned.

Emotions in Cultural Context. Make a list of the emotions you most often experience. Rank order them in terms of how much you value each. Is the experience of happiness a major priority in your life? Useful expression of anger? Attending to feelings of joy or fear? How did you learn about the importance of these emotions? How might individuals from cultures other than your own feel differently about this ranking? Think about people in your life from different races, genders, religions, or generations—might they have both similarities and differences to you with regard to expression of various emotions?

LIFE ENHANCEMENT STRATEGIES

We encourage you to develop new emotional skills that you can apply in the important domains of your life.

Love

- Practice using more "feeling words" when interacting with friends and family. Adding this to your daily communication will encourage a more emotional approach.
- Set new goals for important relationships that might promote your emotional growth and that of the other person. Think about how your plans and those of others might differ depending on their cultural facets. Are there gender differences in terms of what may be most beneficial, for example? This might enhance the quality of the relationship over time.

Work

- Acknowledge the emotional undercurrents of communication at work. Share these observations in a nonconfrontational way with your coworkers and bosses and facilitate a dialogue about the roles of emotions in the workplace.
- Seek "emotional intelligence at work" seminars. Many human resources offices or local consulting services offer this type of seminar, and anecdotal evidence suggests that participants feel more efficacious in their use of emotional intelligence skills once they complete such training.

Play

- Become an emotional storyteller. Write down the stories of your good times and bad in a journal or share them with trusted friends. Storytelling may distance you from negative experiences in your life and bring you closer to people who are important to you.
- Learn and practice meditation skills. These skills are believed to "suspend time" and help us engage our emotional experiences more deeply.

KEY TERMS

Cool Intelligence
Emotional approach
Emotional avoidance
Emotional expression
Emotional intelligence
Emotional processing
Emotional storytelling
Hot Intelligence
Pennebaker paradigm
Poignancy
Socioemotional selectivity theory

STATES AND PROCESSES

8 SEEING OUR FUTURES THROUGH SELF-EFFICACY, OPTIMISM, AND HOPE

LEARNING OBJECTIVES

After reading this chapter, you should be able to:

8.1 Discuss the origins and core components of the constructs of self-efficacy, optimism, and hope

8.2 Describe the psychological benefits of self-efficacy, optimism, and hope

8.3 Recognize common psychological instruments measuring self-efficacy, optimism, and hope

8.4 Discuss cultural differences and similarities across self-efficacy, optimism, and hope research and measurement

8.5 Identify neurological and biological factors associated with self-efficacy, optimism, and hope

FASCINATION WITH THE FUTURE

What does the future hold? The answer to this question can tell us a lot about a person's views of themselves and the world. Positive psychology has spent decades studying **future orientations**. In the present chapter, we first examine three major future-oriented perspectives in positive psychology—**self-efficacy**, optimism, and **hope**. We explore the theories that guide these concepts, along with the scales that measure them and various research findings. We also comment on how these future-oriented concepts may (or may not) apply to samples other than the White Western individuals where these theories originated.

SELF-EFFICACY

I Think I Can, I Think I Can . . .

After Stanford University psychologist Albert Bandura (1925-2021) published his 1977 *Psychological Review* article titled "Self-Efficacy: Toward a Unifying Theory of Behavior Change," the self-efficacy concept spread in popularity to the point that it now may have produced more empirical research than any other topic in positive psychology (Bandura, 1977, 1982, 1997). What exactly is this concept that has proven so influential? To understand self-efficacy, some people have used the sentiments of the little train engine (from Watty Piper's [1930/1989] children's story, *The Little Engine That Could*) to epitomize self-efficacy. Recall that the tiny engine, thinking about how the children on the other side of the mountain would not have their toys unless she helped, uttered the now-famous motivational words, "I think I can. I think I can. I think I can"—and then proceeded to chug successfully up the mountainside to deliver her payload. This belief that you can accomplish what you want if you believe you can do it is at the core of the self-efficacy idea.

Children's books aside, the self-efficacy construct rests upon a long line of historical thinking related to the sense of personal control. Famous thinkers such as John Locke, David Hume, William James, and Gilbert Ryle have focused on willfulness, or volition, in human thinking (Vessey, 1967). Similar ideas have appeared in theories on achievement motivation (McClelland et al., 1953), effectance motivation (White, 1959), and social learning (Rotter, 1966). It was this classic line of control-related scholarship upon which Bandura drew in defining the self-efficacy concept.

A Definition

Bandura (1997) defined self-efficacy as "people's beliefs in their capabilities to produce desired effects by their own actions" (p. vii). Similarly, Maddux (2009a) has described self-efficacy as "what I believe I can do with my skills under certain conditions" (p. 336). Based on examining what needs to be done to reach a desired goal (these are called *outcome expectancies*), the person analyzes their capability to complete the necessary actions (these are called *efficacy expectancies*). For Bandura, outcome expectancies are viewed as far less important than efficacy expectancies (Maddux, 1991; Maddux & Kleiman, 2021). Thus, situation-specific self-efficacy thoughts are proposed to be the last and most crucial cognitive step before people launch goal-directed actions.

Childhood Antecedents: Where Does Self-Efficacy Come From?

Self-efficacy is a learned human pattern of thinking rather than a genetically endowed one. It begins in infancy and continues throughout the life span. Self-efficacy is based on **social cognitive theory**, which holds that humans actively shape their lives rather than passively reacting to environmental forces (Bandura, 1986; Barone et al., 1997).

Social cognitive theory, in turn, is built on three ideas. First, humans have powerful symbolizing capacities for cognitively creating models of their experiences. Second, by observing themselves in relation to these cognitive models, people become skilled at self-regulating their actions as they navigate ongoing environmental events. Thus, cognitive reactions influence the surrounding environmental forces that, in turn, shape subsequent thoughts and actions (i.e., there is a back-and-forth interchange of environmental and thinking forces). Third, people (i.e., their self-concepts) and their personalities result from these situation-specific, reciprocal interactions of thoughts. → environment. → thoughts. Given these social cognitive ideas, therefore, a developing child uses symbolic thinking, with specific reference to the understanding of cause-and-effect relationships, and learns self-efficacious, self-referential thinking by observing how they can influence the surrounding circumstances (Maddux, 2009a; Maddux & Kleiman, 2021).

Bandura (1977, 1989a, 1989b, 1997) proposed that the developmental antecedents of self-efficacy include the following:

1. Previous successes in similar situations (calling on the wellspring of positive thoughts about how well one has done in earlier circumstances)
2. Modeling others in the same situations (watching other people who have succeeded in a given arena and copying their actions)
3. Imagining oneself behaving effectively (visualizing acting effectively to secure a wanted goal)
4. Arousal and emotion (when physiologically aroused and experiencing negative emotions, our self-efficacy may be undermined, whereas such arousal paired with positive emotions heightens the sense of self-efficacy)
5. Undergoing verbal persuasion by powerful, trustworthy, expert, and attractive other people (being influenced by a helper's words to behave in a given manner)

Measurement of Self-Efficacy

Bandura (1977, 1982, 1997) has held staunchly to the **situational perspective** that self-efficacy should reflect beliefs about using abilities and skills to reach given goals *in specific circumstances or domains,* stating that "efficacy beliefs should be measured in terms of particularized judgments of capacity that may vary across realms of activity, under different levels of task demands within a given domain, and under different situational circumstances" (Bandura, 1997, p. 42). Accordingly, there are more self-efficacy self-report questionnaires for specific domains than we can sufficiently cover in this chapter (possibly this entire book). For example, researchers have developed a variety of self-efficacy measures for general health behaviors or health management (Sallis et al., 1988), interpersonal relationship functioning (Zullig et al, 2011), and mental health (Alessandri et al., 2015; Pool & Qualter, 2012). Researchers also developed measures of self-efficacy in more specific domains such as career counseling (Betz & Klein Voyten, 1997), alcohol abstinence (McKiernan et al. 2011), internet use (Kim & Glassman, 2013), childbirth (Lowe, 1993), memory ability (Berry et al., 1989), and many more.

Noting the proliferation of self-efficacy scale development projects in the literature, Bandura (2005) published a best practice guide for creating new measures and argued for the following criteria. First, efficacy items should have adequate content validity (i.e., they should be phrased as *can do* rather than *will do*). Second, they must relate to domains where a person has some degree of perceived control. Third, they must reflect a solid conceptual analysis of a particular domain (i.e., they must reflect the most relevant behaviors that one should master).

Fourth, they should represent different levels of challenge in a particular domain (i.e., items should not simply cover the hardest or easiest behaviors—they should have a gradation of challenge). Finally, items should have sufficient response scales to allow variability. The standard set forth by Bandura (2005) was to present a specific task (e.g., working out each day) and then have respondents mark their level of self-efficacy for this task on a 0 (*cannot do at all*) to 10 (*highly certain can do*) rating scale. We should note that not all domain-specific self-efficacy instruments follow these guidelines. Still, if you are searching for a measure, we encourage you to look at the items and see if they fit with these best practice recommendations (see also Chapter 3 for a list of recommendations for selecting measurement tools in positive psychology).

While heavily promoting the concept of domain-specific self-efficacy, Bandura (2005) consistently argued against the **trait perspective** (in which psychological phenomena are viewed as enduring over time and circumstances). Nevertheless, researchers have developed such dispositional measures of self-efficacy (e.g., Sherer et al., 1982; see also Tipton & Worthington, 1984). Citing evidence that self-efficacy experiences involving personal mastery can generalize to actions that transcend any given target behavior (e.g., Bandura et al., 1977) and that some people are especially likely to have high self-efficacy expectations across several situations, Sherer et al. (1982) developed and validated a trait-like index called the Sherer's General Self-Efficacy Scale (SGSES).

The SGSES consists of 17 items to which respondents rate their agreement on a 5-point Likert scale (1 = *strongly disagree* to 5 = *strongly agree*). Examples of some items include the following: "When I make plans, I am certain I can make them work," "If I can't do a job the first time, I keep trying till I can," and "When I have something unpleasant to do, I stick to it until I finish it." The internal consistency of the scale (i.e., the degree to which individual items aggregate together—see Chapter 3) has generally been acceptable (i.e., alphas were greater than .70) in a variety of different populations (Chen et al., 2001). Last, the concurrent validity of the Self-Efficacy Scale has been supported by its positive correlations with scores on measures of personal control, ego strength, interpersonal competency, and self-esteem (Chen et al., 2001; Sherer et al., 1982). Other researchers have also developed dispositional measures of self-efficacy that have good reliability and validity evidence and have been used widely over time. For example, the General Perceived Self-Efficacy Scale (GPSES, also known as the General Self-Efficacy Scale [GSE]; Schwarzer & Jerusalem, 1995) consists of 10 self-report items (e.g., "I am certain I can accomplish my goals"). The GPSES is scored using a 1 (*not at all true*) to 4 (*exactly true*) scale.

Some investigators have endeavored to make shorter and more refined measures of general self-efficacy. Chen et al. (2001) developed an eight-item New General Self-Efficacy Scale (NGSES), and its scores appear to relate positively to those on the Self-Efficacy Scale of Sherer et al. (1982) (although there are exceptions). More recently, Romppel and colleagues (2013) shortened the GSE to just six items (i.e., the GSE-6) and found that the shorter scale evidenced similar reliability and validity coefficients as the GPSES. Rigorous psychometric analyses at the item-level of the SGSES, NGSES, the GSE, and the GSE-6 have all supported the ability of these instruments to capture general self-efficacy, especially at lower levels. In other words, evidence suggests these instruments may be especially good at identifying issues related to a *lack* of self-efficacy (Peter et al., 2014; Scherbaum et al., 2006).

Measuring self-efficacy has also become a more common cross-cultural endeavor in recent years. For example, Israelashvili and Socher (2007) focused on self-efficacy in counselors in an Israeli sample, and self-efficacy scales for children in Brazil (De Cássia et al., 2009) and Poland (Gambin & Swieçicka, 2012) also have been developed. Other researchers have endeavored to examine self-efficacy across various countries (e.g., Klassen et al., 2009; Wu, 2009). Indeed, measuring general self-efficacy has been a particularly productive area of research in China (Ji-liang & Dan, 2004; Leung & Leung, 2011; Sun et al., 2021). These and other similar studies point to the global relevance of strength-based research and applications of this construct and may lead us to a better understanding of how self-efficacy is developed and maintained in various cultural contexts.

Self-Efficacy's Influence in Life Arenas

Self-efficacy has produced huge bodies of research both inside and outside of psychology. In this section, we explore some of this research. For the interested reader, see Maddux and Kleiman (2021) for a detailed review of the self-efficacy literature.

Psychological Adjustment

Bandura (1997) was one of the first to take a positive, strengths-based approach by arguing that self-efficacy can play a protective role in dealing with psychological problems. Over time, this assertion has been consistently supported in the scientific literature. Self-efficacy has been implicated in successful coping with a variety of psychological problems (Maddux & Kleiman, 2021). Lower self-efficacies have been linked with depression (Bandura, 1977; Locke et al., 2017; O'Shea et al., 2017; Pickett et al., 2012) and avoidance and anxiety (Bertrams et al., 2016). Higher self-efficacy is helpful in overcoming eating disorders and abuse (Byrne et al., 2015), and it has also been linked with life satisfaction in a variety of populations (see Charrow, 2006; Dahlbeck & Lightsey, 2008; Danielson et al., 2009). Research also suggests that self-efficacy may play a role in the success of treatment aimed at interpersonal behavior of outpatients dealing with schizophrenia (Morimoto et al., 2012; Vaskinn et al., 2015). Additionally, decreases in self-efficacy may drive increases in depression over time in patients who have suffered a stroke (Volz et al., 2019). Thus, the ability to have agency in one's life, as represented by self-efficacy, may be a core component of psychological health (Maddux & Kleiman, 2021).

Physical Health

Maddux (2009a) has suggested that self-efficacy can influence positive physical health in two ways. First, elevated self-efficacy increases health-related behaviors and decreases unhealthy ones; moreover, self-efficacy helps to maintain these changes (Lee et al., 2012; Maddux & Kleiman, 2021). In this regard, theories pertaining to health behaviors all showcase self-efficacy. Examples of these theories include the protection motivation theory (Rogers & Prentice-Dunn, 1997), the theory of planned behavior (Ajzen, 1991), and the health belief model (Strecher et al., 1997). Second, self-efficacy has an impact on various biological processes that relate to better physical health. Included in such adaptive biological processes are immune functioning (O'Leary

& Brown, 1995), susceptibility to infections, the neurotransmitters that are implicated in stress management (i.e., catecholamines), and the endorphins for muting pain (Bandura, 1997).

Finally, self-efficacy may be particularly useful in dealing with individuals coping with disease. Many researchers have attempted to leverage self-efficacy to inform *mHealth* applications. Smart phone apps and other interactive technologies can help individuals manage their medical conditions, in part, by increasing efficacy beliefs about important medical management skills. In a recent meta-analysis of randomized control trials of smart-phone based applications for the management of Type 2 diabetes, for example, researchers found large effects for mHealth, suggesting this technology dramatically increases self-efficacy and positive health management behaviors (Aminuddin et al., 2021).

Psychotherapy

Self-efficacy is a common factor across various psychological interventions (Bandura, 1986; Maddux & Lewis, 1995; Maddux & Kleiman, 2021). As such, self-efficacy enhancement in the context of psychotherapy not only bolsters efficacious thinking for specific circumstances but also shows how to apply such thinking across situations that the client may encounter (Maddux & Kleiman, 2021). Psychotherapy may use one or more of the following five strategies for enhancing self-efficacy:

1. Building successes, often through the use of goal setting and the incremental meeting of those goals (Hollon & Beck, 1994)
2. Using models to teach the person to overcome difficulties (e.g., Bandura, 1986)
3. Allowing the client to imagine themselves behaving effectively (Kazdin, 1979)
4. Using verbal persuasion by a trustworthy psychotherapist (Ingram et al., 1991; Maddux & Kleiman, 2021)
5. Teaching techniques for lowering arousal (e.g., meditation, mindfulness, biofeedback, hypnosis, relaxation) to increase the likelihood of more adaptive, self-efficacious thinking

Cultural Context and Self-Efficacy

Given that self-efficacy was identified and measured primarily by White Western researchers, a logical question arises as to whether it is applicable to other cultural groups. Teo and Kam (2014) were among some of the first to rigorously test whether general self-efficacy represented the same construct across Western and Eastern samples. They found evidence that self-efficacy may have the same meaning across cultures but that there may be differences in the way it is expressed. Specifically, Asian participants appeared to be less likely to endorse self-efficacy beliefs compared to their Western peers, likely due to Asian cultural norms of modesty. Similar results have been identified for domain-specific forms of self-efficacy. For example, Scherer and colleagues (2016) examined teacher self-efficacy across 32 different Western and Eastern countries and found support for the generalizability of the construct but noted differences in the way it was endorsed. Although research on the cultural applicability of self-efficacy is ongoing, it is possible that the ability to have mastery or a sense of agency is fundamental to positive psychology in all cultures, but how one expresses self-efficacy may be culturally determined.

Within-group cultural differences in self-efficacy have also been noted. In a meta-analysis, women were found to exhibit higher self-efficacy in language arts than their male counterparts, whereas men had higher self-efficacy than women in areas of study such as math, social sciences, and computer sciences (Huang, 2013). Cultural norms, expectations, and stereotype threat (defined by Claude Steele as the threat one feels at being judged on performance in relation to negative stereotypes that exist about one's group) may be at work in the development (or lack thereof) of self-efficacy in these instances. Interestingly, other research has found that biological sex may not be the determining factor in the development of self-efficacy in the domains of math, science, or language arts. Instead, it appears that gender roles may be the main influence. Huffman et al. (2013) found in their study that masculinity (i.e., a more masculine gender expression and role assumption) predicted self-efficacy for technological pursuits regardless of biological sex. This means that both men and women who had more masculine gender role traits had higher self-efficacy in technology, whereas those of both genders with less masculinity had lower self-efficacy in this same area. This type of research is important in helping us to understand the role cultural context may have in determining personal beliefs about one's abilities.

The Neurobiology of Self-Efficacy

It is likely that the frontal and prefrontal lobes of the human brain evolved to facilitate the prioritization of goals and the planful thinking that are crucial for self-efficacy (as well as hope, discussed later in this chapter). When faced with goal-directed tasks, especially the problem solving that is inherent in much of self-efficacy thinking, the right hemisphere of the brain reacts to the dilemmas as relayed by the linguistic and abstract left hemisphere processes (Newberg et al., 2000).

Experiments, most of which have been conducted on animals, also reveal that self-efficacy or perceived control can be traced to underlying biological variables that facilitate coping (Bandura, 1997). Self efficacy yields a sense of control that leads to the production of neuroendocrines and catecholamines (neurotransmitters that govern automatic activities related to stress) (Bandura, 1991; Maier et al., 1985). These later catecholamines have been found to mirror the level of felt self-efficacy (Bandura et al., 1985).

In one study involving human participants, individuals who were attempting to stop smoking were exposed to one of three different treatment conditions, one of which involved increasing self-efficacy to avoid cravings to smoke (Ono et al., 2018). In this self-efficacy condition, cravings were significantly reduced, and neuroimaging showed "increased activation in the rostral medial prefrontal cortex and the pregenual anterior cingulate cortex in smokers compared with ex-smokers" (p. 1), as well as increased connections between the hippocampus with the pregenual anterior cingulate cortex and parahippocampus gyrus when participants were using the self-efficacy strategies to avoid cravings. These areas are related to craving and the ability to regulate it and, as such, may provide some interesting starting places for studying the neural impacts of self-efficacy.

Collective Efficacy

Although the great majority of work on the self-efficacy concept has centered on individuals reacting to given circumstances, self-efficacy can also operate at the collective level and involve large numbers of people who are pursuing shared objectives (Bandura, 1997). **Collective efficacy** has been defined as "the extent to which we believe that we can work together effectively to accomplish our shared goals" (Maddux, 2009a, p. 340). Although there is no agreement about how to measure this collective efficacy, some evidence suggests that it plays a helpful role in marriages, competitive sports, and education (Maddux & Kleiman, 2021).

Many investigators have also examined collective efficacy at a community level and found it to be an important contributor to mental health (Barnett et al., 2018) and community safety (Gearhart, 2022; Lanfear, 2022). For example, in a large longitudinal study of community environments, Pei and colleagues (2022) found that collective efficacy was integrally linked to increases in social cohesion and informal social control (i.e., residents getting together to intervene in various situations to prevent crime or violence). These findings are consistent with research suggesting that collective efficacy may spur community residents to action in an effort to address social ills, such as reducing child maltreatment (Spilsbury et al., 2022). In addition to recognizing collective efficacy as an important community-level variable, several researchers have investigated collective efficacy in relation to social action and change such as reducing health disparities (Butel & Braun, 2019). Recent research also suggests that collective self-efficacy may help individuals sacrifice their personal interests for the betterment of the environment (Doran & Hanss, 2022). Given the multitude of sociopolitical challenges facing us at the moment (e.g., inequality, climate change, political division), finding ways to tap into our collective efficacy may be vital for the future.

OPTIMISM

In this section, we discuss two theories that have received the most attention regarding the construct of optimism. The first is **learned optimism** as studied by Martin Seligman and colleagues, and the second is the view of **dispositional optimism** as advanced by Michael Scheier and Charles Carver.

Learned Optimism—Seligman and Colleagues

The Historical Basis of Learned Optimism

Abramson and colleagues (1978) reformulated their model of helplessness (see also Peterson et al., 1992) to incorporate the attributions (explanations) that people make for the bad and good things that happen to them. University of Pennsylvania psychologist Martin Seligman (Seligman, 1991, 1998b; see also Seligman et al., 1995) later used this attributional or explanatory process as the basis for a theory of learned optimism.

A Definition of Learned Optimism

In the Seligman theory of learned optimism, the optimist uses adaptive causal attributions to explain negative experiences or events. Thus, the person answers the question, "Why did that bad thing happen to me?" In technical terms, the optimist makes external, variable, and specific attributions for failure-like events rather than the internal, stable, and global attributions of the pessimist. Stated more simply, the optimist explains bad things in such a manner as (1) to account for the role of other people and environments in producing bad outcomes (i.e., an external attribution), (2) to interpret the bad event as not likely to happen again (i.e., a variable attribution), and (3) to constrain the bad outcome to just one performance area and not others (i.e., a specific attribution).

Thus, the optimistic student who has received a poor grade in a high school class would say, (1) "It was a poorly worded exam" (external attribution), (2) "I have done better on previous exams" (variable attribution), and (3) "I am doing better in other areas of my life such as my relationships and sports achievements" (specific attribution). Conversely, the pessimistic student who has received a poor grade would say, (1) "I messed up" (internal attribution), (2) "I have done lousy on previous exams" (stable attribution), and (3) "I also am not doing well in other areas of my life" (global attribution).

Seligman's theory implicitly places great emphasis on negative outcomes in determining one's attributional explanations. Therefore, as shown in Figure 8.1, Seligman's theory uses an excuse-like process of "distancing" from bad things that have happened in the past rather than the more usual notion of optimism involving the connection to positive outcomes desired in the future. Within the learned optimism perspective, therefore, the optimistic goal-directed cognitions are aimed at distancing the person from negative outcomes of high importance.

Childhood Antecedents of Learned Optimism

Seligman and colleagues (Abramson et al., 2000; Gillham, 2000; Seligman, 1991, 2018; Seligman et al., 1995, 1998b) carefully described the developmental roots of the optimistic explanatory style. To begin, there appears to be some genetic component of explanatory style, with learned optimism scores more highly correlated for monozygotic than dizygotic twins (correlations =.48 vs.0; Schulman et al., 1993).

FIGURE 8.1 ■ Learned Optimism Theory Viewed in Terms of Its Past Temporally Oriented Excusing Qualities as Compared to Future Temporally Oriented Optimism Qualities

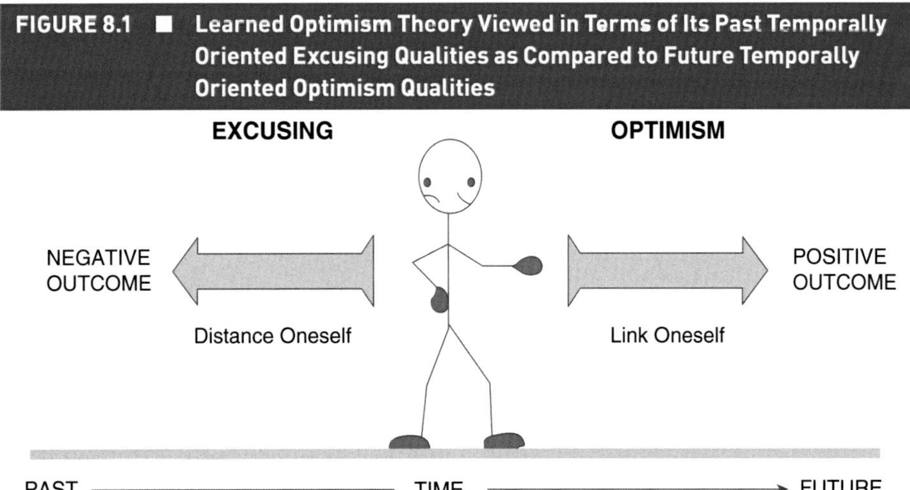

Additionally, learned optimism appears to have roots in the environment (or learning). For example, parents who provide safe, coherent environments are likely to promote the learned optimism style in their offspring (Franz, et al., 1994). Likewise, the parents of optimists are portrayed as modeling optimism for their children (Bamford & Lagattuta, 2012), often by making explanations for negative events that enable the offspring to continue to feel good about themselves (i.e., external, variable, and specific attributions) and by providing explanations for positive events that help the offspring feel extra-good about themselves (i.e., internal, stable, and global attributions; Forgeard & Seligman, 2012). Moreover, children who grow up with learned optimism are characterized as having parents who understood their failures and generally attributed those failures to external rather than internal factors (i.e., they taught their children adaptive excusing; see Snyder et al., 1983/2005). On the other hand, pessimistic people had parents who also were pessimistic or grew up in an unsafe environment (Peterson & Steen, 2021).

Scales: Can Learned Optimism Be Measured?

The instrument most often used to measure an optimistic attributional style in adults is called the Attributional Style Questionnaire (ASQ; Peterson et al., 1982; Seligman et al., 1979); the instrument for children is the Children's Attributional Style Questionnaire (CASQ; Kaslow et al., 1978; Seligman et al., 1995; Seligman et al., 1984). The most recent version of the CASQ is the CASQ-R (Kaslow & Nolen-Hoeksema, 1991). The ASQ poses negative or positive life events, and respondents are asked to indicate what they believe to be the causal explanation of those events on the dimensions of internal/external, stable/transient, and global/specific. Since the development of the ASQ, however, researchers have begun using expanded versions with more items (E-ASQ; see Metalsky et al., 1987; Peterson & Villanova, 1988).

Beyond the explanatory style scales for adults and children, University of Michigan psychologist Chris Peterson and his colleagues (Peterson et al., 1985) developed the Content Analysis of Verbal Explanation (CAVE) approach for deriving ratings of optimism and pessimism from written or spoken words (Peterson et al., 1992). The advantage of the CAVE technique is that it allows an unobtrusive means of rating a person's explanatory style based on language usage. In this latter regard, one can go back and explore the optimism/pessimism of famous historical figures in their speeches, diaries, or newspaper interviews from earlier decades (e.g., Satterfield, 2000).

What Learned Optimism Predicts

The various indices of learned optimism have spawned a large amount of research (see Carr, 2004; Peterson & Steen, 2021 for reviews), with the learned optimistic rather than pessimistic explanatory style associated with some of the following:

1. Better academic performances (Beard et al., 2010; Feldman & Kubota, 2015; Seligman, 1998b; Tetzner & Becker, 2017)
2. Superior athletic performances (Ortin-Montero et al., 2018; Seligman et al.,1990)
3. More productive work records (Rabenu & Yaniv, 2017; Seligman & Schulman, 1986)

4. Greater satisfaction in interpersonal relationships (Crocker et al., 2017; Fincham, 2000; Fitzpatrick, 2017)

5. More effective coping with life stressors (Nolen-Hoeksema, 2000; Reed, 2016)

6. Less vulnerability to depression (Abramson et al., 2000; Ji et al., 2017) and suicidal ideation (Huffman et al., 2016; Yu & Chang, 2016)

7. Superior physical health (Peterson, 2000; Puig-Perez et al., 2017)

8. Greater life satisfaction (Heo et al., 2016; Moreno & Marrero, 2015; Szczesniak & Soares, 2011)

Dispositional Optimism—Scheier and Carver

Defining Optimism as Expectancies of Reaching a Desired Goal

In their seminal article published in *Health Psychology*, psychologists Michael Scheier and Charles Carver (1985) presented their new definition of dispositional optimism, which they described as the stable tendency "[to] believe that good rather than bad things will happen" (p. 219). Scheier and Carver assumed that when a goal was of sufficient value, then the individual would produce an expectancy about attaining that goal.

In their definition of optimism, Scheier and Carver (1985) purposefully do not emphasize the role of personal efficacy. They wrote,

> Our own theoretical approach emphasizes a person's expectancies of good or bad outcomes. It is our position that outcome expectancies per se are the best predictors of behavior rather than the bases from which those expectancies were derived. A person may hold favorable expectancies for a number of reasons—personal ability, because the person is lucky, or because others favor him. The result should be an optimistic outlook—expectations that good things will happen. (p. 223)

Thus, these generalized outcome expectancies may involve perceptions about being able to move toward desirable goals or to move away from undesirable goals (Carver & Scheier, 1999). The consensus is that there is a genetic basis to optimism as defined by Scheier and Carver (see also Plomin et al., 1992). Likewise, borrowing from Erikson's (1963, 1982) theory of development, Carver and Scheier (1999) suggest that their form of optimism stems from early childhood experiences that foster trust and secure attachments to parental figures (Bowlby, 1988). Parents have a role in the development of optimism on the "nurture side" of things. Various types of childhood experiences may lead a child to develop less optimism for the future. Some researchers have noted that children born to parents who live in a lower socioeconomic status may be exposed to more stress and a greater amount of negative emotional states due to this; exposure to socioeconomic difficulties in childhood predicts lower adult optimism as well (Heinonen et al., 2006). Sadly, children in these cases may expect the worst throughout life because they've often been right; this lower level of optimism appears to be somewhat stable throughout life, even if socioeconomic status becomes higher in adulthood (Heinonen et al., 2006; Pedrotti, 2013a).

In a study asking college students why they scored high on a scale of dispositional optimism, participants credited factors such as belief in a higher power, feelings that the world was just, personal privileges and benefits in life, and feelings of hope as major reasons with regard to *why* they were optimistic overall (Sohl et al., 2011). Many of these types of factors might find their origin in positive childhood experiences and beneficial parenting practices, thus giving a bit more evidence for a positive childhood leading to the development of optimism.

Scales: Can Optimism Be Measured?

Scheier and Carver (1985) introduced their index of optimism, the Life Orientation Test (LOT), as including positive ("I'm always optimistic about my future") and negative ("I rarely count on good things happening to me") expectancies. The LOT has displayed acceptable internal consistency (alpha of .76 in the original sample) and a test–retest correlation of .79 over 1 month. In support of its concurrent validity, the LOT correlated positively with expectancy for success and negatively with hopelessness and depression. The LOT has been used in numerous studies.

After years of extensive research using the LOT, criticism arose about its overlap with neuroticism (see Smith et al., 1989). In response to this concern, Scheier et al. (1994) validated a shorter, revised version of the LOT known as the LOT-Revised (LOT-R). The LOT-R eliminated items that caused the neuroticism overlap concerns. Furthermore, relative to neuroticism, trait anxiety, self-mastery, self-esteem, and optimism (as measured by the LOT-R) have shown superior capabilities in predicting various outcome markers related to superior coping. For example, higher scores on the LOT-R have been related to better recovery in coronary bypass surgery, dealing more effectively with AIDS, enduring cancer biopsies more easily, having better adjustment to pregnancy, and continuing treatment for alcohol abuse (see Mens et al., 2021; Carver & Scheier, 2002; for a good review of the many beneficial correlates of optimism). Additionally, the internal consistency of the LOT-R equals or exceeds the original LOT (alpha of .78); its test–retest correlations are .68 to.79 for intervals of 4 to 28 months. Further, confirmatory factor analyses have substantiated the two-factor structure of the LOT-R and showed similarities in structure across participants of different ages and genders (Hinz et al., 2017).

In addition, some discussion has been generated regarding whether optimism should be considered a *unidimensional* characteristic (i.e., with optimism at one end of the continuum and pessimism at the other) versus a *bidimensional* construct (i.e., two different factors on two different continua). Studies have found varying results on the factor structure of the LOT-R, with Scheier et al. (1994) finding one factor (optimism) and Affleck and Tennen (1996) finding the two independent factors of optimism and pessimism. This may be a function of cultural context, as differing results have been found when looking cross-culturally. Findings show that the LOT-R seems to measure two factors (optimism and pessimism) in its Spanish translation and with Brazilian Portuguese individuals as well (Ribeiro et al., 2012), though some evidence also suggests that these two factors may be driven by a higher-level general optimism factor (Cano-García et al., 2015). Differing reliability coefficients have been found in different samples; specifically, English-language versions of the LOT have been found to have reliability estimates that are higher than non-English-language versions (Vassar & Bradley, 2010).

Given this finding, it is important to acknowledge that measurement does not appear to be consistent across varying groups at this time; more research is needed in this area.

Other scales of optimism have also been developed, including a measure of personal and social optimism called the Questionnaire for the Assessment of Personal Optimism and Social Optimism–Extended (POSO-E; Schweizer & Koch, 2001). A scale created in Italy in 2017 by Ginevra and colleagues called the Visions About Future (VAF) scale has also shown some potential in use with adolescents. In addition, versions of the LOT for children have been developed, including the Youth Life Orientation Test (YLOT; Ey et al., 2004) and the Parent-Rated Life Orientation Test (PLOT; Lemola et al., 2010). For the PLOT, parents rate the optimism of their young children. Thus, the assessment of optimism in children and adults continues to be an active area of research and development.

What Optimism Predicts

The LOT-R, like the LOT, has generated a large amount of research (Mens et al., 2021). When coping with stressors, optimists (in mostly White samples) appear to take a problem-solving approach[1] (Scheier et al., 1986) and are more planful than pessimists (Fontaine et al., 1993). Furthermore, optimists tend to use the approach-oriented coping strategies of positive reframing and seeing the best in situations, whereas pessimists are more avoidant and use denial tactics (Carver & Scheier, 2002). Optimists appraise daily stresses in terms of potential growth and tension reduction more than their pessimistic counterparts. Also, when faced with truly uncontrollable circumstances, optimists tend to accept their plights, whereas pessimists actively deny their problems and thereby tend to make them worse (Carver & Scheier, 1998; Carver et al., 2010; Scheier & Carver, 2001). In other words, an optimist knows when to give up and when to keep plugging on, whereas the pessimist still pursues a goal, even when it may no longer be beneficial to do so.

On the whole, the LOT-R has produced robust predictive relationships with a variety of outcome markers (Carver & Scheier, 1999, 2002; Carver et al., 2009). For example, optimists, as compared to pessimists, fare better in the following situations:

1. Starting college (Aspinwall & Taylor, 1992)
2. Work performance (Long, 1993; Rabenu & Yaniv, 2017), vocational identity (Shin & Kelly, 2013), and avoiding work-related burnout (Garrosa et al., 2022)
3. Managing traumatic events such as enduring a missile attack (Zeidner & Hammer, 1992), experiencing other traumatic events in war (Thomas et al., 2011), coping with college sexual assault trauma (Kumar et al., 2022), or coping during the COVID-19 pandemic (Singleton et al., 2022)
4. Caring for patients with dementia (Yehene et al., 2022) and patients with cancer (Given et al., 1993)
5. Undergoing coronary bypass surgeries (Ai & Smyth, 2021) and bone marrow transplants (Curbow et al., 1993)

6. Coping with cancer (Carver et al., 1993; Colby & Shifren, 2013), AIDS (Taylor et al., 1992), and chronic pain (Ramírez-Maestre et al., 2012)

7. Coping in general (Harris et al., 2022)

8. Dealing with health issues in later life (Ruthig et al., 2011)

Given that optimism has a variety of positive correlates and theorized outcomes, a logical question emerges as to whether one can increase this important positive psychological disposition. A meta-analysis looked at a variety of studies that aimed to increase optimism because of its clear links to both psychological and physical health. Malouff and Schutte (2017) found that across 29 studies, optimism can be increased in interventions aimed at this goal. Some moderators of the increase were found, including the use of the Best Possible Selves intervention, using an expectancy measure of positive and negative outcomes (as opposed to a quantitative measure such as the LOT-R), and providing the intervention in person as opposed to other methods of administration. While a number of different facets may impact the effect size found in these interventions, an overall meta-analytic effect size of .41 was found when looking at the studies together. This was a significant effect size and points to the attainability of increasing optimism via intervention.

Edward C. Chang

Optimism and Culture

Is optimism universal? In one of the most comprehensive studies of optimism worldwide to date, Gallagher and colleagues (2013) provided one answer to this question. They examined a measure of future-oriented optimism in representative samples across 142 countries and 150,148 participants. While there were some cross-cultural differences, their results indicated that most countries and people were optimistic. Specifically, the most optimistic individuals may be young, economically secure, and educated women in Ireland, Brazil, Denmark, New Zealand, and the United States; however, the effect sizes of these apparent advantages in optimism were very small. Thus, Gallagher and colleagues' findings point to more similarities than differences regarding cross-cultural levels of optimism. Moreover, similar results were noted with respect to the relationship between optimism and indicators of well-being and health across and within each country (Gallagher et al., 2013). These results generally conform to other, more recent, studies of positive future orientation worldwide. For example, in an analysis of archival data collected across more than 100 countries, Busseri (2022) found that most people reported a positive future outlook on life and that this outlook could be linked to objective and subjective levels of societal functioning in each country (e.g., life expectancy, educational attainment, political freedom, and income). In countries with more positive societal indicators, individuals reported feeling as though their life circumstances had improved in the past and were likely to continue improving in the future. Likewise, in countries with fewer positive indicators, individuals had a less optimistic view of their past experience, but they still reported a positive outlook on the future (Busseri, 2022).

While large, worldwide studies of optimism seem to highlight more cultural similarities than differences, smaller studies comparing Western and Eastern cultural backgrounds yield somewhat different findings. Using the learned optimism construct as measured by the ASQ, for example, Lee and Seligman (1997) found that Asian Americans and White Americans had similar levels of optimism, but the mainland Chinese students were less optimistic. Using the Scheier and Carver approach to operationalizing optimism (along with a version of the LOT), Edward Chang of the University of Michigan (1996a) found that Asian American and non-Asian American students did not differ in optimism, but Asian Americans were higher in pessimism than their non-Asian peers. In this same study, Chang found that, for non-Asian Americans, their higher pessimism was associated with less problem solving. For Asian Americans, on the other hand, *their higher pessimism was associated with greater problem solving.* In the words of Chang (2001), "Thus, what 'works' for Asians relative to [White] Americans simply might be different, *not necessarily more effective*" (p. 226, emphasis added). (See Chapter 4 for a related discussion of Chang's work.) Thus, in Asian American samples, optimism and pessimism seem to interact differently than they do in White or Black samples. One possibility for these differences is that the LOT-R may be measuring a slightly different set of constructs in Asian Samples based on the findings from rigorous measurement invariance analyses between Eastern and Western participants (Long Lu, et al., 2020).

Chang and colleagues (Yu & Chang, 2016) also found that suicidal ideation might be differently related to optimism and pessimism in Asian American samples in comparison to other cultural groups. Yu and Chang measured optimism and pessimism in Asian American, Latinx, and Black college students and found that pessimism and lack of ability to orient oneself toward the future were related to suicidal thoughts in both Black and Latinx students. This finding was not present in the Asian American college student participants, however, furthering the evidence that optimism and pessimism may not have the same links with depression as they do in other cultural groups (Yu & Chang, 2016).

More recently, Chang and colleagues (2020) extended their work on optimism to lesser studied Asian populations. In a recent study of 462 Asian Indian college students recruited across six colleges in Northern India, optimism explained unique variation in well-being even when controlling for adaptive coping behaviors. This study was the first to link optimism to well-being in a large sample of Asian Indian students. While more research is needed, particularly to examine differences between Asian Indian, East Asian, and Western individuals, these results suggest that optimism may be important to well-being across a variety of Asian cultures, even if its expression may be somewhat unique compared to Western cultures.

Optimism and Race and Gender

In Black American samples, optimism seems to mirror White samples' usual associations with other constructs, including positive correlations to resilience (Baldwin et al., 2011) and effective parenting practices (Taylor et al., 2010), as well as spirituality and faith (Mattis et al., 2017), and negative relationships to depressive symptoms (Odom & Vernon-Feagans, 2010; Taylor et al., 2011) and stress/distress (Baldwin et al., 2011; Taylor et al., 2011). Researchers have also found that dispositional optimism is associated with a decreased risk for mortality in Black American samples over time (Lee et al., 2022). However, the biological effects of optimism, such as increased cell telomere length, were not supported (Lee et al., 2021), suggesting that optimism's life-extending properties in Black Americans may be due to other qualities. One possibility is that optimism may be a buffer (along with other factors such as church-related support) against racism and discrimination experiences for Black Americans (Odom & Vernon-Feagans, 2010). Indeed, experiences of discrimination have been robustly linked to adverse health outcomes (Hardeman et al., 2022; Williams et al., 2019), and thus any factor that protects against those experiences may be especially important to Black Americans' health and well-being.

Research on gender differences also suggests similarities in optimism and its correlates between cisgender men and cisgender women. Using measurement invariance analyses, researchers have identified that several measures of optimism evidence metric invariance between these groups in Western samples (i.e., the same latent constructs are being measured for each group), thus indicating that cisgender men and women shared the same meaning of optimism (Hinz et al., 2017; Webber & Smokowski, 2018). To date, researchers have not conducted these kinds of rigorous psychometric evaluations with gender minorities (e.g., transgender or nonbinary individuals). However, there is some evidence that optimism may be a protective factor for transgender individuals. Specifically, in a sample of mostly trans women of color, researchers found a significant association between greater optimism and sexual health prevention behaviors (Forbes et al., 2016). Optimism also emerged as a significant predictor of mental health help seeking for both cisgender and transgender participants (Howell & Maguire, 2019) and was a prominent theme identified in a sample of community-engaged trans women of color (Logie et al., 2022). It is well documented that transgender and gender nonconforming individuals face significant hardships (Guidelines for Psychological Practice With Transgender and Gender Nonconforming People, 2015). Thus, understanding the positive psychology of these groups, particularly with respect to optimism, will continue to be a productive and important area of inquiry.

Although optimism may have the same conceptual meaning for cisgender men and women, some researchers have found differences in the self-reported levels of optimism between men and women. However, the magnitude of these differences is often small, and in some studies males report more optimism than females (Black & Reynolds, 2013; Chang et al., 2010; Jacobsen et al., 2014), and in other studies females report more optimism than males (Webber & Smokowski, 2018). Moreover, meta-analyses of optimism and specific psychological issues suggest that the benefits of optimism, such as bouncing back from trauma, are not conditional on gender (Gallagher et al., 2020; Prati & Pietrantoni, 2009). Additionally, most gender difference studies of optimism use biological sex as a proxy for gender identity. Thus, while some studies may find sex or gender differences, and there are likely cultural factors that boost or suppress optimism in any group, we conclude that there are more similarities than differences between cisgender men and women on this construct. At the very least, the mixed findings point toward more within-group variability than between-group variability in optimism, which is consistent with theories of sex differences in psychology (Hyde, 2005, 2014). Said another way, there may be some men that have more optimism than women, but within men and women as a group, respectively, there is a great deal of individual variability in one's level of optimism. Still, it is currently unclear if such similarities extend to understudied gender minority groups.

Optimism and Biology

Optimism has received considerable attention from a biological lens. Indeed, it is beyond the scope of this chapter to review every study linking optimism to biological functions, and thus, we review some of what we see as the core findings to consider. First, and perhaps most strikingly, indicators of optimism (as evidenced by predictable behaviors consistent with optimism) have been identified in nonhuman animals such as cows (Crump et al., 2021), pigs (Douglas et al., 2012), and even fish (Espigares et al., 2021). There appears to be some universal nature to optimism in this respect, possibly because it may hold an evolutionary advantage. For instance, optimistic fish may live longer than pessimistic fish (Espigares et al. 2021). Optimistic people may also enjoy a longer life. In an analysis of two longitudinal cohort studies (one of female nurses and one of male veterans), Lee and colleagues (2019) found that optimism was specifically related to 11% to 15% longer life span, as well as greater odds of achieving exceptional longevity (i.e., living to age 85 or beyond) across two cohort studies of men and women. The beneficial effects of optimism were present even when controlling for socioeconomic status, health conditions, depression, social integration, and health behaviors (e.g., smoking, diet, and alcohol use). One possible contributor to this potential longevity effect is that optimistic people may be buffered against the daily hassles of life. For example, individuals high in optimism tend to have a weaker cortisol response upon waking up in the morning compared to those lower in dispositional optimism; this result was found after holding other influencing factors constant (e.g., waking time, depressive symptoms, gender; Endrighi et al., 2011). This may also help explain why more optimism is often associated with less stress in general (Baumgartner et al., 2018).

Second, optimism may be somewhat hardwired into our brains. For example, fMRI and other neuroimaging studies of dispositional optimism suggest that frontal areas of the brain may be driving optimistic thinking. In a systematic review of 14 brain imaging studies, the most consistent evidence pointed to two key areas: the anterior cingulate cortex (ACC), involved in imagining the future and processing self-relevant data, and the inferior frontal gyrus (IFG), involved in response inhibition and processing relevant cues (Erthal et al., 2021).

Finally, some researchers have been investigating the biological underpinnings of *unrealistic optimism* (i.e., optimism for a good outcome in the face of a difficult reality; Ruthig et al., 2017). Unrealistic optimism can be a protective factor but also problematic, depending on the context. Most recently, for example, researchers have linked it to *underestimating* the risk of COVID-19 infection for self and others (Gassen et al., 2021; Salgado & Berntsen, 2021). Thus, an important question emerges: What are the neurological mechanisms that appear to keep some of us optimistic even when we really shouldn't be? To help answer this question, Sharot et al. (2011) asked participants to rate their risk of developing various medical problems in the future (e.g., kidney stones, Alzheimer's disease) and then presented these same participants with the actual calculated risk of someone similar to them in terms of physicality and lifestyle developing these problems. The participants were then asked at a second interview to again estimate their likelihood of risk for these various diseases and medical conditions. When participants were allowed to become more optimistic as a result of the actual prediction offered to them (i.e., they had *over*estimated their likelihood of developing these problems), they were much more likely to move to a more accurate position in terms of assessing their risk in the second interview. When participants should logically have revised their view in a more pessimistic direction (i.e., they had *under*estimated their likelihood of developing these problems in the face of the actual probability), they did not change as much in their predictions from the first interview to the second (Sharot et al., 2011). Neurologically, less activity was noted in many brain regions in the unrealistically optimistic individuals. This provides interesting evidence for the *optimism bias* discussed by many researchers in this area of the field (see Sharot's [2011] book *The Optimism Bias: A Tour of the Irrationally Positive Brain*). Many researchers have pondered the evolutionary benefits of optimism (e.g., its positive correlations to coping and resiliency); findings such as these ask us to delve further into this very interesting area of study (Izuma & Adophs, 2011; Shah, 2012; Whelan & Garavan, 2013).

HOPE

The final future-oriented perspective we review in this chapter is the concept of hope. Many years ago, at the University of Kansas, C. R. Snyder was investigating excuse-making with a group of colleagues. In the process of studying how people explained away the outcomes they did not want, Snyder started to become interested in how people explained the outcomes

C. R. Snyder

they *did* want. This eventually led to Snyder's theory of hope (e.g., Snyder, 1994; Snyder et al., 1991), which has received considerable attention in the literature since it was first proposed. We (Teramoto Pedrotti and McDermott) are fortunate to be able to relay to you some of Snyder's original work in this chapter, as he was an author of this text before his death in 2006. Thus, we explore this approach to explaining hopeful thinking in some detail. An overview of the other theories of hope is set forth in Appendix A. Additionally, the book *Making Hope Happen* by Shane J. Lopez (2013) and a recent chapter by Rand and Touza (2021) in the *Oxford Handbook of Positive Psychology 3rd Edition* (Snyder et al., 2021) provide additional information on hope theory.

A Definition

Both the Snyder hope theory and the dictionary definition of hope emphasize cognitions that are built on goal-directed thought. Snyder defined hope as goal-directed thinking in which the person uses **pathways thinking** (the perceived capacity to find routes to desired goals) and **agency thinking** (the requisite motivations to use those routes and beliefs that one can be successful). Those who see themselves as having a greater capacity for agency thinking endorse energetic personal agency-focused self-talk statements (e.g., "I will keep going"; Snyder et al., 1998), and they are especially likely to produce and use such motivational talk when encountering impediments. Likewise, pathways thinking has been shown to relate to the production of alternate routes when original ones are blocked (Snyder et al., 1991), as has positive self-talk about finding routes to desired goals (e.g., "I'll find a way to solve this"; Lopez, 2013; Snyder et al., 1998).

While hopeful thinking can connect, in theory, to any goal-related activity, Snyder was most interested in how we pursue those goals with considerable value to the individual. These goals can vary temporally—from those that will be reached in the next few minutes (short-term goals) to those that will take months or even years to reach (long-term goals). Likewise, the goals entailed in hoping may be approach oriented (aimed at reaching a desired goal) or preventative (aimed at stopping an undesired event) (Hellman et al., 2013; Snyder, Ilardi, Cheavens et al., 2000; Snyder, Ilardi, Michael et al., 2000). Last, goals can vary in relation to the difficulty of attainment, with some quite easy and others extremely difficult. Even with purportedly impossible goals, however, people may work with others to succeed through supreme planning and persistent efforts. On this latter issue, coordinated and successful group efforts illustrate why we should refrain from characterizing extremely difficult goals as being based on "false hopes" (Snyder, Rand et al., 2002).

Hope Theory

The various components of hope theory can be viewed in Figure 8.2, with the iterative relationship of pathways and agency thoughts on the far left. Moving left to right, we start with the *learning history phase* of the model. Developmentally derived agency–pathways thoughts influence the emotional sets that are taken to follow specific goal pursuit activities. That is, high hopers (people who have a great deal of agency and pathways thinking) have positive emotional sets (joy and confidence) and a sense of zest that stems from their histories of success in goal pursuits. By contrast, low hopers have negative emotional sets and a sense of emotional flatness that stems from their histories of having failed in goal pursuits. High- or low-hope people bring these overriding emotional sets with them as they undertake specific goal-related activities.

Next, in Figure 8.2, we enter the *pre-event phase* of the model. This phase focuses on the values associated with specific goal pursuits. As noted previously, sufficient value must be attached to a goal pursuit before the individual will continue the hoping process. If the goal is considered of sufficient value to pursue, then we enter the *event-sequence phase* of the model.

FIGURE 8.2 ■ The Feedforward and Feedback Functions in Hope Theory

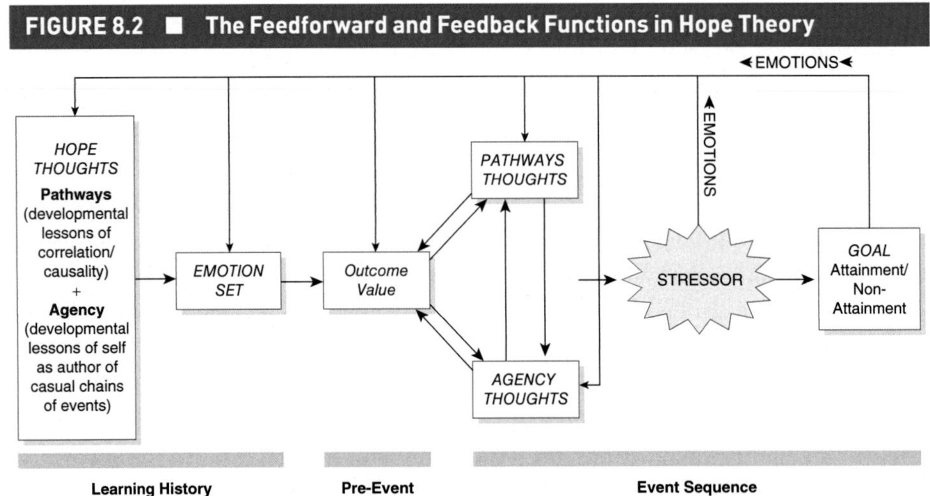

At this point, the pathways and agency thoughts are applied to the desired goal repeatedly as the goal pursuit continues. Importantly, hopeful thinking continually references the outcome values in this model (hence arrows leading to and from agency and pathways thinking) because the value of the outcome is routinely assessed as we encounter obstacles and barriers (i.e., the "stressor" in this model) to our goals. Finally, once an obstacle is broken through or overcome and a goal is met, this success feeds back to the start of the model and feeds forward for other goal pursuits. Said another way, more goal attainment leads to more hopeful thinking and positive emotions that, in turn, build hope and increase the chances one can persist on the next goal. By contrast, if a person's goal pursuit is not successful (often because that person cannot navigate around blockages), then negative emotions can result, and the goal pursuit process can be undermined.

Childhood Antecedents of Hope

More details on the developmental antecedents of the hope process can be found in Snyder (1994, pp. 75–114) and Snyder, McDermott et al. (2002, pp. 1–32). In brief, Snyder (1994) proposes that hope has no hereditary contributions but rather is entirely a learned cognitive set of goal-directed thinking. The teaching of pathways and agency goal-directed thinking is an inherent part of parenting, and the components of hopeful thought are in place in a child by age 2. Pathways thinking reflects basic cause-and-effect learning that the child acquires from caregivers and others. Such pathways thought is acquired before agency thinking, with the latter being posited to begin around age 1. Agency thought reflects the baby's increasing insights as to the fact that they are the causal force in many of the cause-and-effect sequences in their surrounding environment.

Snyder (1994, 2000a) has proposed that strong attachment to caregivers is crucial for imparting hope, and available research is consistent with this speculation (Shorey et al., 2003). Parents who are securely attached themselves also have children who are higher in hope (Blake & Norton, 2014; Goldner et al., 2015; Otis et al., 2016). Researchers have even found positive associations between hope and adult attachment (i.e., attachments in our adult romantic relationships; McDermott et al., 2015).

Traumatic events across the course of childhood may negatively impact hope (Rodriguez-Hanley & Snyder, 2000; Weinberg et al., 2016), and there is research support for the negative impacts of some of these traumas (e.g., the loss of parents; Westburg, 2001). That said, research has found that even in cases of trauma, high-hope individuals are less susceptible to depression and other negative psychological consequences as compared to those lower in hope (Chang. Yu et al., 2016). Indeed, Chang, Yu, and colleagues (2016) found that the level of impact a traumatic event had on the development of depressive symptoms in high hopers was closer to the rate of depression in participants in a no-trauma condition. Others have found that hope interventions might be successfully used to help deal with trauma. Camp HOPE America is an example of one intervention that attempts to treat exposure to trauma in school-aged children who have been exposed to violence in their homes (Hellman & Gwinn, 2017). Best of all, hope is contagious, meaning that when children are around adults who exude hope, they benefit from learning how to be hopeful as well (Best & de Alwis, 2017).

Scales: Can Hope Be Measured?

Using hope theory, Snyder and his colleagues developed several self-report scales. First, Snyder et al. (1991) developed a 12-item trait measure for adults ages 16 and older in which four items reflect pathways, four items reflect agency, and four items are distracters that are not included in the calculation of scale scores. An example pathways item is "I can think of many ways to get out of a jam," and an example agency item is "I energetically pursue my goals." Individuals respond to each item on an 8-point Likert continuum (1 = *definitely false* to 8 = *definitely true*). This version of the Hope Scale is the most widely used and has been translated into many different languages (Rand & Touza, 2021).

The internal consistency (alpha level) typically has been in the .80 range, and test–retest reliabilities have been .80 or above over time periods of 8 to 10 weeks (Snyder et al., 1991). Internal consistency is typically found to be higher for the 8-item test (alpha =.82) as compared to a shorter 4-item version (alpha =.77) of the Hope Scale, although both are at adequate levels (Hellman et al., 2013). Furthermore, there is extensive data on the concurrent validity of the Hope Scale in regard to its predicted positive correlations with scales tapping such similar concepts as optimism, expectancy for attaining goals, expected control, and self-esteem, and there have been negative correlations with scales reflecting such opposite constructs as hopelessness, depression, and pathologies (Rand & Touza, 2021). Finally, several factor-analytic studies provide support for the pathways and agency components of the Hope Scale (Babyak et al., 1993; Feldman & Dreher, 2012; Hellman et al., 2013). Consistent with hope theory, researchers have also found support for the unique contribution of a general hope factor consisting of the combination of agency and pathways, suggesting that hope is best conceptualized and measured as *both* agency and pathways thinking rather than measuring either form of hopeful thinking independently (Gomez et al., 2015). The same support for a general hope factor has been identified in translated versions of the hope scale (e.g., Chinese Hope Scale; Li et al., 2018; and a Spanish version, Galiana et al., 2015).

The Children's Hope Scale (CHS; Snyder et al., 1997) is a 6-item self-report trait measure appropriate for children aged 8 to 15. Three of the six items reflect agency thinking (e.g., "I think I am doing pretty well"), and three reflect pathways thinking (e.g., "When I have a problem, I can come up with lots of ways to solve it"). Children respond to the items on a 6-point Likert continuum (1 = *none of the time* to 6 = *all of the time*). The alphas have been close to .80 across several samples, and the test–retest reliabilities for 1-month intervals have been .70 to .80. (Hellman et al., 2013). The CHS has shown convergent validity in terms of its positive relationships with other indices of strengths (e.g., self-worth) and negative relationships with indices of problems (e.g., depression). Last, factor analyses have corroborated the two-factor structure of the CHS (Snyder et al., 1997). Both Portuguese (Marques et al., 2009) and Spanish (L. M. Edwards, personal communication, November 14, 2013) language versions of the CHS have been developed and determined psychometrically valid as well. The CHS has also been found to be valid cross-culturally with children in Burundi, Indonesia, and Nepal (Haroz et al., 2017) and with Native American children as well (Shadlow et al., 2015). However, a recent investigation of the CHS found some measurement differences between Chinese and youth in the United States, suggesting that cultural differences in response styles (e.g., reluctance to endorse high scores) may superficially suppress Chinese children's hope compared to their American peers (Yang et al., 2021).

Snyder and colleagues (Snyder et al., 1996) also developed the State Hope Scale (SHS), a 6-item self-report scale that taps here-and-now goal-directed thinking. Three items reflect pathways thinking (e.g., "There are lots of ways around any problem that I am facing now"), and three items reflect agency thinking ("At the present time, I am energetically pursuing my goals"). The response range is 1 = *definitely false* to 8 = *definitely true.* Internal reliabilities are quite high (alphas often in the .90 range). Strong concurrent validity results also show that SHS scores correlate positively with state indices of self-esteem and positive affect and negatively with state indices of negative affect. Likewise, manipulation-based studies reveal that SHS scores increase or decrease according to situational successes or failures in goal-directed activities. Factor analysis has supported the two-factor structure of the SHS (Snyder et al., 1996). Finally, hope scales have also been created involving specific domains of life (e.g., the Academic Hope Scale and the Math Hope Scale), and many of these measures have also been found to be psychometrically valid (Robinson & Rose, 2010).

What Hope Predicts

For a detailed review of the predictions flowing from Hope Scale scores, see Snyder (2002a), Hellman and colleagues (2013), or Rand & Touza (2021). What is noteworthy about the results related to these predictions is that the statistically significant findings typically remain, even after mathematical correction for the influences of a variety of other self-report psychological measures, such as optimism, self-efficacy, personal growth initiative, and self-esteem are taken into account (Rand & Touza, 2021). In general, Hope Scale scores have predicted outcomes in academics, sports, physical health, adjustment, and psychotherapy. For example, in the area of academics, higher Hope Scale scores obtained at the beginning of college have predicted better cumulative grade point averages and whether students remain in school (Feldman & Kubota, 2015; Snyder, Shorey, et al., 2002). More recent research has found that although other positive constructs are also related to academic achievement (e.g., self-efficacy, engagement), hope is "the only factor that had unique effects when examining predictors simultaneously and controlling for academic history" (Gallagher et al., 2017, p. 341). In addition, hope has been linked with other academically beneficial constructs such as grit (Anderson et al., 2016). Unsurprisingly, those highest in overall hope and in agency have had the best academic outcomes, and no significant differences were found with socioeconomic status or gender (Dixson et al., 2017). However, some differences have been found in the links between hope and a number of variables, including academic achievement, when looking at different racial and ethnic groups (Pedrotti, 2018). In some populations, hope in combination with ethnic identity provides the best predictor of academic achievement such that those high in ethnic identity are often also high in hope (Adelabu, 2008).

In the area of sports achievement, higher Hope Scale scores obtained at the beginning of college track season have predicted the superior performances of male athletes and have done so beyond the coach's rating of natural athletic abilities (Curry et al., 1997). Some studies show that hope appears to be active in decision making about potential wins or losses in sports and is distinct from just being optimistic about winning (Bury et al., 2016). This shows that hope is more than just a positive expectation or belief and may be present and particularly useful in situations where it is hard to have optimism (low possibility of winning; Bury et al., 2016).

With regard to adjustment, higher Hope Scale scores are related to various indices of elevated happiness, satisfaction, positive emotions, persistence and engagement, self-worth, dealing with change, and getting along with others, to name a few (Marques et al., 2013; McDavid et al., 2015; McDermott et al., 2016; Snyder et al., 1991); Yeung et al., 2015). Recent research suggests that hope may be a critical factor in predicting adjustment during the COVID-19 pandemic (Laslo-Roth et al., 2022). Additionally, hope has been advanced as the common factor underlying the positive changes that happen in psychological treatments (Howell et al., 2015; Owens et al., 2015; Snyder, Ilardi, Michael et al., 2000), even in an online counseling program (Dowling & Rickwood, 2016).

Many researchers have also tested the basic premise that Snyder's scale predicts goal attainment. For example, Feldman and colleagues (2009) found the agency portion of the Hope Scale was the most successful predictor of goal attainment in college students. The seemingly greater strength of agency (as compared to pathways and, at times, overall hope) in predicting other positive outcomes is something that has been found in other samples as well (e.g., Tong et al., 2010; Gomez et al., 2015).

Physical health is also linked to hope, and some studies have found that it may help individuals cope with a variety of illnesses and health difficulties in general, including physical effects of stress, chronic illnesses, chronic pain, breast cancer, and other diseases (Eaves et al., 2016; Hirsch & Sirois, 2016; Larsen et al., 2015; Yadav & Jhamb, 2015). In addition, hope may be linked to well-being in older adults who are struggling with a dwindling amount of time left (Ferguson et al., 2017) and may help promote a future orientation in older adults (Barnett, 2014) and may even reduce suicide risk in this population (Lucas et al., 2020).

The Neurobiology of Hope

Although Snyder and colleagues have held that hope is a learned mental set, this does not preclude the idea that the operations of hopeful thinking have neurobiological underpinnings, especially as related to goal-directed behaviors. Norman Cousins, in his 1991 best-selling book *Head First: The Biology of Hope and the Healing Power of the Human Spirit*, wrote the following apt description of the brain and hope-related thinking:

> Hope, purpose, and determination are not merely mental states. They have electrochemical connections that play a large part in the workings of the immune system and, indeed, in the entire economy of the total human organism. In short, I learned that it is not unscientific to talk about a biology of hope. (p. 73)

One exciting idea here is that goal-directed actions are guided by opposing control processes in the central nervous system. According to Pickering and Gray (1999), these processes are regulated by the *behavioral inhibition system* (*BIS*) and the *behavioral activation system* (*BAS*). The BIS is thought to be responsive to punishment, and it signals the organism to stop, whereas the BAS is governed by rewards, and it sends the message to go forward. A related body of research suggests a *behavioral facilitation system (BFS)* that drives incentive-seeking actions of organisms (see Depue, 1996). The BFS is thought to include the dopamine pathways of the midbrain that connect to the limbic system and the amygdala.

Another concept discussed by Lopez (2013) is the idea of the "prospection pipeline" (p. 41). Lopez discusses the process of hope as it may occur neurologically in the brain. Neuroscientists can track in the brain the process of a good idea or a future plan by watching the parts of the brain that light up as the idea forms and becomes realized. Lopez talks about creating hopes from memories, and thus the prospection pipeline begins in the hippocampus, where memories are examined and often used as the basis for new imaginings. Hope, a form of imagining in some ways, may start here as we begin to take stock of what has happened before and what that might mean we could do in the future. Once the ideas have been examined, the next stop along the pipeline might be the rostral anterior cingulate cortex (rACC), which works with the amygdala to determine how important our various mental images and plans are and to attach emotional meaning to them. As Lopez says, "It pushes you to make smart choices" (p. 43). The last stop on the pipeline is the prefrontal cortex. Thoughts and ideas that are deemed meaningful and emotionally provocative change into action in the prefrontal cortex. It is here that the hopeful pathway begins to emerge in a way that looks like Snyder and colleagues' (1991) operationalization of hope. Ideas about pathways, obstacles, and ways around obstacles begin to emerge in our minds, and we can then begin our journey along these pathways, motivated by that prospection pipeline that got us started on the process. Using neuroscience to understand processes such as this is invaluable in helping us to understand how to shape our future as we would like.

Some researchers have explored the medial orbitofrontal cortex and its potential role in buffering against anxiety. In this research, scientists found that hope as a trait construct appeared to mediate the relationship between anxiety and spontaneous activity in this area of the brain (Wang et al., 2017). As the authors state, this study may "provide the first evidence for functional brain substrates underlying trait hope" (p. 439). More recently, Wang et al. (2020) examined dispositional hope in relation to gray matter volume (GMV) and subjective well-being in a sample of 231 high school graduates using brain imaging technologies. The study team identified that higher dispositional hope was associated with greater GMV in the left supplementary motor area (SMA), an area critical for linking thoughts to actions. Dispositional hope also mediated (i.e., explained) the association between left SMA volume and subjective well-being. These findings provide further evidence that hopeful thinking, as defined by Snyder, may use specific areas of the brain.

Hope and Cultural Context

Hope has been investigated in many different cultures (Rand & Touza, 2021), and the results begin to elucidate our understanding of the contextual influences on this construct (Vela et al., 2016). Chang and Banks (2007) were some of the first to investigate the applicability of Snyder's (1994, 2002) hope model in a diverse population and found that predictors of hope and its factors of pathways and agency might vary between racial or ethnic groups. For example, in European Americans in this study, life satisfaction was the strongest predictor of agentic thinking, but it had no significant predictive power toward agentic thinking in the Asian American portion of the sample (Chang & Banks, 2007). Among Latinx individuals in Chang and Banks's sample, rational problem solving (i.e., a deliberate and rational approach to solving problems) was the strongest significant predictor of agentic thinking; this construct was not significantly predictive of this trait in European Americans. Positive affect was the strongest predictor of agentic thinking in Asian Americans, but it was not a significant predictor for Latinx or European Americans.

Differences between racial and ethnic groups in terms of the mean overall hope, agency, and pathways scores were also found in this comprehensive study (Chang & Banks, 2007). Some racial and ethnic minority groups appear to have higher mean scores in agentic and pathways thinking when compared to majority groups. Chang and Banks (2007) hypothesized that the types of obstacles faced by these different cultural groups (e.g., racism, discrimination) may differ substantially, and these experiences may lead some individuals to have more practice at dealing with obstacles in life, which may in turn lead to higher scores.

Other researchers have looked at hope in a racially diverse sample within the context of the relationship between depression and suicidal behavior (Hirsch et al., 2012). These researchers measured trait hope (via Snyder and colleagues' [1991] model), hopelessness, depression, and suicidal thoughts/behavior (including ideation, attempts, etc., over a lifetime). Findings showed different patterns of data when comparing different racial groups. In Latinx and White samples, higher-hope individuals were less likely to have many suicidal behaviors as a result of their depression, but this was not found in the Black American or Asian American participants. In these cases, hope (either high or low) was a better predictor of suicidal behavior than hopelessness (Hirsch et al., 2012). In addition, lack of hope (measured by the Beck Hopelessness Scale) was a better predictor of suicidal behavior (as opposed to depression) for both Black and White participants, although this was not found in the Latinx or Asian samples. (Note: Some of Hirsch and colleagues' [2012] conclusions about Asian Americans must be tempered, as the sample size was small compared to the other racial groups.) Thus, this study provides more evidence for the fact that hope may interact with other psychological constructs differently across racial groups.

Hirsch and colleagues (2012) are not the only ones to discover that hope may not hold the same protective properties for some racial minorities (at least not in the short term). My (McDermott) students and I found that hope interacted with stress in the context of racial discrimination for Black college students in a unique way. Students with high levels of hope evidenced a stronger *positive* relationship between discrimination and psychological stress, whereas students lower in stress evidenced a weaker relationship (McDermott et al., 2020). This means that students with higher levels of hope reported the most stress from racial discrimination. Moreover, this paradoxical effect of hope on stress was only found in the context of *psychological* distress. When we examined academic distress, we found that hope had an overwhelmingly beneficial effect for Black college students. Thus, we speculated that high-hope Black college students may be especially distressed when they encounter an obstacle that cannot be easily overcome (such as racial discrimination). These findings highlight the need for more longitudinal research on hope and racial discrimination, as we believe that stress from racial discrimination among high-hope Black college students may be especially distressing at first, but it may eventually translate to focused action and advocacy. That is, we expect hope to have an overall beneficial psychological effect for Black college students (or any other racial group) in the long run.

Additionally, although there may be differences in the way hope operates among different cultural groups, it has also been found to be effective in many groups. Shogren and colleagues (2015) found that hope assists in the cultivation of self-determination and well-being in people with disabilities. Additionally, hope may weaken the relationship between suicidal thoughts and belongingness, as well as feelings of being a burden to others in Black American populations (Hollingsworth et al., 2016).

Regarding interventions to enhance hope, we recommend reading Snyder's (2000a) original edited volume, *Handbook of Hope*, or its latest edition edited by Gallagher and Lopez (2018), *The Oxford Handbook of Hope* for the reader with a strong background in psychotherapy. For the reader with less experience in psychotherapy, "how-to" descriptions for enhancing adults' hopes can be found in Lopez's (2013) *Making Hope Happen* and in Snyder's (1994/2000c) *The Psychology of Hope: You Can Get There From Here.* "How-to" descriptions for raising children's hopes are described in McDermott and Snyder's (2000) *The Great Big Book of Hope* and in Snyder, McDermott, et al.'s (2002) *Hope for the Journey: Helping Children Through the Good Times and the Bad.* In general, hope interventions involve building and facilitating agency and pathways thinking through psychoeducation and daily practice. For example, one that I (McDermott) use frequently is to fill my to-do list with things that I know I will get done each day (e.g., eat breakfast, watch TV, or exercise). Crossing these tasks off each day builds my sense of agency. Likewise, when I am dealing with a difficult obstacle, I look for ways around that obstacle, and I recall how I have solved similar problems in the past. These interventions have been very helpful. You can try some of this out yourself via our personal mini experiments and life enhancement strategies.

LIFE ENHANCEMENT STRATEGIES

Self-efficacy, optimism, and hope provide the momentum needed to pursue a good life. Therefore, we encourage you to use the self-efficacy, optimism, and hope you already possess to improve functioning in important domains of your life.

Love

- Build new confidence in your relationships by observing someone who is quite skilled in managing friendships and romantic relationships. Emulate their behavior as appropriate.
- Approach your next visit with extended family with a flexible explanatory style. When positive events occur, be sure to identify your role in the family success.
- Set goals for important relationships that will help you grow closer to others. Be sure to identify multiple pathways and sources of agency for pursuing these aims.

Work

- Develop new skills for work or school by attending training or study sessions that will help you approach your assignments with increased confidence.

- When a new project is assigned to you, expect that the best will happen. Nurture those optimistic thoughts daily as you work toward the successful completion of the project.
- Break down a big task into small goals and direct your energy toward pursuing small goal after small goal until the big task is completed.

Play

- Watch an hour of educational television for children. Attempt to identify the many messages designed to enhance self-efficacy.
- Play a board game or a sport with a friend and attempt to respond to a poor outcome with a flexible explanatory approach.
- Identify a personal goal associated with your favorite leisure activity that you hope to attain in the next month. Identify and procure all the resources you need to make progress toward that goal.

PERSONAL MINI-EXPERIMENTS

INCREASING SELF-EFFICACY, OPTIMISM, AND HOPE VIA SMART GOALS

In this chapter, we discuss the benefits of self-efficacy, optimism, and hope. Each of these constructs involves meeting your goals for the future. How do you set goals, and are there ways of setting goals that can help you increase these positive psychological characteristics? Yes, and we hope (no pun intended) this personal mini experiment, in conjunction with the life enhancement strategies described above, will allow you to experience the connections between goal attainment and greater self-efficacy, optimism, and hope in your daily activities.

To do this experiment, you need to think of a goal. However, we don't want you to think of just any old goal. We want you to make your goal SMART. That is, your goal should be specific (S), measurable (M), achievable (A), relevant (R), and time-bound (T). A good example of a SMART goal that I (McDermott) have made recently is to try to go to bed a little earlier each night. While I would ideally like to get 8 hours of sleep per night instead of the five or six I have been getting, I know that saying I am going to go to bed at 10 p.m. is not likely to happen when I have been accustomed to going to bed at 1 a.m. Thus, my SMART goal is to go to bed 30 minutes earlier than normal for a couple of days (e.g., 12:30 instead of 1 a.m.), and then when that feels comfortable, I will move it back another 30 minutes and so on. This goal is measurable (I can record the time I head to bed each night), achievable (30 minutes seems quite reasonable), relevant (I want to have more energy and be more productive), and time-bound (I can check back in on myself in a week and evaluate my progress).

After you have made your SMART goal, we would like you to execute your plan for one week and note how you feel when you meet (or do not meet) your chosen benchmarks along the way. If you find that you are consistently struggling to meet that goal, simply make it more achievable. For instance, if I was really struggling to hit that 30-minute-earlier bedtime, then I might try 20 (or even 10) minutes earlier. The idea here is to give yourself a win by finding that sweet spot where you can probably meet your goal, but it still will take some effort.

Prior to executing this plan, take a moment to jot down how much efficacy, optimism, and hope you feel toward your ability to meet this goal on a 1 (none) to 10 (a great amount) scale. Save those notes somewhere. Then, once you've been doing this for one week, review what you wrote down originally. Reflect on how your perspectives have changed or haven't changed over the past week. Consider what may have led to any changes. Likewise, be sure to evaluate your progress. Celebrate your successes, and analyze your failures without judgment. That is, even when we fail, we can learn something about why we failed. Perhaps a barrier came up that you didn't anticipate. If so, make a note of that so you can plan accordingly. If time allows, try this process for another week and reflect again at the end of that time. This process of self-evaluating your goal progress and modifying what you need to meet your goals is extremely valuable, and we hope this experiment helps you better understand what you need to meet your future goals.

APPENDIX A: A SUMMARY OF HOPE THEORIES

Averill

Averill et al. (1990) define hope in cognitive terms as appropriate when goals are (1) reasonably attainable (i.e., have an intermediate level of difficulty), (2) under control, (3) viewed as important, and (4) acceptable at social and moral levels.

Breznitz

Breznitz (1986) proposed five metaphors to capture the operations of hope in response to stressors, with hope as (1) a protected area, (2) a bridge, (3) an intention, (4) a performance, and (5) an end in itself. He also cautioned that hope may be an illusion akin to denial.

Erikson

Erikson (1964) defined hope as "the enduring belief in the attainability of fervent wishes" (p. 118) and posed dialectics between hope and other motives, one of the strongest and most important being trust/hope versus mistrust, which is the infant's first task. Another broad dialectic, according to Erikson (1982), pertains to the generativity of hope versus stagnation.

Gottschalk

For Gottschalk (1974), hope involves positive expectancies about specific favorable outcomes, and it impels a person to move through psychological problems. He developed a hope scale to analyze the content of 5-minute segments of spoken words. This hope measurement has concurrent validity in terms of its positive correlations with positive human relations and achievement and its negative relationships to higher anxiety, hostility, and social alienation.

Marcel

Basing his definition on the coping of prisoners of war, Marcel (see Godfrey, 1987) concluded that hope gives people the power to cope with helpless circumstances.

Mowrer

Mowrer (1960) proposed that hope was an emotion that occurred when rats observed a stimulus that was linked with something pleasurable. Mowrer also described the antithesis of hope, or fear, which he said entailed a type of dread in which the animal lessened its activity level and that, as such, fear impedes their goal pursuits.

Staats

Staats (1989) defined hope as "the interaction between wishes and expectations" (p. 367). Staats and colleagues developed instruments for tapping the affective and cognitive aspects of hope. To measure affective hope, the Expected Balance Scale (EBS; Staats, 1989) entails 18 items for which respondents use a 5-point Likert continuum. To measure cognitive hope, the Hope Index (Staats & Stassen, as cited in Staats, 1989) focuses on particular events and their outcomes and contains the subscales of Hope-Self, Hope-Other, Wish, and Expect. The Hope Index contains 16 items, and respondents use a 6-point Likert continuum (0 = *not at all* to 5 = *very much*) to rate both the degree to which they "wish this to occur" and "expect this to occur."

Stotland

Stotland (1969) explored the role of expectancies and cognitive schemas and described hope as involving important goals for which there is a reasonably high perceived probability of attainment. Using Stotland's (1969) model, Erickson et al. (1975) designed a hope scale that consists of 20 general and common (i.e., not situation-specific) goals. This hope scale yields scores of average importance and average probability across these goals. There is little reported research, however, using this scale.

Source: Zimbardo, P. G. & Boyd, J. N. (1999). Putting time in perspective: A valid, reliable individual-differences metric. *Journal of Personality and Social Psychology, 77*(6), 1271–1288. Copyright © 1999 by the American Psychological Association. Reproduced with permission.

KEY TERMS

Agency thinking
Collective efficacy
Dispositional optimism
Future orientations
Hope
Learned optimism
Pathways thinking
Self-efficacy
Situational perspective
Social cognitive theory
Trait perspective

NOTE

1. As noted later in this chapter and in Chapter 4, Asian Americans who are higher in pessimism are also higher in problem solving (Chang, 2001).

9 WISDOM AND COURAGE

Characteristics of the Wise and the Brave

LEARNING OBJECTIVES

After reading this chapter, you will be able to:

9.1 Understand the definitions and research associated with wisdom and courage

9.2 Identify top theories (both implicit and explicit) of wisdom and courage

9.3 Differentiate a wise response from one lacking in wisdom

9.4 Classify measures of wisdom and courage

9.5 Apply a cultural lens to theories of wisdom and courage

> God grant me the serenity to accept the things I cannot change, courage to change the things I can, and the wisdom to know the difference.
>
> —**Attributed to Reinhold Niebuhr**

The serenity prayer has become the credo for many ordinary people who are struggling with life challenges. We open with this reference because it makes two points that we examine throughout this chapter. First, as the prayer reveals, the notions of wisdom and courage have been intermingled, historically, in literature. We will examine this link and the reasons for it. Second, the prayer suggests that the extraordinary qualities of wisdom and courage are available to everyone. This point is discussed in the context of the reviews pertaining to wisdom and courage.

WISDOM AND COURAGE: TWO OF A KIND

Some philosophers and theologians consider wisdom (prudence) and courage (fortitude) to be two of the four cardinal virtues (along with justice and temperance). These primary virtues are traditionally ranked in the order of prudence, justice, fortitude, and temperance and are meant to be examples of dispositions that blend moral characteristics with generative behavior (Baltes et al., 2002). The cardinal virtues facilitate personal development; good living through practicing them may foster the development of social resources that spark the growth of other people. Both wisdom and courage can inform human choices and fuel pursuits that lead to enhanced personal functioning and communal good. Courage also can help overcome obstacles that make the practice of other virtues more difficult.

Wisdom and courage often have been studied together, although their intermingling may cause difficulties in distinguishing them. This construct confusion is captured in a statement from the movie *The Wizard of Oz* (Haley & Fleming, 1939), in which the Wizard says to the Cowardly Lion, "As for you, my fine friend, you are a victim of disorganized thinking. You are under the unfortunate delusion that, simply because you run away from danger, you have no courage. You're confusing courage with wisdom."

Wisdom and strength both exemplify human excellence; they involve a challenge, they require sound decision making, they are culturally bound, and they typically contribute to the common good. Furthermore, as mentioned in the introduction to this chapter, ordinary people can demonstrate both of these extraordinary qualities. Without question, however, the scholarly discussion aimed at clarifying the relationship between wisdom and courage will be complex. In some cases, wisdom is characterized as the predecessor of courage. Moreover, in the strongest form of the argument, St. Ambrose believed that "fortitude without justice is a level of evil" (cited in Pieper, 1966, p. 125). But courage has also been portrayed as a precursor of wisdom. The logic here is that the capacity for courageous action is necessary before one can pursue a noble outcome or common good that is defined by wisdom. Courage sometimes is viewed as the

The Cowardly Lion (played by Bert Lahr)

Bettmann/Contributor/via Getty Images

virtue that makes all virtuous behaviors possible. Irrespective of their relative power or import, we believe that a discussion of **implicit** and **explicit theories** of wisdom and courage will help in understanding their importance in our daily lives.

THEORIES OF WISDOM

Wisdom often is referenced in ancient maxims (e.g., Yang, 2001) and in philosophical reviews. For example, early Western classical dialogues, specifically Aristotle noted three distinct conceptualizations of wisdom: (1) that found in persons seeking a contemplative life (the Greek term *sophia*); (2) that of a practical nature, as displayed by great statesmen (*phronesis*); and (3) scientific understanding (*episteme*). Aristotle added to the list of types of wisdom by describing *theoretikes*, the theoretical thought and knowledge devoted to truth, and distinguishing it from *phronesis* (practical wisdom).

During the 15th, 16th, and 17th centuries in the Western world, two issues dominated the scholarly discussion of wisdom. Philosophers, religious scholars, and cultural anthropologists still debate the philosophical versus pragmatic applications of virtue, along with the divine or human nature of the quality. Both issues relate to the question of whether wisdom is a form of excellence in living as displayed by ordinary people or is more aptly seen as a fuzzy philosophical quality possessed only by sages. These issues have yet to be resolved, although psychology scholars have suggested recently that ordinary people are capable of living a good life by applying wisdom. As an example today, as explained in just a moment, researchers such as Glück and Westrate (2022) have described a new model that situates wisdom into the context of real life.

Although our understanding of wisdom has progressed slowly over modern times, this started to change during the late 20th century. The first president of the American Psychological Association, G. Stanley Hall, wrote a book in 1922 in which he addressed the wisdom gained during the aging process that was considered the main authority on the subject until about 1975, when psychologists began to scrutinize the concept of wisdom. These scholarly efforts produced a better commonsense psychological understanding of wisdom. Implicit theories (folk theories of a construct that describe its basic elements) of wisdom first were described by Clayton (1975; Clayton & Birren, 1980) and then further explicated by German psychologist Paul Baltes's (1993) analysis of cultural-historical occurrences. Knowledge gained from these recent studies has informed the development of explicit theories (theories detailing the observable manifestations of a construct) of wisdom. Recent studies show that there tends to be much overlap between implicit and explicit theories of wisdom (Weststrate et al., 2016). In the next section, we explore these implicit and explicit theories of wisdom.

Implicit Theories of Wisdom

Throughout the history of psychology researchers have conducted studies in which they ask participants to give their implicit ideas of what exactly wisdom is. As you can see in Table 9.1, there is overlap and dissent between various theories in this regard. While some answers address everyday life and problem-solving behaviors, other themes focus more on characteristics that

TABLE 9.1 ■ Historical Implicit Theories of Wisdom

Researcher	Method	Dimensions
Clayton (1975)	Participants were asked to pair the following words associated with wisdom: experienced, intelligent, introspective, intuitive, knowledgeable, observant.	1. Affective (empathy and compassion) 2. Reflective (intuition and introspection) 3. Cognitive (experience and intelligence)
Sternberg (1985)	Card sort of 40 wise behaviors	1. Reasoning ability 2. Sagacity (profound knowledge and understanding) 3. Learning from ideas and environment 4. Judgment 5. Expeditious use of information 6. Perspicacity (discernment and perception)
Baltes (1993)	Analysis of cultural-historical and philosophical writings	Wisdom: 1. Addresses important/difficult matters of life 2. Involves special or superior knowledge, judgment, and advice 3. Reflects knowledge with extraordinary scope, depth, and balance applicable to real life 4. Is well intended and combines mind and virtue 5. Is very difficult to achieve but easily recognized.

seem possible for only a few to possess. Though much research has been conducted on college students, some researchers have asked school children about their ideas of what makes someone wise. Researchers have asked children what *wisdom* means to them. (Glück et al., 2012). Children in this study listed attributes that fell into the categories of (1) cognitive aspects (e.g., "clever," "astute"), (2) characteristics that addressed thinking of others (e.g., "friendly," "helpful"), (3) facets involved in appearance (e.g., "green eyes," "gray beard"), and (4) possession of real-world abilities (e.g., "gives good advice," "can teach you things"). They also listed some characteristics such as "old" in specific relation to age. As you might notice, much overlap exists between the ideas of these children and those of adults discussed previously. One area of difference that Glück and colleagues (2012) note between these younger children is the absence of a "reflective" component of wisdom (e.g., life experience or perspective taking; p. 596). It may be that increased age comes with a better understanding of the value of these other, more abstract components.

Last, as will be discussed more fully in the following sections, in the consensus gained by the Wisdom Task Force (a group of 44 wisdom experts from across the world), implicit definitions of wisdom also differ by cultural context. Sternberg (2012) specifically argues that cultural context must be consulted with regard to both conceptualization of this construct and in terms of its measurement as a result of this. Although some similarities exist across cultures, followers of Western and Eastern ideology differ on their views of what makes someone wise (Benedikovicová & Ardelt, 2008; Yang, 2008). Those from Eastern traditions may take the affective side (e.g., compassion/altruism, open-mindedness, humility) into account in equal balance with the cognitive side of wisdom, whereas Westerners appear to stress cognition (e.g., intelligence, problem solving, planning) over affective dimensions (Yang, 2008). As always, culture counts in how people think of different constructs.

Explicit Theories of Wisdom

Although informed by implicit theories, explicit theories of wisdom focus more on behavioral manifestations of the construct. Such founding scholars as Erikson and Piaget note wisdom as a part of their developmental theories in terms of how children first learn to think logically and solve problems and how maturity brings a more nuanced assessment of how to make life decisions. And other historical theories tout the application of pragmatic knowledge in pursuit of exceptional human functioning (Baltes & Staudinger, 1993, 2000; Sternberg, 1998a).

Both Sternberg's (1998a) **balance theory** and Baltes's (Baltes & Smith, 1990; Baltes & Staudinger, 1993, 2000) **Berlin wisdom paradigm** are historically important theories and similar in that they emphasize the organization and application of pragmatic knowledge. Furthermore, both views of wisdom propose that wise people can discern views of others, develop a rich understanding of the world, craft meaningful solutions to difficult problems, and direct their actions toward achieving a common good.

Yale psychologist Robert Sternberg built on his previous work on intelligence and creativity (Sternberg, 1985, 1990) and proposed the balance theory of wisdom, theorizing that the tacit knowledge underlying practical intelligence (i.e., "knowing how" rather than "knowing what") is used in balancing self and other interests within the environmental context to achieve a common good (R. Sternberg, personal communication, October 8, 2003). See Figure 9.1 for a diagram of Sternberg's wisdom model. In this model, the wise person goes through a process in which they are challenged by a real-life dilemma that activates the reasoning abilities that were first developed in adolescence and then refined in adulthood. Then, the person's life history and personal values bear on their use of available tacit knowledge in balancing interests and generating wise responses. The person striving to be wise then examines possible responses to determine the extent to which solutions require adaptation to the environmental and cultural context, the shaping of the environment to fit the solutions, or the selection of a new environment where the solutions might work, as well as taking into account competing interests. Finally, if balance is achieved, then the common good is addressed with the proposed solution.

In the Berlin Wisdom Paradigm, Baltes and his colleagues (Baltes & Smith, 1990; Baltes & Staudinger, 1993, 2000) defined wisdom as the "ways and means of planning, managing, and understanding a good life" (Baltes & Staudinger, 2000, p. 124). The Baltes group (Baltes & Smith, 1990; Staudinger & Baltes, 1994) has identified five criteria that characterize wisdom (excellence) and wisdom-related (near-excellence) performance (see Table 9.2).

FIGURE 9.1 ■ Sternberg's Balance Theory of Wisdom

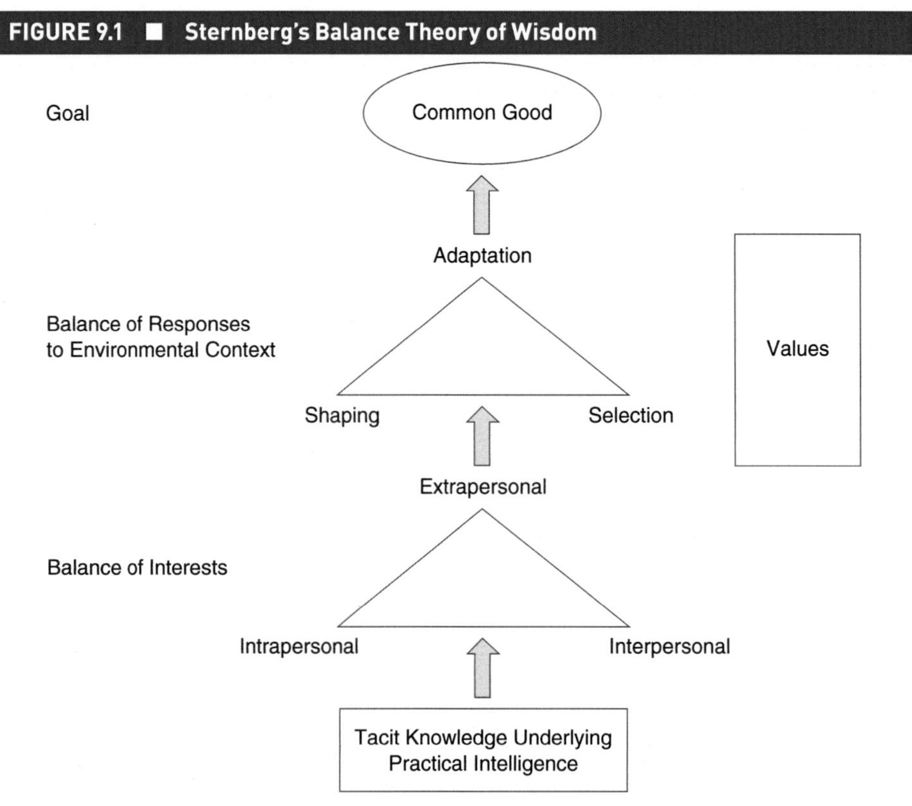

From Sternberg, R., A balance theory of wisdom. In *Review of general psychology*, 1998. Reprinted with permission.

TABLE 9.2 ■ Five Factors in Baltes's Wisdom Paradigm

Factual knowledge	"Know what"; having knowledge about topics such as human nature, development, individual differences, social relationships and norms, etc.
Procedural knowledge	"Know how"; the ability to develop strategies for dealing with problems, giving advice, resolving life conflicts, and planning for and overcoming obstacles
Life span contextualism	Ability to consider contexts of life, cultural values, and relevance of developmental stages related to age
Relativism of values	Awareness of different perspectives, life priorities, and societies
Managing uncertainty	Decision-making flexibility necessary for processing difficult information and coming up with appropriate solutions

To determine the quality of wisdom, Baltes's paradigm challenges people with questions about resolving real-life problems. Then, the responses to such questions are transcribed and rated according to the five criteria of wisdom. For example, people are asked to consider the following: "In reflecting over their lives, people sometimes realize that they have not achieved what they had once planned to achieve. What should they do and consider?" (Baltes & Staudinger, 2000, p. 126). Here is an example of a "high-level" (i.e., wise) response to this question that demonstrates the value perspective plays in drawing meaning from life:

> First, I would want to say that only very few and most likely uncritical people would say that they are completely satisfied with what they have achieved. . . . It depends very much on the type of goals we are considering, whether they are more of the materialistic or more of the idealistic kind. It also depends on the age of the person and the life circumstances in which he/she is embedded. . . . Next, one would start to analyze possible reasons for why certain goals are not attained. Often, it is the case that multiple goals were pursued at the same time without setting priorities and, therefore, in the end, things get lost. . . . It is important to gradually become realistic about goals. Often, it is helpful to talk to others about it. . . . Conditions external and internal to the person could be at work or sometimes it is also the match between the two that can lead to difficulties in life. (Staudinger & Leipold, 2003, p. 182)

The models of Sternberg and Baltes are still widely used and are important foundations for current models that exist today. Here, we note two more recent models: (1) the Integrative Model of Wise Behavior (Glück & Weststrate, 2022) which integrates several models into a dynamic framework, and (2) the Common Wisdom Model (CWM; Grossman et al., 2020) that integrates culture fully into the model.

Glück and Westrate (2022) describe previous wisdom research as similar to the story told in the Indian proverb which tells the story of blind men describing an elephant. In this proverb, each describes the elephant from the portion they are able to touch because of its size. As a result, the descriptions vary widely. In these researchers' estimations, a major reason that wisdom research has many different and conflicting findings with regard to correlations, processes, and definitions is because of the different perspectives others have taken to research one construct; this may be resulting in descriptions of different constructs, while calling all *wisdom*. In their integrative model, Glück and Westrate (2022) posit that both cognitive and noncognitive components of wisdom factor into the process of successful solving of real-life challenges. The basic premise in this model is that components like concern for others and regulation of emotion (described as *noncognitive components* in this model) moderate the impact of components like self-reflection, metacognition, and basic knowledge (described as *cognitive components* in this model) on behavior described as wise. Both types of components are necessary for wise reasoning and wise behavior to take place. See Figure 9.2 for a tree diagram depicting the process from "Wisdom-Requiring Situation" to "Wise (or Unwise) Behavior." This model represents a new way of thinking that shows the effect of both cognitive and noncognitive components on success of wisdom-related behavior (Glück & Westrate, 2022).

Finally, the CWM was built by the Wisdom Task Force who asked a group of 44 wisdom experts from across the world about their understandings of wisdom today based on the current and emerging research. Though this type of gathering of wisdom researchers had been done before, a notable difference from the previous gathering was that researchers from non-Western cultural groups were also brought into the discussion including those from Asia, the Caribbean, the Middle East, and South America, in addition to those from Europe, North

FIGURE 9.2 ■ Making a Wise Decision

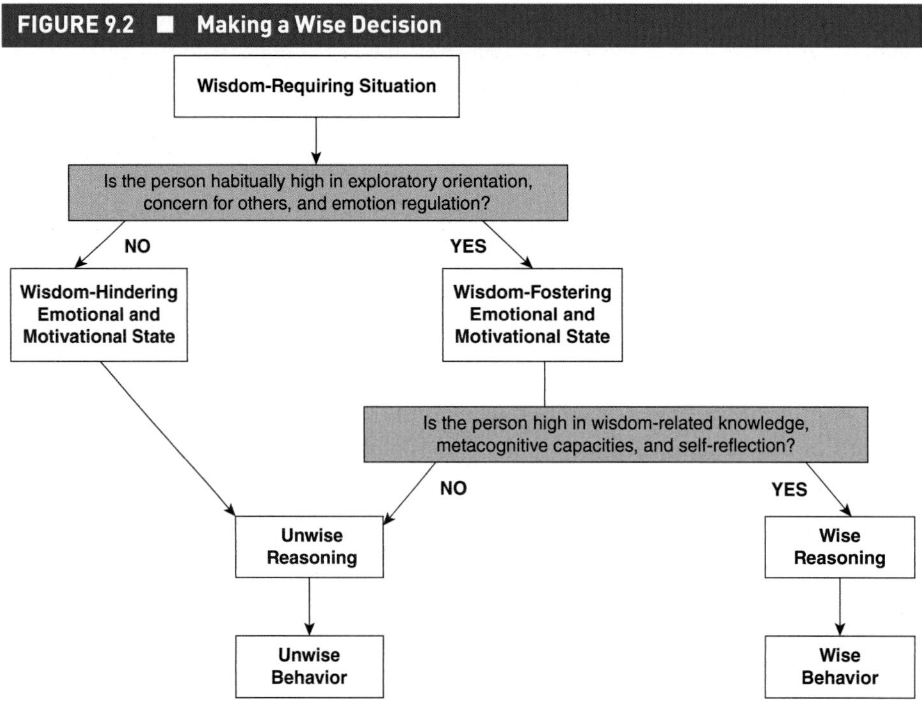

Source: Glück, J., & Weststrate, N. M. (2022). The Wisdom Researchers and the Elephant: An integrative model of wise behavior. *Personality and Social Psychology Review, 26,* 342–374.

America, and Australia (Grossman et al., 2020). The CWM has two main components: perspectival meta-cognition (PMC) and moral aspirations. PMC includes four components: balance of viewpoints, epistemic humility, context adaptability, and multiple perspectives. The basic uniting factors of the differing thoughts on wisdom from the Task Force members was that these four components play a strong role in allowing wise people to understand a situation in a more balanced, and less biased, way (Grossman et al. 2020). For a full discussion of the different elements of wisdom reviewed and debated, please see Grossman and colleagues' (2020) overview, but basic conclusions were as follows. We spend a bit of time on this study here as it has important implications for a more full understanding of wisdom. In some ways, this study spans both implicit and explicit theory distinctions—researchers were asked their views (implicit) about theories and research about wisdom that exist currently (explicitly), so we finish with this.

First, some discussion about the differences between philosophical definitions and those created in the field of psychology ensued, and conclusions drawn were that the diversity existing in the different types of wisdom must be acknowledged before lumping all theories into the same construct. We would caution the same: Looking closely at what is called *wisdom* is necessary when organizing thoughts or drawing conclusions about the variety of topics called wisdom. Second, findings pointed to a general agreement from this varied group of wisdom researchers around the idea that wisdom as a construct must include some "morally-grounded aspects of metacognition as a common psychological signature of wisdom" (Grossman et al., 2020, p. 125) and by this appear to mean that there must be some level of excellence in one deemed "wise" that relates to their ability to reason well and to apply that reasoning within a social context to make good decisions and assessments. Thus, put in more plain terms, those who are wise are strong in PMC and thus are able to look at the different pieces of a situation or problem and apply their skill in assessing the situation in a reasoned way while paying attention to context and while keeping in mind that solutions must be grounded within a morality that takes others into account and strives to do the right thing.

Third, the 2020 findings of Grossman and colleagues did something that previous large discussions have not always done: paid attention to social identity facets as they may impact the way in which characteristics of wisdom might be observed and assessed. This adds significantly to previous research that may have made assumptions about who was wise (and who wasn't) that were influenced by the cultural bias of the researcher. This final question asked of the wisdom experts was, *Do various cultural groups display different patterns of performance on wisdom tests and, if so, what might explain those differences?* In looking cross-culturally, it has been found that Japanese individuals, who are young and or middle-age, appear to display greater wisdom in comparison to their United States-based counterparts, and that wisdom is less varied across the age groups (in the United States, older adults have significantly higher wisdom than younger adults; Grossman et al., 2020). The experts here agreed that the focus on social context emphasized in Eastern countries is likely the reason for these differences. In looking at class differences that have been found in the past (namely that lower socioeconomic groups are often found to be less wise than those that have higher socioeconomic status; SES), you may not be surprised to note that the experts determined that these differences likely have to do with access to resources. Interestingly, however, these differences were more prominent in interpersonal wisdom and not as prevalent in wisdom about society at large. Finally, some differences have been found between male and female genders[1] in past research though this may be a function of the situation and, if it involves different genders, of the social situation in which wisdom is required. This area of research must be examined more fully to better understand gender differences in wisdom. Grossman and colleagues (2020) note something that you have likely already ascertained in reading about these differences: There is strong evidence "calling for a culturally grounded understanding of wisdom-related performance" (p. 120), and thus, as with other constructs we have discussed, paying attention to cultural differences is important in making decisions about wisdom as a characteristic. This assertion is highlighted in the work of Grossman, Dorfman, and Oakes (2020) as well, noting that wisdom cannot be accurately measured or defined when it is focused on a *person* but must include a *socioecological framework* before one can determine whether behavior is wise or unwise. Grossman and colleagues state "wise reasoning . . . varies dramatically across cultures, regions, economic strata, and situational contexts" (Grossman, Dorfman, & Oakes, 2020, p. 66). Thus, an ecological perspective that takes context into account is essential.

[1] Though we view gender as existing along a continuum, past psychological research has often used a binary distinction (e.g., male *or* female). Thus, some studies throughout the text reflect binary results when writing about gender.

BECOMING AND BEING WISE

Developing Wisdom and Wise Characteristics

Influential developmental theorists such as Piaget (1932), Jung (1953), and Erikson (1959) provided building blocks for 20th-century wisdom theorists, giving modern theorists clues about how resolving conflict leads to enhanced discernment and judgment. In this regard, Erikson emphasized that wisdom is gained through resolving daily crises, specifically those involving integrity and despair. Other theorists such as Baltes (1993), Labouvie-Vief (1990), and Sternberg (1998a) suggest that wisdom builds on knowledge, cognitive skills, and personality characteristics and that it requires an understanding of culture and the surrounding environment. Moreover, wisdom develops slowly through exposure to wise role models. Sternberg proposed that knowledge, judicial thinking style, personality, motivation, and environmental context precede wisdom, and Baltes and Staudinger (2000) suggested that fluid intelligence, creativity, openness to experience, psychological-mindedness, and general life experiences "orchestrate" to produce wisdom. Others, such as Ardelt, Pridgen, and Nutter-Pridgen (2019) suggest that some research asserts that wisdom is itself a personality type that correlates with aspects of the Big 5 personality traits. Importantly, it appears to be related to openness to experience, conscientiousness, agreeableness, extraversion, and low neuroticism (emotional stability). Additionally, wisdom as defined by these personality traits is related to a greater sense of well-being (psychological and subjective; Ardelt et al., 2019). These ideas are backed by the previously discussed Integrative Model by Glück and Westrate (2022). In Taiwan, general agreement exists on similar factors believed to underlie wisdom, and a list of several facilitative factors of wisdom in this culture has been developed. Ideas similar to those found in Western contexts include life and work experiences, observation and social interaction, and professional development and reading (Chen et al., 2011). Also included in this list, however, are unique ideas more normative of Eastern culture, including "family teaching" and religion (Chen et al., 2011, p. 178). In addition, this study found that experts believed in certain types of conditions or scenarios as being more conducive to the development of wisdom (similar to Sternberg's ideas that environmental context plays a role).

Life experience appeared to be positively correlated with the idea that emotional challenge was included in the development of wisdom, although growing older in and of itself did not factor into the explanations offered (Glück & Bluck, 2011). Some research shows that difficult or adverse experiences may provide an opportunity to use wisdom as a sort of coping strategy. In a study with adolescents who had experienced very difficult and stressful situations, those who were higher in thinking of these incidents as "turning points" or chances to gain wisdom had higher well-being and also showed higher wisdom later on than those who did not view these hurdles in this way (Jayawickreme et al., 2017). In a similar study with a different population, adults who processed difficult events in their lives by thinking of them as opportunities for personal growth or tried to make these events have beneficial meaning in their lives were higher in wisdom overall (Weststrate & Glück, 2017). Being wise may thus help some people to move forward in positive directions after troubling events.

Wisdom grows as people learn to think flexibly to solve problems, and such problem solving entails recognizing ideas according to place and culture. In turn, by recognizing that the answers to questions depend both on contextual factors and on the balancing of many interests, people become even more flexible in their thinking. While some take a more cognitive view of wisdom, others believe that wisdom may have an affective component that is neglected by this conceptualization (Benedikovicová & Ardelt, 2008; Labouvie-Vief, 1990; Levenson, 2009). These researchers believe that those who are truly wise integrate these two components. Some slight gender differences have been found, pointing toward a more cognitive bent in wise men and a more affective bent in wise women (Ardelt, 2010); this difference was larger when dealing with true-life contexts as opposed to being asked to abstractly think about a situation (Glück et al., 2009). More recently, Glück and Westrate (2022) list a number of traits and skills, both cognitive and noncognitive, that seem to lead one to being a more wise individual (see Table 9.3).

TABLE 9.3 ■ Noncognitive and Cognitive Components of Wisdom

Noncognitive	
Exploratory orientation:	A mindset that involves looking to learn and grow from experiences
Desire for understanding:	Tendency to be curious and an interest in philosophical questions
Open-mindedness:	Open to ideas, values, and opinions that are different from their own
Concern for others:	Caring about the well-being of others
Empathic concern:	Ability to discern accurately feelings of others
Common-good orientation:	General motivation to think of the "big picture" and the good of the group
Emotion regulation:	Ability to manage and control their emotions
Cognitive Components	
Life knowledge:	Learned expertise about life in general based on experience
Self-knowledge	Understanding of one's strengths and weaknesses in an accurate sense
Metacognitive capacities:	Ability to think about the quality of one's thinking, including identifying the limitations of one's knowledge
Awareness and consideration of uncertainty and uncontrollability:	Possessing the knowledge that the future cannot be predicted
Awareness and consideration of divergent perspectives:	Knowledge of differing views and the ability to consider them
Self-reflection	Ability to look inward during times of trouble

Adapted from Glück, J., & Weststrate, N. M. (2022). The wisdom researchers and the elephant: An integrative model of wise behavior. *Personality and Social Psychology Review, 26*, 342–374.

Some evidence also points to *collective wisdom* (i.e., wisdom that is generated by a group of people discussing solutions to a dilemma) as a precursor toward more accurate (i.e., wise) decisions being made (Eckstein et al., 2012). Some research has found that discussing a problem with a loved one led to an increase in subsequent wisdom-related performances and that this was even more beneficial for older participants in comparison to those who were younger (Staudinger & Baletes, 1996). And other research notes that wisdom may be able to be transmitted from generation to generation, not only through advice but through the modeling of listening behavior and flexible thinking (Edmondson, 2012). All of these studies point to wisdom as something that can grow over time and that can occur in people at different ages throughout the life span.

It may also be that certain characteristics related to wisdom are cultivated more purposefully in some cultures. In investigating differences in wise strategies used to handle conflicts, samples from Japan and the Midwestern United States were compared. Researchers found that individuals in Japan showed evidence of wise traits throughout their life span (whereas those in the United States exhibited increased wisdom with increased age) and that younger and middle-aged Japanese adults showed greater utilization of wise strategies when compared to their U.S. counterparts (Grossman et al., 2012). These authors hypothesized that, due to the strong motivation within Japanese culture to avoid conflict, Japanese individuals become skilled at resolving conflicts in wise ways at an earlier age due to normative pressure to maintain group harmony. Individuals in the United States, however, may not have as much motivation to resolve conflicts, and as such, they may not practice these strategies as frequently; wisdom related to resolving conflict accrues more quickly in Japanese individuals but takes a lifetime to develop in U.S. adults (Grossman et al., 2012). This provides more evidence for the old adage, "culture matters."

The Measurement of Wisdom

Several measurement approaches have been used in the models of wisdom described in this chapter. For example, developmental and personality theories of wisdom have yielded self-report questions and sentence completion tasks. The forms of wisdom involving expertise in the conduct and meaning of life have been tapped via problem-solving tasks. Sternberg (1998b) has proposed that wisdom problems require a person to resolve conflicts. Consistent with his emphasis on pragmatism, Baltes (Baltes & Smith, 1990; Baltes & Staudinger, 1993) has constructed a series of difficult life problems such as the following: "Someone receives a telephone call from a good friend, who says that he or she cannot go on like this and has decided to commit suicide. What might one/the person take into consideration and do in such a situation?" (Baltes & Staudinger, 1993, p. 126). Respondents are encouraged to "think aloud" while considering the resolution of this problem. Their comments and solutions to the problem are evaluated by trained raters, based on the five criteria identified by the Baltes group (factual and procedural knowledge, **life-span contextualism**, **relativism of values**, and recognition and management of uncertainty).

A second and very commonly used wisdom scale was developed by Monica Ardelt in 2003: the three-dimensional wisdom scale or 3D-WS. This scale consists of 39 items divided into three different subscales: Cognitive ("In this complicated world of ours, the only way we can know what's going on is to rely on leaders or experts who can be trusted"), Reflective ("When I'm upset with someone, I usually try to put myself in his or her shoes for a while"), and Affective ("There are some people I know I would never like") components of wisdom. This measure has been used with multiple populations, including Korean adults (Kim & Knight, 2015) and Iranian adults (Cheraghi et al., 2015). A short form of this measure, the 3D-WS-12, was developed in 2017, which uses just 12 items and has been shown to have good psychometric properties for its length (Thomas, M. L. et al., 2017). Its authors caution that the longer 3D-WS does show stronger psychometric properties, however.

Finally, Brienza and colleagues (2018) have developed a 21-item scale called the Situated WIse Reasoning Scale (SWIS). This scale asks participants to first think of an example of a situation in which a conflict occurred at a single time (not a recurring problem) and then reflect on their emotions and thoughts at that time. Answers to the items are then based on the experience chosen. Brienza and colleagues (2018) developed this scale after research showed evidence of bias and lack of correlation between many other wisdom-related measures. Specifically, the majority asked about global wisdom, without looking at specific circumstances. In the SWIS, this bias was found to be reduced, and the measure appears to better measure the ability to balance interests. Different questions on the scale look at intellectual humility, the ability to consider perspectives of others and a broader context, skills in being able to recognize change and uncertainty as a part of any problem, and the ability to integrate these contexts and perspectives into a final decision or compromise (Brienza et al., 2018). This scale shows much promise in being a more full measurement of wisdom as a whole.

Benefits of Wisdom

As may be expected, wisdom is associated with many other positive psychological constructs. Studies with young adults have found that wisdom is related to having a coherent sense of self and a solid and consistent ego, which may be linked to other beneficial qualities both inter- and intrapersonally (Webster, 2010). In addition, wise individuals appear to have less investment in hedonistic pursuits (e.g., seeking pleasure) and more interest in reflection and personal growth (Bergsma & Ardelt, 2012; Webster, 2010). The wise also tend to reserve social judgment in favor of making attempts to understand the whole situation and its context before making conclusions; this may have implications for decreasing prejudice and the making of ultimate attributional errors (i.e., assuming that actions of all members of a group can be attributed to internal and stable conditions).

Recent studies have also found moderate and positive links to happiness and life satisfaction (Cheung & Chow, 2020; Le, 2011; Walsh, 2012), particularly with relevance to wise reasoning (Brienza et al., 2018; Brocato et al., 2020). One reason for this may be the fact that wise individuals appear to be more open to experience in general, as well as open to various attributions for different life experiences (both bad and good; Le, 2011). In addition, as others have suggested, having a wise outlook on life may allow an individual to be more flexible, adapting and changing as life requires (Glück, 2020; Sternberg, 2012). Some have also found that gratitude and appreciation of life and its experiences are also related to a wise outlook on life (König & Glück, 2014).

Many of the studies conducted on the construct of wisdom have taken place with older and aging adults, and several point to the finding that wisdom is something that is best accumulated over the life span (Ardelt, 2016; Ardelt & Edwards, 2016). If this is achieved, then wise adults seem to have other types of strengths and personality characteristics that may also affect a more positive experience in older adulthood. Even after controlling for demographic factors such as gender, race, physical health, socioeconomic status, marital status, and social involvement, connections are found between wisdom and subjective well-being (Ardelt & Edwards, 2016), as well as other positive personal traits such as generativity and a desire for personal growth and maturity (Wink & Staudinger, 2016). In addition, links between wisdom and a feeling of mastery over and a sense of purpose in life exist in multiple studies of older adults (Ardelt, 2016; Ardelt & Edwards, 2016). Finally, wise individuals also have been found to have greater humility (Grossman et al., 2016; Krause, 2016). Thus, wisdom appears to be related to many positive factors, beneficial over the life span and clearly something that is worth cultivating toward the aim of a more positive experience toward the end of one's life.

The Neurobiology of Wisdom

Although it would seem to fit naturally in the discussion, wisdom often has not been included in neuroscience for various reasons, one of which is the perception that it falls outside the realm of biological science (Jeste & Harris, 2010). Recently, however, some researchers have begun to discuss brain regions that appear to be fundamental to the development of wisdom. In cases where traumatic brain injuries have been centralized in the frontotemporal lobe, deficits are found in the ability to be socially appropriate, process emotions effectively, and control impulsivity; all of these are, as Jeste and Harris (2010) state, "the antithesis of wisdom" (p. 1603). In a recent study of wisdom, Brennan and colleagues (2021) found that activity in the temporoparietal junction (TPJ) was increased when participants were stimulated to have happy emotions while using wisdom to solve a problem. Additionally, wisdom correlated more with greater speed of processing when positive emotions were induced during thinking. Thus, emotions appear to have a fairly strong interaction with wise behavior neurologically. More research is needed in this developing area, but we are hopeful that wisdom will be included in future neurobiological discussions.

Future Study of Wisdom

One area that must still be attended to in more detail is the study of wisdom in cultural groups other than the U.S. majority. Although some studies exist on Asian and Asian American populations with regard to wisdom, there is very little information about how wisdom might be used, is developed, or differs in construct in Latinx and Black populations. In our last edition, we remarked, "When searching in PsycInfo for articles on these populations using the keyword of "wisdom," there are virtually no articles that address Latino or Hispanic populations and very few that discuss Black Americans in regard to this construct (see Bang, 2015, for one example with this population)." Unfortunately, a search conducted today shows much the same. White and colleagues (2023) have a very recently published chapter in which criticisms are made against the stereotypic depiction of Latinx adolescents by focusing on resilience and other positive characteristics of Latinx communities that are imparted to their youth, noting that much research focuses only on this population as "damaged by structural racism" (p. 325). White and colleagues (2023) instead emphasize capacities for hope and self-determination, the ability to share and have vision and wisdom, and other positive benefits of growing up in a Latinx community. We know that sometimes stereotypes exist with regard to intelligence and certain cultural groups—namely, that Asian populations are often depicted as high in wisdom and intelligence (Aronson et al., 1999), while other underrepresented groups have been pathologized as less intelligent throughout history (see Steele, 1994 for an overview of the concept of stereotype threat in this regard). Studying strengths in these populations may provide an additional benefit of positive psychology in that we can work to decrease stereotypes and begin to see all populations as able to possess wisdom.

THEORIES OF COURAGE

Like wisdom, courage is appreciated in many cultures. Go to any corner of the earth, and you will find that courage is valued, although potentially manifested in very different ways in different cultures. Read the works of Eastern and Western thinkers, and you will find that even the wisest people in the history of the world marveled at courage. Socrates is one of many who sought to understand this noble quality, as illustrated in his question to Laches: "Suppose we set about determining the nature of courage and in the second place, proceed to inquire how the young men may attain this quality by the help of study and pursuits. Tell me, if you can, what is courage," implored Socrates (Plato, trans., 1953, p. 85). Although this age-old question has long intrigued scholars and laypeople, it is only in the past few decades that researchers from many different fields (e.g., Finfgeld, 1995; Gal & Rucker, 2021; Kelley et al., 2019; Pury & Saylors, 2018; Rachman, 1984) have established the requisite theoretical and scientific springboards needed for launching more comprehensive examinations of courage.

Hemingway defined courage as "Grace under pressure" (Parker, 1929), whereas Hobbes was critical of courage, stating, "The contempt of wounds and violent death. It inclines men to private revenges, and sometimes to endeavor the unsettling of public peace" (cited in Rorty, 1988, p. x). See Table 9.4 for a few more famous quotes about courage. One other scholarly description, that of the Roman statesman Cicero (as summarized by Houser, 2002), may be the view of courage that best transcends time (as suggested by a comparison to implicit and explicit views on courage detailed later in this chapter). Houser noted that Cicero saw courage as

> (1) magnificence, the planning and execution of great and expansive projects by putting forth ample and splendid effort of mind; (2) confidence, that through which, on great and honorable projects, the mind self-confidently collects itself with sure hope; (3) patience, the voluntary and lengthy endurance of arduous and difficult things, whether the case be honorable or useful, and (4) perseverance, ongoing persistence in a well-considered plan. (p. 305)

More recently, authors have philosophized that courage is a virtue that all teachers should aim to engender and that it, along with other virtues such as justice and truthfulness, is inspired

TABLE 9.4 ■ Quotes on Courage

Maya Angelou	"Courage is the most important of all the virtues because without courage you can't practice any other virtue consistently."
John F. Kennedy	"Moral courage is a more rare commodity than bravery in a battle or great intelligence."
Martin Luther King, Jr.	"Courage is the power of the mind to overcome fear."
Nelson Mandela, speaking about his imprisonment	"I learned that courage was not the absence of fear but the triumph over it. The brave man is not he who does not feel afraid but he who conquers that fear."
Anais Nin, in her 3rd diary	"Life shrinks or expands according to one's courage."

by *phronesis* or the practical aspect of knowledge (Kreber, 2015). Courage here is linked to the other moral virtues as being an antecedent of teaching one *how* one should act based on accumulated knowledge. This idea of teachers needing courage, perhaps particularly in terms of having the courage to represent history accurately and to include the voices of the disenfranchised along with majority culture groups, is perhaps particularly salient at this time in the United States as legislatures across the country have been seeking to control the curriculum. Being a scholar, that is, one who is dedicated to the accumulation of knowledge, bears with it a responsibility to represent that information correctly despite the desire of some to keep certain kinds of knowledge hidden; courage is a necessity in today's classroom. In their curriculum guide for teachers addressing the Civil Rights Movement in their classroom, the National Museum of Civil Rights (2014) notes that three components must be present for courage to occur: will ("courage is no accident," p. 11), risk ("fear is . . . an inherent component of courage," p. 11), and morals ("courage involves a noble or worthy cause," p. 11).

Implicit Theories of Courage

To examine laypeople's views of courage, O'Byrne and colleagues (2000) surveyed 97 people and found considerable variation. While some perceive courage as an attitude (e.g., optimism or sustaining well-being in the face of hardship), others see it as a behavior (e.g., saving someone's life or standing up for one's faith or beliefs). Some refer to mental strength; others write of physical strength. Many claim that courage involves taking a risk (e.g., facing a challenge when success is uncertain), whereas others accentuate the role of fear or one's ability to control it and continue to act. Interestingly, neither the risk component nor the fear component, however, is found in all descriptions of courage. Additionally, some research suggests that being willing or eager to engage in one type of courage does not necessarily translate to all other types of courage, suggesting that courage is truly multidimensional (Howard et al., 2017).

Across history and cultures, courage has been regarded as a great virtue because it helps people to face their challenges. Philosophers offered the earliest views on understanding courage. Over the past centuries, efforts to construct socially relevant views of courage have transported it from the hearts of the warriors on the battlefields to the daily experiences and thoughts of every person. In today's discussions of social justice, it is often discussed in relation to making the decision to stand up for others who are more vulnerable. Whereas Aristotle analyzed the physical courage of his "brave soldier," Plato marveled at the moral courage of his mentors. The philosophical focus seemed to shift to the deeds and traits of veterans of moral wars with Aquinas's (1273/1948) attention paid to steadfastness in the face of difficulty. These latter two types of courage (physical and moral) have captured most philosophers' attentions, and the classification of courageous behavior has broadened over the years.

After reviewing work on courage, two groups of researchers developed similar classifications of courage. In their Values in Action classification system, Peterson and Seligman (2004) conceptualized courage as a core human virtue comprising such strengths as **valor** (taking physical, intellectual, and emotional stances in the face of danger), **authenticity** (representing oneself to others and the self in a sincere fashion), **enthusiasm/zest** (thriving/having a sense of vitality in a challenging situation), and **industry/perseverance** (undertaking tasks and challenges and finishing them).

In a similar model, O'Byrne et al. (2000) identified the three types of courage as physical, moral, and health/change (now referred to as *vital courage*). **Physical courage** involves the attempted maintenance of societal good by the expression of physical behavior grounded in the pursuit of socially valued goals (e.g., a firefighter saving a child from a burning building). **Moral courage** is the behavioral expression of authenticity in the face of the discomfort of dissension, disapproval, or rejection (e.g., a politician invested in a "greater good" places an unpopular vote in a meeting). **Vital courage** refers to the perseverance through a disease or disability even when the outcome is ambiguous (e.g., a child with a heart transplant maintaining their intensive treatment regimen even though the prognosis is uncertain). Discussions of **psychological courage** (linked to vital courage) and **civil courage** (linked to moral courage) are also found in the next sections.

Physical courage has evolved slowly from the Greek *andreia*, the military courage of the brave soldier in ancient Greece. Finding the rugged path between cowardice and foolhardiness distinguished a Greek soldier as courageous. This disposition to act appropriately in situations involving fear and confidence in the face of physical danger has been valued in many cultures for centuries (Rorty, 1988). For example, Ernest Hemingway was a major writer on the topic of courage in the 20th-century within the United States. His fascination with physical courage in a variety of arenas, such as the battlefield, the open sea, and the bullfighting arena, seemed to mirror the fascination with staring danger in the face and persevering often attributed to "American culture" within the United States. In fact, the "Hemingway code" of living a life characterized by strength, knowledge, and courage provided a code of conduct for many.

Jack Rachman's research on courage stemmed from his realization that courage was the mirror image of fear. He noticed that, when faced with physical jeopardy, some people dealt with the perceived danger better than others. Therefore, Rachman (1984) worked with paratroopers, decorated soldiers, and bomb squad members to gather information on the nature of fear and its counterpart, courage. He found that courageous people persevere when facing fear and thereafter make quick physiological recoveries. He also suggested that courageous acts are not necessarily confined to a special few, nor do they always take place in public.

One recent example of this physical courage may be the 19 Granite Mountain Hotshot firefighters who lost their lives fighting the Arizona wildfire in June 2013, which can be held up as examples of bravery and courage. These men knew the danger they were in and still pressed forward to try to stop the raging fire. Another might be the story of Officer Eugene Goodman, who lead violent rioters away from the Senate chambers during the January 6th, 2021 insurrection at the U.S. Capitol, despite potential grave risk to himself. Other examples would of course include the tens of thousands of service people in our armed forces who leave their families and friends to go to fight for our country every day, sometimes volunteering for extended tours of duty despite the daily threat of death. These individuals must feel the bite of fear on a regular basis and yet press onward due to their great courage. Similarly, others have noted that even in the face of significant fear, the importance of the task held by the actor may sometimes influence a physically courageous behavior (Chocklingam & Norton, 2019).

The study of physical courage has in some ways lagged behind other forms, according to some researchers, perhaps especially as many view acts of this type of courage as relegated to specific occupations as noted previously by our examples of first responders and service members (Howard & Reiley, 2020). Howard and Reiley (2020), however, say this view of physical courage is narrow and should also include workers who work in other types of dangerous situations on a daily basis, such as miners or other blue collar workers. These authors pull away from the idea of physical courage being an "in the moment" kind of act and note that courage might be staying in a dangerous situation for a longer period of time in order to contribute to an overall good outcome. Interestingly, some have posited that watching acts of physical courage might inspire others to enact broader social change (Sekerka et al., 2009).

Moral courage involves the preservation of justice and service for the common good. Fascinated by moral courage, President John F. Kennedy spent years gathering stories of statesmen who followed their hearts and principles when determining what was "best" for the United States as a people—even when constituents did not agree with their decisions or value their representations. Although Kennedy himself was a military hero, in his *Profiles in Courage* (1956), he seemed to give more attention and reverence to moral courage than to physical courage. As a testament to his interest in courage, as you'll read a bit later in this chapter, Kennedy's daughter, Caroline Kennedy Schlossberg and her son have recently created a campaign to honor this passion.

Authenticity and integrity are closely associated with the expression of personal views and values in the face of dissension and rejection. Exactly when should one take a stand? In one example, Rosa Parks said that she took a seat at the front of a bus because it was time to do so. Doctors and nurses, when facing difficult situations with patients and families, must be truthful and straightforward even when it would be easier, emotionally, to sugarcoat diagnoses and prognoses (see Finfgeld, 1998; Pury and Saylors, 2018). Not only does it take courage to speak the truth, but it also takes courage to hear the truth. Moral courage can take yet another form when an individual stands up for the rights of the disenfranchised or voiceless and confronts someone with power over them. It can also take the form of those with privilege being willing to hear that their experiences may not include reference to those who are different from them in some way.

Moral courage might be considered the "equal opportunity" form of this virtue; we all experience situations in which a morally courageous response is provoked, and any of us may encounter discomfort or dissension and be challenged by the task of maintaining authenticity and integrity in those situations. So, how does a common person like you or me respond to situations that challenge our core assumptions about the world and about people? When prudence suggests that a stand needs to be taken, we have the opportunity to engage in behavior consistent with moral courage. Unfortunately, any one of us may encounter situations in which a person (who is present or not present) is not getting a "fair shake" because of someone's prejudice, be it racism, ableism, ageism, sexism, or others. In a recent study by Thoroughgood and colleagues (2021), the impact of speaking up in the face of this type of situation was studied. These researchers interviewed transgender employees about the impact of cisgender colleagues speaking publicly about their support for the transgender community and found that the moral courage these allies demonstrated was significantly and positively related to job satisfaction and negatively related to psychological factors such as emotional exhaustion (Thoroughgood et al., 2021). Cultivating your ability to muster up the moral courage to address perceived injustices can make a difference for those around you.

Courage can occur at any age. Most of us will never have to summon the type of courage shown by activists like Malala Yousafzai. All of us should be relieved that such a brave girl recovered after being shot by the Taliban at age 15 in an effort to silence her and has moved forward toward becoming one of the world's strongest advocates of education of girls and women (Bailey, 2014). In following the footsteps of this youngest winner of the Nobel Peace Prize in history, perhaps we can use her unfailing courage as an inspiration to be courageous in our own ways. Another outspoken and courageous young person is Greta Thunberg, being willing to speak up for environmental activism. Pictures of Thunberg as she began her quest toward urging action on climate change often show her protesting alone at first. Being a sole voice to a cause takes courage as well (see the article in this chapter talking about Yousafzai, Thunberg, and other young activists using their moral courage compasses to speak up about important topics).

THE EMERGING VOICES OF YOUTH ACTIVISTS

We are living in the midst of a wave of worldwide cultural change. Peaceful global activism led by young people is gaining momentum, challenging power structures at every level of society. But, as yet, this potential opportunity has not been seized for health. What more could be done to infuse energy and constructive anger into campaigns for a better health?

Led with remarkable poise by 16-year-old Swede Greta Thunberg, today's young activists demand urgent action on climate change. As many as 1 million young people now participate in the weekly worldwide school strikes on Fridays, which she initiated in 2018, encouraging countries to adhere to the Paris Agreement and Intergovernmental Panel on Climate Change recommendations and calling for measures to ensure that our planet has a future in the face of decades of neglect and abuse. In the aftermath of the Arab Spring, the 2012 Taliban shooting of 15-year-old Malala Yousafzai in Pakistan brought her leadership for the right to education into global view. Her Nobel Peace Prize award implicitly endorsed youth activism. Other leaders include the teenage period poverty campaigner

Amika George, whose #FreePeriods crusade convinced the U.K. Government to provide free menstrual products in schools across the country from September, 2019. The impassioned 20-year-old Syrian wheelchair-bound Nujeen Mustafa spoke in April to the U.N. Security Council about the profound neglect experienced by disabled people, such as herself, in conflict zones. In the United States, the Parkland shooting survivors' defiant voices against gun violence arose out of the 2018 school shootings in which 17 students and staff were killed.

Cultural change led by young people is sweeping across society, and young activists are becoming legitimised, but these emerging youth movements have yet to turn their attention to health emergencies. Younger populations have shown their capacity to respond, as demonstrated by the youth commissioners' input to the Lancet Commission on Adolescent Health and Wellbeing. But even stronger voices are needed (Lancet, 2019).

Vital courage is at work as a patient battles illness through surgery and treatment regimens. Many researchers have examined vital courage (although not calling it such), and their work has captured the phenomenon that captivates us when we hear about someone facing chronic illness. Haase (1987) interviewed nine chronically ill adolescents to answer the question, "What is the essential structure of the lived-experience of courage in chronically ill adolescents?" She found that courage involves developing a deep personal awareness of the potential short-term and long-term effects of the illness.

The courage of physicians is also studied in the literature on vital courage, and Shelp (1984) found that this virtue, along with competence and compassion, is a very desirable characteristic of health care providers. Moreover, instilling courage through "encouragement" (p. 358) is required of anyone in a profession that exemplifies care and concern. Furthermore, Shelp states that the necessary components of courage are freedom of choice, fear of a situation, and the willingness to take risks in a situation with an uncertain but morally worthy end. There has perhaps been no other time in recent history where physicians, nurses, and other frontline health workers have had to persevere so courageously as in the face of the COVID-19 pandemic. We have been moved by pictures of health care workers with tears in their eyes, bruising from personal protective equipment on their faces, as they work tirelessly to care for the scores and scores of people who were hospitalized in the United States with COVID-19 in these past years. Thus, we believe that vital courage frequently is exhibited by people who are suffering, by the health care providers who treat them, *and* by the many significant others who care for loved ones during hard times. During the COVID-19 pandemic, the John F. Kennedy Library, under the ambassadorship of Caroline Kennedy and her son, Jack Schlossberg, created a public nomination campaign for examples of "COVID Courage." This campaign resulted in thousands of nomination from across the country, "sharing moving stories about the commitment and sacrifice of members of their communities who put their own health at risk to help" (John F. Kennedy Library and Museum, 2021, para 1). If you visit the website of the library, you will see stories of Dr. Amy Acton, the former director of the State Health Department in Ohio, who was nominated for her ability to remain compassionate and to give truthful and essential information during the pandemic. Darrell R. Marks, a Native American Academic Advisor from Arizona, is another winner who advocated for the Navajo and Hopi tribal communities during the pandemic due to health disparities that were especially prominent during the pandemic, despite suffering some personal losses due to COVID in his own family. We have seen, and perhaps you have as well, that sometimes a crisis brings out strength in people. These examples of COVID courage provide evidence of that.

Psychological courage, as Putman (1997) described it, is strength in facing one's destructive habits. This form of vital courage may be quite common in that we all struggle with psychological challenges in the forms of stress, sadness, and dysfunctional or unhealthy relationships. In light of these threats to our psychological stabilities, we stand up to our dysfunctions by restructuring our beliefs or systematically desensitizing ourselves to our fears. One psychological challenge that plagues many in the United States and across the world is that of addiction. Di Maggio and colleagues (2019) conducted a mixed-methods study in which they interviewed adults currently in treatment for substance abuse about times during their lives in which they would characterize themselves as having acted courageously. When the qualitative data from these interviews was analyzed, Di Maggio and colleagues noted several themes that existed regarding the courageous experiences recounted. First of all, more than half of the participants relayed courageous stories associated with their addiction, with 23% of participants stating they had to show courage in order to begin treatment, and another 33% citing that they needed courage to "accept difficult past behaviors [related to addiction]" (Di Maggio et al., 2019, p. 4). In addition, most stories (76.3%) focused specifically on psychological courage with participants sharing experiences such as being courageous enough to "[admit that] I was not able to look after my son. Leaving him in the care of others for his good and mine" (Di Maggio et al., 2019, p. 4). These findings are in line with what Putman and others have found in similar studies. Thinking of the courage it takes to pull oneself away from an addiction might allow such

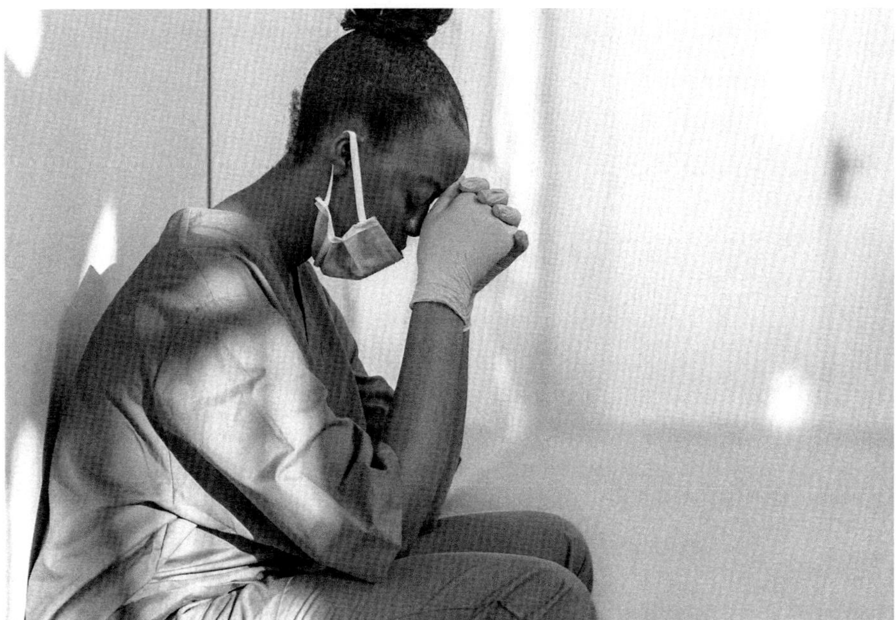

iStockphoto.com/insta_photos

individuals to tell a different story in their lives, one that may assist them in additional courageous pursuits as they move forward in their lives.

One striking argument that Putman advanced about psychological courage is that there is a paucity of training for psychological courage as compared to physical and moral courage. Putman goes on to say that pop culture presents many physically and morally courageous icons in literary works and movies, but exemplars of psychological courage are rare. Perhaps this is due to the negative stigma surrounding mental health problems and destructive behaviors. In fact, some researchers say that psychological courage might be viewed as a form of moral courage in some ways as individuals possessing this trait are often asked to stand up against this stigma (Pury et al., 2014). This seems true as being open about mental illness is a relatively new social phenomenon, and diagnoses of this sort still carry with them stigma in society. It is also possible, however, that the language surrounding vital courage is new relative to that for moral and physical courage (the latter having been acknowledged since the ancient Greeks). Rosa Parks, firefighters, and Elie Wiesel exemplify moral, physical, and vital courage. Some recently have called for training for therapists in terms of developing higher levels of courage, specifically the psychological courage to deal with conflict, to be able to witness a client's recounting (or reliving) of particularly traumatic moments, and to remain present despite difficulty (Vargas, 2019). This relation to psychotherapy in particular is a valuable course of future study.

Moral Courage: Rosa Parks stood up to injustice when she sat in a seat in the front of a Birmingham bus during a time of extreme prejudice.

Bettmann/Contributor/via Getty Images

Physical Courage: Firefighters completing a training exercise prepare for their life-threatening work.
iStockphoto.com/monkeybusinessimages

Vital Courage: Elie Wiesel devoted his life to fighting for human rights after he survived youth in a concentration camp.
Consolidated News Pictures/Contributor/via Getty Images

Other researchers have discussed the construct of civil courage, which is defined by Greitemeyer and others (2007) as "brave behavior accompanied by anger and indignation that intends to enforce societal and ethical norms without considering one's own social costs" (p. 115). This form of courage is thought to combine facets of physical courage and moral courage, as defined by O'Byrne et al. (2000) and Pury and others (2007; Greitemeyer et al., 2007). As an example, someone exhibiting civil courage may decide to intervene in a situation where someone is under physical attack as a result of prejudice. Greitemeyer and colleagues (2007) state that this type of courage is separate from helping behaviors more commonly labeled as altruism (e.g., helping an individual who has dropped something) because of the common cost experienced by the individual who decides to help in these circumstances. In the example given here, the "helper" who is exhibiting civil courage risks bodily harm in helping to fend off attackers but feels angered and morally and civilly obligated to stand up for what is right. Additionally, there are many works devoted today to "courageous conversations" about race, gender, and other topics that sometimes lead to differences in perceptions, emotions, and understandings (McCormick et al., 2019; Sue, 2015). Glen E. Singleton (2021) recently published his newest edition of his seminal work *Courageous Conversations About Race: A Field Guide for Achieving Equity in Schools and Beyond*, which details ways in which authentic dialogues can occur between groups with different identity statuses and different views. This type of work calls for courage as many avoid such topics out of fear of being "wrong" or found lacking in knowledge, but using a concept like courage to push oneself to engage in conversations that may lead to a better understanding of oneself and others is a laudable task to undertake.

BECOMING AND BEING COURAGEOUS

Courageous behaviors follow the identification of a threat, after which there is a shift away from defining the problem as an insurmountable obstacle (Finfgeld 1995, 1998). Behavioral expectations, role models, and value systems also appear to determine if, when, and how courage unfolds. Courageous behavior may result in a sense of equanimity, or calmness; an absence of regret about one's life; and personal integrity.

Using structured individual interviews, Szagun (1992) asked children ages 5 to 12 to rate the courage associated with 12 different risks (on a 5-point scale ranging from 1 = *not courageous* to 5 = *very courageous*); moreover, the researcher asked the children to judge courage vignettes. The younger children (ages 5 to 6) likened courage to the difficulty of the task at hand, along with being fearless. The older children (ages 8 to 9) likened courage to subjective risk taking and overcoming fear. Still older children (ages 11 to 12) reported that being fully aware of a risk at the time of acting is a necessary component of courage. Not surprisingly, given their developmental stages, the younger group rated physical risks as entailing more courage than other risks (e.g., psychological risks). These results have been repeated in other studies by Szagun and others (e.g., Piht et al., 2016; Szagun & Schauble, 1997), and many have replicated the results that younger children think of courage separate from fear, while adolescents and adults tend to think of fear as a necessary precursor for having "true" courage. Some studies also find that more developmentally mature conceptualizations of courage include an urge to act (Piht et al., 2016). Additionally, older children were able to differentiate between courageous acts and mere "risky" acts. Piht et al. (2016) state that older children understood this difference through statements like, "When they're jumping on a trampoline and doing tricks and you don't dare, you don't have to" (p. 1935). This type of risk was clearly not the same as standing up for a friend or doing some important, but potentially frightening, task together.

Interestingly, studies have shown that one precursor to the development of some kinds of courage (namely civic courage) is some reminder of the risks of *not* being courageous. Readers might remember Milgram's famous study in which participants showed blind obedience to a researcher asking them to deliver shocks to individuals who got answers to questions wrong, even when these shocks appeared to gravely harm the recipients. In a study by Graupmann and Frey (2014), researchers showed their participants a documentary on Milgram's study and then assessed their feelings with regard to personal responsibility, civil courage, and societal engagement. Results showed that these factors increased after being primed by the lack of civil courage present in the Milgram study. When the behavior of the participants in the Milgram study was attributed to personal traits, intentions to volunteer and to stand up in the face of wrong were increased the most (Graupmann & Frey, 2014). Thus, reminding ourselves of what can sometimes happen when we decide *not* to act in times that call for courage may bolster our resolve to act in courageous and generative ways.

Several researchers have attempted to determine how people become courageous or decide upon courageous action in the face of certain circumstances (Goodwin et al., 2020; Haase, 1987). Trait moral courage as well as lack of narcissism were consistent predictors of those who decided to report or call out sexual harassment in a work environment in a recent study by Goodwin and colleagues (2020). In this study, the researchers measured trait moral courage as "ability to interpret, and willingness to violate, social norms" (p. 1). Corrupt times often test our courageous mettle, and perhaps in no other historical era was this more evident than during the Jewish Holocaust. Fagin-Jones and Midlarsky (2007) interviewed two groups of individuals: (1) non-Jewish "rescuers" who assisted and/or saved the lives of Jews during this time, despite the obvious threat to their own personal safety, and (2) non-Jewish "bystanders" who did not make efforts to assist Jews, although they also did not participate in direct persecution of them (p. 139). These researchers aimed to better understand the effect of various positive characteristics of personality (e.g., social responsibility) on the "courageous altruism" that took place during this time (Fagin-Jones & Midlarsky, 2007, p. 136). Results showed that rescuers could be distinguished from bystanders on measures of social responsibility, empathic concern, and risk taking, as well as altruistic moral reasoning. These findings further exemplify the idea that personal traits may lead some individuals toward more courageous actions. In January 2010, one of the most famous of these rescuers passed away. Miep Gies, one of the incredible individuals who helped to hide Anne Frank and who was the keeper of Anne's diary, remained humble about the civil courage she showed by her involvement in helping the Franks until her death at 100 years old. Gies considered helping Anne Frank and her family to be not a choice but a duty (a key component of the concept of civil courage) and has been quoted as saying, "I am not a hero" (Goldstein, 2010). Nonetheless, history will always remember her as one.

Some findings regarding courage point to the development of attitudes and coping methods rather than descriptions of so-called born heroes. Howard (2019) found that individuals thinking of social or civil courage through the lens of an "approach/avoidance" framework might be beneficial in determining who acts in courageous ways. Teaching coping skills related to approaching situations, as opposed to avoiding them, may be one way to obtain more courageous outcomes. In looking at adolescents with chronic illness, Haase (1987) found that, through daily encounters with "mini-situations" of courage (e.g., treatment, procedures, physical changes, and others that result from the illness), these adolescents came to an awareness and resolution of the experience as one of courage. Increasingly, over time and experiences, the situation is viewed as difficult but not impossible. Some psychologists have spoken of the use of courage in therapeutic treatment, specifically with regard to having the "courage to risk positive change" (Campos, 2012, p. 209). As a part of transactional analysis, therapists who are proponents of this style of treatment state that one must take some risks to seek out change in one's life, which requires courage.

Campos (2012) and others write about building a "culture of courage" in which clients are encouraged to try to change themselves or their community in some way (p. 215). This relates to more recent research that looked at likelihood of standing up against disparaging jokes made at the expense of others (Thomas et al., 2020). In this study, Thomas and colleagues (2022) found that the willingness to stand up against such a joke was related to how other bystanders reacted to it. When the participants were told that other bystanders reacted with anger as opposed to amusement, they were more willing to stand against the disparagement. Interestingly, those who found a disparaging joke humorous were not more likely to collaborate with others to support the humor, and this is consistent with other findings related to this; the shared anger appeared to invoke the courageous response (Sasse et al., 2022; Thomas et al., 2020). These researchers concluded that "even a small minority of bystanders expressing anger at disparagement humor may help to promote its rejection" (Thomas et al., 2020, p. 6). These findings may be particularly useful during this time in our culture where allyship is being learned by many in majority cultural group. If you are an ally yourself, or even an ally-in-training, it may help you to know that standing up against injustice yourself may encourage others to do the same!

Other researchers talk about ways in which leaders can support expressions of moral courage. Simola (2016) posits that, at times, expressions of moral courage can be met with initial discomfort from the group. Bucking the system and standing against a policy or incident can be extremely beneficial but also carry with them a push for change. This can be something that an organization, for example, may initially resist, even if the moral courage shown is on the side of right. Simola states that leaders can challenge themselves to behave in authentic ways when faced with change and that this may assist others in letting go of their discomfort and encourage them to be more authentic as well. The end result in an organization that practices these skills is that moral courage may instead increase vitality of the organization and foster collective growth (Simola, 2016). Other research supports this idea that modeling courage through leadership is a beneficial way to increase courage in a group overall (Mansur et al., 2020; Palanski et al., 2015).

Sean Hannah and colleagues (2007) have proposed a theory explaining how the individual may experience courage on a subjective level and how these experiences may lead to the development of what they call "a courageous mindset" (p. 129). In Hannah et al.'s model (see Figure 9.3), factors such as the perception of risk are affected by external constructs such as social forces (e.g., normative influences) and positive states (such as hope, efficacy, or the experience of positive emotions), as well as more internal characteristics such as positive traits (e.g., openness to experience and conscientiousness) and values and beliefs (e.g., valor, loyalty, honor). Hannah and colleagues posit that these influences have a collective effect on how risk is perceived, how fear is experienced, and whether courageous behaviors are exhibited. In addition, they theorize that the subjective experience of these courageous behaviors may lead the individual to develop the "courageous mindset" (Hannah et al., 2007, p. 129) that in turn affects the occurrence of courageous action in future endeavors. Some research has shown that using writing interventions might be one way in which to encourage creative mindset. Kramer and Zinbarg (2019) asked some individuals in their study to think about times in which they acted with courage, facing their fears. Findings showed that those who were asked to recall courage were more willing to state that they would act similarly in a different related scenario. Though effect sizes were small in this study, Kramer and Zinbarg (2019) provide some important evidence for the impact of remembering past courageous incidents in order to spur likelihood of future ones.

Other studies in this vein have shown that general helping behavior and moral courage helping behavior may have differential predictors (Kayser et al., 2009). Some have shown that certain emotions are more impactful at promoting morally courageous behavior. Although we

FIGURE 9.3 ■ Subjective Experience of Courage

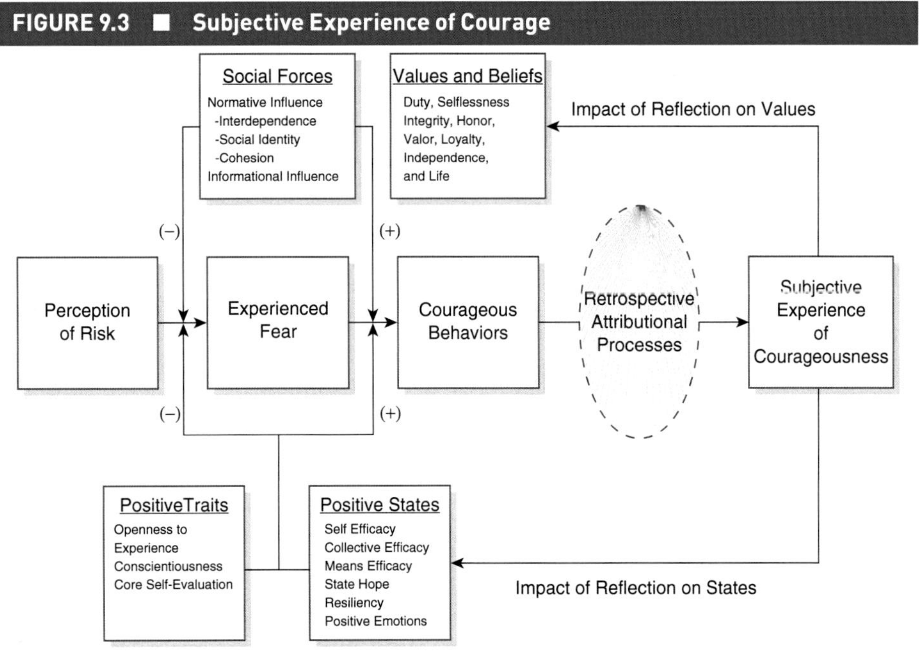

From Hannah, S. T., Sweeney, P. J., & Lester, P. B. Toward a courageous mindset: The subject act and experience of courage, *The Journal of Positive Psychology, 2,* 129–135, 2007. Figure on p. 130.

might often think of some emotions as "negative" and others as "positive," the fact remains that all emotions are potential stimulators of positive action. Research has shown that anger, sometimes thought to be a problematic emotion, is actually an incredible motivator of moral courage and more effective at this task than emotions such as guilt or overall mood (Halmburger et al., 2015). This emotion may propel some individuals into action.

In *The Courage Quotient,* Robert Biswas-Diener (2012) talks more about courage for the layperson. Biswas-Diener states that most people think first of *physical* courage when the word is mentioned. Images of people rescuing babies from burning buildings or daredevils willing to risk death to perform physical feats are often the first things that come to our minds. When we compare everyday actions of ourselves or others we know to these types of images, it seems that courage is a scarce thing, something not often seen. Biswas-Diener makes the point, however, that courage can mean more than this, stating,

> When we understand courage as 'a quality of spirit or mind,' we can see that this mental attitude can apply as easily to a child facing her first day of school as to an executive who is willing to gamble on a new product. In the end courage is not found only in physical acts; it is fundamentally an attitude toward facing intimidating situations. (p. 5)

If we are able to identify more courageous acts, we might also be able to emulate them in everyday situations. Bravery in trying something new, for example, is something that might be attempted in the workplace, in our relationships, and in setting difficult goals for ourselves. As we are able to pay more attention to more courageous acts in these domains, we may be better situated to become more courageous ourselves.

Teaching courage and supporting courageous acts are things that we can do with children as well. Heiner (2019) evaluated a training program for fourth- and fifth-grade students called "The Hero Construction Company" developed in 2006 by Langdon. This program teaches students about heroism as a concept, and follows a curriculum designed to help school-aged children to see themselves as "heroes" and to act accordingly in their everyday lives. Heiner (2019) found that this program appeared to increase courage in children and that this increase was sustained a month after the curriculum was completed. Though not a formal program, we can teach our own children about courage in various ways as well. When my (JTP) children were very young, we occasionally put up "The Bravery Tree" when inspiration for trying challenging new things seem to be needed. The Bravery Tree was just a makeshift shape of a tree, drawn with ribbons on our sliding glass door. Everyone in the family had a different branch, and each could earn Bravery Leaves for attempting acts of courage. A child might try a new food at the dinner table even though she thought she wouldn't like it. Another might challenge himself by playing in the "big kids" basketball game at recess. A third might try her best not to cry, although she misses her mother while she is at school. We talked about "brave faces" and what we could do to make ourselves feel brave. One of my children used to like to roar in her loudest voice, "I am not afraid!" Another just lifted her chin ever so subtly. As they have gotten older, we've fallen into a practice of setting a "Scary Goal" each year as a new year's resolution. The Scary Goal isn't something that is physically threatening but instead involves trying something that we might be nervous to do. This could be trying out for a team despite not making it in a previous year or deciding to remain positive about something and leaning into hope for success fully even though we might be disappointed in the end. It could be deciding to submit a book proposal for the first time or applying for a new job. Praising acts of bravery in our children (and ourselves) that involve these more everyday feats may instill in them (and us) the idea that they are courageous individuals, that this is something *inside* of them. There is no telling what they might do with this mindset in the future.

U.S. SENATOR JOHN MCCAIN'S VIEW ON STRENGTHENING COURAGE—APRIL 2004

"Moral courage we can strengthen. The first time you stand up to a bully, it's hard. The second time, it's not so hard. Physical courage sometimes you run out of. And when I ran out of courage and came back to my cell and tapped on my wall, it was my comrades that picked me up, that lifted me up, that sustained me, that gave me strength to go back and fight again." (Transcript of MSNBC's *Hardball With Chris Matthews*)

COURAGE RESEARCH

The Measurement of Courage

Over the past 30 years, numerous brief self-report measures of courage have been created for research purposes. Although several of these measures have some strong points, all warrant additional development.

In 1976, Larsen and Giles developed a scale to measure existential (akin to moral) and social (related to physical) courage. The existential courage domain is tapped by 28 items, and 22 items examine social courage. Psychometric support for this measure is limited, and little if any work has been done to refine the scale.

Schmidt and Koselka (2000) constructed a seven-item measure of courage. Three items relate to general courage, and four assess what is considered panic-specific courage (possibly a subtype of vital courage). This scale meets basic standards for reliability, but evidence for its validity is limited.

Woodard (2004) used a carefully researched definition of courage as the willingness to act for a meaningful (noble, good, or practical) cause, despite experiencing fear (associated with perceived threat exceeding available resources), to develop a different measurement of courage. This psychometrically sound scale has since been revised (now called the Woodard-Pury Courage Scale [WPCS-23]), and new scoring calls for analysis of the items that address the willingness piece of this construct in four factors. These factors include the willingness to act in a courageous way for (1) one's job or self-interest, (2) one's beliefs (e.g., religious, patriotic), (3) individual social and/or moral situations, and (4) situations relevant to family

(Woodard & Pury, 2007). Recent scale development has been completed by positive psychology research teams who were working on what originally were called "wellsprings" measures and now referred to as the Values in Action Inventory of Strengths (Peterson & Seligman, 2004). The first version of a wellsprings measure included five items (e.g., "I have taken a stand in the face of strong resistance") that tapped courage. The current version measures four types of courage, including valor, authenticity, enthusiasm/zest, and industry/perseverance. Norton and Weiss (2009) have developed a final measure more recently that consists of items that ask individuals to judge their likelihood of acting when experiencing fear, regardless of situational characteristics. More research on psychometric characteristics must be conducted to determine its utility (Pury & Lopez, 2009), but this appears to be another promising research tool for assessing the construct of courage.

In addition, measures of distinct types of courage exist. Kastenmüller and colleagues (2007) have developed a scale that specifically measures the construct of civil courage (see previous sections for a discussion of this concept). Although at the time of publication, this scale is only offered in German, it provides more information about this type of courage and appears to be psychometrically sound (Kastenmüller et al., 2007). Measures for specific domains also exist, with two for the workplace (Workplace Social Courage Scale, Howard et al., 2017 and the Physical Courage at Work Scale, Howard & Reiley, 2020) and another specifically for use with students in high school (Student Courage Scale; Fabio, 2014).

The Courage Measure for Children (CM-C; Norton & Weiss, 2009) is a 12-item scale that asks Likert-based questions regarding the likelihood of a participant acting in a courageous way (e.g., "If I am anxious about something, I will do it anyway" and "If something scares me, I try to get away from it") and is commonly used in research on courage in this age group. In addition to a self-report version, a parent version of the CM-C is also available for corroboration (Muris et al., 2010). Some suggestions with regard to increasing validity with this measure are detailed in a more recent study, including the removal of some reverse-coded items on this scale (Howard & Alipour, 2014). It is unclear at present if this measure truly measures *courage* or the closely related concept of *persistence despite fear.* More research on this distinction would be beneficial.

Neurological Factors in Courage

Some studies have begun to look at brain activity with regard to courageous acts. Studying this phenomenon is somewhat difficult, because many acts of courage are more spontaneous and occur when a situation arises. Nili et al. (2010) asked participants to overcome a fear to simulate a courageous act and then measured brain activity associated with this action. Participants (all of whom reported a fear of snakes) were presented with a live snake on a conveyor belt and asked to control the distance of the proximity of the snake to be as close to them as possible. These individuals had total control over moving the conveyor belt; thus, choices to move the snake forward on the belt despite fear were defined as acts of courage. In this study, activity was shown in the subgenual anterior cingulate cortex (sgACC) and the right temporal pole when individuals engaged in this act of courage. Making a choice to overcome fear when fear was high was correlated strongly with activity in the sgACC. Some other research has shown that this type of reaction may be limited to certain tasks (Holec et al., 2014). In some of these studies, data suggest that the sgACC may be particularly related to persevering in the face of fear and in learning how to move forward in these instances. More research is needed in this exciting area.

Benefits of Courage

Many beneficial characteristics seem to be correlated with the construct of courage. For example, in personality research, individuals who have the positive traits of agreeableness and openness also score higher on measures of courage (Muris et al., 2010). Courage was also found to correlate with the Big 5 personality trait of extraversion in this study and to have a negative relationship with the trait of anxiety. In addition, courage exhibited in certain scenarios (e.g., educational settings), even in the face of fear of failure, has other positive correlates, including a more adaptive coping style and higher levels of confidence, although there is a question of whether or not courage and confidence are distinct enough to be called different constructs (Martin, 2011). As more research is done on this interesting construct, it is likely that other positive correlates could emerge. Gal and Rucker (2021) write that there can be opportunities to choose courage via risk taking during various points in life, for example, when a new job opportunity presents itself. These authors talk about the benefits of choosing a courageous step forward and note that being willing to take risks might be more common that some other literature suggests. We might think of this as *being brave enough to be brave*, and you might think of ways to do this in your daily life as well.

Courage and Culture

In closing, we would like to highlight the fact that there is a dearth of literature on the subject of courage and its manifestations in different cultures. Acts deemed "courageous" might differ from culture to culture. For example, the acts of suicide bombers in some areas of the world, or of those who choose to bomb abortion clinics within the United States, are at times considered courageous by the proponents of these cultural groups (e.g., extremist members of some religions). It is safe to say, however, that these might not be considered acts of courage by members of other cultural groups (Orsini, 2015; Pury et al., 2015; Sörman et al., 2016). In some cultural groups (e.g., Asian cultures), deciding to keep a personal opinion quiet in service of the pursuit of harmony of the group might be viewed as courageous, although speaking up at all costs might be viewed as courageous in other groups (e.g., Western cultures; Pedrotti et al., 2009). Some research shows that conceptual understandings of courage may differ between individuals in China and people in the United States. While similar elements were likely to inspire courage in both groups (e.g., self-confidence, support of social network, anger) some facets of courage, such as responsibility, may be unique to the Chinese individuals' conceptualization of the need for a courageous act (Cheng & Huang, 2017). Gender stereotypes may also build expectations of courage as a trait in men in particular. Some research has shown that using techniques that build traits like courage that may be seen as "acceptable" may assist in psychotherapy processes as well (Dvorkin, 2015).

In addition, some cultural groups might find courage to be *necessary* more often than others. For instance, the young Pakistani hero Malala Yousafzai, discussed previously, was faced with extreme discrimination and danger, the likes of which might not be present for members of many other cultural groups. Within the United States, problematic race relations may require a basic level of courage from racial, ethnic, and other minorities to live day to day in our country despite violence directed disproportionately at these groups. As an example, the most recent Federal Bureau of Investigation (2020) statistics regarding hate crimes in the United States show that in the 4,939 incidents of racial bias crimes in 2020, 55.8% were victims of anti-Black bias, versus 15.6% being victims of anti-White bias. The same report noted acts of antireligious bias numbered 1,174 in 2020, with 57.6% being anti-Jewish, and another 8.9% anti-Islamic. Of the 1,051 hate crimes perpetrated because of sexual orientation bias, over 99% were due to bias against LGBT individuals, in comparison to less than 1% of heterosexual individuals being targeted due to this type of bias. In addition, individuals who identify as lesbian, gay, transgender, or bisexual may have more adverse reactions to their identities and as a result may have more necessity to engage in courageous acts. Research with this group shows that strength in courage may emerge as a result of resilience in the face of adversity (Higgins et al., 2016). This said, it must be acknowledged that LGBTQ individuals are not the only group who has *opportunity* to engage in courageous acts in standing up for the LGBTQ community. People who were not LGBTQ but who intervened when threat was levied on this community were shown to be higher in courage and other positive attributes such as altruism, leadership, and justice sensitivity (Poteat & Vecho, 2016). Finally, courage may be a necessary component of life for women across the world as their safety is not commensurate to that enjoyed by men in most areas of the world (National Organization for Women, 2012; Safe World for Women, 2013). Gender differences have been found as well in terms of which genders are willing to act courageously and in which situations. Goodwin and colleagues (2020) found that women were more likely, for instance, to report sexual harassment of other women as compared to men witnessing the same behaviors, though this may be mediated by the finding that women are also more likely to notice sexual harassment. In researching this necessary, although perhaps more quiet, courage that many of these individuals may need to live their daily lives, many of those who strive to be allies may discover a new source of strength to emulate.

FINDING WISDOM AND COURAGE IN DAILY LIFE

Wisdom and courage, probably the most valued of the virtues, are in high demand in our world, and fortunately there is not a limited supply. Indeed, we believe that most people, through a mindful approach to life, can develop wisdom and courage. Feel free to test this hypothesis by completing the Personal Mini-Experiments. Then, create some mini-situations of wisdom and courage by implementing the Life Enhancement Strategies. We want to end this chapter by acknowledging that during this moment in history, our world is in turmoil due to political upheaval and disagreement in the United States and other countries, due to the global pandemic of COVID-19 and its aftermath, due to rising temperatures and calls for urgency regarding climate change, and due to the racial tension and reckoning currently occurring in the United States following the murder of George Floyd. These times call for both courage and wisdom. Many will look back upon this momentous time in history and will judge the courage and the wisdom of all of us. With this in mind, we urge you to read more about these important topics and to work to develop these attributes during this tumultuous time.

PERSONAL MINI-EXPERIMENTS

IN SEARCH OF THE WISDOM AND COURAGE OF EVERYDAY PEOPLE . . . INCLUDING YOURSELF

In this chapter, we discuss two of the most celebrated human strengths, wisdom and courage. Our review suggests that both these qualities, although extraordinary, are manifested in one's daily life. Here are a few ideas for finding wisdom and courage in everyday people.

The Wisdom Challenge. Consider your views on the following life event. Think aloud and write them down. "A 15-year-old girl wants to get married right away. What should one/she consider and do?" (Baltes, 1993, p. 587). What questions would you want to ask before offering a comment? Write them down. Then, informally evaluate how well your questions address the five criteria of wisdom (factual and procedural knowledge, life-span contextualism, relativism of values, and recognition and management of uncertainty).

Today's Superheroes. Identify real-life superheroes, people you know, who exemplify each type of courage—physical, moral, vital, and civil. Write a brief biography of each person, and, if you are inclined, write a note to these people telling them why you think they possess courage. You may be surprised by how easy it is to find people who demonstrate courage, as well as how uncomfortable courageous people are with the label.

Everyday Courage. Look for opportunities to be courageous in your everyday life, and watch for examples from others as well. Don't just focus on big and loud acts; look for quiet courage and bravery as well. Challenge yourself to be brave, and start now! Focus on personal and cultural definitions of courage and on ideas about whose common good needs to be considered when identifying courage. Sometimes a great deal of wisdom is needed in determining this. Invite children, a partner, siblings, or other family members to join you in forming courageous goals, and check in on a regular basis to support one another.

LIFE ENHANCEMENT STRATEGIES

Pursuits of wisdom and courage have been chronicled in many historical and fictional accounts. For example, Buddha abandoned everything that he knew and loved to seek enlightenment, a state of wisdom and love that has defined the Buddhist traditions. And, as we referenced at the beginning of this chapter, the Cowardly Lion trekked through the magical forest in hopes that the Wizard of Oz would grant him the courage that he thought he lacked.

We believe that, over the journey that is your life, you can develop the wisdom and courage to make your life more fulfilling and to contribute to a greater good. By no means do we think it is easy to develop these qualities, but other ordinary people have been able to do so by facing life's challenges . . . and with mindful practice, so can you.

As in most chapters, we categorize the life enhancement strategies across three of life's important domains—love, work, and play. We share two suggestions for each domain, one related to wisdom and one to courage.

Love

- Balancing your love life with your work life will take a tremendous amount of wisdom. Identify one person in your family who is the best role model for using wisdom to balance their love life with their work life. Interview this person, and determine the four wise acts in which they engage to maintain that balance.
- Face the fear often associated with dating and making new friends by introducing yourself to twice as many people today as you did yesterday. You can increase and broaden the impact of this challenge to yourself by making sure that some of these new faces look different from your own.

Work

- Share your wisdom about succeeding academically and socially with freshmen at your college or university. Your perspective on how to adapt may prove valuable to other students, particularly those who may not have others in their lives to share this type of wisdom (e.g., first-generation college students).
- Stand up for what is just when your rights or the rights of others are violated. Take opportunities to display your moral and civil courage, especially in situations where someone who has less power than you is being mistreated (e.g., situations involving racism, sexism, heterosexism, ageism, ableism, etc.).

Play

- Balance your work or school demands with your leisure activities. Reflect on the past week and determine how well you balanced your daily living.
- Pursue recreational interests with a passion, and cultivate new ones, but do not confuse rashness or fearlessness with courage.

THE VALUE OF WISDOM AND COURAGE

"To understand wisdom fully and correctly probably requires more wisdom than any of us have" (Sternberg, 1990, p. 3). Likewise, to understand courage may require a good bit of wisdom. This chapter provides a brief review of what we know about these strengths. Undoubtedly, despite our effort to demonstrate that everyday people embody both of these extraordinary characteristics, the number of times that you are exposed either directly or by the media to images of unwise and rash behavior may outnumber the times that you see virtuous behavior. Given some of the recent developments around our globe, including brashness in leaders threatening war against other nations and a rise in populism in many countries that seems to demean the struggles of refugees and undocumented immigrants, we feel compelled to make an even stronger case for celebrating virtue: Wisdom and courage have evolutionary value, whereas stupidity and rash fearlessness thin the herd. Risky decisions should not be made without careful and wise decision making, and making bold statements to gain attention or to see a reaction are not acts of courage.

A clear argument for the adaptive value of wisdom is made by Csikszentmihalyi and Rathunde (1990). Wisdom guides our action, and through that wisdom, we make good choices when challenged by the social and physical world. This practiced wisdom is intrinsically rewarding and beneficial to the common good; it promotes the survival of good ideas, of oneself, and of others. Indeed, wise ideas and wise people may stand the test of time. A similar case can be made for courage. Physical courage and vital courage often extend lives. So, too, do moral and civil courage preserve the ideals of justice and fairness. Perhaps now more than ever we need to cultivate these important strengths in our children to prepare them for the world that awaits them. In closing, we ask you to look for opportunities to exhibit *creative* courage and leave you with a quote from Rollo May, a formative psychologist in the field who is known for his work in developing the existential orientation. May is quoted as saying "Whereas moral courage is the righting of wrongs, creative courage, in contrast, is the discovering of new forms, new symbols, new patterns on which a new society can be built" (May, 1975, p. 21).

KEY TERMS

Authenticity
Balance theory of wisdom
Berlin wisdom paradigm
Civil courage
Enthusiasm/zest
Explicit theories
Implicit theories
Industry/perseverance
Life-span contextualism
Moral courage
Physical courage
Psychological courage
Relativism of values
Valor
Vital courage

10 MINDFULNESS, FLOW, AND SPIRITUALITY

In Search of Optimal Experiences

LEARNING OBJECTIVES

After reading this chapter, you will be able to:

10.1 Describe the difference between mindfulness and mindlessness

10.2 Identify how mindfulness is both a skill and a dispositional trait

10.3 Describe the benefits of mindfulness practice

10.4 List the core characteristics of a flow state

10.5 Recognize the differences and similarities between religion and spirituality

10.6 Discuss cultural considerations for mindfulness, flow, and spirituality research and practice

Perhaps our favorite definition of *insanity* is "doing the same thing over and over again and expecting different results" (attributed to Albert Einstein and Benjamin Franklin). Why would we engage in the same behavior repeatedly if we know that the eventual outcome will be negative? Well, passive habits are easy to establish and hard to break (see Bargh & Chartrand, 2014). For example, many of us have done this more than once: scrolled through social media on our phones for hours and then wished we had those minutes back. That habitual, mind-numbing experience may have some short-lived, stress-relieving benefits, but it often distracts us from what matters in our lives. Mindless pursuit of less-than-meaningful goals or unchallenging ones can sometimes leave people feeling bored and empty. Mindlessness can even harm others, such as relying on stereotypes instead of getting to know someone different from us (Anālayo, 2020). Conversely, intentional, moment-to-moment searches for optimal experiences give us joy and fulfillment and allow us to have novel experiences (Langer & Ngnoumen, 2021). These positive pursuits may bring about sanity in daily life that is grounded in competence (Pagnini et al., 2016) and happiness (Allen et al., 2017; Hsu & Langer, 2013).

This chapter directs your attention to the moment-to-moment experiences that make up every day of our lives. We frame the discussion of **mindfulness**, flow, and **spirituality** as a search for optimal experiences. We believe that too many of us walk through everyday life unaware, eyes trained on our phones instead of taking in our surroundings. This often causes us to be out of sync with the significance of our experiences and our emotional selves. Hence, we need to learn more about the psychology of deeper living, a psychology with many applications that teaches about the depths of enjoyment, contentment, and meaningfulness that can be achieved through engagement with everyday life.

MINDFULNESS: IN SEARCH OF NOVELTY AND EMBRACING UNCERTAINTY

In a fast-paced, 21st-century world, it is easy to lose sight of the thousands of moments passing in front of our eyes. However, each of these moments is accessible (or can be captured) and has untapped potential. To test our contention that each moment of life is novel and potentially packed, try slowing down your day a bit by taking a stroll through a neighborhood . . . with a 3-year-old child! A 3-year-old (who is well rested and generally content) can turn a two-block walk into a grand adventure that lasts about five times longer than you expected. The typical child will attend to everything in their line of vision and will happily share thoughts about what is being experienced. When the next "moment" arrives (e.g., another child runs across the path), this child can move on to experience it without any "analysis paralysis" (i.e., "Should I attend to that or to this?"). Undoubtedly, sauntering through a neighborhood with a toddler will draw your attention to the slices of life that are there to be experienced. By adding a bit of intentionality to your belief that each moment has potential, we believe you can actively pursue a richer life experience.

Mindfulness as a State of Mind

One aspect of mindfulness is focusing one's attention intentionally on specific moments. Indeed, mindfulness meditative practices date back at least 2,500 years and are a feature of Hindu and Buddhist traditions. This said, there are some important differences between Westernized mindfulness and its use in the Buddhist tradition (Keng et al., 2011). Whereas in Westernized ideas of mindfulness, this construct may be studied independently, it is often viewed as only one component on the road to true enlightenment within Buddhism. In addition, mindfulness must be introspective in Buddhist teachings as opposed to more of an external awareness of surroundings in Western teachings (Keng et al., 2011).

Within Western psychology, mindfulness interventions (i.e., learning to be more mindful or engaging in mindful meditative practices) are a core component of many psychotherapy interventions (Karl & Fischer, 2022). A related body of research has integrated mindfulness into a broader view of holistic well-being and positive psychological characteristics. For these researchers, mindfulness can be conceptualized as the "general tendency of a person to show characteristics of non-judgmental awareness of present-moment experience in their everyday life" (Krägeloh, 2020, p. 64). One widely used measure of mindfulness as a trait is the Five Factor Mindfulness Questionnaire (FFMQ; Baer et al., 2006). Participants respond to 39 items covering five facets of mindfulness on a 1 (*never or very rarely true*) to five (*very or often always true*) scale: (1) Observing (e.g., "When I'm walking, I deliberately notice the sensations of my body moving), (2) Describing (e.g., "I'm good at finding words to describe my feelings"), (3) Acting with Awareness (e.g., "When I do things, my mind wanders off, and I'm easily distracted" [reverse scored]), (4) Non-judging (e.g., "I criticize myself for having irrational or inappropriate emotions" [reverse scored]), and (5) Nonreactivity (e.g., "I perceive my feelings and emotions without having to react to them"). Thus, mindfulness can be viewed as both a learnable skill and a measurable trait.

Ellen Langer, a social psychologist at Harvard University, is credited with being the "mother of mindfulness" and has examined mindfulness as both a skill and a trait. She argues that people engaged in mindfulness exhibit a certain state of mind. Moreover, she differentiates mindfulness from mindlessness. For example, Langer's (2009a) definition of mindfulness included the following:

> It is a flexible state of mind—an openness to novelty, a process of actively drawing novel distinctions. When we are mindful, we become sensitive to context and perspective; we are situated in the present. When we are mindless, we are trapped in rigid mind-sets, oblivious to context or perspective. When we are mindless, our behavior is rule and routine governed. In contrast, when mindful, our behavior may be guided rather than governed by rules and routines . . . mindfulness requires or generates novelty. (p. 214)

Thus, Langer (2009a) highlights how mindful attention is a search for novelty in our experiences, whereas mindlessness involves passively zoning out to everyday life. Indeed, being on "automatic pilot" is a form of mindlessness attributable to repeated behaviors. Some of you may have experienced this in an extreme form via highway hypnosis (Cerezuela et al., 2004). You are driving alone, and suddenly, you cannot recollect the last several miles. This can be very disconcerting. Finding the novelty in your surroundings as you drive, however, may prevent highway hypnosis from occurring.

Langer argues that identifying novel distinctions (being mindful) requires us (1) to overcome the desire to reduce uncertainty in daily life, (2) to override a tendency to engage in automatic behavior, and (3) to engage less frequently in evaluations of self, others, and situations (Langer & Ngnoumen, 2021). Regarding uncertainty, Langer and Ngnoumen (2021) argue that "aspects of our culture currently push us to try to reduce uncertainty" (p. 380). However, our desire to control our surroundings by reducing uncertainty often leads to more uncertainty. For example, a child's effort to hold a spirited kitten or puppy demonstrates this point well. The more the child attempts to hold the little pet still, the more it tries to wriggle away. This also happens in daily life when we attempt to hold things (and people's behavior) still in our attempt to reduce uncertainty. Given that life is not static, Langer and Ngnoumen (2021) contend that we should exploit the uncertainty. Specifically, they propose that mindfulness "makes clear that things change and loosens the grip of our evaluative mind-sets so that these changes need not be feared" (p. 380). In other words, uncertainty keeps us grounded in the present.

Embracing uncertainty also allows us to break out of automatic thought and behavioral patterns. For example, mindfulness may battle our evaluative nature and lead us to make fewer unnecessary judgments while encouraging in-the-moment adaptation to one's surroundings (Bercovitz et al., 2017; Pagnini et al., 2016). This trait can potentially assist with being in unfamiliar situations or being better at working with people who are different from you in some way—a valuable skill for today's world of work. For example, on a walk through a park, a statue may catch your eye and grab a few minutes of your attention. During that short span of time, you may mindfully make numerous observations that discriminate between weathered portions of the statue and less weathered portions, or you may notice that it looks taller from one perspective than another. There is no need or benefit for you to mindlessly activate your criteria for quality artwork and pass judgment on the statue, labeling it as either good art or bad art. The same is true for people. Noticing someone's skin color or gender or that they dress or talk a certain way does not need to lead to confirmation of stereotypes about the group to which a person belongs (Anālayo, 2020). Sometimes, there is also a push to ignore differences among people to avoid making judgments altogether. However, mindfulness shows us we can notice differences and similarities without judging the person.

Mindfulness as a Skill

Turning from Langer's (2009b) definitions and discussions of mindfulness, we consider a nuts-and-bolts operationalization of mindfulness that often is used by mindfulness meditation practitioners (Kabat-Zinn, 1990; Shapiro, 2009; Shapiro et al., 2002). In the practice community, mindfulness is parsimoniously described as attending nonjudgmentally to all stimuli in the internal and external environments. Jon Kabat-Zinn (1982, 2005) of the University of Massachusetts is widely credited as being the first to adapt ancient Eastern meditation practices into a deliverable intervention. Specifically, Kabat-Zinn created a form of mindfulness meditation that has been used in many successful mindfulness-based stress reduction (MBSR) programs (see Figure 10.1 for a simple, introductory example of mindfulness meditation instructions that I [McDermott] have been using for years for myself and my clients).

A traditional MBSR program is 8 weeks long with 2.5-hour weekly classes and a one-day full retreat, all taught by a certified trainer. MBSR teaches a variety of relaxation skills, including mindfulness meditation and a variety of stretching and posture techniques. While traditional MBSR is time consuming, aspects of the training have been adapted to fit specific population needs and time constraints. Indeed, some form of MBSR has become a standard offering at almost every college counseling center and has gained significant popularity in the medical field (Niazi & Niazi, 2011). MBSR and related programs may be especially helpful for individuals in high-stress fields or situations. For example, several researchers have found significant psychological benefits for MBSR among practicing nurses (Ghawadra et al., 2019) and other healthcare professionals (Kriakous et al., 2021).

In moments of mindfulness, some "mindfulness qualities" (Shapiro et al., 2002) come into consciousness (e.g., openness, acceptance, and empathy). Many of these qualities are positive psychological processes discussed elsewhere in this text. Thus, it is not surprising that mindfulness-based interventions have become popular in the practice community and have been used to

FIGURE 10.1 ■ Mindfulness Meditation Practice Steps

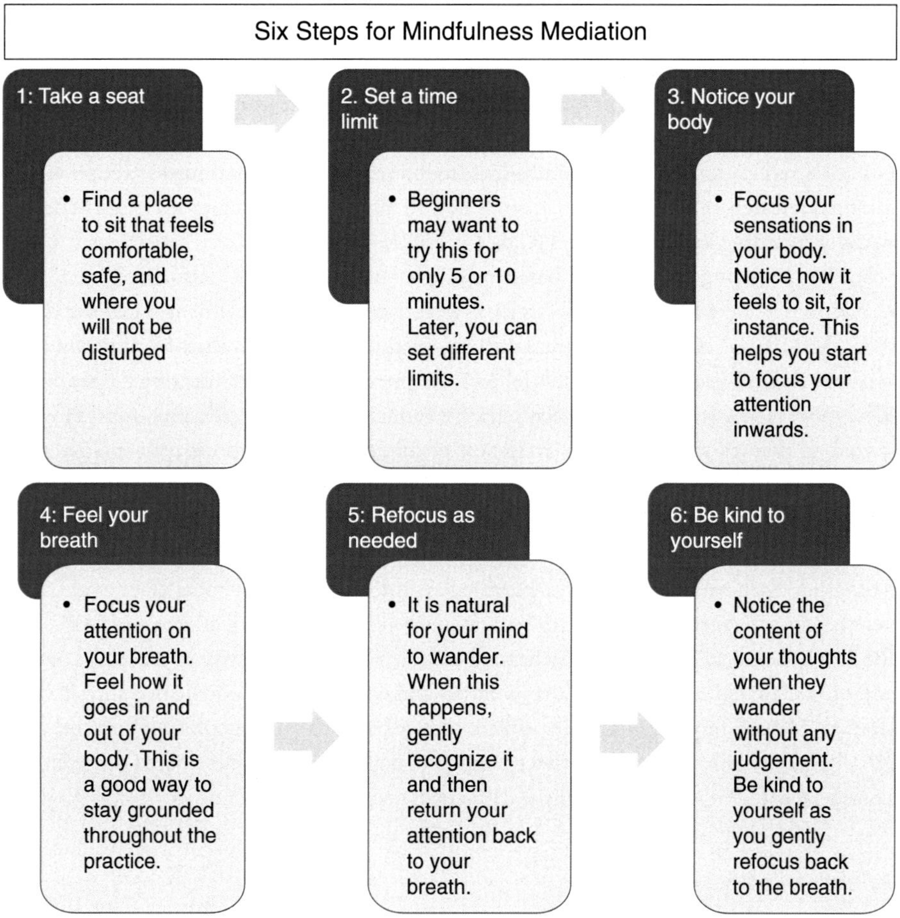

combat a variety of psychological problems such as chronic pain, insomnia, smoking cessation, work-related stress, and many more. This body of research was criticized in the past because few rigorous, randomized, controlled studies had been published (Bishop, 2002). However, more randomized clinical trials (RCTs) have been conducted today in the United States and worldwide. There is now a rich body of evidence supporting the psychological and health benefits of mindfulness meditation practices for a variety of issues and across a wide range of delivery methods (Bamber & Morpeth, 2019; Gong et al., 2016; Heckenberg et al., 2018; Hilton et al., 2017; Maglione et al., 2017; Millett et al., 2021). There are also several popular mobile applications to train individuals in mindfulness practices (Crandall et al., 2019), and some show psychological benefits if used correctly (Flett et al., 2019).

Although the benefits of mindfulness-based interventions are evident across a wide variety of RCTs, the positive effects range in size, and there is a great deal of heterogeneity in the findings (i.e., there are likely several moderating factors yet to be discovered). In one recent example,

Gál and colleagues (2021) examined data from 34 RCTs on the effectiveness of self-use mindfulness applications (i.e., published between 2015 and 2020). When compared to the control condition, they found that participants using mindfulness applications evidenced significant small to moderate decreases in depression and perceived stress. However, they also noted variability across studies and that the long-term effects of these applications were questionable, suggesting that certain variables may enhance the effectiveness and longevity of mindfulness-based meditation applications. Thus, as mindfulness mobile applications continue to gain popularity, additional research will be needed to identify how to make this technology even more effective, especially regarding long-term effects (Gál et al., 2021).

Studies involving mindfulness-based cognitive therapy (MBCT) also have led to positive discoveries. Like MBSR, MBCT is an 8-week, standardized treatment. However, unlike MBSR, MBCT was developed to attempt to hold depression at bay in cases of remission (Segal et al., 2002). This group intervention follows the premises of general cognitive therapy. The goal is to weaken associations between negative thoughts and depressive emotions. However, it differs in that it focuses more on awareness of thoughts and emotions than evaluating the legitimacy of these thoughts (Keng et al., 2011). Many beneficial outcomes have been observed through MBCT, including reductions in depressive relapse (Teasdale et al., 2000), decreasing depressive symptoms (Costa & Barnhofer, 2016; Williams et al., 2008), treating sexual dysfunction (Stephenson, 2017), and lessening symptoms of social phobia (Piet et al., 2010). Interestingly, in a recent systematic review and meta-analysis of the effectiveness of MBCT and MBSR in nonclinical samples, researchers noted that both were effective at reducing cognitive symptoms of anxiety and stress (e.g., rumination and worry) and improving overall well-being. However, MBCT produced stronger effects than MBSR on all outcomes (Querstret et al., 2020). MBCT and MBSR are just two examples of popular mindfulness-based programs. We recommend exploring these programs and practices and seeing which one works best for you.

Benefits of Mindfulness

Mindfulness meditation can be beneficial across the life span. Children, for example, report more feelings of calmness following a brief mindfulness practice (Nadler et al., 2017). In addition, Duncan and colleagues (2009) proposed a model of mindful parenting that includes "moment-to-moment awareness" (p. 255) of the parent–child relationship to interact with more compassion toward our children. This may be something that children start to internalize as well, as they have more exposure to mindfulness techniques through watching their parents cope with difficult situations. Researchers have also found that mindful adults are preferred by children, perhaps because of their more compassionate approach, and may have less self-devaluation following these interactions (Langer et al., 2012).

As you might guess, given the other benefits of mindfulness, there have been significant positive correlations between mindfulness and various types of well-being in a number of different situations. It is beyond the scope of this text to discuss every area of research related to mindfulness practices and traits. Indeed, a PsychInfo search for mindfulness returns more than 13,000 hits! Many of these studies examine how dispositional (i.e., trait) mindfulness moderates or mediates the links between other positive constructs and indicators of well-being. In a study looking at relationships between mindfulness, attachment, and well-being, for example, mindfulness played a moderating role in the connection between attachment and well-being, such that being a mindful person lessened the effects of insecure attachment on well-being (Davis et al., 2016) and relationship dissatisfaction (Zhou et al., 2022). Relatedly, other studies have found that mindfulness may also assist couples in dealing with high-conflict situations, with those higher in mindfulness having increased positive affect during conflict, allowing them to better cope with the circumstance (Laurent et al., 2016). This makes sense as a conflict can be viewed as a "novel experience" to some extent, and those more mindful may be better at adapting and changing direction if necessary, without a decrease in their positive affect.

Mindfulness may also assist with self-acceptance and reaction to stigma. In a study conducted in Singapore, a population of gender-nonconforming adults was sampled and measured on various characteristics. Gender nonconformity, or "the incongruence between the biological sex assigned at birth, and the socially prescribed gender role" (Keng & Liew, 2017, p. 615), is often associated with a lower well-being due to the stigma that is often aimed at this population. In the study by Keng and Liew (2017), however, it was found that mindfulness appeared to moderate the connections found between gender nonconformity and depression, anxiety, and other characteristics associated with lower well-being. This finding and others led the authors to state that "trait mindfulness [may have a role as] a protective factor against psychological distress" in this population (Keng & Liew, 2017, p. 626). A similar finding was discovered in a study looking at parents of children with Autism spectrum disorder (who are often the subjects of public stigma). In this study, trait mindfulness again appeared to buffer or protect these parents from depression, anxiety, and other negative emotions that might be felt as a result of stigma (Chan & Lam, 2017).

Although many studies suggest that trait mindfulness may explain (mediate) or condition (moderate) the links between other trait positive psychology constructs, we recommend caution when interpreting those findings. Studies suggesting a mediating or moderating role of mindfulness often rely on cross-sectional data. Such studies cannot adequately infer causality. Far fewer researchers have examined mindfulness longitudinally. For example, a PsychInfo search for longitudinal mindfulness research returned only about 350 hits. These studies are more rigorous and require more resources, so there are far fewer of them than cross-sectional studies.

In general, longitudinal studies support the benefits of trait mindfulness and mindfulness practices. For instance, in a study combining six different longitudinal studies in the U.S. military, researchers found evidence that mindfulness training protected soldiers from working memory problems, which can become imperiled in high-stress or high-demand situations common in military combat (Jha et al., 2021). However, the findings from longitudinal studies do not always match those from cross-sectional investigations. For instance, although many researchers have focused on mindfulness as an important mediating or moderating variable between various positive psychological characteristics and well-being in cross-sectional studies, one longitudinal study found a different set of casual relationships. Specifically, in a large longitudinal study examining the links between self-connection and meaning of life on well-being in a sample of 465 (predominantly White) men and women, Klussman and colleagues (2022) found that mindfulness may not be an intermediate variable filtering the effect of positive psychological characteristics into greater well-being. Instead, counter to what may be suggested via cross-sectional data; longitudinal analyses suggest that positive psychological characteristics may filter the effects of dispositional mindfulness into greater well-being over time (Klussman et al., 2022). Thus, the true mechanisms that explain the benefits of mindfulness are still up for debate, and more longitudinal research is needed going forward.

Mindfulness and Cultural Factors

As mindfulness-based therapies and treatments have become more common and popular, researchers are beginning to study their relevance and use across multiple populations. Research on this front has been somewhat mixed. For instance, Karl and colleagues (2020) examined trait mindfulness, as measured by the FFMQ, for measurement invariance across 16 different countries. They found that FFMQ scores appeared to be measuring a different construct in each culture. The FFMQ appeared to be better at measuring trait mindfulness in Western, individualistic cultures than in Eastern, collectivistic cultures. Indeed, Karl and colleagues cautioned against making conclusions about the generalization of mindfulness across cultures based on the FFMQ. Clearly, more research is needed to understand how culture shapes definitions, experiences, and expressions of mindfulness (Karl et al., 2022).

While cultural differences in mindfulness exist, this does not negate the benefits of mindfulness practices or trait mindfulness across cultures (Karl et al., 2022). Moreover, mindfulness may be important for the health and well-being of marginalized individuals within a culture. As some individuals in underserved populations (e.g., racial and ethnic minorities and/or those in lower socioeconomic status groups) might face a greater amount of adversity due to discrimination, acculturative stress, or poverty, mindfulness-based treatments may provide an excellent opportunity to enhance resilience and limit the negative impacts of those experiences. Indeed, some researchers suggest that mindfulness may be a protective factor against the negative health consequences of racism for Black college students (Zapolski et al., 2019) and may reduce the links between perceived discrimination and depression (Brown-Iannuzzi et al., 2014; Watson-Singleton et al., 2019).

Neurological Findings and Mindfulness

Much attention has been paid to the neuroscience behind mindfulness, particularly its neurological benefits (Chow et al., 2017; Tang & Posner, 2013). Improving mindfulness is related to better spatial abilities regardless of gender (Chiesa et al., 2011; Geng et al., 2011), increased ability for awareness (Jerath et al., 2012), and potential increased neuroplasticity in the brain (Berkovich-Ohana et al., 2012). To delineate clinical implications, some studies have mapped the neurological process of mindfulness, although there is no consistent agreement in this area. In neuroscience, emotional regulation is thought to occur in two distinct ways. A "top-down" approach to this is where cognitive reappraisal of a situation occurs to modulate the emotional impact of the stimulus; this contrasts with a "bottom-up" approach in which the base reaction to the stimulus is modulated without the need to cognitively reappraise and use higher order functioning (Chiesa et al., 2013). Researchers disagree on whether mindfulness follows a bottom-up or a top-down procedure, and research on controlled laboratory experiments suggests mindfulness skills may have a small (and somewhat unstable) effect on down-regulating negative emotions overall (Zangri et al., 2022). Thus, more research is needed to understand the cognitive mechanisms of mindfulness.

While investigators are still identifying the exact cognitive mechanisms of mindfulness, there may be less debate about how mindfulness operates at a neurological level. Using functional magnetic resonance imaging (fMRI) techniques, several studies suggest that individuals actively engaging in mindfulness meditation in the laboratory use frontal regions of the brain that govern focused attention to a greater extent than people not engaging in mindfulness meditation (Falcone & Jerram, 2018). This result is unsurprising, given that focused attention is critical to mindfulness meditation. However, one interesting finding from the fMRI literature is that there are significant differences in brain functioning between people who have practiced mindfulness meditation for a long time and those who are new to the process. Thus, the more you practice mindfulness, the more it may change your brain functioning over time (Falcone & Jerram, 2018).

Cultivating Mindfulness

The fostering and encouragement of mindfulness is something that many groups have been doing throughout history. In some Native American traditions (specifically Cherokee), the practice of *ayeli* is described as a "centering technique" that can be used to help individuals to become more mindful (Garrett et al., 2011; Garrett & Garrett, 2002). This practice involves breathing and meditation techniques that allow participants to sit in the moment and allow balance and integration to assist them in increasing personal wellness. A large part of this technique involves orienting oneself to value relations to other things.

It may be difficult for today's busy adults to find time for lengthy training on mindfulness, but less intense interventions may also be effective. In a study employing a brief online mindfulness training, researchers offered participants three different online modules: "Mindfulness in Daily Life," "Introduction to Mindfulness," and "Mindful Breathing and Walking" (Kemper, 2017). Most participants took all three 1-hour modules, and results showed that small but significant increases were found in mindfulness in this relatively short time. This may be one way to make small incremental changes in mindfulness quickly. In a second study, researchers found that even self-guided work on mindfulness via a workbook using Mindfulness-Based Stress Reduction (MBSR) techniques successfully reduced stress (Hazlett-Stevens & Oren, 2017). Again, this treatment may more easily fit into one's busy lifestyle but still delivers good results.

Mindfulness may also be of interest in looking at the development of what Thomas (2006) calls "cultural intelligence (CQ)" (p. 78). Speaking primarily of CQ's use in business settings, Thomas discusses mindfulness as a primary ingredient in developing this useful construct.

Similar in some ways to social intelligence (Kihlstrom & Cantor, 2000) and emotional intelligence (Goleman, 1995), Thomas defines CQ as "the ability to interact effectively with people who are culturally different" (p. 80). This concept views mindfulness as a link between behavior and knowledge that accounts for the ability to have awareness in the moment, which can assist one in achieving an effective cross-cultural interaction. This mindful behavior may be manifested in different ways, such as being aware of one's biases, noting context in various situations, and tuning in to different worldviews and perspectives as they may affect these interactions (Thomas, 2006). Thus, mindfulness may be a construct of particular use in our increasingly diverse society today.

Last, mindfulness is something that can be taught to children as well as adults. A number of studies have amassed in the past decade examining mindfulness interventions in children. In one study, children were encouraged to reflect moment to moment on various experiences. Results showed that children who were taught these strategies had better self-regulation skills and were also able to solve problems and think more creatively (Zelazo & Lyons, 2012). Other studies with children show that they report more feelings of "calmness" after learning mindfulness techniques (Nadler et al., 2017). Aggregate findings of the effectiveness of mindfulness-based interventions for children and adolescents paint a somewhat more nuanced picture; effectiveness may be conditional on other psychological and contextual factors. Nevertheless, evidence generally supports the short-term effectiveness of mindfulness training for children and adolescents (Chimiklis et al., 2018; Dunning et al., 2022; Odgers et al., 2020).

FLOW: IN SEARCH OF ABSORPTION

Flow experiences have been observed throughout time, across cultures, and in countless creative and competitive endeavors. Such experiences are vividly described in accounts of the responses of the world's great artists, scientists, and religious figures to the challenge of seemingly overwhelming tasks. For example, historical accounts suggest that Michelangelo worked on the Vatican's Sistine Chapel ceiling for days at a time. Totally absorbed in his work, he would go without food and sleep and push through discomfort until he ultimately passed out from exhaustion. He was consumed by work, neglecting self-care and the needs of others. (Legend says that Michelangelo went weeks without changing his clothes, including his boots. One of his assistants supposedly observed the skin of his foot peel down as a boot was removed.)

Mihaly Csikszentmihalyi was intrigued by the stories about artists who lost themselves in their work. Studying the creative process in the 1960s (Getzels & Csikszentmihalyi, 1976), Csikszentmihalyi was struck by the fact that, when work on a painting was going well, the artist persisted single-mindedly, disregarding hunger, fatigue, and discomfort—yet rapidly lost interest in the artistic creation once it had been completed (Nakamura & Csikszentmihalyi, 2009, p. 195). Csikszentmihalyi (1975/2000) also noted that forms of play (e.g., chess, rock climbing) and work (e.g., performing surgery, landing a plane) often produced similar states of engagement. Over several decades, Csikszentmihalyi has interviewed and observed thousands of people, which has informed the concept of a flow state.

The Flow State

Decades of qualitative and quantitative research (Nakamura & Csikszentmihalyi, 2021) have explored the underpinnings of intrinsic motivation. Indeed, psychology has grappled with the issue of why people pursue specific goals with great fervor in the absence of external rewards (e.g., money and praise). Csikszentmihalyi (e.g., 1975/2000, 2015) examined this issue to understand "the dynamics of momentary experience and the conditions under which it is optimal" (Nakamura & Csikszentmihalyi, 2021, p. 282). Csikszentmihalyi conducted extensive interviews of people from many walks of life; he also developed and used the **experience sampling method**, in which research participants are equipped with programmable watches, phones, or handheld computers that signal them at preprogrammed times throughout the day, to complete a measure describing the moment at which they were paged. To date, the conditions of flow appear to be remarkably similar across work settings, play settings, and cultures. These conditions of flow include (1) perceived challenges or opportunities for action that stretch (neither too easy nor overwhelming) existing personal skills and (2) clear proximal goals and immediate feedback about progress.

Many of Csikszentmihalyi's early research participants described their optimal momentary experiences as being "in flow." Based on the early interviews, Csikszentmihalyi (1975/2000) mapped out the landscape of deep flow experiences by graphically representing the relationship between perceived challenges and skills. Three regions of momentary experiences were identified: (1) *flow*, where challenges and skills matched; (2) *boredom*, where challenges and opportunities were too easy relative to skills; and (3) *anxiety*, where demands increasingly exceeded capacities for action (see Figure 10.2).

FIGURE 10.2 ■ The Original Model of the Flow State

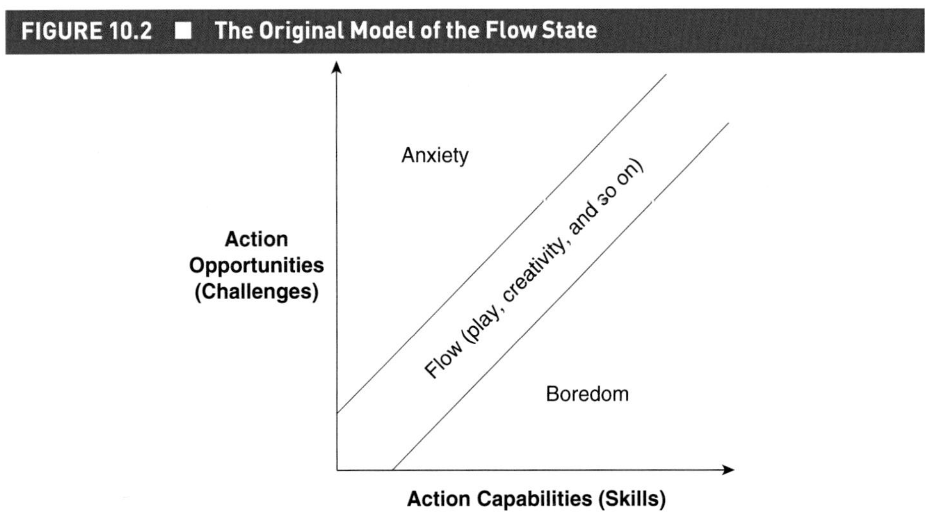

From Csikszentmihalyi, M., *Flow: The psychology of optimal experience.* Copyright © 1990 by Mihaly Csikszentmihalyi.

Under the flow conditions of perceived challenge to skills, clear goals, and feedback on progress, experience unfolds from moment to moment, and the subjective state that emerges has the following characteristics (as listed in Nakamura & Csikszentmihalyi, 2021):

- Intense and focused concentration on what one is doing in the present moment
- Merging of action and awareness
- Loss of reflective self-consciousness (i.e., loss of awareness of oneself as a social actor)
- A sense that one can control one's actions; that is, a sense that one can deal with the situation because one knows how to respond to whatever happens next
- Distortion of temporal experience (typically, a sense that time has passed faster than normal)
- Experience of the activity as intrinsically rewarding, such that often the end goal is just an excuse for the process

The search for absorption in momentary experiences is primarily an intentional attentional process. Intense concentration is dedicated to the present activity, followed by the merging of action and awareness. The loss of self-consciousness occurs as flow emerges. Maintaining the flow state is quite challenging given the many distractions from the outside world and the self-talk that may involve criticism of performance. (Hence, a mindful, nonjudgmental approach to personal performance may be necessary for achieving deep flow.) When considering the quality of a flow state, the variable of interest is time spent absorbed, with more engagement in flow being better for the individual.

The conceptualization of flow has not changed much over the past quarter century of research. The model of balancing perceived challenge and skill has been refined, however, by Delle Fave, Massimini, and colleagues (Delle Fave & Massimini, 1988, 1992), who, by using the experience sampling method, discovered that the quality of a momentary experience intensifies as challenges and skills move beyond a person's *average* levels. For example, if you play chess with a typical 6-year-old, the experience will not present you with an average or above-average challenge that requires higher-level skills. If you play chess with someone with considerably more experience and skill, however, you experience a great challenge, your skills will be stretched, and flow is more likely. See Figure 10.2 for a depiction of a flow model that considers these flow characteristics. Apathy is experienced when perceived challenges and skills are below a person's average levels; when they are above, flow is experienced. The intensity (depicted by the concentric rings) of each experience (e.g., anxiety, arousal, relaxation) increases with distance from a person's average levels of challenge and skill. In addition, interest in the particular activity in which the person is engaging also appears to play a role. Some researchers suggest that interest in the task should "be considered as a precondition for the appearance of flow" (Bricteux et al., 2017). A person, for example, who does not enjoy chess may have a more difficult time gaining a flow state even if their skill level is high enough to theoretically mean that they should be able to be in flow. This makes sense in your personal experience of flow as well, perhaps. You may recall being skilled at a particular task but dislike it, thus finding it tedious. On the other hand, you may be able to reach a flow state quickly when the task is something that also interests you.

A large body of research conducted on flow has focused on experiences during sport. Many have described golfers, basketball players, soccer players, and more who seem to lose time as they play, later reporting reductions in conscious attention to what they are doing and almost effortless ability to anticipate what is coming in their game (Bruya, 2010). The "effortless" piece has been questioned, as neuroimaging studies seem to tell a different story (Ulrich et al., 2016). Some researchers have posited that perhaps better controlled and more efficient attention occurs during flow as opposed to a complete decoupling from attention, even though this may feel "effortless" (Harris et al., 2017). This research has exciting implications, particularly concerning training that could hone one's focus and attention to experience flow (Harris et al., 2017).

Research on flow experiences domains other than sport, such as general flow experiences or other domain-specific experiences (e.g., work or education), continues to evolve. One tricky question is how to best measure a flow experience. Nakamura and Csikszentmihalyi (2021) describe several ways these experiences are assessed in the research literature, including self-report questionnaires, experimental manipulations, and experience sampling (i.e., repeatedly assessing participants multiple times per day or per week). However, each of these approaches may have some drawbacks. For instance, checking in with individuals about whether they are having a flow state inevitably runs the risk of interrupting the flow state (Nakamura & Csikszentmihalyi, 2021). Likewise, self-report questionnaires ask individuals to reflect on their flow experiences, but those experiences may not always generalize to different people. Despite some limitations in terms of generalizability, self-report measures of flow experiences are the most common approach to studying the construct (de Moura & Porto Bellini, 2020). Indeed, researchers have created several instruments to assess flow experiences in a variety of domains including during physical activities (Jackson & Eklund, 2002), at work (Bakker, 2008), and in adult education (Heutte et al., 2021).

The Autotelic Personality

Most flow research has focused on flow states and the dynamics of momentary optimal experiences via self-report questionnaires. However, Csikszentmihalyi (1975/2000) hypothesized that a cluster of personality variables (e.g., curiosity, persistence, low self-centeredness) may be associated with the ability to achieve flow and with the quality of flow that is experienced. This suggests the possible existence of an **autotelic personality** (from the Greek words *autos*, meaning "self," and *telos*, meaning "end"), as exhibited by a person who enjoys life and "generally does things for [their] own sake, rather than in order to achieve some later external goal" (Csikszentmihalyi, 1997, p. 117). The amount of time spent in flow has been used as a rough measure of this personality type (Hektner, 1996), but this operationalization does not account for possible environmental influences on flow. A more nuanced operationalization of the autotelic personality focused on the disposition to be intrinsically motivated in high-challenge, high-skill situations. (Csikszentmihalyi et al., 1993).

FIGURE 10.3 ■ The Current Model of the Flow State

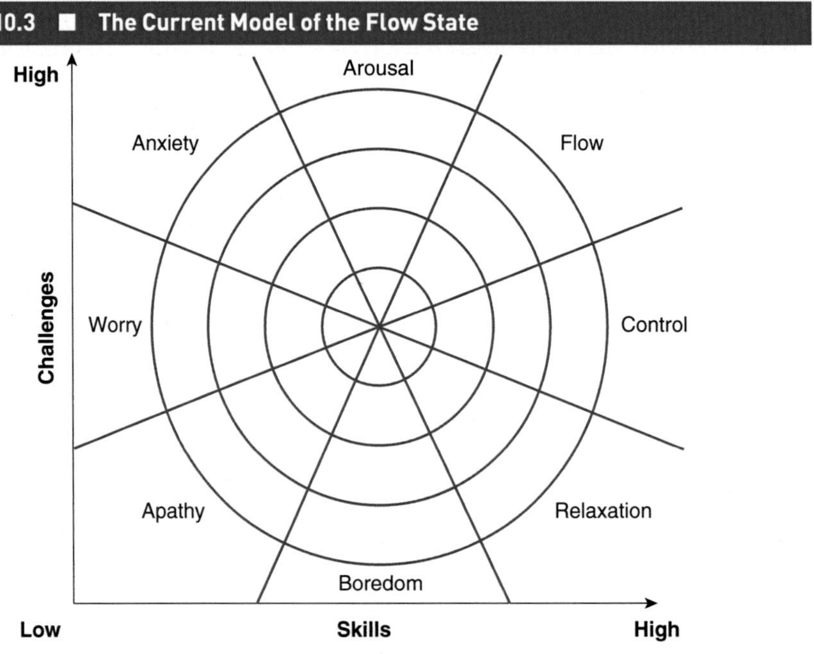

Adapted from Csikszentmihalyi, M., *Finding flow.* Copyright © 1997 by Mihalyi Csikszentmihalyi. Reprinted by permission of Basic Books, a member of Perseus Books, L.L.C.

The autotelic personality in teenagers in the United States appears to be related to positive and affective states and the quality of personal goal statements (Adlai-Gail, 1994). In a sample of adults in the United States, Abuhamdeh (2000) found that, compared to people who do not have autotelic personality characteristics, those with these characteristics prefer high-action-opportunity. These high-skill situations stimulate them and encourage growth. Furthermore, people with the autotelic personality appear to experience little stress when in the flow quadrant (see Figure 10.3), whereas the reverse is true for adults without these characteristics. While comparatively fewer researchers have focused on the autotelic personality compared to other aspects of flow, some investigators continue to refine the definition. For example, Baumann (2021) argues that implicit achievement motivation (i.e., finding a sense of personal purpose in a particular task) may be the most important aspect of an autotelic personality.

Cultural Comparisons and Considerations in the Flow Experience

Although flow has been studied more often in Western contexts (Moneta, 2004a), some cross-cultural differences have been found in looking at various groups. Moneta (2004b) found that Chinese students in Hong Kong did not experience flow by the optimal challenge/skill conditions that Csikszentmihalyi's (1975/2000) model found in Western populations; instead, these participants preferred skill level to be higher than challenge level. They evaluated high-challenge situations negatively, which Moneta (2004b) postulates could be because of this culture's higher values of prudence (among other traits). Similarities have also been found across cultures.

Asakawa (2004) investigated autotelic personality and flow experience in general in Japanese college students and found that Csikszentmihalyi's (1975/2000) flow model was a good fit for these individuals (i.e., high challenge plus high skill produced flow experiences as in Western samples). In 2010, Asakawa found that Japanese college students who were more autotelic and had more flow experiences also scored higher on measures of self-esteem, scored lower on scales measuring anxiety, and had better coping strategies (Asakawa, 2010). Factors that seemed to contribute to flow included college engagement (including academic work and college life in general) and were positively linked to more frequency of the flow experience. In addition, these Japanese participants scored higher in *Jujitsu-kan,* a Japanese concept meaning possession of a sense of fulfillment. Finally, in this study, Japanese individuals experienced flow far less often than in data collected with U.S. and German participants. More research in this area is necessary to fully understand how flow may work in non-Western and non-majority cultural groups (Asakawa, 2010; Ishimura & Kodama, 2006). Again, this contributes to our understanding of how context and cultural values may dictate the necessary circumstances to achieve an actual flow state.

Another interesting finding is what may serve to *prevent* the experience of flow in some individuals. Guizzo and Cadinu (2017) conducted a study in which they investigated the experience of flow for men versus women while attempting to provoke feelings of sexual objectification. Specifically, participants were asked to perform a particular task while a counterfeit of the opposite sex took body pictures of them. Women who had a higher internalization of beauty ideals were found to perform worse while under "the male gaze" and reported less flow experience as well. These results were not found in the male participants. This research provides essential information about the impact of sexual objectification on women and the adverse effects of internalized beauty ideals. In a study conducted in Australia with female college students, participants reported as many as one instance of sexual objectification every 2 days, and they noticed other women being exposed to unwanted sexual gazing on average 1.5 times per day (Holland et al., 2017). If so many women report experiences of the male gaze or objectification daily, more investigation and education are needed on these important topics (Speight & Vera, 2004; Szymanski et al., 2011). In our evolving climate for less tolerance of sexual harassment in the United States (e.g., the MeToo movement), we can have some hope that flow can be experienced more often by more individuals.

Neurological Research on Flow

Some researchers have been working to better understand how flow is instigated and sustained and have turned to neurological studies to illuminate this connection. Researchers have established that there appears to be a heritable component to flow, although it is moderate—specifically, identical twins had approximately a .30 concordance (de Manzano et al., 2013). When investigating which parts of the brain appear to be involved, they have found that the release of dopamine seems key to the flow experience and that this may be one of the reasons flow feels rewarding (de Manzano et al., 2013; Gyurkovics et al., 2016). In addition, some brain areas that control impulses and attention are also involved in a flow state (Ulrich et al., 2016). Consistent with the assertion that flow depends on being intrinsically motivated for a specific task (Baumann, 2021), some research suggests that flow is most evident via fMRI when individuals are intrinsically motivated (Huskey et al., 2018).

More research is being done in this area, but such findings are exciting in several ways. First, because if only a moderate level of concordance exists in identical twins concerning flow, there is much reason to believe that flow can be nurtured and enhanced and, second, because more neurological research might allow us to better understand how flow can be better explicated in its many domains (Cheron, 2016; Gyurkovics et al., 2016) and to identify what variables may explain a personal disposition to experience flow (Baumann, 2021; Huskey et al., 2018).

Fostering Flow and Its Benefits

According to the flow model, experiencing absorption provides intrinsic rewards that encourage persistence and return to an activity. Hence, skills related to that activity might be enhanced over time. Therefore, the goal of intervention researchers interested in the applications of flow is to help people identify those activities that give them flow and encourage them to invest their attention and energies in these activities.

Flow researchers (e.g., Csikszentmihalyi, 1990, 1997; Csikszentmihalyi & Robinson, 1990; Jackson & Csikszentmihalyi, 1999; Nakamura & Csikszentmihalyi, 2009; Perry, 1999) have assisted people in their search for absorption by describing two paths to becoming more engaged with daily life: (1) finding and shaping activities and environments that are more conducive to flow experiences and (2) identifying personal characteristics and attentional skills that can be tweaked to make flow more likely.

Work is a common place for many individuals to experience maximum flow (de Moura & Porto Bellini, 2020), especially when the skill level required for this work is at an optimum level (Bricteux et al., 2017). In addition, when flow is more often experienced at work, higher well-being is reported (Ilies et al., 2017), and more on-the-job coping (with stress, etc.) is more commonly used (Rivkin et al., 2016). In consultation practices, Csikszentmihalyi has modified numerous work environments to increase the chances of producing flow. For example, Csikszentmihalyi worked with the Swedish police to identify obstacles to flow in their daily work routines and make their work more conducive to flow on the beat. (Specifically, officers were encouraged to walk the beat alone occasionally, rather than with their partners, to become more absorbed in their work.) Flow principles have also been incorporated into the design of workplaces and into the organization of displays at art venues, including those at the J. Paul Getty Museum in Southern California, to increase the enjoyment of visits to these sites, and certain parts of the artistic process in general (e.g., sketching) may help to induce flow experiences (Cseh et al., 2016).

Several clinical researchers (e.g., Bassi & Delle Fave, 2016; Inghilleri, 1999) have used the experience sampling method and flow principles to help individuals discover and sustain flow. Using the experience sampling method provides feedback on momentary experiences and identifies activities and environments in which optimal experience can be increased. Perhaps the best application of flow principles has occurred at the Key School in Indianapolis, Indiana, where the goal is to foster flow by influencing both the environment and the individual (Whalen,

1999). In the school's Flow Activities Center, students have regular opportunities to actively choose and engage in activities related to their interests and then pursue these activities without demands or distractions, creating what has been described as "serious play" (Csikszentmihalyi et al., 1993). In support of students' searches for absorption, teachers encourage students to challenge and stretch themselves; teachers also provide new challenges to the children to foster growth. (See the Personal Mini-Experiments for a flow experiment and the Life Enhancement Strategies for tips for enhancing flow within the domains of your life.)

Newer Areas of Investigation Involving Flow: Gaming and Internet Use

The use of the Internet for social media, gaming, and other functions is relevant to flow in numerous contexts. Many people, from professionals to adolescents and children, spend hours online engaging in technological pursuits. While some of these activities may have purposes (e.g., doing research for a school paper or investigating ratings of elementary schools), many people seem to spend time on their devices just to be online. Those who study digital gaming have proposed that the flow state is experienced by some during this type of activity (Boyle et al., 2012; Procci et al., 2012; Sherry, 2004). This same conclusion has been drawn by some who study Internet shopping and browsing behavior (Hsu et al., 2012). Those who engage in these activities report a loss of awareness of time, the desire to keep playing despite physical discomfort, and the experience of action and awareness merging (Procci et al., 2012). However, one distinction that has been made in this literature is that flow is described as a *constructive* or *beneficial* construct. As some of these Internet-related behaviors may take on an almost addiction-like quality, perhaps those engaging in them cannot accurately be described as experiencing flow in the way Csikszentmihalyi describes it (Thatcher et al., 2008; Voiskounsky, 2010). More research and better measurement are needed here (Procci et al., 2012), and future developments may help to clarify this distinction. For example, researchers recently developed a self-report measure of flow experiences while gaming (Cai et al., 2022) that may hold promise for future research.

SPIRITUALITY: IN SEARCH OF THE SACRED

The term *search for the sacred* is a widely accepted description of spirituality. (Religion and religious behaviors represent how the search for the sacred becomes organized and sanctioned in society, such as attending religious services and the frequency and duration of prayer.) In 2000, Hill et al. defined spirituality as "the feelings, thoughts, and behaviors that arise from a search for the sacred" (p. 66). Pargament and Mahoney (2009/2017) also defined spirituality "as a search for the sacred." They elaborated that "people can take a virtually limitless number of pathways in their attempts to discover, conserve, and transform the sacred" (p. 612). These pathways to the sacred also may be described as spiritual strivings, which include personal goals associated with the ultimate concerns of purpose, ethics, and recognition of the transcendent (Emmons et al., 1998). However, this link sometimes becomes weaker when mediators of this relationship are investigated (Holland et al., 2016).

Psychology researchers agree with the foregoing definitions of spirituality, and there is general support for the belief that spirituality is a positive state of mind experienced by most people. Peterson and Seligman (2004) contend that spirituality is a strength of transcendence, stating, "Although the specific content of spiritual beliefs varies, all cultures have a concept of an ultimate, transcendent, sacred, and divine force" (p. 601). Similarly, Pargament and Mahoney (2009/2017) argue that spirituality is a vital part of society and psychology within the United States:

> First, spirituality is a "cultural fact" (cf. Shafranske & Malony, 1990): The vast majority of Americans believe in God (95%), believe that God can be reached through prayer (86%), and feel that religion is important or very important to them (86%) (Gallup Organization, 1995; Hoge, 1996). Second, in a growing empirical body of literature, the important implications of spirituality for a number of aspects of human functioning are being noted . . . There are, in short, some very good reasons why psychologists should attend more carefully to the spiritual dimension of peoples' lives. (p. 647)

The statistics cited by Pargament and Mahoney (2009/2017) are outdated at this point. More recent survey data suggest that the percentage of individuals identifying as religious has declined in recent decades (about 65% of respondents in the United States reported that religion played an important part in their lives; Pew Research Center, 2022). This said, despite widespread agreement on the definition of what it means to be "religious," psychological researchers and the general public continue to muddy the waters when discussing spirituality. For example, Peterson and Seligman's (2004) Values in Action Classifications of Strengths lumped spirituality with similar, yet different, concepts such as religion and faith. Although many think of the two as the same, many within the United States describe themselves as spiritual but not religious (Sperry, 2016). Sperry (2016) and others call this concept "secular spirituality" (p. 221). The fuzziness of the construct undermines efforts to understand the actual effects of searching for the sacred on a person's functioning.

THE TRUE BENEFITS OF SPIRITUALITY?

Many positive psychologists (e.g., Lopez & Snyder, 2009; Peterson & Seligman, 2004) have hypothesized that our search for the sacred enhances a deep understanding of ourselves and our lives. Indeed, as noted previously, spirituality is associated with mental health, managing substance abuse, marital functioning, parenting, coping, and mortality (summarized in Pargament & Mahoney, 2009/2017; Thoresen et al., 2001). One examination of spiritual strivings reveals that these pathways to the sacred may lead to (or at least are associated with) well-being (Emmons et al., 1998). Although much research in this area has been conducted with individuals who identify with a variety of Christian religions, the same links have been found between religiosity and happiness in other Western religions, such as Islam (Ghorbani et al., 2016; Sahraian et al., 2013). Better overall mental health may be another benefit, although the function of spirituality in a cultural context is important to distinguish here (Dein et al., 2012). In a 2017 study with a very culturally diverse sample, researchers investigated several different positive constructs in terms of their effect on mental health. They found that despite different cultural definitions of "spirituality" as a construct among the group, those who reported "living in accordance with one's spiritual values" were correlated with better mental health (Moore, 2017, p. 21). Another examination of spiritual strivings suggests that the search for the sacred may lead to what we consider to be the actual benefits of spirituality in our lives: purpose and meaning (Mahoney et al., 2005). Finally, a higher level of spiritual commitment may increase hope and optimism (over and above variance predicted by personality measures; Ciarrocchi et al., 2008) and may help in successful aging (Ahmad & Khan, 2016; Tomás et al., 2016).

Despite the findings demonstrating the benefits of searching for the sacred, the mechanisms by which spirituality leads to positive life outcomes are unclear. Other studies show no link between spirituality and well-being or other positive constructs. In a study looking at direct and indirect connections between spirituality and mental and physical health, researchers found neither direct nor indirect links between these types of health and spirituality. However, when looking at social health (i.e., having a perceived healthy level of social interaction), some links were found between this construct and a moderate level of spirituality (Cragun et al., 2016). As one's religious affiliation got more intense in this sample, however, some of the social facets of participating in a religious community became less common and thus the correlation disappeared. One interesting feature in this study, which may partly explain these results, is that the researchers used a measure specifically designed not to conflate spirituality and well-being. In some scales designed to measure spirituality, questions such as "I experience joy from my prayers" assume a positive connection between spirituality and well-being that might provide misleading results (Garssen et al., 2016). In other studies, links between spirituality and well-being were found, but the connection was completely mediated by a third variable: a sense of community (Ng & Fisher, 2016). However, this sample was collected in Hong Kong, so the potential effects of the collectivism present in that culture may be partially at work. In any case, the links between spirituality and well-being may be more nuanced than we have previously thought, and more research would be beneficial (Cragun et al., 2016; Garssen et al., 2021; Tong, 2017).

Other research shows that spirituality and religiosity may be particularly beneficial in times of strife or when coping is necessary. Links have been found between these constructs and better coping in patients dealing with schizophrenia (Mohr et al., 2011), struggling with cancer (George & Park, 2017; Holt et al., 2011; Lai et al., 2017; LoPresti et al/, 2016), dealing with chronic illness (Biccheri et al., 2016; Dalmida et al., 2012; Harvey & Cook, 2010), living with chronically ill children (Allen & Marshall, 2010), dealing with trauma (Gubkin, 2016; Santoro et al., 2016), and taking care of elders (Koerner et al., 2013). Some research also looks at its benefits in aging and care. Many clinicians and practitioners advocate for more training focused on treating clients with various issues. Some, like Sperry (2016), are focused mainly on the idea of secular spirituality and promote the idea of helping clients to develop self-transcendence as a part of treatment, while others advocate for information about more traditional ideas of religiosity and spirituality to be included in training as a part of cultural competence (Currier et al., 2022). Many clinical researchers offer suggestions for what may be included in a training program (for example, see Currier et al., 2022; Vieten et al., 2016).

Spirituality and Cultural Context

Spirituality may be useful in therapeutic treatment in many cultural groups—for example, Black (Alawiyah et al., 2011; Boyd-Franklin, 2010) and Latinx American (Koerner et al., 2013) individuals. Research investigating women of color dealing with postpartum depression found that spirituality played a strong role in helping Black and Latinx mothers to think differently about various stressors, particularly those that often contribute to postpartum depression (Keefe et al., 2016). In addition, a study looking at religiosity and spirituality in Black urban youth showed that religious and spiritual beliefs appeared to help inspire stronger academic goals, participation, and achievement in general (Holland, 2016). Similarly, emergent research suggests that spirituality and religious participation may be especially important for Black Americans' relational health and well-being (Balkin et al., 2022).

It is important to consider spirituality broadly when interpreting these results and when looking to implement various strategies to help individuals gain from the reported benefits of spirituality. In American Indian culture, for example, spirituality may take many forms and look very different in some ways from Christianity or other organized religions. Nevertheless, involvement in spiritual life benefited American Indian youth in a sample of adolescents from several different acculturation levels (Kulis et al., 2016). Remembering that culture influences the definitions of various positive constructs can help us find benefits across groups.

Race and ethnicity are not the only cultural facets to consider when thinking about spirituality and religion. Individuals with low socioeconomic status who are also religious show better physical health and higher well-being than expected given their environments (Steffen, 2012). It is also important not to give in to stereotypes regarding "who" we think of as religious, spiritual, or not involved in these beliefs. We might think of individuals within the LGBTQ community, for example, as having less conservative religious beliefs (Barrow & Kuvalanka, 2011), but "[LGBTQ individuals] report praying as frequently as heterosexuals; further, gay and lesbian-identified individuals attend religious services at the same rates as heterosexual men" (Rostosky et al., 2017, p. 437). Similar correlations are found in some LGBTQ individuals and their families between spirituality in general and some psychological and health benefits (Rostosky et al., 2017) but may also cause problems concerning these same areas depending on the way religion is perceived and feelings about potential negative religious rhetoric that can be aimed at LGBTQ individuals (Garrett-Walker & Torres, 2017). Along this same vein, much of what is reported on and researched within the United States with regard to religiousness is based on Judeo-Christian religions. Research is beginning to be more common with other groups as well, however, and several studies discussing Muslim individuals and their connection to spirituality and religion have been conducted. As with other groups, spirituality can benefit Muslim individuals in several ways, including healthier aging (Ahmad & Khan, 2016) and better adjustment (Ghorbani et al., 2016).

The Neural Circuitry of Spirituality

Over the past few decades, researchers have paid more attention to neurological aspects of spirituality and religion. Using brain imaging techniques, for example, the underlying mechanisms by which spiritual and religious practices influence the body begin taking shape. However, there is still much left to learn and many methodological hurdles to overcome

(McClintock et al., 2019; Newberg, 2014). Some brain regions associated with focused attention activated via mindfulness meditation are also activated during spiritual meditative practices (Barnby et al., 2015). However, across a series of studies summarized by McClintock and colleagues (2019), individuals with high self-reported spirituality may be biologically protected from stress or trauma in unique ways, as evidenced by decreased activity in brain regions traditionally activated during a stress response (e.g., hippocampus, brain stem, ventral striatum, and thalamus) (McClintock et al., 2019). Additionally, researchers recently discovered a possible "neural circuit" for spirituality and religion using a dataset of individuals with brain lesions. Across two independent samples of patients with brain lesions, Ferguson and colleagues (2022) found evidence that spirituality and religiosity may be linked to a brain circuit centered on the periaqueductal gray. This brainstem region is associated with fear conditioning, pain modulation, and altruistic behavior. Moreover, lesions in this area corresponded with self-report measures of religiosity. While researchers have only skimmed the surface about how our brain functions when we search for the sacred, these findings suggest that variation in self-report measures of religion and spirituality may be traced back to variation in brain functioning.

RESEARCHER SPOTLIGHT: STUDYING THE PSYCHOLOGY OF RELIGION AND SPIRITUALITY WITH JOSEPH CURRIER

I (McDermott) sat down with a prolific researcher in the psychology of religion and spirituality, Dr. Joseph Currier, at the University of South Alabama to get an insider's perspective of what it is like to do this work.

Dr. Joseph Currier
Courtesy of Joseph Currier

How long have you been studying the psychology of religion and spirituality, and what got you interested in the subject? What are you most proud of about this work to date?

My research has squarely focused on the applied psychology of religion and spirituality (R/S) for almost 15 years. Dating back to adolescence, I have long been intellectually fascinated by the intersection between religion, spirituality, and mental health. Also, while I certainly experience my doubts and struggles with faith, Christianity has long had a powerful role in shaping my identity and vocation as a psychologist.

However, as a scholar and researcher, I was initially hesitant to study the psychology of R/S. Under the mentorship of Robert Neimeyer, I was initially focused on understanding facilitators and processes by which people make meaning of bereavement and trauma. Drawing on a variety of qualitative and quantitative methods, we learned from bereaved parents, survivors of suicide and other tragic events that many people turn to R/S for resilience, healing, and transformation. As such, much of my research has attempted to illumine the possible strengths and resources R/S can provide in the aftermath of trauma and how to translate this knowledge into clinical practice. Whether focusing on specific beliefs, practices, or relationships related to R/S, I have collaborated with amazing colleagues and students over the years to advance scientific knowledge along these lines.

What is one moment from your clinical or research work that really stands out to you as a good example of the positive psychology of religion and/or spirituality?

About a decade ago, I partnered closely with Dr. Kent Drescher, a mentor and former Presbyterian Pastor who was serving as the lead psychologist in a VA PTSD residential treatment program, to include the Brief Multidimensional Measure of Religiousness and Spirituality in intake, discharge, and follow-up assessments over a multiyear period. Focusing on over 500 veterans with PTSD who completed the program, we found those who with more engagement in prayer and other R/S practices, organizational religiousness, positive religious coping, and daily spiritual experiences at pretreatment actually experienced greater reductions in PTSD symptoms over the course of their treatment (Currier et al., 2015). Also, we found these same adaptive dimensions of R/S were highly predictive of well-being (Currier et al., 2016). Specifically, even though many of these veterans had experienced unspeakable traumas in Vietnam and other service eras, R/S beliefs, practices, and relationships appeared to strengthen enjoyment and meaning in life in many ways.

I understand Division 36, Society for the Psychology of Religion and Spirituality, of the American Psychological Association is working on a set of best practice guidelines for spiritual and religious populations. Why do you think psychologists need such guidance at this time, and what do you think is an important thing for aspiring psychologists to know/think about if they are interested in the psychology of religion and spirituality?

Led by Drs. Cassandra Vieten and Kari O'Grady, APA Division 36 recently commissioned a task force to develop Professional Practice Guidelines for addressing R/S in professional psychology. Along with about 20 other colleagues working in this area, we identified six guidelines that every psychologist will ideally aspire to in their professional endeavors. For example, we believe that psychologists will ideally possess knowledge about the interrelated but distinct associations between R/S and how these core areas of diversity may affect mental health. Second, psychologists should be self-aware about their own R/S background and how their own worldview or lived experiences with R/S might influence or bias internal reactions to clients. Third, psychologists should understand ways R/S might support resilience, recovery, and well-being and incorporate these possible strengths and resources in their interventions when clinically indicated and acceptable to a given client. Fourth, we also hope that psychologists will be able to identify and address ways that dimensions of a person's R/S might cause harm, and interfere with or hinder their resilience, recovery, and well-being. Fifth, we hope that psychologists cultivate the necessary awareness, knowledge, and skill to discuss or inquire about peoples' R/S in their assessment, case formulation, and treatment planning process. Last, just as psychologists should partner with other healthcare professionals, we hope they will be willing to collaborate with clergy and other faith leaders when such collaborative care may benefit their clients.

Finally, you've successfully secured external funding from the John Templeton Foundation, a philanthropic organization dedicated to studying virtues, religion, spirituality, and other positive psychological constructs. What funded work are you doing right now, and where do you hope to go in the future?

We were recently awarded a 3-year grant from the John Templeton Foundation to promote training in R/S competencies that we call the "Spiritual and Religious Competencies Project." This project's impetus is to improve mental health care by ensuring that psychologists and other mental health professionals cultivate the foundational awareness, knowledge, and skills to attend to spiritual and/or religious aspects of peoples' lives. Focusing on disciples providing most of the mental health services in the United States (counseling, marriage and family therapy, psychology, and social work), we are seeking to increase spiritually competent care via five aims: (1) generating strategies and tools for defining, studying, and assessing R/S competencies; (2) establishing effective methods of promoting R/S competencies in graduate and postgraduate training; (3) understanding graduate faculty views, experiences, supports, and barriers related to training R/S competencies across these disciplines; (4) synergizing diverse stakeholders with a commitment to promoting R/S competencies; and (5) fueling momentum for systemic and cultural changes in ways that R/S are addressed in mental health care. Looking ahead, we hope this project will catalyze cultural and systemic changes in training, research, and practice that will be part of a larger solution to reducing the persisting mental health crisis in the United States (for more details, see srcproject.org).

THE SEARCH CONTINUES

"Zoning out," experiencing apathy and boredom, staying glued to our technological devices, and feeling as though we lack direction in our lives are signs that we are not actively engaged with daily experiences. What if we use these signs of disengagement as prompts to initiate searches for novelty, absorption, and the sacred? For example, next time you are driving and lose track of a stretch of road, take that as a nudge to search for novelty in the next few miles of highway. Seek out new experiences with people who are different from you. When you find yourself thinking, "I'm bored," try to lose yourself in an activity that brings you the most flow and commit to engaging in activities such as this more regularly. Finally, when you feel aimless, turn your attention to your search for the sacred, or use the benefits of spirituality when dealing with strife or frustration.

Practicing mindfulness, flow, and engaging with spirituality may benefit your psychological and physical health, academic or work performance, and sociocultural well-being. Thus, we urge you to engage in this chapter's personal mini-experiments and explore the suggested life enhancement strategies. These practices may have a more profound effect on us. Indeed, these searches may lead us to a greater appreciation for diversity and a more profound meaning-filled existence.

PERSONAL MINI-EXPERIMENTS

IN SEARCH OF OPTIMAL EXPERIENCES

In this chapter, we discuss mindfulness, flow, and spirituality. Our review suggests that intentional pursuits of novelty, absorption, and the sacred can lead you to the good life. Here are a few ideas for experiments aimed at helping you initiate these searches and explore the benefits.

Searching for Novelty: Increasing Mindfulness in Your Relationships. Numerous behaviors are associated with mindfulness. For example, *nonjudging* is impartial witnessing, observing the present moment by moment without evaluation and categorization. *Nonstriving* involves nongoal-oriented behavior, remaining unattached to outcome or achievement, and not forcing things. What would happen if you practiced these behaviors in a significant relationship for one day? Try no judgments and no "forcing things." Be an impartial witness, remain unattached to outcomes for one day, and attempt careful introspection. Then, at the end of the day, ask your partner what differences they have noticed in your behavior.

Searching for Absorption: Finding Flow in Your School Day. Have you ever wondered how much your screen time (time in front of television, surfing the Internet, instant messaging) affects your ability to immerse yourself in schoolwork? Take a break from all screen time (except academic use of computers) for 2 days, and determine whether your ability to concentrate increases or decreases. If focused attention increases during this trial period, be sure to decrease screen time during busy times in your academic semester.

Searching for the Sacred: Being More Spiritual in Daily Life. The search for the sacred is often cast as a grand journey toward a life-changing goal, but it actually requires small daily steps. Jon Haidt at New York University (http://people.stern.nyu.edu/jhaidt/) created the following exercises to help folks start the search. Try these brief exercises and see how they work for you:

- For 5 minutes a day, relax and think about the purpose of life and where you fit in.
- For 5 minutes a day, think about what you can do to improve the world or your community.
- Read a religious or spiritual book or go to a religious service once a week.
- Explore different religions. You can do this by visiting a library, looking on the Internet, or asking your friends about their religions.
- Spend a few minutes a day in meditation or prayer.
- Invest in a book of affirmations or optimistic quotes. Read a few every day.

LIFE ENHANCEMENT STRATEGIES

Every day, you make thousands of choices about how to focus your attention and spend your time. We hope that you choose to become more intentional in your searches for novelty, for absorption, and for the sacred (as you define it in your life.)

As in most chapters, we categorize the life enhancement strategies across three of life's important domains—love, work, and play. Three suggestions for each domain are shared here, one related to each of the topics of this chapter.

Love

- Orient yourself to the mindfulness relationship skills presented in Chapter 12.
- Identify an activity that helps you and a friend achieve flow at the same time. Then, spend more time jointly engaged in that activity.
- Find out how a significant other defines the sacred, and ask that person how they pursue it.

Work

- Practice making nonjudgmental observations when working with classmates or colleagues.
- Volunteer for assignments and projects that challenge or stretch your existing skills. These tasks are more likely to bring about flow than are easy assignments.
- Find a spiritual haven at work or school that allows you to pursue the sacred during your breaks in the day.

Play

- Read a book on mindfulness meditation (e.g., Kabat-Zinn, 1990), and practice some of the basic skills.
- Pursue recreational activities that are known to induce flow: playing chess, riding a mountain bike, climbing a rock wall, learning a second language, and so on.
- Make your search for the sacred a communal experience; invite friends to join you in your favorite spiritual pursuit.

KEY TERMS

Autotelic personality
Experience sampling method
Mindfulness
Spirituality

PART V

PROSOCIAL BEHAVIOR

11 EMPATHY AND EGOTISM

Portals to Altruism and Gratitude

LEARNING OBJECTIVES

After reading this chapter, you will be able to:

11.1 Understand the definitions and research associated with altruism and gratitude

11.2 Understand cultural differences in benefits and manifestations of altruism and gratitude

11.3 Define the egoism and empathy motives

11.4 Identify the different types of altruism

11.5 Describe the neurological underpinnings of altruism and gratitude

11.6 Classify measures of altruism and gratitude

In this chapter, we explore how empathy and **egotism** can lead to altruism and **gratitude.** Think of incidents in your childhood or your life today that have inspired empathy in you for someone who is different from you in some way. Seeing someone who doesn't have enough money for a home might cause you to want to reach out to help or may make you feel grateful for the home that you have, however small or large it is. Watching a friend struggle with a health issue might make you decide to help raise money for that cause and may make you value your own health all the more. You may do and feel these things because of **empathy**, the emotional response to the perceived plight of another person, and this may be the driving factor behind your desire to help and your gratitude. At other times, you may do and feel these things for a different reason. For some, imagining that they themselves could experience a similar health issue later in life, for example, might spur them on to donate so that more research can be done prior to their coming in contact with such a plight. In this case, the altruistic act of donating might be more focused on egoism, as your motive is focused on more personal gain. Here, we discuss both motives and research surrounding the important constructs of altruism and gratitude.

ALTRUISM

In this section, we begin by defining **altruism.** Next, we explore the egotism motive and show that it also can drive various types of altruistic actions. We then discuss the **empathy–altruism hypothesis** and follow with discussions of the genetic and neural underpinnings of empathy and of cultural variations of this construct. We close with approaches for enhancing and measuring altruism.

Defining Altruism

Altruism is behavior that is aimed at benefiting another person. As discussed in the previous examples, this type of prosocial behavior can be motivated by personal egotism, or it can be prompted by "pure" empathy, or the desire to benefit another person irrespective of personal gain (for overviews, see Batson, 1991; Batson et al., 2011). Egotism and empathy are the two main areas discussed as motivations toward helping behavior; however, Batson and colleagues (2011) suggest that collectivism, described as valuing the group above oneself, and **principlism,** usually described as moral integrity, may be viewed as two other potential contributors to some altruistic actions.

Several types of altruism have been distinguished in the literature, and motivations behind each appear to be different from one another in some ways, although they may overlap in others (Maner & Gailliot, 2007). Three of these types of altruism will be discussed here: (a) reciprocity-based, (b) care-based, and (c) kin-based. **Reciprocity-based altruism** was described by Trivers (1971) several decades ago and involves the type of helping behavior that seems to be motivated by the likelihood of reciprocity of the person in need—for example, deciding to help a classmate with a project at school because you know you may need help on your own project in the future. This type of altruism is most often discussed as an egoistic type of altruism. Others have argued that this is not necessarily altruism per se, as it requires the benefits to the helper to outweigh their costs over the longer term if it is to be sustained (Kurzban et al., 2015). **Care-based altruism** is believed to take place because of feelings of empathy for the recipient of the help offered. Researchers discuss this type of altruism occurring as a result of a connection being formed between the helper and helpee or because of a perceived or actual relativeness to the helper. As an example, care-based altruism may involve a helper being willing to take on personal cost to help a close friend. Friendships cannot be explained entirely by reciprocity as they are not usually viewed by people as "exchanges"; in fact, when friendships are viewed in this way (e.g., when people keep careful track of helps and hurts in a relationship), they often fail (Xue & Silk, 2012). Thus, this type of altruism represents more of an empathy-based motivation to help. Finally, **kin-based altruism** is similar to care-based altruism in that a connection exists between helper and helpee but is relegated only to altruism directed toward family. This area seems to span the gap of egoism and empathy to some extent, as a closer personal relationship is often present, perhaps making the helper desire to ease the helpee's distress, but at the same time some egoistic protection of genes may be involved in the motivation (Marsh, 2016). Regardless, it is important to note that humans are rather unique in the involved level of care (and high level of investment despite cost; think of the amount of sleep parents are willing to lose with their newborn) they give their offspring, which goes far beyond what is ordinarily seen in animals with regard to their young. Thus, this type of altruism cannot be completely explained by a pure sense of motivation directed toward the protection of genes (Kurzban et al., 2015).

The Egotism Motive

Egotism is the motive to pursue some sort of personal gain or benefit through targeted behavior and has been heralded as one of the most influential of all human motives. Not surprisingly, therefore, egotism is seen as driving a variety of human actions, including altruism. In this regard, noted Western thinkers such as Aristotle (384–322 BCE), St. Thomas Aquinas (1125–1274), Thomas Hobbes (1588–1679), David Hume (1711–1776), Adam Smith (1723–1790), Jeremy Bentham (1748–1832), Friedrich Nietzsche (1844–1900), and Sigmund Freud (1856–1939) have weighed in on the debate as to whether egotism, the sense of empathy, or both fuel altruistic human actions (see Batson et al., 2009).

Since the Renaissance, a prevailing view in the West has been that altruism is best explained by the motive of egotism. So, too, have several modern Western scholars reasoned that egotism fuels altruistic behavior (for review, see Wallach & Wallach, 1983). The essence of this position is that we care for other people because it benefits us to do so (Mansbridge, 1990). Furthermore, no matter how noble the altruism may appear, those in the egotism–altruism camp believe that all altruistic actions produce an underlying benefit to the person who is doing the good deeds. Thus, the prevailing motive here is, "I help because it benefits me." As an aside, we note that these ideas are rooted in *Western* thought. As you have already seen in Chapter 2, it is likely that collectivist cultural groups may be motivated differently.

The forms of such self-beneficial egotism may be straightforward, as when helping another person results in public praise for the individual rendering the aid. In another variant of praise, the helper may receive material rewards or honors for altruistic deeds. In 2020, as the world was racing to develop a reliable vaccine against COVID-19, it was made public that country musician Dolly Parton had given $1 million to fund production of the Moderna vaccine. Fans, new and old, took to social media praising Parton for her altruism. It possibly inspired sales of Dolly Parton music and other positive outcomes regardless of the motivation.

There are other examples of self-benefits where the helpers receive no external rewards for their altruistic actions. For example, it is distressing to see another person in some sort of anguishing situation; accordingly, we may help that person to lessen our own sense of personal torment or to escape a sense of guilt for not helping when we step in and lend a hand to a needy person. Yet another possibility is that we simply may feel good about ourselves when we act kindly toward another individual. Being known as a "generous person," for example, may assist us in self-esteem or in the esteem of others. Although this might not be something that directs every individual action in our day, we might find ourselves almost habit bound to this type of action as a part of our desire to be seen a certain way (Locey & Rachlin, 2015).

Several examples in the literature exist that appear to provide evidence that some seemingly selfless behavior actually comes from an egoist motive (for a review, see Dovidio et al., 2006). Some of these studies appear to suggest that when no one is watching or help given is anonymous, there are fewer acts of such altruism (Locey & Rachlin, 2015). Others support the idea

iStockphoto.com/jacoblund

that it is escaping increased sadness (not increased empathy) brought on by witnessing a person in need that spurs helping (Cialdini et al., 1987; Ferguson et al., 2021).

Although we have posed several variants, such egotistical or self-benefiting actions involving altruism basically take one of the following three forms:

1. The helping person gets public praise or even a monetary reward, along with self-praise for having done that which is good.
2. The helping person avoids social or personal punishments for failing to help.
3. The helping person may lessen their personal distress at seeing another's trauma.

In posing these various ego-based explanations, we do not mean to be cynical about the helping actions of people. Rather, we are uncovering the many subtle forms that such egotism-based helping can take. Remember also that, even though the helping person is motivated by personal egotism, the bottom line is that the person renders aid to a fellow human being in need. The benefit exists, regardless of the motive.

The Empathy Motive and the Empathy–Altruism Hypothesis

Empathy is an emotional response to the perceived plight of another person. One view of empathy is that it involves the ability to match another person's emotions. Instead of this mimic-like reproduction of another person's emotions, however, empathy may entail a sense of tenderheartedness toward that other person. Social psychologist and University of Kansas, professor emeritus C. Daniel Batson described this latter empathy in his 1991 book, *The Altruism Question*, and more recently in his 2011 follow-up, *Altruism in Humans.* For Batson, altruism involves human behaviors that are aimed at promoting another person's well-being.

Batson and colleagues do not deny that some forms of altruism may occur because of egotism, but their shared view is that, under some circumstances, these egotistical motives cannot account for the helping (see Batson et al., 2009). Indeed, in careful tests of what has come to be called the empathy–altruism hypothesis (see Batson, 1991), findings show that there are instances in which egotism does *not* appear to explain such helping behaviors. One example addresses the argument that people help at least partially to avoid aversive arousal and negative emotions that may occur as a result of not helping another. Much support has been found, however, for the idea that even when physical (Batson, 1991; Batson et al., 2011) or psychological (Stocks et al., 2009) escape from such a situation is made easy, individuals higher in empathy still help those in need. Thus, the evidence appears to strongly support the view that having empathy for another leads to a greater likelihood of helping that other person (for reviews, see Batson, 1991; Batson et al., 2009; Dovidio et al., 1990)

Because of the efforts of Batson and other recent scholars, "pure" altruism arising from human empathy has been viewed as a viable underlying motive for helping, in contrast to the previous emphasis on egotism as the sole motive. Void of egotistical gains, therefore, humans at times are sufficiently moved by their empathies to help other people. If we ever need an example of positive psychology in action, this surely is it.

Genetic and Neural Foundations Related to Altruism Empathy

The method for measuring genetic heritability is to compare the concordances of empathy scores in monozygotic (identical) twins with the scores of dizygotic (fraternal) twins. For adult males, the empathy correlations for monozygotic and dizygotic twins were found to be .41 and .05, respectively (Matthews et al., 1981; for similar results, see Rushton et al., 1986). Although both of these studies have been criticized because of concerns that their analytic procedures produced overly elevated heritability scores (e.g., Davis et al., 1994), other studies have found monozygotic correlations in the range of.22 to .30, as compared to dizygotic correlations of .05 to .09 (Davis et al., 1994; Zahn-Wexler et al., 1992). The latter correlations still suggest a modest level of heritability for empathy.

Several specific brain structures and substances are thought to participate in the process of altruistic behavior. Some research has revealed that areas of the prefrontal and parietal cortices are essential for empathy (Damasio, 2002). For example, damage to the prefrontal cortex leads to impairments in appraising the emotions of other people (Bechara et al., 1996), and asymmetry in the right frontal lobe has been linked to empathic concern (Duan & Sager, 2021; Tullet et al, 2012). Furthermore, beginning in the 1990s, researchers discovered "mirror neurons" that react identically when an animal performs an action or witnesses another animal performing the same action (Winerman, 2005). In the words of neuroscientist Giacomo Rizzolatti, who was the first to discover these mirror neurons, "The neurons could help to explain how and why we . . . feel empathy" (in Winerman, 2005, p. 49), and other researchers agree (Duan & Sager, 2021). We must be careful in generalizing these findings to humans, however, because much research on mirror neurons has been conducted in monkeys. In some work done with human participants, some suggest that relationships between the observer and the target of the empathy are important to take into consideration (de Vignemont & Singer, 2006), though there are likely other neurological processes that are also being activated in order for empathy to be experienced (Duan & Sager, 2021). More recently, research done with participants on the Autism spectrum (a disorder that notably is distinguished in part by a lack of display of empathy) has shown lower activity in the fusiform gyrus structure within the temporal lobe (Greimel et al., 2010). Each of these findings points to empathy being at least in part tied to structural differences in the brain.

Along these same lines, Fetchenhauer and colleagues (2010) posit that altruism could be the result of trait-like behavior, as opposed to being state-like, leading people to act in this way more frequently. These researchers theorize that altruists may be actually able to recognize the trait of altruism in one another and benefit evolutionarily from selecting a similarly altruistic mate. These ideas present another view of altruism as something more than just learned behavior within the current time of a single individual's life; rather, it may be an evolutionary benefit developed over time. What is even more fascinating in this line of research is empathy at the trait level appears to motivate actual helping behavior in a way that a tendency toward personal distress does not (FeldmanHall et al., 2015). Researchers in this study measured both trait empathic concern and trait personal distress by way of self-report questionnaires and then tested whether high scorers in one group were more likely to behave altruistically in comparison to high scorers in the other. Findings showed that "trait empathic concern—and not trait personal distress—motivates costly altruism" (FeldmanHall et al., 2015, p. 347). This finding was supported by more activity shown in several areas of the brain (the ventral tegmental area, caudate, and subgenual anterior cingulate regions) that are often linked with caregiving and social attachment in those who are higher in trait empathic concern. A unique piece of this research is that the investigators supported the behavioral findings with actual neurological data, giving us a clearer picture of how altruism might be promoted. For a more complete overview of the neural correlates in the empathy–altruism process, see Buchanan and Preston (2016).

Correlates of Altruism

Many beneficial qualities have been linked to the presence of altruism in a variety of individuals (Duan & Sager, 2021). Specifically, helping others seems to be linked to feelings of well-being for a variety of reasons. Research shows that positive mood or affect often stimulates altruism and other types of helping behavior (Isen, 2000). In addition, even when people are experiencing negative moods, helping others seems to help them self-regulate these negative emotions in the moment, thus leading to more positive moods at home, in the workplace (Glomb et al., 2011), and in the face of disaster (Yang & Chen, 2011). In addition, helping individuals to feel and act in ways that are more empathic appears to increase well-being in general. Whereas much literature surrounding well-being is specific to hedonic happiness (i.e., pleasurable feelings; see Chapter 6 for an overview), the type of well-being linked to altruism is instead eudaemonic (i.e., well-being tied to purpose in life and fulfillment; Konrath, 2014; Xi et al., 2016). When viewing the links between altruism and this second type of well-being, the research is clear that a strong relationship exists. Konrath (2014) discusses the "positive feedback loop" (p. 399) that is created between helping and well-being such that people who feel happy are more likely to help others, and, in turn, helping others seems to further increase overall well-being and lower negative affect. These types of benefits are found across many different cultures, although certain types of volunteering or helping may be particularly beneficial depending on culture. In addition, research finds that when helping behavior is motivated by a true desire to help others in need (as opposed to being motivated by feeling good about oneself or gaining praise), returns on well-being are greater (Konrath, 2014), and benefits begin to drop when one puts too much strain on personal resources of time and money (Windsor et al., 2008). Again, some of these benefits will vary with regard to cultural norms and practices (Brethel-Haurwitz & Marsh, 2014). Regardless, it appears that helping others helps ourselves in many conditions.

Altruistic acts might also make us happier than we anticipate ahead of the deed. Dunn and colleagues (2014) conducted a study in which they gave either $5 or $20 to college-aged research participants and asked some of them to spend that money by the end of the day. Some participants were told to spend the money on themselves, while others were asked to spend it on someone else. Those who spent the money on others were higher in well-being at the end of the day. When these researchers asked other participants to predict if they would be happier spending $5 or $20 on either themselves or someone else, participants assumed that they would be happiest if spending the higher amount and spending it on themselves, but the opposite was true on both counts! In reality, those who spent $5 and on someone else were those with the highest well-being at the end of the day (Dunn et al., 2014). This is important information because it highlights the fact that we sometimes make mistakes when guessing what would make us truly happy. Knowing that the "return" on altruism is higher than that on self-gain in this type of situation might make some more willing to help others.

Other research shows that those with more compassionate tendencies also tend to be more altruistic. This likely comes as no surprise, as compassion is often thought to be a precursor to deciding to help someone. Findings in this area have shown that more compassionate people are more likely to help someone identified as a victim of an unfair situation but are no more or less likely to punish the transgressor in these cases (Weng et al., 2015). For those participants who did decide to punish the transgressor, however, those higher in empathic concern made those punishments lighter. Results were similar when some participants were trained in a compassion meditation prior to asking them to help an identified victim even when the personal cost was rather high. This compassion did not seem to extend to those identified as the transgressors in this instance, however. Those who were and were not trained in compassion training were equally likely to punish the transgressors in these instances (Weng et al., 2015). Thus, it may be that compassion only extends so far in some cases, although it may account for some leniency even when punishment is seen as an acceptable outcome of a transgression. The idea of compassionate empathy moves beyond an emotional experience to one that involves a desire to protect the person and may therefore elicit some sort of action (Duan & Sager, 2021). In this line of thinking, "compassionate empathy will help not only in supporting individuals, but also in addressing social, cultural, and environmental issues that can adversely affect individuals" (Duan & Sager, 2021, p. 543).

Finally, and perhaps unsurprisingly given the grouping of these constructs in this chapter, altruism is also positively correlated with gratitude. In a study that compared groups who were induced experimentally to feel gratitude versus those induced to feel happiness, researchers found that those in the gratitude group were most likely to voluntarily help others, and other studies have replicated this finding (Kong & Belkin, 2019). When thinking about the link between gratitude and altruism in an evolutionary context, some researchers posit that gratitude is actually the catalyst that promotes reciprocal helping behavior (McCullough et al., 2008; Hoffman et al., 2020). Thus, when one feels grateful, they may be more likely to view future helping behavior with a pay-it-forward mindset.

Cultural Variations in Altruism

As always, we as researchers and scholars must be careful about generalizing findings across cultural groups. Many have discussed the idea that personal identities and values may determine the definition of constructs and the manifestation of them, as well as the value of various constructs as being beneficial (Chang, 2001; Leu et al., 2011; Pedrotti et al., 2009; Uchida et al., 2004). In the following section, we report differences found between cultural definitions of altruism and differences found in those from different genders, cultural ideologies, and religious backgrounds.

Some research shows that different cultural groups use different definitions when using the term *altruism*. In a study comparing Indian (more collectivistic) and Italian (more individualistic) participants on their thoughts regarding altruism, results showed that Indians more often used words that represented a duty to help others at the cost of oneself (Soosai-Nathan et al., 2013). In qualitative analysis of phrases used when defining an altruistic person, Indian participants talked about the role of that person within the society ("what the person is"), whereas Italian participants talked more about the emotions of the person ("what the person feels"; Soosai-Nathan et al., 2013, p. 110). Furthermore, when asked about what makes altruism difficult, the Indian participants focused more on overwhelment of tasks/commitments or feeling a time crunch in helping all, whereas the Italian participants emphasized overcoming a desire to be selfish instead of selfless. Both of these differences appear guided by the nature of the type of cultural society from which the participants hailed: The collectivistic Indian participants felt duty bound, whereas the individualistic Italians felt altruism was more of a choice (Soosai-Nathan et al., 2013). This difference between collectivist and individualist views of altruism reinforces the idea that helping behavior can become a norm within a society.

The concepts of altruism and empathy have been investigated with regard to gender in several recent studies, although only in a binary way. Altruism is more often found in female participants in comparison to males, and these data are fairly consistent across age groups (Angerer et al., 2015). Visser and Roelofs (2011) conducted a study in which participants of male and female genders were asked to distribute a fixed number of tokens between themselves and a fictional other person based on different scenarios (often called a Dictator Game). Part of the information given to the participants was the ingroup or outgroup status of the other in relation to them. Here, women as a group were found to be less sensitive to the "price of giving" in making decisions about dividing the tokens, meaning that they gave altruistically more often than did men (Visser & Roelofs, 2011, p. 490). This effect, however, appeared to be heightened by possession of particular Big 5 personality factors (e.g., Agreeableness, Conscientiousness, etc.), leading to a conclusion that gender may explain only part of the equation about this seeming tendency toward being more altruistic in this setting. More recent research shows that there may also be cultural and social gender norms that expect more altruism from women as compared to men

(Rand & Brescoll, 2016). In a carefully executed study, women were encouraged to behave intuitively or to spend some time thinking about how to behave with regard to helping someone else. Results showed that women more often behaved altruistically when acting intuitively, particularly when they identified more strongly with character attributes that are thought of as traditionally feminine (e.g., nurturance, compassion). When women were encouraged to deliberate more about their behavior before acting, those who identified more strongly with qualities more often valued in men (e.g., competitiveness, power) exhibited less altruism (Rand & Brescoll, 2016). Thus, some of the differences found with regard to gender and altruism may depend on cultural context and social norms regarding gender-appropriate behaviors. Other research has shown that altruism appears to be a more common trait found in women (in comparison to men; other genders were not examined in this study) in the United States, which appeared to facilitate a greater degree of purpose in life in these women (Xi et al., 2022). To this final point, Xi and colleagues (2022) found that men displaying less altruism might be partially due to norms valuing competition over altruism within United States culture. Finally, altruism may be an appreciated trait in choosing a partner in participants who identify as female (Barclay, 2010).

Cultural variations may also be found in looking at different norms and ideologies between groups. Batson and colleagues (Batson et al., 2009; Batson et al., 2011) posit that *collectivism* as an ideology may in fact be a form of altruism or prosocial behavior that affects an entire community. In prioritizing the welfare of others above one's own welfare, helping behavior becomes a part of the normed social structure; not behaving in a way that serves the greater good is punished, while engaging in helping behavior is rewarded. Looking toward cultures who model this WE perspective rather than a ME perspective may reveal other routes toward cultivating altruistic behaviors (see Chapter 2). Research conducted by Oda and others (2011) supports this premise, as can be seen in their study of Japanese undergraduates. Oda and colleagues looked at both external and internal factors determining a prosocial mindset and found that individuals who exhibited prosociality toward others received significantly more social support from mothers, siblings, and friends/acquaintances. These results were found with regard to prosocial behavior directed at friends and acquaintances but in some cases also extended to prosocial behavior toward strangers. In addition, internal traits such as self-sacrifice and private self-consciousness were found to be related to prosocial behavior. Oda and colleagues (2011) term this collectivist society an "altruism niche" (p. 283) and state that it is the function of prosociality being rewarded and valued within the Japanese society. Related to this area of study is the concept of **parochial altruism** (i.e., prosocial behavior that is shown toward an ingroup that preferences and values them over any outgroup members despite potential detriment to the self) (Everett et al., 2015). This type of altruism may explain some cultural connections with regard to helping behavior, and more research would be beneficial in this area (Simpson & Willer, 2015). Others have argued that altruism toward an ingroup is not truly altruism, as the actions likely benefit the individual as well (Galen, 2012). Additionally, though some note that links between religiosity and spirituality and altruism make ideological sense (Huber & MacDonald, 2012; Saroglou, 2021), others have stated that scientific evidence for this link is lacking (Galen, 2012). Thus, the relationships between religiousness, spirituality, and these prosocial tendencies may be more nuanced than previously assumed.

Last, generational and cohort effects may exist for the value or practice of altruism at particular times in history. In recent times, global and national crises have provided both opportunities and surprising evidence for altruism as it relates to volunteerism. First, during the economic downturn in the United States known as the Great Recession, many expected volunteerism to wane, however others within specific states suggested that practices related to economic difficulties (e.g., mandatory furlough days, shortened workweeks) provided volunteering opportunities for some individuals. *USA Today* ("Four-day workweek," 2009) reported that in Utah, mandatory flex schedules that called for state workers to work four 10-hour days per week to save on electricity and maintenance costs in 2009 left many of these workers free to volunteer on their nonworking Fridays. In California, the Office of the Governor (2009) reported that "800,000 more Californians volunteered their time in 2008 than in the previous year" (para. 1). As the U.S. economy has begun to heal and unemployment dropped, rates of volunteerism dropped as well (Sullivan, 2015). More recently, in the wake of the COVID-19 pandemic, many again expected volunteerism to decrease. The exact opposite was found, however, with volunteerism dipping slightly in the beginning of the pandemic, only to return to normal levels and to keep moving upward, such that volunteerism and behaviors related to altruism are at the highest rates ever across the world (Helliwell et al., 2022). Specifically the helping of strangers doubled from 2020 to 2021 according to Gallup World Happiness Report data (Helliwell et al., 2022) and was joined shortly after by large increases in donations and volunteering overall. Though the United States and Western Europe are usually found to have the highest rates of prosocial behavior in comparison to the rest of the world, data from 2020 and 2021 showed that the gap between these countries and others was effectively erased due to greater participation in Eastern Europe and other non-Western countries (Helliwell et al., 2021). These findings point us to a renewed global value of altruistic acts and bode well for a more benevolent global future.

Cultivating Altruism

For clues to how to help someone become more altruistic, we call upon the very processes of egotism and empathy that we have used to explain altruism.

Egotism-Based Approaches to Enhancing Altruistic Actions

In our experiences working with clients in psychotherapy, we have found that people often may incorrectly assume that feeling good about themselves is not part of rendering help. At least for some individuals living in the United States, this attitude may reflect the Puritan heritage with its emphasis on suffering and total human sacrifice for the good of others. Whatever the historical roots, however, it is inaccurate to conclude that helping another and feeling good about oneself are incompatible. Thus, this is one of the first lessons we use in enabling people to realize that they can help and, because of such actions, have higher self-esteem. Furthermore, we have found that people seem to take delight in learning that it is legitimate to feel good about helping others.

One way to unleash such positive feelings is to have the person engage in community volunteer work. Local agencies assisting children, people with disabilities, older people who are alone, the homeless and other low-income groups, and hospitals all need volunteers to render aid. Although this form of helping may begin as a voluntary experience, we have witnessed instances in which our clients have changed their professions to involve activities where they support others *and get paid for it.* Our more general point, however, is that it feels good to help other people, and this simple premise has guided some of our efforts at channeling people into volunteer positions.

One note of caution with these egoistically based approaches must be stated, however. Although it is true that egoistic approaches result in benefits to others as much as those that are based more purely on helping, the benefits *to the helper* may differ. Research shows that there may be some distinction between those who set out to help another to attain this sort of egoistic gain and those who act due to less egoistic motivation. Konrath and others (2012) studied motivations in older adults toward volunteer work and found that those whose primary motivations were for self-gain had higher mortality risk 4 years after the study was conducted in comparison to those whose primary motivations were more directed at helping others. This finding was supported in subsequent study of these factors (e.g., Konrath, 2014) and was especially true in individuals who volunteered on a more regular basis. Thus, although egoistic motivations may provide some of the same benefits that "true" altruists obtain, there may still be greater benefits from acting outside of self-interest.

Empathy-Based Approaches to Enhancing Altruistic Actions

A way to increase people's likelihood of helping is to teach them to have greater empathy for the circumstances of other people. How can such empathy be promoted? People act in altruistic ways most often when they have some sort of affiliation with the person they are helping (Hauser et al., 2014). One simple approach is to have a person interact more frequently with people who need help. Then, once the individual truly begins to understand the perspectives and motives of the people who are being helped, this insight breaks down the propensity to view interpersonal matters in terms of "us versus them." This research can also help us as individuals and as a society by further investigating the use of empathy within multicultural and cross-cultural interactions. As one gets to know another's plight or situation, it may be that feelings of empathy come more easily. Thus, in interacting with individuals from cultural backgrounds other than your own, *ethnocultural empathy* may be cultivated and measured (see Wang et al., 2003). Wang and colleagues (2003) define this concept as "empathy directed toward people from racial and ethnic cultural groups who are different from one's own ethnocultural group" (p. 221). Development of this type of empathy seems to be aided by close interactions with members of groups who are different from oneself (Pedrotti & Sweatt, 2007) and can avoid things like scapegoating and stereotyping that are often found when limited interactions occur between cultural groups (Mio et al., 2015; Pedrotti & Isom, 2021). By engaging with others from different backgrounds, we learn about history and ways in which certain groups and individuals have been treated and mistreated. Interestingly, peer support was a predictor of White college students' ethnocultural empathy for Asian Americans during the COVID-19 pandemic (when anti-Asian racism and scapegoating were higher than usual), thus bringing social norms into play in this relationship as well (Kim & Tausen, 2021). In helping to cultivate ethnocultural empathy in our children, ourselves, and in serving as models for others to set empathic norms, we lay a foundation for a more understanding world (Pedrotti & Isom, 2021).

Ethnocultural empathy may be particularly important today as there is a strong perception of more overt racism being present in the United States in recent years (Horowitz et al., 2019). In our day-to-day life, the word *different* is often used synonymously with *strange* or some other negative trait. From a young age, we train children to spot similarities and highlight differences, but at the same time we often pretend that differences, specifically those pertaining to facets such as race or disability, are invisible. Many researchers have shown that difference is not invisible, even to very small children (e.g., Bigler & Liben, 2006), but in acting as though it is, we as parents and educators accidentally malign the idea of "difference" in general. As Bigler and Liben (2006) have discussed in their research, this may make it less likely for dissimilar individuals to spend time with one another, even during childhood. We would take this one step further and posit that this lack of closeness may in turn decrease empathy. If we can help our children to develop wide and diverse social circles, perhaps we can allow empathy to develop toward a broader group of people. This may mean that altruistic acts have a farther reach as well.

Values-Based Approaches to Enhancing Altruistic Actions

Personal values may affect altruistic behavior and examples of historical accounts of "helpers" such as those who protested against Nazi ideology and practices or who engaged in the civil rights movement may show this link (Fagin-Jones & Midlarsky, 2007; Hitlin, 2007; see discussion of altruistic courage in Chapter 9). Researchers have found some individuals may incorporate helping into their personal identity such that anything other than altruistic behavior in these types of situations does not feel authentic and thus isn't considered a viable behavioral option (Colby & Damon, 1995). Public servant occupations such as firefighters, ambulance workers, and the police, who put themselves in harm's way for others on a regular basis (Zimbardo, 2007), may also tend to draw individuals who already value prosocial behavior to them, at the same time promoting further development of prosocial qualities in those individuals who choose such positions. Emulating these real-life heroes may have an effect on the development of altruism as well. Franco and colleagues (2011) believe we can stimulate our "heroic imagination," which is "a collection of attitudes about helping others in need, beginning with caring for others in compassionate ways, but also moving toward a willingness to sacrifice or take risks on behalf of others or in defense of a moral cause" (p. 11). Maybe anyone has the capacity to act in a heroic way.

Finally, these values may be passed along. Even after taking parental volunteer action into account, Rosen and Sims (2011) found that those children who volunteered or were involved in some kind of fundraising during childhood were 8.3% and 6%, respectively, more likely to volunteer their time as adults. Thus, involving children in altruistic actions when they are young may have important implications for continuation of this prosocial behavior. We explore yet more ways to increase altruism in the following Personal Mini-Experiments.

PERSONAL MINI-EXPERIMENTS

EXERCISES IN ALTRUISM AND GRATITUDE

As suggested in previous exercises, experiment and see what works for you.

Altruism for Thy Neighbor. If you look around your local neighborhood, you will find people who could use a helping hand. The key is to surprise other people and do them favors that they are not expecting. Here are some suggestions:

- Volunteer to babysit for a single parent who is working hard to make ends meet.
- Speak up for someone whose voice is not as likely to be heard as yours. Put any privilege you have (e.g., socioeconomically, racially, gender-wise) to good use to help others.
- Give blood or go to a local hospital and see what volunteer work can be done there.

You get the idea. Do for others, and make a note of the feelings that altruism engenders in you.

Count Your Blessings (see Emmons & McCullough, 2003). At the beginning and end of each day, list five things for which you are grateful, and then take a few minutes to meditate on the gift inherent in each. One means of elucidating this sense of appreciation is to use the stem phrases, "I appreciate ___________ because_____________." In the first blank, list the person, event, or thing for which you are grateful, and in the second blank, state the reasons for each of the things for which you have expressed gratitude. Discuss the effects of 1 week of this practice with a classmate, and tweak the exercise as you wish.

Put Yourself in Someone Else's Shoes. Although we can never quite experience what someone else is feeling or thinking, we can make efforts to try to have empathy for others even when we are annoyed or upset. This may be particularly important and helpful when working with someone different from ourselves in some way or hearing about a different perspective. Next time you find yourself feeling annoyed with something that doesn't fit with your way of thinking or feeling, stop for a moment to try some conscious empathic concern. You can do this even if you aren't changing your own perspective, but it might help to understand theirs even if you don't agree with it. Try asking yourself, "If I believed what they believe, how might that feel?" Sometimes more understanding assists us with managing negative feelings about differences of opinion or experience.

Measuring Altruism

A variety of self-report instruments exist to assess altruism in people from childhood through adulthood. Perhaps the best-known self-report instrument is the Self-Report Altruism Scale, a validated 20-item index for adults (Rushton et al., 1981). If one desires an observational index, the Prosocial Behavior Questionnaire (Weir & Duveen, 1981) is a 20-item rating index that can be used by teachers to report prosocial behaviors (using a 3-point continuum of applicability ranging from "does not apply" to "applies somewhat" to "definitely applies"). (For a similar index to the Prosocial Behavior Questionnaire, see the Ethical Behavior Rating Scale, a 15-item teacher rating instrument by Hill and Swanson [1985].) Finally, the Altruism subscale of the

iStockphoto.com/Daisy-Daisy

Prosocial Tendencies Measure-Revised (Carlo & Randall, 2002), and the Helping Attitude Scale (Nickell, 1998; see Appendix A) are popular for related studies.

As discussed previously, researchers often use various decision-making games of give-and-take borrowed from the field of economics (such as "The Dictator Game") to determine if participants in their studies are likely to act in a more prosocial way or a more egoistic way in various scenarios. These scenarios attempt to measure altruism from a more behavioral standpoint by asking participants to make decisions on how to disperse a set amount of tokens to others in the game based on various circumstances (e.g., the other person is a member of the same group or another group, the other person holds all the tokens or the participant holds all the tokens, etc.)

Future Directions

Thinking of ways to enhance our understanding of efforts to become more prosocial becomes a valued goal in our current global and local communities. Developing more ethnocultural empathy, for example, might assist us toward a higher level of connection to those who are different from us and can aid in social change and pursuit of true equality across racial and ethnic groups. More study in groups that seem to develop empathy and prosocial behavior as a part of their social norms, such as the previously discussed collectivist societies, may also assist in developing a kinder world. Finally, thinking about emulating the strength of empathy from various groups that seem to exhibit more of this (e.g., women, older populations) or exposing children to the idea of "giving back" may assist us in "borrowing" this strength of altruism. Many scholars and writers have spoken about altruism, but we will leave you here with a quotes for further pondering. The Dalai Lama is quoted as saying, "The root of happiness is altruism—the wish to be of service to others."

GRATITUDE

We now turn to discussion of the concept of gratitude, first defining it and discussing its potential physiological bases. We next turn to discussion of gratitude in cultural variations of this construct, and then ways in which it can be cultivated and measured.

Defining Gratitude

The term *gratitude* is derived from the Latin concept *gratia*, which entails some variant of grace, gratefulness, and graciousness. In the words of noted University of California, Davis researcher Robert Emmons (personal communication, 2005), gratitude emerges upon recognizing that one has obtained a positive outcome from another individual who behaved in a way that was (1) costly to the giver, (2) valuable to the recipient, and (3) intentionally rendered. As such, gratitude taps into the propensity to appreciate and savor everyday events and experiences (Armenta et al., 2022; Borelli et al., 2022; Langston, 1994).

In Emmons's definition, the positive outcome is defined as coming from another person; however, the benefit may also be derived from a nonhuman action or event. For example, the individual who has undergone a traumatic natural event, such as a family member's survival of a hurricane (Ai & Smyth, 2021; see also Coffman, 1996), feels a profound sense of gratitude. In a related vein, it has been suggested that events of larger magnitude also should produce higher levels of gratitude (Trivers, 1971). Other researchers have found that *quality*, not quantity, is more important in gratitude experiences. For example, Wood and colleagues (2011) found that participants in their study ranked their level of gratitude in any one particular instance relevant to other situations in which they had been thankful for something. When participants were not used to getting help from friends, they felt more grateful when someone did help them and vice versa. Interestingly, an unexpected present or gift might interact differently on the type of gratitude expressed. In a study by Weiss and colleagues (2020), an unexpected gift (as opposed to one that was expected) resulted in being more strongly correlated with a focus on praising the giver, as opposed to a focus on the benefit of the gift to the recipient.

In yet another example of gratitude, a person may come through a major medical crisis or problem and discover benefits in that experience (Affleck & Tennen, 1996). This process is called *benefit finding*. This may be especially helpful in the short term in dealing with the stress that occurs as a result of some trauma (Wood et al., 2012). Some very recent research suggests that one can derive positive emotional consequences by practicing preemptive benefit finding while waiting for possible bad news (e.g., waiting for test results to see if one has cancer but thinking of benefits in the situation even if the news is bad; Rankin & Sweeny, 2022). An example might be to focus on the fact of catching a disease early, even if one receives the bad news that they are diagnosed with something frightening.

Gratitude is viewed as a prized human propensity in the Hindu, Buddhist, Muslim, Christian, and Jewish traditions (Emmons & McCullough, 2003). On this point, philosopher David Hume (1888) went so far as to say that *in*gratitude is "the most horrible and unnatural of all crimes that humans are capable of committing" (p. 466). According to medieval scholar Thomas Aquinas (1273/1981), not only was gratitude seen as beneficial to the individual, but it also serves as a motivational force for human altruism. Tudge and colleagues (2021) note that gratitude is better explained as a moral virtue, than as a trait.

The Psychophysiological Underpinnings of Gratitude

Some research relating directly to neural and physical underpinnings of gratitude is beginning to emerge in the past few years. First, current research has begun to study the role of the cingulate cortex in the brain in terms of its relation to the generation of gratitude neurally. In one study by Yu and colleagues (2018), the perigenual anterior cingulate cortex (pgACC) was found to play a role in the stimulation of gratitude. In another study, led by the same researcher (Yu et al., 2017), activation of the posterior cingulate cortex appeared to align with self-reported gratitude in participants. Fox et al. (2015) have uncovered some very interesting findings while trying to observe brain activity after gratitude has been evoked. In this study, Fox and colleagues found that activity in the anterior cingulate cortex (thought to be responsible for emotional regulation and other impulse control) and the medial prefrontal cortex (often associated with social cognition and decision making) was found during the experience of gratitude. The type of brain activity observed is similar to what appears to happen in the brain when moral issues are analyzed. In addition, Fox and colleagues found that areas of the brain that usually deal with social relationships and bonding, as well as social rewards, also appeared to be activated while experiencing gratitude. More research is needed as there are overlaps with gratitude and other types of emotions when receiving a gift or service. Fox and colleagues (2015) urge caution in interpretation of these findings because of these overlaps, but these are exciting new strides in this part of the field and help us to have a better understanding of what underlies the concept of gratitude.

Other research appears to further support this finding of the role of the prefrontal cortex in better understanding the neural underpinnings of gratitude as well (Zhu et al., 2021). Activation of the prefrontal cortex was also shown to occur in a study by Tori and colleagues (2020) during the experience of being thanked. In this study, partners wrote gratitude letters to one another and then read them aloud while brain activity was monitored. Those listening to letters of gratitude showed activation in their prefrontal cortex (Tori et al., 2020). As more research in this area emerges, ideas surrounding the neurology associated with gratitude will bring more understanding to these cognitive processes and structures.

Correlates of Gratitude

Feeling grateful and exhibiting it helps people to develop other characteristics that assist them in their daily lives. Grateful people have many other positive mental and physical health characteristics (Emmons & Mishra, 2011; Puente-Diaz & Cavazos-Arroyo, 2016). Higher scores on gratitude assessments have correlated positively with elevated positive emotions, vitality, optimism, hope, and satisfaction with life (McCullough et al., 2002; Szcześniak & Soares, 2011). Those higher in gratitude are generally higher in physical, psychological, and spiritual well-being (Lamas et al., 2014; O'Leary & Dockray, 2015) and life satisfaction (Toepfer et al., 2012), and this connection to well-being and life satisfaction appears to exist across several cultures

iStockphoto.com/fizkes

as well (Kong et al., 2015). Moreover, higher gratitude has correlated positively with empathy, sharing, forgiving, and giving one's time for the benefit of others. Other researchers have found that grateful reframing of negative events assisted individuals in developing emotional closure toward unpleasant memories of these events (Watkins et al., 2008). Gratitude is also a predictor of less depression in life (Lambert et al., 2012; Petrocchi & Couyoumdjian, 2016) and linked to a perception of more meaning in life (Kashdan et al., 2006). Additionally, the COVID-19 pandemic was a time for many to feel grateful despite hardships imposed by the lockdowns across the globe. Consider the words of one mother of three:

> Even though things have been difficult with having the children participate in online schooling, worrying about my elderly parents catching COVID, and the stress of having to work from home, I find myself feeling so grateful at the same time. Grateful that my children have each other to socialize with since we can't interact with very many other families right now, grateful for our backyard so that the kids can still get exercise when I know so many people don't have that, grateful for the space in my house so that the kids can be in separate rooms while they are online for school and that my husband and I still have space to do our work from home as well. I've caught myself feeling a little guilty that some of these things haven't evoked as much gratitude in me as they are now. It's like the benefits of these things are clearer to me during this hard time.

Other studies reinforced some of the ideas put forward by the story above in that statements of public gratitude appeared to increase in online forums at this time, particularly in areas related to growth opportunities (Nguyen & Gordon, 2022). Some other research conducted during this time showed that college students in their first year, who had higher levels of hope, self-efficacy, and gratitude, had a buffering effect on some of the negative psychological impacts of being a new college student during the pandemic (Ang et al., 2022). Similarly, another study found that well-being was "protected" by gratitude and other positive traits during COVID (Mead et al., 2021). It will be interesting to see how the pandemic impacts individuals with regard to positive traits like gratitude in a long-term way as well. Other studies have shown that cohort effects can influence the level of gratitude that people feel toward various sources. In a study looking at differences in gratitude in children pre- and post-9/11, Gordon, Musher-Eizenman, and colleagues (2004) found that mention of gratitude toward rescue workers (such as police and firefighters), the United States and its values (e.g., freedom), and people other than family members were each significantly higher in children after the 9/11 terrorist attacks. In addition, post-9/11 discussions of gratitude included less reference to material items (such as toys), leading Gordon and colleagues to hypothesize that "at least in the months following the terrorist attacks, children may have reprioritized their lives in a manner similar to adults" (p. 549) with regard to gratitude. The same may occur following the pandemic. Thus, times of strife may lead to emphasis of different priorities and might offer opportunities to build on positive traits such as gratitude.

One area with which gratitude seems to assist those who are high in this strength is within the social realm. Grateful people often have qualities that allow them to develop and maintain strong relationships with others, including a higher level of forgiveness (Mooney et al., 2016) and overall attachment (Dwiwardani et al., 2014). In addition, grateful people are shown to be higher in patience (Dickens & DeSteno, 2016), often perceive that they have more social support, and have more satisfaction in their social relationships (Algoe, 2012). Interestingly, the way in which participants are asked to recall things for which they feel grateful may also influence the strength of gratitude. In a study by Puente-Diaz and Cavazos-Arroyo (2016), researchers asked some participants to recall just two things for which they were grateful and others to recall six. Results in this study showed that state gratitude was positively affected when only two items were requested, and subsequent analysis seemed to show that this was directly related to the ease of recall. Relatedly, a study in China involved experimental groups in which some participants felt responsible for receiving a donation and others felt the donation was unprompted (Li et al., 2019). In the group who did not feel responsible for receiving help, gratitude was found to be at a greater level. These last two studies provide helpful tips for the layperson as well. The Puente-Diaz and Cavazos-Arroyo study shows that thinking of even one thing for which one is grateful can be beneficial in the moment. In reading the second study by Li and colleagues, a layperson might recognize that making a recipient of help feel as though the decision to help was initiated by themselves instead of freely given, might result in a less grateful response.

Cultural Variations in Gratitude

Research focused on cross-cultural comparisons between East Asian participants from Korea and Japan and participants from the United States (primarily White American samples) shows that expressions of gratitude and reactions to these expressions may differ between East and West. The words "thank you," for example, are shown to produce more positive reactions in the

U.S. samples as compared with those participants from Korea, especially when the attention of the recipient of the gratitude is drawn specifically toward the use of these words (Park & Lee, 2012). Other research found that Koreans preferred the use of apology phrases as opposed to a "thank you," whereas those in the United States (again, primarily White Americans) had the opposite reaction (Lee & Park, 2011). Lee and Park (2011) state that this preference has to do with perception of which words would help soothe a threat to personal "face" (i.e., saving face); while Koreans felt that "I'm sorry" best accomplished this task, those in the United States felt that "thank you" was more effective. Similar results were found in the samples in Japan (Ide, 1998; Long, 2010).

Differences have been found between racial groups within the multicultural context of the United States as well. The use of gratitude-enhancing strategies to influence happiness or well-being also appears to differ between Asian Americans and their White American counterparts. In a study by Boehm et al. (2011), researchers assigned participants to groups that employed different happiness-enhancing techniques. In the condition using gratitude expression as a vehicle for increasing happiness, marked differences were found between these cultural groups, with White Americans benefiting much more greatly from these techniques as compared with the Asian American participants. This may be because Asian Americans hold similar beliefs regarding gratitude to those in Asian countries, as suggested previously by Lee, Park, and others (Long, 2010; Park & Lee, 2012). In addition, a follow-up study investigated the practice of gratitude journaling's effect on well-being in a diverse U.S.-based group of participants and compared their results to a second group in South Korea (Layous et al., 2013). Both groups were asked to keep gratitude journals, but while this resulted in a spike in well-being for the U.S. participants, it resulted in a decreased well-being for the South Korean participants. Layous and colleagues (2013) speculate that due to cultural rules in Asian cultures regarding the necessity of reciprocity and the value of a balance of both positive and negative experiences in life, South Koreans are perhaps more "likely to experience conflicting emotions (such as guilt) when they are grateful" (p. 1299). This doesn't mean that gratitude is problematic for Asian cultures; in fact, much evidence points to the idea that gratitude is strongly valued by collectivist cultures in general. That said, the practice of recounting the reasons one has to feel grateful, and perhaps in the absence of balance that exists in only recounting these positive occurrences, may be what is affecting well-being in the South Korean individuals. This has special significance for practitioners in terms of reminding them to consider the value placed on particular constructs and cultural norms that may exist in different cultures when working with clients from non-Western (and especially Eastern) racial and ethnic backgrounds and perhaps especially when devising interventions to promote various characteristics.

Having a cultural identity as someone who is religious may also affect one's levels of gratitude in life (Tsang & Martin, 2016). Research has found that religiousness is positively correlated with gratitude in general (Sandage et al., 2011; Tsang et al., 2012) and that specific gratitude toward God (within Western Christian religion) "enhances the psychological benefit of gratitude" (Rosmarin et al., 2011, p. 389). Findings looking at adult followers of six major religions (Hindus, Muslims, Christians, Sikhs, Buddhists, and Jains; majority of sample was Christian) found that gratitude appears to mediate the relationship between spirituality and well-being, via altruism and forgiveness (Sharma & Singh, 2019). Thus, this cultural facet may be both protective and generative in the lives of those who use it.

Some research seems to imply that different genders may not benefit from gratitude in the same way or experience it with the same frequency. Kashdan et al. (2009) found that in adult samples, those who identified as women appear to benefit from gratitude more and experience it more often and more comfortably overall. Some of these results have been replicated more recently in terms of connections to certain genes that may be more or less prevalent in different biological sexes (VanOyen Witvliet et al., 2019). At the same time, Froh, Yurkewicz, and colleagues (2009) found that in adolescents, these differences between genders may not hold, particularly in families where social support is high; in these families, boys benefited most from experiencing gratitude. More study is needed in this area, but it seems highly likely that societal expectations and gender norms play a role in these correlations. Additionally, most studies that have investigated links between gratitude and gender define it in an outdated way as a binary. In positive psychology as a whole, it will be important in the coming years that we learn more about gender overall, its fluidity, and its connections to various strengths.

Additionally, it must be noted that multiple cultural facets (e.g., race + religious affiliation) may also play a dynamic role in affecting understanding, manifestation, and utility of various constructs. In light of the benefits purported to be received as a result of spiritual gratitude, Krause (2012) studied the role of gratitude toward God in the Western Christian tradition within elderly populations from three different racial and ethnic groups: African Americans, White Americans, and Mexican Americans. Older African Americans and older Mexican Americans reported feeling more grateful to God than older White Americans, but although the reason for this gratitude among African Americans and White Americans appeared to be a function of perception of the receipt of spiritual support, this model did not hold true for the Mexican American sample. Krause calls for more research into this area of Mexican American religiosity and gratitude, as it appears that ethnicity may play a role in the use of gratitude in a religious setting.

Cultivating Gratitude

We begin this section with the words of Deepak Chopra, "Gratitude opens the door to . . . the power, the wisdom, the creativity of the universe. You open the door through gratitude," (Chopra, 2015). This leads us into our discussion surrounding the question: What can you do to cultivate gratitude in your own life? Psychologists Robert Emmons and Michael McCullough have explored a variety of ways to help people enhance their sense of gratitude (for reviews, see Bono et al., 2004). These benefits have been shown for those young in age (Bono et al., 2014) and those toward the end of their lives (Killen & Macaskill, 2015). These interventions aimed at enhancing gratitude also have resulted in benefits in other areas. For example, in comparison to people who recorded either neutral or negative life stresses in their diaries, those who kept weekly gratitude journals were superior in terms of (1) the amount of exercise undertaken, (2) optimism about the upcoming week, and (3) feeling better about their lives (Emmons & McCullough, 2003). Furthermore, those who kept gratitude journals reported greater enthusiasm, alertness, and determination, and they were significantly more likely to make progress toward important goals pertaining to their health, interpersonal relationships, and academic performances. Those who were in the "count your blessings" diary condition also were more likely to have helped another person. Finally, in a third study in Emmons and McCullough's (2003) trilogy, people with neuromuscular conditions were randomly assigned to either a gratitude condition or a control condition. Results showed that those in the former condition were (1) more optimistic, (2) more energetic, (3) more connected to other people, and (4) more likely to have restful sleep. It is important to note that these results were found in a United States population (recall that gratitude journaling was not as helpful for those in Layous and colleagues' [2013] study in a South Korean population), but for this cultural group journaling about gratitude held a multitude of benefits.

In recent years, researchers have begun to investigate interventions carried out within the platform of social media. Valdez and colleagues (2022) designed a Facebook-based intervention aimed at Filipino high school students with the goal of increasing academic motivation, engagement, and achievement in school. In this study, the students joined a private Facebook group where they were asked to complete certain tasks daily. Examples included posting five things for which they were grateful, writing and sharing a gratitude letter about someone they knew, posting quotes about gratitude, and so on. Students in the group were also encouraged to be in community with the others in the group and to "like" or comment on others' posts as well. A control group was also employed in this study, and its members did similar tasks about more neutral topics (e.g., posting a quote they liked or writing a letter to themselves). In this mixed-methods study, quantitative results showed significant impacts for the gratitude group that involved increased independent motivation in school, more cognitive engagement, and increased controlled motivation, while qualitative results found increased desire in these students to give back to their parents, more positive thinking, and other related benefits (Valdez et al., 2022). At times it is easy to decry social media as solely negative or counterproductive, but interventions like this show the benefit of developing an online community toward the amplification of a positive trait like gratitude.

Chan (2010, 2011) designed a culturally competent gratitude intervention to be used with school teachers in Hong Kong. Chan used a very similar procedure to the studies discussed previously, although he changed the format somewhat, using elements of Naikan meditation questions (Chan, 2010). In addition, he emphasized a less self-focused attention with regard to thinking about gratitude to accommodate cultural norms in these participants (Chan, 2011). In both of these studies, Chan showed that as gratitude increased, life satisfaction did as well. In addition, emotional exhaustion was found to decrease, thus revealing an additional benefit of gratitude. Chan's studies are to be emulated in their careful attention to cultural differences; here these changes in the intervention were able to help show the beneficial impact of gratitude in this non-Western population. In summary, there are multiple ways in which formal interventions can increase feelings of gratitude and their beneficial correlates.

One additional study showed that gratitude interventions alone might be amplified with the use of coaching. Life coaching has gained popularity in recent years, but is not to be confused with actual clinical therapeutic practice or psychotherapy. In most cases in positive psychology, life coaches might deliver positive interventions via a coaching style, but in a study by Trom and Burke (2022), coaching was used to further encourage the development of gratitude gained in a traditional intervention. Those in the coaching experimental group showed higher levels of eudaimonic well-being and dispositional gratitude, as opposed to an increase of subjective well-being only in the no-coaching control group (Trom and Burke, 2022). This opens up new ways that coaching can be used to further gains in positive interventions.

The effectiveness of gratitude interventions may be moderated by the level of positive affect in the lives of participants (Froh, Kashdan et al., 2009). Jeffrey Froh, Kashdan, and colleagues (2009) asked a sample of children and adolescents to write a letter of thanks to someone for whom they were grateful and to then deliver that letter in person. They then compared youth in their study who were high in positive affect with those who were low in positive affect in terms of the effectiveness of this gratitude exercise. Results showed that those youth who were low in positive affect were able to make greater increases in their level of gratefulness and had higher positive affect postintervention. Thus, gratitude may be even more important to cultivate in individuals who are lower in regular positive emotional experiences. This said, individuals who are higher in depression and already lower in trait gratitude, might have a hard time expressing gratitude or engaging with it in the moment (Enko et al., 2021). For these individuals, gratitude expression is related to stress and elevated cardiac activity (Enko et al., 2021). As such, it is important to be thoughtful in thinking of gratitude interventions as a "cure all" for negative affect and other problems in one's life and to pay attention to what Enko and colleagues (2021) refer to as "person-activity fit" (p. 49).

THANKING YOUR HEROES

RICK SNYDER

It was 1972, and I had just taken a job as an assistant professor at KU. There was one person who had sacrificed her whole life to make it possible for me to reach this point. She worked her regular job, along with part-time jobs, to see that I could go to college. She was a hero in every sense, giving so that I could have a better life than what she had experienced.

This hero was my mother. She told me that my life as an academician was to be her reward. She planned to visit Lawrence later that year, but that visit never happened. Diagnosed with a form of quickly spreading cancer, she spent her last months bedridden in Dallas, Texas.

I visited as much as I could, and we talked about things that were important to both of us. Unfortunately, I never told her that she was my hero. Almost every day over the past 30 years, I have regretted this omission. If you still have a chance to deliver this message to an important hero in your life, do it right now.

Source: From Snyder, C. R., Thanking your heroes, *Lawrence Journal-World*, October 4, 2004.

As Chopra stated in the quote in the beginning of this chapter, cultivating gratitude is an active process in which someone must choose to engage. We share some of the clinical approaches we have used to facilitate it in the Personal Mini-Experiments (see also Bono et al., 2004).

Measuring Gratitude

Several approaches have been taken to measure gratitude. One tactic has been to ask people to list the things about which they felt grateful (*Gallup Poll Monthly*, 1996). This simple method allowed researchers to find those events that produced gratefulness. Another strategy often used is to take the stories that people wrote about their lives and code these vignettes for gratefulness themes. Some attempts also have been made to measure gratitude behaviorally. For example, whether children said "thank you" during their door-to-door Halloween trick-or-treat rounds was used as an unprompted index of gratitude (Becker & Smenner, 1986). Similarly, the grateful responses of people receiving food in a soup kitchen have been quantified (Stein, 1989).

Self-report measures of trait gratitude are perhaps among the most common methods to measure this important construct. The Gratitude, Resentment, and Appreciation Test (GRAT), a 44-item index developed and validated by Watkins et al. (1998), taps the three factors of resentment, simple appreciation, and social appreciation. A second scale is the Gratitude Adjective Checklist (GAC; McCullough et al., 2002), which asks participants to state how well three adjectives (grateful, appreciative, and thankful) describe them. This scale is often used as a secondary measure of gratitude in conjunction with some other inventory.

The trait self-report index that has been most promising across the years and most commonly used is the Gratitude Questionnaire (GQ-6) (McCullough et al., 2002; see also Emmons et al., 2003). The GQ-6 is a six-item questionnaire (see Appendix B for the entire scale) on which respondents endorse each item on a 7-point Likert scale (1 = *strongly disagree* to 7 = *strongly agree*). Results show that the six items correlate strongly with each other, and one overall factor seems to tap the scale content. Scores of the GQ-6 correlate reliably with peers' rating of target persons' gratitude levels; people scoring high on this scale report feeling more thankful and more grateful (Gray et al., 2001). Additionally, this sense of appreciation as tapped by the GQ-6 endured over a 21-day interval (McCullough et al., 2004).

Froh and colleagues (2011) assessed the validity of all three of the above adult-normed scales (the GQ-6, GAC, and the GRAT–short form) for use with children and adolescents. Results showed that similar relationships were found as with adult research participants on positive affect and life satisfaction but that age appeared to mediate the relationships with depression and negative affect. Additionally cross-cultural validations with some Asian populations have been established (Valdez et al., 2017). One finding to be aware of in using the GQ-6 with different aged populations is that there exists some violations of metric invariance (i.e., the items appear to be responded to in differing ways in different age groups; Allemand et al., 2021). As such, comparisons across age groups should be interpreted cautiously.

THE SOCIETAL IMPLICATIONS OF ALTRUISM AND GRATITUDE

In this portion of the chapter, we turn to the societal repercussions of altruism and gratitude. As you will learn in this section, these constructs play crucial roles in helping groups of people live together with greater stability and interpersonal accord.

Empathy/Egotism, Altruism, and Gratitude

First turning to the role of egotism-based benefits as they are implicated in the altruism process, our view is that it would be wise to teach people that there is nothing wrong with deriving benefits from feeling good about helping others. In fact, it is unrealistic to expect that people always will engage in pure, non-ego-based motives as they go about their helping activities. In other words, if people indeed do feel good about themselves in rendering aid to others, then we should convey the societal message that this is perfectly legitimate and does not take away from the help that is given. Although it certainly is worthwhile to engender the desire to help because it is the right thing to do, we also can impart the legitimacy of rendering help on the grounds that it is a means of deriving some sense of gratification. We should remember both the former and the latter lessons as we educate our children about the process of helping other people.

Unfortunately, however, we often act either consciously or unconsciously so as to mute our sense of empathy toward other people. Consider, for example, the residents in so many towns and cities today who walk down the street and do not even appear to see people who are homeless stretched out on the pavement or sidewalk. Faced daily with such sights, it may be that we learn to avoid eye contact to mute our empathies, which gives us fewer opportunities to practice altruism, gratitude, and other related constructs.

Realize, however, that even professionals whose training and job descriptions entail helping others may undergo similar muting of their sensibilities. For example, both nurses and school teachers may experience burnout when they feel blocked and overworked; both of these populations were particularly burdened during the COVID-19 pandemic. Nurses who watched patient after patient die from COVID-19 reported feeling less empathic as time went on in the pandemic out of self-preservation. A nurse in New York City talked about her experience caring for an elderly man at the height of the pandemic,

> I want to spend time with him, but more patients, much younger patients, keep arriving, struggling to breathe. I have to tend to them instead. The disease has won against him; these new patients have a chance. I don't want to think that way, but it is the dismal truth of our new situation. . . . Too concerned about the new patients, I never take the time to check on him again. Too exhausted at the end of my shift, I don't say goodbye to him either. He dies later that night. (Anzaldua & Halpern, 2021, p. 22.)

Additionally, article after article notes that empathy was important to display toward our teachers in the pandemic, despite the hardships parents had from teaching from home or that college students had with being online with potential novices at virtual teaching. And yet, parents across the country called teachers lazy and challenged their teaching methods repeatedly. Empathy seemed to disappear in the face of the individual hardships so many felt during this time.

If we can understand and take the perspective of another person to a greater degree, it is more likely that we will express our sense of gratitude for that other person's actions. Research shows that taking time to voice appreciation for one's friends, spouse, and family can have large benefits for these relationships. Those who feel that their romantic partners appreciate them report that they in turn feel more grateful back, creating a context of gratitude within the relationship (Gordon et al., 2012). In the words of a first grade teacher teaching at the height of the pandemic,

> [During the pandemic] I was stressed about my own children and the impact on them, and about my students who were struggling to remain engaged. And all the while so many parents were angry with the way that school was being conducted. Then this one day a parent came into frame on the computer at the end of the lesson and I braced myself for what she was going to say. But she said, "I am really grateful for all you're doing for our children. I am sure it is really hard and I appreciate you trying so hard." I almost burst into tears. It gave me a boost that day and it was something to think about and derive energy from other days, too.

Being more appreciative of a partner is associated with more commitment and more responsivity to a partner's needs, and this may extend to other partnerships in our lives (Bartlett et al., 2012; Gordon et al., 2012). In addition, expressing gratitude toward a partner has been found to improve not only the recipient's perception of the relationship but the *expresser's* perception of the relationship as well (Lambert et al., 2010). Thus, gratitude can be good for many aspects of relationships.

In our estimation, positive psychology must find ways to help people to remain empathic so they can continue to help others and be kind to others as well, perhaps through mindfulness training and self-reflection (Burks & Kobus, 2012) or perhaps through various gratitude interventions as we have discussed here. Furthermore, we should explore avenues for enhancing empathy to address some of the divides we have recently experienced in the United States with regard to issues like immigration, which might be better understood via a lens of empathy. For those of us whose families have been in this country for more than a few generations, the issues that immigrants deal with on a daily basis may be lost to us. Depending on where our families originated, they may also have come to the United States in different circumstances as well and thus have less personal understanding about populations in our country such as those who are undocumented or who are fleeing dire situations. Other issues, like the experience of racism directed toward people of color, or the biases and vitriol that can be aimed at transgender individuals on a daily basis, might decrease if more empathy was applied. One of the main sources of empathy for those who are different from ourselves is close interaction with individuals from these groups (Wang et al., 2003). Working to increase our friendship and community networks to include a diverse array of individuals may also help us to increase the number of different groups for which we can develop empathy. Additionally, taking the time to appreciate what we have and working to develop this type of everyday gratitude for these rights and commodities are things we can all do toward building a more grateful attitude. This, of course, has benefits for others and for ourselves.

Martin Luther King, Jr.
Michael Ochs Archives /Stringer/via Getty Images

LIFE ENHANCEMENT STRATEGIES

Altruism and gratitude can help you to live a more satisfying life. Here, we offer some tips for being more giving and grateful in all three life arenas.

Love

- Doing things for others can help others to feel love, even if they are outside your normal social context. Spreading this goodwill to those who are different from you can begin to foster true connections between you and others.
- A loving relationship is built on praise for one's mate when they do positive things; therefore, it is crucial to say "thank you" and to not take the positive for granted. Your expressed gratitude for your partner keeps the sense of caring alive through an atmosphere of appreciation.

Work

- Help others when they need it and without the expectation of help in return. Assisting a new parent coworker by offering empathy at the difficulty of beginning stages of parenthood, or agreeing to a worse shift time-wise to help a college student you know is struggling to finish their studying, can go a long way toward developing an empathic and altruistic workplace.

- Gratitude can be even more important than money as management's way of rewarding workers. If you are given the responsibility of leading a team, give daily thanks for the contributions of others.

Play

- By their very nature, play and leisure activities entail a sense of freedom. Give that sense of freedom to others by making sure that time for play and recharging is afforded to people of all socioeconomic groups.
- Sometimes we are given peeks into others' pleasure. When friends and family are having fun around the house, don't be shy about expressing your gratitude for the "good times" and help others savor them.

"I HAVE A DREAM": TOWARD A KINDER, GENTLER HUMANKIND

Dr. Martin Luther King, Jr. once said, "Life's most persistent and urgent question is, 'What are you doing for others?'" This chapter covers some of the finest behaviors of people—altruism and gratitude. It appears that empathy for the target person often is an important precursor to these behaviors. When we have empathy for another, we are more likely to help that person, to feel grateful for their actions, and perhaps to use that information to act kindly in the future. But in feeling such empathy, people also can fulfill their egotism needs. Thus, it need not be an either–or proposition when it comes to the motives of empathy and egotism that unleash altruism and gratitude.

An implication here is that a kinder and gentler humankind will be one where each of us can understand the actions of others, feel their pains and sorrows, and yet also feel good about our own motives as we help our neighbors. In addition, working hard to channel that empathy toward actions that give equal rights to all helps us to stand up for those who need assistance and calls us to lend power to those who have less. These are all ideas that stem from the legacy left to our country by Dr. King. A large part of development of this empathy might be broadening our circles of interaction with those who we perceive to be dissimilar to us and encouraging our children to do the same. Indeed, much of the future of positive psychology will be built upon people who can attend to their own egotism needs and also get along with and respect each other. Relationships are at the core of positive psychology, and our goal is a more "civilized" humankind in which altruism and gratitude are the expected, rather than the unexpected, reactions between interacting people.

In what may be one of the most famous oral discourses of modern times, the "I Have a Dream" speech of Dr. King, his empathy and altruism/gratitude thoughts and feelings were captured in his call for brotherhood and sisterhood (King, 1968). If positive psychology is to share in such a dream, as it surely aspires to do, then we must continue our quest to understand the science and applications that flow from the concepts of helping and showing thanks for help and benefits given.

APPENDIX A: THE HELPING ATTITUDE SCALE

Instructions: This instrument is designed to measure your feelings, beliefs, and behaviors concerning your interactions with others. It is not a test, so there are no right or wrong answers.

Please answer the questions as honestly as possible. Using the scale below, indicate your level of agreement or disagreement in the space which is next to each statement.

1	2	3	4	5
Strongly Disagree	*Disagree*	*Undecided*	*Agree*	*Strongly Agree*

_____ 1. Helping others is usually a waste of time.

_____ 2. When given the opportunity, I enjoy aiding others who are in need.

_____ 3. If possible, I would return lost money to the rightful owner.

_____ 4. Helping friends and family is one of the great joys in life.

_____ 5. I would avoid aiding someone in a medical emergency if I could.

_____ 6. It feels wonderful to assist others in need.

_____ 7. Volunteering to help someone is very rewarding.

_____ 8. I dislike giving directions to strangers who are lost.

_____ 9. Doing volunteer work makes me feel happy.

_____ 10. I donate time or money to charities every month.

_____ 11. Unless they are part of my family, helping the elderly isn't my responsibility.

_____ 12. Children should be taught about the importance of helping others.

_____ 13. I plan to donate my organs when I die, with the hope that they will help someone else live.

_____ 14. I try to offer my help with any activities my community or school groups are carrying out.

_____ 15. I feel at peace with myself when I have helped others.

_____ 16. If the person in front of me in the checkout line at a store was a few cents short, I would pay the difference.

_____ 17. I feel proud when I know that my generosity has benefited a needy person.

_____ 18. Helping people does more harm than good because they come to rely on others and not themselves.

_____ 19. I rarely contribute money to a worthy cause.

_____ 20. Giving aid to the poor is the right thing to do.

To score the Helping Attitude Scale, reverse the scores for items 1, 5, 8, 11, 18, and 19, then add all items to obtain the total score. Scores range from 20 to 100, with a neutral score of 60.

Source: From Nickell, G. S., "The Helping Attitude Scale," presented at the 106th Annual Convention of the American Psychological Association. Reprinted by permission of Dr. Gary Nickell.

APPENDIX B: THE GRATITUDE QUESTIONNAIRE—SIX ITEMS FROM GQ-6

Instructions: Using the scale below as a guide, write a number beside each statement to indicate how much you agree with it.

1	2	3	4	5	6	7
Strongly Disagree	*Disagree*	*Slightly Disagree*	*Neutral*	*Slightly Agree*	*Agree*	*Strongly Agree*

_____1. I have so much in life to be thankful for.

_____2. If I had to list everything that I felt grateful for, it would be a very long list.

_____3. When I look at the world, I don't see much to be grateful for.*

_____4. I am grateful to a wide variety of people.

_____5. As I get older, I find myself more able to appreciate the people, events, and situations that have been part of my life history.

_____6. Long amounts of time can go by before I feel grateful to something or someone.*

Source: McCullough, M. E., Emmons, R. A., & Tsang, J.-A. "The grateful disposition: A conceptual and empirical topography," in *Journal of Personality and Social Psychology, 82*(1), 112–127. Copyright © 2002 by the American Psychological Association. Reproduced with permission.

* Items 3 and 6 are reverse scored.

KEY TERMS

Altruism
Care-based altruism
Egotism
Empathy
Empathy–altruism hypothesis
Gratitude
Kin-based altruism
Parochial altruism
Principlism
Reciprocity-based altruism

12 ATTACHMENT, LOVE, FLOURISHING RELATIONSHIPS, AND FORGIVENESS

LEARNING OBJECTIVES

After reading this chapter, you will be able to:

12.1 Discuss the attachment system in infancy and childhood and describe how it sets a foundation for adult relationships

12.2 Describe the characteristics of adult attachment security

12.3 Recognize how culture impacts the attachment system

12.4 Describe the characteristics of flourishing relationships and identify ways to help relationships thrive

12.5 Identify different ways of expressing love in relationships

12.6 Discuss the psychological and interpersonal benefits of forgiveness

12.7 Recognize the biological and evolutionary factors influencing close relationships

In our clinical work, we see people from all walks of life who talk about feelings of loneliness. For some clients, the conversation focuses on longing for loved ones "back home" and concerns about finding good friends in a new place. For too many, the loneliness and a sense of alienation stem from relationships that have soured. There are adult children who do not feel connected to their fathers, boyfriends who feel invisible to their partners, wives who "don't know" their partners anymore, and aging parents who haven't seen their children in years. All these people tell painful stories of loss. We feel lonely and worthless when our basic needs for love, affection, and belongingness are unmet (Maslow, 1970; see Figure 12.1). This pain has long-term effects because our growth is stymied when we feel detached and unloved.

We start our discussion of attachment, love, and **flourishing relationships** with comments on loneliness because much of the psychology of social connection was built on scholarship about traumatic separation (Bowlby, 1969) and failed relationships (Carrere & Gottman, 1999). Positive psychology provides the other side to this equation. Rather than focusing on what causes relationships to fail or examining the negative sequelae of traumatic loss, positive psychology illuminates the characteristics and correlates of healthy, loving, and successful relationships. This information can enhance our relationships and make the most out of those connections.

FIGURE 12.1 ■ The Fulfillment of Needs for Love and Belongingness Is Considered a Prerequisite for Esteem and Self-Actualization

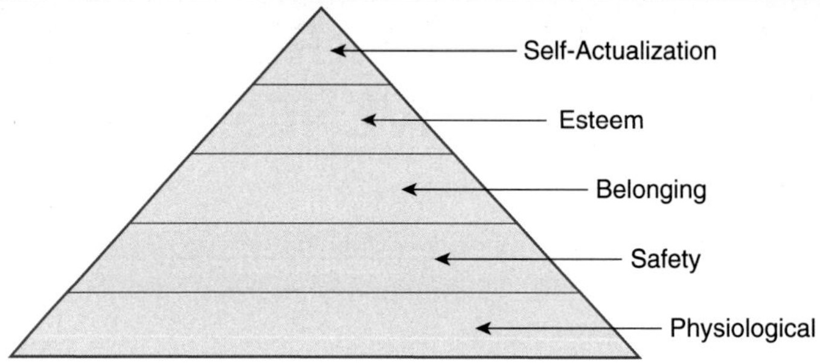

In this chapter, we discuss the *infant-to-caregiver attachment* that forms the foundation for future relationships, the *adult attachment security* that is closely linked to healthy relationship development, the *love* that is often considered a marker of the quality of relationships, and the *purposeful positive relationship behaviors* that sustain interpersonal connections over time and contribute to *flourishing relationships.* Along the way, we describe a hierarchy of social needs that demonstrates how meaningful relationships develop into flourishing relationships. Important to note as well is the impact of cultural context on our experience of love, its manifestations, and the emotions that accompany it (de Munck et al., 2011; Gareis & Wilkins, 2011; Shiota et al., 2010). We also describe real-life exemplars of "person-growing" relationships (i.e., relationships that promote the optimal functioning of both participants). Moreover, we discuss people who have experienced the best aspects of the interpersonal world and summarize the findings on the biology of social support. We also touch upon the other side of relationships—what do we do when mistakes are made, transgressions are enacted, or betrayal occurs? Part of being in a relationship, whether it be romantic or platonic, means making ourselves vulnerable in some way, and this vulnerability can open us up to both love and hurt. Thus, in the final section in this chapter, we will discuss forgiveness and research about this important, and very human, construct.

INFANT AND CHILDHOOD ATTACHMENT

Attachment is a process that is thought to start in the first moment of an infant's life. It is the emotional link that forms between a child and a caregiver, and it physically binds people together over time (Ainsworth et al., 1992). John Bowlby (1969), a clinician who worked with troubled and orphaned children, identified numerous **maladaptive parental behaviors** (chaotic, unplanned attempts to meet a child's needs; lack of physical availability) and **adaptive parental behaviors** (responsiveness to a child's behavioral cues, e.g., smiling and being nurturing) that were believed to be causally linked to functional behavior and emotional experiences of children. For example, inconsistency in responses to children is associated with children's frustration and later anxiety. On the other hand, consistency in caregivers' responses to children's cues is linked to children's contentment and later development of trust. Environmental factors can also play a role. Being witness at a young age to stressors (e.g., violence between parents) can lead to future insecure attachment (Gustafsson et al., 2017).

Through the study of children who became disconnected from their caregivers, Bowlby (1969) realized that insecure attachment is a precursor to numerous developmental struggles. A child with insecure attachment to at least one caregiver may have difficulty in cooperating with others and in regulating moods. These problems make existing relationships fragile and new relationships hard to build. Conversely, children with sound attachment systems become more appealing to their caregivers and other people. Over time, that attachment system becomes more sophisticated, and mutually beneficial patterns of interaction facilitate the psychological development of such children and their caregivers.

In summary, adaptive and maladaptive parental behaviors influence an **attachment system** that regulates the proximity-seeking behaviors connecting infants and caregivers in physical and emotional space. When this system is disrupted, formative social and emotional milestones may not be met (Howard et al., 2011). This two-way connection has been described as "a unique, evolutionarily-based motivational system . . . whose primary function is the provision of protection and emotional security" (Lopez, 2003, p. 286). Moreover, as we describe in greater detail later, attachment security is the relational scaffolding that supports positive views of self and others. That is, the attachment system is where fundamental working models (i.e., mental representations) of the self and others likely originate. If children are successful in meeting their innate attachment needs (i.e., they receive love and support from their parents in a safe and stable environment), they are likely to develop a positive working model of self and a positive working model of others. However, if a child is unable to meet their attachment-related needs, the child may develop a negative view of self or a negative view of others. These fundamental working models are the scaffolding upon which other relationships are developed over time (Lopez, 2003; Mikulincer & Shaver, 2021).

Attachment and The "Strange Situation"

A classic behavioral assessment strategy designed by Mary Ainsworth (1979) has allowed psychologists to look into the attachment phenomenon in early life. In the **Strange Situation** assessment, a child is exposed to a novel situation in the company of their caregiver, and then the caregiver is removed and reintroduced to the situation twice. During this process, the child participant's reactions are assessed. Here are the basic steps in the assessment paradigm (Steps 2 through 7 last 3 minutes each):

1. Caregiver and child are invited into a novel room.
2. The caregiver and child are left alone. The child is free to explore.
3. The stranger enters, sits down, talks to the caregiver, and then tries to engage the child in play.
4. Caregiver leaves. The stranger and child are alone.
5. The caregiver returns for the first reunion, and the stranger leaves unobtrusively. The caregiver settles the child, if necessary, and then withdraws to a chair in the room.

6. Caregiver leaves. The child is alone.
7. The stranger returns and tries to settle the child, if necessary, and then withdraws to the chair.
8. The caregiver returns for the second reunion, and the stranger leaves unobtrusively. The caregiver settles the child and then withdraws to the chair.

Trained observers code behavioral responses in this strange situation and render one of the following assessments of the quality of the attachment: **secure attachment**, **insecure-avoidant attachment**, or **insecure-resistant/ambivalent attachment**. The secure attachment pattern is characterized by a balance between exploration of the environment and contact with the caregiver. A securely attached child will explore the room using the caregiver as a secure base. Said another way, as the Strange Situation unfolds, the child will engage in more proximity-seeking and contact-maintaining behavior with the caregiver, exploring the environment only to return for comfort when necessary. Importantly, the child will be visibly happy and comforted when the caregiver returns and then will quickly settle. Insecure patterns involve increasing tension between the child and caregiver over the course of the strange situation. Children with insecure-avoidant patterns avoid the caregiver when they are reintroduced into the situation, and those with the insecure-resistant/ambivalent pattern passively or actively demonstrate hostility toward the caregiver while simultaneously wanting to be held and comforted. See if you can spot these patterns when observing children and their caregivers by conducting the Personal Mini-Experiment for this chapter.

Parent-child attachment appears to be fairly stable and can have lifelong consequences. In one seminal longitudinal study, for instance, 72% of adults who, as children, were assessed via the strange situation received the same attachment classification 20 years later, suggesting that attachment orientations are relatively stable over time (Waters et al., 2000). Other researchers (e.g., Belsky & Nezworski, 1988; Howard et al., 2011; Sprecher & Fehr, 2010) have identified long-term consequences of insecure attachment, such as relationship problems, emotional disorders, mental disorders, and conduct problems. Emerging evidence even suggests that attachment insecurity in infancy may predict health vulnerabilities in toddlers (Nelson et al., 2020), early and middle childhood (Bernard et al., 2019), and adulthood (Farrell et al., 2019).

ADULT ATTACHMENT

Personal perspectives on attachment are carried through childhood and adolescence and into stages of adulthood in the form of an internal working model of self and others (Bowlby, 1988; Shaver et al., 1988). Early in their social development, children integrate perceptions of their social competence, appeal, and lovability (the model of self) with their expectations regarding the accessibility, responsiveness, and consistency of caregivers (the model of other). These models are relatively stable over developmental periods because they are self-reinforcing. That is, the internal models consist of a set of cognitive schemas through which people see the world, gather information about self and others, and make interpersonal decisions. The model is a "conscious 'mindful state' of generalized expectations and preferences regarding relationship intimacy that guide participants' information processing of relationship experiences as well as their behavioral response patterns" (Lopez, 2003,

p. 289). If people carry forward a secure, mindful state, they see the world as safe and others as reliable. Unfortunately, negative or insecure schemas may also be perpetuated. For example, people who see the social world as unpredictable and other people as unreliable have difficulty overcoming their desires to keep others at a distance, and they may falter in participating in high-quality love relationships later in adulthood (McCarthy & Maughan, 2010).

Numerous theorists (e.g., Bartholomew & Horowitz, 1991; Dugan & Fraley, 2022; Hazan & Shaver, 1987; Main & Goldwyn, 1984, 1998; Shaver & Mikulincer, 2006; Sprecher & Fehr, 2010) have extended attachment theory across the life span to understand how adults relate to other adults, as well as to the children for whom they will serve as caregivers. Table 12.1 provides a list of three of the most influential classification systems. For example, developmental psychologists Mary Main and colleagues have conducted interviews of mothers who participated in the Strange Situation assessment and found that adult attachment can best be described by a system comprising four categories: secure/autonomous, dismissing, preoccupied, and unresolved/disorganized.

TABLE 12.1 ■ Three Prominent Classification Systems of Adult Attachment Styles

Main & Goldwyn (1984, 1998)	*Description*
Secure/Autonomous	Interviewee demonstrates coherent, collaborative discourse. Interviewee values attachment but seems objective regarding any particular event/relationship. Description and evaluation of attachment-related experiences are consistent whether experiences are favorable or unfavorable.
Dismissing	Interview is not coherent, and interviewee is dismissing of attachment-related experiences and relationships. Interviewee "normalizes" these experiences with generalized representations of history unsupported or actively contradicted by episodes recounted. Transcripts also tend to be excessively brief, violating the maxim of quantity.
Preoccupied	Interview is not coherent, and interviewee is preoccupied with or by past attachment relationships/experiences. Interviewee appears angry, passive, or fearful and uses sentences that are often long, grammatically entangled, or filled with vague uses. Transcripts are often excessively long, violating the maxim of quantity.
Unresolved/Disorganized	During discussions of loss or abuse, interviewee shows striking lapse in the monitoring of reasoning or discourse. For example, the person may briefly indicate a belief that a dead person is still alive in the physical sense or that this person was killed by a childhood thought. Interviewee may lapse into prolonged silence or eulogistic speech.

(Continued)

TABLE 12.1 ■ Three Prominent Classification Systems of Adult Attachment Styles (*Continued*)

Hazan & Shaver (1987)	*Description*
Secure	I find it relatively easy to get close to others and am comfortable depending on them and having them depend on me. I don't often worry about being abandoned or about someone getting too close to me.
Avoidant	I am somewhat uncomfortable being close to others; I find it difficult to trust them completely, difficult to allow myself to depend on them. I am nervous when anyone gets too close, and often love partners want me to be more intimate than I feel comfortable being.
Anxious/Ambivalent	I find that others are reluctant to get as close as I would like. I often worry that my partner doesn't really love me or won't want to stay with me. I want to merge completely with another person, and this desire sometimes scares people away.
Bartholomew & Horowitz (1991)	***Description***
Secure	It is easy for me to become emotionally close to others. I am comfortable depending on others and having others depend on me. I don't worry about being alone or having others not accept me.
Dismissing	I am comfortable without close emotional relationships. It is very important for me to feel independent and self-sufficient, and I prefer not to depend on others or have others depend on me.
Preoccupied	I want to be completely emotionally intimate with others, but I often find that others are reluctant to get as close as I would like. I am uncomfortable being without close relationships, but I sometimes worry that others don't value me as much as I value them.
Fearful	I am uncomfortable getting close to others. I want emotionally close relationships, but I find it difficult to trust others completely, or to depend on them. I worry that I will be hurt if I allow myself to become too close to others.

Source: From Hazan & Shaver (1987). Adapted from E. Hesse in *Handbook of attachment: Theory, research, and clinical applications*. Copyright 1999 by Guilford Press. Also appeared in Lopez & Snyder (2003) *Positive Psychology Assessment*.

Social psychologists Cindy Hazan and Phillip Shaver have studied attachment in the context of adult romantic relationships. They found (Hazan & Shaver, 1987) that the three categories of secure, avoidant, and anxious, akin to Ainsworth's (1979) groups, effectively described the nature of adult attachments to a significant other. In 1991, Bartholomew and Horowitz expanded the three categories of adult attachment to four by differentiating two types of avoidant attachment: dismissive and fearful.

In a ground-breaking study, Brennan et al. (1998) considered Bartholomew and Horowitz's system from a different perspective. Specifically, Brennan et al. (1998) examined the items from several popular self-report measures of adult attachment styles via factor analysis. Rather than finding several distinct styles, they discovered two independent dimensions: **attachment anxiety** (i.e., marked by a compulsive need for closeness in times of distress, hyper-activating emotion regulation strategies, fears of abandonment, and a negative view of self) and **attachment avoidance** (i.e., marked by a compulsive need for self-reliance, avoidance of intimacy, and a tendency to push partners away) that seemed to underlie the four possible styles. This conceptualization of attachment has become one of the well-supported views of adult attachment in the extant literature (Mikulincer & Shaver, 2017) and can be assessed via a popular self-report measure, The Experiences in Close Relationships Scale (ECR; Brennan et al., 1998). The ECR has undergone several refinement processes and evidences strong psychometric properties. It has also been extensively studied across many different populations. One researcher, Chris Fraley, at the University of Illinois, has been at the forefront of adult attachment measurement and conceptualization research for decades using the ECR. We strongly encourage you to check out your attachment style using the free assessment tools, including different versions of the ECR, available through Dr. Fraley's website (http://labs.psychology.illinois.edu/~rcfraley/resources.html). We should also note that the attachment literature has grown far beyond adult romantic relationships and now includes attachment to peers (Gorrese & Ruggieri, 2012), pets (Beck & Madresh, 2008), God (Stulp et al., 2019), and a variety of other attachment targets.

Figure 12.2 illustrates how attachment dimensions identified by Brennan and colleagues (1998) may underly common attachment styles. According to this dimensional perspective of attachment, the secure style is low on both dimensions of anxiety and avoidance, the dismissing/avoidant style is high on avoidance and low on anxiety, the preoccupied/anxious style is low on avoidance and high on anxiety, and the fearful style is high on both avoidance and attachment anxiety.

Secure adult attachment, as characterized by low attachment avoidance and anxiety, involves comfort with emotional closeness and a healthy balance of autonomy and dependence (i.e., a securely attached person can share when needed in the relationship and can be alone when needed without getting angry or fearful). Feeling secure in one's attachment to other significant adults has numerous benefits. Most importantly, this approach provides the pathways to survival and healthy development. By successfully recruiting care from significant others, children and adults become stronger and more able to cope with threats (Bowlby, 1988). Adults who are lower in attachment anxiety may also have less intense and prolonged grieving experiences (Jerga et al., 2011) and even a higher amount of physical energy (Luke et al., 2012). Moreover, by pursuing growth experiences within the context of safe, secure relationships, we can pursue optimal human functioning or flourishing (Lopez & Brennan, 2000; Luke et al., 2012).

FIGURE 12.2 ■ Attachment Dimensions

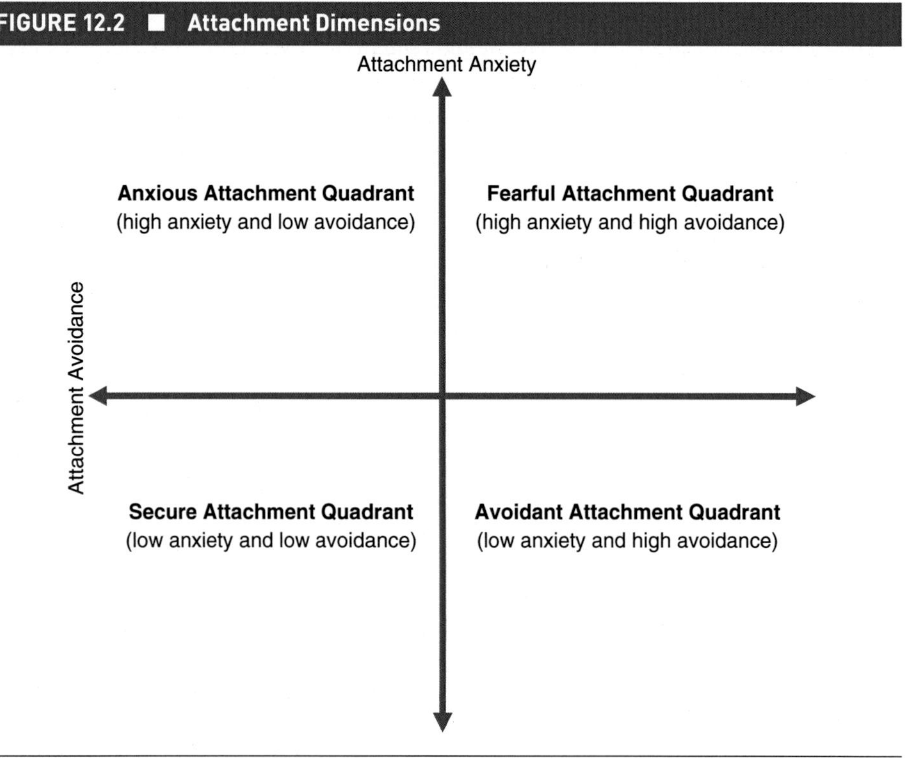

Source: Brennan, K. A., Clark, C. L, & Shaver, P. R. (1998).

Attachment dimensions are also linked to emotional regulation and experiences of happiness and positive affect. Adults who were classified as secure in their attachment style were found to have higher levels of well-being in comparison to those who exhibited a preoccupied/anxious style of attachment (Karreman & Vingerhoets, 2012). This appears to be due in part to the higher levels of resilience exhibited by securely attached adults and their ability to cognitively reframe various situations (e.g., reevaluate an emotional circumstance as less emotional). Indeed, greater adult attachment security has been associated with greater self-compassion (Brophy et al., 2020; Wei et al., 2011), self-esteem (Marrero-Quevedo et al., 2019), and a variety of other positive psychological constructs (Mikulincer & Shaver, 2021).

While the precise mechanisms by which adult attachment security promotes personal and relational well-being and health are more complicated than we can adequately describe in this volume, a simplified version is that individuals who are low in attachment anxiety and low in attachment avoidance (i.e., securely attached) have at their disposal a vast array of positive cognitive, behavioral, and affective self-regulation strategies that contribute to their overall resilience. Attachment security in childhood may set a foundation for healthier relationships in adulthood, thus creating a positive feedback loop that maintains attachment security over time (Mikulincer & Shaver, 2017). Said another way, attachment security helps people make more adaptive relationship choices. Securely attached individuals are likely to choose partners that meet their emotional needs (Mikulincer & Shaver, 2017). By contrast, attachment insecurity (i.e., higher anxiety, high avoidance, or high levels of both anxiety and avoidance) also creates a feedback loop, but this time, insecurely attached individuals are drawn to romantic partners that further perpetuate their attachment insecurity. Fortunately, there are ways of changing one's attachment orientation via therapy and learning to recognize automatic attachment-related emotions, beliefs, and behaviors. Levine and Heller (2012) wrote a book that I (McDermott) recommend as a resource for individuals who would like to learn how to become more securely attached in their adult romantic relationships: *Attached: The New Science of Adult Attachment and How It Can Help You Find—and Keep—Love.* Next, we provide a brief case example to illustrate how adult attachment works in romantic relationships and what it takes to move from a less secure to a more secure attachment orientation.

Journey Toward a Secure Attachment: A Case Example

I (McDermott) recall the case of "Derek," a White, cisgender 35-year-old heterosexual man who came to me concerned about his relationship with his current wife. Upon our first session, Derek lamented that he was falling into the same pattern of relationship dysfunction that had led to a divorce from his first wife a few years prior. He described several instances in which he perceived his partner "pulling away." He identified that this contributed to feelings and thoughts of anger ("Why won't she love me!?") and fear ("What is wrong with me that this keeps happening?"). In addition to mindfulness skills to help him get some perspective on these emotions and thoughts (see Chapter 10), Derek benefited from learning about his attachment orientation. His scores on the ECR suggested he was anxiously attached, and when I described the pattern of maladaptive and anxious proximity seeking associated with this attachment orientation, Derek felt like it fit his experiences perfectly. We also explored his childhood and discovered past traumatic events that may have contributed to a fundamentally negative view of himself—a hallmark of anxious adult attachment (Mikulincer & Shaver, 2017).

Over time, Derek learned to recognize attachment-related cues that triggered automatic thoughts and feelings of anger and fear. He noticed that these feelings were most present when his partner was spending time with other people outside of the relationship. She also had a busy career and often had to work long hours. Thus, she would not come home until late in the evening most nights of the week. Derek realized that his anger and fear translated into behaviors that were aversive to his relationship. For example, he would repeatedly call his partner at work to see what time she would be home, and then he would engage in a variety of passive-aggressive behaviors when she arrived, such as not leaving any lights on after he went to bed or ignoring her the next morning. Most importantly, Derek realized that these ways of coping with attachment-related distress were pushing his partner away. This, in turn, contributed to even more feelings of anger and fear and made him vigilant for any attachment cues that she was going to leave him. He identified that he had the same issues with his first wife, and ultimately, she did leave him.

Following the recommendations of Levine and Heller (2012), Derek learned to stop his maladaptive cycle. It was not easy, and if it were not for him giving me an update many years later, I would not know that he was successful in that endeavor. One of my favorite correspondences a few years later was when he explained to me that his scores on the ECR were now squarely in the secure range.

When I look back at Derek's journey, I believe the most important factor contributing to his success was the awareness of his attachment patterns. He learned to recognize his maladaptive responses to perceived abandonments from his partner and to cope with those experiences more effectively. In other words, he learned to engage the way a securely attached person would function in those instances. Of note, this is just one example of how the knowledge of an attachment orientation can be harnessed to effect important changes in one's relationships. This example was with someone who scored high on attachment anxiety—marked by fear of abandonment, a compulsive need for proximity, and anger/controlling behaviors in response to attachment-related threats. However, I have also worked extensively with individuals who score high on attachment avoidance—marked by a compulsive need for self-reliance and difficulty with emotional expression. The same processes of generating insight and then learning to behave in a more secure fashion over time have been equally effective with these clients.

Attachment Theory and Cultural Considerations

Attachment theory is based almost entirely on White, Western populations. More research is needed with participants of different cultural groups to see if these theories hold true in groups with more collectivistic orientations. For example, although a one-on-one or two-on-one ratio of caregiver to child is often thought of as "normal" in Western cultural groups, there may be more caregivers involved in the lives of children raised in a collectivist society. Grandparents, aunts, uncles, older cousins, and other extended family may more commonly provide regular caregiving for children in addition to parents in non-Western cultural groups, and children and mothers may remain more physically close in these cultural groups. Supporting this cultural influence, some have found that parental absence and other factors may have different meanings for these children (Rothbaum et al., 2000). Other studies have found that there may be some similar characteristics of reaction to the Strange Situation assessment that exist across cultures. Jin and colleagues (2012) conducted a study in which Korean infants were exposed to the same parameters as in Ainsworth's original assessment. Korean infants reacted similarly to the children in the Ainsworth sample, although some differences existed in both babies' and mothers' behavior following the situation. In addition, the incidence of some *insecure* attachment styles (particularly avoidant classifications) has been found to be significantly lower in both Korean (Jin et al., 2012) and Japanese samples (Miyake et al., 1985), as well as Asian American–born samples (Huang et al., 2010). Although more research is needed, it appears that at least some factors of the development of parent-child attachment may be culture-specific.

Cultural differences between Western and Eastern groups may also be present for adult romantic attachment. One researcher, Chiachih DC Wang at the University of North Texas, has studied the cross-cultural applications of adult attachment theory for decades. In a recent study, Dr. Wang, in partnership with a group of colleagues (Zhu et al., 2021), examined the effects of adult romantic attachment dimensions on relationship sacrifice (e.g., willingness to move to another city for your partner's career) using a cross-cultural sample (115 dating couples in the United States and 99 dating couples in China). These researchers found some similarities between the U.S. and Chinese respondents. Mainly, avoidantly attached partners were less likely to sacrifice in both cultural groups. However, they also noted some significant differences. In the U.S. sample, attachment anxiety was associated with a greater likelihood of making major sacrifices for one's partner, which is consistent with the proximity-seeking (i.e., dependent) behaviors associated with an anxious attachment style. In the Chinese sample, however, attachment anxiety had no relationship with sacrifice. Additionally, the authors noted that the link between couples' attachment and their emotional reactions to sacrifice was conditional on the sample. In a related study examining U.S. (n = 401) and Korean (n = 673) participants, Wang and colleagues (2022) found a number of differences in the relationships between attachment insecurity and depressive symptoms on a series of self-report questionnaires. Specifically, the relationship between attachment insecurity and depression was explained by different variables for U.S. versus Korean participants. In conclusion, the authors cautioned that their, "findings highlight the necessity of learning the nuances regarding how the same cultural factor may interact with attachment constructs differently in two cultural contexts to produce variable impacts on people's mental health." (p. 308). These studies remind us that attachment may be a universal human need, but how it is expressed, and its personal or relational impact, is determined by our cultural context.

Cultural context may also impact attachment dynamics across other identity factors. For example, in two large samples of mostly cisgender and heterosexual participants, small (but statistically significant) gender differences were noted on two common self-report measures of attachment security via measurement invariance analyses (Gray & Dunlop, 2019). These findings are consistent with a previous meta-analysis, suggesting that when gender differences are present, cisgender men may score slightly higher in attachment avoidance and lower in attachment anxiety than cisgender women (Del Giudice, 2011). However, more research is needed to see how adult attachment functions in transgender and nonbinary individuals. For instance, in a sample of trans women of color, investigators found that attachment security was associated with better mental health, but only 12.7% of the sample fell in the securely attached range (Sizemore et al., 2019). Sizemore and colleagues (2022) also found that securely attached trans women who had been sexually victimized as children reported better mental health (less depression and less substance use) than their insecurely attached peers. So far, these findings are in line with what would be expected from adult attachment theory even though it was developed entirely with cisgender and heterosexual couples. Nevertheless, more research is needed to identify how attachment theory may need to be adjusted for transgender and nonbinary gender identities.

LOVE

The capacity for love is a central component of all human societies. Love in all its manifestations, whether for children, parents, friends, or romantic partners, gives depth to human relationships. Specifically, love brings people closer to each other physically and emotionally. When experienced intensely, it makes people think expansively about themselves and the world.

Notable scholars, such as Texas Tech University psychologists Susan Hendrick and Clyde Hendrick (1992, 2009), hypothesized that only during the past 300 years or so have cultural forces led people to develop a sense of self that has made them capable of loving and caring for a romantic partner over a lifetime. Despite the uncertainty about the place of romantic love in history, its role in the future of the world is clear. Indeed, love for a companion is considered central to a life well lived, as described in this quotation:

> Romantic love may not be essential in life, but it may be essential to joy. Life without love would be for many people like a black-and-white movie full of events and activities but without the color that gives vibrancy and provides a sense of celebration. (Hendrick & Hendrick, 1992, p. 117)

There is even some research that suggests that romantic love may be evolutionarily beneficial in that it binds us more securely to a mate and that this bond may lead to better parenting to our offspring (Fletcher et al., 2015). Given the intense interest in romantic love, we next provide a brief overview of a few core theories in the field (for more information on additional love theories and research see Hendrick & Hendrick, 2021).

Passionate and Companionate Aspects of Romantic Love

Romantic love is a complex emotion that may be best parsed into *passionate* and *companionate* forms (Berscheid & Walster, 1978; Hatfield, 1988), both of which are valued by most people. **Passionate love** (the intense arousal that fuels a romantic union) involves a state of absorption between two people that is often accompanied by moods ranging from ecstasy to anguish. **Companionate love** (the soothing, steady warmth that sustains a relationship) is manifested in a strong bond and an intertwining of lives that brings about feelings of comfort and peace. These two forms can occur simultaneously or intermittently rather than sequentially (from passionate to companionate). Romantic love is characterized by intense arousal and warm affection. Sexual satisfaction may be a part of this passionate love and has been found to be a very strong predictor of relationship well-being in both same-sex couples and opposite-sex couples (Holmberg et al., 2010).

Love Prototypes

Psychologist, Beverly Fehr at the University of Winnipeg (1993, 1994) studied love by asking individuals to identify or rank its most salient or representative features. These *love prototypes* often revolved around honesty, trust, and other characteristics of companionate love. Interestingly, research using a love prototypes framework has demonstrated that what we often associate with romance in pop culture (e.g., sexual intimacy, passion, or desire) is important, but companionship is equally important. Indeed, one interpretation is that prototypical romantic love is a combination of passionate and companionate love (Hendrick & Hendrick, 2021).

Triangular Theory of Love

In developing the **triangular theory of love**, psychologist Robert Sternberg (1986) theorized that love is a mix of three components: (1) passion, or physical attractiveness and romantic drives; (2) intimacy, or feelings of closeness and connectedness; and (3) commitment, involving the decision to initiate and sustain a relationship. Various combinations of these three components yield eight forms of love. For example, intimacy and passion combined produce romantic love, whereas intimacy and commitment together constitute companionate love. **Consummate love**, the most durable type, is manifested when all three components (passion, intimacy, commitment) are present at high levels and in balance across both partners.

Self-Expansion Theory of Love

Informed by Eastern conceptualizations of love, Arthur Aron and Elaine Aron (1986) developed a theory that humans have a basic motivation to expand the self; moreover, they posited that the emotions, cognitions, and behaviors of love fuel such self-expansion. People seek to expand themselves through love: "The idea is that the self expands toward knowing or becoming that which includes everything and everyone, the Self. The steps along the way are ones of including one person or thing, then another, then still another" (Aron & Aron, 1996, pp. 45–46). People often look to expand themselves by choosing people who are similar to them in some perceived way, and this has been linked to greater attraction in a mate as well (Sprecher et al., 2015). Thus, according to the **self-expansion theory of romantic love** (Aron & Aron, 1996), relationship satisfaction is a natural by-product of self-expansive love. Being in a loving relationship makes people feel good. They then associate those positive feelings with the relationship, thereby reinforcing their commitment to the relationship.

Love Styles

Many contemporary researchers studying romantic love use some variation of a love styles typology. Building from early research on love (e.g., Lee, 1973), Hendrick and colleagues have focused on six love styles: **Eros**, Ludus, Storge, Pragma, Mania, and **Agape** (see Hendrick & Hendrick, 2021 for review). *Eros* is a passionate, lustful, and intense love. *Ludus*, sometimes also referred to as game-playing, is love played as a consensual game without the same intensity as Eros love. *Ludus* love is typically short-lived and not entirely monogamous. *Storge* represents companionship or friendship love. *Pragma* is a pragmatic (e.g., realistic or practical) love style. Someone with this style may connect with a mate for practical reasons (e.g., they meet a certain set of requirements). *Mania* is "manic" love. A person with a manic love style both craves and fears intimacy. This style is marked by cycles of jealousy and dramatic breakups and reconciliations. Finally, the *Agape* style is characterized by a "selfless and giving love where the person is fully concerned with the partner's welfare" (Hendrick & Hendrick, 2021, p. 589). This form of love is sometimes called "altruistic love."

Love and Cultural Context

Cultural context can sharply define how love is expressed and the value it has in romantic relationships, as well as how it is defined as a construct. Landis and O'Shea (2000) examined the concept of passionate love across several countries (as well as comparing locations within those countries) and found that this construct appeared to have unique factor structures across different cultural groupings. It is important to recognize that different cultural practices, such as arranged marriages, may dictate to some extent the value love has within a society. Some researchers have found differences in constructs such as emotional investment (Schmitt et al., 2009) or in the experiences of passionate or companionate love among different cultural groups (Gao, 2001). In addition, using the words "I love you" may be more common in some cultures than in others. Gareis and Wilkins (2011) found that verbal expression of love, particularly a public declaration of this love, was much less common in Germany when compared with U.S. participants. Gender differences may be present in some aspects of romantic love as well. A recent meta-analysis of gender differences in love types across 51 studies and 21,395 participants revealed that men tended to endorse more agape love than women, and that women tended to report more mania and pragma love styles (Tehrani & Yamini, 2020). Additionally, there may be some interactions between gender differences and cultural differences, as the same meta-analysis identified that women in individualistic cultures reported more pragmatic love than men, but these differences disappeared in collectivistic cultures. These findings highlight a need for additional research to understand how love may be expressed and defined across (and within) different cultures.

FLOURISHING RELATIONSHIPS: A SERIES OF PURPOSEFUL POSITIVE RELATIONSHIP BEHAVIORS

Positive psychologists specializing in close relationships (Harvey et al., 2001; Reis & Gable, 2003) have explored what makes existing relationships flourish and what skills can be taught directly to partners to enhance their interpersonal connections (try to develop some of these behaviors by completing the brief exercises in the Life Enhancement Strategies section at the end of this chapter). In this section, we discuss theories and research evidence on flourishing relationships, which are good relationships that continue to get better due to the concerted effort of both partners.

Building a Mindful Relationship Connection

Well-minded relationships are healthy and long-lasting. This belief led University of Iowa social psychologist John Harvey and his colleagues (Harvey & Ormarzu, 1997; Harvey et al., 2001) to develop a five-component model of **minding** relationships. This model shows how closeness, or the satisfaction and relationship behaviors that contribute to one another's goals in life, may be enhanced. (See Table 12.2 for a summary of these components and their maladaptive counterparts).

Minding is the "reciprocal knowing process involving the nonstop, interrelated thoughts, feelings, and behaviors of persons in a relationship" (Harvey et al., 2001, p. 424). As described in Chapter 10, mindfulness is a conscious process that requires moment-to-moment effort. This need for consciousness in minding relationships is reflected in the first component of the model, *knowing and being known.* According to the model, each partner in the relationship must want to know the other person's hopes, dreams, fears, vulnerabilities, and uncertainties. Furthermore, each partner must monitor the balance between their own self-expression and that of the partner and give preference to learning about the other person rather than focusing on their own personal information. People who are successful at knowing and being known in their relationships demonstrate an understanding of how time brings about change and of how change necessitates renewed opportunities and attempts to learn about the other person.

TABLE 12.2 ■ Minding Relationship Behavior: Adaptive and Nonadaptive Steps

Adaptive	*Nonadaptive*
Via an in-depth knowing process, both partners in step in seeking to know and be known by the other.	One or both partners are out of step in seeking to know and be known by the other.
Both partners use the knowledge gained to enhance the relationship.	Knowledge gained in the knowing process is not used or not used well (may be used to hurt others).
Both partners accept what they learn and respect the other for the person they learn about.	Acceptance of what is learned is low, as is respect for the other person.
Both partners are motivated to continue this process and do so indefinitely, such that synchrony and synergy of thought, feeling, and action emerge.	One or both partners are not motivated to engage in the overall minding process or do so sporadically; little synchrony and synergy emerge.
Both partners, in time, develop a sense of being special and appreciated in the relationship.	One or both partners fail to develop a sense of being special and appreciated in the relationship.

From Harvey, J. H., Pauwels, B. G., & Zicklund, S., Relationship connection: The role of minding in the enhancement of closeness, in C. R. Snyder & S. J. Lopez (Eds.), *The Handbook of Positive Psychology.* Copyright © 2002 by Oxford University Press, Inc. Used by permission of Oxford University Press, Inc.

The second component of relationship minding involves partners *making relationship-enhancing attributions for behaviors.* Attributing positive behaviors to dispositional causes and negative behaviors to external, situational causes may be the most adaptive approach to making sense of another person's behavior. Over time, people in well-minded relationships develop the proper mixture of internal and external attributions and become more willing to reexamine attributions when explanations for a partner's behavior don't jibe with what is known about the loved one. Making charitable attributions (i.e., going beyond the benefit of the doubt) can occasionally resolve conflicts before they become divisive.

Accepting and respecting, the third component of the minding model, requires an empathic connection (see Chapter 11), along with refined social skills (such as those described in the next section). As partners become more intimate in their knowledge of one another and share some good and bad experiences, mindful acceptance of personal strengths and weaknesses is necessary for the continued development of the relationship. When this acceptance is linked with respect, it serves as an antidote for contemptuous behavior that can dissolve a relationship (Gottman, 1994).

The final components of the model are *maintaining reciprocity and continuity in minding.* Regarding reciprocity in minding, "Each partner's active participation and involvement in relationship-enhancing thoughts and behaviors" (Harvey et al., 2001, p. 428) is necessary for maintaining a mutually beneficial relationship. A lack of conscious engagement displayed by one partner can lead to frustration or contempt on the part of the other partner. Continuity in minding also may require planning and strategizing to become closer as the relationship matures. Mindfulness is a skill that can be taught, and as such, relationship minding can be enhanced (Harvey & Ormarzu,

1997). The mutual practice of mindfulness techniques (discussed in Chapter 10) could benefit partners who are attempting to apply Harvey's relationship-enhancing guidance.

It is important to recognize that the way in which we start relationships and mind them may look different as our society's use of technology continues to increase. In a study looking at the popular social media networking site, Facebook, researchers found that couples who were more authentic about their relationship in real life tended to also be more likely to represent themselves as part of a couple on Facebook when posting and tended to have a stronger relationship quality in general as compared to those who were less likely to post about their relationships (Steers et al., 2016). The link between this authenticity and the quality of the relationship seemed to be mediated by the factor of *relationship awareness*. Thus, it may be that technology in the form of Facebook, in this case, may be a tool one uses to *mind* their relationship.

At the same time, Northrup and Smith (2016) have found that couples who report a high level of love in their relationships also spend less time on Facebook maintenance behaviors (such as posting on one another's feed, making comments to one another, or "liking" pictures or comments on each other's feeds). Although the authors note that this might seem illogical at first, they conclude that couples who are engaged in healthy relationships are likely complimenting each other or making loving comments in person, "so there is no need to repeat these behaviors via Facebook" (Northrup & Smith, 2016, p. 249). Finally, some research on online dating shows that couples whose relationships exist primarily online probably unsurprisingly have less commitment to one another and a lower quality of relationship compared to couples who have an actual physical relationship (Haack & Falcke, 2014). These researchers conclude that "the Internet is a great tool for people to meet, but for the development of intimacy and commitment, it is important for the relationship to develop in a physical context" (Haack & Falcke, 2014, p. 111). Additionally, some research suggests that the perceived availability of partners (e.g., the sheer number of possible partners available on dating apps such as Tinder) may increase the chances of later relationship infidelity (Alexopoulos et al., 2020). Thus, as we increasingly move away from in-person connections toward online profiles, further research will be needed to understand how those dynamics influence relationship behaviors over time.

Creating a Culture of Appreciation

John Gottman (1994, 1999, 2015) has spent a lifetime "thin-slicing" relationship behavior (Gladwell, 2005). He measures the bodily sensations of partners, "reads" the faces of couples as they interact, and watches people talk about difficult issues while dissecting every aspect of the exchange. After watching only a brief interaction, Gottman's methods can predict relationship success (divorce versus continued marriage) with over 90% accuracy several years later (Gottman, 2015).

Gottman achieved this feat of prediction by studying thousands of heterosexual married couples across many years of their relationships. The standard research protocol involves a husband and wife entering the "love lab" and engaging in a 15-minute conversation while being closely observed by the researchers and monitored by blood pressure cuffs, electrocardiograms, and other devices. Gottman's seminal finding from observations of couples was derived with the assistance of mathematicians (Gottman, Murray et al., 2003) who helped him discover what is referred to as the "magic ratio" for marriages. Five positive interactions to one negative interaction (5:1) are needed to maintain a healthy relationship. As the ratio approaches 1:1, however, divorce is likely. Importantly, achieving the 5:1 ratio in a relationship does not require avoiding all arguments. Partners in master marriages can talk about difficult subjects and do so by infusing warmth, affection, and humor into the conversation. On the other hand, a lack of positive interactions during challenging discussions can lead couples to emotional disconnections and mild forms of contempt.

Drawing from decades of research and a "sound marital house" theory, Gottman and colleagues (2002) developed a multidimensional therapeutic approach to couples counseling that moves partners from conflict to comfortable exchanges. The goals of the therapy include the enhancement of basic social skills and the development of an awareness of the interpersonal pitfalls associated with the relationship behaviors of criticism, contempt, defensiveness, and stonewalling. Over time, these four behaviors that undermine relationships are replaced with complaint (i.e., a more civil form of expressing disapproval), a culture of appreciation, acceptance of responsibility for a part of the problem, and self-soothing. These skills are also mentioned in Gottman's (1999) book, *The Seven Principles for Making Marriage Work* and the more recent *Principia Amoris: The New Science of Love* (Gottman, 2015). The Gottman Institute continues to grow, now offering many online learning opportunities for professionals who want to help couples, as well as resources and a newsletter for couples themselves (you can find more information here: https://www.gottman.com/). Additionally, although most of Gottman's core work revolved around heterosexual couples, evidence suggests that these findings and their therapeutic implications generalize to same-sex marriages (Garanzini et al. 2017; Gottman, Levenson et al., 2003, 2020).

Based on our reading of Gottman's work, the advice regarding creating a culture of appreciation in a relationship may be the most basic, yet most potent, advice to couples of all ages, backgrounds, and marital statuses. The purposeful, positive relationship behavior of creating a culture of appreciation is potentially powerful because of (1) the positive reception of the partner and the partner's behavior that it promotes and (2) the contemptuous feelings that it prevents. Creating a culture of appreciation helps to establish an environment where positive interactions and a sense of security are the norms. Expressing gratitude (see Chapter 11) to a partner is the primary means of creating a positive culture. Saying thanks for the small behaviors that often go unnoticed (e.g., picking up around the house, taking the trash out, making the morning coffee, cleaning out the refrigerator) makes a partner feel valued for their daily efforts around the home. Sharing appreciation for small favors (e.g., taking an extra turn in the carpool, making a coworker feel welcome in the home) and for big sacrifices (e.g., remembering a least favorite in-law's birthday, giving up "rainy day" money for a home expense) honors a partner's contributions to the relationship and the family.

THE NEUROBIOLOGY OF CLOSE RELATIONSHIPS

Psychologists and other health professionals have long understood that our early experiences shape brain development. Drawing from human and animal samples, researchers have found evidence of the neurobiological bases of the core concepts we have discussed so far in this chapter. Specifically, the mechanisms in our brains that keep us connected to others are generally distinct from brain structures that keep us physically safe (e.g., fight, flight, or freeze behaviors). However, there is evidence that both serve an important biological role. Close relationships, for example, allow us to use less cognitive resources, as we can rely on our partners (Long, Verbeke et al., 2020). In this section, we review some key developments in the neurobiology of close relationships.

Attachment and the Developing Brain

Neuropsychoanalyst Allan Schore (1994, 2003) and health psychologist Shelley Taylor (Taylor et al., 2002) have gathered and integrated indirect and direct evidence on the neurobiology of interpersonal connection from their own laboratories, as well as from other researchers. Schore, building on the assumptions of attachment theory, argues that the social environment, mediated by actions of and attachment to the primary caregiver, influences the evolution of structures in a child's brain. More specifically, Schore proposed that the maturation of a region of the right cortex, the orbitofrontal cortex (which may store the internal working models of attachment), is influenced by interactions between the child and the caregiver. As the orbitofrontal cortex matures, self-regulation of emotions is enhanced. The brain–behavior interactions suggest that an upward spiral of growth may explain how infant attachment sometimes produces emotionally healthy adults. That is, when a child and their caregiver have a secure attachment, the part of the brain that helps with the regulation of emotions and behavior is stimulated. As the child's security is maintained, brain development is promoted, and the abilities to empathize with others and to regulate intrapersonal and interpersonal stress are enhanced. Equipped with well-honed self-regulation skills, the child can develop and sustain healthy friendships and, eventually, healthy adult relationships.

Taylor and colleagues (Taylor et al., 2002), intrigued by the health benefits of social contact and social support, reviewed research on social animals and humans to determine the biological mechanisms associated with interpersonal experiences. Like Schore (1994, 2003), Taylor et al. (2002) hypothesized that a nurturing relationship between a child and a caregiver promotes the development of regulatory activity, in this case in the hypothalamic-pituitary-adrenocortical (HPA) system (which is activated via hormone secretion). Additionally, the hormone, oxytocin, has been consistently implicated in the development of a secure attachment. Oxytocin is a hormone released into the bloodstream via the pituitary gland in the brain. In pregnant women, it induces labor, but both men and women secrete oxytocin during close physical contact. In a recent systematic review of 17 studies of mothers, fathers, and their infant children, researchers found that greater maternal oxytocin was significantly associated with more caregiver responsiveness to an infant's needs and greater caregiver engagement (Scatliffe et al., 2019). Likewise, the same review of the literature identified a similar connection in fathers, particularly with skin-to-skin contact. Similar increases were noted in the infants, suggesting that higher caregiver oxytocin is associated with greater infant oxytocin.

Neural Mechanisms of Love

Some researchers have studied the neural links to long-term romantic love. When participants involved in intense romantic relationships lasting more than 10 years were shown pictures of their loved partner, effects occurred in many areas of the brain that are associated with bonding and attachment, including regions rich in dopamine, and this finding has been replicated in other studies (Acevedo et al., 2012; Takahashi et al., 2015). These effects were not found when participants were shown pictures of other close individuals (e.g., long-term friends) or strangers, and thus it was not merely a preference for familiarity but a response related specifically to a loved one. Activation in this study was also found in the dorsal striatum, which is an area of the brain linked to behavior aimed at achieving goals that lead to rewards. This "suggests regions that are active when partners enact behaviors that maintain and enhance their relationships" (Acevedo et al., 2012, p. 157). In other research, areas of the brain associated with value estimation (i.e., how much one subjectively values certain objects) were activated when participants were shown objects related to their loved ones (Wang et al., 2016). These results point to the close association between attachment and the development of long-term romantic relationships and give more insight into what neural correlates may sustain this type of relationship.

In addition, the experience of being in love may protect individuals from stress at the biological level and lead to better responses to negative emotions (Schneiderman et al., 2011). The vagus nerve, which is the 10th cranial nerve, plays a key role in regulating the amount of physiological stress felt by an individual. Strong reactivity of this nerve leads to better protection of other bodily processes from the effect of stress. Researchers have found that individuals in love seem to have better regulation of their vagal-cardiac response and that this may "be one mechanism through which love and attachment reduce stress and promote well-being and health" (Schneiderman et al., 2011, p. 1314). Other research shows that individuals dealing with physical pain who are also in passion-filled relationships have reported that focusing on a picture of their partner can decrease the experience of pain (Nilakantan et al., 2014). Companionate love and a feeling of harmony in the relationship may help buffer against depression and other negative emotions across many different cultures (Smith & Bryant, 2016). Neuroscientists and psychologists will continue to explore how neurobiology and positive social behavior are intertwined. As the positive psychology of close relationships incorporates neurobiological findings, we will draw closer to knowing how good relationships become great.

POSITIVE PSYCHOLOGY AS ACCEPTANCE

Humans have a long and storied history of reacting with suspicion and fear to groups or practices that we don't understand, particularly when it comes to different ways of expressing romantic love. For example, same-sex couples in the United States fought and won the right to be legally married in 2015; however, discrimination against LGBTQ couples still exists. Indeed, to mitigate the possibility that the Supreme Court of the United States may overturn its 2015 ruling supporting same-sex marriage, President Joseph R. Biden signed a bill codifying same-sex and interracial marriage protections on December 13, 2022.

Love is complex and nuanced. Fortunately, positive psychology offers a framework to study and understand *all* positive relationships. Specifically, it teaches us to recognize the antecedents and legitimacy of positive relationships, to use positive behaviors and emotions for combating negative feelings associated with stigma and prejudice, and it moves us toward acceptance of positive and loving relationships between consenting adults. For example, researchers are beginning to explore romantic love in more complex forms, such as consensual nonmonogamy (i.e., being romantically involved with more than one partner at a time). Findings on this new research frontier suggest that, contrary to many negative stereotypes, individuals engaged in consensual nonmonogamy appear to have the same personal and relational benefits of monogamous relationships, as well as some unique challenges (Wood et al., 2021) and benefits (Balzarini & Muise, 2020). As psychological research grows to account for the increasing diversity in who we love, positive psychology will provide valuable insights that we can use to help strengthen and understand positive relationships between consenting adults.

FORGIVENESS

We now turn our attention toward the concept of **forgiveness,** though one could easily make an argument that love and forgiveness go hand-in-hand in successful romantic relationships. Still, the psychological study of forgiveness goes beyond simply not holding a grudge against one's romantic partner. Indeed, there has been an explosion of interest in forgiveness since the 1990s. Part of the reason for this tremendous expansion of theory and research relates to the fact that philanthropist John Templeton initiated calls for grants involving research on forgiveness from the Templeton Foundation. In this section, we first introduce the various definitions of forgiveness and discuss its individual and cultural variations; then, we describe how it can be cultivated, review its measurement, and end with an overview of its evolutionary and neurobiological bases.

Defining Forgiveness

Scholars have differed in their definitions of forgiveness (Tsang & Martin, 2021). Although views of the exact nature of forgiveness vary, the consensus is that it is beneficial to people (see Worthington, 2005). We discuss the major ways of defining forgiveness in the remainder of this section, starting with the most liberal and inclusive definition and moving to relatively more circumscribed ones.

McCullough and Colleagues

According to McCullough (2000; McCullough et al., 1998), forgiveness reflects increases in prosocial motivation toward another such that there is (1) less desire to avoid the transgressing person and to harm or seek revenge toward that individual and (2) increased desire to act positively toward the transgressing person. Changes in motivation are viewed as being at the core of this theory (McCullough et al., 2000a, 2000b), with the person becoming more benevolent over time; moreover, forgiveness is seen as applicable only when there is another person who has engaged in a transgression.

Enright and Colleagues

The scholar with the longest track record in studying forgiveness is Robert Enright, who defined forgiveness as "a willingness to abandon one's right to resentment, negative judgment, and indifferent behavior toward one who unjustly hurt us, while fostering the undeserved qualities of compassion, generosity, and even love toward him or her" (Enright et al., 1998, pp. 46–47). For Enright (2000; Enright et al., 1998), it is crucial that the forgiving person develop a benevolent stance toward the transgressing person. As he put it, "The fruition of forgiveness is entering into a loving community with others" (Enright & Zell, 1989, p. 99). Furthermore, Enright was adamant in stating that forgiveness cannot be extended to situations and thus must be directed only at people. On this, Enright wrote, "Forgiveness is between people. One does not forgive tornadoes or floods. How could one, for instance, again join in a loving community with a tornado?" (Enright & Zell, 1989, p. 53).

Tangney and Colleagues

In 1999, Tangney and her colleagues (1999) suggested that forgiveness reflected three key aspects: "(1) cognitive-affective transformation following a transgression in which (2) the victim makes a realistic assessment of the harm done and acknowledges the perpetrator's responsibility, but (3) freely chooses to "cancel the debt," giving up the need for revenge or deserved punishments and any quest for restitution" (p. 2). This "canceling of the debt" also involves a "cancellation of negative emotions" directly related to the transgression. In particular, by engaging in the act of forgiving, the harmed individual can remove themselves from the victim role. Thus, the Tangney model suggests that the act of letting go of negative emotions is the crux of the forgiving process.

Self-Report Measures of Forgiveness

Several self-report measures of forgiveness have been created over the years. Some of the more common ones include the Enright Forgiveness Inventory (EFI; Enright et al., 2022), the Rye Forgiveness Scale (RFS; Rye, Loiacono et al., 2001), the Transgression-Related Inventory of Motivations (TRIM; McCullough et al., 1998), and Worthington's Decision and Emotional Forgiveness Scales (DEF; Worthington et al., 2007). We have also included the Heartland Forgiveness scale (HFS; Thompson et al., 2005) in its entirety as an appendix to this chapter. These instruments provide important information about forgiveness as a trait or a behavior. At the same time, Tsang and Martin (2021) warn that it is essential to supplement self-report forgiveness measures with other assessments, such as physiological measures (e.g., facial expressions, skin conductance levels, blood pressure, or heart rate) that are less susceptible to socially desirable response bias. That is, most people are going to say they are more forgiving than they truly are, because being forgiving is a socially desirable trait (Tsang & Martin, 2021).

Correlates of Forgiveness

Several lines of evidence suggest that individuals who have empathy for the transgressor and display certain personality characteristics (e.g., are highly agreeable) or identify as religious are likely to forgive (Tsang & Martin, 2021). Empathy may help victims relate to their transgressors and the situational variables contributing to the transgression. Likewise, individuals high in the personality characteristic of agreeableness value social harmony, and thus, it is not surprising that they may prefer to forgive their transgressors (Tsang & Martin, 2021).

In terms of the possible outcomes of forgiveness, many researchers have found correlations between forgiveness and well-being (Moorhead et al., 2012), as well as between forgiveness and physical health (Green et al., 2012; Hannon et al., 2012; Lavelock et al., 2015). In addition, those who forgive are said to be less ruminative, are less depressed, and possess less narcissistic entitlement (Strelan, 2007; Takaku, 2001). Other research has found that longevity is also associated with practicing forgiveness (Toussaint et al., 2012), as is satisfaction within relationships (Aalgaard et al., 2016; Braithwaite et al., 2011) and the maintaining of a romantic relationship over time (Kato, 2016), both of which might be linked to health as well. Some research shows that forgiveness might provide somewhat of a buffer against stress over a transgression and the mental health implications that can follow over the course of a lifetime (Toussaint et al., 2016). Several studies have also found that self-forgiveness may protect individuals from engaging in self-harming behaviors (Cleare et al., 2019). Interestingly, the consequences of forgiveness may not always be positive (Wohl & Thompson, 2011; Tsang & Martin, 2021). According to Gordon, Burton, and Porter (2004), victims of domestic violence who were able to forgive their abusive partners were more likely to return to the violent situation. This finding held even when other factors (e.g., lack of belief in divorce and concerns about alternatives to the relationship) were controlled. Based on this pattern of data, these researchers caution clinicians to take care in linking the ideas of forgiveness and reconciliation. As discussed above, many may find these two concepts to be joined, and in these situations, this belief that reconciliation is necessary may drive an abused woman toward returning as a component of her forgiveness process (Gordon, Burton, & Porter, 2004). In addition, other studies have found that the tendency to forgive a violent partner is predictive of continued aggression (both physical and psychological) within marriages (McNulty, 2011). Therefore, although forgiveness can lead to positive outcomes for many, caution must be taken in looking carefully at the situation before employing strategies in this area.

Newer Areas of Forgiveness Research

Tsang and Martin (2021) highlight two newer areas of forgiveness research that have taken off over the last 10 to 15 years. These concepts expand beyond the typical dyadic (i.e., person and transgressor) form of forgiveness discussed so far. Specifically, concepts such as self-forgiveness and intergroup forgiveness have become increasingly popular in the extant literature.

The definition of self-forgiveness may seem self-explanatory, though it was once described as the "step-child" of forgiveness research due to a lack of sound theoretical and empirical foundations (Hall & Fincham, 2005). We now know that self-forgiveness is a distinct form of forgiveness with unique correlates and outcomes (Tsang & Marting, 2021). Webb and colleagues (2017) provide the following definition:

> Self-forgiveness . . . is a deliberate, volitional process initiated in response to one's own negative feelings in the context of a personally acknowledged self-instigated wrong, that results in ready accountability for said wrong and a fundamental, constructive shift in one's relationship to, reconciliation with, and acceptance of the self through human connectedness and commitment to change. (p. 217)

This definition somewhat resembles the concept of self-compassion, and it is possible self-forgiveness may be a component of self-compassion. Indeed, we will all go through life making mistakes along the way. Sometimes, those mistakes hurt others or ourselves. Self-forgiveness and self-compassion allow us to reduce negative emotions toward the self and develop a sense of closure so we can move forward when we make mistakes. Not surprisingly, studies conducted in the United States and abroad suggest that self-forgiveness is associated with a wide variety of positive outcomes (Tsang & Martin, 2021). For example, a systematic review of 18 published studies worldwide found evidence that higher self-forgiveness was associated with lower levels of self-harm and suicidal ideation (Cleare et al., 2019). Likewise, self-forgiveness was associated with less social exclusion and internet addiction in Turkish college students (Arslan & Coşkun, 2022) and was uniquely associated with fewer depression symptoms in U.S. participants over a 10-week interval (Fincham & May, 2020). Emerging evidence also suggests that a self-forgiveness writing intervention may be beneficial in treating trauma over time in a randomized control treatment study of sexually traumatized Korean participants (Ha et al., 2019).

Some researchers have shown that there may be some less positive antecedents to self-forgiveness as well. Wohl and Thompson (2011) found that some maladaptive behaviors may be maintained through the process of self-forgiveness. In their study, these researchers looked at smokers and found that those higher in self-forgiveness were more likely to continue smoking and resist change toward a healthier lifestyle. This may be in part because the negative emotion associated with not forgiving oneself for this type of behavior spurs the individual to change; when the negative emotion is dissipated by self-forgiveness, the need to change is no longer warranted (Wohl & Thompson, 2011).

Forgiveness of groups of individuals (e.g., intergroup forgiveness) is another area of research that has become increasingly more popular (Tsang & Martin, 2021). Van Tongeren and colleagues (2013) defined this form of forgiveness as, "an internal transformation of motivation toward a perceived perpetrating out-group that is situated within a specific collective, political, or societal context" (p. 81). There are many examples of groups extending apologies to other groups. Specific to psychology, the American Psychological Association adopted a formal resolution on October 29, 2021 to issue an apology for its role in legitimizing anti-Black racism via biased science and clinical practices over the years. Research on intergroup forgiveness shows us that such apologies are, unfortunately, not very effective in facilitating forgiveness (Tsang & Martin, 2021). Nevertheless, intergroup forgiveness can be achieved in some instances. In their seminal meta-analysis of intergroup forgiveness, Van Tongeren and colleagues noted that greater empathy, outgroup expressions of collective guilt and trustworthiness, and more outgroup contact were associated with greater intergroup forgiveness. Thus, it is not enough for one group to apologize to another for transgressions; several group dynamics and contextual factors on both sides need to be present for forgiveness to occur.

Cultivating Forgiveness

In this section, we explore how forgiveness can be taught or encouraged. Accordingly, we show how two sources—another person and a situation or circumstance—can be used as targets in forgiveness instruction.

Forgiving Another Person

Making the decision to forgive another, perhaps particularly when the relationship we have with a person is very meaningful to us, often requires some perspective-taking. In the previous chapter, we read about *empathy* and some of its benefits. Consider, for example, the person who is filled with anger at something hurtful that another person has done and who must first learn to see the issue from the perspective of that other person (i.e., empathize) before coming to the point of forgiving them.

In a situation related to this point, a woman, Anna, who received a very dire medical diagnosis, chose not to impart the seriousness of this diagnosis or its life-threatening nature to her close friends, among whom were this author (JTP) and her family. Upon Anna's death, many of us felt anger mixed with sadness at losing this great friend in a way that felt very sudden. We felt cheated, at some level, at not being able to say goodbye and instead were jolted by the suddenness (to us) of her death. In light of Anna's very caring and nurturing nature, however, it was likely her true belief was that she was sparing her friends from worry during the time that she was ill, especially as her death was inevitable. Reframing this "transgression" as a caring gesture toward loved companions allowed us to "forgive" Anna for not telling us the truth.

In our therapy experiences with couples dealing with forgiveness in the wake of infidelities, we have found that the model of Gordon and colleagues is a useful one (Gordon, Burton, & Porter, 2004, 2005; Gordon & Baucom, 1998). In this model, in which forgiveness is the goal, the first step is to promote a nondistorted, realistic appraisal of the relationship. The second step is the attempt to facilitate a release from the bond of ruminative, negative affect held toward the violating (transgressing) partner. Finally, the third step is to help the victimized partner lessen their desire to punish the transgressing partner. Over time, forgiveness makes it possible for the hurt and the outpouring of negative feelings to diminish—especially for the victimized partner. Likewise, the treatment enhances the empathy for the transgressing partner, and the therapist tries to make both people feel better about themselves. Other research supports this idea of loosening the hold of the negative memory of a negative transgression. Sell (2016) conducted a study in which she employed methods of *intentional forgetting* of a particular transgression in some participants via a series of exercises. Findings showed that those who practiced this intentional forgetting were more likely to show feelings of forgiveness for someone they felt had done something negative to them (Sell, 2016). Finally, mindfulness may be linked to a higher propensity of forgiving a partner for infidelity, and the literature shows this may be due to an ability to stay in the present (as opposed to hashing over the past; Johns et al., 2015).

Another productive approach for helping couples to deal with infidelity is the forgiveness model of Everett Worthington of Virginia Commonwealth University (see Ripley & Worthington, 2002; Worthington, 1998; Worthington & Drinkard, 2000). This model is based on helping the partners through the five steps of the acronym REACH: Recall the hurt and the nature of the injury caused, promote Empathy in both partners, Altruistically give the gift of forgiveness between partners, Commit verbally to forgive the partner, and Hold onto the forgiveness for each other. The REACH program has been successfully used across a number of different cultural groups within the United States and found to be helpful in several ways (Lin et al., 2014).

Forgiveness of a Situation

Recall the Enright position (described previously) that forgiveness should be applied only to people, not to inanimate objects such as tornadoes. We disagree with this premise; our views are consistent with the Snyder model of forgiveness, in which the target can be another person, oneself, or a situation.

C. R. Snyder's recounting of a psychotherapy case he had some 20 years after the publication of the first edition of this book shows how forgiveness can be applied to a situation. Dr. Snyder resided in Lawrence, Kansas, at the time, where tornadoes occasionally descend on the local community. In this particular instance, a tornado had damaged houses and injured the inhabitants. After this tornado, Dr. Snyder saw a cisgender, White man in therapy who held severe angry and bitter thoughts toward the tornado for destroying his house and making him feel psychologically victimized. In the course of treatment, the goal was to help this man to stop ruminating about the tornado and to stop blaming it for having ruined his life (Snyder, 2003). Therefore, the man was taught to let go of his resentment toward the tornado. This was part of a larger treatment goal aimed at teaching this person to release the bitterness he felt about a series of "bad breaks" that he had received in life. Moreover, he came to understand that the tornado had struck other houses and families, but those people had picked up the pieces and moved on with their lives. For this client, ruminations about the tornado kept him stuck in the past, and he realized that letting go was part of moving forward so as to have hope in his life (see Lopez et al., 2004; Snyder, 1989).

For professionals who have done considerable psychotherapy, this case will not seem unusual. Clients often point to their life circumstances as the causes of their problems (i.e., they blame the happenings in their lives). For such clients, therefore, a crucial part of their treatment entails instruction in stopping thoughts about earlier negative life events so that they can instead look ahead toward their futures (Michael & Snyder, 2005; Wade, 2010).

Individual and Cultural Variations in Forgiveness

Researchers suggest that the way in which individuals conceptualize forgiveness plays an important role in their assignment of value to this construct and ultimately their use of it in their daily lives. Ballester and colleagues (2009) state that differences may occur in how one defines forgiveness (e.g., as "pardoning" or agreeing with the offender versus moving on with a relationship after a transgressor has seen the error of their ways) and that having different conceptualizations may interfere with healthy relationships between transgressors and victims. If, for example, a transgressor knows that a victim feels that forgiveness is a pardoning of behavior, they may be able to work harder to emphasize their fault in the situation or assure the victim that this type of behavior will not recur, and thus forgiveness may be more comfortably granted as well as received (Ballester et al., 2009).

Actions that the transgressor takes (or decides not to take) may make a difference in whether forgiveness occurs as well. Past research shows that when a transgressor apologizes (either verbally or by offering some kind of compensation), forgiveness is more likely to follow (Exline & Baumeister, 2000; McCullough et al., 2014). This said, the effectiveness of an apology is often influenced by the personality factors of the person who committed the bad act—namely, how much agreeableness they possess (Tabak et al., 2012). In addition, others have shown that apologies are more effective when they are in line with the victim's self-construal. For example, Fehr and Gelfand (2010) found that those individuals who are more independent in their self-construal tend to be more forgiving when a transgressor clearly states what they will do to "make things right" and recreate equality in the relationship. Individuals in this study who were more relational in their construal responded more positively to empathy as opposed to compensation. Other work has found that **restorative justice** can also lead to forgiveness and more strongly than just seeking retribution, suggesting that a victim may feel more able to forgive when a transgressor agrees they were wrong (Wenzel & Okimoto, 2014). Studies have also found that even children were more likely to reconcile with a brother or sister who has committed some "crime" against them when the sibling apologized and when that apology was not mandated by parents or authority figures (Schleien et al., 2010). Thus, knowing the mindset from which the victim comes might make a difference in whether forgiveness occurs. The function of an apology may also differ based on the amount of power the victim perceives the transgressor to have. To this point, some research has found that an apology, or remorse for wrongdoing, is less believable to a victim when coming from a high-power transgressor (Zheng et al., 2016).

Finally, differences across developmental stages account for the qualitative experience and likelihood of forgiveness. Most studies find that the older you are, the more willing you are to forgive and that this tendency to forgive becomes more dispositional (as opposed to situational) with age (Steiner et al., 2011, 2012). Other studies, however, show that as a rule, the number and seriousness of transgressions seem to decrease in older adulthood, and thus this may partially explain these findings (Steiner et al., 2011).

Identification with various cultural facets and contexts (e.g., race, ethnicity, gender, religion) may also drive different definitions or values placed on forgiveness as a concept. In some cultures, forgiveness may be more of an interpersonal process, and in others, it may be more of an intrapersonal process; these different conceptualizations may have implications for cross-cultural interactions with regard to forgiveness (Hook et al., 2012; Kadiangandu et al., 2007). Others have stated that forgiveness may be more common in Eastern cultures as compared to Western cultures and that situational factors and cultural norms (such as a value of harmony) may play more of a role in the likelihood of forgiving in certain cultures as well (Paz et al., 2008). Karremans and colleagues (2011) found that in collectivist nations such as Japan and China, norms of social harmony dictated forgiveness, even in situations where Western-oriented individuals would be less likely to forgive. In addition, in these collectivist societies, people believe that some sort of reconciliation attempt or conciliatory behavior is a necessary precursor to forgiveness (Hook et al., 2012; Watkins et al., 2011). Engaging in regular acts of forgiveness may also enhance our social relationships within our communities (Hook et al., 2009). In cultures whose ideologies are more collectivistic, forgiveness is a necessary part of achieving social harmony, which is highly valued within these groups. Hook and colleagues (2009) present the concept of "collective forgiveness" (p. 821) and discuss its usefulness in maintaining and repairing relationships that have been ruptured due to some transgression. With this type of forgiveness, the decision to forgive may be "largely to promote and maintain group harmony rather than [attain] inner peace" (Hook et al., 2009, p. 821).

Some personal and social identity facets may bring up more opportunities to forgive, particularly in the case of exposure to bias and discrimination. In a study looking at the measurement of forgiveness of race-related offenses, Davis and colleagues (2015) found that relationship closeness and value and belief that a similar event would not be perpetrated by the transgressor in the future were associated with a higher likelihood of forgiving. Those who did not feel a desire for revenge against their transgressor also were found to have more strength in the form of ethnic identity development in this study. It may be that knowing who one is allows these individuals to buffer themselves from some of the negative emotions that might come with deciding not to forgive. Racial identity development was also shown to have some effect on willingness and propensity to forgive in another study by Leach and colleagues (2011), which found that African American participants' propensity to forgive White transgressors was predicted at least in part by their current stage of Cross's (1971) Black racial identity development model. This may be true for other cultural identity facets as well. Other studies have found that the link between forgiveness and health may be stronger in African Americans as compared to White Americans (McFarland et al., 2012).

Other cultural facets may affect the propensity and experience of forgiveness as well. With regard to gender, results have been mixed. One study found that men have stronger initial responses to forgiveness prompts than women (Root & Exline, 2011). However, other studies have found that forgiveness is "a more manifest subject in everyday life" for adult women (Ghaemmaghami et al., 2011, p. 192). In another study, women in heterosexual marriages reported perceptions that their partners were more forgiving, in comparison with male partners' perception of their female partners' forgiveness (Miller & Worthington, 2010). Interestingly, men seem to benefit in terms of cardiovascular health when they are forgiving people overall (i.e., high in trait forgiveness); this same benefit does not appear to extend to women with high trait forgiveness (Fincham et al., 2015). The reasons behind these findings are not well understood to date, with more recent studies finding more similarities than differences between men and women on emotional correlates of forgiveness (Kaleta & Mróz, 2022), and thus, this is an area that may benefit from more study.

Level of economic stability may also determine the amount of well-being associated with forgiveness at the country level. In less-developed nations (with regard to socioeconomics), forgiveness and well-being were not found to be significantly related in a study encompassing 30 different countries (Hanke & Vauclair, 2016). This brings up interesting questions about the value of forgiveness and asks for more research focused on what conditions are necessary, both economically and in terms of stability, to make a positive construct like forgiveness more of a priority.

Finally, having a personal identity that includes religiosity may affect propensity to forgive and the definition associated with this concept. As many religions, including Christianity, Hinduism, and Buddhism, promote forgiveness, this is unsurprising; however, religious beliefs may dictate what forgiveness means, and this meaning may differ from the way in which the field of psychology defines it. For example, in many religious traditions, the idea of "forgive and forget" (i.e., forgive and then reconcile) goes hand in hand. In the field of psychology, particularly in the majority culture, however, forgiveness does not always include the reconciliation piece of this concept (Frise & McMinn, 2010). Moreover, the centrality of the role religion plays in the life of an individual is likely to mediate the relationship between whether or not the idea of forgiveness necessarily translates to everyday life outside of the individual's religious experience (Huber et al., 2011). Interestingly, however, newer research has shown that the link between spirituality and forgiveness may be mediated at least partially by one's positioning on the cultural indicator of the collectivist/individualist continuum (Edara, 2015). Those results showed that "people who are high both in spirituality and collectivistic orientation are highly motivated to forgive their offenders" (Edara, 2015, p. 34).

The Evolutionary and Neurobiological Bases of Forgiveness

In many places throughout this book, we emphasize the communal nature of human beings. We live in groups, and part of such contact unfortunately involves instances in which one person strikes out against another in an injurious manner. In subhuman creatures, animals may at times engage in submissive gestures that stop the aggression cycle (deWaal & Pokorny, 2005; Newberg et al., 2000). In an analogous fashion, forgiveness may break the violence cycle in humans. Lacking such mechanisms to lessen the potential for aggression and retaliative counter aggression, humans may risk an escalating cycle that threatens the demise of the entire group. In this sense, there is an evolutionary advantage to forgiving actions in that they lower the overall level of hostility and increase access to important resources (Enright, 1996; Komorita et al., 1991; Tsang & Martin, 2021), thereby enhancing the survival chances of the larger group. Indeed, people who display forgiveness toward their transgressors produce positive feelings in surrounding people who were in no way involved in the confrontation (Kanekar & Merchant, 1982), thereby stabilizing the social order. In short, forgiveness represents a process that has an adaptive evolutionary advantage in that it helps to preserve the social structure.

Newberg et al. (2000) have described the underlying neurophysiology of the forgiveness process. First, by necessity, forgiveness involves a person's sense of self because it is this source that is damaged during transgression by another. (Incidentally, perception of the self is crucial from an evolutionary standpoint because it is the self that the person strives to preserve over time.) The sense of self is believed to be located in the frontal, parietal, and temporal lobes, which receive input from the sensory system and the hippocampus. Second, injury to the self is registered via sensorimotor input, and this input is mediated by the limbic system, the sympathetic nervous system, and the hypothalamus. Third, initiation of the reconciliation process by the person transgressed against involves activation of the temporal, parietal, and frontal lobes, along with limbic system input. Offering further support to Newberg and colleagues' (2000) observations, more recent research suggests that the ventromedial prefrontal cortex plays a key role when deciding to forgive a deception (Hayashi et al., 2010). Relatedly, greater gray matter volumes in several structures of the prefrontal cortex and parietal lobe were positively associated with higher self-reported dispositional and emotional forgiveness (Rao et al., 2022). Such findings suggest that, in a way, we may be hard-wired to forgive in some instances.

ATTACHMENT, LOVE, AND FORGIVENESS: BUILDING A POSITIVE PSYCHOLOGY OF CLOSE RELATIONSHIPS

As we have described throughout this chapter, healthy and supportive relationships are essential to positive psychological functioning. Attachment early in life provides the fertile field upon which love can grow, and at times forgiveness is needed as a salve to harsh conditions in a relationship. Moreover, any relationship in which we invest brings both benefits and potential risks. We would posit here, however, that the benefits of love and attachment usually outweigh the cost that a need for forgiveness might pose from time to time. Additionally, in our current times, exhibiting love and forgiveness may heal some of our current woes within our world by facilitating forgiveness between groups. Positive psychology research that focuses on these building blocks of strong relationships and promotion of caring and empathy across groups may help to set an agenda for the future—an agenda that will hopefully produce a society that will help all individuals to flourish and live together. We hope you will see some of the benefits of these concepts in your own life as you engage in the following personal mini-experiment and life enhancement strategies.

PERSONAL MINI-EXPERIMENTS

IN SEARCH OF LOVE AND FLOURISHING RELATIONSHIPS

In this chapter, we discuss attachment, love, and flourishing relationships. Our review suggests that sound relationships are built on a foundation of secure attachments and that they are maintained with love and purposeful positive relationship behaviors. Here are a few ideas for personal experiments aimed at helping you develop a better understanding of secure, loving relationships—including your own.

The Jungle Gym Observations of Attachment. Conduct your own Strange Situation (Ainsworth, 1979) observations at a jungle gym at the local playground. As a child begins to play and is separated from the caregiver by physical distance, note the frequency of proximity-seeking and contact-maintaining behavior exhibited by that child. Hypothesize how the child will react when they take a break from playing . . . or when the caregiver roams a little farther away from the jungle gym (to supervise another child or find a bench). Note whether the child's behavior is consistent with your attachment-related hypotheses. Remember to integrate cultural context into your observation. Are you using an ethnocentric bias with your assumptions?

The Relationship of Two Circles. According to self-expansion theorists (Aron, Aron, & Smollan, 1992), a relationship between two people can be evaluated based on the degree of overlap of two circles representing the two persons in the relationship. To consider the degree of expansion and inclusion in your relationship (the less the two circles overlap, the less inclusion; the more they overlap, the more inclusion), draw a circle that represents your partner, and then draw a circle that represents you and your relationship to your partner. Consider the meaningfulness of the degree of overlap (inclusion and self-expansion) by discussing it with your partner. Note that the optimal degree of overlap may vary as a function of cultural context.

Making the Most of Good News. Over the course of your relationship, you may become a master of capitalizing on joyful occurrences by providing active/constructive responses (see Table 12.3) to your partner's attempts to share positive events. To foster this purposeful positive relationship skill, do the following to make the most of the positive daily events in your romantic partner's life:

- Listen actively and empathically to the account of the positive event.
- Make efforts to understand the significance of the event for your partner's cultural context (e.g., Does this have special significance for this person as a part of a particular religion? Does this have special significance for the person as a racial or ethnic minority? Other cultural significance?).
- Mirror your partner's enthusiasm about the positive event (while they share it with you) by engaging in authentic expressions of excitement and delight (e.g., smiling, saying "Great!" or "Wow!," reaching for your partner's hand).
- Ask two constructive questions about the positive event ("How did you feel when it happened?" "How did it happen? Tell me everything!" and other, more specific questions).
- Reintroduce the positive event into conversation later in the day or the next day to stretch out the benefits of something good having happened in your partner's life.

TABLE 12.3 ■ Capitalizing on Daily Positive Events

How would your friend/relative/partner characterize your habitual responses to their good news?

Active/Constructive

My friend/relative/partner reacts to the positive event enthusiastically.

My friend/relative/partner seems even more happy and excited than I am.

My friend/relative/partner often asks a lot of questions and shows genuine concern about the good event.

Passive/Constructive

My friend/relative/partner tries not to make a big deal out of it but is happy for me.

My friend/relative/partner is usually silently supportive of the good things that occur to me.

My friend/relative/partner says little, but I know he/she is happy for me.

Active/Destructive

My friend/relative/partner often finds a problem with it.

My friend/relative/partner reminds me that most good things have their bad aspects as well.

My friend/relative/partner points out the potential down sides of the good event.

Passive/Destructive

Sometimes I get the impression that my friend/relative/partner doesn't care much.

My friend/relative/partner doesn't pay much attention to me.

My friend/relative/partner often seems uninterested.

Modified portion of the Perceived Responses to Capitalization Attempts Scale. From Gable, S. L., Reis, H. T., Impett, E. A., & Asher, E. R., Capitalizing on daily positive events, *Journal of Personality and Social Psychology, 87*. Copyright © 2004. Reprinted with permission.

Note: Shelly Gable of UCLA divides the possible responses into the four categories described previously. She has found that the first response style is central to capitalizing on, or amplifying, the pleasure of the good situation and contributing to an upward spiral of positive emotion.

LIFE ENHANCEMENT STRATEGIES

Additional tips for bringing more security and love into your life are listed here. Although we focus on aspects of romantic love in this chapter, we address many forms of love in this list of strategies.

Love

- Identify a couple in your life that you believe has an excellent relationship. Arrange to spend some time with them so you can observe relationship behaviors that work for them. If you know the couple well, ask them specific questions about how they maintain their relationship. Emulate some of these behaviors in your own significant relationships.
- When you are in an ongoing relationship, develop a list of what makes your partner feel appreciated and attempt to enhance the culture of appreciation in your relationship with five purposeful acts each day.

Work

- Take a mindfulness meditation course (see Chapter 10 for a description) with a partner, and apply your newfound skills when attending to your own behavior and to the relationship. Generalize these skills to behavior with colleagues at work.
- Ignore old advice about not making friends at work. Vital friendships in the workplace can enhance your engagement with your work.

Play

- Children benefit socially and emotionally from having at least one caring adult in their lives. Volunteer some time with a child or youth service and attempt to form a connection with at least one young person. Over time, the benefits of the relationship may become increasingly mutual.
- We often become friends with people who are similar to us. While this "birds of a feather flock together" tendency is natural, we may be able to capitalize more via self-expansion when we stretch ourselves to include dissimilar others in our close social circles or romantic relationships. Challenge yourself to step outside of your usual social circles and to extend yourself to others who are different than from you in some ways.

APPENDIX: THE HEARTLAND FORGIVENESS SCALE (HFS)

Directions: In the course of our lives, negative things may occur because of our own actions, the actions of others, or circumstances beyond our control. For some time after these events, we may have negative thoughts or feelings about ourselves, others, or the situation. Think about how you *typically* respond to such negative events. In the blank lines before each of the following items, please write the number (using the 7-point scale below) that best describes how you *typically* respond to the type of negative situation described. There are no right or wrong answers. Please be as honest as possible.

1	2	3	4	5	6	7
Almost Always False		*More Often False of Me*		*More Often True of Me*		*Almost Always True*

_____ 1. Although I feel badly at first when I mess up, over time I can give myself some slack.

_____ 2. I hold grudges against myself for negative things I've done.

_____ 3. Learning from bad things that I've done helps me get over them.

_____ 4. It is really hard for me to accept myself once I've messed up.

_____ 5. With time, I am understanding of myself for mistakes I've made.

_____ 6. I don't stop criticizing myself for negative things I've felt, thought, said, or done.

_____ 7. I continue to punish a person who has done something that I think is wrong.

_____ 8. With time, I am understanding of others for the mistakes they've made.

_____ 9. I continue to be hard on others who have hurt me.

_____10. Although others have hurt me in the past, I have eventually been able to see them as good people.

_____11. If others mistreat me, I continue to think badly of them.

_____12. When someone disappoints me, I can eventually move past it.

_____13. When things go wrong for reasons that can't be controlled, I get stuck in negative thoughts about it.

_____14. With time, I can be understanding of bad circumstances in my life.

_____15. If I'm disappointed by uncontrollable circumstances in my life, I continue to think negatively about them.

_____16. I eventually make peace with bad situations in my life.

_____17. It's really hard for me to accept negative situations that aren't anybody's fault.

_____18. Eventually, I let go of negative thoughts about bad circumstances that are beyond anyone's control.

From Thompson, L., Snyder, C. R., Hoffman, L., Michael, S., Rasmussen, H., Billings, L., Heinze, L., Neufeld, J., Shorey, H., Roberts, J., & Roberts, D., "Dispositional forgiveness of self, others, and situations," in *Journal of Personality, 73*.

Reverse-Scored Items

Items 2, 4, 6, 7, 9, 11, 13, 15, and 17 are reverse scored.

Overall HFS Score

A total forgiveness score is derived by summing the numbers given in response to items 1 through 18 (using the reverse scores for items 2, 4, 6, 7, 9, 11, 13, 15, and 17).

Subscales

Self: Items 1 through 6 compose the forgiveness-of-self subscale.

Other: Items 7 through 12 compose the forgiveness-of-other subscale.

Situations: Items 13 through 18 compose the forgiveness-of-situations subscale.

KEY TERMS

Adaptive parental behaviors
Agape
Attachment Anxiety (Brennan et al., 1998)
Attachment Avoidance (Brennan et al., 1998)
Attachment system
Companionate love
Consummate love
Eros
Flourishing relationships
Forgiveness (as defined by Enright and colleagues)
Forgiveness (as defined by McCullough and colleagues)
Forgiveness (as defined by Tangney and colleagues)
Forgiveness (as defined by Thompson and colleagues)
Insecure-avoidant attachment
Insecure-resistant/ambivalent attachment
Maladaptive parental behaviors
Minding
Passionate love
Restorative justice
Secure attachment
Self-expansion theory of romantic love
Strange Situation
Triangular theory of love

PART VI

UNDERSTANDING AND CHANGING HUMAN BEHAVIOR

13 PREVENTING THE BAD AND PROMOTING THE GOOD

LEARNING OBJECTIVES

After reading this chapter, you will be able to:

13.1 Understand the differences between primary and secondary prevention

13.2 Understand the differences between primary and secondary enhancement

13.3 Distinguish between correlates of psychological and physical health

13.4 Critique uses of enhancement and prevention for different groups

13.5 Apply knowledge and skills about enhancement toward making these accessible to all populations

Eager to get started, a new psychotherapy client passionately announced, "I want to stop the bad things that keep happening, but that's not all. . . . I want more good!" Their words tap the two broad topics that we explore in this chapter.

The first category, stopping the bad, involves efforts to prevent negative things from occurring later, and it can be divided into primary and secondary preventions. As we describe in greater detail in the following sections, **primary prevention** lessens or eliminates physical or psychological problems *before* they appear. **Secondary prevention** lessens or eliminates problems *after* they have appeared. The latter process often is called tertiary prevention (APA, 2014).

The second category, making more good, involves enhancing what people want in their lives; it, too, can be divided into primary and secondary types. **Primary enhancements** establish optimal functioning and satisfaction. **Secondary enhancements** go even further to build upon already optimal functioning and satisfaction and achieve *peak* experiences. In other words, primary enhancements make things good (create optimal experiences), whereas secondary enhancements make things the very best that they can be (create peak experiences).

PRIMARY PREVENTION: "STOP THE BAD BEFORE IT HAPPENS"

Primary prevention (see Figure 13.1) reflects actions that people take to lessen or remove the likelihood of problems (Hiller et al., 2017; Kaplan, 2000) before those issues develop. With primary prevention, people are not yet manifesting any problems, and it is only later that such

FIGURE 13.1 ■ Primary and Secondary Preventions

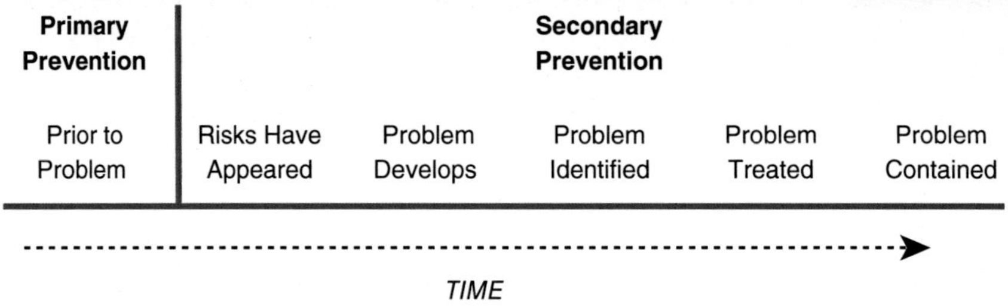

Primary Prevention	Secondary Prevention				
Prior to Problem	Risks Have Appeared	Problem Develops	Problem Identified	Problem Treated	Problem Contained

TIME →

problems will appear if appropriate protective or preventative steps are not taken (Snyder, Feldman et al., 2000). When primary prevention is aimed at an entire population, it is sometimes called **universal prevention** (e.g., childhood immunizations); when focused on a particular at-risk group, it is sometimes called **selective prevention** (e.g., home visitations for children with low birth weight).

If each of these primary and secondary approaches to prevention and enhancement were to have a slogan, we would suggest the following:

- Primary prevention: "Stop the bad before it happens."
- Secondary prevention (psychotherapy): "Fix the problem."
- Primary enhancement: "Make life good."
- Secondary enhancement: "Make life the best possible."

Is Primary Prevention Effective?

On the whole, primary preventions can be quite effective (APA, 2014), though it depends on the prevention target. A good example of a successful primary prevention effort is something that we remember each time we get in a vehicle. Specifically, until the mid-1970s, it was legal in most states to not wear a seatbelt in the front seat. After compulsory seatbelt laws were enacted, traffic fatalities dropped dramatically over time (Wagenaar et al., 1988). Currently, it is estimated that seatbelts save close to 15,000 lives annually and that about 90% of vehicle occupants wear a seatbelt (National Center for Statistics and Analysis, 2021). While seatbelt laws have arguably been effective, another (more recent) universal primary prevention effort highlights the challenges to successful implementation. Despite clear evidence that vaccines prevent serious COVID-19, and a data trend suggesting the rate of vaccines uptake is increasing, many of those in the United States still refuse to get vaccinated as of January 2023 (Centers for Disease Control and Prevention, May 2023).

As these two universal prevention efforts illustrate, some issues are easier to prevent than others. In the case of seatbelts, the political will was sufficient to pass laws that made wearing a seatbelt compulsory nationwide. The political will has not been sufficient to make COVID-19 vaccines mandatory in the same fashion. While these are national (universal) prevention efforts, similar successes and setbacks occur at the local level. Even the most well-planned prevention program can succeed or fail due to contextual factors outside of the scope of the program. In Chapter 5, for example, we provided a balanced review of several positive youth development programs and noted that their effectiveness has been somewhat mixed. Next, we briefly touch on possible ways to increase the effectiveness of primary prevention.

Components of Effective Primary Preventions

Heller and colleagues (2000) offered five suggestions for implementing successful primary preventions that still hold weight more than two decades later. Indeed, many of the five components mentioned here are present in the American Psychological Association's Guidelines for Prevention in Psychology (APA, 2014), a professional consensus document that will be revised in 2024. First, the targeted populations should be given knowledge about the risky behavior to be prevented. Second, the program should be attractive; it should motivate potential participants to increase the desirable behaviors and decrease the undesirable ones. Third, the program should teach problem-solving skills, as well as how to resist regressing into previous counterproductive patterns. Fourth, the program should change any norms or social structures that reinforce counterproductive behaviors. On this latter point, social support and approval often are needed to overcome the rewarding qualities of problematic behaviors. Fifth, data should be gathered to enable evaluation of the program's accomplishments. These evaluation data then can be used to make a case for implementing primary prevention programs in other settings.

Other researchers have investigated various components in prevention programs as specific "active ingredients" in the change process. Collins and Dozois (2008) list (1) inclusion of parents in treatment, (2) approaches that focus on interpersonal interactions, and (3) incorporation of cognitive–behavioral interventions as offering specific benefits toward effective prevention programs. Studies such as this that investigate particular mechanisms of change are particularly helpful at determining future evidence-based treatments and programming (Kazdin, 2008).

We would add one further component: that programs should be culturally competent. As has been discussed in other chapters, many constructs are culture specific, and some are not necessarily equivalent across cultural groups (Pedrotti & Edwards, 2014, 2017). As such, making sure that programs take culture into account is a necessity to provide equity in both physical and psychological health. In addition, some problems may exist in different frequencies across different populations (Mattingly & Andresen, 2016), thus necessitating more programing in these cultural groups.

SECONDARY PREVENTION (PSYCHOTHERAPY): "FIX THE PROBLEM"

Secondary prevention addresses a problem as it begins to unfold (see Figure 13.1). There are many examples of secondary prevention for various societal problems. Domestic violence shelters, for example, help individuals (mostly women) reduce the chances that they will experience death or serious injury from their abusive partners. These shelters do not prevent intimate partner violence, but they do reduce the harm it causes. Likewise, shelters for homeless individuals do not prevent homelessness, but they provide a bed and a hot meal for those in need for a limited amount of time.

When secondary prevention focuses on psychological functioning, it is generally synonymous with psychotherapy intervention. We view psychotherapy as a prime example of secondary prevention because people who come for such treatments know that they have specific problems that are beyond their capabilities to handle, and this is what leads them to obtain help (Snyder & Ingram, 2000a). Indeed, the related literature reveals that specific problems and life stressors trigger the seeking of psychological assistance (Norcross & Prochaska, 1986; Wills & DePaulo, 1991). Of course, when psychotherapy is successful, it also may produce the primary prevention characteristic of lessening or preventing recurrence of similar problems in the future. Accordingly, in this section, we will focus primarily on secondary prevention in the form of psychotherapy.

Is Secondary Prevention Effective?

From the earliest summaries of the effectiveness of psychotherapies (e.g., Smith et al., 1980) to more contemporary ones (see Moore et al., 2017; Wampold, 2011, 2013), there is consistent evidence that psychotherapy improves the lives of adults and children. When we say that psychotherapy "works," we mean that there is a lessening of the severity and/or frequency of the client's problem and symptoms. The highest level of evidence supporting a particular treatment comes from a randomized control trial (RCT). Participants are carefully screened and then randomly assigned to either a treatment condition or some kind of a control group. After a period of time, the two groups are compared on a variety of outcomes. Division 12, Society for Clinical Psychology, of the American Psychological Association maintains a growing list of evidence-based treatments (EBTs) that have been demonstrated as effective via RCTs. Division 12's list is an excellent resource for identifying what kind of treatment you may need or want; you can check it out here: https://div12.org/psychological-treatments/.

It is important to note that psychologists have long debated the exact cause of treatment effectiveness. Is it the treatment, the therapist, or both? For example, counseling psychologist, Bruce Wampold, professor emeritus at the University of Wisconsin, made a ground-breaking assertion that the biggest piece of the puzzle of whether therapy is actually effective in any given situation is the level of effectiveness of the *therapist*. In a symposium given in 2011 to the American Psychological Association at its annual convention, Wampold cited characteristics such as strong interpersonal skills, powers of persuasion, and the abilities to be reflective and offer optimism as key traits that an effective therapist must possess. Wampold's work, which moved beyond a symposium to include numerous journal articles, books, and edited volumes, led to the concept of empirically supported therapy relationships (ESTRs; Ackerman et al., 2001). ESTRs are those qualities of a therapist or the therapeutic relationship that explain variation in psychotherapy outcome. Qualities such as empathy and warmth appear to be critical to the therapeutic relationship based on several lines of research (Norcross & Hill, 2004; Norcross & Lambert, 2019). Researchers have also begun to focus on ESTRs specific to multiculturally sensitive and effective psychotherapy (Davis et al., 2018). Today, ESTRs are believed to compliment EBTs, such that the combination of both is critical for overall evidence-based practice (Norcross & Lambert, 2019).

All this said, throughout the history of psychotherapy, there have been varying opinions on which treatments are "best" (e.g., Eysenck, 1952; Strupp, 1964), and as many have noted, the "evidence" used in these studies that appears to back one type of treatment or another is often fraught with error (Wampold, 2013). Wampold (2013), in a seminal paper titled "The Good, the Bad, and the Ugly: A 50-Year Perspective on the Outcome Problem," notes that defining what is a "good outcome" is inherently culturally based and thus can often be flawed. Wampold uses Strupp's (1964) list of what constitutes a good outcome of therapy as an example here, noting that one criterion of positive functioning listed at this time was "full *heterosexual* functioning with potency and pleasure" (p. 10, italics added). Today we would not consider this to be a universally positive outcome and recognize that heterosexual functioning is not the only healthy expression of sexuality. This said, there are very likely other criteria we might use today that are still culturally biased and contained and that we might someday come to believe are also wrong. Thus, all discussions of "effective" treatment must be couched in a discussion of cultural context (Kirmayer, 2012).

Looking ahead to the future, one final point that must be made here is the fact that secondary prevention in the form of psychotherapy is not always accessible to all populations that may benefit from it. Lower socioeconomic groups of both adults and children have been shown to benefit from secondary prevention as much as other groups, but they participate in therapeutic interventions less often (Santiago et al., 2013). Part of our ethics code as psychologists calls for us to make sure that the profession is accessible to all; therefore, we have work to do in this area. Determining strategies to alter programs to make them more culturally competent across socioeconomic groups and attractive and available to all is necessary for future work in this area.

Hope as a Core Component of Psychotherapy

Predating concepts such as EBTs or EBTRs, psychotherapy researcher Jerome Frank (1968, 1973, 1975) suggested that *hope* was the underlying process common to all successful psychotherapy approaches. Building on Frank's pioneering ideas, Snyder and his colleagues (Snyder, Ilardi, Cheavens et al., 2000; Snyder, Ilardi, Michael, & Cheavens, 2000; Snyder Parenteau et al., 2002) have used hope theory (see Chapter 8) to show how pathways and agency goal-directed thinking facilitate successful outcomes in psychotherapy. In this same vein, Conoley and Scheel (2018) advocate for goal-focused positive psychotherapy (GFPP), noting that style of therapy is based on four processes, including "(1) the identification and enhancement of client strengths, (2) the promotion of positive emotions, (3) the formation of approach goals, and (4) engendering hope" (p. viii). Their book provides a solid overview of this style of psychotherapy and its connection to hope and other positive constructs. Other investigations of the role of hope as a part of psychotherapy can be found in Ouer (2016), Chamodraka and colleagues (2017), and Bartholomew and colleagues (2019).

Given that hope is a critical aspect of psychotherapy process and outcome, some researchers have developed ways of explicitly working with it in the therapy room. As shown in the Appendix, which is a worksheet for use in implementing hope therapy for adults, the client undergoing the therapy initially is probed for their goals in differing life arenas. Next, the client

FIGURE 13.2 ■ Primary and Secondary Enhancements

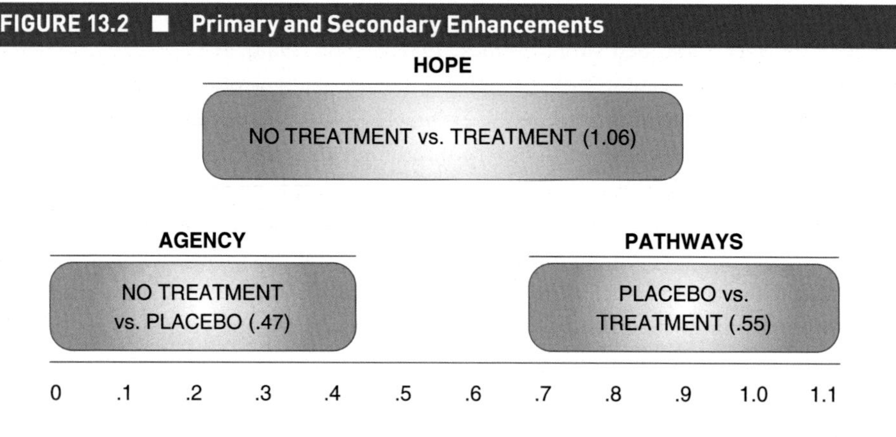

is asked to select a particular life domain on which to work. Over the ensuing sessions, the therapist then helps the client to clarify the goals by making lucid marker points for assessing progress in attaining these goals. Various pathways for reaching the goals are then taught, along with ways to motivate the person to actually use those routes. Impediments to the desired goals are anticipated, and the clients are given instructions on how to institute backup routes to the goals. As reaching different goals is practiced over time, the clients learn how to apply hope therapy naturally in their everyday goal pursuits. The overall purpose is to teach clients how to use hope therapy principles to attain ongoing life goals, especially when they encounter blockages (Cheavens Feldman, Woodward, & Snyder, 2006; Cheavens & Gum, 2010).

Secondary Prevention Psychotherapy for Racial and Ethnic Minorities

Members of non-White groups represent roughly 40% of the U.S. population (U.S. Census Bureau, 2020), but they make up a much smaller percentage of those who seek mental health care services (Jimenez et al., 2013). This problem is magnified by the fact that the members of some racial and ethnic minority groups who do enter psychotherapy are more likely than White clients to terminate treatment early (Cooper & Conklin, 2015; Gray-Little & Kaplan, 2000). Some studies have also found that racial and ethnic minorities may receive less benefit from some mental health programs potentially due to lack of cultural competence (Patterson et al., 2016). Some of this may have to do with linguistic or other differences, but another hypothesis is that we still have some way to go with regard to multicultural competence in understanding folks from different racial groups than our own (Patterson et al., 2016). Thus, good education in this area for all therapists is a must when trying to broadly enhance the benefits of secondary prevention.

More recent studies seem to suggest that treatment outcomes are more similar between White and non-White therapy participants as of late, but the authors of a meta-analysis suggest caution in warranted in accepting some of these results (Cougle & Grubaugh, 2022). Some of this caution is due to methods used to obtain these results. For example, many studies still do not classify demographics in viewing results from effectiveness studies or do not include representative samples of racial and ethnic minorities (Cougle & Grubaugh, 2022). Others distinguish between "White" and "non-White" but lump all racial and ethnic minorities into one group as opposed to looking at differences between non-White groups. It is evident more critical and rigorous research is needed in assessing whether equitable psychotherapy is available for racial and ethnic minorities today.

We mention these facts in part to highlight that the system has not always been effective in reaching and helping people of color. Furthermore, so little research has been done with psychotherapy clients who are Black American, American Indian, Latino/a/x, or Asian American that we presently cannot make statements about the best approaches for treatments for these groups. An article by Whaley and Davis (2007) is still considered to be a strong source in terms of providing suggestions for increasing cultural competence in evidence-based practice and discussing making cultural adaptations with non-White populations. These authors posit that the move toward *effectiveness* studies (as opposed to the former focus on *efficacy*) may assist cultural adaptations as well. Some researchers state that inclusion of more non-White individuals in the samples of empirical studies regarding effective treatments will address this dearth in the literature, while others argue that adaptations to treatments are necessary for true cultural competence with diverse individuals (Whaley & Davis, 2007). Additionally, three suggestions are made by Burque (2017) toward the goal of equity in care: "(1) Acknowledging and affirming the humanity of people of color; (2) Requiring providers to intentionally assess their own racial identity, racial biases, and racial prejudices; and (3) Expecting service providers to act as agents of social change." The interested reader may look toward a review conducted by Miranda and colleagues (2005) titled "State of the Science on Psychosocial Interventions for Ethnic Minorities" or Hall and Ibaraki's (2016) chapter, "Multicultural Issues in Cognitive-Behavioral Therapy."

Though the focus here is on those seeking therapy, understanding that care may also be necessary for therapists themselves who are from historically marginalized groups may also be important in thinking about this topic. The chapter "When Racism Is Reversed: Therapists of Color Speak About Their Experiences With Racism From Clients, Supervisees, and Supervisors" (Ali et al, 2005) discusses the dilemmas that can occur when a client exhibits racism or uses slurs while in therapy with a non-White therapist. These can be slurs related to identities the therapist holds, which may make forming a connection with a client difficult. Therapists are often cautioned not to let their personal feelings enter the therapy process, and yet Ali and colleagues (2005) note that this type of interaction may make therapists feel unsafe and may be hard to ignore. This same instance could also occur with gender or with identities that can be less visible such as sexual orientation, disability, or social class. This is a topic that deserves more treatment in the literature.

Obviously, one of the missions of positive psychology should be to understand the reasons for the underutilization of mental health professionals by members of racial and ethnic minority groups, as well as to increase the propensity of minoritized individuals to seek such services and remain in treatment. No less important is to encourage diversity in terms of those seeking to become therapists which may, in and of itself, increase equity of care. In 2020, the National Science Foundation (2022) reported that 61% of doctoral degrees in counseling psychology and 69% of doctoral degrees in clinical psychology were awarded to White recipients. Black Americans were the second highest group of recipients of counseling psychology doctoral degrees at 15.3%, while the second largest group of doctoral degree recipients in clinical psychology was Hispanic/Latinx individuals at approximately 11%. Though racial and ethnic diversity has increased, these numbers are still sorely lacking. More efforts to increase applications toward educational pipelines that produce therapist are essential if we as a field are to adequately provide for all clients.

PRIMARY ENHANCEMENT: "MAKE LIFE GOOD"

Primary enhancement involves the effort to establish optimal functioning and satisfaction. As shown on the left side of Figure 13.3, primary enhancement involves attempts either to increase hedonic well-being by maximizing the pleasurable or to increase eudaemonic well-being by setting and reaching goals (Davids et al., 2017; Ryan & Deci, 2001). Whereas **hedonic primary enhancements** tap indulgence in pleasure and the satisfaction of appetites and needs, **eudaemonic primary enhancements** emphasize effective functioning and happiness as a desirable result of the goal-pursuit process (Marrero et al., 2016; Seligman, 2002). In this regard, it should be noted that factor-analytic research has supported the distinction between hedonic and eudaemonic human motives (Compton et al., 1996; Joshanloo, 2016; Keyes et al., 2000).

Before describing various routes to primary enhancement, some comments are necessary about the role of evolution. In an evolutionary sense, particular activities are biologically predisposed to produce satisfaction (Buss, 2000; Gailliot, 2012; Pinker, 1997). An evolutionary premise is that people experience pleasure under the circumstances favorable to the propagation of the human species (Carr, 2004; Cohn & Fredrickson, 2009). Accordingly, happiness results from close interpersonal ties, especially those that lead to mating and the protection of offspring. Indeed, research shows that happiness stems from (1) a safe and supportive living unit with people who work together, (2) an environment that is fertile and productive of food, (3) the "stretching" of our bodies through exercise, and (4) the pursuit of meaningful goals in one's work (Diener, 2000; Kahneman et al., 1999).

One more caveat is warranted. Many of the experiences placed in the category of primary enhancement also could fit into the category of secondary enhancement, which involves peak

FIGURE 13.3 ■ Common Components of Successful Psychotherapy: The Agency and Pathways of Hope

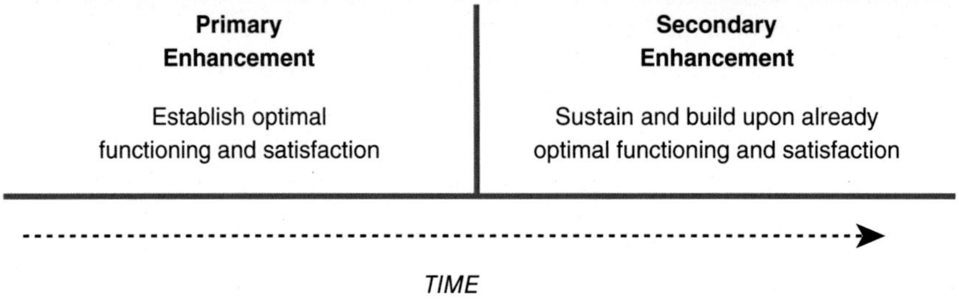

Primary Enhancement	Secondary Enhancement
Establish optimal functioning and satisfaction	Sustain and build upon already optimal functioning and satisfaction

TIME →

experiences. The line between an optimal experience and a peak experience may be very subtle. In addition, experiences and their magnitude and value vary across cultures. Keeping in mind cultural facets such as socioeconomic status, nation of origin, gender, and others is important in understanding these concepts.

Primary Enhancement: Psychological Health Through Relationships, Employment, and Leisure

For most people, interpersonal relationships with lovers, family, and good friends provide the most powerful sources of well-being and life satisfaction (Berscheid & Reis, 1998; Prati et al., 2016; Reis & Gable, 2003). Engaging in shared activities that are enjoyable enhances psychological well-being, especially if such joint participation entails arousing and novel activities (Aron et al., 2000; Tomlinson & Aron, 2013). Likewise, it is beneficial for couples to tackle intrinsically motivated activities in which they can share aspects of their lives and become absorbed in the ongoing flow of their behaviors (Csikszentmihalyi, 1990; Graham, 2008; Le et al., 2018).

Beyond the relationship with one's mate, primary enhancement satisfactions also come from a variety of sources, such as relationships with family and friends. Arranging living circumstances to be within close physical proximity to kin can produce the social supports that are so crucial for happiness. So, too, can the close network of a few friends produce contentment. There are compelling evolutionary arguments (Argyle, 2001) and supportive empirical research (Demir & Davidson, 2012; Diener & Seligman, 2002; Prati et al., 2016) as to why such kin and friend relationships are crucial for happiness.

Another relationship that produces happiness for many people is involvement in religion and spiritual matters (Delle Fave et al., 2013; Myers, 2000; Piedmont, 2004), though the effect may be smaller than we once thought (Garssen et al., 2021). In part, the positive psychological benefits of religion may reflect the facts that religiosity and prayer are related to higher hope (DiPierro et al., 2017; Laird et al., 2004; Snyder, 2004b) and that religious faith and various other religious practices can be predictive of hope and optimism (Ciarrocchi et al., 2008). Additionally, some of the satisfaction from religion probably stems from the social contacts it provides (Carr, 2004; Garssen et al., 2021). And it may be particularly beneficial when the religion one practices is thought of as the normative one within a country's national context (Stavrova et al., 2013). Happiness also may result from the spirituality stemming from the individual's relationship with a higher power (Cohen & Johnson, 2017; Saroglou et al., 2008). On this point, there is some scientific evidence of a possible genetic and biological link to human spirituality needs (Hamer, 2004; Ferguson et al., 2022).

Gainful employment also is an important source of happiness (Rothausen & Henderson, 2019). To the degree to which people are satisfied with their work, they also are happier (see Bowling et al., 2010 for a meta-analysis). The reason for this finding is that, for many people, work provides a social network, and it also allows for the testing of talents and skills. It also can provide a source of meaning and purpose (Rothausen & Henderson, 2019). Along similar lines, education and academic achievement are also linked to happiness and well-being in some research. Nikolaev (2017) investigated links between participation in higher education and eudaemonic, hedonic, and evaluative life satisfaction and found that those with higher education are more satisfied with their lives in many areas (e.g., employment, children, neighborhood), although somewhat less satisfied with the amount of free time they have.

Leisure activities can also bring pleasure (Argyle, 2001; Hood & Carruthers, 2007). Iwasaki (2007) noted that leisure seems to be connected to quality of life overall in both multicultural and cross-cultural contexts. Relaxing, resting, and eating a good meal all have the short-term effect of making people feel better. Recreational activities such as sports, dancing, and listening to music allow people to make enjoyable contacts with others. Thus, sometimes happiness comes from stimulation and a sense of positive arousal, whereas at other times, happiness reflects a quiet, recharging process. Interestingly, although we sometimes only hear about the negative effects of involvement in social media and use of mobile devices as a form of leisure activity, some studies have shown that this form of leisure may also promote well-being by brokering social capital via "friending" and "likes" (Chen & Li, 2017).

Certain types of leisure activities may be more beneficial than others. In a study looking across several nations, activities such as listening to music, attending a sporting or cultural event, getting together with family, and reading books all showed a positive effect on happiness (Wang & Wong, 2013). In some groups, such as Asian Americans (Nagata et al., 2017) and Latinos (DiPierro et al., 2017), there is little research, but findings point toward similar conclusions as for White Americans. Making sure that life satisfaction and happiness are accessible to all can have profound effects on our society as a whole, especially perhaps for disenfranchised populations (Pedrotti & Edwards, 2017).

Primary Enhancement Through Flow, Mindfulness, Savoring, and Enhancing Positive Emotions

Whatever the primary enhancement activities may be, those actions that are totally absorbing tend to be the most enjoyable. As we describe in greater detail of Chapter 10 of this text, Csikszentmihalyi and colleagues (Csikszentmihalyi, 1990, 2015; Nakamura & Csikszentmihalyi, 2009) have studied the circumstances that lead to a sense of total engagement. Such activities typically are intrinsically fascinating, and they stretch talents to satisfying levels in which persons lose track of themselves and the passage of time. This type of primary enhancement has been called a *flow experience*, and artists, surgeons, and other professionals report such flow in their work.

Yet another route to attaining a sense of contentment is through here-and-now contemplation of one's external or internal environment. Indeed, a common thread in Eastern thought is that immense pleasure is to be attained through "being" or experiencing. Even in Western societies, **meditation** upon internal experiences or thoughts has gained many followers (Shapiro et al., 2002). Meditation has been defined as "a family of techniques which have in common a conscious attempt to focus attention in a nonanalytic way, and an attempt not to dwell on discursive, ruminating thought" (Shapiro, 1980, p. 14). For example, mindfulness meditation (Langer, 2009a) involves a nonjudgmental attention that allows a sense of peacefulness, serenity, and pleasure. Kabat-Zinn (1990) has posed the following seven qualities of mindfulness meditation: nonjudging, acceptance, openness, nonstriving, patience, trust, and letting go (see Chapter 10). Likewise, in what is called *concentrative meditation*, awareness is restricted by focusing on a single thought or object, such as a personal mantra, breath, word (Benson &

Proctor, 1984), or even a sound (Carrington, 1998). Interestingly, people who have just engaged in mindfulness meditation or who are experts in this type of meditation appear happier even to others who observe them (Choi et al., 2012)!

Another process that is meditation-like in its operation is **savoring**. Savoring involves thoughts or actions that are aimed at appreciating and perhaps amplifying a positive experience of some sort (see Bryant, 2004; Bryant & Veroff, 2006), and it appears to be "an important mechanism through which people derive happiness from positive events" (Jose et al., 2012, p. 176). This can be beneficial at many points in the life span (Geiger et al., 2017; Smith & Bryant, 2016). According to Fred Bryant (2004; Bryant & Smith, 2015), who is the psychologist who coined this term and produced the major theory and research on it, savoring can take three temporal forms:

1. Anticipation, or the enjoyment of a forthcoming positive event
2. Being in the moment, or thinking and doing things to intensify and perhaps prolong a positive event as it occurs
3. Reminiscing, or looking back at a positive event to rekindle the favorable feelings or thoughts

Furthermore, savoring can take the form of

- Sharing with others
- Taking "mental photographs" to build one's memory
- Congratulating oneself
- Comparing with what one has felt in other circumstances
- Sharpening senses through concentration
- Becoming absorbed in the moment
- Expressing oneself through behavior (laughing, shouting, pumping one's fist in the air)
- Realizing how fleeting and precious the experience is
- Counting one's blessings

Savoring can be an activity that comes naturally to some, or it can be intentional as well. One of the authors (JTP) recounts the exceptional skill that Dr. Lopez had at savoring:

> When good things happened, no one could savor them like Shane. When our class graduated from the University of Kansas, we all walked out of the auditorium, exhilarated to be done with our degrees, our families trailing us. He led us right over to his car where he had filled the trunk with beer and snacks and we had a tailgate right there in the parking lot. It must have looked so funny from the outside: a bunch of newly minted PhDs surrounded by professors wearing funny hats, everyone in black robes, drinking

beer out of the back of a car. Others walked by us and you could tell they wished they knew him, too. But Shane invited them in—gave them beers too—congratulated them—celebrated them. He was the best at doing that.

You, too, can savor things for yourself and also for others who are important to you in your life. When a partner gets a promotion, take some time to ask good questions, to talk about how excited you are for them, to ask what they are looking forward to about the change. We can also teach our children to do this, modeling for them how to ask questions about an exciting event and how to show their joy for their friends or family. What is wonderful about savoring is the extended feeling you gain from retelling the story, and this is something that happens when you are asking someone else to recount their story, too. Positive affect, as we know, is contagious, and savoring things others have done with them can also increase our own positive feelings.

To this exact point, there is yet more that people can do beyond savoring. In this regard, University of North Carolina psychologist Barbara Fredrickson (2001) developed her pioneering broaden-and-build model (see Chapter 6 for a more detailed discussion of the model) after observing that negative emotions such as anger and anxiety tend to constrict a person's thought and action repertoires. That is to say, when feeling negative emotions, people become concerned with protection, and their thoughts and actions become limited to a few narrow options aimed at remaining "safe." On the other hand, Fredrickson proposed that, when experiencing positive emotions, people open up and become flexible in their thinking and behaviors. Thus, positive emotions help to produce a "broaden-and-build" mentality in which there is a positive carousel of subsequent emotions, thoughts, and actions. Therefore, anything a person can do to experience joy, perhaps through play or other activities, can yield psychological benefits.

Martin Seligman and colleagues have also undertaken a program of research aimed at finding interventions that are effective as primary enhancements (see Seligman et al., 2005). In particular, Seligman recruited 577 adults who visited the website of his book *Authentic Happiness* (Seligman, 2002). Most of these people were White Americans who had some college education and were between 35 and 54 years old, and 58% were women. Before and after undergoing the primary enhancement intervention, each participant took self-report measures of happiness. (Although participants were randomly assigned to several conditions, we focus on one control and three primary enhancement intervention conditions.)

The control comparison condition was a placebo exercise in which the participants wrote for a week about their early memories. Participants assigned to the gratitude intervention were given a week to "deliver a letter of gratitude in person to someone who had been especially kind to them but had never been properly thanked" (Seligman et al., 2005, p. 416). Participants assigned to the condition involving three good things in life were to write for a week about three things that went well each day, noting the underlying causes of each positive thing. Last, a group of participants was asked to examine their character strengths in a new way for a week.

Results showed that each of these three primary enhancement interventions had robust positive effects in terms of raising the participants' happiness levels relative to the levels of the participants in the placebo control condition. The gratitude activity produced the largest increases in happiness, but these lasted for only a month. The writing about three good things that had happened and the use of the signature strengths in a new way also made people happier, and these positive changes endured for as long as 6 months.

Extending Seligman's work, several interventions have been developed to increase gratitude, as well as other positive psychological variables from a primary enhancement framework. On the website, PositivePsychology.com, a resource founded in the Netherlands and dedicated to disseminating positive knowledge regarding positive psychological interventions for clinicians and laypeople, Chowdhury (2019) describes 19 primary enhancement interventions. Today, researchers are beginning to amass enough data to look at the effectiveness of these interventions in a rigorous fashion. For example, in a meta-analysis, gratitude interventions (e.g., writing a gratitude letter or expressing gratitude in a systematic way) performed better than controls on participants' psychological well-being overall (Davis et al., 2016). However, the effects sizes were generally small to moderate in magnitude. Thus, engaging in gratitude in a systematic way does have some moderately beneficial aspects. These effect sizes are similar to other meta-analytic findings of positive psychology-based interventions aggregated together (Carr et al., 2021). Thus, as you may have already discovered by engaging in the personal mini-experiments for this text, some of the benefits of these primary enhancement strategies may be subtle or may take some time to develop. Nevertheless, research findings suggest that psychologists can help in the development and implementation of enhancement interventions that promote subjective well-being. In their closing comments about these pioneering findings, Seligman et al. (2005) concluded, "Psychotherapy has long been where you go to talk about your troubles. . . . We suggest that psychotherapy of the future may also be where you go to talk about your strengths" (p. 421).

Before we close this section on primary enhancement in psychological health, the following observation may surprise you: One goal that does not appear to qualify for primary enhancement is the pursuit of personal financial wealth. Beyond providing for life's basic necessities, money does little to raise well-being (Diener & Biswas-Diener, 2002; Diener et al., 2010; Myers, 2000; Sengupta et al., 2012), and even when increases are shown, they are so slight as to lack any impact (Boyce et al., 2017). Think about the people you know. Chances are that the ones who are consumed with acquiring wealth probably are not all that happy. Indeed, as we noted in our earlier chapter on the antecedents of happiness (Chapter 6), acquiring great monetary riches is not the royal road to satisfaction in life.

Primary Enhancement: Physical Health & Health Promotion

Exercise is a common route for attaining a sense of physical conditioning, fitness, and stamina. Regular physical activities produce both psychological and physical benefits. For example, physical activity relates to the following benefits (taken from Mutrie & Faulkner, 2004, p. 148): (1) lessened chance of dying prematurely, (2) diminished probability of dying prematurely of heart disease, (3) reduced risk of developing diabetes, (4) less likelihood of developing high blood pressure, (5) smaller chance of developing colon cancer, (6) weight loss and control, and (7) healthy bones, muscles, and joints.

Beyond the physiological improvements that result from exercising, it is also connected to greater well-being in many instances (Biddle et al., 2000; Ryff & Boylan, 2016). Although short-term exercise raises positive moods, it is long-term exercise that produces greater happiness (Argyle, 2001; Sarafino, 2002). In a sample of 1.2 million adults in the United States, for example, researchers found that individuals who exercised reported 43.2% fewer days of poorer mental health than individuals who did not exercise, and that these benefits were similar across demographics (Chekroud et al., 2018). It is important to note, however, that not all physical activity may be associated with positive mental health. In one systematic review and meta-analysis of 98 studies, physical activity for leisure or pleasure was positively associated with mental health; however, the same kind of activities performed as part of one's job were inversely associated with mental health (White et al., 2017). These findings suggest that the link between exercise and mental health is complex and may be dependent on our underlying reasons for performing those activities. Working long hours where physical activity is required may not contribute to happiness in the same positive way as intentionally exercising for pleasure or leisure, though either are likely beneficial for one's physical health.

Given the benefits of physical health (either through diet or through exercise), it is a common intervention target. While there are numerous interventions to increase individual health behaviors, health promotion research has focused intently on how to develop healthier systems in which we reside (e.g., safer and healthier workplaces, schools, or other institutions). The overarching goal of health promotion has not changed much since it was first introduced by the World Health Organization in 1986: advocate (to boost the factors which encourage health), enable (allowing all people to achieve health equity) and mediate (through collaboration across all sectors) (World Health Organization, 2023). Currently, health promotion can be found in a variety of public and private sectors. One common area of research and intervention is health promotion via the workplace. According to the Centers for Disease Control and Prevention (2023), workplace health promotion may consist of classes or seminars on health topics (e.g., fitness, nutrition, tobacco cessation, or stress management), weight loss programs (e.g., counseling and education), exercise classes, ergonomic equipment, and employee assistance programs (EAPs). Having access to such health promoting resources serves an important primary enhancement function; however, such programs are difficult to apply successfully and may interact with a variety of other contextual factors that influence their effectiveness (Jarman et al., 2016; Proper & van Oostrom, 2019). Additionally, study design or program quality can also impact the generalizability of results from workplace health promotion programs (Rongen et al., 2013), as well as health promotion in other domains such as school (Feiss et al., 2019).

A Caveat About Primary Enhancement

People should take care in primary enhancements not to overdo these activities. When seduced by the pleasures derived from building strengths, a person may lose a sense of balance in their life activities. As with any activity, moderation may be needed. It is also important for us in the field of psychology (and in other fields) to remember that activities that produce primary enhancement may not be equally accessible to all individuals. Socioeconomic status and income level may affect whether someone is able to afford leisure time, good nutrition, education, or access to good mental health care. Such factors may be especially relevant to health promotion intervention. Thus, one of our missions in the field can be to make sure that we try to make these types of benefits as available to all as they can be so that anyone might benefit from primary enhancement.

SECONDARY ENHANCEMENT: "MAKE LIFE THE BEST POSSIBLE"

Compared to primary enhancement, in which the person seeks optimal performance and satisfaction via the pursuit of desired goals and health, in secondary enhancement, the goal is to augment already positive levels to reach the ultimate in performance and satisfaction (see the right side of Figure 13.3). In a temporal sense, secondary enhancement activities take place after basic levels of performance and satisfaction have been reached in primary enhancement. Again, variation in different cultural contexts or between individuals with different status on various cultural facets (e.g., socioeconomic status) is inevitable.

Secondary Enhancement: Psychological Health

Secondary enhancement of psychological health enables people to maximize their pleasures by building on their preexisting positive mental health. Peak psychological moments often involve important human connections, such as the birth of a child, a wedding, the graduation of a loved one, or perhaps the passionate and companionate love of one's mate.

Psychological group experiences are used to help people achieve the extreme pleasures of indepth relating with others. As early as the 1950s, for example, the training groups, or T-groups, as they were called (Benne, 1964), emphasized how people could gather together to fully experience their positive emotions (Forsyth & Corazzini, 2000). Such groups were sometimes called "sensitivity training" (F. Johnson, 1988).

The existentialist contemplation of the meaning in life is yet another approach to achieving a transcendently gratifying experience. Viktor Frankl (1966, 1992), in considering the question "What is the nature of meaning?" concluded that the ultimate in experienced life meaning comes from thinking about our goals and purposes. Furthermore, he speculated that the ultimate satisfaction comes from contemplating our purpose during times in which we are suffering. Recently researchers have looked more closely at the phenomenon of **Black joy** and the way joy has been used as an act of resistance in the face of suffering in Black communities since the time of slavery. Chanté Joseph (2020) recently penned an op-ed for British Vogue entitled "What Black Joy Means—and Why It's More Important Than Ever," in which she details the refusal of the Black people as a collective to live without joy even in a world that has often tried to eradicate them as a population. As a part of her article, Joseph interviewed Kleaver Cruz, a New York writer who began the "Black Joy Project" in 2015, a project designed to highlight and center Black joy. Joseph writes about this interview:

> "When we acknowledge that we exist in an anti-black world that is set up to ensure we do not live, to choose life and to choose to enjoy any aspect of that life is a radical act," Cruz tells me over Instagram DM. "Amplifying black joy is not about dismissing or creating an 'alternative' black narrative that ignores the realities of our collective pain; rather, it is about holding the pain and injustices we experience as black folks around the world in tension with the joy we experience in pain's midst. It's about using that joy as an entry into understanding the oppressive forces we navigate through as a means to imagine and create a world free of them."

Using joy in this way is an excellent example of how secondary enhancement can occur within a community, even when that community has been plagued by strife and suffering. Note, that though some work around this area focuses on "resilience," Black joy is beyond this concept in that it is the ability to experience and exhibit not just happiness, but *joy*—a clear testament to psychological strength. Dunbar (2022) calls for more research to be conducted on this concept as do Lu and Steele (2019). Some researchers also have focused on the precursors or correlates that might bring a greater meaning of life to an individual and have included such areas as a personal understanding of what matters most in one's life, a positive attitude in general, and a decision to live freely even in the face of stressors or barriers (Koskinen et al., 2023). These researchers found that the recognition of vulnerability via suffering might in part be responsible for a deeper understanding of the meaning in life, which in turn is linked to a more enhanced happiness overall.

Other positive psychology researchers have reported that such meaning in life is linked to very high hope (Feldman & Snyder, 2005). In addition, studies have found that having stability in daily meaning in life appears to be related to higher life satisfaction (both personal and in relationships), more social connectedness, higher overall positive affect (Steger & Kashdan, 2013), and better coping with stress (Ward et al., 2023).

Occasionally, the very highest levels of pleasure are derived from involvements that are larger than any one person alone can attain (Destine & Destine, 2021; Snyder & Feldman, 2000). This may be particularly true in collectivist contexts (San-Martín et al., 2017). Working together, people can strive for achievements that would be unthinkable for any one individual. Then, as part of this collective unit, people can experience a sense of meaning and

iStockphoto.com/FG Trade

emotions that are of the grandest scale. History is filled with such instances of collective triumph in the face of adversity. Examples like the more frequent political activism we have seen throughout the country such as the Women's March, the March on Science in Washington, DC, the #metoo movement to end sexual harassment, and the #BlackLivesMatter movement to end police brutality, or the protests in Iran calling for women's rights show the energy we can create when we come together in shared ideas. In each of these cases, allies and stakeholders came together to raise their voices together. This type of banding together to make change is a part of our country's fabric and that of many others as well. Likewise, literature often details the sheer ecstasy experienced by the people who have worked together to overcome difficult and challenging blockages to reach their collective goals. When the U.S. Supreme Court ruled that same-sex marriage was to be allowed at the federal level, the hashtag #LoveWins, accompanied by rainbow heart emojis, was used 284,730 times in the first hour (Lafferty, 2015). Those who fought for this marriage equality were experiencing a high level of positive emotion. Some psychologists have begun using wilderness coping experiences in which a small group of people learn the supreme joys of cooperating as a group to successfully complete various challenges (e.g., diving, kayaking, rafting, mountain climbing) in raw, natural settings.

Finally, through the arts—such as music, dancing, theater, and painting—great pleasures are afforded to the masses. The viewing of stellar artistic performances can lift audiences to the highest levels of satisfaction and enjoyment (Snyder & Feldman, 2000). We also encourage older adults to recapture some of the joys and pleasures that came with the exploration and attainment of new skills when they were younger. (See the Personal Mini-Experiment, "Renewing the 'Wonder Years,'" for suggestions for recapturing the amazement of acquiring new skills.)

One concluding thought, before we leave you to find joy and awe in your own life: There are likely many who find it almost impossible to attain basic psychological health and as such have less access to enhancing positive emotions and experiences in their lives. Note that this makes the discussion of Black joy all the more impressive, and at the same time, those without community or those who have fewer psychological strengths overall may be far from experiencing secondary enhancement in their lives. A question we ask ourselves, and pass on to you, is, How can we help people across the world to gain basic psychological health so that they can experience the benefits of secondary enhancement in their lives? Positive psychologists, such as Ed Diener's work in creating National Well Being Accounts (see Chapter 6), have been involved in national conversations about how to make life better for all and which constructs might have the most impact, as well as which conditions are essential for achieving this lofty goal. You have likely read about Abraham Maslow's (1954) "Hierarchy of Needs" in other psychology classes and are therefore familiar with the theory that in order for self-actualization to be possible, basic needs must first be satisfied. Thus, in your daily life, consider how you might increase the likelihood of basic need satisfaction for all. We have spoken elsewhere about the importance of not just surviving, but *thriving*, in life as a basic standpoint for the field of positive psychology overall. Now we ask you to think of ways you might bring positive psychology to others in your life and beyond.

PERSONAL MINI-EXPERIMENTS

ENHANCING YOUR DAILY LIFE

Throughout this chapter, we make the case that people can make changes that will make their lives better. You can put this thesis to the test by engaging in these three mini-experiments.

Finding Pleasure in Helping Another. Popular responses to the question "What brings you pleasure?" typically cite engaging in some sort of hedonic activity—watching a good movie, eating a favorite meal, playing a favorite sport or game, or having sex with one's partner. What about helping activities that bring pleasure? Examples of such altruistic actions have included volunteering as an aide at a local hospital, serving as a Big Brother or Big Sister to a grade school student or junior high student, helping an older person with yard work, tutoring a student who is having difficulty in a given subject matter, running an errand for a disabled person, reading to a person who is blind, being an ally for the cause of a disenfranchised group, and taking a child to a sporting event. Certainly, both hedonic and helping activities bring personal pleasure. For you, which type of activity brings more pleasure? Engage in one of each kind of activity (hedonic and helping), and then write a paragraph explaining why you think one brought you more pleasure than the other. Think about what it may mean for the way you spend your time. Although most of us may think we know what brings us pleasure, this exercise shows that we may have some lessons to learn from positive psychology.

Stepping Outside of Your Comfort Zone. While at face value, this title does not seem as though this exercise would produce positive emotion or pleasure, learning about groups that are different from our own can expand our opportunities for pleasurable social involvement. Knowing more about a wide variety of cultural groups can help us to feel more comfortable in cultivating relationships with a larger social circle. In addition, by having a better understanding of the histories of other groups, all of us can more confidently help groups that have traditionally been marginalized or disenfranchised. Strike up a conversation with someone you view as different from you. Visit a religious service or community different from your own. Read a novel about a group to which you do not belong. Stretch yourself.

How can you bring positive psychology to all? As we noted previously, not all may have access to psychological health in a way that allows them to move into secondary enhancement of that construct. This said, thinking of making a difference in this area might be a bit overwhelming due to the magnitude of this issue. Instead of trying to change the world in one step, we ask you to take one step toward changing the world. Think now of your **sphere of influence**. This concept is meant to describe the sphere(s) in your life over which you have control. For some, this might be a small group—you have control over yourself, for example, or over your words and how you use them. For others, you may have a positive level of social control within your circle of friends or colleagues. For still others, you may be in a position to make policy or practice changes to impact a larger group—for example, a teacher over a classroom, or an administrator in higher education. Think of this sphere, and try to impact it toward secondary enhancement in small ways every day. Once you have achieved some small steps in this area, make efforts to enhance your sphere of influence, moving farther and farther outward as you bring positive change to a larger group. Even better, work closely with others in a group to try to achieve this. You can make a difference.

Secondary Enhancement: Physical Health

Secondary enhancement of physical health pertains to the peak levels of physical health—levels that are beyond those of well-conditioned people. People who seek secondary enhancement strive for levels of physical conditioning that far surpass those typically obtained by people who simply engage in exercise. Be clear, however, that such persons need not be Olympic-level athletes who compete against other elite athletes with the goal of achieving the very best performance in a sport. While many athletes who pursue the highest levels of competition may see physical fitness as a means of enhancing the probability of winning, people who typify the secondary enhancement of physical health in and of itself are motivated to reach very high levels of physical prowess per se. This superior level of physical fitness mirrors what Dienstbier (1989, 2015) has defined as *toughness* and may have implications for decreased stress (Gerber et al., 2013). Research on children has shown that thriving in sports may have important psychological consequences as well (Kinoshita et al., 2022).

Some researchers have posited that physical health is a primary basis for psychological health and thus achieving peak levels of physical health may lead to opportunities for peak psychological experiences as well (Winter et al., 2022). These researchers have developed what they term the RICH theory of happiness, with each of the letters standing for a component of overall happiness: R is for resources, I stands for intimacy, C for competence, and H for health. In this research, gains can be made toward wellness and self-efficacy only if health is also in place. More research is needed here on the different precursors for optimal health, and again as noted in the previous section, ways in which we can help a majority to gain base physical health such that they can better access the benefits of enhanced physical health.

THE BALANCE OF PREVENTION AND ENHANCEMENT SYSTEMS

In this chapter, we describe the prevention and enhancement intercessions separately. Primary and secondary preventions entail efforts to see that negative outcomes do not happen, whereas primary and secondary enhancements reflect efforts to ensure that positive outcomes will happen. Unchained from their problems via primary and secondary preventions, people then can turn their attentions to primary and secondary enhancements related to reaching optimal, even peak, experiences and life satisfactions (Snyder, Thompson, & Heinze, 2003). Together, preventions and enhancements form a powerful dyad for coping and excelling, and efforts to expand their access to all is a worthwhile goal.

It is noteworthy that prevention and enhancement parallel the two major motives in all of psychology. Namely, prevention mirrors those processes aimed at avoiding harmful outcomes, and enhancement mirrors the processes that focus upon attaining beneficial outcomes. In many ways this encompasses the very heart of positive psychology—a balanced approach to viewing strengths and weaknesses within a cultural context, both in the environment and in ourselves. Too often, positive psychology is thought of in layperson circles as a focus solely on the positive. Discussing the balance between prevention and enhancement is a good starting point for understanding the important roles knowing about *both* our weaknesses or lacks *and* our strengths and assets.

APPENDIX: HOPE THERAPY WORKSHEET

Domain	*Importance Rating*	*Satisfaction Rating*
Academic		
Family		
Leisure		
Personal growth		
Health/fitness		
Romantic		
Social relationships		
Spiritual		
Work		

My selected domain is:

What would I have to do to increase my satisfaction in this domain?

What is my goal?

What is my pathway to the goal?

How much do I believe that I can make it? (circle one)

A little Medium Very much

How much energy do I have to accomplish my goal? (circle one)

A little Medium Very much

What makes me think I can attain my goal?

What will slow me down or stop me from reaching my goal?

What is my backup plan?

What are the first three steps to my goal?

1.

2.

3.

KEY TERMS

Black joy
Eudaemonic primary enhancements
Hedonic primary enhancements
Meditation
Primary enhancements
Primary preventions
Savoring
Secondary enhancements
Secondary preventions
Selective prevention
Sphere of influence
Universal prevention

POSITIVE ENVIRONMENTS

14 POSITIVE SCHOOLING AND GOOD WORK

The Psychology of Gainful Employment and the Education That Gets Us There

LEARNING OBJECTIVES

After reading this chapter, you will be able to:

14.1 Understand the components of positive schooling

14.2 Analyze and critique schooling from an inclusive and equitable standpoint

14.3 Discuss the current state of education from a positive psychology lens

14.4 Understand the psychological benefits of gainful employment and its characteristics

14.5 Explain and understand the strengths-based approach to work

We spend a large chunk of our lives either in school or at work. Although our values are often set at home, both school and work contribute highly to our understanding of how the world works and what we should be doing in it. In addition, school and work are opportunities for identification of our strengths and our weaknesses. According to Erik Erikson (1959) and his psychosocial stage of Industry versus Inferiority, it is in school that we first start to notice that we are perhaps better than some at reading or not as good as others at playing basketball or doing math equations. This indexing of strengths and skills continues on to adolescence and adulthood when we might begin to lean toward an area of study or an occupation defined in part by the strengths we believe have and the skills we hope to develop. At both school and work, there is potential for further enhancement of strength and skill; there is also, unfortunately, equal chance for stagnation and discouragement depending on the type of environment instilled. In the following, we discuss what components make up a **positive schooling** or *good work* experience.

PERSONAL MINI-EXPERIMENTS

THE POWER OF POSITIVE (AND NEGATIVE) TEACHERS

Throughout this chapter, we are reminded of the powerful effects of teachers on our lives. Here, we ask that you consider the effects of a bad teacher and a good teacher on your life.

Letting Go of a Bad Teacher. Think back over your days in grade school, junior high school, high school, college, and perhaps even graduate school. Think about one teacher in particular who made you feel small or dread going to their classroom. Take a blank piece of paper and see how much you can remember about this teacher. Write down what they looked like, along with the grade and place where you met. Describe how this teacher ran the class. What were the most negative things you can remember this teacher doing? Did this teacher make fun of you or other students? Would this teacher not trust or believe you? Did this teacher make you feel dumb? Did this teacher give you the impression that they couldn't care less about you and your success in life?

Once you have written a fairly good summary of this negative teacher, turn the page over and write what you took away from that class and that instructor. Do messages that started in that class still play in your mind today? Do you think certain things about yourself even now because of something that happened with that teacher? When you have answered these questions, then say to yourself, "I am going to bury any influence this teacher had on the way I think." Then, repeat several times, "I am going to stop the bad lessons that [teacher's name] taught me!" Feel free to make any other statements that you want—just as if this teacher were sitting in a chair across from you.

When you have finished making your statements to this bad teacher, grab a shovel and go outside and dig a hole. That's right, dig a hole! Now, put the shovel down and say goodbye to the bad things you learned from this teacher. Next, take the sheet of paper on which you wrote about this teacher and tear it into many pieces. Then, throw the pieces of paper into the hole and cover it over with dirt. Walk away—don't forget the shovel—and vow to yourself that this lousy teacher never again will influence your life. Finally, buy yourself a treat to celebrate this ritual.

Saying Thank You to a Good Teacher. We again ask that you look back over your school days. But this time, recall those teachers who were superb. They were so good that you looked forward to going to their classes every day. You enjoyed learning from these teachers. They cared about you and treated you with respect. Now, take a blank piece of paper and write the name of a good teacher at the top of the page. Then, write everything you can remember about this teacher. Write down what this teacher looked like, the grade and place where you met, and how this teacher ran the class. What were some of the most positive things that you can remember this teacher doing?

Once you have a good summary of this positive teacher, turn the page over and write what you took away from this teacher. Are there any messages that you still play in your mind that were cultivated in that teacher's class? Because of things that happened with that teacher, do you now hold certain positive views of yourself? Perhaps this teacher made you feel smart or clever. Did this teacher make a point to give you credit when you did well? Did this teacher truly care that you succeeded in life? Do you still practice certain positive behaviors that you owe to your interactions with this teacher?

Once you have completed this assignment for one or more teachers, try to find out where they can be reached today. Some still may be teaching. Others probably will be retired. With the advent of e-mail, it has become easier to contact people whom we met earlier in our lives. Now, write a thank you note to each of these positive teachers. You will feel great for having done this, and we can assure you that the teacher will get a tremendous lift from your message. There is nothing more gratifying to a teacher than to be told that they played a positive role in the life of a former student. We often do not take the time to thank the truly important people in our lives for the things they have done on our behalf. Your former teachers will treasure your note all the more if you describe specific instances where they helped you. So, too, will they cherish hearing about the successes and accomplishments in your life.

POSITIVE SCHOOLING

Because schools play a major role in promoting the tenets of positive psychology, we begin with the topic of schooling. *Schooling*, an older word for "education," conveys the importance of the entire community in teaching children. This is why we use the word *schooling* in the title of this chapter. We begin by doing a deep dive into the components of positive schools. Following this, we take some time to talk about giving back to teachers, and, lastly, discuss some of the current threats to education in the United States.

THE COMPONENTS OF POSITIVE SCHOOLING

Positive schooling is an approach to education that consists of a foundation of care, trust, and respect for diversity, where teachers develop tailored goals for each student to engender learning and then work with them to develop the plans and motivation to reach their goals. Before we review the components of this approach, we acknowledge briefly some of the major educators who have paved the way for it. Noted philosophers such as Benjamin Franklin, John Stuart Mill, Herbert Spencer, and John Dewey focused on the assets of students (Lopez, Janowski, & Wells., 2005). Alfred Binet (Binet & Simon, 1916) often is considered the father of the concept of mental age, but he also emphasized the enhancement of student skills rather than paying attention only to the remediation of weaknesses. Likewise, Elizabeth Hurlock (1925) accentuated praise as more influential than criticism as a determinant of students' efforts. Lewis Terman (Terman & Oden, 1947) spent his whole career exploring the thinking of truly brilliant learners, and Arthur Chickering (1969) sought to understand the evolution of students' talents. More recently, Donald Clifton identified and then expanded on the particular talents of students, rather than focusing on their weaknesses (see Buckingham & Clifton, 2001; Clifton & Anderson, 2002; Clifton & Nelson, 1992; Rath & Clifton, 2004).

We next explore the major components of positive schooling (see Buskist et al., 2005; Lopez, Hodges et al., 2005; Ritschel, 2005). Figure 14.1 is a visual representation of the lessons that are common in positive schooling. This figure shows the positive psychology schoolhouse as being built of six parts, from the ground up. We begin with the foundation, where we describe the importance of care, trust, and diversity. Then, the first and second floors of our positive schoolhouse represent teaching goals, planning, and the motivation of students. The third floor holds hope, and the roof represents the societal contributions and paybacks produced by our positive psychology school graduates.

FIGURE 14.1 ■ The Components of Positive Schooling

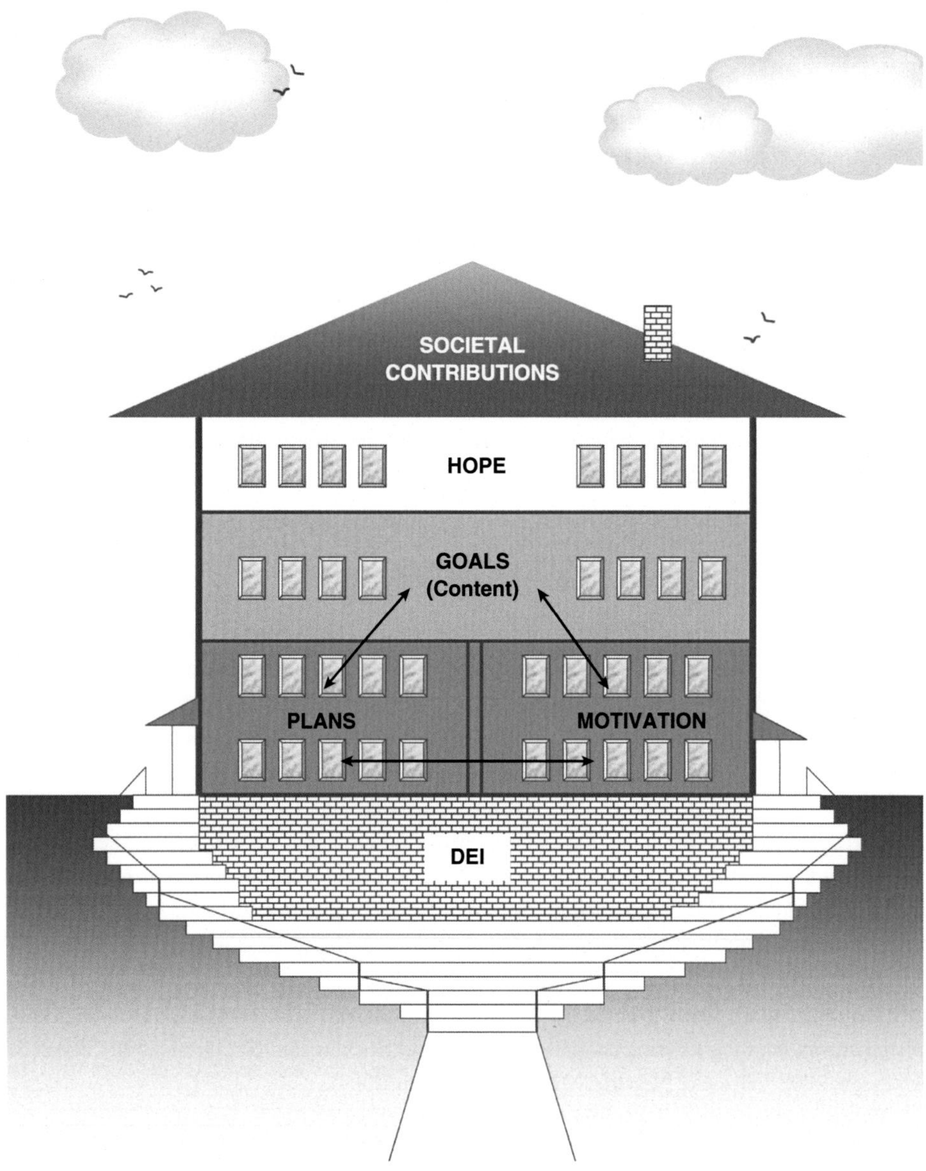

Care, Trust, and Respect for Diversity, Equity, and Inclusion

We begin with a foundation that involves caring, trust, and respect for diversity, equity, and inclusion (DEI). It is absolutely crucial to have a supportive atmosphere of care and trust because students flourish in such an environment. In attending award ceremonies for outstanding teachers, we have noticed that both the teachers and their students typically comment on the importance of a sense of caring. Students need as role models teachers who consistently are responsive and available. Such teacher care and positive emotions provide the secure base that allows young people to explore and find ways to achieve their own important academic and life goals (Shorey et al., 2003). In addition, social acceptance by teachers has been found to contribute to overall school satisfaction (Baker, 1998; Gilman et al., 2008), which has been found to be related to more satisfaction with life (Mahoney et al., 2003) and fewer issues related to mental health (Locke & Newcomb, 2004). Better behavior in class is also linked with perceived acceptance from teachers for both boys and girls (Khan et al., 2010). One final point here, some research has shown that when students have teachers who are like them in some demographic way (e.g., the same race or culture, the same gender, or sexual orientation), they may have even more positive outcomes (Rios et al., 2010). One of our goals as a society should be to have representative work forces of our population, particularly perhaps in any field working with children and adolescents.

Trust in the classroom has received considerable attention among educators, and the consensus is that it yields both psychological and performance benefits for students (Bryk & Schneider, 2002; Collins, 2001). Trust is crucial from the earliest grades on up. In their influential book (now in its second edition in 2019), *Learning to Trust: Attachment Theory and Classroom Management*, Marilyn Watson (an educational psychologist) and Laura Ecken (an elementary school teacher) tackle the thorny problem of classroom management and discipline in a low-income elementary school. Trust is almost nonexistent between Laura and her students at first, partially because many of the children have had a lack of trustworthy relationships in their lives up to this point. Their approach is to establish trusting relationships with the most difficult students, with the logic that this then will have ripple effects that spread to the rest of the class. Watson and Ecken (2019) advocate for what they call **developmental discipline**. This notion is derived from the principles of attachment theory (see Chapter 12), which advocates helping those students who have insecure attachments to caregivers. Laura Ecken recounts many heartwarming stories throughout this book about real life experiences in her classroom. She and Watson (2019) give solid advice on how to work with children from all backgrounds and to establish trust with them toward the goal of a better educational experience overall.

Instructors must make sure that there is a sense of trust in their classrooms. They must avoid becoming cynical about students because this undermines the trust that is so crucial for learning. Often, and particularly at some developmental stages, students would rather misbehave (and suffer any punishment) than look dumb in front of their peers. In their interactions with students, therefore, positive teachers try to find ways to make students look good and to feel good about themselves as well. Without assurance that they can trust a teacher, students may not choose to take the risks that are so important for learning. In addition, teachers must be willing to step outside their own worldviews and make room for ideas that come from backgrounds different from their own. Remembering cultural context in judging ideas, views, and behaviors and avoiding invalidation of experiences (especially those related to experiences of discrimination and prejudice) are essential components of providing an environment of trust. In these cases, affirmation and caring can promote a sense of trust within the classroom (Watson & Ecken, 2019).

Another aspect of the positive psychology foundation for schooling involves the importance of diversity of student backgrounds and worldviews in the classroom and thinking about equity and inclusion in relation to this. This starts by encouraging students to become sensitive to the ideas of people from racial, ethnic, or age cohorts that are different from their own. This can be accomplished by revealing to students that they have much in common with those who are different from them. At the same time, it is important to emphasize that differences between individuals and groups are not necessarily problematic; there is room for more than one viewpoint, and trying to see things from different vantage points can broaden our minds. Along these lines, it is crucial to make certain that the views of all the different constituencies in a class are given voices in the classroom. Ethnocultural empathy (Wang et al., 2003), or the ability to feel for groups outside of our own cultural background, can be established through close contact with others who are different from oneself (see Chapter 11).

Teachers who encourage students to be inclusive in their social circles and equitable in their treatment of others can effectively broaden the cultural experiences of all their students. In addition, teachers can try to help break down barriers for students that make their experiences inequitable. In recent years, several types of graphics have made their rounds on the internet depicting the differences between *equality* and *equity*. In Figure 14.2, equality means giving the same size box to each person reflected in the picture regardless of height, effectively treating all the *same*. In doing this, we often do not assist everyone in such a way as to truly help. In the graphic, the person on the left and the person in the middle can both see over the fence with the help of the same sized box, though the person on the far right still cannot see over the fence. Equity, instead, is to try to create a situation in which all groups have access to an experience or a benefit. In the right hand side of the figure you can see that giving a larger box to the person on the right allows them to see over the fence, a smaller box allows the middle person to see over equitably, and the person on the left can see without any box. All three are able to equitably see over the fence, with different adjustments. One more step can be taken by teachers to ensure full equity, and that is to correct the problem. Though not pictured in Figure 14.2, some graphics now show a third scenario in which the fence would be removed, or made see-through via chain-link, or something similar. In this final scenario, often entitled "justice," there is no need for different sized boxes or same sized boxes as all can see what is on the other side of the fence without any help.

In a positive classroom, teaching with equity might look like having a shared set of school supplies for the class to use instead of asking each family to purchase a set of supplies on their own. It could also be reflected in making sure that letters and information that go home are translated into other languages spoken by the parents in the classroom and not just written in English. In this way, teachers can show their care for the students and their supporters and can establish trust in this way as well.

In addition, there is more to an inclusive and equitable classroom than understanding differences. In her book *The Culturally Inclusive Educator: Preparing for a Multicultural World*, Dena R. Samuels (2014) talks about making purposeful changes in our classrooms from top to bottom as we work toward equity across all students. For example, how many teachers did you have growing up who used the strategy of calling on students in order of who put their hand up first? Although this seems like a fair strategy, research shows that boys raise their hands faster and more often than other genders in a number of different studies (Owens et al., 2003),

FIGURE 14.2 ■ Equality and Equity Concept

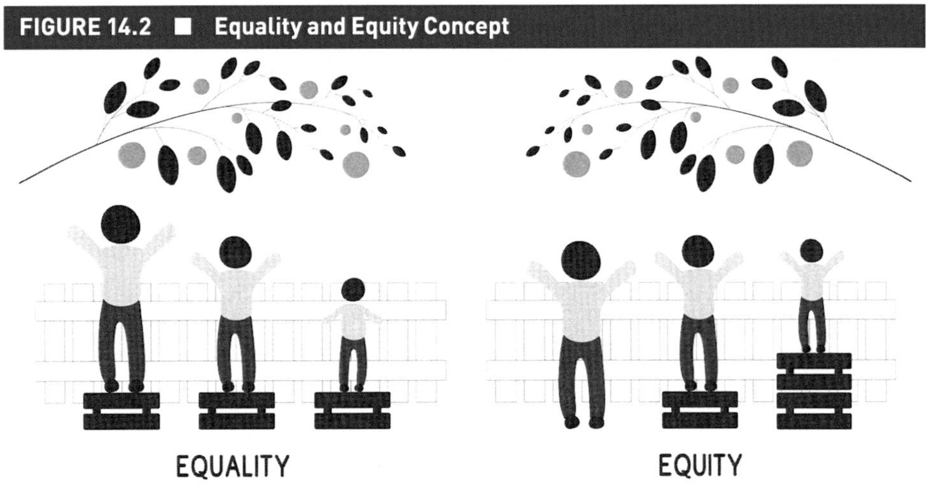

iStockphoto.com/iam2mai

meaning that using a practice such as this likely allows boys to have the right answer first and, more often, perhaps sets the tone of a discussion as well. Calling on students by going back and forth between various genders might be a more equitable way of handling this and an easy fix.

Samuels (2014) also discusses the importance of examining our own biases as teachers. Although we would all like to say we are nonbiased, we know this is not an authentic representation of any of us—everyone has biases, but we can choose not to act upon them. Even as we are working on our own biases against or for people who may be different from us, we must also validate that experiences of bias are a reality for many children of color and other underrepresented backgrounds. Black students were more likely to receive a conduct report for "bad behavior" when compared to White counterparts in a study investigating teacher discipline interventions (Silva et al., 2015). In addition, other studies have shown that Latino and Black students are often expected to perform worse from the beginning and seen as "the root of the problem, not because of who they are as individuals, but because of who they are as a social group" (Silva et al., 2015, p. 790). We bring these more negative experiences up in this section to encourage future and present teachers to work on counteracting automatic and implicit biases and to *believe* children who have experienced these types of incidents and to try to give them coping strategies for dealing with them in the future. This validation can go a long way toward the trust we know is crucial.

Perhaps the words of Dr. LaKimbre Brown, a former instructional superintendent for *Teach for America* say it best:

> One of my main responsibilities [as a former principal] was to help facilitate meaningful relationships. And an essential component of meaningful relationships is trust. Trust is safety. Trust is comfort. Trust is feeling that someone has your back. Trust is an environment where individuals can be their best selves. (2014, para 1)

This is what we want for all children.

Goals

The component of goals is represented by the second floor of the strengths schoolhouse (see Figure 14.1). Through exploring the responses of students from kindergarten to college, Stanford University professor Carol Dweck has put together an impressive program of research showing that goals provide a means of targeting students' learning efforts. Moreover, goals are especially helpful if agreed upon by the teacher and students (Bardach et al., 2018; Dweck, 1999). Perhaps the most conducive targets are the **stretch goals**, in which the student seeks a slightly more difficult learning goal than attained previously. Reasonably challenging goals engender productive learning, especially if the goals can be tailored to particular students (or groups of students). One of the biggest benefits of completing stretch goals is that they have been shown to increase willingness to take risks (Gary et al., 2017).

It is important for students to feel some sense of input in regard to their teachers' conduct of classes. Of course, the instructors set the classroom goals, but in doing so, they are wise to consider the reactions of their previous students. The success of class goals involves making the materials relevant to students' real-life experiences whenever possible (Snyder & Shorey, 2002) and making sure that students know that their teachers believe that they can achieve their goals and do not underestimate their efforts and abilities (Cherng, 2017). Additionally, some research has shown that child agency is a large factor in determining the benefits of growth mindsets. In research by Hargreaves and others (2021), it was found that even when lower-achieving children in a classroom showed beneficial curiosity, creative learning, and engagement, as well as capacity for using these skills in active ways, set rules in the classroom at times got in the way of children using these important skills. Thinking of ways to have order in a classroom but not to stifle so much as to remove all agency is a lesson worth paying attention to.

It also helps to make the goals understandable and concrete, as well as to take a larger learning goal and divide it into smaller subgoals that can be tackled in stages. Likewise, as we noted with respect to diversity issues in the previous section, goal setting is facilitated when teachers allow part of students' grades to be determined by group activities in which cooperation with other students is essential.

Plans and Motivation

In Figure 14.1, the first floor of the strengths schoolhouse is divided into plans and motivation, both of which interact with the educational goals on the second floor (and with content). Like building science on accumulating ideas, teaching necessitates a careful planning process on the part of instructors.

One planning approach we will discuss is championed by noted social psychologist Robert Cialdini, emeritus at Arizona State University (see Cialdini, 2005, and his works compiled by Kenrick et al., 2012). Once Professor Cialdini has established a teaching goal regarding given psychological content, he then poses mystery stories for students. Through solving the mystery, the student learns the particular content. The inherent need for closure (see Schumpe et al., 2017) regarding the mysteries also motivates the students; motivation is the companion to planning, which we discuss in the next section. Likewise, because the mystery stories have beginnings, middles, and ends, there is the inherent desire on the part of students to get to the conclusion (see Green et al. [2002] on the drive to traverse a narrative). Others have emulated this work with other topics. Schmaltz (2016), for example, discusses using heavy metal music as a way to introduce the tenets of scientific thinking. In Schmaltz's examples, students investigate claims that certain heavy metal music has led to crimes or other negative behavior. Students may be more motivated to delve into a topic such as this and to thus practice scientific thinking while investigating this type of claim.

Most of these previous studies discuss raising students' motivations by making the material relevant to them (Buskist et al., 2005). At the most basic level, when the course information is relevant, students are more likely to attend class, pay attention, and make comments during the lectures (Harackiewicz et al., 2016). To increase the relevance of material, instructors can develop classroom demonstrations and at-home exploration (such as the Personal Mini-Experiments and Life Enhancement Strategies in this book) of various phenomena applicable to situations that the students encounter outside the classroom. Even with topics like statistics that students may find challenging, asking students for their ideas on what data would be interesting to collect or toward examples of questions to which one might want to find answers can assist with greater learning and motivation (Childers & Taylor, 2021). This tactic may also assist in providing a diversity of examples as students from different backgrounds may add their voice to the table if they wish, even if they are from groups that have been historically marginalized.

Teachers must be enthused about their materials in order to carry out the plans that they have made for their classes (see the interactive arrow between plans and motivation on the first floor of Figure 14.1). Instructors are models of enthusiasm for their students. Therefore, when instructors make lesson goals and plans interesting to themselves, their students easily can pick up on this energy. Motivated teachers are sensitive to the needs and reactions of their students. Strengths-based instructors also take students' questions very seriously and make every effort to give their best answers. If the teacher does not know the answer to a student question in the moment, they should make every effort to find it. When teachers follow through to locate the answer to a question and present it at the next class period, students typically are very appreciative of such responsiveness.

Both teacher enthusiasm and student academic motivation were sorely challenged during the COVID-19 pandemic, and this provided a unique opportunity to study factors that impact motivation in times of such a crisis. Some of the research conducted at this time was specific to online learning and the closing of schools, regardless, many provided information beyond this that could be applied beyond this paradigmatic shift. Following the pandemic it is likely that more digital technology and online learning will continue as so many more teachers and students gained increased self-efficacy with this type of pedagogy and learning (Beardsley et al., 2021). Some findings related to motivation and online learning pointed to making asynchronous materials as close to real-life experiences as possible. Medical students who were asked to investigate case studies via e-learning that were close to real-life incidents were much more motivated to complete them, versus those that investigated less current or relevant material (Rahm et al. 2021). Other studies found that adolescents' academic motivation was impacted positively by more positive mood and more parental support (Klootwijk et al., 2021).

This finding is unsurprising as it mirrors the impact of these factors in noncrisis times as well, but it is an important reminder that in times of crisis, attending to positive emotions and providing as much support as possible can impact academic outcomes as well. Additionally, those students during the pandemic who were able to keep up with their extracurricular activities in some way were found to have higher motivation toward academics during this time as compared to those who were not (Zaccoletti et al., 2020). These findings are particularly important to keep in mind as we work with students from backgrounds that may not provide as much support as is ideal and who may not have funds to participate in extracurriculars. Making sure that students have equitable experiences in these ways can assist with more equitable academic outcomes.

Finally, we have often found in our own teaching that students will perform at whatever level you expect; this is true if a teacher's expectations are high . . . or low. Working in groups may have this same effect on accountability. Students who worked together in a cooperative learning program for physical education increased both intrinsic motivation and students' enjoyment in the process, among others (Fernandez-Rio et al., 2017). Additionally, students whose teachers and parents praise them (though sometimes private praise is preferred), who believe in them, and give positive and accurate feedback are more motivated to succeed (Hellmich & Hoya, 2017). The opportunities for appropriately interacting with and motivating students are many, and positive teachers often try to convey energizing feedback.

Hope

If the previously mentioned lessons regarding goals, planning, and motivation have been applied in a classroom, then there will be a spirit of inquiry that students will pick up on (Ritschel, 2005). As Auburn University award-winning teacher William Buskist and his colleagues (2005) put it,

> An essential aspect of our teaching is to pass the torch—to share our academic values, curiosities, and discipline-focused enthusiasm and to encourage students to embrace these values and qualities and to own them. Teaching is not about being dispassionate dispensers of facts and figures. Teaching is about influence. It is about caring deeply about ideas and how those ideas are derived, understood, and expressed. It is about caring deeply for the subject matter and for those students with whom we are sharing it. And it is through such passionate caring that we inspire students. (p. 116)

When students acquire this spirit, their learning expands to increase their sense of empowerment. Thus, students are empowered to become lifelong problem solvers. This "learning how to learn" pulls from goals-directed pathways thinking as well as from the "I can" motivation. Therefore, positive psychology schooling not only imparts the course contents but also produces a sense of hope in the student learners. (See Chapter 8 for a detailed discussion of hope and *Making Hope Happen*, Lopez, 2013.) Hope is depicted in the attic of the positive schoolhouse in Figure 14.1. A hopeful student believes that she or he will continue to learn long after stepping out of the classroom. Or perhaps it is more apt to say that hopeful thinking knows no walls or boundaries in the life of a student who never stops learning.

Societal Contributions

A final positive psychology lesson is that students understand that they are part of a larger societal scheme in which they share what they have learned with other people. As shown in the potentially nourishing cloud above the metaphorical schoolhouse in Figure 14.1, these societal contributions represent the lasting "paybacks" that educated people give to those around them—whether this means teaching children to think positively or sharing insights and excitement with the multitude of others with whom they come into contact over the course of their lifetimes. Consider this comment from a student involved in one of our (JTP's) diversity-focused courses in college:

> By learning more about how to be multiculturally competent myself, I can now share that information with my friends and family. When my friends judge based solely on their own worldviews, I can be the one who says, "Have you thought about it from this perspective?" This makes me feel like I am making a difference as an ally out there in the world!

The feeling of empowerment is obvious in her tone. Positive education thus turns students into teachers who continue to share what they have learned with others and who have an appreciation for diversity in thoughts and ideas. In this way, the benefits of the learning process are passed on to a wide range of other people. In positive schooling, therefore, students become teachers of others.

TEACHING AS A CALLING

Though we sometimes hear more about the impact of negative teachers on the learning process, there is much evidence that positive teachers unleash the enthusiasm and joys of education. These teachers in positive schooling see their efforts as a **calling** rather than work (Wrzesniewski et al., 1997). A calling is defined as a strong motivation in which a person repeatedly takes a course of action that is intrinsically satisfying (see Buskist et al., 2005). When positive psychology tenets are applied to teaching, we believe that the instructors behave as if they had callings in that they demonstrate a profound and strong love for teaching.

Every year, the Council of Chief State School Officers (CCSSO) gives out its National Teacher of the Year Award. Past winners include teachers at all grade levels and from towns all over the United States. The 2022 winner of this prestigious award was Kurt Russell, a high school history teacher in Oberlin, Ohio in the same high school he attended as an adolescent. For 25 years, Russell has impacted young minds as the selection committee stated "[by being] a powerful advocate who always puts students at the center of his work" (Walker, 2022, para 2). Russell, a Black man, was inspired to become a teacher after having his first Black teacher, Larry Thomas. Must research supports the wise words "If you can see it, you can be it" and this was true for Russell (Rios et al, 2010). In addition to teaching topics related to social justice, oppression, and race and injustice in his classes, Russsell supports students as the advisor to the Black Student Union at his high school and has used restorative justice to impact behavior for the better (Walker, 2022). Enrollment of both White students and students of color in his courses

Kurt Russell, 2022 National Teacher of the Year

Courtesy of Kurt Russell

on these topics have made strides toward a more inclusive community at school. Read about his journey in the following story. (As an aside, the 2016 Teacher of the Year that we profiled in the 4th edition of this textbook, Jahana Hayes, went on to become a United States Congresswoman in the state of Connecticut, and at the time of publication was on the verge of being elected to her third term in office! Having a teacher help to make decisions about schooling at the national level is a benefit to us all).

GIVING BACK TO TEACHERS

Our final observations about positive schooling pertain to the role that you can play in making teachers better. You can do several things to help teachers in particular and the school system in general. First, you can work with teachers to help in whatever ways possible to improve your own children's learning. Learning obviously happens outside of school hours as well, and we encourage you to try various activities with the children in your life to reinforce and practice the ongoing lessons taught at school.

Teach your children that their viewpoint is not the only one and to appreciate differences as well as similarities between themselves and others. Likewise, if you are able, volunteer to help with various school activities. Your children and their friends and classmates will be impressed by the fact that learning is not something about which only their teachers care.

You also can visit with the teachers in your local elementary, junior high, and high schools and ask them what they need to make their teaching more effective. Teachers often pay for school supplies out of their own pockets as so many schools are often underfunded across the country. If larger items like computers or other electronics are needed, perhaps a crowdfunding or donation drive by parents and community members could raise the necessary money. If you are in a position to do so, donate your old books to the school library. Additionally, regardless of your background, ask that teachers be multiculturally competent in their teaching and equity minded in their classrooms. If you have expertise in this area, share it with your local schools. If you have special skills in other areas, volunteer to come into class and give demonstrations to students. You may want to become politically active to increase local school taxes in order to raise teacher pay and benefits, build new classrooms, or to help get more relevant curricula approved. In a similar spirit, we ask that you look toward the end of this chapter at an exercise aimed at saying thank you to those special teachers in your local community. Please try "Saying Thank You to a Good Teacher" (in the Personal Mini-Experiments). This payback takes very little time, but it would be tremendously meaningful to the teacher(s) whom you remember. Don't forget that these teachers were there for you at many crucial points in your life, so take some time now and reach out to them. Retired or still working, a thank you at any time is greatly appreciated by your former teachers.

CURRENT THREATS TO EDUCATION

Though long ago in many societies across the world education was only accessible or even deemed appropriate for the wealthy, the ideal within the United States has been that public education should make one's life outcomes less dependent upon family status and more dependent on the use of public education. Thus, schools were idealized as making huge differences in the lives of our children.

Unfortunately, this romanticized view of schools in the United States often has been more a dream than a reality. Though segregation explicitly based on race no longer legally exists, we still today see incredible differences between school districts or campuses based on the socioeconomic status of the neighborhoods from which they draw. As schools are funded in part based on the tax money of those within their boundaries, this means some schools receive much less support than others. Author Jonathan Kozol, in several books devoted to the topic, depicts the extreme differences in schools attended by poor children or minoritized children in comparison to those who are White and wealthy (see *Savage Inequalities* [2012] or *Amazing Grace* [2005] for close accounts of these inequities). As with many issues, money appears to play an important role here, with relevant research showing that school districts with higher salaries and better physical facilities are likely to attract and keep the higher-quality teachers (Hanushek et al., 2004). Murnane and Steele stated in 2007 that "the most urgent problem facing American education . . . is the unequal distribution of high-quality teachers" (p. 18) and discussed the trend for children in lower socioeconomic brackets and in non-White groups to more often be the recipients of low-quality teaching. While it must be acknowledged that teaching in schools with fewer resources is difficult at best, this leaves less privileged children at a lifelong disadvantage.

In more recent years, many teachers have left the profession due to a number of factors. During the large-scale school shutdowns across the United States as a part of the COVID-19 pandemic, teachers were criticized roundly by parents largely as a part of the frustration many felt at the fact that their children were not physically in school at the time. In fact, in a survey conducted by RAND in early 2021, approximately 25% of teachers noted that they hoped to leave their teaching job at the end of the 2020-2021 school year (Zamarro et al., 2021). The main reason noted by teachers as to their defection from the field was stress (Diliberti et al., 2021). Additionally, new laws established to prosecute teachers who discuss topics that parents in some states say should be "off limits" in classrooms (e.g., racial issues, sexual orientation, gender, social-emotional learning, etc.) have contributed to many teachers feeling attacked and leaving the profession. We agree that parents and experts should have a say in what is being taught in schools, but sanitizing history or erasing experiences of those who have been historically marginalized is not part of solid educational theories supported by research. Likewise, hearing different perspectives than your own is beneficial to understanding others. You can be part of the positive psychology solution to making the schools better in your community by remaining engaged in these topics, educating yourself on topics brought up for criticism (as opposed to listening to sound bytes on curated news channels), and continuing to support measures that increase funding for our schools. Our school system is at a crossroads right now, and our children's future education is at stake. Positive schooling and its tenets toward a broad educational mindset may be the antidote during this dark time.

GAINFUL EMPLOYMENT

It was Sigmund Freud who first made the bold statement that a healthy life is one in which a person has the ability to love and to work (O'Brien, 2003). In the many decades since Freud presented these ideas, the psychological literature has reinforced the importance of positive interpersonal relationships and employment. After reviewing the growing body of literature on the role of one's job in producing a healthy life, we searched for a phrase that captured the essence of the many benefits that can flow from work. In the end, we decided to use the phrase ***gainful employment.***

Although often popular culture in movies shows people awaken in the morning only to dread getting up and going to work, gainfully employed people actually look forward to it. Gainful employment is work that is characterized by the nine benefits displayed in Figure 14.3. In recent years, the idea of what "work" looks like has shifted for many. For some, a work week now includes some days working from home via virtual meetings while others are in person. For others, the shift to virtual was impossible due to duties needed to be performed. And finally, though our unemployment rates remain low in the United States, labor shortages exist across the country as many have hypothesized that for some the COVID pandemic precipitated permanent life changes with regard to work and its value in our daily lives.

FIGURE 14.3 ■ Nine Characteristics of Gainful Employment

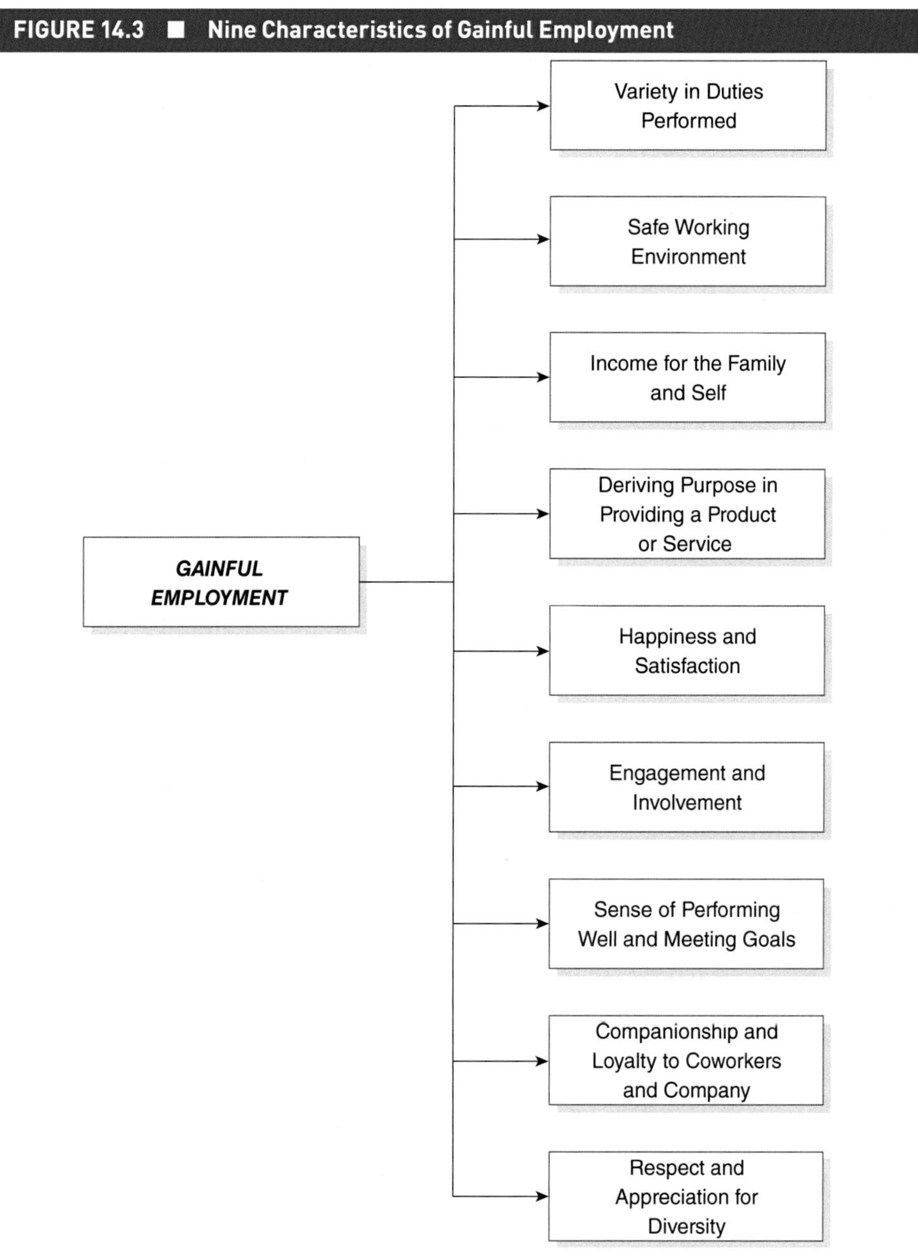

In the remainder of this chapter, we explore the growing body of positive psychology findings related to work and look at gainful employment from the perspectives of the employee, the leadership, and the organization. We finish with some findings related to what gainful employment looks like in today's world.

GAINFUL EMPLOYMENT: HAPPINESS, SATISFACTION, AND BEYOND

As shown in Figure 14.3, nine benefits are derived from gainful employment. We place happiness and satisfaction at the center because of their key role (see Allen & McCarthy, 2016; Amick et al., 2002; Burnette & Pollack, 2013; Keller & Semmer, 2013). As Jane Henry (2004) describes it,

> The centrality of work to well-being is not surprising when you think of the number of benefits it offers, notably: an identity, opportunities for social interaction and support, purpose, time filling, engaging challenges, and possibilities for status apart from the provision of income. (p. 270)

If a person is happy at work, chances are that their overall satisfaction with life will be higher (Douglass, Duffy, & Autin, 2016; Hart, 1999). The correlation of job satisfaction with overall happiness is about .40 (Diener & Lucas, 1999). Employed people consistently report being happier than their counterparts without jobs (Argyle, 2001; Warr, 1999), and those who have been taken out of the community due to jailtime (Cherney & Fitzgerald, 2016; Lageson & Uggen, 2013) or military service report that employment may help them integrate better back into their prior life and could potentially help physical health for some individuals as well (Starmer et al., 2016).

Why should work, happiness, and satisfaction go hand in hand? In the next sections, we explore the various work factors that appear to be linked to greater happiness. Although we acknowledge the strong role that gainful employment plays in overall happiness and satisfaction, we hasten to add that there often is a reciprocal relationship in that factors may influence each other to produce a sense of gainful employment. For example, as we explain in the next section, performing well at work heightens the sense of satisfaction. But so, too, does the sense of satisfaction contribute to an employee's better performance in the work arena.

Performing Well and Meeting Goals

How often has someone commented to you, "You are really grumpy. Did you have a bad day at work?" Or it can go the other way: "Wow, you are in a great mood. Did things go well at the office?" Without question, perhaps particularly in the career-focused culture of the United States, what happens at work spills over into various other aspects of our lives.

One school of thought about the happy worker is that such an employee has a sense of effectiveness and efficiency in performing their work activities (Herzberg, 1966). To test the notion that performance on the job relates to satisfaction, Judge et al. (2001) performed a meta-analysis (a statistical procedure for testing the robustness of results across many studies) of 300 samples (about 55,000 workers). They found a reliable relationship of approximately .30 between performance and general satisfaction. This type of result has been replicated more recently as well, with bidirectional relationships between happiness and occupational success (Allen & McCarthy, 2016).

By far the most research related to the sense of performing well has emerged from Bandura's influential self-efficacy construct (see Chapter 8 for a review of the role of self-efficacy in promoting work happiness). **Career Decision-Making Self-Efficacy (CDMSE),** which is defined as the personal confidence in one's capacity to handle career development and work-related goal activities, has been significantly related to both success and satisfaction with one's occupational efforts and decisions (Glessner et al., 2017; Sari, 2017; Wang & Jiao, 2022). CDMSE can be built in individuals through a variety of means. Student athletes who had more support from various academic services felt more confident in making decisions about possible career choices (Burns et al., 2013). Other investigations have shown that students who have family members who contribute meaningfully (both financially and in terms of advice and help) to the career decision-making process, as well as certain styles of parenting, develop higher levels of CDMSE (Alexander & Harris, 2022; Guan et al., 2016). Finally, CDMSE has been studied in several different racial and ethnic groups. We now know that level of acculturation may positively affect development of feelings of self-efficacy with regard to career in Latinx youth (Ojeda et al., 2012). Additionally, recent qualitative work has been done with scholastically successful Latinx adolescents to ask them directly what they thought helped maintain or enhance their career self-efficacy. Martinez and Baker (2023) conducted interviews with Latinx adolescents aged 16 to 18 and found four themes that came from questions related to how self-efficacy in this sphere can be maintained: "(a) beating the stigma through resistance, (b) aspirations and hope, (c) a state of perpetual transition (i.e., being flexible and nimble), and (d) with confidence (*con confianza*)" (p. 6). Recall the work of Yosso (2005) in Chapter 4 regarding the Cultural Wealth model, and you may see similarities to this work. Helping Latinx adolescents to feel hopeful and confident about their work may assist them in maximizing development of career self-efficacy. For Asian Americans and African Americans, programs designed to increase career self-efficacy were successful when they contained constructivist approaches—that is, when participants were able to make personal meaning out of various factors that influenced career choice and decisions (Grier-Reed & Ganuza, 2011). Finally, doing this type of intervention early on (i.e., in high school), particularly for STEM fields when attempting to increase representation in Black adolescents, may assist in developing more diverse talent pipelines and pathways (Fletcher et al., 2022).

Performing well at work is more likely to occur when workers have clear goals. As shown in relevant literature (see the seminal works of Emmons, 1992 or Snyder, 2000c in this area), lucid goals offer satisfaction when they are met. Accordingly, when work goals are clearly delineated and employees can meet established standards, heightened personal pleasure and a sense of accomplishment result. In past research, focus was often placed on the goal-setting behavior of a boss or supervisor in an organization (Snyder & Shorey, 2004). While having a high-hope boss who sets clear goals is likely still a positive thing in any work environment, many companies today are instead moving to high-performance work systems (HPWSs). HPWSs are defined as management initiatives that help to broaden decision-making capability across their workers as opposed to centralizing all decisions through a boss (Fu et al., 2020; Pak & Kim, 2018). In these systems, workers are carefully selected during the application process for their fit to a particular company. Questions specific to why an applicant wants to work at a particular company lead to securing workers that are committed to the company upon hiring. Additionally, workers in HPWSs have a voice in making decisions but are also very well trained and have access to key information such that they have the skills to do so. Finally, workers at HPWSs are more motivated at work and feel more secured and appreciated in their jobs (Awardaroo, 2022; Caldwell & Floyd, 2014). All of these factors lead to more profitability and company success.

Most research in this area has investigated the links between happiness and successful work performance by looking at success as the predictor and the happiness of the individual as the result (i.e., good work performance leads to a happier life). Boehm and Lyubomirsky (2008) investigated this relationship in the other direction, asking instead if happy people might have more career success overall. After reviewing a number of different studies in this area of research, they concluded that it is often the case that happiness is a precursor to career success. Others agree, including some studies that show that happy people make more money overall, even after controlling for personal circumstances (Kansky & Diener, 2020). Other more recent research has also found that happiness not only makes for more successful employees but more successful organizations in the long run (Thompson & Bruk-Lee, 2019). These researchers found that, especially in high demand jobs, happy employees appear to impact overall positive organizational outcomes. Evidence across many nations shows that the causal relationship between happiness and career success exists cross-culturally (Kansky & Diener, 2020).

Deriving Purpose by Providing a Product or Service

One's work is an important potential source of purpose in life. A major underlying force that drives such purpose is the sense of providing needed products or services to customers. Workers want, sometimes in very small ways, to feel that they are making a contribution to other people and to their society. Part of this might include feeling as though their presence and skills are valued at their place of work. Credit should be given to Amy Wrzesniewski of New York University for her groundbreaking research on the notion of calling (Wrzesniewski et al., 1997) describing how workers, from the very highest organizational status to the lowest, can perceive their work as a calling (a vocation to which the employee brings a passion—a **commitment** to the work for its own sake). Researcher Martin Seligman (2002) on Wrzesniewski's notion of calling:

> Individuals with a calling see their work as contributing to the greater good, to something larger than they are, and hence the religious connotation is entirely appropriate. The work is fulfilling in its own right, without regard for money or for advancement. When the money stops and the promotions end, the work goes on.
>
> Traditionally, callings were reserved to very prestigious and rarified work—priests, Supreme Court justices, physicians, and scientists. But there has been an important discovery in the field: Any job can become a calling, and any calling can become a job. (p. 168).

In a study from 2016, Dutton and colleagues asked hospital cleaners to share their experiences of being valued and found that it was clear that feeling valued helped these individuals to derive meaning from their work that provided positivity in their life.

In recent years, many have studied whether this type of passion could provide a buffering effect during times of stress. As we emerge from the COVID-19 pandemic, even those of us that did not suffer long-term health effects may find ourselves a bit more careworn and battered due to stress. Some research has found that those who have a strong level of work fulfillment, especially those who felt more autonomy in their lives, had more sustained levels of satisfaction in their work life, even during a time such as the pandemic. In a recent study, Bitter and McCrea (2022) found that "higher levels of fulfillment predicted greater quality of work" (p. 6) in professors during the pandemic. Conversely, those that did not feel this fulfillment were less productive overall.

Engagement and Involvement

Engagement is the employee's involvement with their work, whereas satisfaction is what we might call employee enthusiasm at work (Harter & Schmidt, 2002). Engagement is said to occur when employees find that their needs are being met. Specifically, engagement reflects those circumstances in which employees "know what is expected of them, have what they need to do their work, have opportunities to feel something significant with coworkers whom they trust, and have chances to improve and develop" (Harter & Schmidt, 2002, p. 269). Bakker and Oerlemans (2016) found that "those with high levels of work engagement satisfy their daily needs and stay happy" (p. 755) in comparison to those who do not experience this level of engagement. For example, in a meta-analysis of roughly 300,000 employees in more than 50 companies, responding positively to the engagement item, "I have the opportunity to do what I do best," was related reliably to work productivity and success (Harter & Schmidt, 2002). When there is a good match between the required activities and the skills and personalities of the employees, there are more opportunities for workers to use their strengths, and this may lead to more engagement overall. Some workers may even do this intentionally by job crafting, that is, choosing to interact with their work duties in ways that allow them to use personal strengths more often, which can lead to greater well-being in workers who use this strategy (Barclay et al., 2021). Berg and colleagues (2007) offer the example of a computer technician who has the strength of relationship development being more likely to be engaged when they can complete tasks such as helping other employees directly with their tech needs or working to train other technicians. This would differ from someone with the same job without these strengths who might choose to craft their job such that little in-person interaction is had.

Targeting individuals who are low in engagement may be a very effective way of increasing positive feelings about work and self-efficacy for various work-related tasks (Ouweneel et al., 2013). Cognitive engagement, in particular, has accounted for up to 50% of the variance in psychological well-being in workers who are able to experience this (Joo et al., 2017). Other studies show that when employees feel like they have a good work–family balance, there is a positive effect on their well-being at work (Yu, Zhou et al., 2016). Thus, finding ways to allow a balance to occur may increase engagement and well-being.

Variety in Job Duties

If the tasks performed at work are sufficiently varied, satisfactions come more easily. Indeed, boredom at work can cast a pall. People should maintain as much variety and stimulation as possible in their work activities (Hackman & Oldham, 1980). Lacking variability in work, the employee may lapse into what recently has been called *presenteeism* (in contrast to *absenteeism*). In **presenteeism**, the employee may physically be at work, but because of either physical or somatic issues, or mental health problems that often result from aversive and repetitive work experiences, they are unproductive and unhappy (Rivkin et al., 2022). Those who are less engaged at work or who may be faced with repetitious and tedious tasks and inflexible schedules can become demoralized and lose their motivation even if they are present (Burton et al., 2017). Some note that social support from colleagues and supervisors seems to combat the negative effects of presenteeism, elevating quality of life overall (Magalhães et al., 2022). Presenteeism may look different across cultures (Garczynski et al., 2013; Lu et al., 2013). Presenteeism is also something to think about with regard to what we ask our students to do in university settings. Some research shows that this phenomenon can occur in this venue as well (Matsushita et al., 2011).

This said, you might have had some experience with presenteeism as a student that was positive in some scenarios. Each of the authors remembers an incident in which we felt illness coming on . . . right before final exams during our college experiences. You might have experienced this yourself and know the mild panic that might ensue as you contemplate missing an exam or struggling to study with a cold. Sometimes in high stakes circumstances like this, both students and employees are able to engage in presenteeism in such a way that one's illness does not impede one's performance as much as it might if less were on the line (Wang et al., 2022). Instead, we're able to sort of rally ourselves using presenteeism as a strength to get through a difficult time.

Income for Family and Self

Without question, a minimum income is necessary to provide for the needs of one's family and oneself. It is the balance of increasing income to benefit oneself and one's family beyond these basic needs, and maintaining a positive quality of life, that becomes important to this aspect of gainful employment.

In past years, many families adhered to a traditional breadwinner–caregiver model aligned along traditional gender roles in opposite-sex relationships. Thus, often women in these partnerships were the ones charged with maintaining relationships. As more and more women enjoy higher levels and salaries, the balance has changed. Some of these ideas are being modeled to their children, who watch them carry out the day-to-day balancing act of work and home. Daughters in families who have mothers with less traditional and more prestigious careers gain more ideas about how to balance family and work early on in their developmental trajectory (Fulcher & Coyle, 2011). It will be important for us to advantage our children of any gender with these same flexible attitudes in the future if we are to maximize the preservation of relationships of any kind while still maintaining a sense of self-efficacy about these important life roles. As a personal story, one of the authors (JTP) who is a parent and has a two-income family recalls her three children playing "house" when they were very little. She remembers that a large portion of the conversation in the game focused on deciding "who would pick the kids up" and "who would do the grocery shopping" as well as "who could stay home that day with the sick baby." This is no doubt because her children had watched her and her husband negotiate these types of scenarios multiple times throughout their lives.

Thinking about ways to ensure a higher level of happiness due to pursuit of income/family time balance for all families can start at a national level. The United States is part of the Organisation for Economic Co-operation and Development (OECD), which is a collective of a number of different countries that share data, policy ideas, and other resources toward the goal of improving the health and well-being of the individuals in their specific nations (OECD, 2017). In a prepandemic study of 22 OECD countries, researchers looked at differences in parental happiness as a function of different work–family policies and practices, such as maternity or paternity leave, childcare options, and others (Glass et al., 2016). Unsurprisingly, the countries with policies that provide more help for parents also have less discrepancies in happiness between parents and nonparents (Glass et al., 2016). What may be surprising to U.S. readers, however, is that the United States was lowest on the list of 22 countries, behind Russia, Germany, the Czech Republic, Israel, and many others. As Glass and colleagues (2016) note, "The United States is exceptional in its failure to develop policies that help offset the financial and opportunity costs associated with raising children, making parenthood unusually expensive in the United States" (p. 891). Bolton and colleagues (2020) offer suggestions and an example of a culture (Norway) that allows both income and personal life to have import in the lives of everyday individuals.

As we share toward the end of this section, a different sense of work-life balance may be more common now due to experiences during the COVID-19 pandemic and beyond. But not all families have the ability to make choices about how many hours to work due to potential to meet basic needs. Importantly, making sure that some level of balance is accessible to families from ALL economic groups will be an important step toward equity in ability to help one's family to thrive.

Companionship and Loyalty to Coworkers and Bosses: Friends at Work

Another reason that work may be associated with happiness is seen in the case of people whose friendship networks are located entirely within the employment setting. Work offers people a chance to get out of the house and interact with others. Because workers may share experiences such as encountering obstacles and celebrating triumphs in the work setting, there are reasons for them to form bonds with each other.

Corporate culture in the United States has traditionally discouraged the development of friendships at work. This practice was based on the assumption that socializing among coworkers, especially fraternizing between a worker and a manager, would lead to poor productivity. This assumption was not carefully examined by systematic research until Tom Rath and colleagues at Gallup developed the Vital Friends Assessment and surveyed 1,009 people about the effects of friendships on their happiness, satisfaction, and productivity (Rath, 2006). Among other results, Rath found that if you have a best friend at work, you are likely to have fewer accidents, increased safety, more engaged customers, and increased achievement and productivity. These findings are attributable to the fact that people with a best friend at work are seven times more likely to be psychologically and physically engaged on the job (Rath, 2006).

The work of the Gallup researchers, presented in the book *Vital Friends*, and subsequent research has confirmed that the sense of community at a given workplace is a contributing factor to happiness and satisfaction on the job (Mahan et al., 2002; Rumens, 2017). See the sidebar interview with one of the authors (JTP) on her views and experiences with friends at work.

INTERVIEW WITH ONE OF THE AUTHORS: JENNIFER TERAMOTO PEDROTTI ON FRIENDSHIP AT WORK

How does friendship with coworkers manifest itself in your workplace?
I think there is room for friendship at work in a different way within academia as opposed to how it might look in more of a corporate business, particularly at the faculty level. At a university, you are often organized by a particular field, and you might have some similarities to others in your area of research right off the bat. Additionally, there might be opportunities to "do work" together as you collaborate on research or other tasks. You can succeed while also helping someone else to succeed. Though there is still some competition between professors, it isn't like a more corporate environment where maybe only one person gets "the promotion" at the faculty level. All professors are working on their own personal trajectory toward promotion or tenure because of standards set up by the university. Bottom line—you can be friends with people at work a little more easily maybe.

What are the benefits of having friends at work?
When I was a newer professor in my field, I enjoyed having a large network of others experiencing the same thing I was—learning to be a better professor each year, balancing children and partners with work, learning how to be successful at publication, and so on. There were a lot of us going through the same steps, and we interacted a lot both at work and outside of work, too. I remember several parties where several "mom professors" brought their kids to one house or another, and the kids played, and the moms talked—it was a nice break!
Now, as an administrator and associate dean, I have a smaller network of people in a similar position to me, but my friends in this new role are very important to me as well. They're a place to go for advice and listening and confidential ears for work problems. This last part is much more important to me now, as some of the things I might be dealing with require absolute confidentiality. My administrator friends are under the same pressures I am, and so we're able to relate and understand each other well.

What has having friends at work meant to you in your career?
As a woman of color who is also in a leadership role, and on a predominantly White campus, I have gravitated toward other women of color in similar roles as our experience is unique. I have a small group of friends that fit this description, and our friendships run very deep, in part because some of the things that we've experienced as women of color in the workplace have been hard. I rely on these friends, and they make a big difference to my well-being on my campus. If one of us has a tough meeting or an experience with a microaggression, we have each other to turn to and to seek solace, comfort, and to find the humor in hard situations. I'm lucky to have them!

Safe Work Environments

Part of happiness at work is a safe and healthy physical environment where it is obvious that management cares about the welfare of workers. In the previously discussed meta-analytic report by Harter and Schmidt (2002), perceived safety of the workplace was one of the most robust predictors of employee satisfaction. More recently, in a study of Latinx farmworkers, researchers found that "workplace safety is directly associated with the health and well-being of [these] workers" (Ramos et al., 2021, p. 1). Unsurprisingly, those in this study who felt safe in their workplace also had less stress and depression.

Are there reasons to be concerned about work and actual physical health? The answer to this question is a resounding yes. Many physical injuries occur at work; moreover, there are high-risk professions where serious accidents are quite prevalent. Keeping workers physically safe and injury free leads to better physical health in other areas of life (Hofmann & Tetrick, 2003; Ramos et al., 2021; Tetrick & Peiró, 2012). We do not leave the pain and suffering of a workplace-induced physical impediment at the door of the factory at quitting time.

Respect and Appreciation for Diversity in the Workplace

As racial and ethnic diversity continues to increase in the workplace, a discussion of the relationship between the presence of this diversity and other factors (e.g., job performance, workplace climate, job satisfaction) becomes necessary. The seminal work done on the concept of "diversity management" (Thomas, 1990, p. 107) describes using various management techniques that increase the positive outcomes associated with having more diversity in the workplace. Pitts (2009) conducted a study in which results showed that proper use of diversity management was predictive of better group performance in the workplace and higher levels of job satisfaction for all employees (although particularly for people of color). In addition, Cunningham (2009) found in measuring responses from 75 National Collegiate Athletic Association athletic departments across the United States that racial diversity and overall performance were positively associated. This study found that the relationship was stronger in athletic departments that used "proactive diversity management" strategies (p. 1448). These strategies include viewing diversity as a broad and multifaceted concept, keeping communications lines open, and making sure that diversity is emphasized as a part of mission statements and organizational goals.

One additional way of respecting diversity in the workplace is for organizational heads to pay attention to representation at different levels throughout a company or organization. In workplaces where gender diversity was present at middle management levels, it actually lead to more profits (Ferrary & Déo, 2022). This result was found, in part, to be due to opportunities provided for women that had previously only been accessible for men. Though this study looked at gender in a binary way, more current thinking would support all genders at all levels of an organization as a positive change. Making sure that leaders are heterogeneous in their cultural backgrounds ensures that responsibility for important decisions is spread across a number of different types of individuals (Cunningham, 2009). It is important to note that diversity management means more than constructing groups with different races represented. Instead, engagement with diversity from the top level of management down is often the most effective approach (Howarth & Andreouli, 2016). More recently, other skills in DEI have been highly sought after across corporate, private, and public arenas. Developing skills in working with those who are different than you in terms of race, ethnicity, sexual orientation, nation of origin, gender, and other social identities is vital to increasing a positive work experience for all groups, especially as diversity continues to increase in the workplace.

A Positive Workplace Example

At the 2014 Asia-Pacific Conference on Applied Positive Psychology held at the City University of Hong Kong, a presentation was offered by Rainbow Cheung, the general manager of Employee Development Service of Hong Kong Christian Service and Four Dimensions Consulting, Ltd. Ms. Cheung and her colleagues developed a survey entitled the Positive Organizational Index that is designed to measure the level of use of good practices in an organization that lead to a more positive experience for its employees (please see Appendix for a detailed description of this index and its uses). As an example of an organization that scored high in this area, Ms. Cheung noted the Hong Kong–based company Richform Holdings, Ltd. The CEO of this organization, Dr. Jimmy Lau Fu-Shing, stated in Richform's promotional materials, "We are not a charity—we are a small company and we have to make profits. But we have found that [using positive organizational strategies] can be competitive and advantageous." At Richform, employees (or associates, as they are called) enjoy longer lunch breaks; paternity leave; access to free, healthy snacks; and various self-care perks such as Chinese medicine consultations. In addition, Richform provides a "parents gratitude" allowance, which is offered in response to the cultural expectations in China that grown children will take care of their aging parents. This particular allowance provides extra salary when an employee's parent reaches the age of 65 (R. Cheung, personal communication, January 9, 2014). The results of the efforts made at Richform are obvious in employees' satisfaction with their positions. As Dr. Lau noted, "What is the single best thing done as a company? We have differentiated our company by caring for stakeholders." These stakeholders—their employees—appear more than grateful for these benefits, which is shown partially in very low turnover in staff and a very high level of employee satisfaction (Cheung, 2014).

A Final Note on Working Qualities and the COVID Pandemic

In summary, the good news is that several factors in the work setting can contribute to a greater sense of happiness and satisfaction in particular and to gainful employment in general. Equally important is the fact that unhappiness with one's work is not inevitable; we expand on this theme in the remainder of this chapter. Caring about employees and their families can be mutually beneficial for workers and the companies with which they are affiliated. This may be even more important in recent times.

According to Pew Research (Parker et al., 2022) more people in the United States are working from home than ever before. Early in the pandemic, approximately 64% of those surveyed by Pew said they were working from home due to office closure or their workplace being inaccessible to them, with 36% saying that working from home was their choice. This is in sharp contrast to early in 2022 when these percentages flipped, with 38% saying that work from home was because of an office closure, while 61% noting that they are working from home due to their own choice (Parker et al., 2022).

Many workers state that they have more work-life balance in their current hybrid or work-from-home scenario in their job (Parker et al., 2022). This, in turn, can influence well-being in positive directions as we know from other research. But this link may be at least in part due to the way in which workers perceive their supervisors feel about their working from home. In a study looking at stress-relief due to a work-from-home environment, researchers found that when supervisors were perceived to trust workers to be productive at home, work-life balance increased, and this in turn was significantly related to higher well-being (Chu et al., 2022). Work-life balance was the only significant indicator of well-being in this study. On the other hand, many more workers who telecommute have less of a feeling of connection to their coworkers (Parker et al., 2022; see Figure 14.4).

During the country's shutdown, you might have heard workers you know complaining about the inability to "turn work off" since their work environment was also their home environment or about being distracted by something as simple as a pile of unfolded laundry while one was supposed to be working. Some studies have found that people who work more from home also do more nonrelated work tasks during work hours, which might not be surprising. The fact that some studies found that this doesn't seem to impact productivity much is an interesting related finding, however (Chu et al., 2022; Parker et al., 2022). Other studies, however, found that the lack of segmentation into "work" and "home" tasks and domains resulted in an

FIGURE 14.4 ■ Work-Life Balance and Connection since COVID

For workers who've made the switch to teleworking, most have found more balance but less connection with co-workers

Among employed adults who rarely or never worked from home before COVID-19 and are working from home at least some of the time now, % saying...

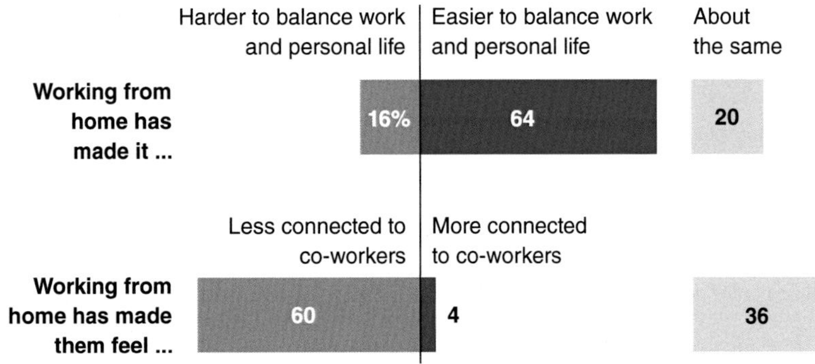

Note: Based on those who say, for the most part, the responsibilities of their job can be done from home. Share of respondents who didn't offer an answer not shown.

Source: "For workers who've made the switch to teleworking, most have found more balance but less connection with co-workers." Pew Research Center, Washington, D.C. (FEBRUARY 14, 2022) https://www.pewresearch.org/social-trends/psdt_2-16-22_covidandwork_0_1/.

increase of unfinished tasks in both domains. This seemed to occur regardless of a worker's preference for having separation between work or not.

More research is needed, but it seems clear that there is no going back to a time when telework is an anomaly. This may also be dependent on generation and so shifts may be seen as one generation leaves the workplace and another begins to join it. Though one might expect that each generation, perhaps in part due to more comfort with technology, may prefer more work-from-home positions. Interestingly, however, Gen Z (i.e., the generation who was at a developmental stage to enter the workforce during the middle of the pandemic) has shown a preference for in-person work, though flexibility with schedule is still desired (York, 2023). Some of these preferences will likely shape the workplace for decades to come.

Lastly, before we close this section, it is important to acknowledge that not everyone had choices of working from home during the height of the pandemic, and many lost their jobs or clients during this time. As university professors and administrators, we enjoy a level of privilege with regard to at-home work that those on the front lines of the medical field, or those in the service industry or other related fields, did not. Additionally, many women found themselves pushed out of the workforce during the worst parts of the shut down due to lack of childcare or assistance from school regarding the education of their children (U.S. Census Bureau, 2023). Though this impacted parents in many circumstances, it was women who took the brunt of this from a workforce perspective (Woodbridge et al., 2021). It is easy to become myopic about the trials and tribulations of the daily grind, but we must also take a moment to be grateful that we have gainful employment for all of the reasons discussed in this chapter and, of course, so that we can afford those basic needs of shelter, food, and safety, that many in our country do not have.

Top 10 Characteristics Common to the Very Best Bosses:

- They provide clear goals and job duties to employees.
- They have personal awareness of biases and power differentials and strive toward cultural competency.
- They are genuine and authentic in their interactions with everyone.
- They are ethical and demonstrate moral and equity-based values in their interactions with people.
- They are honest and model integrity.
- They find employee talents and strengths and build on them.
- They trust workers and facilitate their employees' trust in them.
- They encourage diverse views from diverse employees and can take feedback about themselves.
- They set high but reasonable standards for employees and for themselves.
- They are not just friends to employees but can deliver corrective feedback so that it is heard.

THE STRENGTHS-BASED APPROACH TO WORK

In this section, we describe and explore a bold, trend-setting approach for matching employee duties to their strengths and talents that was spearheaded at Gallup. Gallup has been a longtime champion of the strengths-based approach, and its leaders practice a "strengths-finder" strategy to hiring and cultivating employees. In these next sections we relay some of the main points of this approach delineated in the important research of Clifton and Harter (2003).

The underlying premise of the strengths-based approach to work is a simple one: Instead of "fixing" all employees so that each has the same basic level of skills, find out what a worker's talents are and then assign the worker to jobs where those talents can be used, or shape the job activities around the workers' talents and skills. As obvious as this approach may seem, many are still focused on weaknesses in thinking about their work performance. You might understand this tendency if you think about the last evaluation you got at work or the last feedback you got from a professor if you are still a student. Many of us tend to look at an overall positive result by spending a bit too much time thinking about the one piece of feedback that suggested working on a weakness.

There are three stages in the **strengths-based approach to gainful employment**. The first stage is the identification of talents, which involves increasing the employee's awareness of their own natural or learned talents. The second stage is the integration of the talents into the employee's self-image; the person learns to define themselves according to these talents. The third stage is the actual behavioral change, in which the individual learns to attribute any successes to their special talents. In this stage, people report being more satisfied and productive precisely because they have begun to own and accentuate their strengths. See the Gallup book *CliftonStrengths for Students* (2017) for a good introduction to this model and to develop ways that you might turn your strengths into a positive employment experience (note: this book includes a code to take Gallup's online assessment the StrengthsFinder).

Does the strengths-based approach work for the betterment of employees? The answer appears to be a firm yes. Researchers have looked at three different types of strengths and their predictive quality of positive work-related outcomes: signature strengths (those that people feel are their top strengths), personally lowest strengths (those areas in which people feel they are not skilled), and happiness strengths (those shown by research to be good predictors of life satisfaction in a variety of people, for example, hope or zest (Littman-Ovadia, Lavy, & Boiman-Meshita, 2017). Results in this study showed that happiness strengths were the best predictors of success at work (including markers of engagement, job satisfaction, performance, and other positive work outcomes), followed closely by signature strengths. Additionally, the relationship between signature strengths and the outcomes was separate from the effect of positive affect pointing to the particular power behind signature strengths (Littman-Ovadia et al., 2017). Even without positive affect as a catalyst or spark, they allow us to be more engaged at work and to have better performance.

WHAT CAN BE DONE TO IMPROVE YOUR WORK?

To help you think somewhat more deeply about your job, we encourage you to study Figure 14.5. We use the boxes in this figure as an aid in going through the steps to improve one's work.

FIGURE 14.5 ■ A Decision Tree for Improving One's Work

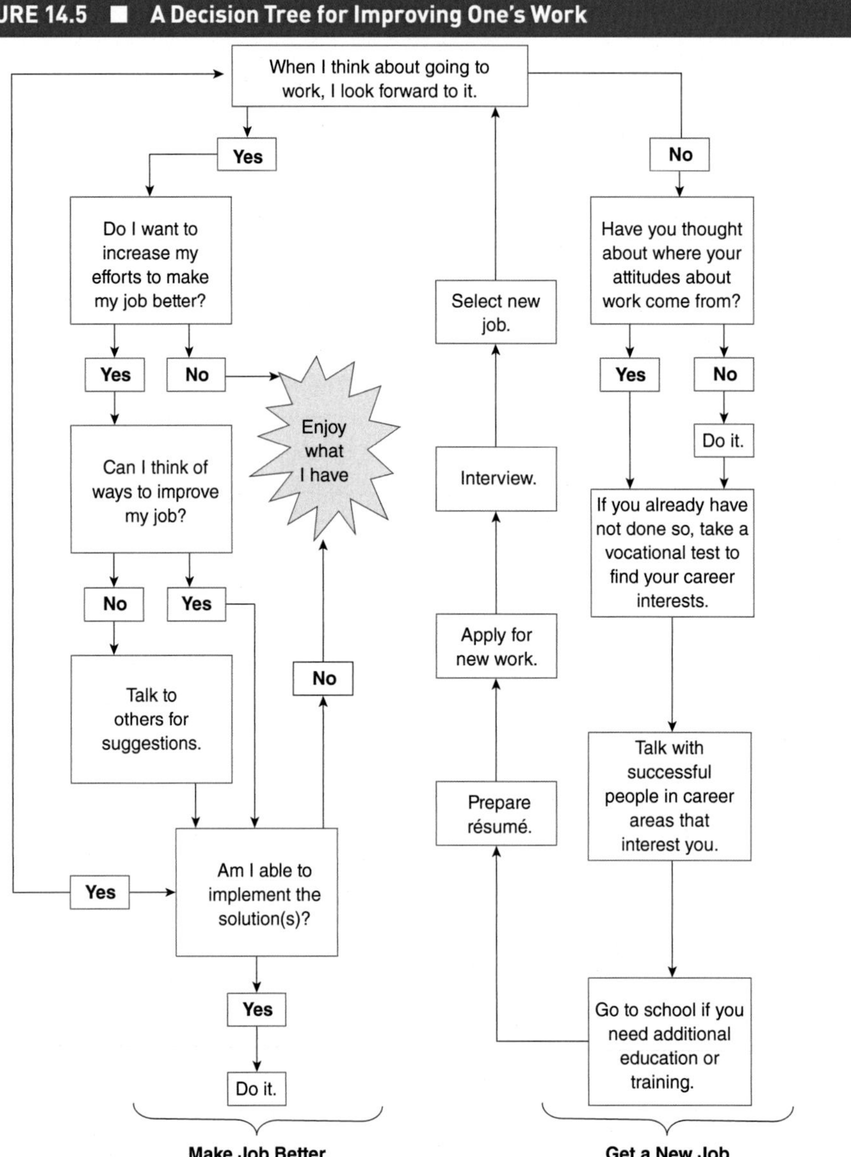

Making the Job Better

In our clinical interactions with people who were exploring issues related to their work, we have found it useful to ask about the first thoughts that a person has, early in the morning, about going to work. If you feel good about your job and look forward to work, we congratulate you on this fortuitous state of affairs. Even if you do like your job, however, we suggest that it helps to look constantly for ways to make it better. In Figure 14.5, this is represented by the left-hand route, labeled "Make Job Better."

Workers across the spectrum often have much more power and latitude than they typically realize in making positive changes in their jobs. This is especially true if you have performed well in your job. Your value to your organization may be far greater than you think. Though many think that getting a raise would greatly increase satisfaction with a job, you already know from our previous discussion that this might not be enough.

If a raise is not a panacea, are there other changes in your job that would make your life more enjoyable? Perhaps you could ask for a more flexible schedule that allows you to increase your work-life balance, more staff support at work, a larger expense account or budget to do the work you want to do, or some company assistance with phone or car. Some other keys to improving your job might be things you don't have to ask for but can do yourself regardless of where you are in the hierarchy of your organization. Making a decision to put a standing time for lunch on your calendar or building in a 15-minute walk in the afternoon can boost your energy both physically and mentally. Waking up 30 minutes earlier than you need to in order to get mentally set for your day, to enjoy a cup of tea as you scroll through the news before kids wake, or to walk your dog might decrease the stress of the morning rush. See the Personal Mini-Experiments to explore other possibilities as well.

A good guide for improving your work situation is to consider the various factors that we have discussed previously as contributing to gainful employment and to see which of these hold the most import for you (see again Figure 14.3). If you are feeling bored with your day-to-day work, talking to a boss about varying your duties or taking on a new project might assist with this area. Is a "stretch position" available for you, in which you take on a set of new duties for some extra salary. If you are a social person, ask a friend to join you on your afternoon walk, or consider carpooling to work with a coworker who's companionship you enjoy. If you are a person who likes to feel like you've accomplished something each day, try making a "have done" list at the end of the day, as opposed to relying only on "to do" lists. Lastly, if you are a person in a job that you must stay in for the money to meet basic needs, regardless of your interest in the position, try to control what you can. If interacting with others is a strength for you, focus on giving the very best customer service you can. If some of your tasks are tedious or repetitive, try setting small goals for yourself and rewarding yourself for each completion. Finally, if there is nothing you like about your job, try not to take it home with you. Thugh it may sound cheesy, imagine your job is like a cape around your shoulders, and as you are walking out the door let that imaginary cape fall to the ground and stay at work. You're free from it until tomorrow. If you are a leader or boss at work, you might consider these nine factors as well. Paying attention to the opportunities you are giving your workers and making sure that these opportunities are provided to many different types of people might assist you at creating a work environment that is protective against burnout and that thrives on hope, creativity, and resilience.

A last strategy that comes from the "Make Job Better" side of Figure 14.5 is to learn to enjoy what you have. Appreciation and savoring (Borelli et al., 2022; Bryant & Veroff, 2006; Hurley & Kwon, 2013) are important positive psychology attributes in many cultural groups, and you may want to take more time to simply realize and enjoy what you have.

PERSONAL MINI-EXPERIMENTS

BECOMING GAINFULLY EMPLOYED

We hope you have realized how crucial work is to our personal well-being and satisfaction. The following activities encourage you to consider the roots of some of your vocational interests and to experiment with the ideas for making your work situation better.

Can You Work From Home? Whether you are working (or will work) part- or full-time, perhaps you should consider what more and more professionals are doing—spending at least some time working virtually. If your reaction to this suggestion is that the activities of your job necessitate your physical presence, then this may not be a good idea. But if your concern is something along the lines of "My boss wouldn't even consider that," or "I would be too distracted to work at home," there are ways to address this. Keep in mind that productivity is a primary concern for most bosses; how or where you get the job done is often less important than that you do. Eliminating the commute from your daily routine and increasing the flexibility of your schedule may lead to greater productivity. It may also allow you to feel more balanced between work and family, which may in turn benefit your productivity by making you more focused and less guilt ridden. If you are a supervisor reading this section, consider your potential biases or concerns at allowing workers to work from home. Regular check-ins with employees in person, meeting virtually over a video platform, and setting clear weekly goals might assuage some of these concerns. Being open to this type of work schedule might increase your ability to find people from all walks of life to staff your organization, particularly postpandemic.

Are You a "Chip Off the Old Block" When It Comes to Work Attitudes? As you think about your own work and your attitudes toward it, have you ever thought about where and how you got your work beliefs? The answer, as with many things, may come from your developmental experiences. Here is an exercise that we have used with our clients to help them to uncover the roots of their work attitudes. Begin by writing down your answers to the following questions:

1. How important is work in your life? (Give details.)
2. What has been your attitude about work throughout your life? (Give details.)
3. Do you enjoy working? If so, why? If not, why not?
4. If you have children, what are you trying (or what did you try) to teach them about the role of work in their lives?

Once you have answered these questions, think about the people who raised you, whether these are your biological parents, stepparents, or a multitude of others who you may think of as one of your caregivers. Think about the caregiver who was the biggest influence on you when you were growing up. Once you have a good image in your mind of this person, do a mental role-play in which you ask that person the same questions you just answered. Write down the answers that you expect your primary caregiver to give to these questions.

At this point, you can see whether or not you are a "chip off the old block." Write each of the questions in a column on the left side of a piece of paper, then make a second columns to the right. Head the first column "My Attitudes About Work"; the second column, "My Caregiver's Attitudes About Work." In our experience, most people are amazed at the similarity of the attitudes across the two columns. This means that we truly do adopt the attitudes and beliefs of our primary caregivers when it comes to work. You could add a third column, if you are a parent or a caregiver yourself, asking the questions again, but changing the answers slightly to what you would *like* them to be. Workaholic caregivers will impart their values about work to their offspring. Likewise, caregivers who have found great meaning in a calling often transmit the quest for a purpose-driven life to their offspring. Remember, if you do not particularly like the attitudes that you have about work, this exercise also provides an excellent starting point for making some changes.

Applying for a New Job

As you can see in Figure 14.5, if your answer is "no" to the question of awakening and looking forward to work, then you go to the right side of the guide, labeled "Get a New Job," and follow the steps outlined there.

It may take courage to launch a search for a new position. A key to this process is to remain flexible as you consider various options. You can use some of the exercises in the Personal Mini-Experiments such as "Chip Off the Old Block" to try to align your new options with the values you've noted you'd like to hold.

The next step in Figure 14.5 is to take a vocational/interest test (if you have not already done so) to see how your interests align with various career trajectories; many exist online for free, but you could also consider talking to a career counselor. If you are a student reading this book you likely have a Career Counseling Center as a part of your campus with counselors and many other resources. The key notion here is that you should be pursuing a career in which the activities truly tap your interests (and strengths, as noted previously). Vocational tests, such as those you might take at a center like this, have been carefully validated to give you a sense of what your career interests may be. They can also give you an idea of how your particular interests may relate to those of people who are happy and successful in various careers (for general overviews of this work, see work by vocational psychologist, Dr. Nadya Fouad). The counselor will talk with you about your pattern of interests and give you helpful feedback about how your interests fit with various professions. The decision about what direction to take will remain yours, but it will be an informed one.

Assuming that you do know what jobs are appropriate for you based on your interests and talents, then it may help to conduct informational interviews with people who are doing well in such careers. Find out what their jobs really entail, and then ask their advice about finding jobs in the same area. Though you may worry about bothering someone with these types of questions, most people enjoy talking about the ways in which they've made their decisions to follow a particular career path and may tell you about the steps (and missteps!) that brought them to this point. Look through Figure 14.5 for additional steps about going back to school, updating or preparing a resumé, and getting ready for interviews. Remember that it is natural to have some anxiety about making a change that might seem large or taking steps in a totally different direction. Also remember, however, that the payoff of a job that feels meaningful and satisfying is a great one. As with other previous suggestions, such as dismissing working virtually out of hand, consider thinking broadly about options before you make your decisions. Going back to school is a big step, but there are many online education programs these days that could allow you to achieve a higher degree while still working. Professors, teachers, mentors, and former coworkers might be able to help with this process. When you get to the point of securing a new job offer, pay attention to the gainful employment factors shown in Figure 14.3 as you negotiate with your potential new employer. Finally, select the job you want to take—the one that best fulfills your gainful employment needs.

THE PSYCHOLOGY OF GAINFUL EMPLOYMENT AND THE EDUCATION THAT GETS US THERE

As mentioned in the beginning of this chapter, much of our life is spent in either a work or school setting. Many friends are made through these venues, and the experiences we have in them shape our lives. Therefore, if you are unhappy in your original choice of major, your current line of work, or just the specific scholastic or workplace environment in which you currently exist, take time to look into other options. As noted previously, change can help us find our true callings or direct us along the path that can help us to find these callings. If you are a current or future teacher reading this book, be mindful of the impact, be it good or bad, that you may have on the lives of countless children. If you are a current or future boss of any kind, take care to infuse the tenets of positive workplaces into your practices and policies. And, regardless of your position, take chances to find your callings and to do your best at serving them.

APPENDIX: POSITIVE WORKPLACES IN HONG KONG: BUILDING POSITIVE ORGANIZATIONS, ENGAGING THE HEART OF EMPLOYEES

Building Positive Organizations, Engaging the Heart of Employees—Insights Gained From the Survey on Positive Organizational Index

In recent years, every business has been facing a lot of social and economic challenges. This causes many managers and employees to suffer varying degrees of difficulty and work pressure. In fact, it is an indisputable fact that Hong Kong "wage earners" have to face long working hours, demanding work, office interpersonal tensions, and work pressure. Failure to respond positively will easily provoke labor conflicts and inevitably, employees will harbor thoughts of leaving the organizations. In the face of all these challenges, we need to strive to change whatever is changeable and at the same time learn to face the unchangeable realities with a positive mindset.

Hong Kong's First Positive Organizational Index

As a pioneer and leading provider of "Employee Assistance Program" in Hong Kong, the Employee Development Service (EDS) of Hong Kong Christian Service recognizes that the operation of an organization not only affects the economic development of the organization itself or society but also the physical and mental well-being of its employees. In order to promote sustainable development in organizations so that they can utilize their positive energy and resilience to manage difficulties in the domains of corporate governance, employee relations, staff quality, leadership, and staff's personal well-being, the EDS and Four Dimensions Consulting Limited had conducted a comprehensive literature review on research and theories related to positive organization from the international community including *Positive Organizational Scholarship: Foundations of a New Discipline* (Cameron et al., 2003) and *The Oxford Handbook of Positive Organizational Scholarship* (Cameron and Spreitzer, 2012) and developed a "Positive Organizational Index." This is the first set of indicators in Hong Kong and overseas designed to measure the level of positivity among organizations. The Index is deduced from a rigorous analysis and the insights gained from literature survey of theories and researches conducted by over 150 experts and scholars on positive organizations. This index consists of 69 effective positive strategies grouped under five core areas, namely P.R.I.D.E., where P stands for Positive Practice, R for Relationship Enhancement, I for Individual Attributes, D for Dynamic Leadership and E for Emotional Well-being.

What Is a Positive Organization?

A positive organization is a fresh lens that focuses on good practice of an organization without ignoring the negatives. It emphasizes on building strengths and capabilities of an organization leading to "generative positive cycles" that enhance it to move toward sustainable excellence. The five core dimensions of Positive Organization are as follows:

> ***P***ositive Practice: Effective measures are taken to maximize the organization's positive corporate governance, human resource management, and sustainable development even under constraints or undesirable situations.
>
> ***R***elationship Enhancement: Good relationships, high quality connection and positive team synergy are maintained among employees in the workplace.
>
> ***I***ndividual Attributes: The best of human conditions are nurtured in the workplace by building on employees' strengths and cultivating corporate and individual integrity.
>
> ***D***ynamic Leadership. Positive leadership strategies are implemented in the process of change to maximize the workforce's positive energy and resilience.
>
> ***E***motional Well-being: Concerted efforts are made to keep up the employees' physical and psychological well-being and boost their positive emotions.

As a matter of fact, the survey has provided evidence indicating that the higher an organization's score on positive organizational index, the better performance it has at organizational level (significance level: $p < 0.01$). This includes effectiveness, efficiency, quality, business ethics, interpersonal relationships, adaptability and profitability, and so on. At the same time, the employees' physical and mental health statuses are comparatively better (significance level: $p < 0.01$). To sustain excellence and retain employees, it is imperative for organizations to invest in both "hardware" and "software" and foster balanced development of the positive strategies in the five areas of the Index. Additionally, organizations should be more proactive in enhancing their employees' psychological capital and positive energy on a regular basis, instead of solving problems when they come up. By doing so, employees can probably possess higher resilience and enthusiasm in the face of challenges and adversity.

About the Writer

Ms. Rainbow K. H. Cheung is the general manager of Employee Development Service of Hong Kong Christian Service and Four Dimensions Consulting, Ltd. She is an experienced registered social worker who is one of the promoters for establishing the very first employee assistance program in Hong Kong. She specializes in positive organizational psychology, motivational interviewing, employee counseling, mental health first aid, and critical incident stress management.

KEY TERMS

Calling
Career decision-making self-efficacy (CDMSE)
Commitment
Developmental discipline
Engagement
Gainful employment
Positive schooling
Presenteeism
Strengths-based approach to gainful employment
Stretch goals

PART VII

FINDING STRENGTHS IN OTHERS

Embodying Strengths in Everyday Life

15 THE FUTURE OF POSITIVE PSYCHOLOGY FOR THE PUBLIC GOOD

A Dialogue Between the Authors

LEARNING OBJECTIVES

After reading this chapter, you will be able to:

15.1 Understand the basic tenets covered in this book that (a) strengths are all around you, (b) strengths are also within you, and (c) strengths can be shared and borrowed

15.2 Critically examine some current issues from a positive psychology lens

15.3 Apply strengths in a variety of situations in one's own life

Throughout this book, we have tried to give you scientifically based evidence for the existence of strengths and for our ability as humans to develop and enhance them. We have shared examples from our own lives and talked about others who have developed strengths despite hard circumstances. Finally, we have tried to remind and encourage you to look at strengths from all domains within a cultural context so as to be able to see a diverse array of people as having both strengths and weaknesses. Here, in this final chapter, we wanted to provide you with a few summary points as you think about how you might choose to use positive psychology in your future.

In the history of this book, the final chapter has changed from edition to edition. In the first and second editions, we asked prominent and fledgling researchers and teachers in the field of positive psychology to share with us their visions of the future of the field. In the third edition, we changed that into a conversation between the two authors at the time (SJL and JTP) to take some time to think about where we felt we were as a field, how we used positive psychology in our daily lives, and to dream a bit about where positive psychology was to go.

In the fourth edition, so close to losing Shane Lopez, I (JTP) felt that the future of positive psychology could not be envisioned without turning first to the past. In the past edition, I asked researchers and teachers of positive psychology for their stories about Shane to provide you with an example in which we can develop, enhance, and ultimately share a multitude of strengths and how we all as individuals can learn from each other's signature strengths. In this fifth edition, we (JTP and RCM) moved these stories to an Appendix following this chapter and hope you will take the time to read through this section as well. For now, however, we leave you with some concluding thoughts to summarize what we hope you have learned, and offer some of our own ideas for the future of positive psychology around some current issues from today.

BASIC TENETS OF POSITIVE PSYCHOLOGY

"Strengths Are All Around You"

This is the truth, and we hope you are starting to be able to see this in your own life as well! Sometimes it is hard to be balanced in our recognition and observance of strengths at the same level as we recognize and observe weakness around us. There are some evolutionary reasons for noticing danger and strife, before turning our attention to beauty and hope. And yet, a balance is necessary in order for us to fully appreciate our lives. We hope that throughout the pages of this book, you have learned to be a better "strengths spotter" in the sense that you have begun to appreciate strengths that exist in both people around you and the environments you are in. This takes work to shift our focus in this way and is not always easy.

You may recall from other psychology courses you have taken that it is sometimes hard to view an object in more than one way until someone shows you how to do it. Look at Figure 15.1, a picture used often in beginning psychology courses. If you look closely, the picture is drawn so that if you look at it in one way, you see an older woman, but focusing on it slightly differently reveals a picture of a younger woman. Can you see the older woman as she looks down, the slope of her large nose and pointed chin, her downturned lips? Now refocus. Can you see the young

FIGURE 15.1 ■ Shifting Our Focus May Allow Us to See Things in Different Ways

woman? She looks away from the artist, the older woman's nose becomes the younger woman's sculpted jaw, and a black ribbon lays against her neck. Once you can see both women, try looking at one for a few moments and then the other, then back to the first, then back to the second. Is it getting easier? Can you see things differently more easily? This is what we must do with positive psychology in general. For a long time, our field has seen more weakness than strength, even though strength too existed all the time. And this may be a habit we have picked up as well: looking at weaknesses more often than strengths. We challenge you to look for strengths around you now as you have learned that they are there. To shift your vision to see both a positive picture and a negative picture is not easy at first, but we promise that as you do it more frequently you will be able to see both more clearly and more easily just as you can with the picture in Figure 15.1. Strengths are all around you.

"Strengths Are Also Within You"

Turning your focus to yourself is also an important part of having a better understanding of positive psychology and the strength that humans can embody. Similar to what we see in the environment, we may have a tendency to focus more on our weaknesses as opposed to our strengths. Consider this scenario: You are evaluated at your place of work by your boss, who provides you with rankings on several criteria or a written summary of how you are doing on the job. What pieces do you look at first? If you are like most people, you focus first on the weaknesses, sometimes focusing more heavily on the one area of improvement and ignoring the seven other areas where you showed strength. Although this may be a common way of imbibing information, it does not have to be the only way. We can work instead to see our own strengths more clearly and to think about ways that we can enhance and develop them. Remember some of the suggestions from Chapter 13 regarding primary and secondary enhancement and think of ways that we might use our own positive traits to move ourselves into a more positive life experience. This might start with a simple measure such as those found in Chapter 3, in which you find out more about your own signature strengths. Once you do this, you might look to find out more about what that particular strength means. If you turn out to be a Maximizer (one of the themes in the Clifton StrengthsFinder 2.0; Rath, 2007), you might think of ways in which you can place yourself into situations to use this ability. Teaching, for example, might be a calling for you as you would be in a position to use your ability to bring children to their best selves. Another example might be a person who is high on the strength of Empathy. An individual in this area might use this ability to help out in times of conflict or use this strength in their work life as a therapist or mediator. Another opportunity to use empathy might show itself within discussions or dialogues between people with different social identity facets such as race, ethnicity, gender, or others. Once you begin to see strengths within yourself more clearly, you might see other positive changes in your life—namely, that you might begin to view yourself in a more positive light, developing confidence and self-efficacy. These are qualities that can help you to have more confidence in pursuing goals and may lead to more hope in your life. Perhaps you will be better able to achieve these goals, leading you to more life satisfaction and positive affect on a daily basis. Regardless of the types of strengths you uncover, knowing that you possess them may be the key to the good life in many ways.

"Strengths Can Be Shared and Borrowed"

Last, we can be purposeful about sharing strengths that we know we possess and about emulating them in others who are close to us. You may already be sharing your strengths with others in your life without even knowing it, but being planful about how to share and how to maximize strengths in others can be an even more beneficial experience for both you and the person with whom you are sharing. In thinking about building your strengths repertoire, turn to the people you admire most and think more about what you see as their greatest strengths. Perhaps they are particularly brave and exhibit courage on a regular basis, or maybe they show gratitude or appreciation for beauty in their daily life. Whatever the strength you see, you might decide to use a "fake it 'til you make it" strategy. Consider this story from a graduate student regarding borrowing a strength from her mentor:

> When I was a new graduate student I was not very skilled at public speaking. My tongue would get twisted or I would sound monotone and too prepared and stiff. One day I was watching my mentor give a talk at a conference and preparing to follow him as the next presenter. My heart sank as I compared the way he did his presentation to the way I "knew" I would give mine. All at once I remembered the "Fake it 'til you make it" advice he had given me once with regard to a different situation. I watched him carefully as he finished his talk, memorizing the cadence and style he used. When I walked up to the podium, I took a deep breath, put my carefully planned notes down, smiled big, and started to talk. I pretended I was him the entire speech! Any time I started to get nervous again, I used my inner voice to chide myself, "No! He wouldn't be nervous. You're him. Pretend you're him." The talk finished to much more appreciative applause than I usually received—I had done it! I used that strategy for a while until I found my own style and gained more comfort with public speaking in general. Watching my mentor excel helped me to follow in his footsteps.

We hope that these concluding thoughts can organize some of your future ideas about the field, and that you might look for ways to bring these ideas to others in your life as well. We now turn to an important question: What does the future hold for positive psychology as a discipline? While it is impossible to make a perfect prediction, psychology exists to serve the public good, and there are many societal and public health problems that need to be solved. Positive psychology provides a framework for addressing these issues. Most importantly, rather than focusing only on what variables need to be changed or removed (i.e., prevent the bad), positive psychology teaches us what variables need to be enhanced or leveraged to address these issues (i.e., increase the good). Both perspectives will be essential in meeting the demands of the future.

In this final chapter, we (JTP and RCM) share our perspectives on a few of these issues via a constructive dialogue. In some ways, the ideas expressed through this conversation represent our aspirational goals for the field, but we also are speaking based on our knowledge of the extant theory and research. Each dialogue follows the same format. First, we provide some information about a societal or public health challenge. Then, we take turns briefly answering the following question: "*How can positive psychology be leveraged to address this issue going forward?*" Lastly, we will close this chapter with a short discussion and review of research illustrating how technological advancements are also shaping the future of positive psychology research and practice for the public good.

CURRENT ISSUES FOR EXAMINATION

Political Division in the United States

The United States has become increasingly more polarized over the years (Dimock & Wike, 2020), possibly due to the rise of equally polarized social media ecosystems (Kubin & von Sikorski, 2021). Some researchers draw a distinction between ideological polarization (e.g., differences in political opinions, beliefs, and attitudes) and affective polarization (e.g., the degree to which one generates their identity from their political affiliation). The latter reflects the degree of warmth or likability one feels toward political outgroups. While more political polarization sometimes means more involvement in the democratic process (Wagner, 2021), it can also be bad for society at large. Congressional gridlock (Thurber & Yoshinaka, 2015), political violence, and the general dehumanizing of political opponents can all be traced back to political polarization (Piazza, 2023). Recognizing these dangers, psychologists have placed considerable attention toward understanding political polarization (e.g., Moore-Berg et al., 2020), and thus this area of research will continue to grow in the future.

The Role of Positive Psychology

Dr. McDermott: This issue hits close to home for me. I have seen firsthand the ugly side of political polarization. In particular, one part of my research program focuses on the psychology of men and masculinities. For example, I have served as the president of Division 51 of the American Psychological Association (Society for the Psychological Study of Men and Masculinities). I was also one of the core organizers and contributors to the American Psychological Association's (2018) *Guidelines for Psychological Practice With Men and Boys*. When we released those guidelines, the polarized political responses were fierce. I was personally attacked by Fox News and several right-wing news outlets, and I was praised or elevated by left-wing organizations and outlets. I was even asked to be on the Today Show to talk about the controversy, though I turned it down, as I did not want to be the poster person for this issue. I confess that I was unaware of the political implications of our research showing that rigid and restrictive constructions of masculinity contributed to the problems men and boys experience. I did not come to that field of research for political reasons; I came to it to better serve my male clients. However, I received death threats for my work and ended up having to hire a company to scrub any identifying or personal information off the Internet until the controversy subsided. It was a difficult time in my life, to say the least.

As this story illustrates, people get very angry these days when they encounter information perceived as threatening to their political worldview. Likewise, others will rush to defend perspectives if they conform to their political worldview. Indeed, I have since discovered that certain masculinity ideologies (i.e., rigid beliefs about what men are supposed to be and do) are strongly related to political conservatism (McDermott et al., 2021). Relatedly, endorsement of liberal attitudes tends to be associated with greater gender role ideology flexibility and rejection of rigid masculinity stereotypes (McDermott et al., 2022). These findings helped me understand how masculinity itself had become a politically polarizing issue. It saddens me that masculinity has become such a divisive topic, because the very men who may most benefit from the insights gained from our research are those that may dismiss our work as being ideologically biased and unhelpful.

I believe positive psychology could have helped turn this story around (at least in part). Specifically, there are evidence-based ways of avoiding political polarization when presenting information that may challenge a person's political world view. *Moral reframing* is the process of finding ways of connecting potentially threatening or challenging information to the underlying values of the recipient of that information (Feinberg & Willer, 2015, 2019; Voelkel & Feinberg, 2018). In other words, one must have enough *empathy* (see Chapter 11 of this text) to understand the worldview of the person you are trying to persuade. Over the last 10 years, studies of moral reframing suggest that it may help in the discussion of politically polarizing topics (Feinberg & Willer, 2015, 2019; Voelkel & Feinberg, 2018). Perhaps if we can find ways of framing the topic of masculinities research in a way that is consistent with the values of different audiences we would like to reach, we could have a meaningful dialogue that does not trigger polarized defenses. For example, my research team is currently studying whether we can frame therapy for men as an avenue to help them be more successful in life. We developed this approach after interviewing and talking with very traditional, conservative men and identifying their values. Hard work, success, and being a provider for their families were at the top of the list. Thus, if we can help men understand that therapy can help them meet those values, my hope is that they will be more likely to seriously consider therapy rather than dismissing it offhand due to right-wing propaganda that psychologists are leftists who want to erase their masculinity.

Dr. Teramoto Pedrotti: These are good examples, Ryon, and I remember when this happened to you. It always seems to me like one of the main problems in healing some of the divisions within the political realm is that we've stopped listening to one another and have resorted to group think in so many circumstances. I think you know that I have taught a course on Intergroup Dialogues (from the University of Michigan, adapted from Charles Behling's original program), and in this course, I teach about how to have a *dialogue* about difficult topics as opposed to a *debate*. The United States values debating and we probably assign good debating skills as a strength more often that good dialoguing skills—we even judge our elected officials on debating. What would it be like if we weighed their skills on dialoguing instead? The concept of dialoguing is to present an idea, a view, an opinion, but not with the goal of convincing someone that we are right. Instead, the idea is to present this in a way such that the other person or group can hear us without immediately reacting, and that they might understand that another perspective exists, even if they don't agree with it. To me, if dialoguing was more valued as a strength we might get a little closer to healing some of our divisions.

I had the opportunity to listen to the renowned social psychologist, Dr. Claude Steele, speak at an event at my university recently, and he talked about something else that might start to make a difference here. He talked about the fact that we have little trust for those unlike ourselves these days because of the sharp divides that exist politically. He noted that it's hard to give trust to someone else, but that when we don't, we miss out on what can be gained by not having to have our guard up all the time. That said, he said this might be harder for minoritized populations to do—we've been burned before here—but he said that if we as a society could get to a place where we are all working to be more trustworthy, we might be able to get there.

Racial and Gender-Based Inequities

For decades, researchers have studied the effects of racial and gender inequality in a variety of domains such as healthcare (Chan et al., 2020; Institute of Medicine, 2003), education (Iruka & Hawkins, 2022; Kozol, 2012), economic access (Clouston et al., 2021; McLoyd, 1998; Noble et al., 2021), and the justice system (Alexander, 2012; Marlowe et al., 2020). Not only do these inequalities have a significant societal impact, they carry an enormous personal cost for racial and gender minorities in the form of race or gender-based discrimination experiences (see Sue et al., 2022). The adverse mental and physical health effects of racial and gender-based discrimination on racial and gender minorities are well-documented (Sue et al., 2022). Of note, we recognize that there are numerous forms of discrimination and "isms" in our current society (e.g., heterosexism, ableism, ageism, and others). For the purposes of this section of the text, we have limited our discussion to race and gender-based discrimination, as racism and sexism have received considerable attention in the literature and continue to be active areas of inquiry.

Brandon Bell/Stringer/via Getty Images

The Role of Positive Psychology

Dr. Teramoto Pedrotti: There's so much to be talked about here. I think the most important place to start is the fact that despite all the hardships that people of color and others have faced, they have also shown incredible strength and resilience at dealing with these kinds of things. Positive psychology has begun to study some of this (e.g., Romero et al., 2014) with regard to the way Black, Indigenous, and people of color (BIPOC) deal with discrimination in their lives, but we can learn much more from historically marginalized groups. We talked about this a little bit in Chapter 13, but the immense power of the Black community in using joy—not just happiness, but *joy*—as a form of resistance is something that needs to be studied more and emulated. Additionally, I think we can learn from the ways in which BIPOC talk about difficult issues like racism and other structural inequalities. We've heard much from DiAngelo (2011) and others in the past few years about White fragility and the difficulty that White people sometimes have in speaking about race due to lack of experience and discomfort. Those of us who are White can learn from those of us who are BIPOC in better understanding that these tough issues *need* to be discussed for solutions to be found.

I also think that many in BIPOC communities use their family history with different experiences with racism to assist them in recognizing and making use of their strengths. I think I've told you before that my father's family was incarcerated in the Japanese American camps during World War II. That was an awful time, and I know it took immense strength for my family to go through that and to come back from that experience. It helps me sometimes to know that that strength is in my blood. I come from very strong people who survived and then thrived. That makes me feel like I can do the same when I face hardships, and I've tried to pass that to my children as well.

I do want to give one caveat to this, however. Sometimes, because I'm someone who's dealt with some discrimination in my personal life, I am less surprised about it than some of my non-marginalized friends or colleagues, and so I think my reactions are more muted at times. It's not that it affects me less, but like many BIPOC, I have stronger and maybe more effective coping responses to discrimination because I've experienced it before. BIPOC can't fall down each time something racist happens, because they'd be on the ground all the time! Sometimes, I've had non-marginalized friends say, "I can't. This is too hard to look at and too frustrating. You're stronger and seem fine, but I need to step back." Now, I'm obviously all for self-care, and we need to monitor this in our own lives, but I also think it's really important to recognize that for stakeholders (meaning those who are from representative groups) "stepping back" often isn't an option, so we might keep going regardless. And sometimes you can't tell all of that on the outside. It's awful for us, too, we just know we need to keep moving forward. If we are part of a group that is not marginalized in a situation, we need to support our friends, and if that means taking a little more, so that they can take a little less, that's a really important move toward allyship.

Lastly, all of us can also use our strengths toward making positive change to end discrimination (Duan & Sager, 2021). Social justice work is hard, but it's fueled by optimism and hope, as well as self-efficacy and courage. You have to believe that a better future is actually possible in order to keep trying. We can use the hope model to plot out a path and to deal with obstacles in our way. We can use moral courage to speak up when we see something that's not right, whether we're a stakeholder in that fight or an ally. We can use things like compassion and empathy to better understand the situations of others who are different from us in some way (Wang et al., 2003). I think positive psychology has always provided the power beneath change—understanding that, developing the strengths we need, and then using those toward equity and justice is a laudable goal for all of us. I've talked a lot about race here, but I know you have much to say about gender as well due to your own research, Ryon.

Dr. McDermott: Yes, and this is an issue close to my heart and my values as a counseling psychologist. Additionally, as a White cisgender, heterosexual man who teaches multicultural counseling at the masters and doctoral level, I have had to explore my experiences and socialization regarding these topics in sometimes uncomfortable ways. I didn't always welcome that kind of self-reflection, but I've learned to appreciate moments where I can grow intellectually and culturally.

Counseling psychology has been at the forefront of research and theory addressing racial and gender-based inequities for many years. Social justice counseling, for example, considers the societal and systemic factors impacting a person rather than focusing solely on the internal psychology of the person (Ratts et al., 2016). This balanced and ecologically sensitive approach reduces the chances that we may pathologize a healthy response to a sick system, and it provides a framework for advocacy and other activities necessary to change a client's system. At the same time, most psychological research on these issues focuses almost exclusively on unhealthy responses or the distress stemming from a sick system. By doing so, our field makes two fundamental mistakes (in my opinion). First, focusing mainly on what is wrong with racial and gender minorities or the systems in which they reside only tells us what needs to be removed or prevented to improve their experiences. It offers little information about the strengths or characteristics that could be enhanced. Second, researchers tend to paint all minorities as being victims, or as one-dimensional beings. While we don't want to ignore racial and gender disparities in different areas, we need an equal focus on what is going well in those systems and the various strengths of these populations. As your research with Lisa Edwards says (see Pedrotti & Edwards, 2014), minoritized individuals are in a sort of "double jeopardy" in the field of psychology at times: both ignored as a viable population to study, and then when studied, weaknesses are emphasized.

Additionally, we need to be mindful of how psychology itself perpetuates disparities. Psychology has a long history of contributing to racial and ethnic disparities through research and theory that pathologized those groups or justified systemic inequalities (Winston, 2020). Today, cultural issues and social justice are common in some areas of psychology, but there is evidence that even these good intentions may create bias in psychological research such that we now may overemphasize cultural differences or cultural explanations for different behaviors (Causadias et al., 2018). Thus, we have to strike a balance between *etic* (common to all people/humans) and *emic* (specific to a particular cultural sphere) explanations for behavior. This is easier said than done, and it is an area where I see a lot of potential in positive psychology going forward. Specifically, many of the instruments we use in the field were developed and validated based primarily on White men. While the newer instruments certainly were developed on a more diverse sample (with respect to gender), those samples are still primarily White, cisgender, and middle class.

As we have illustrated throughout this text, there are clear differences between Western and Eastern cultures, and sometimes these differences are statistically evident on the measures we use in positive psychology. What is less known at this point, however, is how our measures (and by extension the theories upon which they are based) generalize to racial and gender minority groups. We can use sophisticated analyses to determine the degree of measurement equivalence between majority and minority groups (Kline, 2016), and this is a major focus of my research in positive psychology. I hope to see more of this kind of work in the future, but I also hope to see more inclusion of racial and gender minorities in terms of the theory building process going forward.

Climate Change

Climate change is defined as the shift in climate patterns mainly caused by greenhouse gas emissions from natural and human sources (see Fawzy et al., 2020 for a review). Greenhouse gas emissions from natural systems (e.g., forest fires, earthquakes, oceans, and volcanoes) and human sources (e.g. burning of fossil fuels and other energy production) trap heat in the atmosphere, which is the main contributor to global warming. Indeed, researchers have analyzed the contributions of both natural and human sources of climate change and have concluded that the Earth's natural systems are self-balancing, and thus human contributions are additive (Yue and Gao, 2018). The long-term effects of climate change vary based on different models but range from more severe and volatile weather systems all the way to a runaway greenhouse effect where the Earth becomes uninhabitable (Goldblatt & Watson, 2012). Thus, this is a significant problem that needs to be addressed through a variety of technological, political, social, and personal means (Fawzy et al., 2020). Naturally, it is also an important area for future research in psychology (Nielsen et al., 2021).

The Role of Positive Psychology

Dr. McDermott: The psychology of climate change attitudes and behaviors is fascinating to me, and I think it is one area where positive psychology may be beneficial. Specifically, most psychology has focused on the science of climate change denial or how negative variables (e.g., shame and guilt) may be driving behaviors such as trying to live a sustainable lifestyle. By contrast, positive psychology encourages us to look at the good variables (e.g. virtues and strengths) that may drive environmental consciousness and reinforce sustainable living behaviors necessary to mitigate climate change (Corral Verdugo, 2012).

Along these lines, one somewhat recent study gives me hope for the future (no pun intended). Li and Monroe (2019) surveyed 728 high school students on their hope for climate change action. In other words, they modified the Adult Hope Scale (Snyder et al., 1991) to focus specifically on beliefs that one can positively impact or reduce climate change. These researchers used structural equation modeling to examine the interrelationships between environmental concern, scientific literacy about climate change, efficacy regarding climate change (e.g., recognizing it can be prevented and that they can make a difference as the next generation going forward), and hope for climate change action. A few findings from this study stuck out to me. First, the relationship between climate change concern and climate change hope was statistically significant, even when controlling for a variety of demographic factors and the other variables in the model. Higher levels of concern were positively associated with greater hope for climate change action. Second, scientific literacy or knowledge about climate change alone was not directly related to hope for climate change action. Instead, the most salient predictor of climate change action was the knowledge that there are things one can do to mitigate climate change. This last point is critical because it means that young people (i.e., the ones who will most be impacted by climate change) may benefit most from hearing about the ways that they can engage in positive climate change actions. Said another way, focusing on the solutions to the problem rather than hammering home the dire consequences may generate more hope for the future. Considering that higher levels of hope are generally associated with goal success, I can only imagine what could happen if we had an entire generation of high-hope young people focused on the goal of mitigating or reversing climate change. What do you think, Jennifer?

Dr. Teramoto Pedrotti: You're so right about this, and if we can teach our kids to look at a problem like climate change as something that can be achieved, I think that's key. I saw a recent phenomenon happen in my own community that surprised me a little and that I think is relevant here. One of my teenagers took a quiz in class regarding political issues just before the presidential election—the point was to answer questions about how you felt about a variety of issues and then the quiz would total your scores to show which party you leaned more strongly toward. I know the political leanings of some of my children's friends' parents as well and the results the kids were talking about were pretty in line with parents' political parties in terms of how they turned out. But one thing that I thought was really interesting, and that the teacher pointed out as well, was how strongly the group was in favor of sustainable and environmentally-related actions and values. You know that I live in California, and in the elementary schools they have a lot of presentations on recycling and composting, or the value of solar and wind power, and there are many state programs set up so that these kinds of things are sort of normalized as something everyone does. I thought it was great that this was separate from political party in this quiz. It was a value the group had because of the education they've received on these topics about how we can reverse some of the environmental problems that exist out there.

Secondly, I think Erikson's (1963) ideas about generativity can be applied here as a positive characteristic. Caring about what you're leaving behind you is a sign, according to Erikson's model, of successful aging. In trying to make things safer and healthier for future generations we're using that strength and maybe there are benefits to us as we age as well in terms of the knowledge that we're committed to making things better in some way. Depoliticizing something like this is so important in moving forward toward positive change that can impact us all. It can give us the strength to work together with hope and optimism toward a better future.

CONCLUDING THOUGHTS

We hope you have enjoyed hearing some of our thoughts about the future and that you might think more on some of these important topics. We write this book for you: the future of positive psychology. And we depend on you to think of your own strengths as both offensive and defensive tools for moving toward a more positive world. Over the years, we've had students tell us that this textbook is one of the only ones they end up keeping. There are things within these pages that can help you to live your life in balanced way, and we hope they will continue to stick with you for years to come.

APPENDIX

Remembering Shane: Real Strengths in a Real Person

For the rest of this chapter, we would like to share with you examples of how a single person can share strengths and to give you some examples of how you might borrow these strengths in your own life.

REMEMBERING SHANE J. LOPEZ

We leave here for you stories about Shane J. Lopez, one of the original authors of this book in its first edition, from researchers and teachers of positive psychology, to provide you with an example in which we can develop, enhance, and ultimately share a multitude of strengths and how we all as individuals can learn from each other's signature strengths. We hope that you can gain some words of wisdom and appreciation from the words of our colleagues here and also that you might discover ways in which you can share your own strengths with your sphere of influence, as well as to look to borrow and emulate them from others around you. What would you like others to say about you when you are gone?

Lisa M. Edwards, Marquette University

There are not enough pages in this book to describe the strengths that Shane possessed and the ways that he continually brought out strengths in others. He inspired, supported, and challenged, and his personality was like a magnet; everyone wanted to work with him and learn from him. Shane was creative and successful, yet always humble. The last time I saw Shane was during a visit he made to Marquette University to give a keynote address, "Hope for Tomorrow." After his amazing talk and an hour-long book signing, he came to have dinner with my family at our home. My mom was in town, and we all started asking Shane about his latest travels and the people he had been meeting on his book tour. He told us about some of the celebrity authors and researchers he had met and the exciting new situations in which he had found himself. We were in awe, but he quickly reminded us that these famous people were just people and that oftentimes the most moving encounters he had with others were with teachers and community members. He was also honest in saying that while he enjoyed all the recent opportunities in his work life, he also missed being at home with his family. He never bragged about his accomplishments, although he easily could have. Shane was just Shane: full of humility and authenticity. That's how I'll always remember him.

Jeana L. Magyar, University of Wisconsin, Steven's Point

From the moment I met him, Shane Lopez was a positive influence in my life. I will never forget his bright eyes and warm smile as he introduced himself to me while I was nervously awaiting my graduate school interview at the University of Kansas. Shane was in his final year of graduate school at that time. He saw me sitting in the department office and did not hesitate to come over to me and help to ease my nerves. Little did I know then that he would be my graduate school mentor! His first year as a professor at KU was my first year as a doctoral student. I was thrilled to meet this new faculty person, only to realize it was the kind graduate student who had left such a wonderful impression on me months earlier. Shane was the best mentor any student could ask for, and he also become a great friend. Words cannot even describe how important a role he played in my career and personal development. He always knew just what to say to help with whatever I may have been dealing with. From active-constructive responding to the good times to framing struggles from a hope perspective, he was simply wonderful. I am proud to say that I was his first graduate student mentee, and I will be forever grateful to have had his positive and supportive influence in my life. Thank you for everything, Shane. I will always love you.

Heather Rasmussen, University of Kansas

Admittedly, this is one of the most difficult paragraphs I have ever written. I have struggled because I have found it nearly impossible to put into words the importance that Shane Lopez had on positive psychological research, the careers of many students, and, really, the world due to his research at Gallup and his many presentations. As a person, he had an uncanny ability to make a person feel special. He would greet people with an enthusiastic smile and would remember an interesting anecdote or funny story about everyone he associated with. His excitement for positive psychology was contagious. One example of this is when he took several graduate students to the International Positive Psychology conference in Washington, DC. Most professors had one or two students with them, if any. Not Shane! He had 12 students with him. It was not a large conference, and the enthusiasm and sheer number of students that came with him had many people noting how remarkable this was. It may sound cliché, but he really did spread ripples of hope; he embodied positive emotion, hope, courage, and flourishing. I currently teach a doctoral-level class in which several videos of Shane's talks on hope are part of the curriculum. I continue to be touched and amazed at the impact his ideas and words have on students every term. They get excited to (as Shane often noted) "make hope happen" in their lives and to "create memories of the future." Students consistently remark that his words and ideas were the most inspiring to them that term. He continues to make ripples of hope. Shane was a gift to us all, and I am grateful to have known him.

Danny Singley, The Center for Men's Excellence

Shane once wrote an article for the APA Division 17's Section on Positive Psychology *Naming & Nurturing* newsletter describing how his father had held a position of esteem and respect in his hometown. In that piece, he noted that his "Poppy" always had time to talk with someone to share a story or offer assistance however he could, and I remember reading that article and thinking to myself that that must be a dominant trait in the Lopez clan. No matter how much he had on his plate, Shane was pretty much always up for hearing out whatever crazy research idea I was excited about—and was unerringly able to connect me with another like-minded "positive psycho" to team up with and carry the idea forward.

His genuineness and incisive humor were also key pieces of what made Shane so authentic in positive psychology. I once had the misfortune of spiking a 103-degree fever the day of a symposium at a positive psychology conference and was so sick that I could barely concentrate on my presentation and was literally hearing my own words on a delay, wondering the whole time, "Am I making sense?" Immediately after the talk ended, Shane walked up to me, gave me a big smile and pat on the back, and confirmed my worst feverish fears by saying, "Well Danny, it's too bad you couldn't be here to give your talk today . . . " It was real, I knew he was right, and his droll delivery was so perfect that I'm smiling all over again just thinking about it.

His friendship and mentorship began when I was in graduate school, and many of my closest friends and colleagues today began with Shane hearing me out about my passion du jour and then saying, "OK, that means you need to talk to [X]." His legacy is one of connection and building, and beyond his scholarly brilliance, he accomplished so much because he was just a great guy who always had time to share a story or offer to help out friends, colleagues, and strangers however he could.

Cynthia Pury, Clemson University

The day I met Shane Lopez was one of the best days of my professional life. I had brought a poster to the 3rd Positive Psychology Summit in Washington, DC, about the first study we'd ever done on courage. We had been strongly influenced by Shane's chapter in *Positive Psychological Assessment*, which was the only work on the psychology of courage at the time that didn't focus almost exclusively on fear. I walked into a session, and as I was sitting down, I saw his nametag and almost fell over. That was THE psychologist I most wanted to talk to. Imagine how surprised I was when he noticed my name tag and said he really wanted to talk to me about the work on the poster! We met up after the talk, and the discussion that we had was one of the most influential talks of my career. Shane knew everyone and what they were working on. He knew who I should talk to next and took the kernel of an idea ("I'd like to see more people doing research on courage") and quickly proposed a symposium, a conference, and a book. We knocked out all three in the next couple of years, and I'm convinced that much of the work we see today in courage stems from him. He was generative, generous, and an all-around delightful person.

Kevin Rand, Indiana University–Purdue University Indianapolis

Before I started graduate school at the University of Kansas in the summer of 2000, I had been corresponding with Shane's colleague (and my mentor), Rick Snyder, via e-mail. We had been tossing some ideas about hope back and forth. Next thing I knew, Rick sent an e-mail asking Shane to include me as a coauthor on a chapter in the *Handbook of Hope* they were putting together at the time. I remember feeling sheepish about this, because it was clear to me that Shane and his coauthors had already put a lot of work into this chapter, and here I was being added as Johnny-Come-Lately (and me a lowly grad student at that!). Shane immediately sent me an e-mail welcoming me to the project and gave me an itemized list of things to do for the chapter, including some new sections to write. Excited to have my first official project as a grad student, I dove into the work with fervor. Shane edited several of my drafts and offered constructive feedback each time. Before the summer was over, the chapter was finished and the book went to the publisher. Months later, after I moved to Lawrence and officially started in the clinical psychology program, I finally had the chance to meet Shane face to face. I introduced myself and confessed to him that I felt a bit awkward about being added as a coauthor to his chapter at such a late date. I said that I hoped that he didn't have any hard feelings about it. An impish grin began to show on his face and quickly grew so big that it seemed like the corners of his mouth were pushing his eyes shut. "Oh, I had no problem adding you as a coauthor," Shane said, "but I was going to make sure you earned it!" That image of Shane's wide smile is still vivid in my mind and always reminds me of how he was able to kindly challenge people to rise to the occasion. To me, that is the essence of engendering hope.

Connie Clifton Rath, Gallup

Shane led strengths research for The Clifton Foundation and was a senior scientist with Gallup. I had the privilege of working with him from the day he came to the first Positive Psychology conference in Lincoln, Nebraska, in 2000. He was the best at gathering people around important ideas and could bring findings that matter to light.

One summer, he brought together a group of dynamic graduate students for the summer—from Kansas, Nebraska, California, and Portugal—to create a way to capture hope, engagement, and well-being in young people. His group created and tested a survey that became the Gallup Student Poll. For 10 years, students have voiced their feelings and opinions about school and their lives. Shane's work showed that year by year, from 5th grade through 12th, students feel less appreciation, belongingness, and recognition. Their enthusiasm for school declines.

He had a mission to help school leaders and teachers reverse this course. He brilliantly engaged audiences in imagining ways school could be better and students could have more hope. He designed studies to identify what was or wasn't working inside schools. He encouraged his colleagues by knowing them very well and recommending ways for each to learn and contribute.

One of his last strengths research projects set up a student coaching model that showed important gains in student confidence and retention at a Midwest university. His models, discoveries, and relationships continue with important results.

Barbara L. Fredrickson, University of North Carolina, Chapel Hill

My own friendship with Shane grew and was enacted almost entirely through the positive psychology meetings that we each attended, from 2000 onward. In the early days, these were in the small-group and fine-weather context of the Akumal meetings and subsequently through the Gallup Organization's much appreciated efforts to incubate the nascent scientific discipline that we were each drawn to. Indeed, Shane eventually became master of ceremonies at the Gallup events, a role that seemed a good fit for his welcoming and generous modus operandi.

What was remarkable about Shane's career path and impact was that, unlike most of us, Shane had one foot firmly rooted within basic science and the other within application. He was ever on the lookout for ways to use the theories and findings of basic science in real-world contexts, like classrooms, in ways that could directly improve the welfare of others. He was also an impeccable communicator and teacher—he made the scientific study of hope, of courage, and of strengths come alive for so many. I sorely miss Shane and his impact on our field and the world. Yet I am also heartened when I see the profound and lasting legacy of his life's work and the continuing ripple effects of it.

Sarah Pressman, University of California, Irvine

As a health psychologist, I know that the effects of social isolation can be as harmful as smoking, but that having good quality and supportive relationships can help you conquer stress and live a happier, healthier, and more successful life. Despite this, it wasn't until I met Dr. Shane Lopez that I saw someone who epitomized how a supportive person in your life can make a monumental difference. Shane valued social relationships above all else. His family and close friends were priceless to him, but he had a way of making every person he met feel special and cared for. Waiters who served Shane would not escape without their name being learned and personal tidbits being disclosed. Coffee baristas developed warm inside jokes with him and couldn't help but smile in their interactions with Shane. Even the casual stranger sitting next to him wouldn't stay a stranger for long.

Thanks in no small part to Shane, I pay extra close attention to the type of mentor and supporter that I am. He talked me through my biggest stressors, propelled me to great success, and was simply the type of mentor that I hope to be to my own students. The world is inevitably stressful, but with care from others, it can be a lot less terrible. While I doubt that I could ever generate the incredible warmth and love that he bestowed upon others or the opportunities that he created for so many, if we try our best to emulate the super-duper supporter that he was, we can certainly make the world a happier and healthier place. I know he would love that.

Kristin Koetting O'Byrne, Abilene Christian University

Shane walked the walk; he was a strengths spotter. For example, he supported my fearlessness about striking up a conversation with anyone. But as much as a strengths spotter, there were times, all in good fun, he preyed on my weaknesses. Shane appreciated my range of knowledge in different areas, but he knew there was an area of knowledge in which I was particularly deficient: college athletics. This is somewhat embarrassing in its own right, but it was especially embarrassing when I was employed at the University of Kansas, an NCAA Division I school.

One day, Shane and I were at lunch near campus, and he pointed to a man a couple of tables over and asked me if I knew who the man was. I said no. Shane teased me for not knowing and said the man is an amazing athlete and that I should introduce myself to him and tell him he had a great football season. I never shied away from a conversation with a stranger, so I did. Something didn't seem right as the man, who was so gracious, by the way, stood up to shake my hand. He was much taller and leaner than I would have expected for a football player. Suddenly, I hear Shane laughing and out of the corner of my eye, I can see Shane shaking because he was laughing so hard. The man was so kind. He introduced himself and explained I must have him confused with another athlete. It turns out this man was Wayne Simien, an All-American KU basketball player, BIG 12 Player of the Year, who would later become a NBA champion. I don't think Shane (or I) stopped laughing for the rest of the day, and neither did the other faculty members and students who Shane would soon tell.

Matt Englar-Carlson, California State University, Fullerton

When asked about my reaction to the job interview at the University of Kansas, I instead immediately started talking about meeting Shane Lopez. It started with "What a nice and kind guy!" and quickly moved to envisioning a future of having Shane as my colleague and friend. My wife had to redirect me to the actual job. But I was more drawn to Shane as he was the type of person that I wanted to be surrounded by in work and life—honest, expressive, and present. We both shared so much in that first interaction. I did not take the job, but the bonus was that Shane still became my colleague and friend—all of that came from 48 hours together during a job interview. Small windows of time can be transformative and extend disproportionately outward. From the moment we met face-to-face, Shane's smile, optimism, and boyish nature became a part of me, and I would like to think that it was mutual as there was reciprocity in our connection. Over the years, we would see each other at conferences and speak on the phone, and our relationship together always felt a bit deeper. Through life, geographical, and work changes, I always appreciated how Shane cultivated our relationship, building on kindness and genuineness. Shane embodied what he studied; his research became action-oriented me-search in so many ways, but certainly through his relationships with others and what he modeled and offered to those who were lucky enough to spend time in his orbit. I also noticed over the years that many of Shane's close friends and colleagues were also some of my favorite people to be around, and that was no coincidence. In my mind, being a friend of Shane's indicated a special somethingness and credibility. To this day, thinking of Shane always results in a smile, a pause, a lowering of my heart rate, and a deep feeling of gratitude for all that he was.

Brian Cole, University of Kansas

Meeting Shane was pure happenstance. As an undergraduate student, I had been paired with him in a mentoring program for first-generation college students. As a student of the late Rick Snyder, I was so enthusiastic about hope, but it wasn't until I met Shane and learned about counseling psychology that I figured out how to make it a career. Shane taught me a great deal about the science of hope during my time in the MS program at the University of Kansas, but one of the biggest lessons came after I graduated and moved on to doctoral training. One day I was feeling particularly discouraged by the lack of interest in positive psychology in my new program. As always, Shane listened intently, exuded warmth and humor, and provided a laser focus that made me feel heard, supported, and cared for. Then he challenged me. I had to walk back into my doctoral program and "be the hope guy." Shane was many things, a prolific researcher, a great mentor, and a good friend, but in all of his personal and professional pursuits, he was definitely "the hope guy." In that moment, I was challenged to be more hopeful about the situation. Together we reflected on my past experiences, which provided a great boost to my agency. We then had a wonderful conversation about pathways to my goals. Over the years that followed, the culture of the program changed. Students and faculty conducted positive psychology research and used positive psychology constructs in therapy, and positive psychology courses were being offered. When I graduated, I had become "the hope guy" in my doctoral program, but more important, like Shane, I had spread ripples of hope.

Matthew Gallagher, University of Houston

Shane had a passion and unique capacity for sharing positive psychology beyond academia. He was particularly passionate about helping students of all ages discover their strengths and learn how to leverage their hope and strengths to achieve their goals for the future. One of my fondest memories of Shane is from an event that Shane organized in the summer of 2007 on the campus of the Clifton Strengths Institute at Gallup headquarters in Omaha. Shane brought together junior researchers in positive psychology from around the world for a week of brainstorming about how best to promote strengths research. During this event, we had the opportunity to witness Shane in action as area students learned about their character strengths.

I can still picture the smile on Shane's face as he went around the room and helped students of diverse backgrounds understand their strengths and how they could harness them both inside and outside the classroom, and Shane's efforts with the Gallup Student Poll have helped millions of students to better understand how to flourish in schools. Shane truly had a unique gift for sharing positive psychology. I was fortunate to witness that in person that day in Omaha and in many other locations, and this textbook is just another example of Shane's legacy of sharing positive psychology with the world.

Ryon McDermott, University of Alabama

Shane was a positive presence in my life throughout high school and while I was getting my BA at the University of Kansas. For most of my time in high school, I only had a vague understanding that he was working under my mom, Diane McDermott [pioneer hope researcher], to get his PhD. I just assumed he was her colleague, although eventually he became one. That background, positive presence became an increasingly important foreground source of personal and professional advice as I progressed toward my own PhD in counseling psychology. Shane consulted on the very first research study I ever completed independently, read/edited my graduate school application materials, and gave me inside knowledge of life as an academic. I am incredibly grateful for his help. He never called in any favors from me, and seeing him at APA each year was always a blast. He had an infectious laugh and an incredibly warm smile. The last time I saw Shane was at my mother's funeral. Although it was certainly a difficult time for me, seeing him there and hearing his words of support as her former student was incredibly powerful. He said that she gave him hope. Shane gave me hope, and he was, at his core, a good person. I am honored to continue in his research and mentorship footsteps.

Jennifer Teramoto Pedrotti, California Polytechnic State University

Some of my favorite memories from graduate school are the times I spent with Shane and Lisa Edwards in coffeehouses like Java Dive or La Prima Tazza off Massachusetts St. in Lawrence, Kansas. Shane, a brand-new assistant professor at the time, liked to get off campus, and so we often met in these locations for our research meetings. It was at one of these coffeehouses that Shane, Lisa, and I conceived of the Making Hope Happen program, which we administered in several local schools. We would start at Point A and somehow end up at Point Z in a matter of hours—it would start with an idea, usually voiced by Shane, and then one of us would start figuring out how to put that idea into practice. Lisa would add something, or I would add something, and the three of us would find ourselves spinning off into the atmosphere, envisioning the program, finishing each other's sentences, gaining energy and strength from each other. It was pure synergy. We were in each other's zones. It was exhilarating. I had never felt like that before—like we could do anything. And Shane was the catalyst, the spark that set us off to dream, to think, to plan. When we met up later after we graduated, at conferences, or any time we were together, it was always the same. Even now, I can hear him egging us on, telling us to reach further, to dream bigger. He was a Maximizer in the purest sense. Anything was possible with Shane.

We miss you, Shane.

REFERENCES

Aalgaard, R. A., Bolen, R. M., & Nugent, W. R. (2016). A literature review of forgiveness as a beneficial intervention to increase relationship satisfaction in couples therapy. *Journal of Human Behavior in the Social Environment, 26*, 46–55.

Abramson, L. Y., Alloy, L., B., Hankin, B. L., Clements, C. M., Zhu, L., Hogan, M. E., & Whitehouse, W. G. (2000). Optimistic cognitive style and invulnerability to depression. In J. Gillham (Ed.), *The science of optimism and hope* (pp. 75–98). Templeton Foundation Press.

Abramson, L. Y., Seligman, M. E. P., & Teasdale, J. D. (1978). Learned helplessness in humans: Critique and reformulation. *Journal of Abnormal Psychology, 87*, 49–74.

Abuhamdeh, S. (2000). *The autotelic personality: An exploratory investigation*. Unpublished manuscript, University of Chicago.

Acevedo, B. P., Aron, A., Fisher, H. E., & Brown, L. L. (2012). Neural correlates of long-term intense romantic love. *Social Cognitive and Affective Neuroscience, 7*, 145–159.

Ackerman, S. J., Benjamin, L. S., Beutler, L. E., Gelso, C. J., Goldfried, M. R., Hill, C., Lambert, M. J., Norcross, J. C., Orlinsky, D. E., & Rainer, J. (2001). Empirically supported therapy relationships: Conclusions and recommendations of the Division 29

Adelabu, D. H. (2008). Future time perspective, hope, and ethnic identity among African American adolescents. *Urban Education, 43*, 347–360.

Adlai-Gail, W. (1994). *Exploring the autotelic personality*. Unpublished doctoral dissertation, University of Chicago.

Affleck, G., & Tennen, H. (1996). Construing benefit from adversity: Adaptational significance and dispositional underpinnings. *Journal of Personality, 64*, 899–922.

Ahmad, M., & Khan, S. (2016). A model of spirituality for ageing Muslims. *Journal of Religion and Health, 55*, 830–843.

Ahmed, A. S. (1999). *Islam today: A short introduction to the Muslim world*. I. B. Tauris & Co.

Ai, A. L., & Smyth, S. S. (2021). Depression after open heart surgery: Influences of optimism, sex, and event-related medical factors. *Journal of Nervous and Mental Disease, 209*(3), 212–217.

Ainsworth, M. D. S. (1979). Infant–mother attachment. *American Psychologist, 34*, 932–937.

Ainsworth, M. D. S., Bell, S. M., & Stayton, D. J. (1992). Infant-mother attachment and social development: "Socialization" as a product of reciprocal responsiveness to signals. In M. Woodhead, R. Carr, & P. Light (Eds.), *Becoming a person* (pp. 30–55). Routledge.

Ajibade, A., Hook, J. N., Utsey, S. O., Davis, D. E., & Van Tongeren, D. R. (2016). Racial/ethnic identity, religious commitment, and well-being in African Americans. *Journal of Black Psychology, 42*, 244–258.

Ajzen, I. (1991). The theory of planned behavior. *Theories of Cognitive Self-Regulation, 50*(2), 179–211.

Alarcon, G. M., Bowling, N. A., & Khazon, S. (2013). Great expectations: A meta-analytic examination of optimism and hope. *Personality and Individual Differences, 54*(7), 821–827.

Alawiyah, T., Bell, H., Pyles, L., & Runnels, R. C. (2011). Spirituality and faith-based interventions: Pathways to disaster resilience for African American Hurricane Katrina survivors. *Journal of Religion and Spirituality in Social Work: Social Thought, 30*, 294–319.

Alessandri, G., Vecchione, M., & Caprara, G. V. (2015). Assessment of regulatory emotional self-efficacy beliefs: A review of the status of the art and some suggestions to move the field forward. *Journal of Psychoeducational Assessment, 33*, 24–32.

Alexander, J. D., & Harris, C. (2022). Parenting styles'

effects on college students' career decision-making self-efficacy. *The Career Development Quarterly, 70*, 229-236.

Alexander, M. (2012). *The new Jim Crow*. The New Press.

Alexopoulos, C., Timmermans, E., & McNallie, J. (2020). Swiping more, committing less: Unraveling the links among dating app use, dating app success, and intention to commit infidelity. *Computers in Human Behavior, 102*, 172–180.

Algoe, S. B. (2012). Find, remind, and bind: The functions of gratitude in everyday relationships. *Social and Personality Psychology Compass, 6*, 455–469.

Ali, S. R., Flojo, J. R., Chronister, K. M., Hayashino, D., Smiling, Q. R., Torres, D., & McWhirter, E. H. (2005). When racism is reversed: Therapists of color speak about their experiences with racism from clients, supervisees, and supervisors. In M. Rastogi, & E. Wieling (Eds.), *Voices of color: First-person accounts of ethnic minority therapists* (pp. 117-1133). Sage.

Allan, B. A., Owens, R. L., Kim, T., Douglass, R. P., & Hintz, J. (2021). Strengths and satisfaction in first year undergraduate students: A longitudinal study. *The Journal of Positive Psychology, 16*(1), 94–104.

Allemand, A., Olaru, G., & Hill, P L. (2021). Age-related psychometrics and differences in gratitude and future time perspective across adulthood. *Personality and Individual Differences, 182*, 1-7.

Allen, D., & Marshall, E. S. (2010). Spirituality as a coping resource for African American parents of chronically ill children. *MCN: The American Journal of Maternal/Child Nursing, 35*, 232–237.

Allen, M. S., & McCarthy, P. J. (2016). Be happy in your work: The role of positive psychology in working with change and performance. *Journal of Change Management, 16*, 55–74.

Allen, T. D., Henderson, T. G., Mancini, V. S., & French, K. A. (2017). Mindfulness and meditation practice as moderators of the relationship between age and subjective wellbeing among working adults. *Mindfulness, 8*, 1055–1063.

Al-Seheel, A. Y., & Noor, N. M. (2016). Effects of an Islamic-based gratitude strategy on Muslim students' level of happiness. *Mental Health, Religion & Culture, 19*, 686–703.

American Indian Health Service of Chicago. (2021). *The seven grandfather teachings*. Retrieved from: https://aihschgo.org/seven-grandfather-teachings/

American Psychiatric Association. (2022). *Diagnostic and statistical manual of mental disorders* (7th ed.). Washington, DC: Author.

American Psychological Association. (2003). Guidelines on multicultural education, training, research, practice, and organizational change for psychologists. *American Psychologist, 58*, 377–402.

American Psychological Association. (2014). Guidelines for prevention in psychology. *American Psychologist, 69*, 285-296.

American Psychological Association, Boys and Men Guidelines Group. (2018). *APA guidelines for psychological practice with boys and men*. Retrieved from http://www.apa.org/about/policy/psychological-practice-boys-men-guidelines.pdf

Amick, B. C., III, McDonough, P., Chang, H., Rogers, W. H., Duncan, G., & Pieper, C. (2002). The relationship between all-cause mortality and cumulative working life course psychosocial and physical exposures in the United States labor market from 1968–1992. *Psychosomatic Medicine, 64*, 370–381.

Aminuddin, H. B., Jiao, N., Jiang, Y., Hong, J., & Wang, W. (2021). Effectiveness of smartphone-based self-management interventions on self-efficacy, self-care activities, health-related quality of life and clinical outcomes in patients with type 2 diabetes: A systematic review and meta-analysis. *International Journal of Nursing Studies, 116*.

Anālayo, B. (2020). Confronting racism with mindfulness. *Mindfulness, 11*(10), 2283–2297.

Anders, S. L., Frazier, P. A., & Shallcross, S. L. (2012). Prevalence and effects of life event exposure among undergraduate and community college students. *Journal of Counseling Psychology, 59*(3), 449–457.

Anderson, C., Turner, A. C., Heath, R. D., & Payne, C. M. (2016). On the meaning of grit . . . and hope . . . and fate control . . . and alienation . . . and locus of control . . . and . . . self-efficacy . . . and . . . effort optimism . . . and . . . .*The Urban Review, 48*, 198–219.

Anderson, L. B., Paul, L. K., & Brown, W. S. (2017). Emotional intelligence in agenesis of the corpus callosum. *Archives of Clinical Neuropsychology, 32*, 267–279.

Andrei, F., Siegling, A. B., Aloe, A. M., Baldaro, B., & Petrides, K. V. (2016). The incremental validity of the Trait Emotional Intelligence Questionnaire (TEIQue): A systematic review and meta-analysis. *Journal of Personality Assessment, 98*(3), 261–276.

Ang, J. Y-Z., Monte, V., & Tsai, W. (2022). First-year college students' adjustment during the COVID-19 pandemic: The protective roles of hope and gratitude. *The Journal of Positive Psychology, 14*, 271-282.

Angerer, S., Glätzle-Rützler, D., Lergetporer, P., & Sutter, M. (2015). Donations, risk attitudes and time preferences: A study on altruism in primary school children. *Journal of Economic Behavior & Organization, 115*, 67–74.

Anonymous. (2021, March 22). The pandemic has changed the shape of global happiness. *The Economist*.

Anzaldua, A., & Halpern, J. (2021). Can clinical empathy survive? Distress, burnout, and malignant duty in the age of COVID-19. *Hastings Center Report, 51*, 22-27.

Argyle, M. (2001). *The psychology of happiness* (2nd ed.). Routledge.

Aquinas, T. (1948). *Introduction to St. Thomas Aquinas: The Summa Theologica, The Summa Contra Gentiles* (A. Pegis, Ed.). Random House. (Original work published 1273)

Aquinas, T. (1981). *Summa theologica*. Christian Classics. (Original work published 1273)

Araújo, L., Ribeiro, O., Teixeira, L., & Paúl, C. (2016). Successful aging at 100 years: The relevance of subjectivity and psychological resources. *International Psychogeriatrics, 28*, 179–188.

Ardelt, M. (2003). Empirical assessment of a three-dimensional wisdom scale. *Research of Aging, 25*, 275–324.

Ardelt, M. (2010). Are older adults wiser than college students? A comparison of two age cohorts. *Journal of Adult Development, 17*, 193–207.

Ardelt, M. (2016). Disentangling the relations between wisdom and different types of well-being in old age: Findings from a short-term longitudinal study. *Journal of Happiness Studies, 17*, 1963–1984.

Ardelt, M., & Edwards, C. A. (2016). Wisdom at the end of life: An analysis of mediating and moderating relations between wisdom and subjective wellbeing. *The Journals of Gerontology: Psychological Sciences and Social Sciences, 71*, 502–513.

Ardelt, M., Pridgen, S., & Nutter-Pridgen, K. L. (2019). Wisdom as a personality type. In R. J. Sternberg & J. Glück (Eds.), *The Cambridge handbook of wisdom* (pp. 144–161). Cambridge University Press.

Argyle, M. (1987). *The psychology of happiness*. Methuen.

Argyle, M. (2001). *The psychology of happiness* (2nd edition). Routledge.

Arman, G., & Adair, C. K. (2012). Cross-cultural differences in perception of time: Implications for multinational teams. *European Journal of Work and Organizational Psychology, 21*(5), 657–680.

Armenta, C. N., Fritz, M. M., & Lyubomirsky, S. (2017). Functions of positive emotions: Gratitude as a motivator of self-improvement and positive change. *Emotion Review, 9*, 183–190.

Armenta, C. N., Fritz, M. M., Walsh, L. C., & Lyubomirsky, S. (2022). Satisfied yet striving: Gratitude fosters life satisfaction and improvement motivation in youth. *Emotion, 22*(5), 1004–1016.

Aron, A., & Aron, E. N. (1986). *Love and the expansion of self: Understanding attraction and satisfaction*. Hemisphere.

Aron, A., Aron, E. N., & Smollan, D. (1992). Inclusion of other in the self scale and the structure of interpersonal closeness. *Journal of Personality and Social Psychology, 63*, 596–612.

Aron, A., Norman, C. C., Aron, E. N., McKenna, C., & Heyman, R. E. (2000). Couples' shared participation in novel and arousing activities and experienced relationship quality. *Journal of Personality and Social Psychology, 78*, 273–284.

Aron, E. N., & Aron, A. (1996). Love and expansion of the self: The state of the model. *Personal Relationships, 3*, 45–58.

Aronson, E. (2003). *The social animal* (9th ed.). Worth.

Aronson, J., Lustina, M. J., Good, C., Keough, K., Steele, C. M., & Brown, J. (1999). When White men can't do math: Necessary and sufficient factors in stereotype threat. *Journal of Experimental Social Psychology, 35*, 29–46.

Aronson, J., & Rogers, L. (2008). Overcoming stereotype threat. In S. J. Lopez (Ed.), *Positive psychology: Exploring the best in people*: Vol. 3. *Growing in the face of adversity* (pp. 109–121). Greenwood.

Arslan, G., & Coşkun, M. (2022). Social exclusion, self-forgiveness, mindfulness, and Internet addiction in college students: A moderated mediation approach. *International Journal of Mental Health and Addiction, 20*(4), 2165–2179.

Asakawa, K. (2004). Flow experience and autotelic personality in Japanese college students: How do they experience challenges in daily life? *Journal of Happiness Studies, 5*, 123–154.

Asakawa, K. (2010). Flow experience, culture, and well-being: How do autotelic Japanese college students feel, behave, and think in their daily lives? *Journal of Happiness Studies, 11*, 205–223.

Ashby, F. G., Isen, A. M., & Turken, A. U. (1999). A neuropsychological theory of positive affect and its influence on cognition. *Psychological Review, 106*, 529–550.

Aspinwall, L. G., & Taylor, S. E. (1992). Modeling cognitive adaptation: A longitudinal investigation of the impact of individual differences and coping on college adjustment and performance. *Journal of Personality and Social Psychology, 61*, 755–765.

Asplund, J., Agrawal, S., Hodges, T., Harter, J., & Lopez, S. J. (2014). *Clifton StrengthsFinder technical report*. Gallup.

Asplund, J., Harter, J. K., Agrawal, S., & Plowman, S. K. (2016). *The relationship between strengths-based employee development and organizational outcomes 2015 strengths meta-analysis*. Gallup.

Aten, J. D., Smith, W. R., Davis, E. B., Van Tongeren, D. R., Hook, J. N., Davis, D. E., Shannonhouse, L., DeBlaere, C., Ranter, J., O'Grady, K., & Hill, P. C. (2019). The psychological study of religion and spirituality in a disaster context: A systematic review. *Psychological trauma: theory, research, practice and policy, 11*(6), 597–613. https://doi.org/10.1037/tra0000431

Austenfeld, J. L., & Stanton, A. L. (2008). Writing about emotions versus goals: Effects on hostility and medical care utilization moderated by emotional approach coping processes. *British Journal of Health Psychology, 13*, 35–38.

Averill, J. R. (1990). Inner feelings, works of the flesh, the beast within, diseases of the mind, driving force, and putting on a show: Six metaphors of emotion and their theoretical extensions. In D. E. Leary (Ed.), *Metaphors in the history of psychology* (pp. 104–132). Cambridge University Press.

Averill, J. R., Catlin, G., & Chon, K. K. (1990). *Rules of hope*. Springer-Verlag.

Awardoo (14 April 2022). What are high performance work systems (HPWS)? https://www.awardaroo.io/blog/what-is-a-high-performance-work-system

Ayed, N., Toner, S., & Priebe, S. (2019). Conceptualizing resilience in adult mental health literature: A systematic review and narrative synthesis. *Psychology and Psychotherapy: Theory, Research and Practice, 92*(3), 299–341.

Babyak, M., Snyder, C. R., & Yoshinobu, L. (1993). Psychometric properties of the Hope Scale: A confirmatory factor analysis. *Journal of Research in Personality, 27*, 154–169.

Bailey, G. (2014). The power of Malala. *International Social Work, 57*, 75.

Baer, R. A., Smith, G. T., Hopkins, J., Krietemeyer, J., & Toney, L. (2006). Using self-report assessment methods to explore facets of mindfulness. *Assessment, 13*(1), 27-45

Baker, J. A. (1998). The social context of school satisfaction among urban, low-income, African-American students. *School Psychology Quarterly, 13*, 25–44.

Bakker, A. B. (2008). The work-related flow inventory: Construction and initial validation of the WOLF. *Journal of Vocational Behavior, 72*(3), 400–414.

Bakker, A. B., & Oerlemans, W. G. M. (2016). Momentary work happiness as a function of enduring burnout and work engagement. *The Journal of Psychology: Interdisciplinary and Applied, 150*, 755–778.

Baldwin, D. R., Jackson, D., Okoh, I., & Cannon, R. L. (2011).

Resiliency and optimism: An African American senior citizen's perspective. *Journal of Black Psychology*, *37*, 24–41.

Balkin, R. S., Neal, S. A., Stewart, K. D., Hendricks, L., & Litam, S. D. A. (2022). Spirituality and relational health among Black Americans. *Journal of Counseling & Development*, *100*(4), 412–420.

Ballester, S., Sastre, M. T. M., & Mullet, E. (2009). Forgivingness and lay conceptualizations of forgiveness. *Personality and Individual Differences*, *47*, 605–609.

Baltes, P. B. (1993). The aging mind: Potential and limits. *The Gerontologist*, *33*, 580–594.

Baltes, P. B., & Smith, J. (1990). The psychology of wisdom and its ontogenesis. In R. J. Sternberg (Ed.), *Wisdom: Its nature, origins, and development* (pp. 87–120). Cambridge University Press.

Baltes, P. B., & Staudinger, U. (1993). The search for a psychology of wisdom. *Current Directions in Psychological Science*, *2*, 75–80.

Baltes, P. B., & Staudinger, U. (2000). Wisdom: A meta-heuristic (pragmatic) to orchestrate mind and virtue toward excellence. *American Psychologist*, *55*, 122–136.

Baltes, P. B., Glück, J., & Kunzmann, U. (2002). Wisdom: Its structure and function in regulating successful life-span development. In C. R. Snyder & S. J. Lopez (Eds.), *The handbook of positive psychology* (pp. 327–347). Oxford University Press.

Balzarini, R. N., & Muise, A. (2020). Beyond the dyad: A review of the novel insights gained from studying consensual non-monogamy. *Current Sexual Health Reports*, *12*(4), 398–404.

Bamber, M. D., & Morpeth, E. (2019). Effects of mindfulness meditation on College student anxiety: A meta-analysis. *Mindfulness*, *10*(2), 203–214.

Bamford, C. M., & Lagattuta, K. H. (2012). Looking on the bright side: Children's knowledge about the benefits of positive versus negative thinking. *Child Development*, *83*, 667–682.

Bandura, A. (1977). Self-efficacy: Toward a unifying theory of behavior change. *Psychological Review*, *84*, 191–215.

Bandura, A. (1982). Self-efficacy mechanism in human agency. *American Psychologist*, *37*, 122–147.

Bandura, A. (1986). *Social foundations of thought and action*. Prentice Hall.

Bandura, A. (1989a). Human agency in social cognitive theory. *American Psychologist*, *44*, 1175–1184.

Bandura, A. (1989b). Regulation of cognitive processes through perceived self-efficacy. *Developmental Psychology*, *25*, 729–735.

Bandura, A. (1991). Self-efficacy mechanism in physiological activation and health-promoting behavior. In J. Madden IV (Ed.), *Neurobiology of learning, emotion and affect* (pp. 229–270). Raven.

Bandura, A. (1997). *Self-efficacy: The exercise of control*. Freeman.

Bandura, A. (2000). Social cognitive theory in context. *Journal of Applied Psychology: An International Review*, *51*, 269–290.

Bandura, A. (2005). The primacy of self-regulation in health promotion. *Applied Psychology: An International Review*, *54*(2), 245–254.

Bandura, A., & Adams, N. E. (1977). Analysis of self-efficacy theory of behavioral change. *Cognitive Therapy and Research*, *1*(4), 287–310.

Bandura, A., Adams, N. E., & Beyer, J. (1977). Cognitive processes mediating behavioral change. *Journal of Personality and Social Psychology*, *35*, 125–139.

Bandura, A., Taylor, C. B., Williams, S. L., Mefford, I. N., & Barchas, J. D. (1985). Catecholamine secretion as a function of perceived coping self-efficacy. *Journal of Consulting and Clinical Psychology*, *53*, 406–414.

Bang, H. (2015). African American undergraduate students' wisdom and ego-identity development: Effects of age, gender, self-esteem, and resilience. *Journal of Black Psychology*, *41*, 95–120.

Bao, K. J., & Lyubomirsky, S. (2013). Making it last: Combating hedonic adaptation in romantic relationships. *The Journal of Positive Psychology*, *8*, 196–206.

Barclay, L. J., & Saldanha, M. F. (2016). Facilitating

forgiveness in organizational contexts: Exploring the injustice gap, emotions, and expressive writing interventions. *Journal of Business Ethics, 137*, 699–720.

Barclay, L. J., Kiefer, T., & El Mansouri, M. (2021). Navigating the era of disruption: How emotions can prompt job crafting behaviors. *Human Resource Management*, Advanced Online.

Barclay, P. (2010). Altruism as a courtship display: Some effects of third-party generosity on audience perceptions. *British Journal of Psychology, 101*, 123–135.

Bardach, L., Khajavy, G. H., Hamedi, S. M., Schober, B., & Lüftenegger, M. (2018). Student-teacher agreement on classroom goal structures and potential predictors. *Teaching and Teacher Education, 74*, 249-260.

Bargh, J. A., & Chartrand, T. L. (2014). The mind in the middle: A practical guide to priming and automaticity research. In H. T. Reis & C. M. Judd (Eds.), *Handbook of research methods in social and personality psychology* (pp. 311–344). Cambridge University Press.

Barnby, J. M., Bailey, N. W., Chambers, R., & Fitzgerald, P. B. (2015). How similar are the changes in neural activity resulting from mindfulness practice in contrast to spiritual practice? *Consciousness and Cognition, 36*, 219–232. https://doi.org/10.1016/j.concog.2015.07.002

Barnett, A., Zhang, C. J. P., Johnston, J. M., & Cerin, E. (2018). Relationships between the neighborhood environment and depression in older adults: A systematic review and meta-analysis. *International Psychogeriatrics, 30*(8), 1153–1176.

Barnett, M. D. (2014). Future orientation and health among older adults: The importance of hope. *Educational Gerontology, 40*, 745–755.

Bar-On, R. (2006). The Bar-On model of emotional-social intelligence (ESI). *Psicothema, 18*, 13–25.

Barone, D., Maddux, J. E., & Snyder, C. R. (1997). The social cognitive construction of difference and disorder. In D. Barone, J. E. Maddux, & C. R. Snyder (Eds.), *Social cognitive psychology: History and current domains* (pp. 397–428). Plenum.

Barrow, K. M., & Kuvalanka, K. A. (2011). To be Jewish and lesbian: An exploration of religion, sexual identity, and familial relationships. *Journal of GLBT Family Studies, 7*, 470–492.

Bartholomew, K., & Horowitz, L. M. (1991). Attachment styles among young adults: A test of a four-category model. *Journal of Personality and Social Psychology, 61*, 226–244.

Bartholomew, T. T., Gundel, B. E., Li, H., Joy, E. E., Kang, E., & Scheel, M. J. (2019). The meaning of therapists' hope for their clients: A phenomenological study. *Journal of Counseling Psychology, 66*, 496–507.

Bartlett, M. Y., Condon, P., Cruz, J., Baumann, J., & Desteno, D. (2012). Gratitude: Prompting behaviours that build relationships. *Cognition and Emotion, 26*, 2–13.

Bassi, M., & Delle Fave, A. (2016). Flow in the context of daily experience fluctuation. In L. Harmat, F. Ø., Andersen, F. Ullén, J. Wright, & G. Sadlo (Eds.), *Flow experience: Empirical research and applications* (pp. 181–196). Springer International.

Batson, C. D. (1991). *The altruism question: Toward a social-psychological answer.* Lawrence Erlbaum.

Batson, C. D. (2011). *Altruism in humans.* Oxford University Press.

Batson, C. D., Ahmad, N., & Lishner, D. A. (2009). Empathy and altruism. In S. J. Lopez & C. R. Snyder (Eds.), *Oxford handbook of positive psychology* (pp. 417–426). Oxford University Press.

Batson, C. D., Ahmad, N., & Stocks, E. L. (2011). Four forms of prosocial motivation: Egoism, altruism, collectivism, and principlism. In D. Dunning (Ed.), *Social motivation* (pp. 103–126). Psychology Press.

Baumann, N. (2021). Autotelic personality. In C. Peifer & S. Engeser (Eds.), *Advances in flow research* (pp. 231–261).

Baumeister, R. F., & Leary, M. R. (1995). The need to belong: Desire for interpersonal attachment as a fundamental human motivation. *Psychological Bulletin, 117*, 497–529.

Baumgartner, J. N., Schneider, T. R., & Capiola, A. (2018). Investigating the relationship between optimism and stress responses: A biopsychosocial perspective. *Personality and*

Individual Differences, 129, 114–118.

Beard, K. S., Hoy, W. K. W., & Hoy, A. (2010). Academic optimism of individual teachers: Confirming a new construct. *Teaching and Teacher Education, 26,* 1136–1144.

Beardsley M, Albó L, Aragón P, Hernández-Leo D. (2021). Emergency education effects on teacher abilities and motivation to use digital technologies. British Journal of Educational Technology, *52,* 1455–1477.

Bechara, A., Tranel, D., Damasio, H., & Damasio, A. R. (1996). Failure to respond autonomically to anticipated future outcomes following damage to prefrontal cortex. *Cerebral Cortex, 6,* 215–225.

Beck, L., & Madresh, E. A. (2008). Romantic partners and four-legged friends: An extension of attachment theory to relationships with pets. *Anthrozoös, 21*(1), 43–56.

Becker, J. A., & Smenner, P. C. (1986). The spontaneous use of *thank you* by preschoolers as a function of sex, socioeconomic status, and listener status. *Language in Society, 15,* 537–546.

Begus, K., Curioni, A., Knoblich, G., & Gergely, G. (2020). Infants understand collaboration: Neural evidence for 9-month-olds' attribution of shared goals to coordinated joint actions. *Social Neuroscience, 15,* 655-667.

Belgrave, F. Z., Chase-Vaughn, G., Gray, F., Addison, J. D., & Cherry, V. R. (2000). The effectiveness of a culture and gender-specific intervention for increasing resiliency among African American preadolescent females. *Journal of Black Psychology, 26,* 133–147.

Belsky, J., & Nezworski, T. (Eds.). (1988). *Clinical implications of attachment.* Lawrence Erlbaum.

Benedikovicová, J., & Ardelt, M. (2008). The three dimensional wisdom scale in cross-cultural context: A comparison between American and Slovak college students. *Studia Psychologica, 50,* 179–190.

Benne, K. D. (1964). History of T-group in the laboratory setting. In L. P. Bradford, J. R. Gibb, & K. D. Benne (Eds.), *T-group and laboratory method: Innovation in re-education* (pp. 80–135). Wiley.

Benson, H., & Proctor, W. (1984). *Beyond the relaxation response.* Putnam/Berkley.

Benson, P. L., Leffert, N., Scales, P. C., & Blyth, D. A. (1998). Beyond the 'village' rhetoric: Creating healthy communities for children and adolescents. *Applied Developmental Science 2*(3), 138–159. doi: 10.1080/10888691.2012.642771

Benson, P. L., & Saito, R. N. (2000). The scientific foundations of youth development. In N. Jaffe (Ed.), *Youth development: Issues, challenges, and directions* (pp. 125–147). Public/Private Ventures.

Benson, P. L., & Scales, P. C. (2009). The definition and preliminary measurement of thriving in adolescence. *Journal of Positive Psychology, 4,* 85–104.

Benton-Banai, E. (1988). *The Mishomis book: The voice of the Ojibway.* Hayward, WI: Indian Country Communications.

Bercovitz, K., Pagnini, F., Phillips, D., & Langer, E. (2017). Utilizing a creative task to assess Langerian mindfulness. *Creativity Research Journal, 29,* 194–199.

Berg, J. M., Dutton, J. E., & Wreisnewski, A. (2007). What is job crafting and why does it matter. *Positive Organizational Scholarship.* Michigan Ross School of Business.

Bergsma, A., & Ardelt, M. (2012). Self-reported wisdom and happiness: An empirical investigation. *Journal of Happiness Studies, 13,* 481–499.

Berkovich-Ohana, A., Glicksohn, J., & Goldstein, A. (2012). Mindfulness-induced changes in gamma band activity—Implications for the default mode network, self-reference, and attention. *Clinical Neurophysiology, 123,* 700–710.

Bernard, K., Hostinar, C. E., & Dozier, M. (2019). Longitudinal associations between attachment quality in infancy, C-reactive protein in early childhood, and BMI in middle childhood: Preliminary evidence from a CPS-referred sample. *Attachment & Human Development, 21*(1), 5–22.

Berry, J. M., West, R. L., & Dennehey, D. M. (1989). Reliability and validity of the Memory Self-Efficacy Questionnaire. *Developmental Psychology, 25,* 701–713.

Berscheid, E., & Reis, H. T. (1998). Attraction and close relationships. In D. T. Gilbert, S. T. Fiske, & G. Lindsey (Eds.), *The handbook of social psychology* (4th ed., Vol. 2, pp. 193–281). McGraw-Hill.

Berscheid, E., & Walster, E. (1978). *Interpersonal attraction* (2nd ed.). Reading, MA: Addison Wesley.

Bertrams, A., Baumeister, R. F., & Englert, C. (2016). Higher self-control capacity predicts lower anxiety-impaired cognition during math examinations. *Frontiers in Psychology, 7*, 485.

Bess, K. D., Fisher, A. T., Sonn, C. C., & Bishop, B. J. (2002). Psychological sense of community. In A. T. Fisher, C. C. Sonn, & B. J. Bishop (Eds.), *Psychological sense of community: Research, applications, and implications* (pp. 3–22). Kluwer Academic/Plenum.

Best, D., & de Alwis, S. (2017). Community recovery as a public health intervention: The contagion of hope. *Alcoholism Treatment Quarterly, 35*, 187–199.

Betz, N. E., & Klein Voyten, K. (1997). Efficacy and outcome expectations influence career exploration and decidedness. *Career Development Quarterly, 46*, 179–189.

Biccheri, E., Roussiau, N., & Mambet-Doué, C. (2016). Fibromyalgia, spirituality, coping and quality of life. *Journal of Religion and Health, 55*, 1189–1197.

Biddle, S. J. H., Fox, K. R., & Boutcher, S. H. (Eds.). (2000). *Physical activity and psychological well-being*. Routledge.

Biddlestone, M., Green, R., & Douglas, K. M. (2020). Cultural orientation, power, belief in conspiracy theories, and intentions to reduce the spread of COVID-19. *British Journal of Social Psychology, 59*, 663-673.

Bieda, A., Hirschfeld, G., Schönfeld, P., Brailovskaia, J., Zhang, X. C., & Margraf, J. (2017). Universal happiness? Cross-cultural measurement invariance of scales assessing positive mental health. *Psychological Assessment, 29*(4), 408–421.

Bigler, R. S., & Liben, L. S. (2006). A developmental intergroup theory of social stereotypes and prejudice. In R. V. Kail (Ed.), *Advances in child development and behaviour* (pp. 39–89). Elsevier Academic Press.

Binet, A., & Simon, T. (1916). *The development of intelligence in children* (E. S. Kit, Trans.). Williams & Williams.

Bishop, S. R. (2002). What do we really know about mind fulness-based stress reduction? *Psychosomatic Medicine, 64*, 71–84.

Biswas-Diener, R. (2012). *The courage quotient: How science can make you braver.* Wiley.

Bitter, A. N., & McCrea, S. M. (2022). "The ship is sinking, yet the band plays on": COVID-19 and academia, *Journal of American College Health.* Advanced Online.

Black, J., & Reynolds, W. M. (2013). Examining the relationship of perfectionism, depression, and optimism: Testing for mediation and moderation. *Personality and Individual Differences, 54*(3), 426-431.

Blake, J., & Norton, C. L. (2014). Examining the relationship between hope and attachment: A meta-analysis. *Psychology, 5*, 556–565.

Blaxton, J. M., Nelson, N. A., & Bergeman, C. S. (2021). The positive and negative affect relation in the context of stress and age. *Emotion, 21*, 1712–1720.

Boateng, G. O., Neilands, T. B., Frongillo, E. A., Melgar-Quiñonez, H. R., & Young, S. L., (2018). *Best practices for developing and validating scales for health, social, and behavioral research: A primer.* Front.

Boehm, J. K., & Lyubormirsky, S. (2008). Does happiness promote career success? *Journal of Career Assessment, 16*, 101–116.

Boehm, J. K., Lyubomirsky, S., & Sheldon, K. M. (2011). A longitudinal experimental study comparing the effectiveness of happiness-enhancing strategies in Anglo Americans and Asian Americans. *Cognition and Emotion, 25*, 1263–1272.

Boer, D., Hanke, K., & He, J. (2018). On detecting systematic measurement error in cross-cultural research: A review and critical reflection on equivalence and invariance tests. *Journal of Cross-Cultural Psychology, 49*(5), 713–734.

Bokser, B. Z. (1989). *The Talmud: Selected writings.* Paulist Press.

Bolton, M., Lobben I., Pruzinsky, T., & Stern, T. A. (2020). Well-being and work-life balance: Cultural, positive psychology, and practical perspectives. In W. W. IsHak (Ed.), *The handbook of wellness medicine.* (pp. 545-552). Cambridge University Press.

Bono, G., Emmons, R. A., & McCullough, M. E. (2004). Gratitude in practice and the practice of gratitude. In P. A. Linley & S. Joseph (Eds.), *Positive psychology in practice* (pp. 464–481). Wiley.

Bono, G., Froh, J. J., & Forrett, R. (2014). Gratitude in school: Benefits to students and schools. In M. J. Furlong, R. Gilman, & E. S. Huber (Eds.), Handbook of positive psychology in schools. (Pp. 67-81). Routledge/Taylor & Francis Group.

Borelli, J. L., Kerr, M. L., Smiley, P. A., Rasmussen, H. F., Hecht, H. K, & Campos, B. (2022). Relational savoring intervention: Positive impacts for mothers and evidence of cultural compatibility for Latinas. *Emotion*. AdvancedOnline.

Borgogna, N. C., & McDermott, R. C. (2022). Is traditional masculinity ideology stable over time in men and women? *Psychology of Men & Masculinities*, *23*, 347–352.

Bowjanowska, A., & Zalewska, A. M. (2016). Lay understanding of happiness and the experience of well-being: Are some conceptions of happiness more beneficial than others? *Journal of Happiness Studies*, *17*, 783–815.

Bowlby, J. (1969). *Attachment and loss: Vol. I. Attachment*. Tavistock.

Bowlby, J. (1988). *A secure base: Parent–child attachment and healthy human development*. Basic Books.

Bowling, N. A., Eschleman, K. J., & Wang, Q. (2010). A meta-analytic examination of the relationship between job satisfaction and subjective well-being. *Journal of Occupational and Organizational Psychology*, *83*, 915-934.

Boyce, C. J., Daly, M., Hounkpatin, H. O., & Wood, A. M. (2017). Money may buy happiness, but often so little that it doesn't matter. *Psychological Science*, *28*, 544–546.

Boyd-Franklin, N. (2010). Incorporating spirituality and religion into the treatment of African American clients. *The Counseling Psychologist*, *38*, 976–1000.

Boyle, E. A., Connolly, T. M., Hainey, T., & Boyle, J. M. (2012). Engagement in digital entertainment games: A systematic review. *Computers in Human Behavior*, *28*, 771–780.

Bradburn, N. M. (1969). *The structure of psychological well-being*. Aldine.

Braithwaite, S., Selby, E. A., & Fincham, F. D. (2011). Forgiveness and relationship satisfaction: Mediating mechanisms. *Journal of Family Psychology*, *25*, 551–559.

Brauer, K., Scherrer, T., & Porter, R. T. (2021). Testing the associations between adult playfulness and sensation seeking: A AEM analysis of librarians and police officers. *Frontiers in Psychology*, *12*.

Brennan, G., Balasubramani, P. P., Alim, F., Zafar-Khan, M., Lee, E. E., Jeste, D. V., & Mishra, J. (2021). Cognitive and neural correlates of loneliness and wisdom during emotional bias. *Cerebral Cortex*, *31*, 3311-3322.

Brennan, K. A., Clark, C. L, & Shaver, P. R. (1998). Self-report measures of adult attachment: An integrative overview. In J. A. Simpson & W. S. Rholes (Eds.), *Attachment theory and close relationships* (pp. 46–76). Guilford.

Brethel-Haurwitz, K. M., & Marsh, A. A. (2014). Geographical differences in subjective well-being predict extraordinary altruism. *Association for Psychological Science*, *25*, 762–771.

Breznitz, S. (1986). The effect of hope on coping with stress. In M. H. Appley & P. Trumbull (Eds.), *Dynamics of stress: Physiological, psychological, and social perspectives* (pp. 295–307). Plenum.

Bricteux, C., Navarro, J., Ceja, L., & Fuerst, G. (2017). Interest as a moderator in the relationship between challenge/skills balance and flow at work: An analysis at within-individual level. *Journal of Happiness Studies*, *18*, 861–880.

Brienza, J. P., Kung, F. Y. H., Santos, H. C., Bobocel, R., & Grossman, I. (2018). *Situated WIse Reasoning Scale (SWIS)* [Database record]. APA PsycTests.

Brocato, N., Hix, L., & Jayawickreme, E. (2020). Challenges in measuring wisdom-relevant constructs in young adult undergraduate students. *Journal of Moral Education*, *49*, 46-70.

Bronfrenbrenner, U. (Ed.). (2005). *Making human beings human: Bioecological perspectives on human development*. Sage

Brooks, J. A., Shablack, H., Gendron, M., Satpute, A. B., Parrish, M. H., & Lindquist, K. A. (2017). The role of language in the experience and perception of emotion: A neuroimaging meta-analysis. *Social Cognitive and Affective Neuroscience, 12*, 169–183.

Brophy, K., Brähler, E., Hinz, A., Schmidt, S., & Körner, A. (2020). The role of self-compassion in the relationship between attachment, depression, and quality of life. *Journal of Affective Disorders, 260*, 45–52.

Brown, L. (28 February 2014). *The importance of trust.* Retrieved from: https://teachforall.org/news/importance-trust

Brown-Iannuzzi, J. L., Adair, K. C., Payne, B. K., Richman, L. S., & Fredrickson, B. L. (2014). Discrimination hurts, but mindfulness may help: Trait mindfulness moderates the relationship between perceived discrimination and depressive symptoms. *Personality and Individual Differences, 56*, 201–205

Bruner, M. W., McLaren, C. D., Sutcliffe, J. T., Gardner, L. A., Lubans, D. R., Smith, J. J., & Vella, S. A. (2021). The effect of sport-based interventions on positive youth development: A systematic review and meta-analysis. *International Review of Sport and Exercise Psychology.* (advanced online publication)

Brunwasser, S. M., & Gillham, J. E. (2018). Identifying moderators of response to the Penn Resiliency Program: A synthesis study. *Prevention Science, 19*(Suppl 1), S38–S48.

Bruya, B. (Ed.). (2010). *Effortless attention: A new perspective in the cognitive science of attention and action.* MIT Press Scholarship Online.

Bryant, F. B. (2004, May). *Capturing the joy of the moment: Savoring as a process in positive psychology.* Invited address at the meeting of the Midwestern Psychological Association, Chicago.

Bryant, F. B., & Smith, J. L. (2015). Appreciating life in the midst of adversity: Savoring in relation to mindfulness, reappraisal, and meaning. *Psychological Inquiry, 26*, 315–321.

Bryant, F. B., & Veroff, J. (2006). *The process of savoring: A new model of positive experience.* Lawrence Erlbaum.

Bryk, A. S., & Schneider, B. (2002). *Trust in schools: A core resource for improvement.* Russell Sage.

Buchanan, T. W., & Preston, S. (2016). When feeling and doing diverge: Neural and physiological correlates of the empathy-altruism divide. In J. D. Greene, I. Morrison, & M. E. P. Seligman (Ed.), *Positive neuroscience* (pp. 85–104). Oxford University Press.

Buckingham, M., & Clifton, D. O. (2001). *Now, discover your strengths.* Free Press.

Bundick, M. J. (2011). Extracurricular activities, positive youth development, and the role of meaningfulness of engagement. *The Journal of Positive Psychology, 6*, 57–74.

Burklund, L. J., Creswell, J. D., Irwin, M., & Lieberman, M. (2014). The common and distinct neural bases of affect labeling and reappraisal in healthy adults. *Frontiers in Psychology, 5*, 73770. https://doi.org/10.3389/fpsyg.2014.00221

Burks, D. J., & Kobus, A. M. (2012). The legacy of altruism in health care: The promotion of empathy, prosociality and humanism. *Medication Education, 46*, 317–325.

Burnette, J. L., & Pollack, J. M. (2013). Implicit theories of work and job fit: Implications for job and life satisfaction. *Basic and Applied Social Psychology, 35*, 360–372.

Burns, G. N., Jasinski, D., Dunn, S., & Fletcher, D. (2013). Academic support services and career decision-making self-efficacy in student athletes. *The Career Development Quarterly, 61*, 161–167.

Burque, M. (2017, July). Is psychotherapy for people of color? *Psychology Today.* https://www.psychologytoday.com/blog/unpacking-race/201707/is-psychotherapy-people-color

Burris, C. T., Schrage K. M., & Rempel, J. K. (2016). No country for girly men: High instrumentality men express empathic concern when caring is "manly." *Motivation and Emotion, 40*, 278–289.

Burton, W. N., Chen, C.-Y., Li, X., & Schultz, A. B. (2017). The association of employee engagement at work with health risks and presenteeism. *Journal of Occupational and Environmental Medicine, 59*, 988–992.

Bury, S. M., Wenzel, M., & Woodyatt, L. (2016). Giving hope a sporting chance: Hope as distinct from optimism when events are possible but not probable. *Motivation and Emotion, 40*, 588–601.

Buskist, W., Benson, T., & Sikorski, J. F. (2005). The call to teach. *Journal of Social and Clinical Psychology, 24*, 110–121.

Buss, D. (2000). The evolution of happiness. *American Psychologist, 55*, 15–23.

Busseri, M. A. (2022). The global belief that "life gets better and better": National differences in recollected past, present, and anticipated future life satisfaction around the world, across time, and in relation to societal functioning. *Journal of Personality and Social Psychology, 123*(1), 223–247.

Butel, J., & Braun, K. L. (2019). The role of collective efficacy in reducing health disparities: A systematic review. *Family & Community Health: The Journal of Health Promotion & Maintenance, 42*(1), 8–19.

Butler-Barnes, S. T., Leath, S., Williams, A., Byrd, C., Carter, R., & Chavous, T. M. (2018). Promoting resilience among African American girls: Racial identity as a protective actor. *Child Development, 89*(6), e552–e571.

Byrne, C. E., Accurso, E. C., Arnow, K. D., Lock, J., & Le Grange, D. (2015). An exploratory examination of patient and parental self-efficacy as predictors of weight gain in adolescents with anorexia nervosa. *International Journal of Eating Disorders, 48*, 883–888.

Cabrera, N. L., & Padilla, A. M. (2004). Entering and succeeding in the "Culture of College": The story of two Mexican heritage students. *Hispanic Journal of Behavioral Sciences, 26*, 152–170.

Cai, X., Cebollada, J., & Cortiñas, M. (2022). Self-report measure of dispositional flow experience in the video game context: Conceptualisation and scale development. *International Journal of Human-Computer Studies, 159*, 102–746

Calder, A. J., Novak, L. F., & Fowers, B. J. (2022). Limits of the concept of altruism: Individualism, Batson's theory of altruism, and a social realist alternative. Journal of Theoretical and Philosophical Psychology, *42*, 78–92.

Caldwell, C., & Floyd, L. (2014). High performance work systems: Building commitment to increase profitability. *Graziadio Business Review, 17*, AdvancedOnline.

Cameron, K. S., & Spreitzer, G. M. (2012). *The Oxford handbook of positive organizational scholarship*. Oxford University Press.

Cameron, K. S., Dutton, J., & Quinn, R. E. (Eds.). (2003). *Positive organizational scholarship: Foundations of a new discipline*. Berrett-Koeller.

Campbell, R. L., & Christopher, J. C. (1996a). Beyond formalism and altruism: The prospects for moral personality. *Developmental Review, 16*, 108–123.

Campbell, R. L., & Christopher, J. C. (1996b). Moral development theory: A critique of its Kantian presuppositions. *Developmental Review, 16*, 1–47.

Campbell, R. L., Christopher, J. C., & Bickhard, M. H. (2002). Self and values: An interactivist foundation for moral development. *Theory & Psychology, 12*, 795–822.

Campos, L. P. (2012). Cultivated cultures of courage with transactional analysis. *Transactional Analysis Journal, 42*, 209–219.

Cano-García, F. J., Sanduvete-Chaves, S., Chacón-Moscoso, S., Rodríguez-Franco, L., García-Martínez, J., Antuña-Bellerín, M. A., & Pérez-Gil, J. A. (2015). Factor structure of the Spanish version of the Life Orientation Test-Revised (LOT-R): Testing several models. *International Journal of Clinical and Health Psychology, 15*(2), 139–148.

Card, K. G. (2022). Collectivism, individualism and COVID-19 prevention: A cross sectional study of personality, culture and behaviour among Canadians. *Health Psychology and Behavioral Medicine, 10*, 415–438.

Carlo, G., & Randall, B. A. (2002). The development of a measure of prosocial behaviors for late adolescents. *Journal of Youth and Adolescence, 31*, 31–44.

Carr, A. (2004). *Positive psychology: The science of happiness and human strengths*. Brunner-Routledge.

Carr, A., Cullen, K., Keeney, C., Canning, C., Mooney, O., Chinseallaigh, E., & O'Dowd, A. (2021). Effectiveness of positive psychology interventions: A systematic review and meta-analysis. *The Journal of Positive Psychology, 16*, 749–769.

Carr, K., & Weir, P. L. (2017). A qualitative description of successful aging through different decades of older adulthood. *Aging & Mental Health, 21*, 1317–1325.

Carrere, S., & Gottman, J. (1999). Predicting divorce among newlyweds from the first three minutes of a marital conflict discussion. *Family Process, 38*, 293–301.

Carrington, P. (1998). *The book of meditation*. Element Books.

Carstensen, L. L. (2021). Socioemotional selectivity theory: The role of perceived endings in human motivation. *The Gerontologist, 61*, 1188–1196.

Carstensen, L. L., & Charles, S. T. (1998). Emotion in the second half of life. *Current Directions in Psychological Science, 7*, 144–149.

Carstensen, L. L., & Hershfield, H. E. (2021). Beyond stereotypes: Using socioemotional selectivity theory to improve messaging to older adults. *Current Directions in Psychological Science, 30*(4), 327–334.

Carstensen, L. L., Beals, M. E., & Deevy, M. (2015). Optimizing older workforces. In L. M. Finkelstein, D. M. Truxillo, F. Fraccaroli, & R. Kanfer (Eds.), *Facing the challenges of a multi-age workforce: A use-inspired approach* (pp. 330–335). Routledge/Taylor & Francis Group.

Carstensen, L. L., Pasupathi, M., Mayr, U., & Nesselroade, J. R. (2000). Emotional experience in everyday life across the adult life span. *Journal of Personality and Social Psychology, 79*, 644–655.

Carver, C. S., & Scheier, M. F. (1998). *On the self-regulation of behavior.* Cambridge University Press.

Carver, C. S., & Scheier, M. F. (1999). Optimism. In C. R. Snyder (Ed.), *Coping: The psychology of what works* (pp. 182–204). Oxford University Press.

Carver, C. S., & Scheier, M. F. (2002). Optimism. In C. R. Snyder & S. J. Lopez (Eds.), *The handbook of positive psychology* (pp. 231–243). Oxford University Press.

Carver, C. S., Scheier, M. F., & Segerstrom, S. C. (2010). Optimism. *Clinical psychology review, 30*(7), 879–889. https://doi.org/10.1016/j.cpr.2010.01.006

Carver, C. S., Pozo, C., Harris, S. D., Noriega, V., Scheier, M. F., Robinson, D. S., Ketcham, A. S., Moffat, F. L., & Clark, K. C. (1993). How coping mediates the effect of optimism on distress: A study of women with early stage breast cancer. *Journal of Personality and Social Psychology, 65*, 375–390.

Carver, C. S., Scheier, M. F., & Weintraub, J. K. (1989). Assessing coping strategies: A theoretically based approach. *Journal of Personality and Social Psychology, 56*, 267–283.

Carver, C. S., Scheier, M. F., Miller, C. J., & Fulford, D. (2009). Optimism. In S. J. Lopez & C. R. Snyder (Eds.), *Oxford handbook of positive psychology* (pp. 303–311). Oxford University Press.

Cassell, E. J. (2009). Compassion. In S. J. Lopez & C. R. Snyder (Eds.), *Oxford handbook of positive psychology* (pp. 393–403). Oxford University Press.

Cassell, E. J. (2016). The nature of suffering. In S. J. Younger & R. M. Arnold (Eds.), *Oxford handbook of ethics at the end of life* (pp. 216–226). Oxford University Press.

Cassell, E. J. (2021). Compassion. In C. R. Snyder, S. J. Lopez, L. M. Edwards, & S. C. Marques (Eds.), *Oxford handbook of positive psychology* (pp. 507–532). Oxford University Press.

Catalano, R. F., Berglund, M. L., Ryan, J. A. M., Lonczak, H. S., & Hawkins, J. D.. (2004). Positive youth development in the United States: Research findings on evaluations of positive youth development programs. *Prevention & Treatment, 591*(1), 98–124

Cavalhieri, K. E., & Wilcox, M. M. (2022). The compounded effects of classism and racism on mental health outcomes for African Americans. *Journal of Counseling Psychology, 69*, 111–120.

Ceballo, R., Alers-Rojas, F., Montoro, J. P., & Mora, A. S. (2020). Contextual stressors and the role of religion and spirituality in the mental health of Latino/a immigrant parents and youth. In G. C. Nagayama Hall (Ed.), *Mental and behavioral health of immigrants in the United States*. (pp. 135–155). Elsevier Academic Press.

Cederblad, M., Dahlin, L., Hagnell, O., & Hansson, K. (1995). Intelligence and temperament as protective factors for mental health: A cross-sectional and prospective epidemiological study. *European Archives of Psychiatry and Clinical Neuroscience, 245*, 11–19.

Centers for Disease Control and Prevention. (May, 2023). *COVID data tracker*. https://covid.cdc.gov/covid-data-tracker/#maps_percent-covid-deaths

Centers for Disease Control and Prevention. (2023). *Workplace health promotion*. https://www.cdc.gov/workplacehealthpromotion/index.html

Cerezuela, G. P., Tejero, P., Chóliz, M., Chisvert, M., & Monteagudo, M. J. (2004). Wertheim's hypothesis on 'highway hypnosis': Empirical evidence from a study on motorway and conventional road driving. *Accident Analysis & Prevention, 36*(6), 1045–1054.

Chamodraka, M., FitzpatricK, M. R., & Janzen, J. I. (2017). Hope as empowerment model: A client-based perspective on the process of hope development. *Journal of Positive Psychology, 12*, 232–245.

Chan, D. K. (1994). COLINDEX: A refinement of three collectivism measures. In U. Kim, H. C. Triandis, C. Kagitcibasi, S. Choi, & G. Yoon (Eds.), *Individualism and collectivism: Theory, method, and applications* (pp. 200–210). Sage.

Chan, D. W. (2010). Gratitude intervention and subjective well-being among Chinese school teachers in Hong Kong. *Educational Psychology, 30*, 139–153.

Chan, D. W. (2011). Burnout and life satisfaction: Does gratitude intervention make a difference among Chinese school teachers in Hong Kong? *Educational Psychology, 31*, 809–823.

Chan, K. K. S., & Lam, C. B. (2017). Trait mindfulness attenuates the adverse psychological impact of stigma on parents of children with autism spectrum disorder. *Mindfulness, 8*, 984–994.

Chan, K. S., Parikh, M. A., Thorpe, Jr., R. J. (2020). Health care disparities race-ethnic minority communities and populations: Does the availability of health care providers play a role? *Journal of Racial and Ethnic Health Disparities, 7*, 539–549.

Chancellor, J., & Lyubomirsky, S. (2011). Happiness and thrift: When (spending) less is (hedonically) more. *Journal of Consumer Psychology, 21*, 131–138.

Chang, E. C. (1996). Cultural differences in optimism, pessimism, and coping: Predictors of subsequent adjustment in Asian American and Caucasian American college students. *Journal of Counseling Psychology, 43*, 113–123.

Chang, E. C. (2001). A look at the coping strategies and styles of Asian Americans: Similar and different? In C. R. Snyder (Ed.), *Coping with stress: Effective people and processes* (pp. 222–239). Oxford University Press.

Chang, E. C., & Banks, K. H. (2007). The color and texture of hope: Some preliminary findings and implications for hope theory and counseling among diverse racial/ethnic groups. *Cultural Diversity and Ethnic Minority Psychology, 13*, 94–103.

Chang, E. C., Downey, C. A., Hirsch, J. K, & Lin, N. J. (2016). *Positive psychology in racial and ethnic groups: Theory, research, and practice*. American Psychological Association.

Chang, E. C., Sanna, L. J., Kim, J. M., & Srivastava, K. (2010). Optimistic and pessimistic bias in European Americans and Asian Americans: A preliminary look at distinguishing between predictions for physical and psychological health outcomes. *Journal of Cross-Cultural Psychology, 41*, 465–470.

Chang, E. C., Yi, S., Liu, J., Kamble, S. V., Zhang, Y., Shi, B., Ye, Y., Fang, Y., Cheng, K., Xu, J., Shen, J., Li, M., & Chang, O. D. (2020). Coping behaviors as predictors of hedonic well-being in Asian Indians: Does being optimistic still make a difference? *Journal of Happiness Studies, 21*(1), 289–304.

Chang, E. C., Yu, T., Jilani, Z., Chang, O. D., Du, Y., Hirsch, J. K., & Kamble, S. V. (2016). Happiness among HIV-positive Indian adults: Examining stress-related growth and coping as predictors of positive psychological adjustment. *Asian Journal of Psychiatry, 24*, 147–148.

Chara, P. J., Jr., & Eppright, W. J. (2012). The item-number distortion effect in rank order testing: An example using the Clifton Strengths Finder Inventory. *Psychological Reports, 111*(1), 219–227.

Charles, S. T., Mather, M., & Carstensen, L. L. (2003). Aging and emotional memory: The forgettable nature of negative images for older adults. *Journal of Experimental Psychology: General, 132,* 310–324.

Charrow, C. B. (2006). *Self-efficacy as a predictor of life satisfaction in older adults* (Doctoral dissertation). Retrieved from ProQuest (#AAI3200607)

Cheavens, J. S., & Gum, A. M. (2010). From here to where you want to be: Building the bridges with hope therapy in a case of major depression. In G. W. Burns (Ed.), *Happiness, healing, enhancement: Your casebook collection for applying positive psychology in therapy* (pp. 51–63). Wiley.

Cheavens, J. S., Feldman, D. B., Gum, A., Michael, S. T., & Snyder, C. R. (2006). Hope therapy in a community sample: A pilot investigation. *Social Indicators Research, 77,* 61–78.

Cheavens, J., Feldman, D., Woodward, J. T., & Snyder, C. R. (2006). Hope in cognitive therapies: Working with client strengths. *Journal of Cognitive Psychotherapy: An International Quarterly, 20,* 135–145.

Chekroud, S. R., Gueorguieva, R., Zheutlin, A. B., Paulus, M., Krumholz, H. M., & Krystal, J. H. (2018). Association between physical exercise and mental health in 1.2 million individuals in the USA between 2011 and 2015: A cross-sectional study. *Lancet Psychiatry, 5,* 739–746.

Chen, G., Gully, S. M., & Eden, D. (2001). Validation of a new general self-efficacy scale. *Organizational Research Methods, 4*(1), 62–83.

Chen, H.-T., & Li, X. (2017). The contribution of mobile social media to social capital and psychological well-being. *Computers in Human Behavior, 75,* 958–965.

Chen, L.-M., Wu, P.-J., Cheng, Y.-Y., & Hsueh, H. (2011). A qualitative inquiry of wisdom development: Educators' perspectives. *The International Journal of Aging & Human Development, 72,* 171–187.

Cheng, C., & Huang, X. (2017). An exploration of courage in Chinese individuals. *Journal of Positive Psychology, 12,* 141–150.

Cheng, D. H. (2000). *On Lao Tzu.* Wadsworth.

Cheraghi, F., Kadivar, P., Ardelt, M., Asgari, A., & Farzad, V. (2015). Gender as a moderator of the relation between age cohort and three-dimensional wisdom in Iranian culture. *The International Journal of Aging & Human Development, 81,* 3–26.

Cherney, A., & Fitzgerald, R. (2016). Finding and keeping a job: The value and meaning of employment for parolees. *International Journal of Offender Therapy and Comparative Criminology, 60,* 21–37.

Cherng, S. H. Y. (2017). If they think I can: Teacher bias and youth of color expectations and achievement. *Social Science Research, 66,* 170–186.

Cheron, G. (2016). How to measure the psychological "flow?" A neuroscience perspective. *Frontiers in Psychology, 7,* 1823.

Cheung, R. (2014, January). *Energizing and transforming organizations through positive organizational initiatives.* Plenary session given at the Asian Pacific Conference on Applied Positive Psychology, Hong Kong.

Cheung, C-K, & Chow, E. O-W. (2020). Contribution of wisdom to well-being in Chinese older adults. *Applied Research in Quality of Life, 15,* 913–930.

Chiang, W.-T. (2012). The suppression of emotional expression in interpersonal context. *Bulletin of Educational Psychology, 43,* 657–680.

Chiarelli, T. M., & Batistoni, S. S. T. (2021). An analysis of socioemotional selectivity theory in the context of older adults' use of Facebook. *Educational Gerontology, 47*(1), 13–24.

Chickering, A. W. (1969). *Education and identity.* Jossey-Bass.

Chiesa, A. A., Calati, R., & Serretti, A. (2011). Does mindfulness training improve cognitive abilities? A systematic review of neuropsychological findings. *Clinical Psychology Review, 31,* 449–464.

Chiesa, A. A., Serretti, A., & Jakobsen, J. (2013). Mindfulness: Top-down or bottom-up emotion regulation strategy? *Clinical Psychology Review, 33,* 82–96.

Chiesi, F., Lau, C., Marunic, G., Sanchez-Ruiz, M.-J., Plouffe, R. A., Topa, G., Yan, G., & Saklofske, D. H. (2020). Emotional intelligence in young women from five cultures: A TEIQue-SF invariance study using the omnicultural composite approach inside the IRT framework. *Personality and Individual Differences, 164,* 110128

Childers, A. F., & Taylor, D. G. (2021). Making data collection and analysis fun, fast, and flexible with classroom stats. *PRIMUS: Problems, Resources, and Issues in Mathematics Undergraduate Studies, 31*, 91–98.

Chimiklis, A. L., Dahl, V., Spears, A. P., Goss, K., Fogarty, K., & Chacko, A. (2018). Yoga, mindfulness, and meditation interventions for youth with ADHD: Systematic review and meta-analysis. *Journal of Child and Family Studies, 27*(10), 3155–3168

Cho, H., Guo, Y., & Torelli, C. (2021). Collectivism fosters preventive behaviors to contain the spread of COVID-19: Implications for social marketing. *Psychology & Marketing, 39*, 694–700.

Chockalingam, M., & Norton, P. J. (2019). Facing fear-provoking stimuli: The role of courage and influence of task-importance. *The Journal of Positive Psychology, 14*(5), 603–613.

Choi, E., & Chentsova-Dutton, Y. E. (2017). The relationship between momentary emotions and well-being across European Americans, Hispanic Americans, and Asian Americans. *Cognition and Emotion, 31*, 1277–1285.

Choi, S., Clark, P. G., Gutierrez, V., & Runion, C. (2022). Racial microaggressions and Latinxs' well-being: A systematic review. *Journal of Ethnic a& Cultural Diversity in Social Work: Innovation in Theory*, Research, & Practice, *31*, 16–27.

Choi, Y., Karremans, J. C., & Barendregt, H. (2012). The happy face of mindfulness: Mindfulness medication is associations with perceptions of happiness as rated by outside observers. *Journal of Positive Psychology, 7*, 30–35.

Chopra, D. (2015). *The seven spiritual laws of success: A pocketbook guide to fulfilling your dreams*. Amber-Allen.

Choubisa, R., & Singh, K. (2011). Psychometrics encompassing VIA-IS: A comparative cross cultural analytical and referential reading. *Journal of the Indian Academy of Applied Psychology, 37*, 325–332.

Chow, T., Javan, T., Ros, T., & Frewen, P. (2017). EEG dynamics of mindfulness meditation versus alpha neurofeedback: A sham-controlled study. *Mindfulness, 8*, 572–584.

Chowdhury, M. R. (20 Feb 2019). *19 top positive psychology interventions + how to apply them*. https://positivepsychology.com/positive-psychology-interventions/

Christopher, J. C. (1999). Situating psychological well-being: Exploring the cultural roots of its theory and research. *Journal of Counseling & Development, 77*, 141–152.

Christopher, J. C. (2001). Culture and psychotherapy: Toward a hermeneutic approach. *Psychotherapy: Theory, Research, Practice, and Training, 38*, 115–128.

Christopher, J. C. (2003, October). *The good in positive psychology*. Paper presented at the International Positive Psychology Summit, Washington, DC.

Christopher, J. C. (2004). Moral visions of developmental psychology. In B. Slife, F. C. Richardson, & J. Reber (Eds.), *Critical thinking about psychology: Hidden assumptions and plausible alternatives*. American Psychological Association.

Christopher, J. C. (2005). Situating positive psychology. *Naming and Nurturing, 17*, 3–4.

Christopher, J. C., & Howe, K. (2014). Future directions for a more multiculturally competent (and humble) positive psychology. In J. T. Pedrotti & L. M. Edwards (Eds.), *Perspectives on the intersection of multiculturalism and positive psychology*. Springer Science + Business Media.

Christopher, J. C., Nelson, T., & Nelson, M. D. (2004). Culture and character education: Problems of interpretation in a multicultural society. *Journal of Theoretical and Philosophical Psychology, 23*, 81–101.

Chu, A., Chan, T. W. C., & So, M. K. P. (2022). Learning from work-from-home issues during the COVID-19 pandemic: Balance speaks louder than words. PLoS ONE, *17*, e0261969.

Chung, C., & Lin, Z. (2012). A cross-cultural examination of the positivity effect in memory: United States vs. China. *The International Journal of Aging & Human Development, 75*, 31–44.

Cialdini, R. B. (2005). What's the best secret device for engaging student interest? The answer is in the title. *Journal of Social and Clinical Psychology, 24*, 22–29.

Cialdini, R. B., Schaller, M., Houlihan, D., Arps, K., Fultz, J., & Beaman, A. L. (1987). Empathy-based helping: Is it selflessly or selfishly motivated? *Journal of Personality and Social Psychology, 52*, 749–758.

Ciarrocchi, J. W., Dy-Liacco, G. S., & Deneke, E. (2008). Gods or rituals? Relational faith, spiritual discontent, and religious practices as predictors of hope and optimism. *Journal of Positive Psychology, 3*, 120–136.

Ciocanel, O., Power, K., Eriksen, A., & Gillings, K. (2017). Effectiveness of positive youth development interventions: A meta-analysis of randomized controlled trials. *Journal of Youth and Adolescence, 46*, 483–504.

Clancy, L., & Gubbala, S.(2021, November 23). *What makes life meaningful? Globally, answers sometimes vary by age*. Pew Research Center.

Clauss-Ehlers, C. S. (2008). Sociocultural factors, resilience, and coping: Support for a culturally sensitive measure of resilience. *Journal of Applied Developmental Psychology, 29*, 197–212.

Clayton, V. (1975). Erikson's theory of human development as it applies to the aged: Wisdom as contradictory cognition. *Human Development, 18*, 119–128.

Clayton, V., & Birren, J. E. (1980). The development of wisdom across the life span: A reexamination of an ancient topic. In P. B. Baltes & O. G. Brim (Eds.), *Life-span development and behavior* (Vol. 3, pp. 103–135). Academic Press.

Cleare, S., Gumley, A., & O'Connor, R. C. (2019). Self-compassion, self-forgiveness, suicidal ideation, and self-harm: A systematic review. *Clinical Psychology & Psychotherapy, 26*(5), 511–530.

Clifton, D. O., & Anderson, E. (2002). *StrengthsQuest: Discover and develop your strengths in academics, career, and beyond*. Gallup Organization.

Clifton, D. O., & Harter, J. K. (2003). Strengths investment. In K. S. Cameron, J. E. Dutton, & R. E. Quinn (Eds.), *Positive organizational scholarship* (pp. 111–121). Berrett-Koehler.

Clifton, D. O., & Nelson, P. (1992). *Soar with your strengths*. Delacorte Press.

Clouston, S. A. P., Natale, G., & Link, B. G. (2021). Socioeconomic inequalities in the spread of coronavirus-19 in the United States: An examination of the emergence of social inequalities. *Social Science & Medicine, 268*, 1–6.

Coffman, S. (1996). Parents' struggles to rebuild family life after Hurricane Andrew. *Issues in Mental Health Nursing, 17*, 353–367.

Cohen, A. B., & Johnson, K. A. (2017). The relation between religion and well-being. *Applied Research in Quality of Life, 12*, 533–547.

Cohn, M. A., & Fredrickson, B. L. (2009). Positive emotions. In S. J. Lopez & C. R. Snyder (Eds.), *Oxford handbook of positive psychology* (pp. 13–24). Oxford University Press.

Colby, A., & Damon, W. (1995). The development of extraordinary moral commitment. In M. Killen & D. Hart (Eds.), *Morality in everyday life: Developmental perspectives* (pp. 342–370). Cambridge University Press.

Colby, D. A., & Shifren, K. (2013). Optimism, mental health, and quality of life: A study among breast cancer patients. *Psychology, Health & Medicine, 18*, 10–20.

Collins, J. (2001). *Good to great*. HarperCollins.

Collins, K. A., & Dozois, D. J. A. (2008). What are the active ingredients in preventative interventions for depression? *Clinical Psychology: Science and Practice, 15*, 313–330.

Compton, W., Smith, M., Cornish, K., & Qualls, D. (1996). Factor structure of mental health measures. *Journal of Personality and Social Psychology, 76*, 406–413.

Connor, K. M., & Davidson, J. R. T. (2003). Development of a new resilience scale: The Connor-Davidson Resilience Scale (CD-RISC). *Depression and Anxiety, 18*(2), 76–82.

Conoley, C. W., & Scheel, J. J. (2018). *Goal focused positive psychotherapy: A strength-based approach*. Oxford University Press.

Consortium for Research on Emotional Intelligence in Organizations (2022). *Measures*. https://www.eiconsortium.org/measures/measures.html

Constantine, M., & Sue, D. W. (2006). Factors contributing to optimal human functioning of people of color in the United States. *The Counseling Psychologist, 34*, 228–244.

Cooper, A. A., & Conklin, L. R. (2015). Dropout from individual psychotherapy for major depression: A meta-analysis of randomized clinical trials. *Clinical Psychological Review, 40*, 57–65.

Corral Verdugo, V. (2012). The positive psychology of sustainability. *Environment, Development and Sustainability, 14*(5), 651–666. https://doi.org/10.1007/s10668-012-9346-8

Cosco, T. D., Stephan, B. C. M., Brayne, C., & Muniz, G. (2017). Education and successful aging trajectories: A longitudinal population-based latent variable modelling analysis. *Canadian Journal of Aging, 36*, 427–434.

Costa, A., & Barnhofer, T. (2016). Turning towards or turning away: A comparison of mindfulness meditation and guided imagery relaxation in patients with acute depression. *Behavioural and Cognitive Psychotherapy, 44*, 410–419.

Costa, P. T., & McCrae, R. R. (1992). The five-factor model of personality and its relevance to personality disorders. *Journal of Personality Disorders, 6*(4), 343–359. https://doi.org/10.1521/pedi.1992.6.4.343

Costa, P. T., & McCrae, R. R. (1988). Personality in adulthood: A six-year longitudinal study of self-reports and spouse ratings on the NEO Personality Inventory. *Journal of Personality and Social Psychology, 54*, 853–863.

Cougle, J. R., & Grubaugh, A. L. (2022). Do psychosocial treatment outcomes vary by race or ethnicity? A review of meta-analyses. *Clinical Psychology Review, 96*, 3–7

Cousins, N. (1991). *Head first: The biology of hope and the healing power of the human spirit*. Penguin.

Cragun, D., Cragun, R. T., Nathan, B., Sumerau, J. E., & Nowakowski, A. C. (2016). Do religiosity and spirituality really matter for social, mental, and physical health? A tale of two samples. *Sociological Spectrum, 36*, 359–377.

Crandall, A., Cheung, A., Young, A., & Hooper, A. P. (2019). Theory-based predictors of mindfulness meditation mobile app usage: A survey and cohort study. *JMIR Mhealth Uhealth, 7*(3), e10794.

Crocker, J., Canevello, A., & Lewis, K. A. (2017). Romantic relationships in the ecosystem: Compassionate goals, nonzero-sum beliefs, and change in relationship quality. *Journal of Personality and Social Psychology, 112*, 58.

Cross, W. E. (1971). The Negro to Black conversion experience: Toward a psychology of Black liberation. *Black World, 20*, 13–27.

Crump, A., Jenkins, K., Bethell, E. J., Ferris, C. P., Kabboush, H., Weller, J., & Arnott, G. (2021). Optimism and pasture access in dairy cows. *Scientific Reports, 11*(1), 4882.

Cseh, G. M., Phillips, L. H., & Pearson, D. G. (2016). Mental and perceptual feedback in the development of creative flow. *Consciousness and Cognition, 42*, 150–161.

Csikszentmihalyi, M. (1990). *Flow: The psychology of optimal experience*. Harper & Row.

Csikszentmihalyi, M. (1997). *Finding flow*. Basic Books.

Csikszentmihalyi, M. (2000). *Beyond boredom and anxiety*. Jossey-Bass. (Original work published 1975)

Csikszentmihalyi, M. (2015). *The systems model of creativity: The collected works of Mihalyi Csikszentmihalyi*. Springer.

Csikszentmihalyi, M., & Rathunde, K. (1990). The psychology of wisdom: An evolutionary interpretation. In R. J. Sternberg (Ed.), *Wisdom: Its nature, origins, and development* (pp. 25–51). Cambridge University Press.

Csikszentmihalyi, M., & Robinson, R. (1990). *The art of seeing*. J. Paul Getty Museum and the Getty Center for Education in the Arts.

Csikszentmihalyi, M., Rathunde, K., & Whalen, S. (1993). *Talented teenagers*. Cambridge University Press.

Cunningham, G. B. (2009). The moderating effect of diversity strategy on the relationship between racial diversity and organizational performance. *Journal of Applied Social Psychology, 39*, 1445–1460.

Curbow, B., Somerfield, M. R., Baker, F., Wingard, J. R., & Legro, M. W. (1993). Personal changes, dispositional optimism, and psychological adjustment to bone marrow transplantation. *Journal of Behavioral Medicine, 16*, 423–443.

Currier, J. M., Drescher, K. D., Holland, J. M., Lisman, R., & Foy, D. W. (2016). Spirituality, forgiveness, and quality of life: Testing a mediational model with military veterans with PTSD. *The International Journal for the Psychology of Religion, 26*(2), 167–179.

Currier, J. M., Fox, J., Vieten, C., Pearce, M., & Oxhandler, H. K. (2022). Enhancing competencies for the ethical integration of religion and spirituality in psychological services. *Psychological Services.*

Currier, J. M., Holland, J. M., & Drescher, K. D. (2015). Spirituality factors in the prediction of outcomes of PTSD treatment for U.S. military veterans. *Journal of Traumatic Stress, 28*(1), 57–64. https://doi.org/10.1002/jts.21978

Curry, L. A., Snyder, C. R., Cook, D. L., Ruby, B. C., & Rehm, M. (1997). The role of hope in student-athlete academic and sport achievement. *Journal of Personality and Social Psychology, 73*, 1257–1267.

Curry, O.S., Rowland, L. A. Van Lissa, C. J., Ziotowitz, S., McAlaney, J., & Whitehouse, H. (2018). Happy to help? A systematic review and meta-analysis of the effects of performing acts of kindness on the well-being of the actor. *Journal of Experimental Social Psychology, 76*, 320–329.

Cushman, P. (1990). Why the self is empty: Toward a historically situated psychology. *American Psychologist, 45*, 599–611.

Cutuli, J. J., Gillham, J. E., Chaplin, T. M., Reivich, K. J., Seligman, M. E. P., Gallop, R. J., Abenavoli, R. M., & Freres, D. R. (2013). Preventing adolescents' externalizing and internalizing symptoms: Effects of the Penn Resiliency Program. *The International Journal of Emotional Education, 5*(2), 67–79.

Cutuli, J. J., Herbers, J. E., Masten, A. S., & Reed, M.-G. J. (2021). Resilience in development. In C. R. Snyder, S. J. Lopez, L. M. Edwards, & S. C. Marques (Eds.), *The Oxford handbook of positive psychology., 3rd ed.* (2021-20328-014; pp. 171–188). Oxford University Press.

Dahlbeck, D. T., & Lightsey, O. R., Jr. (2008). Generalized self-efficacy, coping, and self-esteem as predictors of psychological adjustment among children with disabilities or chronic illnesses. *Children's Health Care, 37*, 293–315.

Dahlsgaard, K., Peterson, C., & Seligman, M. E. P. (2005). Shared virtue: The convergences of valued human strengths. *Review of General Psychology, 9*, 203–213.

Dalmida, S., Holstad, M., DiLorio, C., & Laderman, G. (2012). The meaning and use of spirituality among African American women living with HIV/AIDS. *Western Journal of Nursing Research, 34*, 736–765.

Damasio, A. R. (2002). A note on the neurobiology of emotions. In S. G. Post, L. G. Underwood, J. P. Schloss, & W. B. Hurlbut (Eds.), *Altruism & altruistic love: Science, philosophy, & religion in dialogue* (pp. 264–271). Oxford University Press.

Danielson, A. G., Samdal, O., Hetland, J., & Wold, B. (2009). School-related social support and students' perceived life satisfaction. *Journal of Educational Research, 102*, 303–320.

Danner, D. D., Snowdon, D. A., & Friesen, W. V. (2001). Positive emotions in early life and longevity: Findings from the nun study. *Journal of Personality and Social Psychology, 80*, 804–813.

Davids, E. L., Roman, N. V., & Kerchhoff, L. J. (2017). Adolescent goals and aspirations in search of psychological well-being: From the perspective of self-determination theory. *South African Journal of Psychology, 47*, 121–132.

Davis, D. E., DeBlaere, C., Hook, J. N., Burnette, J., Van Tongeren, D. R., Rice, K. G., & Worthington, E. L. (2015). Intergroup forgiveness of race-related offenses. *Journal of Counseling Psychology, 62*, 402–412.

Davis, D. E., Owen, J., Hook, J. N., Rivera, D. P., Choe, El, Van Tongeren, D. R., Worthington, Jr., E. L., and Placeres, V. (2018). The multicultural orientation framework: A narrative review. *Psychotherapy, 55*, 89–100.

Davis, L., & Wu, S. (2019). The taste for status in international comparison. *Journal of Happiness Studies, 21*, 2237–2256.

Davis, M. H., Luce, C., & Kraus, S. J. (1994). The heritability of characteristics associated with dispositional empathy. *Journal of Personality, 62*, 369–391.

Davis, T. J., Morris, M., & Drake, M. M. (2016). The moderation effect of mindfulness on the relationship between adult attachment and wellbeing. *Personality and Individual Differences, 96*, 115–121.

De Cássia Marinelli, S., Bartholomeu, D., Caliatto, S. G., & de Greggi Sassi, A. (2009). Children's self-efficacy scale: Initial psychometric studies. *Journal of Psychoeducational Assessment*, *27*, 145–156.

de Manzano, O., Cervenka, S. Juacaite, A., Hellenäs, O., Farde, L., & Ullén, F. (2013). Individual differences in the proneness to have flow experiences are linked to dopamine receptor availability in the dorsal striatum. *NeuroImage*, *67*, 1–6.

de Moura, P. J. Jr., & Porto Bellini, C. G. (2020). The measurement of flow and social flow at work: A 30-year systematic review of the literature. *Personnel Review*, *49*(2), 537–570.

de Munck, V. C., Korotayev, A., de Munck, J., & Khaltourina, D. (2011). Cross-cultural analysis of models of romantic love among U.S. residents, Russians, and Lithuanians. *The Journal of Comparative Social Science*, *45*, 128–154.

Destine, S. L., & Destine, S. V. (2021). Black joy as emotional resistance. A collaborative auto-ethnography of two Black Queer married academics as contingent labor. In I. Ruffin, and C. Powell (Eds.), *The emotional self at work in higher education* (pp. 195–214). Information Science Reference/IGI Global.

de Tocqueville, A. (2003). *Democracy in America*. Penguin. (Original work published 1835)

Deichert, N. T., Fekete, E. M., & Craven, M. (2021). Gratitude enhances the beneficial effects of social support on psychological well-being. *The Journal of Positive Psychology*, *16*(2), 168–177.

Dein, S., Cook, C. H., & Koenig, H. (2012). Religion, spirituality, and mental health: Current controversies and future decisions. *Journal of Nervous and Mental Disease*, *200*, 852–855.

Dejonckheere, E., Mestdagh, M. Verdonck, S., Lafit, G., Ceulemans, E., Bastian, B., & Kalokerinos, E. K. (2021). The relation between positive and negative affect becomes more negative in response to personally relevant events. *Emotion*, *21*, 326–336.

Del Giudice, M. (2011). Sex differences in romantic attachment: A meta-analysis. *Personality and Social Psychology Bulletin*, *37*(2), 193–214.

Delle Fave, A., & Massimini, F. (1988). Modernization and the changing contexts of flow in work and leisure. In M. Csikszentmihalyi & I. Csikszentmihalyi (Eds.), *Optimal experience* (pp. 193–213). Cambridge University Press.

Delle Fave, A., & Massimini, F. (1992). The experience sampling method and the measurement of clinical change: A case of anxiety disorder. In M. deVries (Ed.), *The experience of psychopathology* (pp. 280–289). Cambridge University Press.

Delle Fave, A., Brdar, I., Vella-Brodrick, D., & Wissing, M. P. (2013). Religion, spirituality, and well-being across nations: The eudaemonic and hedonic happiness investigation. In H. H. Knoop & A. Delle Fave (Eds.), *Well-being and cultures: Perspectives from positive psychology* (pp. 117–134). Springer Science + Business Media.

DeMaris, A. (2018). Marriage advantage in subjective well-being: Causal effect or unmeasured heterogeneity? *Marriage & Family Review*, *54*, 335–350.

Demir, M. (2021). Perceived playfulness in same-sex friendships and happiness. *Current Psychology: A Journal for Diverse Perspectives of Diverse Psychological Issues*, *40*, 2052–2066.

Demir, M., & Davidson, I. (2012). Toward a better understanding of the relationship between friendship and happiness: Perceived responses to capitalization attempts, feelings of mattering, and satisfaction of basic psychological needs in same-sex best friendships as predictors of happiness. *Journal of Happiness Studies*, *14*, 525–550.

Deng, W., & Gadassi Polack, R. (2021). Predicting negative and positive affect during COVID-19: A daily diary study in youths. *Journal of Research on Adolescence*, *31*, 500–516.

Depue, R. (1996). A neurobiological framework for the structure of personality and emotions: Implications for personality disorder. In J. Clarkin & M. Lenzenweger (Eds.), *Major theories of personality* (pp. 347–390). Guilford.

de Vignemont, F., & Singer, T. (2006). The empathic grain: How, when and why? *Trends in Cognitive Sciences*, *10*, 435–441.

DeVellis, R. F. (2017). *Scale development: Theory and applications* (4th ed.). Sage.

deWaal, F. B. M., & Pokorny, J. J. (2005). Primate conflict

and its relations to human forgiveness. In E. L. Worthington (Ed.), *Handbook of forgiveness* (pp. 17–32). Taylor & Francis.

DeWit, D. J., DuBois, D., Erdem, G., Larose, S., Lipman, E. L., & Spencer, R. (2016). Mentoring relationship closures in Big Brothers Big Sisters Community Mentoring Programs: Patterns and associated risk factors. *American Journal of Community Psychology, 57*(1-2), 60–72. https://doi.org/10.1002/ajcp.12023

DiAngelo, R. (2011). White fragility. *International Journal of Critical Pedagogy, 3*, 54–70.

Diaz, T., & Bui, N. H. (2017). Subjective well-being in Mexican and Mexican American women: The role of acculturation, ethnic identity, gender roles, and perceived social support. *Journal of Happiness Studies, 18*, 607–624.

Dickens, L., & DeSteno, D. (2016). The grateful are patient: Heightened daily gratitude is associated with attenuated temporal discounting. *Emotion, 16*, 421–425.

Diener, E. (1984). Subjective well-being. *Psychological Bulletin, 95*, 542–575.

Diener, E. (2000). Subjective well-being: The science of happiness and a proposal for a national index. *American Psychologist, 55*, 34–43.

Diener, E. (2013). The remarkable changes in the science of well-being. *Perspective on Psychological Science, 8*, 663–666.

Diener, E., & Biswas-Diener, R. (2002). Will money increase subjective well-being? *Social Indicators Research, 57*, 119–169.

Diener, E., & Larsen, R. J. (1984). Temporal stability and cross-situational consistency of affective, behavioral, and cognitive responses. *Journal of Personality and Social Psychology, 47*, 871–883.

Diener, E., & Lucas, R. (1999). Personality and subjective well-being. In D. Kahneman, E. Diener, & N. Schwartz (Eds.), *Well-being: The foundations of hedonic psychology* (pp. 213–229). Russell Sage.

Diener, E., & Seligman, M. E. P. (2002). Very happy people. *Psychological Science, 13*, 81–84.

Diener, E., Diener, M., & Diener, C. (1995). Factors predicting the well-being of nations. *Journal of Personality and Social Psychology, 69*, 653–663.

Diener, E., Emmons, R. A., Larsen, R. J., & Griffin, S. (1985). The Satisfaction With Life Scale. *Journal of Personality Assessment, 49*, 71–75.

Diener, E., Lucas, R. E., & Oishi, S. (2002). Subjective well-being: The science of happiness and life satisfaction. In C. R. Snyder & S. J. Lopez (Eds.), *The handbook of positive psychology* (pp. 63–74). Oxford University Press.

Diener, E., Lucas, R., & Scollon, C.N. (2006). Beyond the hedonic treadmill: Revising the adaptation theory of well-being. *American Psychologist, 61*, 305–314.

Diener, E., Ng, W., Harter, J., & Arora, R. (2010). Wealth and happiness across the world: Material prosperity predicts life evaluation, whereas psychosocial prosperity predicts positive feeling. *Journal of Personality and Social Psychology, 99*, 52–61.

Diener, E., Oishi, S., & Lucas, R. E. (2009). Subjective well-being: The science of happiness and life satisfaction. In S. J. Lopez & C. R. Snyder (Eds.), *Oxford handbook of positive psychology* (pp. 187–194). Oxford University Press.

Dienstbier, R. A. (1989). Arousal and physiological toughness: Implication for mental and physical health. *Psychological Review, 96*, 84–100.

Dienstbier, R. A. (2015). *Building resistance to stress and aging: The toughness model.* Palgrave Macmillan.

Diliberti, M. K., Schwartz, H. L., & Grant, D. (2021). *Stress topped the reasons why public school teachers quit even before COVID-10.* RAND Corporation. https://www.rand.org/pubs/research_reports/RRA1121-2.html.

Di Maggio, I., Santilli, S., Nota, L. (2019). Stories of courage in a group of adults with substance use disorder. *Addictive Behaviors Reports, 10*, 1–6.

DiMenichi, B. C., Ceceli, A. O., Bhanji, J. P., & Tricomi, E. (2019). Effects of Expressive writing on neural processing during learning. *Frontiers in Human Neuroscience, 13*.

DiMenichi, B. C., Lempert, K. M., Bejjani, C., & Tricomi, E. (2018). Writing about past failures attenuates cortisol responses and sustained attention deficits following psychosocial stress. *Frontiers in Behavioral Neuroscience, 12*.

Dimock, M., & Wike, R. (13, Nov 2020). America is exceptional in the nature of its political divide. https://www.pewresearch.org/fact-tank/2020/11/13/america-is-exceptional-in-the-nature-of-its-political-divide/

DiPierro, M., Fite, P. J., & Johnson-Motoyama, M. (2017). The role of religion and spirituality in the association between hope and anxiety in a sample of Latino youth. *Child & Youth Care Forum*, *47*, 101–114.

Dixson, D. D., Worrell, F. C., & Mello, Z. (2017). Profiles of hope: How clusters of hope relate to school variables. *Learning and Individual Differences*, *59*, 55–64.

Don, B. P., Fredrickson, G. L., & Algoe, S. B. (2022). Enjoying the sweet moments: Does approach motivation upwardly enhance reactivity to positive interpersonal processes? *Journal of Personality and Social Psychology*, *122*, 1022–1055.

Doran, R., & Hanss, D. (2022). Expectation of others' cooperation, efficacy beliefs, and willingness to sacrifice personal interests for the environment. *Scandinavian Journal of Psychology*, *63*(4), 357–364.

Doty, J. L., Davis, L., & Arditti, J. A. (2017). Cascading resilience: Leverage points in promoting parent and child well-being. *Journal of Family Theory & Review*, *9*, 111–126.

Douglas, C., Bateson, M., Walsh, C., Bédué, A., & Edwards, S. A. (2012). Environmental enrichment induces optimistic cognitive biases in pigs. *Applied Animal Behaviour Science*, *139*(1–2), 65–73.

Douglass, R. P., Duffy, R. D., & Autin, K. L. (2016). Living a calling, nationality, and life satisfaction: A moderated multiple mediator model. *Journal of Career Assessment*, *24*, 253–269.

Dovidio, J. F., Allen, J. L., & Schroeder, D. A. (1990). The specificity of empathy-induced helping: Evidence for altruism motivation. *Journal of Personality and Social Psychology*, *59*, 249–260.

Dovidio, J. F., Piliavin, J. A., Shroeder D. A., & Penner, L. (2006). *The social psychology of prosocial behavior*. Lawrence Erlbaum.

Dowling, M., & Rickwood, D. (2016). Exploring hope and expectations in the youth mental health online counselling environment. *Computers in Human Behavior*, *55*, 62–68.

Duan, C., & Sager, K. (2021). Understanding empathy: Current state and future research challenges (pp. 533–550). In C. R. Snyder, S. J. Lopez, L. M. Edwards, & S. C. Marques (Eds.), *The Oxford handbook of positive psychology*. Oxford University Press.

Duan, W., & Ho, S. M. Y. (2017). Does being mindful of your character strengths enhance psychological wellbeing? A longitudinal mediation analysis. *Journal of Happiness Studies*. Advance online publication.

Duckworth, A. (2016). *Grit: The power of passion and perseverance* (2016-30309-000). Scribner/Simon & Schuster.

Duckworth, A. L., Quirk, A., Gallop, R., Hoyle, R. H., Kelly, D. R., & Matthews, M. D. (2019). Cognitive and noncognitive predictors of success. *PNAS Proceedings of the National Academy of Sciences of the United States of America*, *116*(47), 23499–23504.

Dugan, K. A., & Fraley, R. C. (2022). The roles of parental and partner attachment working models in romantic relationships. *Journal of Social and Personal Relationships*.

Dunbar, A. (2022). Black lives and black research matter: How our collective emotions continue to drive a movement. *Journal of Research on Adolescence*, *32*, 307–313.

Duncan, L. G., Coatsworth, J. D., & Greenberg, M. T. (2009). A model of mindful parenting: Implications for parent–child relationships and prevention research. *Clinical Child Family Psychology Review*, *12*, 255–270.

Dunn, E. W., Aknin, L. B., & Norton, M. I. (2014). Prosocial spending and happiness: Using money to benefit others pays off. *Current Directions in Psychological Science*, *23*, 41–47.

Dunning, D., Tudor, K., Radley, L., Dalrymple, N., Funk, J., Vainre, M., Ford, T., Montero-Marin, J., Kuyken, W., & Dalgleish, T. (2022). Do mindfulness-based programmes improve the cognitive skills, behaviour and mental health of children and adolescents? An updated meta-analysis of randomised controlled trials. *Evidence Based Mental Health*, *25*(3), 135.

Dutton, J. E., Debebe, G., & Wrzesniewski, A. (2016). Being valued and devalued at work: A social valuing perspective. In B. A. Bechky & K. D. Elsbach (Eds.), *Qualitative organizational research: Best papers from the Davis Conference on Qualitative Research* (pp. 9–51). Charlotte, NC: IAP INformation Age Publishing.

Dvorkin, K. (2015). Working with men in therapy. *Group, 39*, 241–250.

Dweck, C. S. (1999). *Self theories: Their role in motivation, personality, and development*. Psychology Press.

Dwiwardani, C., Hill, P. C., Bollinger, R. A., Marks, L. E., Steele, J. R., Doolin, H. N., & Davis, D. E. (2014). Virtues develop from a secure base: Attachment and resilience as predictors of humility, gratitude, and forgiveness. *Journal of Psychology and Theology, 42*, 83–90.

Easterbrook, J. A. (1959). The effects of emotion on cue utilization and the organization of behavior. *Psychological Review, 66*, 183–200.

Eaves, E. R., Nichter, M., & Ritenbaugh, C. (2016). Ways of hoping: Navigating the paradox of hope and despair in chronic pain. *Culture, Medicine, and Psychiatry, 40*, 35–58.

Ebberwein, C. A., Krieshok, T. S., Ulven, J. S., & Prosser, E. C. (2004). Voices in transition: Lessons on career adaptability. *Career Development Quarterly, 52*, 292–308.

Eckstein, M. P., Das, K., Pham, B. T., Peterson, M. F., Abbey, C. K., Sy, J. L., & Giesbrecht, B. (2012). Neural decoding of collective wisdom with multi-brain computing. *NeuroImage, 59*, 94–108.

Edara, I. R. (2015). Mediating role of individualism-collectivism in spirituality's relation to motivational forgiveness. *Asia Pacific Journal of Counseling and Psychotherapy, 6*, 28–40.

Edmondson, R. (2012). Intergenerational relations in the West of Ireland and sociocultural approaches to wisdom. *Journal of Family Issues, 33*, 76–98.

Eichas, K., Albrecht, R. E., Garcia, A. J., Ritchie, R. A., Varela, A., Garcia, A., Rinaldi, R., Wang, R., Montgomery, M. J., Silverman, W. K., Jaccard, J., & Kurtines, W. M. (2010). Mediators of positive youth development intervention change: Promoting change in positive and problem outcomes? *Child & Youth Care Forum, 39*, 211–237.

Eichas, K., Montgomery, M. J., Meca, A., & Kurtines, W. M. (2017). Empowering marginalized youth: A self-transformative intervention for promoting positive youth development. *Child Development, 88*, 1115–1124.

Emmons, R. A. (1992). Abstract versus concrete goals: Personal striving level, physical illness, and psychological well-being. *Journal of Personality and Social Psychology, 62*, 292–300.

Emmons, R. A., & McCullough, M. E. (2003). Counting blessings versus burdens: Experimental studies of gratitude and subjective well-being. *Journal of Personality and Social Psychology, 84*, 377–389.

Emmons, R. A., & Mishra, A. (2011). Why gratitude enhances well-being: What we know, what we need to know. In K. M. Sheldon, T. B. Kashdan, & M. F. Steger (Eds.), *Designing positive psychology: Taking stock and moving forward* (pp. 248–262). Oxford University Press.

Emmons, R. A., Cheung, C., & Tehrani, K. (1998). Assessing spirituality through personal goals: Implications for research on religion and subjective well-being. *Social Indicators Research, 45*, 391–422.

Endrighi, R., Hamer, M., & Steptoe, A. (2011). Associations of trait optimism with diurnal neuroendocrine activity, cortisol responses to mental stress, and subjective stress measures in healthy men and women. *Psychosomatic Medicine, 73*, 672–678.

Enko, J., Behnke, M. Dziekan, M., Kosakowski, M., & Kaczmarek, L. D. (2021). Gratitude texting touches the heart: Challenge/threat cardiovascular responses to gratitude expression predict self-initiation of gratitude interventions in daily life. *Journal of Happiness Studies: An Interdisciplinary Forum on Subjective Well-Being, 22*, 49–69.

Enright, R. D. (1996). Counseling within the forgiveness triad: On forgiving, receiving forgiveness, and self-forgiveness. *Counseling and Values, 40*, 107–126.

Enright, R. D. (2000). *Helping clients forgive: An empirical guide for resolving anger and restoring hope*. American Psychological Association.

Enright, R. D., & Zell, R. L. (1989). Problems encountered when we forgive another. *Journal of Psychology and Christianity, 8*, 52–60.

Enright, R. D., Freedman, S., & Rique, J. (1998). The

psychology of interpersonal forgiveness. In R. D. Enright & J. North (Eds.), *Exploring forgiveness* (pp. 46–62). University of Wisconsin Press.

Enright, R. D., Rique, J., Lustosa, R., Song, J. Y., Komoski, M. C., Batool, I., Bolt, D., Sung, H., Huang, S. T. T., Park, Y., Leer-Salvesen, P. E., Andrade, T., Naeem, A., Viray, J., & Costuna, E. (2022). Validating the Enright Forgiveness Inventory - 30 (EFI-30): International studies. *European Journal of Psychological Assessment, 38*(2), 113–123.

Erickson, R. C., Post, R. D., & Paige, A. B. (1975). Hope as a psychiatric variable. *Journal of Clinical Psychology, 31*, 324–330.

Erikson, E. H. (1950). *Childhood and society.* Norton.

Erikson, E. H. (1959). *Identity and the life cycle.* International Universities Press.

Erikson, E. H. (1963). *Childhood and society* (2nd ed.). Norton.

Erikson, E. H. (1964). *Insight and responsibility.* Norton.

Erikson, E. H. (1982). *The life cycle completed: A review.* Norton.

Ersner-Hershfield, H., Mikels, J. A., Sullivan, S. J., & Carstensen, L. L. (2008). Poignancy: Mixed emotional experience in the face of meaningful endings. *Journal of Personality and Social Psychology, 94*, 158–167.

Erthal, F., Bastos, A., Vilete, L., Oliveira, L., Pereira, M., Mendlowicz, M., Volchan, E., & Figueira, I. (2021). Unveiling the neural underpinnings of optimism: A systematic review. *Cognitive, Affective, & Behavioral Neuroscience, 21*(5), 895–916.

Espigares, F., Abad-Tortosa, D., Varela, S. A. M., Ferreira, M. G., & Oliveira, R. F. (2021). Short telomeres drive pessimistic judgement bias in zebrafish. *Biology Letters, 17*(3), 20200745.

Espinosa, A., Anglin, D. M., & Pandit, S. (2022). Emotional self-efficacy informs the interrelation between discrimination, ethnic identity and psychotic-like experiences. *Emotion, 22*(6), 1347–1358.

Estrada, C. A., Isen, A. M., & Young, M. J. (1997). Positive affect facilitates integration of information and decreases anchoring in reasoning among physicians. *Organizational Behavior and Human Decision Processes, 72*, 117–135.

Evans, A. B., Banerjee, M., Meyer, R., Aldana, A., Foust, M., & Rowley, S. (2012). Racial socialization as a mechanism for positive development among African American youth. *Child Development Perspectives, 6*, 251–257.

Everett, J. A. C., Faber, N. S., & Crockett, M. J. (2015). Preferences and beliefs in ingroup favoritism. *Frontiers in Behavioral Neuroscience, 9*, ArtID: 15.

Exline, J. J., & Baumeister, R. F. (2000). Expressing forgiveness and repentance: Benefits and barriers. In M. E. McCullough (Ed.), *Forgiveness: Theory, research, and practice* (pp. 133–155). Guilford.

Ey, S., Hadley, W., Allen, D. N., Palmer, S., Klosky, J., Deptula, D., Thomas, J., & Cohen, R. (2004). A new measure of children's optimism and pessimism: The youth life orientation test. *Journal of Child Psychology and Psychiatry, 46*, 548–558.

Eysenck, H. J. (1952). The effects of psychotherapy. *Journal of Consulting and Clinical Psychology, 16*, 319–324.

Fabio, A. D. (2014). Student Courage Scale: Psychometric properties of the scale to measure courage in students. *Counseling: Giornale Italiano di Ricerca e Applicazioni, 7*, 327–334.

Fabius, C. D. (2016). Toward an integration of narrative identity, generativity, and storytelling in African American elders. *Journal of Black Studies, 47*, 423–434.

Fagin-Jones, S., & Midlarsky, E. (2007). Courageous altruism: Personal and situational correlates of rescue during the Holocaust. *Journal of Positive Psychology 2*, 136–147.

Falcone, G., & Jerram, M. (2018). Brain activity in mindfulness depends on experience: A meta-analysis of fMRI studies. *Mindfulness, 9*(5), 1319–1329.

Farah, C. E. (1968). *Islam: Beliefs and observances.* Baron's Woodbury Press.

Farley, A., Kennedy-Behr, A., & Brown, T. (2021). An investigation into the relationship between playfulness and well-being in Australian adults: An exploratory study. *OTJR: Occupation, Participation and Health, 41*, 56–64.

Farrell, A. K., Waters, T. E. A., Young, E. S., Englund, M. M., Carlson, E. E., Roisman, G. I.,

& Simpson, J. A. (2019). Early maternal sensitivity, attachment security in young adulthood, and cardiometabolic risk at midlife. *Attachment & human development, 21*(1), 70–86.

Fawzy, A., Osman, A. I., Doran, J., & Rooney, D. W. (2020). Strategies for mitigation of climate change: A review. *Environmental Chemistry Letters, 18*, 2069–2094.

Federal Bureau of Investigation. (2020). *Hate crime statistics*. https://www.justice.gov/crs/highlights/2020-hate-crimes-statistics

Feher, A., Yan, G., Saklofske, D. H., Plouffe, R. A., & Gao, Y. (2019). An investigation of the psychometric properties of the Chinese Trait Emotional Intelligence Questionnaire Short Form (Chinese TEIQue-SF). *Frontiers in Psychology, 10*.

Fehr, B. (1993). How do I love thee? Let me consult my prototype. In S. Duck (Ed.), *Individuals in relationships* (pp. 87–120). Sage. https://doi.org/10.4135/9781483326283.n4

Fehr, B. (1994). Prototype-based assessment of laypeople's views of love. *Personal Relationships, 1*(4), 309–331. https://doi.org/10.1111/j.1475-6811.1994.tb00068.x

Fehr, R., & Gelfand, M. J. (2010). When apologies work: How matching apology components to victims' self-construals facilitates forgiveness. *Organizational Behavior and Human Decision Processes, 113*, 37–50.

Feinberg, M., & Willer, R. (2015). From gulf to bridge: When do moral arguments facilitate political influence? *Personality and Social Psychology Bulletin, 41*, 1665–81.

Feinberg, M., & Willer, R. (2019). Moral reframing: A technique for effective and persuasive communication across political divides. *Social and Personality Psychology Compass, 13(12)*, e12501.

Feinnberg, M., Fang, R., Liu, S., & Peng, K. (2019). A world of blame to go around: Cross-cultural determinants of responsibility and punishment judgments. *Personality and Social Psychology Bulletin, 45*, 634–651.

Feiss, R., Dolinger, S. B., Merritt, M., Reiche, E., Martin, K., Yanes, J. A., Thomas, C. M, & Pangelinan, M. (2019). A systematic review and meta-analysis of school-based stress, anxiety, and depression prevention programs for adolescents. *Journal of Youth and Adolescence, 48*, 1668–1685.

Feldman, D. B., & Dreher, D. E. (2012). Can hope be changed in 90 minutes? Testing the efficacy of a single-session goal-pursuit intervention for college students. *Journal of Happiness Studies, 13*, 745–759.

Feldman, D. B., & Kubota, M. (2015). Hope, self-efficacy, optimism, and academic achievement: Distinguishing constructs and levels of specificity in predicting college grade-point average. *Learning and Individual Differences, 37*, 210–216.

Feldman, D. B., & Snyder, C. R. (2005). Hope and meaning in life. *Journal of Social and Clinical Psychology, 24*, 401–421.

Feldman, D. B., Rand, K. L., & Kahle-Wrobleski, K. (2009). Hope and goal attachment: Testing a basic prediction of hope theory. *Journal of Social and Clinical Psychology, 28*, 479–497.

FeldmanHall, O., Dalgleish, T., Evans, D., & Mobbs, D. (2015). Empathic concern drives costly altruism. *ScienceDirect, 105*, 347–356.

Ferguson, A. M., Cameron, C. D., & Inzlicht, M. (2021). When does empathy feel good? *Current Opinion in Behavioral Sciences, 39*, 125–129.

Ferguson, M. A., Schaper, F. L. W. V. J., Cohen, A., Siddiqi, S., Merrill, S. M., Nielsen, J. A., Grafman, J., Urgesi, C., Fabbro, F., & Fox, M. D. (2022). A neural circuit for spirituality and religiosity derived from patients with brain lesions. *Aging and Neurodegeneration, 91*(4), 380–388.

Ferguson, S. J., Taylor, A. J., & McMahon, C. (2017). Hope for the future and avoidance of the present: Associations with well-being in older adults. *Journal of Happiness Studies: An Interdisciplinary Forum on Subjective Well-Being, 18*(5), 1485–1506. https://doi.org/10.1007/s10902-016-9787-0

Fernandez-Rio, J., Sanz, N., Fernandez-Cando, J., & Santos, L. (2017). Impact of a sustained Cooperative Learning intervention on student motivation. *Physical Education and Sport Pedagogy, 22*, 89–105.

Ferrary, M., & Déo, S. (2023). Gender diversity and firm performance: When diversity at middle management and staff levels matter. *The International Journal of Human Resource Management, 34*, 2797–2831.

Fetchenhauer, D., Groothuis, T., & Pradel, J. (2010). Not only states but traits—Humans can identify permanent altruistic dispositions in 20s. *Evolution and Human Behavior, 31*, 80–86.

Fincham, F. (2000). Optimism and the family. In J. Gillham (Ed.), *The science of optimism and hope* (pp. 271–298). Templeton Foundation Press.

Fincham, F. D., & May, R. W. (2020). Divine, interpersonal and self-forgiveness: Independently related to depressive symptoms? *The Journal of Positive Psychology, 15*(4), 448–454.

Fincham, F. D., May, R. W., & Sanchez-Gonzalez, M. A. (2015). Forgiveness and cardiovascular functioning in married couples. *Couple and Family Psychology: Research and Practice, 4*, 39–48.

Finfgeld, D. L. (1995). Becoming and being courageous in the chronically ill elderly. *Issues in Mental Health Nursing, 16*, 1–11.

Finfgeld, D. L. (1998). Courage in middle-aged adults with long-term health concerns. *Canadian Journal of Nursing Research, 30*(1), 153–169.

Fitzpatrick, K. M. (2017). How positive is their future? Assessing the role of optimism and social support in understanding mental health symptomatology among homeless adults. *Stress and Health, 33*, 92–101.

Fletcher, G. J. O., Simpson, J. A., Campbell, L., & Overall, N. C. (2015). Pair-bonding, romantic love, and evolution: The curious case of Homo sapiens. *Perspectives on Psychological Science, 10*, 20–36.

Fletcher, Jr., E. C., Carroll, T., Hines, E. M., Moore, III, J. L., & Ford, D. Y. (2022). Layering programs: Career academies as a plausible intervention to increase the representation of pre collegiate Black males in STEM. In A. G, Robins, L. Knibbs, T. N. Ingram, M. N., Weaver, Jr., and A. A. Hilton (Eds.). *Young, gifted, and missing: The underrepresentation of African American males in science, technology, engineering, and mathematics disciplines* (pp. 23–36). Emerald Publishing Vol 25.

Flett, J. A. M., Hayne, H., Riordan, B. C., Thompson, L. M., & Conner, T. S. (2019). Mobile mindfulness meditation: A randomised controlled trial of the effect of two popular apps on mental health. *Mindfulness, 10*(5), 863–876.

Flores, W., Laurent, É., & Ruger, J. P. (2020). Well-being as a pathway to equity.In A. L. Plough (Ed.). *Well-being: Expanding the definition of progress: Insights from practitioners, researchers, and innovators from around the globe* (pp. 3–12). Oxford University Press.

Fontaine, K. R., Manstead, A. S. R., & Wagner, H. (1993). Optimism, perceived control over stress, and coping. *European Journal of Psychology, 7*, 267–281.

Forbes, C., Clark, L. F., & Diep, H. (2016). Positive attributes and risk behaviors in young transgender women. *Psychology of Sexual Orientation and Gender Diversity, 3*, 129–134.

Fordyce, M. W. (1977). Development of a program to increase personal happiness. *Journal of Counseling Psychology, 24*, 511–520.

Forgeard, M. J. C., & Seligman, M. E. P. (2012). Seeing the glass half full: A review of the causes and consequences of optimism. *Pratiques Psychologiques, 18*, 107–120.

Forsyth, D. R. (1999). *Group dynamics* (3rd ed.). Brooks/ Cole.

Forsyth, D. R., & Corazzini, J. G. (2000). Groups as change agents. In C. R. Snyder & R. E. Ingram (Eds.), *Handbook of psychological change: Psychotherapy processes and practices for the 21st century* (pp. 309–336). New York: Wiley.

Fouad, N. A. (2002). Cross-cultural differences in vocational interests: Between-group differences on the Strong Interest Inventory. *Journal of Counseling Psychology, 49*, 282–289.

Four-day workweek creates new volunteers in Utah. (2009, July 10). *USA Today*. http://usatoday30.usatoday.com/news/nation/2009-07-10-utah-volunteers_N.htm? csp=15

Fox, G. R., Kaplan, J., Dama sio, H., & Damasio, A. (2015). Neural correlates of gratitude. *Frontiers in Psychology, 6*, ArtID: 1491.

Franco, Z. E., Blau, K., & Zimbardo, P. G. (2011). Heroism: A conceptual analysis and differentiation between heroic action and altruism. *Review of General Psychology, 15*, 99–113.

Frank, J. D. (1968). The role of hope in psychotherapy. *International Journal of Psychiatry, 5*, 383–395.

Frank, J. D. (1973). *Persuasion and healing* (Rev. ed.). Johns Hopkins University Press.

Frank, J. D. (1975). The faith that heals. *Johns Hopkins Medical Journal, 137,* 127–131.

Frankl, V. (1966). What is meant by meaning? *Journal of Existentialism, 7,* 21–28.

Frankl, V. (1992). *Man's search for meaning: An introduction to logotherapy* (I. Lasch, Trans.). Beacon.

Franz, C. E., McClelland, D. C., Weinberger, J., & Peterson, C. (1994). Parenting antecedents of adult adjustment: A longitudinal study. In C. Perris, W. A. Arrindell, & M. Eisemann (Eds.), *Parenting and psychopathology* (pp. 127–144). Academic Press.

Fredricks, J. A., & Simpkins, S. D. (2012). Promoting positive youth development through organized after-school activities: Taking a closer look at participation of ethnic minority youth. *Child Development Perspectives, 6,* 280–287.

Fredrickson, B. L. (2000). Cultivating positive emotions to optimize health and well-being. *Prevention and Treatment, 3,* 1–25.

Fredrickson, B. L. (2001). The role of positive emotions in positive psychology: The broaden-and-build theory of positive emotions. *American Psychologist, 56,* 218–226.

Fredrickson, B. L. (2002). Positive emotions. In C. R. Snyder & S. J. Lopez (Eds.), *The handbook of positive psychology* (pp. 120–134). Oxford University Press.

Fredrickson, B. L. (2016). The eudaimonics of positive emotions. In J. Vittersø (Ed.), *Handbook of eudaimonic well-being* (pp. 183–190). Springer International.

Fredrickson, B. L., & Joiner, T. (2002). Positive emotions trigger upward spirals toward emotional well-being. *Psychological Science, 13,* 172–175.

Fredrickson, B. L., & Losada, M. F. (2005). Positive affect and the complex dynamics of human flourishing. *American Psychologist, 60,* 678–686.

Fredrickson, B. L., Mancuso, R. A., Branigan, C., & Tugade, M. M. (2000). The undoing effects of positive emotions. *Motivation and Emotion, 24,* 237–258.

Freeman, M. A., & Bordia, P. (2001). Assessing alternative models of individualism and collectivism: A confirmatory factor analysis. *European Journal of Personality, 15,* 105–121.

Freud, S. (1936). *The problem of anxiety* (H. A. Bunker, Trans.). Norton. (Original work published 1926)

Friedman, T. L. (2005). *The world is flat: A brief history of the 21st century.* Farrar, Straus & Giroux.

Frijda, N. H. (1999). Emotions and hedonic experience. In D. Kahneman, E. Diener, & N. Schwartz (Eds.), *Well-being: The foundations of hedonic psychology* (pp. 190–210). Russell Sage.

Frise, N. R., & McMinn, M. R. (2010). Forgiveness and reconciliation: The differing perspectives of psychologists and Christian theologians. *Journal of Psychology and Theology, 38,* 83–90.

Froh J. J., Fan J., Emmons R. A., Bono G., Huebner E. S., Watkins P. (2011). Measuring gratitude in youth: Assessing the psychometric properties of adult gratitude scales in children and adolescents. *Psychological Assessment, 23,* 311–324

Froh, J. J., Kashdan, T. B., Ozimkowski, K. M., & Miller, N. (2009). Who benefits the most from a gratitude intervention in children and adolescents? Examining positive affects as a moderator. *Journal of Positive Psychology, 4,* 408–422.

Froh, J. J., Yurkewicz, C., Kashdan, T. B. (2009). Gratitude and subjective well-being in early adolescence: Examining gender differences. *Journal of Adolescence, 32,* 633–650.

Fu, M., & Vong, S. (2016). Social connectedness can lead to happiness: Positive psychology and Asian Americans. In E. C. Chang, C. A. Downey, J. K. Hirsch, & N. J. Lin (Eds.), *Positive psychology in racial and ethnic groups: Theory, research, and practice* (pp. 217–233). American Psychological Association.

Fulcher, M., & Coyle, E. F. (2011). Breadwinner and caregiver: A cross-sectional analysis of children's and emerging adults' visions of their future family roles. *British Journal of Developmental Psychology, 29,* 330–346.

Fung, H. H., Isaacowitz, D. M., Lu, A. Y., Wadlinger, H. A., Goren, D., & Wilson, H. R. (2008). Age-related positivity enhancement is not universal: Older Chinese look away from positive stimuli. *Psychology and Aging, 23,* 440–446.

Gailliot, M. T. (2012). Happiness as surplus or freely

available energy. *Psychology, 3*, 702–712.

Gal, D., & Rucker, D. D. (2021). Act boldly: Important life decisions, courage, and the motivated pursuit of risk. *Journal of Personality and Social Psychology, 120*(6), 1607–1620.

Gál, É., È˜tefan, S., & Cristea, I. A. (2021). The efficacy of mindfulness meditation apps in enhancing users' well-being and mental health related outcomes: A meta-analysis of randomized controlled trials. *Journal of Affective Disorders, 279*, 131–142.

Galen, L. W. (2012). Does religious belief promote prosociality? A critical examination. *Psychological Bulletin, 138*, 876–906.

Galinha, I. C., Garcia-Martin, M. Á., Gomes, C., & Oishi, S. (2016). Criteria for happiness among people living in extreme poverty in Maputo, Mozambique. *International Perspectives in Psychology: Research, Practice, Consultation, 5*, 67–90.

Galiana, L., Oliver, A., Sancho, P., & Tomás, J. M. (2015). Dimensionality and validation of the Dispositional Hope Scale in a Spanish sample. *Social Indicators Research, 120*(1), 297–308.

Gallagher, M. W., & Lopez, S. J. (2018). *Oxford handbook of hope*. Oxford University Press.

Gallagher, M. W., Long, L. J., & Phillips, C. A. (2020). Hope, optimism, self-efficacy, and posttraumatic stress disorder: A meta-analytic review of the protective effects of positive expectancies. *Journal of Clinical Psychology, 76*(3), 329–355.

Gallagher, M. W., Long, L. J., Tsai, W., Stanton, A. L., & Lu, Q. (2018). The unexpected impact of expressive writing on posttraumatic stress and growth in Chinese American breast cancer survivors. *Journal of Clinical Psychology, 74*(10), 1673–1686.

Gallagher, M. W., Lopez, S. J., & Pressman, S. D. (2013). Optimism is universal: Exploring the presence and benefits of optimism in a representative sample of the world. *Journal of Personality, 81*(5), 429–440.

Gallagher, M. W., Marques, S. C., & Lopez, S. J. (2017). Hope and the academic trajectory of college students. *Journal of Happiness Studies, 18*, 341–352.

Gallup. (2017). *CliftonStrengths for students*. Author.

Gallup Organization. (1995). *Disciplining children in America: Survey of attitude and behavior of parents* (Project registration #104438). Author.

Gallup Poll Monthly. (1996, November). Gallup Organization.

Gambin, M., & Swieçicka, M. (2012). Construction and validation of self-efficacy scale for early school-aged children. *European Journal of Developmental Psychology, 9*, 723–729.

Gao, G. (2001). Intimacy, passion, and commitment in Chinese and US American romantic relationships. *International Journal of Intercultural Relations, 25*, 329–342.

Garanzini, S., Yee, A., Gottman, J., Gottman, J., Cole, C., Preciado, M., & Jasculca, C. (2017). Results of Gottman method couples therapy with gay and lesbian couples. *Journal of Marital and Family Therapy, 43*(4), 674–684.

García-Poole, C., Byrne, S., & Rodrigo, M. J. (2019). How do communities intervene with adolescents at psychosocial risk? A systematic review of positive development programs. *Children and Youth Services Review, 99*, 194–209.

Garczynski, A. M., Waldrop, J. S., Rupprecht, E. A., & Grawitch, M. J. (2013). Differentiation between work and nonwork self-aspects as a predictor of presenteeism and engagement: Cross-cultural differences. *Journal of Occupational Health Psychology, 18*, 417–429.

Gareis, E., & Wilkins, R. (2011). Love expression in the United States and Germany. *International Journal of Intercultural Relations, 35*, 391–411.

Garmezy, N. (1985). Stress-resistant children: The search for protective factors. In J. E. Stevenson (Ed.), *Recent research in developmental psychopathology: Journal of Child Psychology and Psychiatry Book Supplement 4* (pp. 213–233). Pergamon.

Garrett, M. T., & Garrett, J. T. (2002). "Ayeli": Centering technique based on Cherokee spiritual traditions. *Counseling and Values, 46*, 149–158.

Garrett, M. T., Brubaker, M. D., Rivera, E. T., Gregory, D. E., & Williams, C. R. (2011). Ayeli: A Native American–based group centering technique for college students. In T. Fitch, & J. L. Marshall (Eds.), *Group work and outreach plans for college counselors*, (pp. 259–264). American Counseling Association.

Garrett-Walker, J. N. J., & Torres, V. M. (2017). Negative religious rhetoric in the lives of Black cisgender queer emerging adult men: A qualitative analysis. *Journal of Homosexuality, 64*, 1816–1831.

Garrosa, E., Blanco-Donoso, L. M., Moreno-Jiménez, J. E., McGrath, E., Cooper-Thomas, H. D., & Ladstätter, F. (2022). Energy loss after daily role stress and work incivility: Caring for oneself with emotional wellness. *Journal of Happiness Studies: An Interdisciplinary Forum on Subjective Well-Being.*

Garssen, B., Visser, A., & de Jager Meezenbroek, E. (2016). Examining whether spirituality predicts subjective well-being: How to avoid tautology. *Psychology of Religion and Spirituality, 8*, 141–148.

Garssen, B., Visser, A., & Pool, G. (2021). Does spirituality or religion positively affect mental health? Meta-analysis of longitudinal studies. *The International Journal for the Psychology of Religion, 31*(1), 4–20.

Gary, M. S., Yang, M. M., Yetton, P. W, & Sterman, J. D. (2017). Stretch goals and the distribution of organizational performance. *Organization Science, 28*, 395–410.

Gassen, J., Nowak, T. J., Henderson, A. D., Weaver, S. P., Baker, E. J., & Muehlenbein, M. P. (2021). Unrealistic optimism and risk for COVID-19 Disease. *Frontiers in Psychology, 12.*

Gearhart, M. (2022). Empowerment and collective efficacy: Insights for community-based crime prevention. *Journal of Human Behavior in the Social Environment.*

Geiger, P. J., Morey, J. N., & Segerstrom, S. C. (2017). Beliefs about savoring in older adulthood: Aging and perceived health affect temporal components of perceived savoring ability. *Personality and Individual Differences, 105*, 164–169.

Geng, L., Zhang, L., & Zhang, D. (2011). Improving spatial abilities through mindfulness: Effects on the mental rotation task. *Consciousness and Cognition: An International Journal, 20*, 801–806.

George, L. S., & Park, C. L. (2017). Does spirituality confer meaning in life among heart failure patients and cancer survivors. *Psychology of Religion and Spirituality, 9*, 131–136.

Gerber, M. K., Nadeem, L., Sakari Clough, P. J., Perry, J. L., Pühse, U., Elliott, C. A., Holsboer-Trachsler, E.,, & Brand, S. (2013). Are adolescents with high mental toughness levels more resilient against stress? *Journal of the International Society for the Investigation of Stress, 29*, 164–171.

Gergen, K. J. (1985). The social constructionist movement in modern psychology. *American Psychologist, 40*, 266–275.

Getzels, J. W., & Csikszentmihalyi, M. (1976). *The creative vision.* Wiley.

Ghaemmaghami, P., Allemand, M., & Martin, M. (2011). Forgiveness in younger, middle-aged, and older adults: Age and gender matters. *Journal of Adult Development, 18*, 192–203.

Ghawadra, S. F., Abdullah, K. L., Choo, W. Y., & Phang, C. K. (2019). Mindfulness-based stress reduction for psychological distress among nurses: A systematic review. *Journal of Clinical Nursing, 28*(21–22), 3747–3758.

Ghorbani, N., Watson, P. J., Madani, M., & Chen, Z. J. (2016). Muslim experiential religiousness: Spirituality relationships with psychological and religious adjustment in Iran. *Journal of Spirituality in Mental Health, 18*, 300–315.

Gilbertson-White, S., Campbell, G., Ward, S., Sherwood, P., & Donovan, H. (2017). Coping with pain severity, distress, and consequences in women with ovarian cancer. *Cancer Nursing, 40*, 117–123.

Gillham, J. (2000). *The science of optimism and hope: Research essays in honor of Martin EP Seligman.* https://works.swarthmore.edu/fac-psychology/542

Gillham, J., & Reivich, K. (2004). Cultivating optimism in childhood and adolescence. *Annals of the American Academy of Political and Social Science, 591*, 146–163.

Gilman, R., Huebner, S., & Buckman, M. (2008). Positive schooling. In S. J. Lopez (Ed.), *Positive psychology exploring the best in people.* Greenwood.

Ginevra, M. C., Sgaramella, T. M., Ferrari, L., Nota, L., Santilli, S., & Soresi, S. (2017). Visions about future: A new scale assessing optimism, pessimism, and hope in adolescents. *International Journal for Educational and Vocational Guidance, 17*, 187–210.

Given, C. W., Stommel, M., Given, B., Osuch, J., Kurtz, M.

E., & Kurtz, J. C. (1993). The influence of cancer patients' symptoms and functional states on patients' depression and family caregivers' reaction and depression. *Health Psychology, 12*, 277–285.

Gladwell, M. (2005). *Blink: The power of thinking without thinking*. Little, Brown.

Glass, J., Simon, R. W., & Andersson, M. A. (2016). Parenthood and happiness: Effects of work-family reconciliation policies in 22 OECD countries. *American Journal of Sociology, 122*, 886–929.

Glass, T. A., Seeman, T. E., Herzog, A. R., Kahn, R., & Berkman, L. F. (1995). Change in productive activity in late adulthood: MacArthur Studies of Successful Aging. *Journal of Gerontology, 50*, 65–76.

Glessner, K., Rockinson-Szapkiw, A. J., & Lopez, M. L. (2017). "Yes, I can": Testing an intervention to increase middle school students' college and career self-efficacy. *The Career Development Quarterly, 65*, 315–325.

Glomb, T. M., Bhave, D. P, Miner, A. G., & Wall, M. (2011). Doing good, feeling good: Examining the role of organizational citizenship behaviors in changing mood. *Personnel Psychology, 64*, 191–223.

Gloria, C. T., & Steinhardt, M. A. (2016). Relationships among positive emotions, coping, resilience and mental health. *Stress and Health: Journal of the International Society for the Investigation of Stress, 32*, 145–156.

Glück, J. (2020). Intelligence and wisdom. In R. J. Sternberg (Ed.), *The Cambridge handbook of intelligence* (pp. 1140–1158). Cambridge University Press.

Glück, J., & Bluck, S. (2011). Laypeople's conceptions of wisdom and its development: Cognitive and integrative views. *The Journals of Gerontology: Series B: Psychological Sciences and Social Sciences, 66B*, 321–324.

Glück, J., Bischof, B., & Siebenhüner, L. (2012). "Knows what is good and bad," "Can teach you things," "Does lots of crosswords": Children's knowledge about wisdom. *European Journal of Developmental Psychology, 9*, 582–598.

Glück, J., Strasser, I., & Bluck, S. (2009). Gender differences in implicit theories of wisdom. *Research in Human Development, 6*, 27–44.

Glück, J., & Weststrate, N. M. (2022). The wisdom researchers and the elephant: An integrative model of wise behavior. *Personality and Social Psychology Review, 26*, 342–374.

Godfrey, J. J. (1987). *A philosophy of human hope*. Martinus Nijhoff.

Goffman, I. (1963). *Stigma: Notes on the management of spoiled identity*. Prentice Hall.

Goldblatt, C., & Watson, A. J. (2012). The runaway greenhouse: Implications for future climate change, geoengineering, and planetary atmospheres. Philosophical transactions of the Royal Society of London. *Series A: Mathematical, physical, and engineering sciences, 370*, 4197–4216.

Goldner, L., Edelstein, M., & Habshush, Y. (2015). A glance at children's family drawings: Associations with children's and parents' hope and attributional style. *The Arts in Psychotherapy, 43*, 7–15.

Goldstein, R. (2010, January 11). Miep Gies, protector of Anne Frank, dies at 100. *The New York Times*.

Goleman, D. (1995). *Emotional intelligence: Why it can matter more than IQ*. Bantam.

Goleman, D. (1998). *Working with emotional intelligence*. Bloomsbury.

Gomez, R., McLaren, S., Sharp, M., Smith, C., Hearn, K., & Turner, L. (2015). Evaluation of the bifactor structure of the Dispositional Hope Scale. *Journal of Personality Assessment, 97*(2), 191–199.

Gong, H., Ni, C.-X., Liu, Y.-Z., Zhang, Y., Su, W.-J., Lian, Y.-J., Peng, W., & Jiang, C.-L. (2016). Mindfulness meditation for insomnia: A meta-analysis of randomized controlled trials. *Journal of Psychosomatic Research, 89*, 1–6.

Gonzalez-Mendez, R., Ramírez-Santana, G., & Hamby, S. (2021). Analyzing Spanish adolescents through the lens of the resilience portfolio model. *Journal of Interpersonal Violence, 36*(9-10), 4472–4489. https://doi.org/10.1177/0886260518790600

Goodwin, R., Graham, J., & Diekmann, K. A. (2020). Good intentions aren't good enough: Moral courage in opposing sexual harassment. *Journal of Experimental Social Psychology, 86*, Article 103894.

Gordon, A. K., Musher-Eizenman, D. R., Holub, S. C., & Dalrymple, J. (2004). What are children thankful for? An archival analysis of gratitude before and after the attacks of September 11. *Applied Developmental Psychology, 25*, 541–553.

Gordon, A. M., Impett, E. A., Kogan, A., Oveis, C., & Keltner, D. (2012). To have and to hold: Gratitude promotes relationship maintenance in intimate bonds. *Journal of Personality and Social Psychology, 103*, 257–274.

Gordon, K. C., & Baucom, D. H. (1998). Understanding betrayals in marriage: A synthesized model of forgiveness. *Family Process, 37*, 425–450.

Gordon, K. C., Baucom, D. H., & Snyder, D. K. (2005). Forgiveness in couples: Divorce, infidelity, and couples therapy. In E. Worthington (Ed.), *Handbook of forgiveness* (pp. 407–422). Routledge.

Gordon, K. C., Burton, S., & Porter, L. (2004). The intentions of women in domestic violence shelters to return to partners: Does forgiveness play a role? *Journal of Family Psychology, 18*, 331–338.

Gorrese, A., & Ruggieri, R. (2012). Peer attachment: A meta-analytic review of gender and age differences and associations with parent attachment. *Journal of Youth and Adolescence, 41*(5), 650–672.

Gottman, J. M. (1994). *Why marriages succeed or fail and how you can make yours last*. Simon & Schuster.

Gottman, J. M. (1999). *The seven principles for making marriage work*. Crown.

Gottman, J. M. (2015). *Principia amoris: The new science of love*. Routledge/Taylor & Francis Group.

Gottman, J. M., Driver, J., & Tabares, A. (2002). Building the sound marital house: An empirically derived couple therapy. In N. S. Jacobsen & A. S. Gurman (Eds.), *Clinical handbook of couple therapy* (3rd ed., pp. 373–399). Guilford.

Gottman, J. M., Gottman, J. S., Cole, C., & Preciado, M. (2020). Gay, lesbian, and heterosexual couples about to begin couples therapy: An online relationship assessment of 40,681 couples. *Journal of Marital and Family Therapy, 46*(2), 218–239.

Gottman, J. M., Levenson, R. W., Gross, J., Frederickson, B. L., McCoy, K., Rosenthal, L., Ruef, A., & Yoshimoto, D. (2003). Correlates of gay and lesbian couples' relationship satisfaction and relationship dissolution. *Journal of Homosexuality, 45*(1), 23–43.

Gottman, J. M., Murray, J. D., Swanson, C., Tyson, R., & Swanson, K. R. (2003). *The mathematics of marriage: Dynamic nonlinear models*. MIT Press.

Gottschalk, L. (1974). A hope scale applicable to verbal samples. *Archives of General Psychiatry, 30*, 779–785.

Gould, S. J. (1996). *The mismeasure of man*. Norton.

Govindji, R., & Linley, P. A. (2007). Strengths use, self-concordance and well-being: Implications for strengths, coaching, and coaching psychologists. *International Coaching Psychology Review, 2*, 143–153.

Graham, J. M. (2008). Self-expansion and flow in couples' momentary experiences: An experience sampling study. *Journal of Personality and Social Psychology, 95*, 679–694.

Graupmann, V., & Frey, D. (2014). Bad examples: How thinking about blind obedience can induce responsibility and courage. *Journal of Peace Psychology, 20*, 124–134.

Gray, J. S., & Dunlop, W. L. (2019). Structure and measurement invariance of adult romantic attachment. *Journal of Personality Assessment, 101*(2), 171–180.

Gray, S. A., Emmons, R. A., & Morrison, A. (2001, August). *Distinguishing gratitude from indebtedness in affect and action tendencies*. Poster session presented at the annual meeting of the American Psychological Association, San Francisco.

Gray-Little, B., & Kaplan, D. (2000). Race and ethnicity in psychotherapy research. In C. R. Snyder & R. E. Ingram (Eds.), *Handbook of psychological change: Psychotherapy processes and practices for the 21st century* (pp. 591–613). Wiley.

Green, D. P., Salovey, P., & Truax, K. M. (1999). Static, dynamic, and causative bipolarity of affect. *Journal of Personal and Social Psychology, 76*, 856–867.

Green, M. C., Strange, J. J., & Brock, T. C. (2002). *Narrative impact: Social and cognitive foundations*. Lawrence Erlbaum.

Green, M., DeCourville, N., & Sadava, S. (2012). Positive affect, negative affect, stress, and social support as mediators of the forgiveness-health relationship. *The Journal of Social Psychology, 152*, 288–307.

Greenbaum, C. A., & Javdani, S. (2017). Expressive writing intervention promotes resilience among juvenile justice-involved youth. *Children and Youth Services Review, 73*, 220–229.

Greimel, E., Schulte-Rüther, M., Kircher, T., Kamp-Becker, I.Remschmidt, H., Fink, G.R., Herpertz-Dahlmann, B. et al. (2010). Neural mechanisms of empathy in adolescents with autism spectrum disorder and their fathers. *NeuroImage,49*, 1055–1065.

Greitemeyer, T., Osswald, S., Fischer, P., & Frey, D. (2007). Civil courage: Implicit theories, related concepts, and measurement. *Journal of Positive Psychology, 2*, 115–119.

Grier-Reed, T., & Ganuza, Z. M. (2011). Constructivism and career decision self-efficacy for Asian Americans and African Americans. *Journal of Counseling & Development, 89*, 200–205.

Grossman, I., Dorfman, A., & Oakes, H. (2020). Wisdom is a social-ecological rather than person-centric phenomenon. *Current Opinion in Psychology, 32*, 66–71.

Grossmann, I., Gerlach, T. M., & Denissen, J. J. A. (2016). Wise reasoning in the face of everyday life challenges. *Social Psychology and Personality Science, 7*, 611–622.

Grossmann, I., Karasawa, M., Izumi, S., Na, J., Varnum, M. E. W., Kitayama, S., & Nisbett, R. E. (2012). Aging and wisdom: Culture matters. *Psychological Science, 23*, 1059–1066.

Grossman, I., Westrate, N. M., Ardlet, M., Brienza, J. P., Dong, M., Ferrari, M., Fournier, M. A., Hu, C. S., Nusbaum, H. C., & Vervaecke, J. (2020). The science of wisdom in a polarized world: Knowns and unknowns. *Psychological Inquiry, 31*, 103–133.

Gruenewald, T. L., Liao, D. H., & Seeman, T. E. (2012). Contributing to others, contributing to oneself: Perceptions of generativity and health in later life. *The Journal of Gerontology: Series B: Psychological Sciences and Social Sciences, 67*, 660–665.

Grych, J., Hamby, S., & Banyard, V. (2015). The resilience portfolio model: Understanding healthy adaptation in victims of violence. *Psychology of Violence, 5*(4), 343–354.

Guan, P., Capezio, A., Restubog, S. L. D., Read, S., Lajom, J. A. L., & Li, M. (2016). The role of traditionality in the relationships among parental support, career decision-making self-efficacy and career adaptability. *Journal of Vocational Behavior, 94*, 114–123.

Gubkin, R. (2016). An exploration of spirituality and the traumatizing experiences of combat. *Journal of Humanistic Psychology, 56*, 311–330.

Guidelines for psychological practice with transgender and gender nonconforming people. (2015). *American Psychologist, 70*(9), 832–864.

Guignon, C. (2002). Hermeneutics, authenticity and the aims of psychology. *Journal of Theoretical & Philosophical Psychology, 22*, 83–102.

Guizzo, F., & Cadinu, M. (2017). Effects of objectifying gaze on female cognitive performance: The role of flow experience and internalization of beauty ideals. *British Journal of Social Psychology, 56*, 281–292.

Gurung, R. A. R., Taylor, S. E., & Seeman, T. E. (2003). Accounting for changes in social support among married older adults: Insights from the MacArthur Studies of Successful Aging. *Psychology and Aging, 18*, 487–496.

Gustafsson, H. C., Brown, G. L., Mills-Koonce, W. R., & Cox, M. J. (2017). Intimate partner violence and children's attachment representations during middle childhood. *Journal of Marriage and Family, 79*, 865–878.

Guzak, J. R. (2015). Affect in ethical decision making: Mood matters. *Ethics & Behavior, 25*, 386–399.

Gyurkovics, M., Kotyuk, E., Katonai, E. R., Horvath, E. Z., Vereczkei, A., & Szekely, A. (2016). Individual differences in flow proneness are linked to a dopamine D2 receptor gene variant. *Consciousness and Cognition, 42*, 1–8.

Ha, N., Bae, S.-M., & Hyun, M.-H. (2019). The effect of forgiveness writing therapy on post-traumatic growth in survivors of sexual abuse. *Sexual and Relationship Therapy, 34*(1), 10–22.

Haack, K. R., & Falcke, D. (2014). Love and marital quality in romantic relationships mediated and non-mediated by Internet. *Paidéia, 24,* 105–113.

Haase, J. E. (1987). Components of courage in chronically ill adolescents: A phenomenological study. *Advances in Nursing Science, 9,* 64–80.

Hackman, J. R., & Oldham, G. R. (1980). *Work design.* Addison-Wesley.

Haley, J. (Producer), & Fleming, V. (Director). (1939). *The wizard of Oz* [Motion picture]. MGM.

Hall, G. C. N., & Ibaraki, A. Y. (2016). Multicultural issues in cognitive-behavioral therapy: Cultural adaptations and goodness of fit. In C. M. Nezu & A. M. Nezu (Eds.), *The Oxford handbook of cognitive and behavioral therapies* (pp. 465–481). Oxford University Press.

Hall, G. S. (1922). *Senescence: The last half of life.* D. Appleton.

Hall, J. H., & Fincham, F. D. (2005). Self-forgiveness: The stepchild of forgiveness research. *Journal of Social and Clinical Psychology, 24(5),* 621–637.

Halmburger, A., Baumert, A., & Schmitt M. (2015). Anger as driving factor of moral courage in comparison with guilt and global mood: A multimethod approach. *European Journal of Social Psychology, 45,* 39–51.

Hamamura, T., Bettache, K., & Xu, Y. (2018). Individualism and collectivism. In V. Zeigler-Hill, and T. K. Shackelford (Eds.), *The SAGE handbook of personality and individual differences: Origins of personality and individual differences* (pp. 365–382). Sage.

Hamby, S., Grych, J., & Banyard, V. (2018). Resilience portfolios and poly-strengths: Identifying protective factors associated with thriving after adversity. *Psychology of Violence, 8*(2), 172–183.

Hamer, D. (2004). *The God gene: How faith is hardwired into our genes.* Doubleday.

Hanke, K., & Vauclair, C.-M. (2016). Investigating the human value "forgiveness": A cross-cultural meta-analysis approach. *Cross-Cultural Research: The Journal of Comparative Social Science, 50,* 215–230.

Hannah, S. T., Sweeney, P. J., & Lester, P. B. (2007). Toward a courageous mindset: The subject act and experience of courage. *Journal of Positive Psychology, 2,* 129–135.

Hannon, P. A., Finkel, E. J., Kumashiro, M., & Rusbult, C. E. (2012). The soothing effects of forgiveness on victims' and perpetrators' blood pressure. *Personal Relationships, 19,* 279–289.

Hanushek, E. A., Kain, J. F., O'Brien, D. M., & Rivkin, S. G. (2004). *The market for teacher quality* (Working Paper 11154). National Bureau of Economic Research.

Harackiewicz, J. M., Canning, E. A., Tibbetts, Y., Priniski, S. J., & Hyde, J. S. (2016). Closing achievement gaps with a utility-value intervention: Disentangling race and social class. *Journal of Personality and Social Psychology, 111,* 745.

Hardball With Chris Matthews. (2004). https://www.nbcnews.com/id/wbna4796454

Hardeman, R. R., Kheyfets, A., Mantha, A. B., Cornell, A., Crear-Perry, J., Graves, C., Grobman, W., James-Conterelli, S., Jones, C., Lipscomb, B., Ortique, C., Stuebe, A., Welsh, K., & Howell, E. A. (2022). Developing tools to report racism in maternal health for the CDC Maternal Mortality Review Information Application (MMRIA): Findings from the MMRIA Racism & Discrimination Working Group. *Maternal and Child Health Journal, 26*(4), 661–669.

Hargreaves, E., Quick, L., & Buchanan, D. (2021). Systemic threats to the growth mindset: Classroom experiences of agency among children designated as 'lower-attaining,' *Cambridge Journal of Education, 51,* 283–299.

Haroz, E. E., Jordans, M., de Jong, J., Gross, A., Bass, J., & Tol, W. (2017). Measuring hope among children affected by armed conflict: Cross-cultural construct validity of the Children's Hope Scale. *Assessment, 24,* 528–539.

Harris, D. J., Vine, S. J., & Wilson, M. R. (2017). Is flow really effortless? The complex role ofeffortful attention. *Sport, Exercise, and Performance Psychology, 6,* 103.

8Harris, P. R., Richards, A., & Bond, R. (2022). Individual differences in spontaneous self-affirmation and mental health: Relationships with self-esteem, dispositional optimism and coping. *Self and Identity.*

Hart, P. M. (1999). Predicting employee satisfaction: A coherent model of personality, work, and nonwork experiences, and domain satisfaction. *Journal of Applied Psychology, 84*, 564–584.

Harter, J. K., & Hodges, T. D. (2003). *Construct validity study: StrengthsFinder and the Five Factor Model* [technical report]. Gallup.

Harter, J. K., & Schmidt, F. L. (2002). Employee engagement and business-unit performance. *Psychologist-Manager Journal, 4*, 215–224.

Harvey, I., & Cook, L. (2010). Exploring the role of spirituality in self-management practices among older African American and non-Hispanic White women with chronic conditions. *Chronic Illness, 6*, 111–124.

Harvey, J. H., & Ormarzu, J. (1997). Minding the close relationship. *Personality and Social Psychology Review, 1*, 223–239.

Harvey, J. H., Pauwels, B. G., & Zicklund, S. (2001). Relationship connection: The role of minding in the enhancement of closeness. In C. R. Snyder & S. J. Lopez (Eds.), *The handbook of positive psychology* (pp. 423–433). Oxford University Press.

Hatfield, E. (1988). Passionate and companionate love. In R. J. Sternberg & M. L. Barnes (Eds.), *The psychology of love* (pp. 191–217). Yale University Press.

Hauser, D. J., Preston, S. D., & Stansfield, R. B. (2014). Altruism in the wild: When affiliative motives to help positive people overtake empathetic motives to help the distressed. *Journal of Experimental Psychology: General, 143*, 1295–1305.

Havighurst, R. J. (1961). Successful aging. *The Gerontologist, 1*, 8–13.

Hayashi, A., Abe, N., Ueno, A., Shigemune, Y., Mori, E., Tashiro, M., & Fujii, T. (2010). Neural correlates of forgiveness for moral transgressions involving deception. *Brain Research, 1332*, 90–99.

Hays, P. A. (2016). *Addressing cultural competencies in practice, Assessment, diagnosis, and therapy* (2nd ed.). American Psychological Association. (Original work published 2008)

Hazan, C., & Shaver, P. (1987). Romantic love conceptualized as an attachment process. *Journal of Personality and Social Psychology, 52*, 511–524.

Hazlett-Stevens, H., & Oren, Y. (2017). Effectiveness of mindfulness-based stress reduction bibliotherapy: A preliminary randomized controlled trial. *Journal of Clinical Psychology, 73*, 626–637.

Heckenberg, R. A., Eddy, P., Kent, S., & Wright, B. J. (2018). Do workplace-based mindfulness meditation programs improve physiological indices of stress? A systematic review and meta-analysis. *Journal of Psychosomatic Research, 114*, 62–71.

Heiner, E. K. (2019). Fostering heroism in fourth- and fifth-grade students. *Journal of Humanistic Psychology, 59*, 596–616.

Heinonen, K., Räikkönen, K., Scheier, M. F., Pesonen, A.-K., Keskivaara, P., Järvenpää, A.-L., & Strandberg, T. (2006). Parents' optimism is related to their ratings of their children's behavior. *European Journal of Psychology, 20*, 421–445.

Heintz, S., Kramm, C., & Ruch, W. (2019). "A meta-analysis of gender differences in character strengths and age, nation, and measure as moderators": Corrigendum. *The Journal of Positive Psychology, 14*(1), i.

Hektner, J. (1996). *Exploring optimal personality development: A longitudinal study of adolescents*. Unpublished doctoral dissertation, University of Chicago.

Heller, K., Wyman, M. F., & Allen, S. M. (2000). Future directions for prevention science: From research to adoption. In C. R. Snyder, & R. E. Ingram (Eds.), *Handbook of psychological change: Psychotherapy processes and practices for the 21st century* (pp. 660–680). Wiley.

Helliwell, J. F., Wang, S., Huang, Hl., & Norton, M. (2022). Happiness, benevolence, and trust during COVID-19 and beyond. *The Gallup World Happiness Report*

Hellman, C. M., & Gwinn, C. (2017). Camp HOPE as an intervention for children exposed to domestic violence: A program evaluation of hope, and strength of character. *Child and Adolescent Social Work Journal, 34*, 269–276.

Hellman, C. M., Pittman, M. K., & Munoz, R. T. (2013). The first twenty years of the will and the ways: An examination of score reliability distribution on Snyder's Dispositional Hope Scale. *Journal of Happiness Studies, 14*, 723–729.

Hellmich, F., & Hoya, F. (2017). Primary school students' implicit theories and their reading motivation: The role of parents' and teachers' effort feedback. *Zeitschrift für Psychologie, 225*, 117–126.

Hendrick, C., & Hendrick, S. S. (2009). Love. In S. J. Lopez & C. R. Snyder (Eds.), *Oxford handbook of positive psychology* (pp. 447–454). Oxford University Press.

Hendrick, C., & Hendrick, S. S. (2021). Love. In C. R. Snyder, S. J. Lopez, L. M. Edwards, & S. C. Marques (Eds.), *The Oxford handbook of positive psychology* (pp. 586–598). Oxford University Press.

Hendrick, S. S., & Hendrick, C. (1992). *Romantic love*. Sage.

Hennessy, E. A., Johnson, B. T., Acabchuk, R. L., McCloskey, K., & Stewart-James, J. (2020). Self-regulation mechanisms in health behavior change: A systematic meta-review of meta-analyses, 2006–2017. *Health Psychology Review, 14*(1), 6–42. https://doi.org/10.1080/17437199.2019.1679654

Henry, J. (2004). Positive and creative organization. In P. A. Linley & S. Joseph (Eds.), *Positive psychology in practice* (pp. 269–285). Wiley.

Heo, J., Chun, S., Lee, S., & Kim, J. (2016). Life satisfaction and psychological well-being of older adults with cancer experience: The role of optimism and volunteering. *The International Journal of Aging and Human Development, 83*, 274–289.

Hernandez, R., Carnethon, M., Penedo, F. J., Martinez, L., Boehm, J., & Schueller, S. M. (2016). Exploring well-being among US Hispanics/Latinos in a church-based institution: A qualitative study. *Journal of Positive Psychology, 11*, 511–521.

Herrera, C., Grossman, J. B., Kauh, T. J., & McMaken, J. (2011). Mentoring in schools: An impact study of Big Brothers Big Sisters school-based mentoring. *Child Development, 82(1)*, 346–361.

Herzberg, F. (1966). *Work and the nature of man*. World.

Heutte, J., Fenouillet, F., Martin-Krumm, C., Gute, G., Raes, A., Gute, D., Bachelet, R., & Csikszentmihalyi, M. (2021). Optimal experience in adult learning: Conception and validation of the flow in education scale (EduFlow-2). *Frontiers in Psychology, 12*.

Hibberd, F. J., & Petocz, A. (2022). Philosophy, realism and psychology's disciplinary fragmentation. *Philosophical Psychology*, [s. l.].

Higgins, A., Sharek, D., & Glacken, M. (2016). Building resilience in the face of adversity: Navigation processes used by older lesbian, gay, bisexual and transgender adults living in Ireland. *Journal of Clinical Nursing, 25*, 3652–3664.

Hill, G., & Swanson, H. L. (1985). Construct validity and reliability of the Ethical Behavior Rating Scale. *Educational and Psychological Measurement, 45*, 285–292.

Hill, P. C., Pargament, K. I., Hood, R. W., Jr., McCullough, M. E., Swyers, J. P., Larson, D. B., & Zinnbauer, B. J. (2000). Conceptualizing religion and spirituality: Points of commonality, points of departure. *Journal for the Theory of Social Behavior, 30*, 51–77.

Hiller, J., Schatz, K., & Drexler, H. (2017). Gender influence on health and risk behavior in primary prevention: A systematic review. *Journal of Public Health, 25*, 339–349.

Hilton, L., Hempel, S., Ewing, B. A., Apaydin, E., Xenakis, L., Newberry, S., Colaiaco, B., Maher, A. R., Shanman, R. M., Sorbero, M. E., & Maglione, M. A. (2017). Mindfulness meditation for chronic pain: Systematic review and meta-analysis. *Annals of Behavioral Medicine, 51*(2), 199–213.

Hinz, A., Sander, C., Glaesmer, H., Brähler, E., Zenger, M., Hilbert, A., & Kocalevent, R.-D. (2017). Optimism and pessimism in the general population: Psychometric properties of the Life Orientation Test (LOT-R). *International Journal of Clinical and Health Psychology, 17*(2), 161–170.

Hirsch, J. K., & Sirois, F. M. (2016). Hope and fatigue in chronic illness: The role of perceived stress. *Journal of Health Psychology, 21*, 451–456.

Hirsch, J. K., Visser, P. L., Chang, E. C., & Jeglic, E. L. (2012). Race and ethnic differences in hope and hopelessness as moderators of the association between depressive symptoms and suicidal behavior. *Journal of American College Health, 60*, 115–125.

Hitlin, S. (2007). Doing good, feeling good: Values and the self's moral center. *Journal of Positive Psychology, 2*, 249–259.

Ho, S. M. Y., Rochelle, T. L., Law, L. S. C., Duan, W., Bai,

Y., & Shih, S. (2014). Methodological issues in positive psychology research with diverse populations: Exploring strengths among Chinese adults. In J. T. Pedrotti & L. M. Edwards (Eds.), *Perspectives on the intersection of multiculturalism and positive psychology*. Springer Science + Business Media.

Hodges, T. D., & Clifton, D. O. (2004). Strengths-based development in practice. In P. A. Linley & S. Joseph (Eds.), *Positive psychology in practice* (pp. 256–268). John Wiley & Sons. https://doi.org/10.1002/9780470939338.ch16

Hoffman, E., Gonzalez-Mujica, J., Acosta-Orozco, C., & Compton, W. C. (2020). The psychological benefits of receiving real-life altruism. *Journal of Humanistic Psychology, 60*, 187–204.

Hofmann, D. A., & Tetrick, L. E. (Eds.). (2003). *Health and safety in organizations: A multilevel perspective*. Jossey-Bass.

Hofstede, G. (1980). *Culture's consequences*. Sage.

Hoge, D. R. (1996). Religion in America: The demographics of belief and affiliation. *Religion and the clinical practice of psychology* (pp. 21–42). American Psychological Association.

Hogeveen, J., Salvi, C., & Grafman, J. (2016). 'Emotional intelligence': Lessons from lesions. *Trends in Neurosciences, 39*(10), 694–705.

Holec, V., Pirot, H. L., & Euston, D. R. (2014). Not all effort is equal: The role of the anterior cingulate cortex in different forms of effort-reward decisions. *Frontiers in Behavioral Neuroscience, 8*, 1–17.

Holland, E., Koval, P., Stratemeyer, M., Thomson, F., & Haslam, N. (2017). Sexual objectification in women's daily lives: A smartphone ecological momentary assessment study. *British Journal of Social Psychology, 56*, 314–333.

Holland, K. J., Lee, J. W., Marshak, H. H., & Martin, L. R. (2016). Spiritual intimacy, and physical/psychological well-being: Spiritual meaning as a mediator. *Psychology of Religion and Spirituality, 8*, 218–227.

Holland, N. E. (2016). Partnering with a higher power: Academic engagement, religiosity, and spirituality of African American urban youth. *Education and Urban Society, 48*, 299–323.

Hollingsworth, D. W., Wingate, L. R., Tucker, R. P., O'Keefe, V. M., & Cole, A. B. (2016). Hope as a moderator of the relationship between interpersonal predictors of suicide and suicidal thinking in African Americans. *Journal of Black Psychology, 42*, 175–190.

Hollon, S. D., & Beck, A. T. (1994). Cognitive and cognitive-behavioral therapies. In A. E. Bergin & S. L. Garfield (Eds.), *Handbook of psychotherapy and behavior change* (4th ed., pp. 428–466). Wiley.

Holmberg, D., Blair, K. L., & Phillips, M. (2010). Women's sexual satisfaction as a predictor of well-being in same-sex versus mixed-sex relationships. *Journal of Sex Research, 47*, 1–11.

Holt, C. L., Wang, M., Caplan, L., Schulz, E., Blake, V., & Southward, V. L. (2011). Role of religious involvement and spirituality in functioning among African Americans with cancer: Testing a meditational model. *Journal of Behavioral Medicine, 34*, 437–448.

Holtz, C. A., & Martinez, M. J. (2014). Positive psychological practices in multicultural school settings. In J. T. Pedrotti & L. M. Edwards (Eds.), *Perspectives on the intersection of multiculturalism and positive psychology*. Springer Science + Business Media.

Hood, C. D., & Carruthers, C. (2007). Enhancing leisure experience and developing resources: The leisure and well-being model, Part II. *Therapeutic Recreation Journal, 41*, 298–325.

Hook, J. N., Worthington, E. L., Jr., & Utsey, S. O. (2009). Collectivism, forgiveness, and social harmony. *The Counseling Psychologist, 37*, 821–847.

Hook, J. N., Worthington, E. L., Jr., Utsey, S. O., Davis, D. E., & Burnette, J. L. (2012). Collectivistic self-construal and forgiveness. *Counseling and Values, 57*, 109–124.

Horowitz, J. M., Brown, A., & Cox, K. (2019, April 9). Race in America 2019. *Pew Research Center*. https://www.pewresearch.org/social-trends/2019/04/09/race-in-america-2019/

Hothersall, D. (1995). *History of psychology*. McGraw-Hill.

Houser, R. E. (2002). The virtue of courage. In S. J. Pope (Ed.), *The ethics of Aquinas* (pp. 304–320). Georgetown University Press.

Howard, M. C. (2019). Applying the approach/avoidance framework to understand the relationships between social courage, workplace outcomes, and well-being outcomes. *The Journal of Positive Psychology, 14*, 734–748.

Howard, K., Martin, A., Berlin, L. J., & Brooks-Gunn, J. (2011). Early mother-child separation, parenting, and child well-being in Early Head Start families. *Attachment & Human Development, 13*, 5–26.

Howard, M. C., & Alipour, K. K. (2014). Does the courage measure really measure courage? A theoretical and empirical evaluation. *The Journal of Positive Psychology, 9*, 449–459.

Howard, M. C., Farr, J. L., Grandey, A. A., & Gutworth, M. B. (2017). The creation of the Workplace Social Courage Scale (WSCS): An investigation of internal consistency, psychometric properties, validity, and utility. *Journal of Business and Psychology, 32*, 673–690.

Howard, M. C., & Reiley, P. J. (2020). Physical courage predicts relevant outcomes in associated contexts: The creation of a measure and empirical analysis into the construct. *Journal of Business Research, 110*, 80–94.

Howarth, C., & Andreouli, E. (2016). "Nobody wants to be an outsider": From diversity management to diversity engagement. *Political Psychology, 37*, 327–340.

Howell, A. J., Jacobson, R. M., & Larsen, D. J. (2015). Enhanced psychological health among chronic pain clients engaged in hope-focused group counseling. *The Counseling Psychologist, 43*, 586–613.

Howell, J., & Maguire, R. (2019). Seeking help when transgender: Exploring the difference in mental and physical health seeking behaviors between transgender and cisgender individuals in Ireland. *International Journal of Transgenderism, 20*(4), 421–433.

Howell, R. T., & Howell. C. J. (2008). The relation of economic status to subjective well-being in developing countries: A meta-analysis. *Psychological Bulletin, 134*, 536–560.

Hoyt, M. A., Nelson, C. J., Darabos, K., Marín-Chollom, A., & Stanton, A. L. (2017). Mechanisms of navigating goals after testicular cancer: Meaning and emotion regulation. *Psycho-oncology, 26*, 747–754.

Hoyt, M. A., Wang, A. W., Boggero, I. A., Eisenlohr-Moul, T. A., Stanton, A. L., & Segerstrom, S. C. (2020). Emotional approach coping in older adults as predictor of physical and mental health. *Psychology and aging, 35*(4), 591–603.

Hsu, C., Chang, K., & Chen, M. (2012). Flow experience and Internet shopping behavior: Investigating the moderating effect of consumer characteristics. *Systems Research and Behavioral Science, 29*, 317–332.

Hsu, L. M., & Langer, E. J. (2013). Mindfulness and cultivating well-being in older adults. In S. A. David, I. Boniwell, & A. Conley Ayers (Eds.), *The Oxford handbook of happiness* (pp. 1026–1036). Oxford University Press.

Huang, C. (2013). Gender differences in academic self-efficacy: A meta-analysis. *European Journal of Psychology of Education, 28*, 1–35.

Huang, Z. J., Lewin, A., Mitchell, S. J., & Zhang, J. (2012). Variations in the relationship between maternal depression, maternal sensitivity, and child attachment by race/ethnic and nativity: Findings from a nationally representative cohort study. *Maternal and Child Health Journal, 16*, 40–50.

Huber, J. T., II, & MacDonald, D. A. (2012). An investigation of the relations between altruism, empathy, and spirituality. *Journal of Humanistic Psychology, 52*, 206–221.

Huber, S., Allemand, M., & Huber, O. W. (2011). Forgiveness by God and human forgiveness: The centrality of the religiosity makes the difference. *Psychology of Religions, 33*, 115–134.

Huffman, A., Whetten, J., & Huffman, W. H. (2013). Using technology in higher education: The influence of gender roles on technology self-efficacy. *Computers in Human Behavior, 29*, 1779–1786.

Huffman, J. C., Boehm, J. K., Beach, S. R., Beale, E. E., DuBois, C. M., & Healy, B. C. (2016). Relationship of optimism and suicidal ideation in three groups of patients at varying levels of suicide risk. *Journal of Psychiatric Research, 77*, 76–84.

Hui Gan, G. Z., Hill, A.-M., Yeung, P., Keesing, S., & Netto, J. A. (2020). Pet ownership and its influence on mental health in older adults. *Aging & Mental Health, 24*(10), 1605–1612.

Hui, C. H. (1988). Measurement of individualism–collectivism. *Journal of Research in Personality, 22*, 17–36.

Hume, D. (1888). *A treatise of human nature*. Clarendon.

Huntington, C., Stanley, S. M., Doss, B. D., & Rhoades, G. K. (2022). Happy, healthy, and wedded? How the transition to marriage affects mental and physical health. *Journal of Family Psychology, 36*, 608–617.

Hurley, D. B., & Kwon, P. (2013). Savoring helps most when you have little: Interaction between savoring the moment and uplifts on positive affect and satisfaction with life. *Journal of Happiness Studies, 14*, 1261–1271.

Hurlock, E. B. (1925). An evaluation of certain incentives in school work. *Journal of Educational Psychology, 16*, 145–159.

Huskey, R., Craighead, B., Miller, M. B., & Weber, R. (2018). Does intrinsic reward motivate cognitive control? A naturalistic-fMRI study based on the synchronization theory of flow. *Cognitive, Affective, & Behavioral Neuroscience, 18*(5), 902–924.

Hyde, J. S. (2005). The gender similarities hypothesis. *The American Psychologist, 60*, 581–592.

Hyde, J. S. (2014). Gender similarities and differences. *The Annual Review of Psychology, 65*, 73–98.

Ide, R. (1998). "Sorry for your kindness": Japanese interactional ritual in public discourse. *Journal of Pragmatics, 29*, 509–529.

Ilies, R., Wagner, D., Wilson, K., Ceja, L., Johnson, M., DeRue, S., & Ilgen, D. (2017). Flow at work and basic psychological needs: Effects on well-being. *Applied Psychology, 66*, 3–24.

Iliescu, D., Ilie, A., Ispas, D., & Ion, A. (2013). Examining the psychometric properties of the Mayer-Salovey-Caruso Emotional Intelligence Test: Findings from an Eastern European culture. *European Journal of Psychological Assessment, 29*, 121–128

Inghilleri, P. (1999). *From subjective experience to cultural change*. Cambridge University Press.

Ingram, R. E., Kendall, P. C., & Chen, A. H. (1991). Cognitive-behavioral interventions. In C. R. Snyder & D. R. Forsyth (Eds.), *Handbook of social and clinical psychology: The health perspective* (pp. 509–522). Pergamon.

Institute of Medicine. (2003). Unequal treatment: confronting racial and ethnic disparities in health care. The National Academies Press

Iruka, I. U., & Hawkins, C. (2022). Making the unique experiences of young Black girls visible. In R. D. Mayes, M. C. Shavers, & J. L. Moore (Eds.). *African American young garland women in pre-K12 schools and beyond: Informing research, policy, and practice* (pp. 7–27). Emerald.

Isen, A. M. (1970). Success, failure, attention, and reaction to others: The warm glow of success. *Journal of Personality and Social Psychology, 17*, 107–112.

Isen, A. M. (1987). Positive affect, cognitive processes, and social behavior. *Advances in Experimental Social Psychology, 20*, 203–253.

Isen, A. M. (2000). Some perspectives on positive affect and self-regulation. *Psychological Inquiry, 11*, 184–187.

Isen, A. M., & Levin, P. F. (1972). The effect of feeling good on helping: Cookies and kindness. *Journal of Personality and Social Psychology, 17*, 107–112.

Isen, A. M., Daubman, K. A., & Nowicki, G. P. (1987). Positive affect facilitates creative problem solving. *Journal of Personality and Social Psychology, 21*, 384–388.

Ishimura, I., & Kodama, M. (2006). Flow experiences in everyday activities of Japanese college students: Autotelic people and time management. *Japanese Psychological Research, 51*, 47–54.

Israelashvili, M., & Socher, P. (2007). An examination of a Counsellor Self-Efficacy Scale (COSE) using an Israeli sample. *International Journal for the Advancement of Counselling, 29*, 1–9.

Iwasaki, Y. (2007). Leisure and quality of life in an international and multicultural context: What are major pathways linking leisure to quality of life? *Social Indicators Research, 82*, 233–264.

Izuma, K., & Adolphs, R. (2011). The brain's rose-colored glasses. *Nature Neuroscience, 14*, 1355–1356.

Jackson, J. (2017). Free to be happy: Economic freedom and happiness in US states. *Journal of Happiness Studies, 18*, 1207–1229.

Jackson, S. A., & Eklund, R. C. (2002). Assessing flow in physical activity: The Flow State Scale-2 and Dispositional Flow Scale-2. *Journal of*

Sport & Exercise Psychology, 24(2), 133–150.

Jackson, S., & Csikszentmihalyi, M. (1999). *Flow in sports*. Human Kinetics.

Jacobsen, B., Lee, J. B., Marquering, W., & Zhang, C. Y. (2014). Gender differences in optimism and asset allocation. *Journal of Economic Behavior & Organization, 107*, 630–651.

Jarman, L., Martin, A., Venn, A., Otahal, P., Blizzard, L., Teale, B., & Sanderson, K. (2016). Workplace health promotion and mental health: Three-year findings from Partnering Healthy@Work. *PLOS ONE, 11*, e0156791.

Jayawickreme, E., Brocato, N. W., & Blackie, L. E. R. (2017). Wisdom gained? Assessing relationships between adversity, personality and well-being among a late adolescent sample. *Journal of Youth and Adolescence, 46*, 1179–1199.

Jensen-Johansen, M. B., O'Toole, M. S., Christensen, S., Valdimarsdottir, H., Zakowski, S., Bovbjerg, D. H., Jensen, A. B., & Zachariae, R. (2018). Expressive writing intervention and self-reported physical health out-comes—Results from a nationwide randomized controlled trial with breast cancer patients. *PLoS ONE, 13*(2). APA PsycInfo.

Jerath, R., Barnes, V. A., Dillard-Wright, D., Jerath, S., & Hamilton, B. (2012). Dynamic change of awareness during meditation techniques: Neural and psychological correlates. *Frontiers in Human Neuroscience, 6*, 1–4.

Jerga, A. M., Shaver, P. R., & Wilkinson, R. B. (2011). Attachment insecurities and identification of at-risk individuals following the death of a loved one. *Journal of Social and Personal Relationships, 28*, 891–914.

Jeste, D. V., & Harris, J. C. (2010). Wisdom—A neuroscience perspective. *JAMA: Journal of the American Medical Association, 304*, 1602–1603.

Jew, C. L., Green, K. E., & Kroger, J. (1999). Development and validation of a measure of resiliency. *Measurement and Evaluation in Counseling and Development, 32*, 75–90.

Jha, A. P., Zanesco, A. P., Denkova, E., MacNulty, W. K., & Rogers, S. L. (2021). The effects of mindfulness training on working memory performance in high-demand cohorts: A multi-study investigation. *Journal of Cognitive Enhancement*.

Ji, J. L., Holmes, E. A., & Blackwell, S. E. (2017). Seeing light at the end of the tunnel: Positive prospective mental imagery and optimism in depression. *Psychiatry Research, 247*, 155–162.

Jiang, S., Wei, Q., Zhang, L. (2021). Individualism vs. collectivism and the early-stage transmission of COVID-19. Soc Indic Res., *164*(2): 791–821. doi: 10.1007/s11205-022-02972-z

Ji-liang, S., & Dan, T. (2004). Use of General Self-Efficacy Scale (GSES) in Chinese aged people. *Chinese Journal of Clinical Psychology, 12*(4), 342–344.

Jimenez, D. E., Cook, B., Bartels, S. J., & Alegría, M. (2013). Disparities in mental health service use of racial and ethnic minority elderly adults. *Journal of the American Geriatrics Society, 61*, 18–25.

Jin, M. K., Jacobvitz, D., Hazen, N., & Jung, S. H. (2012). Maternal sensitivity and infant attachment security in Korea: Cross-cultural validation of the Strange Situation. *Attachment & Human Development, 14*, 33–44.

John F. Kennedy Presidential Library and Museum. (2021). *COVID courage*. https://www.jfklibrary.org/events-and-awards/profile-in-courage-award/award-recipients/covid-courage

Johns, K. N., Allen, E. S., & Gordon, K. C. (2015). The relationship between mindfulness and forgiveness of infidelity. *Mindfulness, 6*, 1462–1471.

Johnson, F. (1988). Encounter group therapy. In S. Long (Ed.), *Six group therapies* (pp. 115–158). Plenum.

Johnson, K. J., & Fredrickson, B. L. (2005). "We all look the same to me": Positive emotions eliminate the own race bias in face recognition. *Psychological Science, 16*, 875–881.

Joo, B.-K., Zigarmi, D., Nimon, K., & Shuck, B. (2017). Work cognition and psychological well-being: The role of cognitive engagement as a partial mediator. *The Journal of Applied Behavioral Science, 53*, 446–469.

Jose, P. E., Lim, B. T., & Bryant, F. B. (2012). Does savoring increase happiness? A daily diary study. *Journal of Positive Psychology, 7*, 176–187.

Joseph, C. (29 July, 2020). What Black joy means and why its more important than ever. *British Vogue*. https://www.vog

ue.co.uk/arts-and-lifestyle/article/what-is-black-joy

Joshanloo, M. (2016). Revisiting the empirical distinction between hedonic and eudaimonic aspects of well-being using exploratory structural equation modeling. *Journal of Happiness, 17*, 2023–2036.

Joshanloo, M., & Weijers, D. (2014). Aversion to happiness across cultures: A review of where and why people are averse to happiness. *Journal of Happiness Studies, 15*, 717–735.

Judge, T. A., Thoresen, C. J., Bono, J. E., & Patton, G. K. (2001). The job-satisfaction performance relationship: A qualitative and quantitative review. *Psychological Bulletin, 127*, 376–407.

Jung, C. (1953). *Two essays on analytical psychology*. Pantheon.

Kabat-Zinn, J. (1982). An outpatient program in behavioral medicine for chronic pain patients based on the practice of mindfulness meditation: Theoretical considerations and preliminary results. *General Hospital Psychiatry, 4*, 33–47.

Kabat-Zinn, J. (1990). *Full catastrophe living*. Delacorte.

Kabat-Zinn, J. (2005). *Coming to our senses*. Piatkus.

Kadiangandu, J. K., Gauché, M., Vinsonneau, G., & Mullet, E. (2007). Conceptualizations of forgiveness: Collectivist–Congolese versus individualist–French viewpoints. *Journal of Cross-Cultural Psychology, 38*, 432–437.

Kahneman, D., Diener, E., & Schwartz, N. (1999). *Well-being: The foundations of hedonic psychology*. Russell Sage.

Kaleta, K., & Mróz, J. (2022). Gender differences in forgiveness and its affective correlates. *Journal of Religion and Health, 61*(4), 2819–2837.

Kállay, É. (2015). Physical and psychological benefits of written emotional expression: Review of meta-analyses and recommendations. *European Psychologist, 20*(4), 242–251.

Kanekar, S., & Merchant, S. M. (1982). Aggression, retaliation, and religious affiliation. *Journal of Social Psychology, 117*, 295–296.

Kansky, J., & Diener, E. (2020). National accounts of well-being for public policy. In S. Donaldson, Csikszentmihalyi, & J. Nakamura (Eds.). *Positive psychological science: Improving everyday life, health, work, education, and societies across the globe*. (pp. 15–37). Routledge/Taylor & Francis Group.

Kaplan, J. S., & Sue, S. (1997). Ethnic psychology in the United States. In D. F. Halpern & A. E. Voiskounsky (Eds.), *States of mind: American and post-Soviet perspectives on contemporary issues in psychotherapy* (pp. 349–369). Oxford University Press.

Kaplan, R. M. (2000). Two pathways to prevention. *American Psychologist, 55*, 382–396.

Kardiner, A., & Ovesey, L. (1951). *The mark of oppression: A psychological study of the American Negro*. Norton.

Karim, J., & Weisz, R. (2010). Cross-cultural research on the reliability and validity of the Mayer-Salovey-Caruso Emotional Intelligence Test (MSCEIT). *Cross-Cultural Research, 44*(4), 374–404

Karl, J. A., & Fischer, R. (2022). The state of dispositional mindfulness research. *Mindfulness, 13*(6), 1357–1372.

Karl, J. A., Johnson, F. N., Bucci, L., & Fischer, R. (2022). In search of mindfulness: A review and reconsideration of cultural dynamics from a cognitive perspective. *Journal of the Royal Society of New Zealand, 52*(2), 168–191.

Karl, J. A., Prado, S. M. M., Gračanin, A., Verhaeghen, P., Ramos, A., Mandal, S. P., Michalak, J., Zhang, C.-Q., Schmidt, C., Tran, U. S., Druica, E., Solem, S., Astani, A., Liu, X., Luciano, J. V., Tkalčić, M., Lilja, J. L., Dundas, I., Wong, S. Y. S., & Fischer, R. (2020). The Cross-cultural validity of the Five-Facet Mindfulness Questionnaire across 16 countries. *Mindfulness, 11*(5), 1226–1237.

Karreman, A., & Vingerhoets, Ad. J. J. M. (2012). Attachment and well-being: The mediating role of emotion regulation and resilience. *Personality and Individual Differences, 53*, 821–826.

Karremans, J. C., Regalia, C., Paleari, F. G., Fincham, F. D., Cui, M., Takada, N., Ohbuchi, K-I, Terzino, K., Cross, S. E., & Uskul, A. K. (2011). Maintaining harmony across the globe: The cross-cultural association between closeness and interpersonal forgiveness. *Social Psychological and Personality Science, 2*, 443–451.

Karris, M. A., & Craighead, W. E. (2012). Differences in character among U.S. college students. *Individual Differences Research, 10*(2), 69–80.

Kashdan, T. B., Mishra, A., Breen, W. E., & Froh, J. J. (2009). Gender differences in gratitude: Examining appraisals, narratives, the willingness to express emotions, and changes in psychological needs. *Journal of Personality, 77*, 691–730.

Kashdan, T. B., Uswatte, G., & Julian, T. (2006). Gratitude and hedonic and eudaimonic well-being in Vietnam war veterans. *Behaviour Research and Therapy, 44*, 177–199.

Kaslow, N. J., & Nolen-Hoeksema, S. (1991). *Children's Attributional Style Questionnaire–Revised (CASQ-R)*. Unpublished manuscript. Emory University.

Kaslow, N. J., Tanenbaum, R. L., & Seligman, M. E. P. (1978). *The KASTAN-R: A children's attributional style questionnaire (KASTAN-R-CASQ)*. Unpublished manuscript, University of Pennsylvania.

Kastenmüller, A., Greitemeyer, T., Fischer, P., & Frey, D. (2007). The Munich civil courage instrument (MüZI): Development and validation. *Diagnostica, 53*, 205–217.

Kaszniak, A. W., & Menchola, M. (2012). Behavioral neuroscience of emotion in aging. In M.-C. Pardon & M. W. Bondi (Eds.), *Behavioral neurobiology of aging* (pp. 51–66).

Kato, T. (2016). Effects of partner forgiveness on romantic break-ups in dating relationships: A longitudinal study. *Personality and Individual Differences, 95*, 185–189.

Kaufman, T. M. L., Laninga-Wijnen, L., & Loder, G. M. A. (2022). Are victims of bullying primarily social outcasts? Person-group dissimilarities in relational, socio-behavioral, and physical characteristics. *Child Development, 0*, 1–17.

Kayser, D. N., Greitemeyer, T., Fisher, P., & Frey, D. (2009). Why mood affects help giving, but not moral courage: Comparing two types of prosocial behaviour. *European Journal of Social Psychology, 40*, 1136–1157.

Kazdin, A. E. (1979). Imagery elaboration and self-efficacy in the covert modeling treatment of unassertive behavior. *Journal of Consulting and Clinical Psychology, 47*, 725–733.

Kazdin, A. E. (2008). Evidence-based treatment and practice: New opportunities to bridge clinical research and practice, enhance the knowledge base, and improve patient care. *American Psychologist, 63*, 146–159.

Keefe, R. H., Brownstein-Evans, C., & Rouland Polmanteer, R. (2016). "I find peace there": How faith, church, and spirituality help mothers of colour cope with postpartum depression. *Mental Health, Religion & Culture, 19*, 722–733.

Kehoe, E. G., Toomey, J. M., Balsters, J. H., & Bokde, A. L. W. (2013). Healthy aging is associated with increased neural processing of positive valence but attenuated processing of emotional arousal: An fMRI study. *Neurobiology of Aging, 34*(3), 809–821.

Keller, A. C., & Semmer, N. K. (2013). Changes in situational and dispositional factors as predictors of job satisfaction. *Journal of Vocational Behavior, 83*, 88–98.

Kelley, C. L., Murphy, H. J., Breeden, C. R., Hardy, B. P., Lopez, S. J., O'Byrne, K. K., Leachman, S. P., & Pury, C. L. (2019). Conceptualizing courage. In M. W. Gallagher & S. J. Lopez (Eds.), *Positive psychological assessment: A handbook of models and measures* (pp. 157–176). American Psychological Association.

Kemper, K. J. (2017). Brief online mindfulness training: Immediate impact. *Journal of Evidence-Based Complementary & Alternative Medicine, 22*, 75–80.

Keng, S. L., & Liew, K. W. L. (2017). Trait mindfulness and self-compassion as moderators of the association between gender nonconformity and psychological health. *Mindfulness, 8*, 615–626.

Keng, S., Smoski, M. J., & Robins, C. J. (2011). Effects of mindfulness on psychological health: A review of empirical studies. *Clinical Psychology Review, 31*, 1041–1056.

Kennedy, H. R., Dalla, R. L. (2020). 'It may be legal, but it is not treated equally': Marriage equality and well-being implications for same-sex couples. *Journal of Gay & Lesbian Social Services: The Quarterly Journal of Community & Clinical Practice, 32*, 67–98.

Kennedy, J. F. (1956). *Profiles in courage*. Harper.

Kennedy, Q., Fung, H. H., & Carstensen, L. L. (2001). Aging, time estimation, and emotion. In R. C. Atchley & S. H. McFadden (Eds.), *Aging and the meaning of time: A multidisciplinary exploration* (pp. 51–73). Springer.

Kenrick, D. T., Goldstein, N. J., & Braver, S. L. (Eds.). (2012). *Six degrees of social influence: Science, application, and the psychology of Robert Cialdini.* Oxford University Press.

Kenyon, D., & Hanson, J. D. (2012). Incorporating traditional culture into positive youth development programs with American Indian/Alaska native youth. *Child Development Perspectives, 6,* 272–279.

Kerr, K. L., Ratliff, E. L., Cosgrove, K. T., Bodurka, J., Morris, A. S., & Kyle Simmons, W. (2019). Parental influences on neural mechanisms underlying emotion regulation. *Trends in Neuroscience and Education, 16.*

Keyes, C. L. M., & Lopez, S. J. (2002). Toward a science of mental health: Positive directions in diagnosis and treatment. In C. R. Snyder & S. J. Lopez (Eds.), *The handbook of positive psychology* (pp. 45–59). Oxford University Press.

Keyes, C. L. M., & Magyar-Moe, J. L. (2003). The measurement and utility of adult subjective well-being. In S. J. Lopez & C. R. Snyder (Eds.), *Positive psychological assessment: A handbook of models and measures* (pp. 411–426). American Psychological Association.

Keyes, C. L. M., & Ryff, C. D. (2000). Subjective change and mental health: A self-concept theory. *Social Psychology Quarterly, 63,* 264–279.

Keyes, C. L. M., Hybels, C. F., Milstein, G., & Proeschold-Bell, R. J. (2020). Are changes in positive mental health associated with increased likelihood of depression over a two year period? A test of the mental health promotion and protection hypotheses. *Journal of Affective Disorders, 270,* 136–142.

Keyes, C. L. M., Shmotkin, D., & Ryff, C. (2000). Optimizing well-being: The empirical encounter of two traditions. *Journal of Personality and Social Psychology, 82,* 1007–1022.

Khan, S., Haynes, L., Armstrong, A., & Rohner, R. P. (2010). Perceived teacher acceptance, parental acceptance, academic achievement, and school conduct of middle school students in the Mississippi Delta region of the United States. *Cross-Cultural Research: The Journal of Comparative Social Science, 44,* 283–294.

Kihlstrom, J. F., & Cantor, N. (2000). Social intelligence. In R. J. Sternberg (Ed.), *Handbook of intelligence* (pp. 359–379). Cambridge University Press.

Killen, A., & Macaskill, A. (2015). Using a gratitude intervention to enhance well-being in older adults. *Journal of Happiness Studies, 16,* 947–964.

Kim, P. Y., & Tausen, B. M. (2021). White college student's ethnocultural empathy toward Asians and Asian Americans during the COVID-19 pandemic. *Asian American Journal of Psychology.*

Kim, S., & Knight, B. G. (2015). Adaptation of the three-dimensional wisdom scale (3D-WS) for the Korean cultural context. *International Psychogeriatrics, 27,* 267–278.

Kim, Y., & Glassman, M. (2013). Beyond search and communication: Development and validation of the Internet Self-Efficacy Scale (ISS). *Computers in Human Behavior, 29,* 1421–1429.

King, M. L., Jr. (1968). *The peaceful warrior.* Pocket Books.

Kinshita, K., MacIntosh, E., & Sato, S. (2022). Thriving in youth sport: The antecedents and consequences. *International Journal of Sport and Exercise Psychology, 20,* 356–376.

Kirmayer, L. J. (2012). Cultural competence and evidence-based practice in mental health: Epistemic communities and the politics of pluralism. *Social Sciences & Medicine, 75,* 249–256.

Kitayama, S., & Markus, H. R. (2000). Culture, emotion, and well-being: Good feelings in Japan and in the United States. *Cognition and Emotion, 14,* 99–124.

Kitayama, S., Camp, N. P., & Salvador, C. E. (2022). Culture and the COVID-19 pandemic: Multiple mechanisms and policy implications. *Social Issues and Policy Review, 16,* 164–211.

Kitayama, S., Markus, H. R., Matsumoto, H., & Norasakkunkit, V. (1997). Individual and collective process in the construction of the self: Self-enhancement in the United States and self-criticism in Japan. *Journal of Personality and Social Psychology, 72,* 1245–1267.

Klassen, R. M., Bong, M., Usher, E. L., Chong, W. H., Huan, V. S., Wong, I. Y. F., & Georgiou, T. (2009). Exploring the validity of a teachers' self-efficacy scale in five countries.

Contemporary Educational Psychology, *34*, 67–76.

Kline, R. B. (2016). *Principles and practice of structural equation modeling* (4th ed.). Guilford Press.

Klootwijk, C. L. T., Koele, I. J., van Hoorn, J., Güroğlu, B., & Van Duijvenvoorde, A. C. K. (2021). Parental support and positive mood buffer adolscents' academica motivation during the COVID-19 pandemic. *Journal of Research on Adolescence*, *31*, 780–795.

Klussman, K., Nichols, A. L., Langer, J., Curtin, N., & Lindeman, M. I. H. (2022). The relationship between mindfulness and subjective well-being: Examining the indirect effects of self-connection and meaning in life. *Applied Research in Quality of Life*.

Knowles, E. D., Wearing, J. R., & Campos, B. (2011). Culture and the health benefits of expressive writing. *Social Psychological and Personality Science*, *2*(4), 408–415.

Koerner, S., Shirai, Y., & Pedroza, R. (2013). Role of religious/spiritual beliefs and practices among Latino family caregivers of Mexican descent. *Journal of Latina/o Psychology*, *1*, 95–111.

Koller, S. H., & Verma, S. (2017). Commentary on cross-cultural perspectives on positive youth development with implications for intervention research. *Child Development*, *88*, 1178–1182.

Koltko-Rivera, M. E. (2004). The psychology of worldviews. *Review of General Psychology*, *8*, 3–58.

Komorita, S. S., Hilty, J. A., & Parks, C. D. (1991). Reciprocity and cooperation in social dilemmas. *Journal of Conflict Resolution*, *35*, 494–518.

Kong, D. T., & Belkin, L. Y. (2019). Because I want to share, not because I should: Prosocial implications of gratitude expression in repeated zero-sum resource allocation exchanges. *Motivation and Emotion*, *43*, 824–843.

Kong, F., Ding, K., & Zhao, J. (2015). The relationship among gratitude, self-esteem, social support and life satisfaction among undergraduate students. *Journal of Happiness Studies*, *16*, 477–489.

König, S., & Glück, J. (2014). Editor's choice: "Gratitude is with me all the time": How gratitude relates to wisdom. *The Journals of Gerontology: Series B: Psychological Sciences and Social Sciences*, *69B*, 655–666.

Konrath, S. (2014). The power of philanthropy and volunteering. In F. A. Huppert & C. L. Cooper (Eds.), *Interventions and policies to enhance well-being* (pp. 387–426). Wiley-Blackwell.

Konrath, S., Fuhrel-Forbis, A., Lou, A., & Brown, S. (2012). Motives for volunteering are associated with mortality risk in older adults. *Health Psychology*, *31*, 87–96.

Koskinen, C., Nyholdm, L., Thorkildsen, K. M., Haga, B. M. Wallgren, G. C., & Kaldestad, K. (2023). Health as a movement between suffering of life and meaning of life in men who have experienced transitions in life. *Scandinavian Journal of Caring Sciences*, *37*, 732–739.

Koydemir, S., S,ims,ek, Ö., Schütz, A., & Tipandjan, A. (2013). Differences in how trait emotional intelligence predicts life satisfaction: The role of affect balance versus social support in India and Germany. *Journal of Happiness Studies*, *14*, 51–66.

Kozol, J. (2005). *Amazing grace: The lives of children and the conscience of a nation*. Crown.

Kozol, J. (2012). *Savage inequalities: Children in America's schools*. Crown.

Kraaijkamp, J. J. M., van Dam van Isselt, E. F., Persoon, A., Versluis, A., Chavannes, N. H., & Achterberg, W. P. (2021). eHealth in geriatric rehabilitation: Systematic review of effectiveness, feasibility, and usability. *Journal of Medical Internet Research*, *23*(8).

Kramer, A., & Zinbarg, E. E. (2019). Recalling courage: An initial test of a brief writing intervention to activate a 'courageous mindset' and courageous behavior. *Journal of Positive Psychology*, *14*, 528+537.

Krägeloh, C. (2020). Mindfulness research and terminology science. *Mindful Practice*, *1*, 53–84.

Krause, N. (2012). Feelings of gratitude toward God among older whites, older African Americans, and older Mexican Americans. *Research on Aging*, *34*, 156–173.

Krause, N. (2016). Assessing the relationship among wisdom, humility, and life satisfaction. *Journal of Adult Development, 23*, 140–149.

Kreber, C. (2015). Reviving the ancient virtues in the scholarship of teaching, with a slight critical twist. *Higher Education Research & Development, 34*, 591–598.

Kretzschmar, A., Harzer, C., & Ruch, W. (2022). Character strengths in adults and adolescents: Their measurement and association with well-being. *Journal of Personality Assessment.* (Advance Online publication)

Kriakous, S. A., Elliott, K. A., Lamers, C., & Owen, R. (2021). The effectiveness of mindfulness-based stress reduction on the psychological functioning of healthcare professionals: A systematic review. *Mindfulness, 12*(1), 1–28.

Ku, L.-C., Allen, J. J. B., & Lai, V. T. (2022). Attention and regulation during emotional word comprehension in older adults: Evidence from event-related potentials and brain oscillations. *Brain and Language, 227*, 105086.

Kubin, E., & von Sikorski (22 September, 2021). The role of (social) media in political polarization: A systematic review. Taylor & Francis Online.

Kulis, S. S., Robbins, D. E., Baker, T. M., Denetsosie, S., Parkhurst, D., & Nicholet, A. (2016). A latent class analysis of urban American Indian youth identities. *Cultural Diversity and Ethnic Minority Psychology, 22*, 215–228.

Kumar, A. (2022). Some things aren't better left unsaid: Interpersonal barriers to gratitude expression and prosocial engagement. *Current Opinion in Psychology, 43*, 156–160.

Kurzban, R., Burton-Chellew, M. N., & West, S. A. (2015). The evolution of altruism in humans. *Annual Review of Psychology, 66*, 575–599.

Labouvie-Vief, G. (1990). Wisdom as integrated thought: Historical and developmental perspectives. In R. J. Sternberg (Ed.), *Wisdom: Its nature, origins, and development* (pp. 52–83). Cambridge University Press.

Lachmann, B., Doebler, A., Sindermann, C., Sariyska, R., Cooper, A., Haas, H., & Montag, C. (2021). The molecular genetics of life satisfaction: Extending findings from a recent genome-wide association study and examining the role of the serotonin transporter. *Journal of Happiness Studies: An Interdisciplinary Forum on Subjective Well-Being, 22*, 305–322.

Lafferty, J. (2015). *#LoveWins: How the same-sex marriage decision spread through social.* http://www.adweek.com/digital/lovewins-how-the-same-sex-marriage-decision-spread-through-social/

Lageson, S., & Uggen, C. (2013). How work affects crime—and crime affects work—over the life course. In C. L. Gibson & M. D. Krohn (Eds.), *Handbook of life-course criminology: Emerging trends and directions for future research* (pp. 201–212). Springer Science + Business Media.

Lai, C., Luciani, M., Gallie, F., Morelli, E., Del Prete, F., Ginobbi, P., Penco, I., Aceto, P., & Lombardo, L. (2017). Spirituality and awareness of diagnoses in terminally ill patients with cancer. *American Journal of Hospice & Palliative Medicine, 34*, 505–509.

Laird, S. P., Snyder, C. R., Rapoff, M. A., & Green, S. (2004). Measuring private prayer: The development and validation of the Multidimensional Prayer Inventory. *International Journal for the Psychology of Religion, 14*, 251–272.

Lamas, T., Froh, J. J. Emmons, R. A., Mishra, A., & Bono, G. (2014). Gratitude interventions: A review and future agenda. In A. C. Parks, & S. M. Schueller (Eds.), *The Wiley Blackwell handbook of positive psychological interventions*. pp. 3–19. Wiley Blackwell.

Lambert, N. M., Clark, M. S., Durtschi, J., Fincham, F. D., & Graham, S. M. (2010). Benefits of expressing gratitude: Expressing gratitude to a partner changes one's view of the relationship. *Psychological Science, 21*, 574–580.

Lambert, N. M., Fincham, F. D., & Stillman, T. F. (2012). Gratitude and depressive symptoms: The role of positive reframing and positive emotion. *Cognition and Emotion, 26*, 615–633.

Lancet. (2019). *The emerging voices of youth activists.* DOI: https://doi.org/10.1016/S0140-6736(19)30991-2

Landis, D., & O'Shea, W. A., III. (2000). Cross-cultural aspects of passionate love: An individual differences analysis. *Journal of Cross-Cultural Psychology, 31*, 752–777.

Lanfear, C. C. (2022). Collective efficacy and the built

environment. *Criminology: An Interdisciplinary Journal, 60*(2), 370–396.

Langer, E. (2009a). Mindfulness versus positive evaluation. In S. J. Lopez & C. R. Snyder (Eds.), *Oxford handbook of positive psychology* (pp. 279–294). Oxford University Press.

Langer, E. (2009b). *Counter clockwise: Mindful health and the power of possibility*. Random House.

Langer, E. J., & Ngnoumen, C. T. (2021). Well-being: Mindfulness versus positive evaluation. In C. R. Snyder, S. J. Lopez, L. M. Edwards, & S. C. Marques (Eds.), *The Oxford handbook of positive psychology., 3rd ed.* (2021-20328-028; pp. 379–395). Oxford University Press.

Langer, E. J., Cohen, M., & Djikic, M. (2012). Mindfulness as a psychological attractor: The effect on children. *Journal of Applied Social Psychology, 42,* 1114–1122.

Langston, C. A. (1994). Capitalizing on and coping with daily-life events: Expressive responses to positive events. *Journal of Personality and Social Psychology, 67,* 1112–1125.

Languirand, M. (2016). Who I was, who I am: Gender and generativity in the assessment of older adults. In V. M. Brabender & J. L. Mihura (Eds.), *Handbook of gender and sexuality in psychological assessment* (pp. 578–602). Routledge/ Taylor & Francis Group.

Lardon, C., Wolsko, C., Trickett, E., Henry, D., & Hopkins, S. (2016). Assessing health in an Alaska native cultural context: The Yup'ik Wellness Survey. *Cultural Diversity and Ethnic Minority Psychology, 22,* 126–136.

Larsen, D. J., King, R. L., Stege, R., & Egeli, N. A. (2015). Hope in a strengths-based group activity for individuals with chronic pain. *Counselling Psychology Quarterly, 28,* 175–199.

Larsen, J. T., & McGraw, A. P. (2011). Further evidence for mixed emotions. *Journal of Personality and Social Psychology, 100,* 1095–1110.

Larsen, K. S., & Giles, H. (1976). Survival or courage as human motivation: Development of an attitude scale. *Psychological Reports, 39,* 299–302.

Laslo-Roth, R., George-Levi, S., & Margalit, M. (2022). Social participation and posttraumatic growth: The serial mediation of hope, social support, and reappraisal. *Journal of Community Psychology, 50*(1), 47–63.

Laurent, H. K., Laurent, S. M., Lightcap, A., & Nelson, B. W. (2016). How situational mindfulness during conflict stress relates to well-being. *Mindfulness, 7,* 909–915.

Laurent, J., Catanzaro, S. J., Joiner, T. E., Rudolph, K. D., Potter, K. I., Lambert, S., Osborne, E., Gathright, T. (1999). A measure of positive and negative affect for children: Scale development and preliminary validation. *Psychological Assessment, 11,* 326–338.

Lavelock, C. R., Snipes, D. J., Griffen, B. J., Worthington, E. L., Davis, D. E., Hook., J., N., Benotsch, E. G., &Ritter, J. (2015). A conceptual model of forgiveness and health. In L. L. Toussaint, E. L. Worthington, & D. R. Williams (Eds.), *Forgiveness and health* (pp. 29–42). Springer Netherlands.

Layous, K. L., Lee, H., Choi, I., & Lyubormirsky, S. (2013). Culture matters when designing a successful happiness-increasing activity: A comparison of the United States and South Korea. *Journal of Cross-Cultural Psychology, 44,* 1294–1303.

Layous, K., Sweeney, K., Armenta, C., Na, S., Choi, I, & Lyubomirsky, S. (2017). The proximal experience of gratitude. *PLoS ONE, 12,* 1–26.

Le, B. M., Impett, E. A., Lemay, E. P., Jr., Muise, A, & Tskhay, K. O. (2018). Communal motivation and well-being in interpersonal relationships: An integrative review and meta-analysis. *Psychological Bulletin, 144,* 1–25.

Lee, J. A. (1973). *The colors of love: An exploration of the ways of loving.* New Press.

Le, T. N. (2011). Life satisfaction, openness value, self-transcendence, and wisdom. *Journal of Happiness Studies, 12,* 171–182.

Le, T. N., Lai, M. H., & Wallen, J. (2009). Multiculturalism and subjective happiness as mediated by cultural and relational variables. *Cultural Diversity and Ethnic Minority Psycho1ogy, 15,* 303–313.

Leach, M. M., Baker, A., & Zeigler-Hill, V. (2011). The influence of Black racial identity on the forgiveness of Whites. *Journal of Black Psychology, 37,* 185–209.

LeDoux, J. E. (1996). *The emotional brain: The mysterious underpinnings of emotional life.* Simon & Schuster.

Lee, B.-O. (2013). Ambivalence over emotional expression and symptom attribution are associated with self-reported somatic symptoms in Singaporean school adolescents. *Asian Journal of Social Psychology, 16*, 169–180.

Lee, G. R., Seccombe, K., & Shehan, C. L. (1991). Marital status and personal happiness: An analysis of trend data. *Journal of Marriage and the Family, 53*, 839–844.

Lee, Y.-T., & Seligman, M. E. P. (1997). Are Americans more optimistic than the Chinese? *Personality and Social Psychology Bulletin, 23*(1), 32–40. https://doi.org/10.1177/0146167297231004

Lee, H. E., & Park, H. S. (2011). Why Koreans are more likely to favor "apology" while Americans are more likely to favor "thank you." *Human Communication Research, 37*, 125–146.

Lee, H. H., Kubzansky, L. D., Okuzono, S. S., Trudel-Fitzgerald, C., James, P., Koga, H. K., Kim, E. S., Glover, L. M., Sims, M., & Grodstein, F. (2022). Optimism and risk of mortality among African-Americans: The Jackson heart study. *Preventive Medicine, 154*, 106899.

Lee, H. H., Okuzono, S. S., Kim, E. S., De Vivo, I., Raffield, L. M., Glover, L., Sims, M., Grodstein, F., & Kubzansky, L. D. (2021). Optimism and telomere length among African American adults in the Jackson Heart Study. *Psychoneuroendocrinology, 125*, 105124.

Lee, J. E., Kahana, B., & Kahana, E. (2017). Successful aging from the viewpoint of older adults: Development of a brief Successful Aging Inventory (SAI). *Gerontology, 63*, 359–371.

Lee, L. O., James, P., Zevon, E. S., Kim, E. S., Trudel-Fitzgerald, C., Spiro, A., III, Grodstein, F., & Kubzansky, L. D. (2019). Optimism is associated with exceptional longevity in 2 epidemiologic cohorts of men and women. *PNAS Proceedings of the National Academy of Sciences of the United States of America, 116*(37), 18357–18362.

Lee, L., Kuo, Y., Fanaw, D., Perng, S., & Juang, I. (2012). The effect of an intervention combining self-efficacy theory and pedometers on promoting physical activity among adolescents. *Journal of Clinical Nursing, 21*, 914–922.

Lee, S. W., Kim, I., Yoo, J., Park, S., Jeong, B., & Cha, M. (2016). Insights from an expressive writing intervention on Facebook to help alleviate depressive symptoms. *Computers in Human Behavior, 62*, 613–619.

Lemola, S., Räikkönen, K., Matthews, K. A., Scheier, M. F., Heinonen, K., Pesonen, A., & Lahti, J. (2010). A new measure for dispositional optimism and pessimism in young children. *European Journal of Personality, 24*, 71–84.

Lepore, S. J., & Greenberg, M. A. (2002). Mending broken hearts: Effects of expressive writing on mood, cognitive processing, social adjustment and health following a relationship breakup. *Psychology and Health, 17*, 547–560

Lerner, J. V., Phelps, E., Forman, Y., & Bowers, E. P. (2009). Positive youth development. In R. M. Lerner & L. Steinberg (Eds.), *Handbook of adolescent psychology: Individual bases of adolescent development* (pp. 524–558). John Wiley & Sons.

Lerner, R. M., Lerner, J. V., Urban, J. B., & Zaff, J. (2016). Evaluating programs aimed at promoting positive youth development: A relational development systems-based view. *Applied Developmental Science, 20*, 175–187.

Lerner, R. M., von Eye, A., Lerner, J. V., Lewin-Bizan, S., & Bowers, E. P. (2010). Special issue introduction: The meaning and measurement of thriving: A view of the issues. *Journal of Youth and Adolescence, 39*, 707–719.

Leu, J., Wang, J., & Koo, K. (2011). Are positive emotions just as "positive" across cultures? *Emotion, 11*, 994–999.

Leung, D. Y. P., & Leung, A. Y. M. (2011). Factor structure and gender invariance of the Chinese General Self-Efficacy Scale among soon-to-be-aged adults. *Journal of Advanced Nursing, 67*(6), 1383–1392.

Levenson, M. R. (2009). Gender and wisdom: The roles of compassion and moral development. *Research in Human Development, 6*, 45–59.

Levine, A., & Heller, R. S. F. (2012). *Attached: The science of adult attachment and how it can help you find and keep love.* TeacherPerigee.

Lewis, J. P., & Allen, J. (2017). Alaska native elders in recovery: Linkages between indigenous cultural generativity and sobriety to promote successful aging. *Journal of Cross-Cultural Gerontology, 32*, 209–222.

Lewis, R. K. (2011). Promoting positive youth development by understanding social contexts. *Journal of Prevention & Intervention in the Community, 39*, 273–276.

Li, C. J., & Monroe, M. C. (2019). Exploring the essential psychological factors in fostering hope concerning climate change. *Environmental Education Research, 25*(6), 936–954. https://doi.org/10.1080/13504622.2017.1367916

Li, Y., Luo, L., & Fun, J. (2019). Benefactor intention, perceived helpfulness, and personal responsibility influence gratitude and indebtedness. *Social Behavior and Personality: An International Journal, 47*, 1–15.

Li, Z., Yin, X., Yang, H., & Tian, J. (2018). The measurement structure of dispositional hope: Hierarchical and bifactor models. Social Behavior and Personality: An International Journal, *46*(4), 597–606.

Lin, C.-C., Kao, Y.-T., Chen, Y.-L., & Lu, S.-C. (2016). Fostering change-oriented behaviors: A broaden-and-build model. *Journal of Business and Psychology, 31*, 399–414.

Lin, Y., Worthington, E. L., Griffen, B. J., Greer, C. L., Opare-Henaku, A., Lavelock, C. R., ... Muller, H. (2014). Efficacy of REACH forgiveness across cultures. *Journal of Clinical Psychology, 70*, 781–793.

Lin, Y., Zhang, Y C., & Oyserman, D. (2022). Seeing meaning even when none may exist: Collectivism increases belief in empty claims. *Journal of Personality and Social Psychology, 122*, 351–366.

Linley, P. A., & Harrington, S. (2006). Playing to your strengths. *The Psychologist, 19*, 85–89.

Littman-Ovadia, H., Lavy, S., & Boiman-Meshita, M. (2017). When theory and research collide: Examining correlates of signature strengths use at work. *Journal of Happiness Studies: An Interdisciplinary Forum on Subjective Well-Being, 18*, 527–548

Liu, Q., & Wang, Z. (2021). Perceived stress of the COVID-19 pandemic and adolescents' depression symptoms: The moderating role of character strengths. *Personality and Individual Differences, 182*.

Locey, M. L., & Rachlin, H. (2015). Altruism and anonymity: A behavioral analysis. *Behavioral Processes, 118*, 71–75.

Locke, K. D., Sayegh, L., Penberthy, J. K., Weber, C., Haentjens, K., & Turecki, G. (2017). Interpersonal circumplex profiles of persistent depression: Goals, self-efficacy, problems, and effects of group therapy. *Journal of Clinical Psychology, 73*, 595–611.

Locke, T. F., & Newcomb, M. D. (2004). Adolescent predictors of young adult and adult alcohol involvement and dysphoria in a prospective community sample of women. *Prevention Science, 5*, 151–168.

Logie, C. H., Kinitz, D. J., Gittings, L., Persad, Y., Lacombe-Duncan, A., & Poteat, T. (2022). Eliciting critical hope in community-based HIV research with transgender women in Toronto, Canada: Methodological insights. *Health Promotion International, 37*(Supplement 2), ii37–ii47.

Lomax, Sl, Camaro, C. L., Hassen, N., Whitlow, C., Magid, K., & Jaffe, G. (2022). Centering mental health in society: A human rights approach to well-being for all. *American Journal of Orthopsychiatry, 92*, 364–370.

Long, B. C. (1993). Coping strategies of male managers: A prospective analysis of predictors of psychosomatic symptoms and job satisfaction. *Journal of Vocational Behavior, 42*, 184–199.

Long, C. (2010). Apology in Japanese gratitude situations: The negotiation of interlocutor role-relations. *Journal of Pragmatics, 42*, 1060–1075.

Long, M., Verbeke, W., Ein-Dor, T., & Vrtička, P. (2020). A functional neuro-anatomical model of human attachment (NAMA): Insights from first- and second-person social neuroscience. *Cortex, 126*, 281–321.

Long, L. J., Lu, Q., Walker, R. L., & Gallagher, M. W. (2020). Examining the measurement invariance of the LOT-R Measure of Optimism in the United States and Japan. *Journal of Well-Being Assessment, 4*(3), 447–462.

Lopes, P. N. (2021). Thriving on emotional intelligence? Bridging research and practice. In C. R. Snyder, S. J. Lopez, L. M. Edwards, & S. C. Marques (Eds.), *The Oxford handbook of positive psychology., 3rd ed.* (2021-20328-025; pp. 340–354)

Lopez, F. G. (2003). The assessment of adult attachment security. In S. J. Lopez & C. R. Snyder (Eds.), *Positive psychological assessment: A handbook of models and measures* (pp. 285–299). American Psychological Association.

Lopez, F. G., & Brennan, K. A. (2000). Dynamic processes underlying adult attachment organization: Toward an attachment-theoretical perspective on the healthy and effective self. *Journal of Counseling Psychology, 47*, 283–300.

Lopez, S. J. (2013). *Making hope happen*. Atria.

Lopez, S. J., & Louis, M. C. (2009). The principles of strengths-based education. *Journal of College and Character, 10*(4), 1–8.

Lopez, S. J., & Snyder, C. R. (2009). *Oxford handbook of positive psychology*. Oxford University Press.

Lopez, S. J., Harter, J. K., Juszkiewicz, P. J., & Carr, J. A. (2007). *Clifton Youth StrengthsExplore™ technical report: Development and validation*. Gallup Organization.

Lopez, S. J., Hodges, T. D., & Harter, J. K. (2005). *Clifton StrengthsFinder technical report: Development and validation*. Gallup Organization.

Lopez, S. J., Janowski, K. M., & Wells, K. J. (2005). *Developing strengths in college students: Exploring programs, contents, theories, and research*. Unpublished manuscript, University of Kansas.

LoPresti, M. A., Dement, F., & Gold, H. T. (2016). End-of-life care for people with cancer from ethnic minority groups: a systematic review. *American Journal of Hospice and Palliative Medicine, 33*, 291–305.

Lowe, N. K. (1993). Maternal confidence for labour: Development of the childbirth self-efficacy inventory. *Research in Nursing & Health, 16*, 141–149.

Lu, J. G., & Jin, P. (2021). Collectivism predicts mask use during COVID-19. *Proceedings of the National Academy of Sciences of the United States of America, 118*.

Lu, J. H., & Steele, C. K. (2019). 'Joy is resistance': Cross-platform resilience and (re) invention of Black oral culture online. *Information, Communication & Society, 22*, 823–837.

Lu, L., & Gilmour, R. (2004). Culture and conceptions of happiness: Individual oriented and social oriented SWB. *Journal of Happiness Studies, 5*, 269–291.

Lu, L., Lin, H. Y., & Cooper, C. L. (2013). Unhealthy and present: Motives and consequences of the act of presenteeism among Taiwanese employees. *Journal of Occupational Health Psychology, 18*, 406–416.

Lu, Q., & Stanton, A. L. (2010). How benefits of expressive writing vary as a function of writing instructions, ethnicity and ambivalence over emotional expression. *Psychology & Health, 25*(6), 669–684.

Lucas, A. G., Chang, E. C., Lee, J., & Hirsch, J. K. (2020). Positive expectancies for the future as potential protective factors of suicide risk in adults: Does optimism and hope predict suicidal behaviors in primary care patients? *International Journal of Mental Health and Addiction, 18*(1), 41–53.

Luke, M. A., Sedikides, C., & Carnelley, K. (2012). Your love lifts me higher! The energizing quality of secure relationships. *Personality and Social Psychology Bulletin, 38*, 721–733.

Lynn, M., & Snyder, C. R. (2002). Uniqueness. In C. R. Snyder, & S. J. Lopez (Eds.), *The handbook of positive psychology* (pp.395–401). Oxford University Press.

Lyons, M. D., Edwards, K. D., & Fallavollita, W. L. (2021). Promoting mentoring relationships through joint decisions: Evidence from a national mentoring program. *School Psychology, 36*(4), 214–223.

Lyubomirsky, S., Dickerhoof, R., Boehm, J. K., & Sheldon, K. M. (2011). Becoming happier takes both a will and a proper way: An experimental longitudinal intervention to boost well-being. *Emotion, 11*, 391–402.

Lyubomirsky, S., Sheldon, K. M., & Schkade, D. (2005). Pursuing happiness: The architecture of sustainable change. *Review of General Psychology, 9*, 111–131.

MacCann, C., Jiang, Y., Brown, L. E. R., Double, K. S., Bucich, M., & Minbashian, A. (2020). Emotional intelligence predicts academic performance: A meta-analysis. *Psychological Bulletin, 146*(2), 150–186.

Maddux, J. E. (1991). Self-efficacy. In C. R. Snyder & D. R. Forsyth (Eds.), *Handbook of social and clinical psychology: The health perspective* (pp. 57–58). Pergamon.

Maddux, J. E. (2009a). Self-efficacy: The power of believing you can. In S. J. Lopez & C. R. Snyder (Eds.), *Oxford handbook of positive psychology* (pp. 335–343). Oxford University Press.

Maddux, J. E., & Kleiman, E. M. (2021). Self-efficacy: The power of believing you can. In C. R. Snyder, S. J. Lopez, L. M. Edwards, & S. C. Marques (Eds.), *The Oxford handbook of positive psychology., 3rd ed.* (2021-20328-032; pp. 443–452). Oxford University Press.

Maddux, J. E., & Lewis, J. (1995). Self-efficacy and adjustment: Basic principles and issues. In J. E. Maddux (Ed.), *Self-efficacy, adaptation, and adjustment: Theory, research, and application* (pp. 37–68). Plenum.

Magalhães, S., Barbosa, J., & Borges, E. (2022). The relationship between presenteeism, quality of life and social support in higher education professionals: A cross-sectional path analysis. *PLoS ONE, 17,* Advanced Online.

Maglione, M. A., Maher, A. R., Ewing, B., Colaiaco, B., Newberry, S., Kandrack, R., Shanman, R. M., Sorbero, M. E., & Hempel, S. (2017). Efficacy of mindfulness meditation for smoking cessation: A systematic review and meta-analysis. *Addictive Behaviors, 69,* 27–34.

Magnuson, C. D., & Barnett, L. A. (2013). The playful advantage: How playfulness enhances coping with stress. *Leisure Sciences, 35,* 129–144.

Mahan, B. B., Garrard, W. M., Lewis, S. E., & Newbrough, J. R. (2002). Sense of community in a university setting. In A. T. Fisher, C. C. Sonn, & B. J. Bishop (Eds.), *Psychological sense of community: Research, applications, and implications* (pp. 123–140). Kluwer/Plenum.

Mahoney, A., Pargament, K. I., Cole, B., Jewell, T., Magyar, G. M., Tarakeshwar, N., Murray-Swank, N. A., & Phillips, R. (2005). A higher purpose: The sanctification of strivings in a community sample. *International Journal for the Psychology of Religion, 15,* 239–262.

Mahoney, J. L., Cairns, B. D., & Farmer, T. W. (2003). Promoting interpersonal competence and educational success through extracurricular activity participation. *Journal of Education Psychology, 95,* 409–418.

Maier, S. F., Laudenslager, M. L., & Ryan, S. M. (1985). Stressor controllability, immune function, and endogenous opiates. In F. R. Brush & J. B. Overmier (Eds.), *Affect, conditioning, and cognition: Essays on the determinants of behavior* (pp. 183–201). Lawrence Erlbaum.

Main, M., & Goldwyn, R. (1984). *Adult attachment scoring and classification system.* Unpublished manuscript, University of California at Berkeley.

Main, M., & Goldwyn, R. (1998). *Adult attachment interview scoring and classification system.* Unpublished manuscript, University of California at Berkeley.

Malouff, J. M., & Schutte, N. S. (2017). Can psychological interventions increase optimism? A meta-analysis. *The Journal of Positive Psychology, 12,* 594–604.

Mandler, G. (1975). *Mind and emotion.* Wiley.

Maner, J. K., & Gailliot, M. T. (2007). Altruism and egoism: Prosocial motivations for helping depend on relationship context. *European Journal of Social Psychology, 37,* 347–358.

Mansbridge, J. J. (Ed.). (1990). *Beyond self-interest.* University of Chicago Press.

Mansur, J., Sobral, F., & Islam, G. (2020). Leading with moral courage: The interplay of guild and courage on perceived ethical leadership and group organizational citizenship behaviors. *Business Ethnics: A European Review, 29,* 587–601.

Markus, H. R., & Kitayama, S. (1991). Culture and the self: Implications for cognition, emotion, and motivation. *Psychological Review, 98*(2), 224–253.

Marlowe, D. B., Ho, T., Carey, S. M., & Chadick, C. D. (2020). Employing standardized risk assessment in pretrial release decisions: Association with criminal justice outcomes and racial equity. *Law and Human Behavior, 44,* 361–376.

Marques, S. C., Lopez, S. J., & Mitchell, J. (2013). The role of hope, spirituality, and religious practice in adolescents' life satisfaction: Longitudinal findings. *Journal of Happiness Studies, 14,* 251–261.

Marques, S. C., Pais-Ribeiro, J. L., & Lopez, S. J. (2009). Validation of a Portuguese version of the Children's Hope Scale. *School Psychology International, 30,* 538–551.

Marrero, R. J., Rey, M., & Hernández-Cabrera, J. A.

(2016). Can big five facets distinguish between hedonic and eudaimonic well-being? A dominance analysis. *The Spanish Journal of Psychology, 19*, e84.

Marrero-Quevedo, R. J., Blanco-Hernández, P. J., & Hernández-Cabrera, J. A. (2019). Adult Attachment and Psychological Well-Being: The Mediating Role of Personality. *Journal of Adult Development, 26*(1), 41–56.

Marroquín, B., Czamanski-Cohen, J., Weihs, K. L., & Stanton, A. L. (2016). Implicit loneliness, emotion regulation, and depressive symptoms in breast cancer survivors. *Journal of Behavioral Medicine, 39*, 832–844.

Marsh, A. A. (2016). Neural, cognitive, and evolutionary foundations of human altruism. *WIREs Cognitive Science, 7*, 59–71.

Martin, A. J. (2011). Courage in the classroom: Exploring a new framework predicting academic performance and engagement. *School Psychology Quarterly, 26*, 145–160.

Martinez, Jr., R. R., & Baker, S. (2023). Perspectives on career and college readiness self-efficacy of Latinx adolescents: A thematic analysis. *Journal of Multicultural Counseling and Development*, 51, 158–173.

Maslow, A. (1954). *Motivation and personality*. Harper.

Maslow, A. (1970). *Motivation and personality* (2nd Ed.). Harper & Row.

Matsumoto, D., Kudoh, T., & Takeuchi, S. (1996). Changing patterns of individualism and collectivism in the United States and Japan. *Culture and Psychology, 2*, 77–107.

Matsushita, M., Adachi, H., Arakida, M., Namura, I., Takahashi, Y., Miyata, M., Kumano-go, T., Yamamura, S., Shigedo, Y., Suganuma, N., Mikami, A., Moriyama, T., & Sugita, Y. (2011). Presenteeism in college students: Reliability and validity of the Presenteeism Scale for Students. *Quality of Life Research: An International Journal of Quality of Life Aspects of Treatment, Care, & Rehabilitation, 20*, 439–446.

Matthews, K. A., Batson, C. D., Horn, J., & Rosenman, R. H. (1981). "Principles in his nature which interest him in the fortune of others . . .": The heritability of empathic concern for others. *Journal of Personality, 49*, 237–247.

Mattingly, J. A., & Andresen, P. A. (2016). NAP SACC: Implementation of an obesity prevention intervention in an American Indian Head Start program. *Journal of Community Health Nursing, 33*, 145–153.

Mattingly, V., & Kraiger, K. (2019). Can emotional intelligence be trained? A meta-analytical investigation. *Advancing Training for the 21st Century, 29*(2), 140–155.

Mattis, J. S., Powell, W., Grayman, N. A., Murray, Y., Cole-Lewis, Y. C., & Goodwill, J. R. (2017). What would I know about mercy? Faith and optimistic expectancies among African Americans. *Race and Social Problems, 9*, 42–51.

Mayer, J. D., Caruso, D. R., & Salovey, P. (2016). The ability model of emotional intelligence: Principles and updates. *Emotion Review, 8*(4), 290–300. https://doi.org/10.1177/1754073916639667

Mayer, J. D., DiPaolo, M. T., & Salovey, P. (1990). Perceiving affective content of ambiguous visual stimuli: A component of emotional intelligence. *Journal of Personality Assessment, 54*, 772–781.

Mayer, J. D., Salovey, P., & Caruso, D. (2001). *The Mayer-Salovey-Caruso Emotional Intelligence Test (MSCEIT)*. Multi-Health Systems, Inc.

May, R. (1975). *The courage to create*. W. W. Norton.

McCarthy, G., & Maughan, B. (2010). Negative childhood experiences and adult love relationships: The role of internal working models of attachment. *Attachment & Human Development, 12*, 445–461.

McClelland, D. C., Atkinson, J. W., Clark, R. W., & Lowell, E. L. (1953). *The achievement motive*. Appleton-Century-Crofts.

McClintock, C. H., Worhunsky, P. D., Balodis, I. M., Sinha, R., Miller, L., & Potenza, M. N. (2019). How spirituality may mitigate against stress and related mental disorders: A review and preliminary neurobiological evidence. *Current Behavioral Neuroscience Reports, 6*(4), 253–262.

McCormick, B., Lewis, T., Gonzalez, K., Horton, G., & Barsky, A. E. (2019). Teaching field educators about courageous conversations concerning racism and religious bigotry. *Journal of Baccalaureate Social Work, 24*, 123–138.

McCrae, R. R., & Costa, P. T. (1987). Validation of the five-factor model of personality across instruments and observers. *Journal of Personality and Social Psychology, 52,* 81–90.

McCullough, M. E. (2000). Forgiveness as a human strength: Theory, measurement, and links to well-being. *Journal of Social and Clinical Psychology, 19,* 43–55.

McCullough, M. E., Emmons, R. A., & Tsang, J. (2002). The grateful disposition: A conceptual and empirical topography. *Journal of Personality and Social Psychology, 82,* 112–127.

McCullough, M. E., Kimeldorf, M. B., & Cohen, A. D. (2008). An adaptation for altruism? The social causes, social effects, and social evolution of gratitude. *Current Directions in Psychological Science, 17,* 281–285.

McCullough, M. E., Pargament, K. I., & Thoresen, C. E. (Eds.). (2000a). *Forgiveness: Theory, research, and practice.* Guilford.

McCullough, M. E., Pargament, K. I., & Thoresen, C. E. (2000b). The psychology of forgiveness: History, conceptual issues, and overview. In M. E. McCullough, K. I. Pargament, & C. E. Thoresen (Eds.), *Forgiveness: Theory, research, and practice* (pp. 1–14). Guilford.

McCullough, M. E., Pedersen, E. J., Tabak, B. A., & Carter, E. C. (2014). Conciliatory gestures promote forgiveness and reduce anger in humans. *PNAS Proceedings of the National Academy of Sciences of the United States of America, 111,* 11211–11216.

McCullough, M. E., Rachal, K. C., Sandage, S. J., Worthington, E. L., Jr., Brown, S. W., & Hight, T. L. (1998). Interpersonal forgiving in close relationships: II. Theoretical elaboration and measurement. *Journal of Personality and Social Psychology, 75,* 1586–1603.

McCullough, M. E., Tsang, J., & Emmons, R. A. (2004). Gratitude in intermediate affective terrain: Links of grateful moods to individual differences and daily emotional experience. *Journal of Personality and Social Psychology, 86,* 295–309.

McDavid, L., McDonough, M. H., & Smith, A. L. (2015). An empirical evaluation of two theoretically-based hypotheses on the directional association between self-worth and hope. *Journal of Adolescence, 41,* 25–30.

McDermott, D., & Snyder, C. R. (2000). *The great big book of hope.* New Harbinger.

McDermott, E. R., Donlan, A. E., Zaff, J. F., & Prescott, J. E. (2016). A psychometric analysis of hope, persistence, and engagement among reengaged youth. *Journal of Psychoeducational Assessment, 34,* 136–152.

McDermott, R. C., Berry, A. T., Borgogna, N. C., Cheng, H.-L., Wong, Y. J., Browning, B., & Carr, N. (2020). Revisiting the paradox of hope: The role of discrimination among first-year Black college students. *Journal of Counseling Psychology, 67*(5), 637–644.

McDermott, R. C., Brasil, K. M., Borgogna, N. C., Barinas, J. L., Berry, A. T., & Levant, R. F. (2021). The politics of men's and women's traditional masculinity ideology in the United States. *Psychology of Men & Masculinities, 22,* 627–638.

McDermott, R. C., Brasil, K. M., Borgogna, N. C., Barinas, J., & Levant, R. F. (2022). Traditional masculinity ideology and feminist attitudes: The role of identity foreclosure. Sex Roles: *A Journal of Research.* Advance online publication. https://doi.org/10.1007/s11199-022-01302-4

McDermott, R. C., Cheng, H.-L., Wright, C., Browning, B. R., Upton, A. W., & Sevig, T. D. (2015). Adult attachment dimensions and college student distress: The mediating role of hope. *The Counseling Psychologist, 43*(6), 822–852. https://doi.org/10.1177/0011000015575394

McFarland, M. J., Smith, C. A., Toussaint, L., & Thomas, P. A. (2012). Forgiveness of others and health: Do race and neighborhood matter? *The Journals of Gerontology: Series B: Psychological Sciences and Social Sciences, 67B,* 66–75.

McGrath, R. E. (2015). Character strengths in 75 nations: An update. *The Journal of Positive Psychology, 10*(1), 41–52.

McGrath, R. E. (2016). Measurement invariance in translations of the VIA Inventory of Strengths. *European Journal of Psychological Assessment, 32*(3), 187–194.

McGrath, R. E. (2019). *Technical report: The VIA Assessment Suite for Adults: Development and initial evaluation* (Rev. ed.). VIA Institute on Character.

McGrath, R. E., & Wallace, N. (2021). Cross-validation of the VIA inventory of Strengths-revised and its short forms.

Journal of Personality Assessment, *103*(1), 120–131.

McGrath, R. E., Brown, M., Westrich, B., & Han, H. (2022). Representative sampling of the VIA Assessment Suite for Adults. *Journal of Personality Assessment*, *104*(3), 380–394.

McKiernan, P., Cloud, R., Patterson, D. A., Golder, S., & Besel, K. (2011). Development of a brief abstinence self-efficacy measure. *Journal of Social Work Practice in the Addictions*, *11*, 245–253.

McLoyd, V. C. (1998). Socioeconomic disadvantage and child development. *American Psychologist*, *53*, 185–204.

McNulty, J. K. (2011). The dark side of forgiveness: The tendency to forgive predicts continued psychological and physical aggression in marriage. *Personality and Social Psychology Bulletin*, *37*, 770–783.

Mead, J. P., Fisher, Z., Tree, J. J., Wong, P. T. P., & Kemp, A. H. (2021). Protectors of wellbeing during the COVID-19 pandemic: Key roles for gratitude and tragic optimism in a UK-based cohort. *Frontiers in Psychology*, *12*, 1–11.

Meehl, P. (1975). Hedonic capacity: Some conjectures. *Bulletin of the Menninger Clinic*, *39*, 295–307.

Meissner, C. A., & Brigham, J. C. (2001). Thirty years of investigating the own-race bias in memory for faces: A meta-analytic review. *Psychology, Public Policy, and Law*, *7*, 3–35.

Memarian, N., Torre, J. B., Haltom, K. E., Stanton, A. L., & Lieberman, M. D. (2017). Neural activity during affect labeling predicts expressive writing effects on well-being: GLM and SVM approaches. *Social Cognitive and Affective Neuroscience*, *12*, 1437–1447.

Menninger, K., Mayman, M., & Pruyser, P. W. (1963). *The vital balance*. Viking.

Mens, M. G., Scheier, M. F., & Carver, C. S. (2021). Optimism. In C. R. Snyder, S. J. Lopez, L. M. Edwards, & S. C. Marques (Eds.), *The Oxford handbook of positive psychology., 3rd ed.* (2021-20328-029; pp. 396–412). Oxford University Press

Merrell, K. W. (2011). *Social emotional assets and resilience scales*. PAR

Metalsky, G. I., Halberstadt, J., & Abramson, L. Y. (1987). Vulnerability to depressive mood reactions: Toward a more powerful test of the diathesis-stress and causal mediation components of the reformulated theory of depression. *Journal of Personality and Social Psychology*, *52*, 386–393.

Miao, C., Humphrey, R. H., & Qian, S. (2021). Emotional intelligence and job performance in the hospitality industry: A meta-analytic review. *International Journal of Contemporary Hospitality Management*, *33*(8), 2632–2652

Michael, S. T., & Snyder, C. R. (2005). Getting unstuck: The rules of hope, finding meaning, and rumination in adjustment to bereavement among college students. *Journal of Death Studies*, *29*, 435–458.

Mikulincer, M, Herzliya, I., & Shaver, Pl R. (2020). Broaden-and-build effects of contextually boosting the sense of attachment security in adulthood. *Current Directions in Psychological Science*, *29*, 22–26.

Mikulincer, M., & Shaver, P. R. (2017). *Attachment in adulthood: Structure dynamics and change*. Guilford Press.

Mikulincer, M., & Shaver, P. R. (2021). Attachment theory as a relational framework for positive psychology. In C. R. Snyder, S. J. Lopez, L. M. Edwards, & S. C. Marques (Eds.), *The Oxford handbook of positive psychology, 3rd ed.* (2021-20328-038; pp. 519–532). Oxford University Press

Mikulincer, M., & Shaver, P. R. (2022). Enhancing the 'broaden-and-build' cycle of attachment security as a means of overcoming prejudice, discrimination, and racism. *Attachment & Human Development (online)*.

Miller, A. J., & Worthington, E. L., Jr. (2010). Sex differences in forgiveness and mental health in recently married couples. *The Journal of Positive Psychology*, *5*, 12–23.

Millett, G., D'Amico, D., Amestoy, M. E., Gryspeerdt, C., & Fiocco, A. J. (2021). Do group-based mindfulness meditation programs enhance executive functioning? A systematic review and meta-analysis of the evidence. *Consciousness and Cognition*, *95*, 103195.

Mio, J. S., Barker, L. A., & Domenech-Rodríguez, M. (2015). *Multicultural psychology: Understanding our diverse communities*. Oxford University Press.

Miranda, J., Bernal, G., Lau, A., Kohn, L., Hwang, W. C., &

LaFromboise, T. (2005). State of the science on psychosocial interventions for ethnic minorities. *Annual Review of Clinical Psychology, 1*, 113–142.

Mirkin, M. P., Suyemoto, K. L., & Okun, B. F. (Eds.). (2005). *Psychotherapy with women: Exploring diverse contexts and identities*. The Guilford Press

Miyake, K., Chen, S. J., & Campos, J. J. (1985). Infant temperament, mother's mode of interaction, and attachment in Japan: An interim report. *Monographs of the Society for Research in Child Development, 50*, 276–297.

Mohr, S., Perroud, N., Gillieron, C., Brandt, P. Y., Rieben, I., Borras, L., & Huguelet, P. (2011). Spirituality and religiousness as predictive factors of outcome in schizophrenia and schizo-affective disorders. *Psychiatry Research, 186*, 177–182.

Moneta, G. B. (2004a). The flow experience across cultures. *Journal of Happiness Studies, 5*, 115–121.

Moneta, G. B. (2004b). The flow model of intrinsic motivation in Chinese: Cultural and personal moderators. *Journal of Happiness Studies, 5*, 181–217.

Mooney, L., Strelan, P., & McKee, I. (2016). How forgiveness promotes offender pro-relational intentions: The mediating role of offender gratitude. *British Journal of Social Psychology, 55*, 44–64.

Moore-Berg, S. L. Hameiri, B., & Bruneau, E. (2020). The prime psychological suspects of toxic political polarization. *Current Opinion in Behavioral Sciences, 34*, 199–204.

Moore, J. T. (2017). Multicultural and idiosyncratic considerations for measuring the relationship between religious and secular forms of spirituality with positive global mental health. *Psychology of Religion and Spirituality, 9*, 21.

Moore, L., Carr, A., Hodgins, S., Duffy, D., & Rooney, B. (2017). What works best for reducing symptoms and improving quality of life? A 6-months follow-up study on the effectiveness of group cognitive behaviour therapy and group information and support for adults suffering from depression. *Journal of Contemporary Psychotherapy, 47*, 211–221.

Moorhead, H. J. H., Gill, C., Minton, C. A. B., & Myers, J. E. (2012). Forgive and forget? Forgiveness, personality, and wellness among counselors-in-training. *Counseling and Values, 57*, 81–95.

Moreno, P. I., Wiley, J. F., & Stanton, A. L. (2021). Coping through emotional approach: The utility of processing and expressing emotions in response to stress. In C. R. Snyder, S. J. Lopez, L. M. Edwards, & S. C. Marques (Eds.), *The Oxford handbook of positive psychology., 3rd ed.* (pp. 319–339). Oxford University Press

Moreno, Y., & Marrero, R. J. (2015). Optimism and self-esteem as predictors of personal well-being: Sex differences (Optimismo y autoestima como predictores de bienestar personal: Diferencias de género). *Revista Mexicana de Psicología, 32*, 27–36.

Morimoto, T., Matsuyama, K., Ichihara-Takeda, S., Murakami, R., & Ikeda, N. (2012). Influence of self-efficacy on the interpersonal behavior of schizophrenia patients undergoing rehabilitation in psychiatric day-care services. *Psychiatry and Clinical Neurosciences, 66*, 203–209.

Morse, G. S., McIntyre, J. G., & King, J. (2016). Positive psychology in American Indians. In E. C. Chang, C. A. Downey, J. K. Hirsch, & N. J. Lin (Eds.), *Positive psychology in racial and ethnic groups: Theory, research, and practice* (pp. 109–127). American Psychological Association.

Mowrer, O. H. (1960). *Learning theory and behavior.* Wiley.

Murata, A., Moser, J. S., & Kitayama, S. (2013). Culture shapes electrocortical responses during emotion suppression. *Social Cognitive and Affective Neuroscience, 8*, 595–601.

Muris, P., Mayer, B., & Schubert, T. (2010). "You might belong in Gryffindor": Children's courage and its relationships to anxiety symptoms, Big Five personality traits, and sex roles. *Child Psychiatry and Human Development, 41*, 204–213.

Murnane, R. J., & Steele, J. L. (2007). What is the problem? The challenge of providing effective teachers for all children. *The Future of Children, 17*, 15–43.

Mutrie, N., & Faulkner, G. (2004). Physical activity: Positive psychology in motion. In P. A. Linley, & S. Joseph (Eds.), *Positive psychology in practice* (pp. 146–164). Wiley.

Myers, D. G. (1993). *The pursuit of happiness*. HarperCollins.

Myers, D. G. (2000). The funds, friends, and faith of happy people. *American Psychologist, 55*, 56–67.

Myers, D. G. (2004). Human connections and the good life: Balancing individuality and community in public policy. In P. A. Linley & S. Joseph (Eds.), *Positive psychology in practice* (pp. 641–657). Wiley.

Myers, D. G., & Diener, E. (2018). The scientific pursuit of happiness. *Perspectives on Psychological Science, 13*, 218–225.

Nadler, R., Cordy, M., Stengel, J., Segal, Z. V., & Hayden, E. P. (2017). A brief mindfulness practice increases self-reported calmness in young children: A pilot study. *Mindfulness, 8*, 1088–1095.

Nagata, D. K., Wu, K., & Kim, J. H. J. (2017). Content review of qualitative research on Asian American psychological well-being. *Asian American Journal of Psychology, 8*, 262–295.

Nakamura, J., & Csikszentmihalyi, M. (2009). Flow theory and research. In S. J. Lopez & C. R. Snyder (Eds.), *Oxford handbook of positive psychology* (pp. 195–206). Oxford University Press.

Nakamura, J., & Csikszentmihalyi, M. (2021). The experience of flow: Theory and research. In C. R. Snyder, S. J. Lopez, L. M. Edwards, & S. C. Marques (Eds.), *The Oxford handbook of positive psychology., 3rd ed.* (2021-20328-021; pp. 279–296). Oxford University Press.

Naragon-Gainey, K., & Watson, D. (2019). Positive affectivity: The disposition to experience pleasurable emotional states. In C. R. Snyder, S. J. Lopez, L. M. Edwards, & S. C. Marques (Eds.), *The Oxford handbook of positive psychology*, 3rd edition (pp. 297–305). Oxford University Press.

National Center for Statistics and Analysis. (2021). *Research and data*. https://www.nhtsa.gov/research-data/national-center-statistics-and-analysis-ncsa

National Museum of Civil Rights (2014). *Courage in the civil rights movement: A resource for educators*. https://assets.speakcdn.com/assets/2417/COURAGE.pdf

National Museum of the American Indian. (n.d.). *The seven teachings*. Author.

National Organization for Women. (2012). *Violence against women in the United States: Statistics*. https://now.org/resource/violence-against-women-in-the-united-states-statistic

National Science Foundation. (2022). *Survey of earned doctorates*. https://ncses.nsf.gov/pubs/nsf22300/data-tables

Native Women's Centre (2008). *Traditional teachings booklet*. http://www.nativewomenscentre.com/files/Traditional_Teachings_Booklet.pdf

Negy, C., Shreve, T. L., Jensen, B. J., & Uddin, N. (2003). Ethnic identity, self-esteem, and ethnocentrism: A study of social identity versus multicultural theory of development. *Cultural Diversity and Ethnic Minority Psychology, 9*, 333–344.

Nelson, B. W., Bernstein, R., Allen, N. B., & Laurent, H. K. (2020). The quality of early infant-caregiver relational attachment and longitudinal changes in infant inflammation across 6 months. *Developmental Psychobiology, 62*(5), 674–683.

Nese, R. N., Doerner, E., Romer, N., Kaye, N. C., Merrell, K. W., & Tom, K. M. (2012). Social emotional assets and resilience scales: development of a strength-based short-form behavior rating scale system. *Journal for Educational Research Online, 4*(1), 124–139.

Newberg, A. (2014). The neuroscientific study of spiritual practices. *Frontiers in Psychology, 5*.

Newberg, A. B., d'Aquili, E. G., Newberg, S. K., & deMarici, V. (2000). The neuropsychological correlates of forgiveness. *Forgiveness: Theory, research, and practice*, 91–110.

Newbrough, J. R. (1995). Toward community: A third position. *American Journal of Community Psychology, 23*, 9–31.

Ng, E. C. W., & Fisher, A. T. (2016). Protestant spirituality and well-being of people in Hong Kong: the mediating role of sense of community. *Applied Research in Quality of Life, 11*, 1253–1267.

Nguyen, S.P., & Gordon, C.L. (2022). Gratitude for categories of needs before and during the COVID-19 pandemic. *Journal of Happiness Studies, 23*, 2881–2901.

Niazi, A. K., & Niazi, S. K. (2011). Mindfulness-based stress reduction: A non-pharmacological approach for chronic illnesses. *North*

American journal of medical sciences, 3(1), 20–23.

Nickell, G. S. (1998, August). *The Helping Attitude Scale*. Paper presented at the American Psychological Association Convention, San Francisco.

Niederhoffer, K. G., & Pennebaker, J. W. (2002). Sharing one's story: On the benefits of writing or talking about emotional experience. In C. R. Snyder & S. J. Lopez (Eds.), *The handbook of positive psychology* (pp. 573–583). Oxford University Press.

Nielsen, K. S., Clayton, S., Stern, P. C., Dietz, T., Capstick, S., & Whitmarsh, L. (2021). How psychology can help limit climate change. *American Psychologist, 76*, 130–144.

Nikolaev, B. (2017). Does higher education increase hedonic eudaimonic happiness? *Journal of Happiness Studies, 19*, 483–504.

Nilakantan, A., Younger, J., Aron, A., & Mackey, S. (2014). Preoccupation in an early-romantic relationship predicts experimental pain relief. *Pain Medicine, 15*, 947–953.

Nili, U., Goldberg, H., Weizman, A., & Dudai, Y. (2010). Fear thou not: Activity of frontal and temporal circuits in moments of real-life courage. *Neuron, 66*, 949–962.

Nisbett, R. E. (2003). *The geography of thought: How Asians and Westerners think differently . . . and why*. Free Press.

Noble, K. G., Hart, E. R., & Sperber, J. F. (2021). Socioeconomic disparities and neuroplasticity: Moving toward adaptation, intersectionality, and inclusion. *American Psychologist, 76*, 1486–1495.

Nolen-Hoeksema, S. (2000). Growth and resilience among bereaved people. In J. Gillham (Ed.), *The science of optimism and hope* (pp. 107–127). Templeton Foundation Press.

Norcross, J. C., & Hill, C. E. (2004). Empirically supported therapy relationships. *The Clinical Psychologist, 57*, 19–24.

Norcross, J. C., & Lambert, M. J. (2019). Evidence-based psychotherapy relationships: The third task force. In J. C. Norcross & M. J. Lambert (Eds.), *Psychotherapy relationships that work: Evidence-based therapist contributions* (pp. 1–23). Oxford University Press.

Norcross, J. C., & Prochaska, J. O. (1986). The psychological distress and self-change of psychologists, counselors, and laypersons. *Psychotherapy, 23*, 102–114.

Northrup, J., & Smith, J. (2016). Effects of Facebook maintenance behaviors on partners' experience of love. *Contemporary Family Therapy: An International Journal, 38*, 245–253.

Norton, P. J., & Weiss, B. J. (2009). The role of courage on behavioral approach in a fear-eliciting situation: A proof-of-concept pilot study. *Journal of Anxiety Disorders, 23*, 212–217.

Notthoff, N., & Carstensen, L. L. (2014). Positive messaging promotes walking in older adults. *Psychology and Aging, 29*, 329.

Notthoff, N., & Carstensen, L. L. (2017). Promoting walking in older adults: Perceived neighborhood walkability influences the effectiveness of motivational messages. *Journal of Health Psychology, 22*, 834–843.

Nussbaum, M. (2001). *Upheavals of thought: The intelligence of emotions*. Cambridge University Press.

O'Brien, K. M. (2003). Measuring career self-efficacy: Promoting confidence and happiness at work. In S. J. Lopez & C. R. Snyder (Eds.), *Positive psychological assessment: A handbook of models and measures* (pp. 109–126). American Psychological Association.

O'Byrne, K. K., Lopez, S. J., & Petersen, S. (2000, August). *Building a theory of courage: A precursor to change*? Paper presented at the 108th Annual Convention of the American Psychological Association, Washington, DC.

O'Leary, A., & Brown, S. (1995). Self-efficacy and the physiological stress response. In J. E. Maddux (Ed.), *Self-efficacy, adaptation, and adjustment: Theory, research, and application* (pp. 227–248). Plenum.

O'Leary, K., & Dockray, S. (2015). The effects of two novel gratitude and mindfulness interventions on well-being. *The Journal of Alternative and Complementary Medicine, 21*, 243–245.

O'Shea, D. M., Dotson, V. M., & Fieo, R. A. (2017). Aging perceptions and self-efficacy mediate the association between personality traits and depressive symptoms in older adults. *International Journal* of Geriatric Psychiatry, 32, 1217–1225.

Oda, R., Hiraishi, K., Fukukawa, Y., & Matsumoto-Oda, A. (2011). Human prosociality in altruism niche. *Journal of Evolutionary Psychology, 9*, 283–293.

Odgers, K., Dargue, N., Creswell, C., Jones, M. P., & Hudson, J. L. (2020). The limited effect of mindfulness-based interventions on anxiety in children and adolescents: A meta-analysis. *Clinical Child and Family Psychology Review, 23*(3), 407–426.

Odom, E. C., & Vernon-Feagans, L. (2010). Buffers of racial discrimination: Links with depression among rural African American mothers. *Journal of Marriage and Family, 72*, 346–359.

Office of the Governor. (2009, July 28). *Gov. Schwarzenegger highlights increased volunteerism in the Golden State*. https://californiavolunteers.ca.gov/wp-content/uploads/2017/07/PR090728.pdf

Ojeda, L., Piña-Watson, B., Castillo, L. G., Castillo, R., Khan, N., & Leigh, J. (2012). Acculturation, enculturation, ethnic identity, and conscientiousness as predictors of Latino boys' and girls' career decision self-efficacy. *Journal of Career Development, 39*, 208–228.

Oman, D., & Paranjpe, A. C. (2020). Psychology of Hinduism from the inside out. In T. A. Sisemore, & J. Knabb (Eds.), *The psychology of world religions and spiritualities: An indigenous perspective*. (pp. 165–196). Templeton Press.

Ono, M., Kochiyama, T., Fujino, J., Sozu, T., Kawada, R., Yokoyama, N., ... & Takahashi, H. (2018). Self-efficacy modulates the neural correlates of craving in male smokers and ex-smokers: An fMRI study. *Addiction Biology, 23*(5), 1179–1188

Organisation for Economic Co-operation and Development. (2017). *About the OECD*. http://www.oecd.org/about/

Orsini, A. (2015). Are terrorists courageous? Micro-sociology of extreme left terrorism. *Studies in Conflict & Terrorism, 38*, 179–198.

Ortin-Montero, F. J., Martinez-Rodríguez, A., Reche-García, C., de Los Fayos-Ruiz, E. J. G., & González-Hernández, J. (2018). Relationship between optimism and athletic performance: Systematic review. *Anales de Psicología, 34*, 153–161.

Oshio, A., Taku, K., Hirano, M., & Saeed, G. (2018). Resilience and Big Five personality traits: A meta-analysis. *Personality and Individual Differences, 127*, 54–60.

Otis, K. L., Huebner, E. S., & Hills, K. J. (2016). Origins of early adolescents' hope: Personality, parental attachment, and stressful life events. *Canadian Journal of School Psychology, 31*, 102–121.

Ouer, R. (2016). *Solution-focused brief therapy with the LGBT community: Creating futures through hope and resilience*. Routledge/Taylor & Francis Group.

Outten, R. H., Schmitt, M. T., Garcia, D. M., & Branscombe, N. R. (2009). Coding options: Missing links between minority group identification and psychological well-being. *Applied Psychology: An International Review, 58*, 146–170.

Ouweneel, E., Le Blanc, P. M., & Schaufeli, W. B. (2013). Do-it-yourself: An online positive psychology intervention to promote positive emotions, self-efficacy, and engagement at work. *The Career Development International, 18*, 173–195.

Owens, R. L., Magyar-Moe, J. L., & Lopez, S. J. (2015). Finding balance via positive psychological assessment and conceptualization: Recommendations for practice. *The Counseling Psychologist, 43*, 634–670.

Owens, S. L., Smothers, B. C., & Love, F. E. (2003). Are girls victims of gender bias in our nation's schools? *Journal of Instructional Psychology, 30*, 131.

Oyserman, D. (2017). Culture three ways: Culture and subcultures within countries. *Annual Review of Psychology, 68*, 435–463.

Oyserman, D., & Dawson, A. (2021). Your fake news, our facts: Identity-based motivation shapes what we believe, share, and accept. In R. Greifeneder, M. E. Jaffé, E. J. Newman, & N. Schwarz (Eds.), *The psychology of fake news: Accepting, sharing and correcting misinformation* (pp. 173–195). Routledge/Taylor & Francis Group.

Oyserman, D., Coon, H. M., & Kemmelmeier, M. (2002). Rethinking individualism and collectivism: Evaluation of theoretical assumptions and meta-analyses. *Psychological Bulletin, 128*, 3–72.

Pagnini, F., Bercovitz, K., & Langer, E. (2016). Perceived control and mindfulness: Implications for clinical practice. *Journal of Psychotherapy Integration, 26*, 91–102.

Pak, J., & Kim, S. (2018). Team manager's implementation, high performance work systems intensity, and performance: A multilevel investigation. *Journal of Management, 44*, 2690–2715.

Palanski, M. E., Cullen, K. L., Gentry, W. A., & Nichols, C. M. (2015). Virtuous leadership: Exploring the effects of leader courage and behavioral integrity on leader performance and image. *Journal of Business Ethics, 132*, 297–310.

Panter-Brick, C., Rowley-Conwy, P., & Layton, R. H. (Eds.). (2001). *Hunter-gatherers: An interdisciplinary perspective*. Cambridge University Press.

Paquin, V., Bick, J., Lipschutz, R., Elgbeili, G., Laplante, D. P., Biekman, B., Brunet, A., King, S., & Olson, D. (2021). Unexpected effects of expressive writing on post-disaster distress in the Hurricane Harvey study: A randomized controlled trial in perinatal women. *Psychological Medicine, 12*, 1–9.

Pardeller, S., Frajo-Apor, B., Kemmler, G., & Hofer, A. (2017). Emotional Intelligence and cognitive abilities—associations and sex differences. *Psychology, Health & Medicine, 22*, 1001–1010.

Pargament, K. I., & Mahoney, A. (2017). Spirituality: The search for the sacred. In S. J. Lopez & C. R. Snyder (Eds.), *Oxford handbook of positive psychology* (pp. 611–620). Oxford University Press. (Original work published 2009)

Parham, T. A., White, J. L., & Ajamu, A. (1999). *The psychology of Blacks: An African centered perspective* (3rd ed.). Prentice Hall.

Park, H. S., & Lee, H. E. (2012). Cultural differences in "thank you." *Journal of Language and Social Psychology, 31*, 138–156.

Park, N., Peterson, C., & Seligman, M. E. P. (2006). Character strengths in fifty-four nations and the fifty US states. *Journal of Positive Psychology, 1*, 118–129.

Parker, D. (1929, November). Interview with Ernest Hemingway. *The New Yorker, 30*, n.p.

Parker, K., Horowitz, J. M., & Minkin, R. (16 February, 2022). *COVID-19 pandemic continues to reshape work in America. Pew Research Center.* https://www.pewresearch.org/social-trends/2022/02/16/covid-19-pandemic-continues-to-reshape-work-in-america/

Patterson, D. A., Dulmus, C. N., Maguin, E., & Perkins, J. (2016). Differential outcomes in agency-based mental health care between minority and majority youth. *Research on Social Work Practice, 26*, 260–265.

Pavot, W., & Diener, E. (2008). The satisfaction with life scale and the emerging construct of life satisfaction. *1984*, 137–152.

Paz, R., Neto, F., & Mullet, E. (2008). Forgiveness: A China-Western Europe comparison. *Journal of Psychology, 142*, 147–157.

Pedrotti, J. T. (2013a). Positive psychology, social class, and counseling. In W. M. Liu (Ed.), *Handbook of social class* (pp. 131–143). Oxford University Press.

Pedrotti, J. T. (2013b). Culture and identity: Integrating an understanding of cultural context into a discussion of positive traits. In J. J. Froh & A. C. Parks (Eds.), *Activities for teaching positive psychology: A guide for instructors* (pp. 41–44). American Psychological Association.

Pedrotti, J. T. (2014a, January). *Shifting the lens: Including culture in discussions of positive psychology.* Keynote address presented at the meeting of the Asian Pacific Conference on Applied Positive Psychology, Hong Kong.

Pedrotti, J. T. (2014b). Taking culture into account with psychological interventions. In A. C. Parks (Ed.), *The Wiley-Blackwell handbook of positive psychological interventions*. Wiley Blackwell.

Pedrotti, J. T. (2018). The will and the ways in school: Hope as a factor in academic success. In M. W. Gallagher & S. J. Lopez (Eds.), *Oxford handbook of hope* (pp. 107–116). Oxford University Press.

Pedrotti, J. T., & Edwards, L. M. (2009). The intersection of positive psychology and multiculturalism in counseling. In J. G. Ponterotto, J. M. Casas, L. A. Suzuki, & C. M. Alexander (Eds.), *Handbook of multicultural counseling* (3rd ed., pp. 165–174). Sage.

Pedrotti, J. T., & Edwards, L. M. (2010). The intersection of positive psychology and multiculturalism in counseling. In J. G. Ponterotto, J. M. Casas, L. A. Suzuki, & C. M. Alexander (Eds.), *Handbook of multicultural counseling* (3rd ed., pp. 165–174). Sage.

Pedrotti, J. T., & Edwards, L. M. (Eds.). (2014). *Perspectives on the intersection of multiculturalism and positive psychology*. Springer Science + Business Media.

Pedrotti, J. T., & Edwards, L. M. (2017). Cultural context in positive psychology: History, research, and opportunities for growth. In M. A. Warren & S. I. Donaldson (Eds.), *Scientific advances in positive psychology* (pp. 257–287). Praeger.

Pedrotti, J. T., Edwards, L. M., & Lopez, S. J. (2009). Putting positive psychology into a multicultural context. In S. J. Lopez (Ed.), *Handbook of positive psychology*, 2nd edition. (pp. 49–57). Oxford University Press.

Pedrotti, J. T., Edwards, L. M., & Lopez, S. J. (2021). Positive psychology within a cultural context. In S. J. Lopez, & C. R. Snyder, S. J. Lopez, L. M. Edwards, & S. C. Marques (Eds.), *Oxford handbook of positive psychology* (pp. 549–570). Oxford University Press.

Pedrotti, J. T., & Isom, D. A. (2021). *Multicultural psychology: Self, society, and social change*. Sage.

Pedrotti, J. T., & Sweatt, L. I. (2007, August). *Effects of a multicultural course on undergraduate students*. Poster session presented at the annual meeting of the American Psychological Association, San Francisco.

Pei, F., Li, Z., Maguire-Jack, K., Li, X., & Kleinberg, J. (2022). Changes of perceived neighbourhood environment: A longitudinal study of collective efficacy among vulnerable families. *Health & Social Care in the Community*.

Peña-Sarrionandia, A., Mikolajczak, M., & Gross, J. J. (2015). Integrating emotion regulation and emotional intelligence traditions: A meta-analysis. *Frontiers in Psychology*, *6*, Article 160. https://doi.org/10.3389/fpsyg.2015.00160

Pennebaker, J. W. (1997). *Opening up: The healing power of expressing emotions* (Rev. ed.). Guilford.

Pennebaker, J. W., & Graybeal, A. (2001). Patterns of natural language use: Disclosure, personality, and social integration. *Current Directions in Psychological Science*, *10*(3), 90–93. https://doi.org/10.1111/1467-8721.00123

Pennebaker, J. W., Hughes, C. F., & O'Heeron, R. C. (1987). The psychophysiology of confession: Linking inhibitory and psychosomatic processes. *Journal of Personality & Social Psychology*, *52*, 781–793

Perazzo, M. F., Abreu, L. G., Pérez-Díaz, P. A., Petrides, K. V., Granville-Garcia, A. F., & Paiva, S. M. (2021). Trait Emotional Intelligence Questionnaire-Short Form: Brazilian validation and measurement invariance between the United Kingdom and Latin-American datasets. *Journal of Personality Assessment*, *103*(3), 342–351

Pérez-Díaz, P. A., Manrique-Millones, D., García-Gómez, M., Vásquez-Suyo, M. I., Millones-Rivalles, R., Fernández-Ríos, N., Pérez-González, J. C., & Petrides, K. V. (2022). Invariance of the trait emotional intelligence construct across clinical populations and sociodemographic variables. *Frontiers in psychology*, *13*, 796057.

Perry, S. K. (1999). *Writing in flow.*: Writer's Digest Books.

Peter, C., Cieza, A., & Geyh, S. (2014). Rasch analysis of the General Self-Efficacy Scale in spinal cord injury. *Journal of Health Psychology*, *19*(4), 544–555.

Peters, R. M. (2006). The relationship of racism, chronic stress emotions, and blood pressure. *Journal of Nursing Scholarship*, *38*, 234–340.

Peterson, C. (2000). Optimistic explanatory style and health. In J. Gillham (Ed.), *The science of optimism and hope* (pp. 145–162). Templeton Foundation Press.

Peterson, C., & Seligman, M. E. P. (2004). *Character strengths and virtues: A handbook and classification*. American Psychological Association.

Peterson, C., & Steen, T. A. (2021). Optimistic explanatory style. In C. R. Snyder, S. J. Lopez, L. M. Edwards, & S. C. Marques (Eds.), *The Oxford handbook of positive psychology., 3rd ed.* (2021-20328-030; pp. 413–424). Oxford University Press.

Peterson, C., & Villanova, P. (1988). An expanded attributional style questionnaire.

Journal of Abnormal Psychology, 97, 87–89.

Peterson, C., Bettes, B. A., & Seligman, M. E. P. (1985). Depressive symptoms and unprompted causal attributions: Content analysis. *Behavior Research and Therapy, 23*, 379–382.

Peterson, C., Schulman, P., Castellon, C., & Seligman, M. (1992). CAVE: Content analysis of verbal explanations. In C. Smith (Ed.), *Motivation and personality: Handbook of thematic content analysis* (pp. 383–392). Cambridge University Press.

Peterson, C., Semmel, A., von Baeyer, C., Abramson, L. Y., Metalsky, G. I., & Seligman, M. E. P. (1982). The Attributional Style Questionnaire. *Cognitive Therapy and Research, 6*, 287–299.

Petrides, K. V. (2009). *Technical manual for the Trait Emotional Intelligence Questionnaires (TEIQue)*. London Psychometric Laboratory.

Petrides, K. V., Perez-Gonzalez, J. C., & Furnham, A. (2007). On the criterion and incremental validity of trait emotional intelligence. *Cognition and Emotion, 21*, 26–55.

Petrides, K. V., Pita, R., & Kokkinaki, F. (2007). The location of trait emotional intelligence in personality factor space. *British Journal of Psychology, 98*, 273–289.

Petrocchi, N., & Couyoumdjian, A. (2016). The impact of gratitude on depression and anxiety: The mediating role of criticizing, attacking, and reassuring the self. *Self and Identity, 15*, 191–205.

Pew Research Center (13 September, 2022). *Modeling the future of religion in America*. https://www.pewresearch.org/religion/2022/09/13/modeling-the-future-of-religion-in-america/

Piaget, J. (1932). *The moral judgment of the child*. Routledge and Kegan Paul.

Piazza, J. A. (2023). Political polarization and political violence. *Security Studies, 32*, 476–504.

Pickering, A., & Gray, J. (1999). The neuroscience of personality. In L. Pervin & O. John (Eds.), *Handbook of personality* (2nd ed., pp. 277–299). Guilford.

Pickett, K., Yardley, L., & Kendrick, T. (2012). Physical activity and depression: A multiple mediation analysis. *Mental Health and Physical Activity, 5*, 125–134.

Piedmont, R. (2004, November). *Spirituality predicts psychosocial outcomes: A cross-cultural analysis*. International Society for Quality of Life Studies Conference.

Pieper, J. (1966). *The four cardinal virtues*. Notre Dame Press.

Piet, J., Hougaard, E., Hecksher, M. S., & Rosenberg, N. K. (2010). A randomized pilot study of mindfulness-based cognitive therapy and group cognitive-behavioral therapy for young adults with social phobia. *Scandinavian Journal of Psychology, 51*, 403–410.

Piht, S., Talts, L., & Nigulas, S. (2016). Shaping Estonian primary school pupils' values by using bullying-prevention methods. *Early Child Development and Care, 186*, 1926–1938.

Pinker, S. (1997). *How the mind works*. Norton.

Piper, W. (1989). *The little engine that could*. Platt and Monk. (Original work published 1930)

Pitts, D. (2009). Diversity management, job satisfaction, and performance: Evidence from U.S. federal agencies. *Public Administration Review, 69*, 328–338.

Plato. (1953). *The dialogues of Plato*: Vol. 1. Laches (B. Jowett, Trans.). Modern Library.

Plomin, R., Scheier, M. F., Bergeman, C. S., Pederson, N. L., Nesselroade, J. R., & McClearn, G. E. (1992). Optimism, pessimism, and mental health: A twin/adoption analysis. *Personality and Individual Differences, 13*, 921–930.

Pocnet, C., Popp, J., & Jopp, D. (2021). The power of personality in successful ageing: A comprehensive review of larger quantitative studies. *European Journal of Ageing, 18*(2), 269–285.

Pool, L., & Qualter, P. (2012). The dimensional structure of the Emotional Self-Efficacy Scale (ESES). *Australian Journal of Psychology, 64*, 147–154.

Porzig, R. (2021). *2020 Big Brothers Big Sisters of America annual impact report*.https://www.bbbs.org/wp-content/uploads/2021-BBBSA-Annual-Impact-Report.pdf

Poteat, V. P., & Vecho, O. (2016). Who intervenes against homophobic behavior? Attributes that distinguish active bystanders. *Journal of School Psychology, 54*, 17–28.

Prati, G., & Pietrantoni, L. (2009). Optimism, social support, and coping strategies as factors contributing to posttraumatic growth: A meta-analysis. *Journal of Loss and Trauma, 14*(5), 364–388.

Prati, G., Albanesi, C., & Pietrantoni, L. (2016). The reciprocal relationship between sense of community and social well-being: A cross-lagged panel analysis. *Social Indicators Research, 127*, 1321–1332.

Prince-Embury, S. (2006). *Resiliency scales for adolescents: Profiles of personal strengths*. Harcourt Assessments.

Prisant Lesko, A. (2016). How do you lead the pack? A resource to develop personal strengths for students and practitioners. *Journal of Management Education, 40*, 102–108.

Procci, K., Singer, A. R., Levy, K. R., & Bowers, C. (2012). Measuring the flow experience of gamers: An evaluation of the DFS-2. *Computers in Human Behavior, 28*, 2306–2312.

Proctor, C., Maltby, J., & Linley, P. (2011). Strengths use as a predictor of well-being and health-related quality of life. *Journal of Happiness Studies, 12*, 153–169.

Proper, K. I., & van Oostrom, S. H. (2019). The effectiveness of workplace health promotion interventions on physical and mental health outcomes—A systematic review of reviews. *Scandinavian Journal of Work, Environment & Health, 6*, 546–559.

Proyer, R. T. (2012). Examining playfulness in adults: Testing its correlates with personality, positive psychological functioning, goal aspirations, and multi-methodically assessed ingenuity. *Psychological Test and Assessment Modeling, 54*, 103–127.

Proyer, R. T., Brauer, K., Wolf, A., & Chick, G. (2019). Adult playfulness and relationship satisfaction: An APIM analysis of romantic couples. *Journal of Research in Personality, 79*, 40–48.

Proyer, R. T., & Ruch, W. (2011). The virtuousness of adult playfulness: The relation of playfulness with strengths of character. *Psychology of Well-Being: Theory, Research and Practice, 1*, 4–12.

Proyer, R. T., & Tandler, N. (2020). An update on the study of playfulness in adolescents: Its relationship with academic performance, well-being, anxiety, and roles in bullying-type-situations. *Social Psychology of Education: An International Journal, 23*(1), 73–99. https://doi.org/10.1007/s11218-019-09526-1

Pruchno, R., Heid, A. R., & Wilson-Genderson, M. (2018). Successful aging, social support, and ownership of a companion animal. *Anthrozoös, 31(1)*, 23–39.

Puente-Diaz, R., & Cavazos-Arroyo, J. (2016). How remembering less acts of gratitude can make one feel more grateful and satisfied with close relationships: The role of ease of recall. *European Journal of Social Psychology, 46*, 377–383.

Puig-Perez, S., Hackett, R. A., Salvador, A., & Steptoe, A. (2017). Optimism moderates psychophysiological responses to stress in older people with Type 2 diabetes. *Psychophysiology, 54*, 536–543.

Pury, C. L. S., & Lopez, S. J. (2009). Courage. In S. J. Lopez & C. R. Snyder (Eds.), *Oxford handbook of positive psychology* (pp. 375–382). Oxford University Press.

Pury, C. L. S., Britt, T. W., Zinzow, H. M., & Raymond M. A. (2014). Blended courage: Moral and psychological courage elements in mental health treatment seeking by active duty military personnel. *Journal of Positive Psychology, 9*, 30–41.

Pury, C. L. S., Kowalski, R. M., & Spearman, J. (2007). Distinctions between general and personal courage. *Journal of Positive Psychology, 2*, 99–114.

Pury, C. L. S., & Saylors, S. (2018). Courage, courageous acts, and positive psychology. In D. S. Dunn (Ed.), *Positive psychology: Established and emerging issues* (pp. 153–168). Routledge/Taylor & Francis Group

Pury, C. L. S., Starkey, C. B. Kulik, R. E., Skjerning, K. L., & Sullivan, E. A. (2015). Is courage always a virtue? Suicide, killing, and bad courage. *The Journal of Positive Psychology, 10*, 383–388.

Putman, D. (1997). Psychological courage. *Philosophy, Psychiatry and Psychology, 4*(1), 1–11.

Pyone, J. S., & Isen, A. M. (2011). Positive affect, intertemporal choice, and levels of thinking: Increasing consumers' willingness to wait.

Journal of Marketing Research, 48, 532–543.

Querstret, D., Morison, L.A., Dickinson, S., Cropley, M., & John, M.E. (2020). Mindfulness-based stress reduction and mindfulness-based cognitive therapy for psychological health and well-being in nonclinical samples: A systematic review and meta-analysis. *International Journal of Stress Management, 27*, 394–411.

Rabenu, E., & Yaniv, E. (2017). Psychological resources and strategies to cope with stress at work. *International Journal of Psychological Research, 10*, 8–15.

Rachman, S. J. (1984). Fear and courage. *Behavior Therapy, 15*, 109–120.

Racine, N., Eirich, R., & Madigan, S. (2022). Fostering resilience in children who have been maltreated: A review and call for translational research. *Canadian Psychology / Psychologie Canadienne, 63*(2), 203–213.

Rahm, A-K., Töllner, M., Hubert, M. O., Klein, K., Wehling, C., Sauer, T., Hennemann, H. M., Hein, S., Kender, Z., Günther, J., Wagenlechner, P., Bugaj, T. J., Boldt, S., Nikendei, C., Schultz, J-H. (2021). Effects of realistic e-learning cases on students' learning motivation during COVID-19. *PLoS One, 16*, e0249425.

Ramírez-Esparza, N., & Pennebaker, J. W. (2006). Do good stories produce good health? Exploring words, language, and culture. *Narrative Inquiry, 16*, 211–219.

Ramírez-Maestre, C., Esteve, R., & López, A. E. (2012). The role of optimism and pessimism in chronic pain patients' adjustment. *The Spanish Journal of Psychology, 15*, 286–294.

Ramos, A. K., McGinley, M., & Carlo, G. (2021). The relations of workplace safety, perceived occupational stress, and adjustment among Latino/a immigrant cattle feed yard workers in the United States. *Safety Science, 139*, 1–8.

Rand, D. G., & Brescoll, V. L. (2016). Social heuristics and social roles: Intuition favors altruism for women but not for men. *Journal of Experimental Psychology: General, 145*, 389–396.

Rand, K. L., & Touza, K. K. (2021). Hope theory. In C. R. Snyder, S. J. Lopez, L. M. Edwards, & S. C. Marques (Eds.), *The Oxford handbook of positive psychology, 3rd ed.* (2021-20328-031; pp. 425–442). Oxford University Press.

Randel, A. E., Galvin, B. M., Shore, L. M., Ehrhart, K., H., Chung, B. G., Dean, M. A., & Kedharnath, U. (2017). Inclusive leadership: Realizing positive outcomes through belongingness and being valued for uniqueness. *Human Resource Management Review, 28*, 190–203.

Ranking, K., & Sweeny, K. (2022). Preparing silver linings for a cloudy day: The consequences of preemptive benefit finding. *Personality & Social Psychology Bulletin, 48*, 1255–1268.

Rao, X., Wang, W., Luo, S., Qiu, J., & Li, H. (2022). Brain structures associated with individual differences in decisional and emotional forgiveness. *Neuropsychologia, 170*, 108223.

Raphals, L. (1992). *Knowing words: Wisdom and courage in the classical traditions of China and Greece*. Cornell University Press.

Raposa, E.B., Rhodes, J., Stams, G. J. J. M., Card, N., Burton, S., Schwartz, S., Sykes, L. A. Y., Kanchewa, S., Kupersmidt, J., & Hussain, S. (2019). The effects of youth mentoring programs: A meta-analysis of outcome studies. *Journal of Youth Adolescence, 48*, 423–443.

Rath, T. (2006). *Vital friends: The people you can't afford to live without*. Gallup Organization.

Rath, T. (2007). *StrengthsFinder 2.0*. Gallup.

Rath, T., & Clifton, D. O. (2004). *How full is your bucket? Positive strategies for work and life*. Gallup Organization.

Ratts, M. J., Singh, A. A., Nassar-McMillan, S., Butler, S. K., & McCullough, J. R. (2016). Multicultural and social justice counseling competencies: Guidelines for the counseling profession. *Journal of Multicultural Counseling and Development, 44*, 28–48.

Rauscher, L., & Cooky, C. (2016). Ready for anything the world gives her? A critical look at sports-based positive youth development for girls. *Sex Roles, 74*, 288–298.

Reed, D. J. (2016). Coping with occupational stress: The role of optimism and coping flexibility. *Psychology Research and Behavior Management, 9*, Article 71-79.

Reed, A. E., & Carstensen, L. L. (2012). The theory behind the age-related positivity effect. *Frontiers in Psychology, 3*, 1–9.

Reese, J. B., Lepore, S. J., Handorf, E. A., & Haythornthwaite, J. A. (2017). Emotional approach coping and depressive symptoms in colorectal cancer patients: The role of the intimate relationship. *Journal of Psychosocial Oncology, 35*, 578–596.

Reinhold, M., Bürkner, P. C., & Holling, H. (2018). Effects of expressive writing on depressive symptoms—A meta-analysis. *Clinical Psychology: Science and Practice, 25*, 1–5.

Reis, H. T., & Gable, S. L. (2003). Toward a positive psychology of relationships. In C. L. M. Keyes & J. Haidt (Eds.), *Flourishing: Positive psychology and the life well lived* (pp. 129–159). American Psychological Association.

Reyes, J. A., & Elias, M. J. (2011). Fostering social-emotional resilience among Latino youth. *Psychology in the Schools, 48*, 723–737.

Ribeiro, J., Pedro, L., & Marques, S. (2012). Dispositional optimism is unidimensional or bidimensional? The Portuguese revised Life Orientation Test. *The Spanish Journal of Psychology, 15*, 1259–1271.

Rich, G. J. (2017). The promise of qualitative inquiry for positive psychology: Diversifying methods. *Journal of Positive Psychology, 12*, 220–231.

Riley, R., K., Sweeney, M. M., & Wonder, D. (2015). The growing racial and ethnic divide in U.S. marriage patterns. *The Future of Children, 25*, 89–109.

Rime, B. (1995). Mental rumination, social sharing, and the recovery from emotional exposure. In J. W. Pennebaker (Ed.), *Emotion, disclosure, and health* (pp. 271–291). American Psychological Association.

Rios, D., Stewart, A. J., Winter, & D. G. (2010). 'Thinking she could be the next president': Why identifying with the curriculum matters. *Psychology of Women Quarterly, 34*, 328–338.

Ripley, J. S., & Worthington, E. L., Jr. (2002). Hope-focused and forgiveness-based group interventions to promote marital enrichment. *Journal of Counseling and Development, 80*, 452–472.

Ritschel, L. (2005). Lessons in teaching hope: An interview with C. R. Snyder. *Teaching of Psychology, 32*, 74–78.

Rivkin, W., Diestel, S., Gerpott, F. H., & Unger, D. (2022). Should I stay or should I go? The role of daily presenteeism as an adaptive response to perform at work despite somatic complaints for employee effectiveness. *Journal of Occupational Health Psychology, 27*, 411–425.

Rivkin, W., Diestel, S., & Schmidt, K. H. (2016). Which daily experiences can foster well-being at work? A diary study on the interplay between flow experiences, affective commitment, and self-control demands. *Journal of Occupational Health Psychology, 23*, 99–111.

Roberts, A. L., Gilman, S. E., Breslau, J., Breslau, N., & Koenen, K. C. (2011). Race/ethnic differences in exposure to traumatic events, development of post-traumatic stress disorder, and treatment-seeking for post-traumatic stress disorder in the United States. *Psychological Medicine, 41*(1), 71–83.

Robinson, C., & Rose, S. (2010). Predictive, construct, and convergent validity of general and domain-specific measures of hope for college student academic achievement. *Research in the Schools, 17*, 38–52.

Robinson, F. T., & Golphin, Q. (2021). Culture of family togetherness, emotional resilience, and spiritual lifestyles inherent in African Americans from the time of slavery until now. In M. O. Adekson (Ed.), *African Americans and mental health: Practical and strategic solutions to barriers, needs, and challenges*. (pp. 57–66). Springer Nature Switzerland AG.

Rodriguez-Hanley, A., & Snyder, C. R. (2000). The demise of hope: On losing positive thinking. In C. R. Snyder (Ed.), *Handbook of hope: Theory, measures, and applications* (pp. 39–54). Academic Press. https://doi.org/10.1016/B978-012654050-5/50005-1

Rodriguez, L. M., Young, C. M., Neighbors, C., Tou, R., & Lu, Q. (2016). Cultural differences and shame in an expressive writing alcohol intervention. *Journal of Ethnicity in Substance Abuse, 15*, 252–267.

Rogers, R. W., & Prentice-Dunn, S. (1997). Protection motivation theory. In D. Gochman (Ed.), *Handbook of health behavior research 1: Personal and social determinants* (pp. 113–132). Plenum.

Romero, A. J., Edwards, L. M., Fryberg, S. A., & Orduña, M. (2014). Resilience to discrimination stress across ethnic identity stages of development. *Journal of Applied Social Psychology, 44*, 1–11.

Romppel, M., Herrmann-Lingen, C., Wachter, R., Edelmann, F., Düngen, H.-D., Pieske, B., & Grande, G. (2013). A short form of the General Self-Efficacy Scale (GSE-6): Development, psychometric properties and validity in an intercultural non-clinical sample and a sample of patients at risk for heart failure. *GMS Psycho-Social-Medicine, 10.*

Rongen, A., Robroek, S. J. W., van Lenthe, F. J., & Burdorf, A. (2013). Workplace health promotion: A meta-analysis of effectiveness. *American Journal of Preventative Medicine, 44*, 406–415.

Roos, S., & Haanpää, L. (2017). Decision-making opportunities at school moderate the effects of positive youth development on civic behaviors. *Nordic Psychology*, 69, 217–230.

Root, B. L., & Exline, J. J. (2011). Gender differences in response to experimental forgiveness prompts: Do men show stronger responses than women? *Basic and Applied Social Psychology, 33*, 182–193.

Rorty, A. O. (1988). *Mind in action: Essays in the philosophy of mind.* Beacon.

Rosen, H. S., & Sims, S. T. (2011). Altruistic behavior and habit formation. *Nonprofit Management and Leadership, 21*, 235–253.

Rosmarin, D. H., Pirutinsky, S., Cohen, A. B., Galler, Y., & Krumrei, E. J. (2011). Grateful to God or just plain grateful? A comparison of religious and general gratitude. *The Journal of Positive Psychology, 6*, 389–396.

Ross, K. L. (2003). *Confucius.* http://friesian.com/confuci.htm

Rostosky, S. S., Abreu, R. L., Mahoney, A., & Riggle, E. D. (2017). A qualitative study of parenting and religiosity/spirituality in LBGTQ families. *Psychology of Religion and Spirituality, 9*, 437.

Rothbaum, F., Weisz, J., Pott, M., Miyake, K., & Morelli, G. (2000). Attachment and culture: Security in the United States and Japan. *American Psychologist, 55*, 1093–1104.

Rothausen, T. J., & Henderson, K. E. (2019). Meaning-based job-related well-being: Exploring a meaningful work conceptualization of job satisfaction. *Journal of Business and Psychology, 34*(3), 357–376.

Rotter, J. B. (1966). Generalized expectancies for internal versus external control of reinforcement. *Psychological Monographs, 80*(1), 1–28.

Rowe, J. W., & Kahn, R. L. (1998). *Successful aging.* Pantheon.

Rubinstein, D., & Lahad, M. (2023). Fantastic reality: The role of imagination, playfulness, and creativity in healing trauma. *Traumatology, 29*, 102–111.

Rui, J. R. (2022). Health Information Sharing via Social Network Sites (SNSs): Integrating social support and socioemotional selectivity theory. *Health Communication*, 1–11.

Rumens, N. (2017). Queering lesbian, gay, bisexual and transgender identities in human resource development management education contexts. *Management Learning, 48*, 227–242.

Rushton, J. P., Chrisjohn, R. D., & Fekken, G. C. (1981). The altruistic personality and the Self-Report Altruism Scale. *Personality and Individual Differences, 2*, 293–302.

Rushton, J. P., Fulker, D. W., Neale, M. C., Nias, D. K., & Eysenck, H. J. (1986). Altruism and aggression: The heritability of individual differences. *Journal of Personality and Social Psychology, 50*, 1192–1198.

Russo-Netzer, P., & Cohen, G. L. (2022). 'If you're uncomfortable, go outside your comfort zone': A novel behavioral 'stretch' intervention supports the well-being of unhappy people. *Journal of Positive Psychology*, 1–17.

Ruthig, J. C., Gamblin, B. W., Jones, K., Vanderzanden, K., & Kehn, A. (2017). Concurrently examining unrealistic absolute and comparative optimism: Temporal shifts, individual-difference and event-specific correlates, and behavioural outcomes. *British Journal of Psychology, 108*, 107–126.

Ruthig, J. C., Hanson, B. L., Pedersen, H., Weber, A., & Chipperfield, J. G. (2011). Later life health optimism, pessimism and realism: Psychological contributors and health correlates. *Psychology & Health, 26,* 835–853.

Ruvio, A., Shoham, A., & Brenčič, M. M. (2008). Consumers' need for uniqueness: Short-form scale development and cross-cultural validation. *International Marketing Review, 25,* 33–53.

Ryan, R. M., & Deci, E. L. (2001). On happiness and human potentials: A review of research on hedonic and eudaimonic well-being. *Annual Review of Psychology, 52,* 141–166.

Rye, M. S., Loiacono, D. M., Folck, C. D., Olszewski, B. T., Heim, T. A., & Madia, B. P. (2001). Evaluation of the psychometric properties of two forgiveness scales. *Current Psychology, 20*(3), 260–277.

Ryff, C. D., & Boylan, J. M. (2016). Linking happiness to health: Comparisons between hedonic and eudaimonic well-being. In L. Bruni & P. L. Porta (Eds.), *Handbook of research methods and applications in happiness and quality of life* (pp. 53–70). Edward Elgar.

Ryff, C. D., & Keyes, C. L. M. (1995). The structure of psychological well-being revisited. *Journal of Personality and Social Psychology, 57,* 1069–1081.

Safe World For Women. (2013). The Safeworld International Foundation, Author. http://www.asafeworldforwomen.org/

Sahraian, A., Gholami, A., Javadpour, A., & Omidvar, B. (2013). Association between religiosity and happiness among a group of Muslim undergraduate students. *Journal of Religion and Health, 52,* 450–453.

Sakade, F. (1958). Momotaro. In F. Sakade (Ed.), *Japanese children's favorite stories.* Tuttle.

Salgado, S., & Berntsen, D. (2021). "It Won't Happen to Us": Unrealistic optimism affects COVID-19 risk assessments and attitudes regarding protective behavior. *Journal of Applied Research in Memory and Cognition, 10*(3), 368–380.

Sallis, J. F., Pinski, R. B., Grossman, R. M., Patterson, T. L., & Nader, P. R. (1988). The development of self-efficacy scales for health-related diet and exercise behaviors. *Health Education Research, 3*(3), 283–292.

Salovey, P., & Mayer, J. D. (1990). Emotional intelligence. *Imagination, Cognition, and Personality, 9,* 185–211.

Samanez-Larkin, G. R., Robertson, E. R., Mikels, J. A., Carstensen, L. L., & Gotlib, I. H. (2014). Selective attention to emotion in the aging brain. *Psychology and Aging, 24,* 519–529.

Samuels, D. R. (2014). *The culturally inclusive educator: Preparing for a multicultural world.* Teachers College Press.

Sanchez-Garcia, M., Extremera, N., & Fernandez-Berrocal, P. (2016). The factor structure and psychometric properties of the Spanish version of the Mayer-Salovey-Caruso Emotional Intelligence Test. *Psychological Assessment, 28(11),* 1404–1415.

Sandage, S. J., Hill, P. C., & Vaubel, D. C. (2011). Generativity, relational spirituality, gratitude, and mental health: Relationships and pathways. *International Journal for the Psychology of Religion, 21,* 1–16.

Sandage, S., Hill, P. C., & Vang, H. C. (2003). Toward a multicultural positive psychology: Indigenous forgiveness and Hmong culture. *The Counseling Psychologist, 31,* 564–592.

Sangharakshita. (1991). *The three jewels: An introduction to Buddhism.* Windhorse.

San-Martín, M., Delgado-Bolton, R., & Vivanco, L. (2017). Professionalism and occupational well-being: Similarities and differences among Latin American health professionals. *Frontiers in Psychology, 8,* 1–10.

Santiago, C. D., Kaltman, S., & Miranda, J. (2013). Poverty and mental health: How do low-income adults and children fare in psychotherapy? *Journal of Clinical Psychology, 69,* 115–126.

Santoro, A. F., Suchday, S., Benkhoukha, A., Ramanayake, N., & Kapur, S. (2016). Adverse childhood experiences and religiosity/spirituality in emerging adolescents in India. *Psychology of Religion and Spirituality, 8,* 185–194.

Sarafino, E. (2002). *Health psychology* (4th ed.). Wiley.

Sari, S. V. (2017). Attaining career decision self-efficacy in life: Roles of the meaning in life and the life satisfaction. *Current Psychology.* Advance online publication.

Saroglou, V. (2012). Is religion not prosocial at all? Comment on Galen (2012). *Psychological Bulletin, 138,* 907–912.

Saroglou, V., Buxant, C., & Tilquin, J. (2008). Positive emotions as leading to religion and spirituality. *Journal of Positive Psychology, 3*, 165–173.

Sasse, J., Halmburger, A., Baumert, A. (2022). The functions of anger in moral courage—insights from a behavioral study. *Emotion, 22*, 1321–1335.

Satterfield, J. (2000). Optimism, culture, and history: The roles of explanatory style, integrative complexity, and pessimistic rumination. In J. Gillham (Ed.), *The science of optimism and hope* (pp. 349–378). Templeton Foundation Press.

Scarduzio, J. A., Sheff, S. E., & Smith, M. (2018). Coping and sexual harassment: How victims cope across multiple settings. *Archives of Sexual Behavior, 47*, 327–340.

Scatliffe, N., Casavant, S., Vittner, D., & Cong, X. (2019). Oxytocin and early parent-infant interactions: A systematic review. *International Journal of Nursing Sciences, 6*(4), 445–453.

Schachter, S. (1951). Deviation, rejection, and communication. *Journal of Abnormal and Social Psychology, 46*, 190–207.

Scheier, M. F., & Carver, C. S. (1985). Optimism, coping, and health: Assessment and implications of generalized outcome expectancies. *Health Psychology, 4*, 219–247.

Scheier, M. F., & Carver, C. S. (2001). Adapting to cancer: The importance of hope and purpose. In A. Baum & B. L. Anderson (Eds.), *Psychosocial interventions for cancer* (pp. 15–36). American Psychological Association.

Scheier, M. F., Carver, C. S., & Bridges, M. W. (1994). Distinguishing optimism from neuroticism (and trait anxiety, self-mastery, and self-esteem): A reevaluation of the Life Orientation Test. *Journal of Personality and Social Psychology, 67*, 1063–1078.

Scheier, M. F., Carver, C. S., & Bridges, M. W. (2001). Optimism, pessimism, and psychological well-being. In E. C. Chang (Ed.), *Optimism & pessimism: Implications for theory, research, and practice* (pp. 189–216). American Psychological Association.

Scheier, M. F., Weintraub, J. K., & Carver, C. S. (1986). Coping with stress: Divergent strategies of optimists and pessimists. *Journal of Personality and Social Psychology, 51*, 1257–1264.

Scherbaum, C. A., Cohen-Charash, Y., & Kern, M. J. (2006). Measuring general self-efficacy: A comparison of three measures using item response theory. *Educational and Psychological Measurement, 66*(6), 1047–1063.

Scherer, R., Jansen, M., Nilsen, T., Areepattamannil, S., & Marsh, H. W. (2016). The quest for comparability: Studying the invariance of the teachers' sense of self-efficacy (TSES) measure across countries. *PLoS ONE, 11*(3).

Schlegel, K. (2021). The effects of emotion recognition training on interpersonal effectiveness. *Basic and Applied Social Psychology, 43*(2), 141–153.

Schleien, S., Ross, H., & Ross, M. (2010). Young children's apologies to their siblings. *Social Development, 19*, 170–186.

Schmaltz, R. M. (2016). Bang your head: Using heavy metal music to promote scientific thinking in the classroom. *Frontiers in Psychology, 7*, 1–4.

Schmidt, F. L., & Rader, M. (1999). Exploring the boundary conditions for interview validity: Meta-analytic findings for a new interview type. *Personnel Psychology, 52*, 445–464.

Schmidt, N. B., & Koselka, M. (2000). Gender differences in patients with panic disorder: Evaluating cognitive mediation of phobic avoidance. *Cognitive Therapy and Research, 24*, 531–548.

Schmitt, D. P., Youn, G., Bond, B., Brooks, S., Frye, H., Johnson, S., Kiesman, J., Peplinkski, C., Sampias, J., Sherrill, M., & Stoka, C. (2009). When will I feel love? The effects of culture, personality, and gender on the psychological tendency to love. *Journal of Research in Personality, 43*, 830–846.

Schneiderman, I., Zilberstein-Kra, Y., Leckman, J. F., & Feldman, R. (2011). Love alters autonomic reactivity to emotions. *Emotion, 11*, 1314–1321.

Schore, A. N. (1994). *Affect regulation and the origin of the self: The neurobiology of emotional development*. Lawrence Erlbaum.

Schore, A. N. (2003). *Affect regulation and the repair of the self*. Norton.

Schulman, P., Keith, D., & Seligman, M. E. P. (1993). Is optimism heritable? A study of twins. *Behaviour Research and Therapy, 31*, 569–574.

Schumpe, B. M., Brizi, A., Giacomantonio, M., Panno, A., Kopetz, C., Kosta, M., & Mannetti, L. (2017). Need for cognitive closure decreases risk taking and motivates discounting of delayed rewards. *Personality and Individual Differences, 107*, 66–71.

Schur, E. M. (1969). Reactions to deviance: A critical assessment. *American Journal of Sociology, 75*, 309–322.

Schwartz, S. H. (1994). Beyond individualism and collectivism: New cultural dimensions of values. In U. Kim, H. C. Triandis, C. Kagitcibasi, S.-C. Choi, & G. Yoon (Eds.), *Individualism and collectivism: Theory, method, and applications* (pp. 85–122). Sage.

Schwarzer, R., & M. Jerusalem (1995). Generalized Self-Efficacy scale. In J. Weinman, S. Wright and M. Johnston (Eds.), *Measures in health psychology: A user's portfolio. Causal and control beliefs* (pp. 35–37). Windsor.

Schweizer, K., & Koch, W. (2001). The assessment of components of optimism by POSO-E. *Personality and Individualism, 31*, 563–574.

Seeley, S. H., Yanez, B., Stanton, A. L., & Hoyt, M. A. (2017). An emotional processing writing intervention and heart rate variability: The role of emotional approach. *Cognition and Emotion, 31*, 988–994.

Segal, Z. V., Williams, J. M. G., & Teasdale, J. D. (2002). *Mindfulness-based cognitive therapy for depression: A new approach to preventing relapse.* Guilford.

Sekerka, L. E., Bagozzi, R. P, & Charnigo, R. (2009). Facing ethical challenges in the workplace: Conceptualizing and measuring professional moral courage. *Journal of Business Ethics, 89*, 565–579.

Seligman, M. E. P. (1991). *Learned optimism.*: Knopf.

Seligman, M. E. P. (1994). *What you can change and what you can't.* Knopf.

Seligman, M. E. P. (1998a). Building human strength: Psychology's forgotten mission. *APA Monitor, 29*(1), 2.

Seligman, M. E. P. (1998b). *Learned optimism: How to change your mind and your life.* Pocket Books.

Seligman, M. E. P. (1998c). Work, love, and play. *APA Monitor, 29*, 2. Retrieved from www.apa.org/monitor/aug98/pc.html

Seligman, M. E. P. (2002). *Authentic happiness: Using the new positive psychology to realize your potential for lasting fulfillment.* Free Press.

Seligman, M. E. P. (2018). *The optimistic child: A revolutionary approach to raising resilient children.* Hachette UK.

Seligman, M. E. P., & Csikszentmihalyi, M. (2000). Positive psychology: An introduction. *American Psychologist, 55*, 5–14.

Seligman, M. E. P., & Schulman, P. (1986). Explanatory style as a predictor of performance as a life insurance agent. *Journal of Personality and Social Psychology, 50*, 832–838.

Seligman, M. E. P., Abramson, L. Y., Semmel, A., & von Baeyer, C. (1979). Depressive attributional style. *Journal of Abnormal Psychology, 88*, 242–247.

Seligman, M. E. P., Kaslow, N. J., Alloy, L. B., Peterson, C., Tanenbaum, R., & Abramson, L. Y. (1984). Attributional style and depressive symptoms among children. *Journal of Abnormal Psychology, 93*, 235–238.

Seligman, M. E. P., Nolen-Hoeksema, S., Thornton, N., & Thornton, K. M. (1990). Explanatory style as a mechanism of disappointing athletic performance. *Psychological Science, 1*, 143–146.

Seligman, M. E. P., Reivich, K., Jaycox, L., & Gillham, J. (1995). *The optimistic child.* New York: Houghton Mifflin.

Seligman, M. E. P., Steen, T. A., Park, N., & Peterson, C. (2005). Positive psychology progress: Empirical validation of interventions. *American Psychologist, 60*, 410–421.

Sell, A. J. (2016). Applying the intentional forgetting process to forgiveness. *Journal of Applied Research in Memory and Cognition, 5*, 10–20.

Sellers, R. M., Copeland-Linder, N., Martin, P. P., & Lewis, R. L. (2006). Racial identity matters: The relationship between racial discrimination and psychological functioning in African American adolescents. *Journal of Research on Adolescence, 16*, 187–216.

Selye, H. (1936). A syndrome produced by diverse nocuous agents. *Nature, 138*, 32.

Sengupta, N. K., Osborne, D., Houkamau, C. A., Hoverd, W., Wilson, M., Halliday, L. M., West-Newman, T.,

Barlow, F. K., Armstong, G., Robertson, A., & Sibley, C. G. (2012). How much happiness does money buy? Income and subjective well-being in New Zealand. *New Zealand Journal of Psychology, 41*, 21–34.

Serrat, R., Villar, F., Pratt, M. W., & Stukas, A. A. (2017). On the quality of adjustment to retirement: The longitudinal role of personality traits and generativity. *Journal of Personality Publisher.* Advance online publication.

Shadlow, J. O., Boles, R. E., Roberts, M. C., & Winston, L. (2015). Native American children and their reports of hope: Construct validation of the Children's Hope Scale. *Journal of Child and Family Studies, 24*, 1707–1714.

Shafranske, E. P., & Malony, H. N. (1990). Clinical psychologists' religious and spiritual orientations and their practices of psychotherapy. *Psychotherapy: Theory, Research, Practice, Training, 27*, 72–78.

Shah, P. (2012). Toward a neurobiology of unrealistic optimism. *Frontiers in Psychology, 3*, 344.

Shapiro, D. H. (1980). *Meditation: Self-regulation strategy and altered state of consciousness.* Aldine.

Shapiro, S. L. (2009). The integration of mindfulness and psychology. *Journal of Clinical Psychology, 65*, 555–560.

Shapiro, S. L., Schwartz, G. E. R., & Santerre, C. (2002). Meditation and positive psychology. In C. R. Snyder & S. J. Lopez (Eds.), *The handbook of positive psychology* (pp. 632–645). Oxford University Press.

Sharma, S., & Singh, K. (2019). Religion and well-being: The editing role of positive virtues. *Journal of Religion and Health, 58*, 119–131.

Sharma, S., Biswal, R., Deller, J., & Mandal, M. K. (2009). Emotional intelligence: Factorial structure and construct validity across cultures. *International Journal of Cross Cultural Management, 9*, 217–236.

Sharot, T. (2011). *The optimism bias: A tour of the irrationally positive brain.* Pantheon/Random House.

Sharot, T., Korn, C. W., & Dolan, R. J. (2011). How unrealistic optimism is maintained in the face of reality. *Nature Neuroscience, 14*, 1475–1479.

Shaver, P. R., & Mikulincer, M. (2006). Attachment theory, individual psychodynamics, and relationship functioning. In A. L. Vangelisti & D. Perlman (Eds.), *The Cambridge handbook of personal relationships* (pp. 251–271). Cambridge University Press.

Shaver, P., Hazan, C., & Bradshaw, D. (1988). Love as attachment. In R. J. Sternberg & M. L. Barnes (Eds.), *The psychology of love* (pp. 68–99). Yale University Press.

Shek, D. T., Dou, D., Zhu, X., & Chai, W. (2019). Positive youth development: Current perspectives. *Adolescent health, medicine and therapeutics, 10*, 131–141.

Sheldon, K. M., & Lyubomirsky, S. (2004). Achieving sustainable new happiness: Prospects, practices, and prescriptions. In P. A. Linley & S. Joseph (Eds.), *Positive psychology in practice* (pp. 127–145). Wiley.

Shelp, E. E. (1984). Courage: A neglected virtue in the patient–physician relationship. *Social Science and Medicine, 18*, 351–360.

Sherer, M., Maddux, J. E., Mercandante, B., Prentice-Dunn, S., Jacobs, B., & Rogers, R. (1982). The self-efficacy scale: Construction and validation. *Psychological Reports, 51*, 663–671.

Sherry, J. L. (2004). Flow and media enjoyment. *Communication Theory, 14*, 328–347.

Shin, L. J., & Lyubomirsky, S. (2017). Increasing well-being in independent and interdependent cultures. In M. A. Warren & S. I. Donaldson (Eds.), *Scientific advances in positive psychology* (pp. 11–36). Praeger.

Shin, L. J., Layous, K., Choi, I., Na, S., & Lyubomirsky, S. (2020). Good for self or good for others? The well-being benefits of kindness in two cultures depend on how the kindness is framed. *The Journal of Positive Psychology, 15*, 795–805.

Shin, Y., & Kelly, K. R. (2013). Cross-cultural comparison of the effects of optimism, intrinsic motivation, and family relations on vocational identity. *The Career Department Quarterly, 61*, 141–160.

Shiota, M. N., Campos, B., Gonzaga, G. C., Keltner, D., & Peng, K. (2010). I love you but . . . Cultural differences in complexity of emotional experiences during interaction with a romantic partner. *Cognition and Emotion, 24*, 786–799.

Shiota, M. N., Keltner, D., & John, O. P. (2006). Positive

emotion dispositions differentially associated with Big Five personality and attachment style. *Journal of Positive Psychology, 1*, 61–71.

Shogren, K. A., Wehmeyer, M. L., Palmer, S. B., Forber-Pratt, A. J., Little, T. J., & Lopez, S. (2015). Causal agency theory: Reconceptualizing a functional model of self-determination. *Education and Training in Autism and Developmental Disabilities, 50*, 251–263.

Shorey, H. S., Snyder, C. R., Yang, X., & Lewin, M. R. (2003). The role of hope as a mediator in recollecting parenting, adult attachment, and mental health. *Journal of Social and Clinical Psychology, 22*, 685–715.

Siegling, A. B., Furnham, A., & Petrides, K. V. (2015). Trait emotional intelligence and personality: Gender-invariant linkages across different measures of the Big Five. *Journal of Psychoeducational Assessment, 33(1)*, 57–67.

Silva, J. M., Langhout, R. D., Kohfeldt, D., & Gurrola, E. (2015). "Good" and "bad" kids? A race and gender analysis of effective behavioral support in an elementary school. *Urban Education, 50*, 787–811.

Simola, S. (2016). Fostering collective growth and vitality following acts of moral courage: A general system, relational psychodynamic perspective. *Journal of Business Ethics*. Advance online publication.

Simonton, D. K., & Baumeister, R. F. (2005). Positive psychology at the summit. *Review of General Psychology, 9*, 99–102.

Simpson, B., & Willer, R. (2015). Beyond altruism: Sociopolitical foundations of cooperation and prosocial behavior. *Annual Review of Sociology, 41*, 43–63.

Sin, N. L., & Lyubomirsky, S. (2009). Enhancing well-being and alleviating depressive symptoms with positive psychology interventions: A practice-friendly meta-analysis. *Journal of Clinical Psychology, 65*, 467–487.

Singh, K., Junnarkar, M., & Kaur, J. (2016). *Measures of positive psychology: Development and validation*. Springer Science + Business Media.

Singleton, G. E. (2021). *Courageous conversations about race: A field guide for achieving equity in schools and beyond*. Corwin.

Singleton, G., Johnson, L., Singleton, N., & Li, H. (2022). Covid-19-related anxiety: How do coping and optimism relate to substance use in African-American young adults? *Journal of Community Psychology*.

Sizemore, K. M., Carter, J. A., Millar, B. M., Cain, D., Parsons, J. T., & Rendina, H. J. (2019). Attachment as a predictor of psychological and sexual wellbeing among transgender women in New York City. *The Journal of Sex Research, 56(9)*, 1192–1202.

Sizemore, K. M., Talan, A., Gray, S., Forbes, N., Park, H. H., & Rendina, H. J. (2022). Attachment buffers against the association between childhood sexual abuse, depression, and substance use problems among transgender women: A moderated-mediation model. *Psychology & Sexuality, 13(5)*, 1319–1335.

Smith, A. (2018, November 16). Algorithms in action: The content people see on social media. *Pew Research*. https://www.pewresearch.org/internet/2018/11/16/algorithms-in-action-the-content-people-see-on-social-media/#:~: text=The%20social%20media%20environment%20is%20another%20prominent%20example, he%20or%20she%20might%20find%20relevant%20or%20engaging.

Smith, E. P., Witherspoon, D. P., & Osgood, D. W. (2017). Positive youth development among diverse racial-ethnic children: Quality afterschool contexts as developmental assets. *Child Development, 88*, 1063–1078.

Smith, J. L., & Bryant, F. B. (2016). The benefits of savoring life: Savoring as a moderator of the relationship between health and life satisfaction in older adults. *The International Journal of Aging & Human Development, 84*, 3–23.

Smith, K. D., Türk-Smith, S., & Christopher, J. C. (1998, August). *Prototypes of the ideal person in seven cultures*. Paper presented at the International Congress of the International Association for Cross-Cultural Psychologists, Bellingham, WA.

Smith, M. L., Glass, G. V., & Miller, T. I. (1980). *The benefits of psychotherapy*. Johns Hopkins University Press.

Smith, T. W., Pope, M. K., Rhodewalt, F., & Poulton, J. L. (1989). Optimism, neuroticism, coping, and symptom reports: An alternative interpretation of the Life Orientation Test.

Journal of Personality and Social Psychology, 56, 640–648.

Smyth, J. M., Nazarian, D., & Arigo, D. (2008). Expressive writing in the clinical context. In A. J. J. M. Vingerhoets, I. Nyklíc˘ek, & J. Denollet (Eds.), *Emotion regulation. Conceptual and clinical issues* (pp. 215–233). Springer.

Snyder, C. R. (1989). Reality negotiation: From excuses to hope and beyond. *Journal of Social and Clinical Psychology, 8*, 130–157.

Snyder, C. R. (1992). Product scarcity by need for uniqueness interaction: A consumer catch-22? *Basic and Applied Social Psychology, 13*, 9–24.

Snyder, C. R. (1994). *The psychology of hope: You can get there from here*. Free Press.

Snyder, C. R. (2000a). Genesis: The birth and growth of hope. In C. R. Snyder (Ed.), *Handbook of hope: Theory, measures, and applications* (pp. 25–38). Academic Press.

Snyder, C. R. (2000b). The past and the possible futures of hope. *Journal of Social and Clinical Psychology, 19*, 11–28.

Snyder, C. R. (2000c). *The psychology of hope: You can get there from here*. Free Press. (Original work published 1994)

Snyder, C. R. (2002). Hope theory: Rainbows of the mind. *Psychological Inquiry, 13*, 249–275.

Snyder, C. R. (2003, November). *Forgiveness and hope*. Paper presented at the International Campaign for Forgiveness Conference, Atlanta, GA.

Snyder, C. R. (2004b, November). *Hope and spirituality*. Paper presented at the International Society for Quality of Life Studies Conference, Philadelphia.

Snyder, C. R. (2004c, December 17). Graceful attitude eases adversity. *Lawrence Journal-World*, p. D4.

Snyder, C. R., & Feldman, D. (2000). Hope for the many: An empowering social agenda. In C. R. Snyder (Ed.), *Handbook of hope: Theory, measures, and applications* (pp. 389–412). Academic Press.

Snyder, C. R., & Fromkin, H. L. (1977). Abnormality as a positive characteristic: The development and validation of a scale measuring need for uniqueness. *Journal of Abnormal Psychology, 86*(5), 518–527.

Snyder, C. R., & Fromkin, H. L. (1980). *Uniqueness: The human pursuit of difference*. Plenum.

Snyder, C. R., & Ingram, R. E. (Eds.). (2000a). *Handbook of psychological change: Psychotherapy processes and practices for the 21st century*. Wiley.

Snyder, C. R., & Shorey, H. (2002). Hope in the classroom: The role of positive psychology in academic achievement and psychology curriculum. *Psychology Teacher Network, 12*, 1–9.

Snyder, C. R., & Shorey, H. (2004). Hope and leadership. In G. Goethals, G. J. Sorenson, & J. M. Burns (Eds.), *Encyclopedia of leadership* (pp. 673–675). Sage.

Snyder, C. R., Feldman, D. B., Taylor, J. D., Schroeder, L. L., & Adams, V., III. (2000). The roles of hopeful thinking in preventing problems and promoting strengths. *Applied & Preventive Psychology: Current Scientific Perspectives, 15*, 262–295.

Snyder, C. R., Harris, C., Anderson, J. R., Holleran, S. A., Irving, L. M., Sigmon, S. T., Yoshinobu, J. G., Langelle, C., & Harney, P. (1991). The will and the ways: Development and validation of an individual-differences measure of hope. *Journal of Personality and Social Psychology, 60*, 570–585.

Snyder, C. R., Higgins, R. L., & Stucky, R. J. (2005). *Excuses: Masquerades in search of grace*. Clinton Corners, NY: Percheron. (Original work published 1983)

Snyder, C. R., Hoza, B., Pelham, W. E., Rapoff, M., Ware, L., Danovsky, M., Highberger, L., H. Rubinstein, & Stahl, K. J. (1997). The development and validation of the Children's Hope Scale. *Journal of Pediatric Psychology, 22*, 399–421.

Snyder, C. R., Ilardi, S. S., Cheavens, J., Michael, S. T., Yamhure, L., & Sympson, S. (2000). The role of hope in cognitive behavior therapies. *Cognitive Therapy and Research, 24*, 747–762.

Snyder, C. R., Ilardi, S., Michael, S., & Cheavens, J. (2000). Hope theory: Updating a common process for psychological change. In C. R. Snyder & R. E. Ingram (Eds.), *Handbook of psychological change: Psychotherapy processes and practices for the 21st century* (pp. 128–153). Wiley.

Snyder, C. R., LaPointe, A. B., Crowson, J. J., Jr., & Early, S. (1998). Preferences of high- and low-hope people for self-referential input. *Cognition & Emotion, 12*, 807–823.

Snyder, C. R., Lopez, S. J., Edwards, L. M., & Marques, S. C. (2021). In C. R. Snyder, S. J. Lopez, L. M. Edwards, & S. C. Marques (Eds.), *The Oxford handbook of positive psychology, 3rd ed.* (Oxford University Press.

Snyder, C. R., Lopez, S. J., Edwards, L. M., Pedrotti, J. T., Prosser, E. C., Larue-Walton, S., Spalitto, S. V., & Ulven, J. C. (2003). *Measuring and labeling the positive and the negative. Positive psychological assessment: A handbook of models and measures* (pp. 21–40). American Psychological Association.

Snyder, C. R., McDermott, D., Cook, W., & Rapoff, M. (2002). *Hope for the journey: Helping children through the good times and the bad* (Rev. ed.). Percheron.

Snyder, C. R., Parenteau, S., Shorey, H. S., Kahle, K. E., & Berg, C. (2002). Hope as the underlying process in Gestalt and other psychotherapy approaches. *International Gestalt Therapy Journal, 25,* 11–29.

Snyder, C. R., Rand, K., King, E., Feldman, D., & Taylor, J. (2002). "False" hope. *Journal of Clinical Psychology, 58,* 1003–1022.

Snyder, C. R., Shorey, H., Cheavens, J., Pulvers, K. M., Adams, V. H., III, & Wiklund, C. (2002). Hope and academic success in college. *Journal of Educational Psychology, 94,* 820–826.

Snyder, C. R., Sympson, S. C., Ybasco, F. C., Borders, T. F., Babyak, M. A., & Higgins, R. L. (1996). Development and validation of the State Hope Scale. *Journal of Personality and Social Psychology, 2,* 321–335.

Snyder, C. R., Tennen, H., Affleck, G., & Cheavens, J. (2000). Social, personality, clinical, and health psychology tributaries: The merging of a scholarly "river of dreams." *Personality and Social Psychology Review, 4,* 16–29.

Snyder, C. R., Thompson, L. Y., & Heinze, L. (2003). The hopeful ones. In G. Keinan (Ed.), *Between stress and hope* (pp. 57–80). Greenwood.

Sohl, S. J., Moyer, A., Lukin, K., & Knapp-Oliver, S. K. (2011). Why are optimists optimistic? *Individual Differences Research, 9,* 1–11.

Solomon, L. D. (2006). *From Athens to America: Virtues and formulation of public policy.* Lexington.

Soosai-Nathan, L., Negri, L., & Delle Fave, A. (2013). Beyond pro-social behavior: An exploration of altruism in two cultures. *Psychological Studies, 58,* 103–114.

Soothill, W. E. (1968). *The analects of Confucius.* Paragon.

Soria, K. M., & Stubblefield, R. (2015). Building a strengths-based campus to support student retention. *Journal of College Student Development, 56(6),* 626–631.

Soria, K. M., Laumer, N. L., Morrow, D. J., & Marttinen, G. (2017). Strengths-based advising approaches: Benefits for first-year undergraduates. *NACADA Journal, 37*(2), 55–65.

Sörman, K., Edens, J. F., Smith, S. T., Clark, J. W., & Kristiansson, M. (2016). Boldness and its relation to psychopathic personality: Prototypicality analyses among forensic mental health, criminal justice, and layperson raters. *Law and Human Behavior, 40,* 337–349.

Southwick, S. M., Bonanno, G. A., Masten, A. S., Panter-Brick, C., & Yehuda, R. (2014). Resilience definitions, theory, and challenges: Interdisciplinary perspectives. *European Journal of Psychotraumatology, 5*(1), 1–14.

Spears-Brown, C., & Chu, H. (2012). Discrimination, ethnic identity, and academic outcomes of Mexican immigrant children: The importance of school context. *Child Development, 83,* 1477–1485.

Speight, S. L., & Vera, E. M. (2004). A social justice agenda: Ready or not? *The Counseling Psychologist, 32,* 109–118.

Spencer-Rodgers, J., & Peng, K. (2018). *The psychological and cultural foundations of East Asian cognition: Contradiction, change, and holism.* Oxford University Press.

Spencer-Rodgers, J., Peng, K., & Wang, L. (2010). Dialecticism and the co occurrence of positive and negative emotions across cultures. *Journal of Cross-Cultural Psychology, 41,* 109–115.

Sperry, L. (2016). Secular spirituality and spiritually sensitive clinical practice. *Spirituality in Clinical Practice, 3,* 221.

Spilsbury, J. C., Dalton, J. E., Haas, B. M., & Korbin, J. E. (2022). "A rising tide floats all boats": The role of neighborhood collective efficacy in responding to child maltreatment. *Child Abuse & Neglect, 124*.

Sprecher, S., & Fehr, B. (2010). Dispositional attachment and relationship-specific attachment as predictors of compassionate love for a partner. *Journal of Social and Personal Relationships, 28*, 558–574.

Sprecher, S., Treger, S., Fisher, A., Hilaire, N., & Grzybowski, M. (2015). Associations between self-expansion and actual and perceived (dis)similarity and their joint effects on attraction in initial interactions. *Self and Identity, 14*, 369–389.

Staats, S. R. (1989). Hope: A comparison of two self-report measures for adults. *Journal of Personality Assessment, 53*, 366–375.

Stanton, A. L., Danoff-Burg, S., & Huggins, M. E. (2002). The first year after breast cancer diagnosis: Hope and coping strategies as predictors of adjustment. *Psycho Oncology, 11*(2), 93–102.

Stanton, A. L., Danoff-Burg, S., Cameron, C. L., Bishop, M., Collins, C. A., Kirk, S. B., Sworowski, L. A., & Twillman, R. (2000). Emotionally expressive coping predicts psychological and physical adjustment to breast cancer. *Journal of Consulting and Clinical Psychology, 68*(5), 875–882.

Stanton, A. L., Kirk, S. B., Cameron, C. L., & Danoff-Burg, S. (2000). Coping through emotional approach: Scale construction and validation. *Journal of Personality and Social Psychology, 78*(6), 1150–1169.

Stanton, A. L., & Low, C. A. (2012). Expressing emotions in stressful contexts: Benefits, moderators, and mechanisms. *Current Directions in Psychological Science, 21*(2), 124–128. https://doi.org/10.1177/0963721411434978

Stanton, A. L., Parsa, A., & Austenfeld, J. L. (2002). The adaptive potential of coping through emotional approach. In C. R. Snyder & S. J. Lopez (Eds.), *The handbook of positive psychology* (pp. 148–158). Oxford University Press.

Stanton, K., & Watson, D. (2014). Positive and negative affective dysfunction in psychopathology. *Social and Personality Psychology Compass, 8*, 555–567.

Starmer, A. J., Frintner, M. P., & Freed, G. L. (2016). Work–life balance, burnout, and satisfaction of early career pediatricians. *Pediatrics, 137*, 1–10.

Staudinger, U., & Baltes, P. B. (1994). Psychology of wisdom. In R. J. Sternberg (Ed.), *Encyclopedia of human intelligence* (Vol. 2, pp. 143–152). Macmillan.

Staudinger, U., & Baltes, P. B. (1996). Interactive minds: A facilitative setting for wisdom-related performance? *Journal of Personality and Social Psychology, 71*, 746–762.

Staudinger, U., & Leipold, B. (2003). The assessment of wisdom-related performance. In S. J. Lopez & C. R. Snyder (Eds.), *Positive psychological assessment: A handbook of models and measures* (pp. 171–184). American Psychological Association.

Stavrova, O., Fetchenhauer, D., & Schlösser, T. (2013). Why are religious people happy? The effect of the social norm of religiosity across countries. *Social Science Research, 42*, 90–105.

Steele, C. M. (1994). A threat in the air: How stereotypes shape intellectual identity and performance. *American Psychologist, 52*, 202–233.

Steers, M. L. N., Øverup, C. S., Brunson, J. A., & Acitelli, L. K. (2016). Love online: How relationship awareness on Facebook relates to relationship quality among college students. *Psychology of Popular Media Culture, 5*, 203.

Steffen, P. R. (2012). Approaching religiosity/spirituality and health from the eudaimonic perspective. *Social and Personality Psychology Compass, 6*, 70–82.

Steger, M. F., & Kashdan, T. B. (2013). The unbearable lightness of meaning: Well-being and unstable meaning in life. *Journal of Positive Psychology, 8*, 103–115.

Stein, M. (1989). Gratitude and attitude: A note on emotional welfare. *Social Psychology Quarterly, 52*, 242–248.

Steiner, M., Allemand, M., & McCullough, M. E. (2011). Age differences in forgivingness: The role of transgression frequency and intensity. *Journal of Research in Personality, 45*, 670–678.

Steiner, M., Allemand, M., & McCullough, M. E. (2012). Do agreeableness and neuroticism explain age differences in the tendency to forgive others? *Personality and Social Psychology Bulletin, 38*, 441–453.

Stephenson, K. R. (2017). Mindfulness-based therapies for sexual dysfunction:

A review of potential theory-based mechanisms of change. *Mindfulness, 8*, 527–543.

Sternberg, R. (1985). Implicit theories of intelligence, creativity, and wisdom. *Journal of Personality and Social Psychology, 49*, 607–627.

Sternberg, R. J. (1986). A triangular theory of love. *Psychological Review, 93*, 119–135.

Sternberg, R. (1990). *Wisdom: Its nature, origins, and development*. Cambridge University Press.

Sternberg, R. (1998a). A balance theory of wisdom. *Review of General Psychology, 2*, 347–365.

Sternberg, R. J. (1998b). *Love is a story: A new theory of relationships*. Oxford University Press.

Sternberg, R. J. (2012). Intelligence in its cultural context. In M. J. Gelfand, C. Ciu, & Y. Hong (Eds.), *Advances in culture and psychology* (pp. 205–248). Oxford University Press.

Sternberg, R. J., & Hojjat, M. (1997). *Satisfaction in close relationships*. Guilford.

Stevenson, L., & Haberman, D. L. (1998). *Ten theories of human nature*. Oxford University Press.

Stickney, L. T. (2010). Who benefits from Pennebaker's expressive writing? More research recommendations: A commentary on Range and Jenkins. *Sex Roles, 63*, 165–172.

Stocks, E. L., Lishner, D. A., & Decker, S. K. (2009). Altruism or psychological escape: Why does empathy promote prosocial behavior? *European Journal of Social Psychology, 39*, 649–665.

Storbeck, J., & Maswood, R. (2016). Happiness increases verbal and spatial working memory capacity where sadness does not: Emotion, working memory and executive control. *Cognition and Emotion, 30*(5), 925–938.

Stotland, E. (1969). *The psychology of hope*. Jossey-Bass.

Strecher, V. J., Champion, V. L., & Rosenstock, I. M. (1997). The health belief model and health behavior. In D. Gochman (Ed.), *Handbook of health behavior research 1: Personal and social determinants* (pp. 71–92). Plenum.

Strelan, P. (2007). Who forgives others, themselves, and situations? The roles of narcissism, guilt, self-esteem, and agreeableness. *Personality and Individual Differences, 42*, 259–269.

Strupp, H. H. (1964). *A bibliography of research in psychotherapy*. Unpublished manuscript.

Stulp, H. P., Koelen, J., Schep-Akkerman, A., Glas, G. G., & Eurelings-Bontekoe, L. (2019). God representations and aspects of psychological functioning: A meta-analysis. *Cogent Psychology, 6(1)*, 1647926.

Sue, D. W. (2015). *Race talk and the conspiracy of silence: Understanding and facilitating difficult dialogues on race*. John Wiley & Sons.

Sue, D. W., & Constantine, M. G. (2003). Optimal human functioning in people of color in the United States. In W. B. Walsh (Ed.), *Counseling psychology and optimal human functioning* (pp. 151–169). Lawrence Erlbaum.

Sue, D. W., Sue, D., Neville, H. A., & Smith, L. (2022). *Counseling the culturally diverse: Theory and practice* (9th edition). Wiley.

Suh, E. M., & Koo, J. (2008). Comparing subjective well-being across cultures and nations: The "what" and "why" questions. In M. Eid & R. J. Larsen (Eds.), *The science of subjective well-being* (pp. 414–427). Guilford.

Sullivan, A. L., Pham, A. V., Weeks, M., & Nguyen, T. (2021). Enfranchising socially marginalized students. In P. J. Lazarus, S. M. Suldo, & B. Doll (Eds.), *Fostering the emotional well-being of our youth: A school-based approach* (pp. 375–394). Oxford University Press.

Sullivan, P. (2015, February 5). Jump in employment putting pressure on volunteering rates. *The NonProfit Times*. http://www.thenonprofittimes.com/news-articles/jump-employment-putting-pressure-volunteering-rates/

Sun, X., Zhong, F., Xin, T., & Kang, C. (2021). Item response theory analysis of general self-efficacy scale for senior elementary school students in China. *Current Psychology: A Journal for Diverse Perspectives on Diverse Psychological Issues, 40*(2), 601–610.

Szagun, G. (1992). Age-related changes in children's understanding of courage. *Journal of Genetic Psychology, 153*, 405–420.

Szagun, G., & Schauble, M. (1997). Children's and adults'

understanding of the feeling experience of courage. *Cognition and Emotion, 11*(3), 291–306.

Szczešniak, M., & Soares, E. (2011). Are proneness to forgive, optimism, and gratitude associated with life satisfaction? *Polish Psychological Bulletin, 42*, 20–23.

Szymanski, D. M., Moffitt, L. B., & Carr, E. R. (2011). Sexual objectification of women: Advances to theory and research 1 ψ 7. *The Counseling Psychologist, 39*, 6–38.

Tabak, B. A., McCullough, M. E., Luna, L. R., Bono, G., & Berry, J. W. (2012). Conciliatory gestures facilitate forgiveness and feelings of friendship by making transgressors appear more agreeable. *Journal of Personality, 80*, 503–536.

Takahashi, K., Mizuno, K., Sasaki, A. T., Wada, Y., Tanaka, M., Ishii, A., Tajima, K., Tsuyuguchi, N., Watanabe, K, Zeki, S., & Watanabe, Y. (2015). Imaging the passionate stage of romantic love by dopamine dynamics. *Frontiers in Human Neuroscience, 9*, 1–6.

Takaku, S. (2001). The effects of apology and perspective taking on interpersonal forgiveness: A dissonance-attribution model of interpersonal forgiveness. *The Journal of Social Psycho1ogy, 141*, 494–508.

Tang, Y., & Posner, M. I. (2013). Tools of the trade: Theory and method in mindfulness neuroscience. *Social Cognitive and Affective Neuroscience, 8*, 118–120.

Tangney, J. P., Fee, R., Reinsmith, C., Boone, A. L., & Lee, N. (1999, August). *Assessing individual differences in the propensity to forgive*. Paper presented at the American Psychological Association Convention, Boston.

Tatar, M. (2002). *The annotated classic fairy tales*. W. W. Norton.

Taube, L. N., & Mussap, A. J. (2020). Character strengths in transgender and gender diverse people. *Psychology & Sexuality, 11*(3), 225–242.

Taylor, R. D., Budescu, M., & McGill, R. (2011). Demanding kin relations and depressive symptoms among low-income African American women: Mediating effects of self-esteem and optimism. *Cultural Diversity and Ethnic Minority Psychology, 17*, 303–308.

Taylor, S. E., Dickerson, S. S., & Klein, L. C. (2002). Toward a biology of social support. In C. R. Snyder & S. J. Lopez (Eds.), *The handbook of positive psychology* (pp. 556–572). Oxford University Press.

Taylor, S. E., Kemeny, M. E., Aspinwall, L. G., Schneider, S. G., Rodriguez, R., & Herbert, M. (1992). Optimism, coping, psychological distress, and high-risk sexual behavior among men at risk for acquired immunodeficiency syndrome (AIDS). *Journal of Personality and Social Psychology, 63*, 460–473.

Taylor, Z. E., Larsen-Rife, D., Conger, R. D., Widaman, K. F., & Cutrona, C. E. (2010). Life stress, maternal optimism, and adolescent competence in single mother, African American families. *Journal of Family Psychology, 24*, 468–477.

Teasdale, J. D., Segal, Z. V., Williams, J. M. G., Ridgeway, V. A., Soulsby, J. M., & Lau, M. A. (2000). Prevention of relapse/recurrence in major depression by mindfulness-based cognitive therapy. *Journal of Consulting and Clinical Psychology, 68*, 615–623.

Tedeschi, R. G., & Calhoun, L. G. (1996). The Posttraumatic Growth Inventory: Measuring the positive legacy of trauma. *Journal of Traumatic Stress, 9*(3), 455–472.

Tehrani, H. D., & Yamini, S. (2020). Gender differences concerning love: A meta-analysis. *TPM: Testing, Psychometrics, Methodology in Applied Psychology, 27*(4).

Teo, T., & Kam, C. (2014). A measurement invariance analysis of the General Self-Efficacy Scale on two different cultures. *Journal of Psychoeducational Assessment, 32*(8), 762–767.

Terman, L. M., & Oden, M. H. (1947). *The gifted child grows up: Twenty five years' follow-up of a superior group*. Stanford University Press.

Tetrick, L. E., & Peiró, J. M. (2012). Occupational safety and health. In S. W. J. Kozlowski (Ed.), *The Oxford handbook of organizational psychology* (Vol. 2, pp. 1228–1244). Oxford University Press.

Tetzner, J., & Becker, M. (2017). Think positive? Examining the impact of optimism on academic achievement in early adolescents. *Journal of Personality*. Advance online publication.

Thatcher, A., Wretschko, G., & Fridjhon, P. (2008). Online flow experiences, problematic Internet use and Internet procrastination. *Computers in Human Behavior, 24*, 2236–2254.

Thomas, D. C. (2006). Domain and development of cultural intelligence. *Group & Organizational Management, 31*, 78–99.

Thomas, E. F., McCarty, C., Spears, R., Livingstone, A. G., Plato, M. J., Lala, G., & Mavor, K. (2020). 'That's not funny!' Standing up against disparaging humor. *Journal of Experimental Social Psychology, 86*, Article 103901.

Thomas, J. L., Britt, T. W., Odle-Dusseau, H., & Bliese, P. D. (2011). Dispositional optimism buffers combat veterans from the negative effects of warzone stress on mental health symptoms and work impairment. *Journal of Clinical Psychology, 67*, 866–880.

Thomas, M. L., Bangen, K. J., Ardelt, M., & Jeste, D. V. (2017). Development of a 12-item abbreviated three-dimensional wisdom scale (3D-WS-12): Item selection and psychometric properties. *Assessment, 24*, 71–82.

Thomas, R. R. (1990). From affirmative action to affirming diversity. *Harvard Business Review, 68*, 107–117.

Thomas-Hawkins, C., Zha, P., Flynn, L., & Ando, S. (2022). Effects of race, workplace racism, and COVID worry on the emotional well-being of hospital based nurses: A dual pandemic. *Behavioral Medicine, 48*, 95–108.

Thompson, A., & Bruk-Lee, V. (2021). Employee happiness: Why we should care. *Applied Research in Quality of Life, 16*, 1419–1437.

Thompson, L. Y., Snyder, C. R., Hoffman, L., Michael, S. T., Rasmussen, H. N., Billings, L. S., Heinze, L., Neufeld, J. E., Shorey, H. S., Roberts, J. C., & Roberts, D. E. (2005). Dispositional forgiveness of self, others, and situations: The Heartland Forgiveness Scale. *Journal of Personality, 73*, 313–359.

Thoresen, C. E., Harris, A. H. S., & Oman, D. (2001). Spirituality, religion, and health: Evidence, issues, and concerns. In T. G. Plante & A. C. Sherman (Eds.), *Faith and health: Psychological perspectives* (pp. 15–52). Guilford.

Thoroughgood, C. N., Sawyer, K. B., & Webster, J. R. (2021). Because you're worth the risks: Acts of oppositional courage as symbolic messages of relational value to transgender employees. *Journal of Applied Psychology, 106*(3), 399–421.

Thurber, J. A., & Yoshinaka, A. (2015). *American gridlock*. Cambridge University Press.

Tierney, J. P., & Grossman, J. B. (2000). *Making a difference: An impact study of Big Brothers/Big Sisters*. Public/Private Ventures.

Ting-Toomey, S. (1994). Managing intercultural conflict in intercultural personal relationships. In D. D. Cahn (Ed.), *Intimate conflict in personal relationships* (pp. 47–77). Lawrence Erlbaum.

Tipton, R. M., & Worthington, E. L. (1984). The measurement of generalized self-efficacy: A study of construct validity. *Journal of Personality Assessment, 48*, 545–548.

Toepfer, S. M., Cichy, K., & Peters, P. (2012). Letters of gratitude: Further evidence for author benefits. *Journal of Happiness Studies, 13*, 187–201.

Toikko, T., & Rantanen, T. (2020). Association between individualism and welfare attitudes: An analysis of citizens' attitudes towards the state's welfare responsibility. *Journal of Social and Political Psychology, 8*, 132–150.

Tolan, P. (2016). Positive youth development interventions: Advancing evaluation theory and practice. *Applied Developmental Science, 20*, 147–149.

Tomás, J. M., Sancho, P., Galiana, L., & Oliver, A. (2016). A double test on the importance of spirituality, the "forgotten factor," in successful aging. *Social Indicators Research, 127*, 1377–1389.

Tomlinson, J. M., & Aron, A. (2013). The positive psychology of romantic love. In M. Hojjat & D. Cramer (Eds.), *Positive psychology of love* (pp. 3–15). Oxford University Press.

Toner, E., Haslam, N., Robinson, J., & Williams, P. (2012). Character strengths and wellbeing in adolescence: Structure and correlates of the Values in Action Inventory of Strengths for Children. *Personality and Individual Differences, 52*(5), 637–642.

Tong, E. M. (2017). Spirituality and the temporal dynamics of transcendental positive emotions. *Psychology of Religion and Spirituality, 9*, 70.

Tong, E. W., Fredrickson, B. L., Chang, W., & Lim, Z. (2010). Re-examining hope: The roles of agency thinking and pathways thinking. *Cognition and Emotion, 24*, 1207–1215.

Tori, D., Sasahara, S., Doki, S., Oi, Y., & Matsuzaki, I. (2020). Prefrontal activation while listening to a letter of gratitude read aloud by a coworker face-to-face: A NIRS study. *PLoS One*, *15*, Article 0238715.

Toussaint, L. L., Owen, A. D., & Cheadle, A. (2012). Forgive to live: Forgiveness, health, and longevity. *Journal of Behavioral Medicine*, *35*, 375–386.

Toussaint, L., Shields, G. S., Dorn, G., & Slavich, G. M. (2016). Effects of lifetime stress exposure on mental and physical health in young adulthood: How stress degrades and forgiveness protects health. *Journal of Health Psychology*, *21*, 1004–1014.

Triandis, H. C. (1988). Collectivism v. individualism: A reconceptualization of a basic concept in cross-cultural social psychology. In G. K. Verma & C. Bagley (Eds.), *Cross-cultural studies of personality, attitudes and cognition* (pp. 6–95). Macmillan.

Triandis, H. C. (1990). Cross-cultural studies of individualism and collectivism. In J. Berman (Ed.), *Nebraska Symposium on Motivation* (pp. 41–133). University of Nebraska Press.

Triandis, H. C. (1995). *Individualism and collectivism*. Westview.

Trivers, R. L. (1971). The evolution of reciprocal altruism. *Quarterly Review of Biology*, *46*, 35–57.

Trom, P., & Burke, J. (2022). Positive psychology intervention (PPI) coaching: An experimental application of coaching to improve the effectiveness of a gratitude intervention. *Coaching: An International Journal of Theory, Research and Practice*, *15*, 131–142.

Tsai, W., Lau, A. S., Niles, A. N., Coello, J., Lieberman, M. D., Ko, A. C., Hur, C., & Stanton, A. L. (2015). Ethnicity moderates the outcomes of self-enhancement and self-improvement themes in expressive writing. *Cultural Diversity and Ethnic Minority Psychology*, *21*(4), 584–592.

Tsai, W., & Lu, Q. (2018). Culture, emotion suppression and disclosure, and health. *Social and Personality Psychology Compass*, *12*(3), 1–13. https://doi.org/10.1111/spc3.12373

Tsang, J.-A., & Martin, S. R. (2016). A psychological perspective on gratitude and religion. In D. Carr (Ed.), *Perspectives on gratitude: An interdisciplinary approach* (pp. 154–168). Routledge/Taylor & Francis Group.

Tsang, J.-A., & Martin, S. R. (2021). Forgiveness. In C. R. Snyder, S. J. Lopez, L. M. Edwards, & S. C. Marques (Eds.), *The Oxford handbook of positive psychology., 3rd ed.* (2021-20328-040; pp. 551–570). Oxford University Press

Tsang, J.-A., Schulwitz, A., & Carlisle, R. D. (2012). An experimental test of the relationship between religion and gratitude. *Psychology of Religion and Spirituality*, *4*, 40–55.

Tsaousis, I., & Kazi, S. (2013). Factorial invariance and latent mean differences of scores on trait emotional intelligence across gender and age. *Personality and Individual Differences*, *54*(2), 169–173.

Tudge, J. R. H., Navarro, J. L., Payir, A., Merçon-Vargas, E. A., Cao, H., Zhou, N., Liang, Y., & Mendonça (2021). Using cultural-ecological theory to construct a mid-range theory for the development of gratitude as a virtue. *Journal of Family Theory & Review*, *14*, 151–174.

Tugade, M. M., Devlin, H. C., & Fredrickson, B. L. (2021). Positive emotions. In C. R. Snyder, S. J. Lopez, L. M. Edwards, & S. C. Marques (Eds.), *The Oxford handbook of positive psychology* (pp. 18–32). Oxford University Press

Tullet, A. M., Harmon-Jones, E., & Inzlicht, M. (2012). Right frontal cortical asymmetry predicts empathic reactions: Support for a link between withdrawal motivation and empathy. *Psychophysiology*, *49*, 1145–1153.

U.S. Census Bureau. (2020). *Profile of general population and housing*. https://data.census.gov/table?g=010XX00US&d=DEC+Demographic+Profile.

U.S. Census Bureau. (14 February, 2023). *The disproportionate impact of the COVID-19 pandemic on women in the workforce*. https://www.census.gov/data/academy/webinars/2023/impact-of-the-covid-19-pandemic-on-women-in-the-workforce.html

U.S. Department of Health and Human Services. (1999). *Mental health: A report of the surgeon general*. Author.

U.S. Department of Health and Human Services. (2001). *Mental health: Culture, race, ethnicity*. Supplement to *Mental health: Report of the surgeon general* (Inventory number SMA 01-3613). Author.

U.S. Department of Veterans Affairs. (2023). *How common is PTSD in adults*. https://www.pt

sd.va.gov/understand/common/common_adults.asplt

Uchida, Y., Norasakkunkit, V., & Kitayama, S. (2004). Cultural considerations of happiness: Theory and empirical evidence. *Journal of Happiness Studies, 5*, 223–239.

Ulrich, M., Keller, J., & Grön, G. (2016). Neural signatures of experimentally induced flow experiences identified in a typical fMRI block design with BOLD imaging. *Social Cognitive and Affective Neuroscience, 11*, 496–507.

Ungar, M., & Liebenberg, L. (2011). Assessing resilience across cultures using mixed methods: construction of the Child and Youth Resilience Measure. *Journal of Mixed Methods Research, 5*, 126–149.

Ungar, M., & Theron, L. (2020). Resilience and mental health: How multisystemic processes contribute to positive outcomes. *The Lancet Psychiatry, 7*(5), 441–448.

Unger, J. B., McAvay, G., Bruce, M. L., Berkman, L., & Seeman, T. (1999). Variation in the impact of social network characteristics on physical functioning in elderly persons: MacArthur Studies of Successful Aging. *Journals of Gerontology, 54*, 245–251.

Urry, H. L., Nitschke, J. B., Dolski, I., Jackson, D. C., Dalton, K. M., Mueller, C. J., Rosenkranz, M. A., Ryff, C., D., Burton, H. S., & Davidson, R. J. (2004). Making a life worth living: Neural correlates of well-being. *Psychological Science, 15*, 367–372.

Vaillant, G. E. (1977). *Adaptation to life*. Little, Brown.

Vaillant, G. E. (2002). *Aging well: Surprising guideposts to a happier life from the landmark Harvard Study of Adult Development*. Little, Brown.

Valdez, J. P. M., Datu, J. A. D., & Chu, S. K. W. (2022). Gratitude intervention optimizes effective learning outcomes in Filipino high school students: A mixed-methods study. *Computers & Education, 176*.

Valdez, J. P. M., Yang, W., & Datu, A. D. (2017). Validation of the Gratitude Questionnaire in Filipino secondary students. *The Spanish Journal of Psychology, 20*, E45.

Van Groningen, N., IsHak, W. W., Ganjian, Sl., Ong, M., & Slusser, W. (2020). Work, love, play, and joie de vivre. In, *The handbook of wellness medicine* (pp. 535–544). Cambridge University Press. Doi 10.1017/9781108650182.045

Van de Vyver, J., & Abrams, D. (2017). Is moral elevation an approach-oriented emotion? *The Journal of Positive Psychology, 12*, 178–185.

Van Tongeren, D. R., Burnette, J. L., Boyle, E. O., Worthington, E. L., Jr., & Forsyth, D. R. (2013). A meta-analysis of intergroup forgiveness. *The Journal of Positive Psychology, 9*, 81–95.

Vandello, J. A., & Cohen, D. (1999). Patterns of individualism and collectivism across the United States. *Journal of Personality and Social Psychology, 77*, 279–292.

Vannest, K. J., Ura, S. K., Lavadia, C., & Zolkoski, S. (2021). Self-report measures of resilience in children and youth. *Contemporary School Psychology, 25*(4), 406–415.

VanOyen Witvliet, C., Luna, L. R., VanderStoep, J. L., Gonzalez, T., Griffin, G. (2019). Granting forgiveness: State and trait evidence for genetic and gender indirect effects through empathy. *The Journal of Positive Psychology, 15*, 390–399.

Vargas, H. L. (2019). Enhancing therapist courage and clinical acuity for advancing clinical practice. *Journal of Family Psychotherapy, 30*, 141–152.

Vargas, J. H., & Kemmelmeier, M. (2013). Ethnicity and contemporary American culture: A meta-analytic investigation of horizontal–vertical individualism–collectivism. *Journal of Cross-Cultural Psychology, 44*, 195–222.

Vaskinn, A., Ventura, J., Andreassen, O. A., Melle, I., & Sundet, K. (2015). A social path to functioning in schizophrenia: From social self-efficacy through negative symptoms to social functional capacity. *Psychiatry Research, 228*, 803–807.

Vassar, M., & Bradley, G. (2010). A reliability generalization study of coefficient alpha for the Life Orientation Test. *Journal of Personality Assessment, 92*, 362–370.

Vassillière, C. T., Holahan, C. J., & Holahan, C. K. (2016). Race, perceived discrimination, and emotion-focused coping. *Journal of Community Psychology, 44*, 524–530.

Vela, J. C., Lu, M. T. P., Lenz, A. S., Savage, M. C., & Guardiola, R. (2016). Positive psychology and Mexican American college students' subjective well-being and depression. *Hispanic Journal of Behavioral Sciences, 38*, 324–340.

Versey, S. H., & Newton, N. J. (2013). Generativity and productive pursuits: Pathways to successful aging in late midlife African American and White women. *Journal of Adult Development, 20*, 185–196.

Vespa, J., Medina L., & Armstrong, A. (2020). Demographic turning points for the United States: Population projections for 2020 to 2060.U.S. Census Bureau.

Vessey, G. N. A. (1967). Volition. In P. Edwards (Ed.), *Encyclopedia of philosophy* (Vol. 8). Macmillan.

VIA Institute of Character. (2022). *VIA Inventory of Strengths (VIA-IS) Psychometrics*. https://coachfoundation.com/blog/via-inventory-of-strengths/#:~: text=The%20VIA%20Inventory%20of%20Strengths%20is%20a%20psychological, system%20allows%20you%20to%20measure%20each%20statement%E2%80%99s%20importance.

Vieten, C., Scammell, S., Pierce, A., Pilato, R., Ammondson, I., Pargament, K. I., & Lukoff, D. (2016). Competencies for psychologists in the domains of religion and spirituality. *Spirituality in Clinical Practice, 3*, 92.

Vignoles, V. L. (2009). The motive for distinctness: A universal but flexible human in need. In S. J. Lopez, & C. R. Snyder (Eds.), *Oxford handbook of positive psychology* (pp. 491–499). Oxford University Press.

Visser, M. R., & Roelofs, M. R. (2011). Heterogeneous preferences for altruism: Gender and personality, social status, giving and taking. *Experimental Economics, 14*, 490–506.

Voelkel, J. G., & Feinberg, M. (2018). Morally reframed arguments can affect support for political candidates. *Social Psychological and Personality Science, 9*(8), 917–924.

Voiskounsky, A. E. (2010). Internet addiction in the context of positive psychology. *Psychology in Russia: State of the Art, 35*, 541–549.

Volz, M., Voelkle, M. C., & Werheid, K. (2019). General self-efficacy as a driving factor of post-stroke depression: A longitudinal study. *Neuropsychological Rehabilitation, 29(9)*, 1426–1438.

Wade, N. G. (2010). Introduction to the special issue on forgiveness in therapy. *Journal of Mental Health Counseling, 32*, 1–4.

Wagenaar, A. C., Maybee, R. G., & Sullivan, K. P. (1988). Mandatory seat belt laws in eight states: A time-series evaluation. *Journal of Safety Research, 19*, 51–70.

Wagner, M. (2021). Affective polarization in multiparty systems. *Electoral Studies, 69*, 102199.

Walker, L. J., & Hennig, K. H. (2004). Differing conceptions of moral exemplarity: Just, brave, and caring. *Journal of Personality and Social Psychology, 86*, 629–647.

Walker, L. J., & Pitts, R. C. (1998). Naturalistic conceptions of moral maturity. *Developmental Psychology, 34*, 403–419.

Walker, T. (19 April, 2022). *Meet Kurt Russell, the 2022 national teacher of the year.* https://www.nea.org/nea-today/all-news-articles/meet-kurt-russell-2022-national-teacher-year

Wallach, M. A., & Wallach, L. (1983). *Psychology's sanction for selfishness: The error of egoism in theory and therapy.* Freeman.

Waller, M. A. (2001). Resilience in ecosystemic context: Evolution of the concept. *American Journal of Orthopsychiatry, 71*(3), 290–297.

Walsh, R. (2012). Wisdom: An integral view. *Journal of Integral Theory and Practice, 7*, 1–21.

Wampold, B. E. (2011). Psychotherapy is effective and here's why. *APA Monitor, 42*, 14.

Wampold, B. E. (2013). The good, the bad, and the ugly: A 50-year perspective on the outcome problem. *Psychotherapy, 50*, 16–24.

Wang, H., & Jiao, R. (2022). The relationship between career social support and career management competency: The mediating role of career decision-making self-efficacy. *Current Psychology: A Journal for Diverse Perspectives on Diverse Psychological Issues.* Advanced Online.

Wang, M., & Wong, M. C. S. (2013, February). Happiness and leisure across countries: Evidence from international survey data. *Journal of Happiness Studies, 15*(1), 85–118.

Wang, M., Lu, C-Q, & Lu, L. (2022). The positive potential of presenteeism: An exploration of how presenteeism leads to good performance evaluation. *Journal of Organizational Behavior.* 1–16.

Wang, S., Xu, X., Zhou, M., Chen, T., Yang, X, Chen, G., & Gong, Q. (2017). Hope and the brain: Trait hope mediates the protective role of medial orbitofrontal cortex spontaneous activity against anxiety. *NeuroImage*, *157*, 439–447.

Wang, S., Zhao, Y., Li, J., Lai, H., Qiu, C., Pan, N., & Gong, Q. (2020). Neurostructural correlates of hope: Dispositional hope mediates the impact of the SMA gray matter volume on subjective well-being in late adolescence. *Social Cognitive and Affective Neuroscience*, *15(4)*, 395–404.

Wang, Y., Davidson, M. M., Yakushko, O. F., Savoy, H. B., Tan, J. A., & Bleier, J. K. (2003). The scale of ethnocultural empathy: Development, validation, and reliability. *Journal of Counseling Psychology*, *50*, 221–234.

Wang, Y., Zhang, Y., Chen, Y., Jing, F., Wang, Z., Hao, Y., Lizhuang, Y., Ying, L., Zhou, Y., & Zhang, X. (2016). Modulatory effect of romantic love on value estimation and its neural mechanism. *NeuroReport*, *27*, 323–328.

Ward, S., Womich, J., Titova, L., & King, L. (2023). Meaning in life and coping with everyday stressors. *Personality and Social Psychology Bulletin*, *49*, 460–476.

Warr, P. (1999). Well-being and the workplace. In D. Kahneman, E. Diener, & N. Schwartz (Eds.), *Well-being: The foundations of hedonic psychology* (pp. 393–412). Russell Sage.

Waterman, A. S. (1993). Two conceptions of happiness: Contrasts of personal expressiveness (eudaemonia) and hedonic enjoyment. *Journal of Personality and Social Psychology*, *64*, 678–691.

Waters, E., Merrick, S., Treboux, D., Crowell, J., & Albersheim, L. (2000). Attachment security in infancy and early adulthood: A twenty-year longitudinal study. *Child Development*, *71*(3), 684–689.

Watkins, D. A., Hui, E. K. P., Luo, W., Regmi, M., Worthington, E. L., Jr., Hook, J. N., & Davis, D. E. (2011). Forgiveness and interpersonal relationships: A Nepalese investigation. *The Journal of Social Psychology*, *151*, 150–161.

Watkins, P. C., Cruz, L., Holben, H., & Kolts, R. L. (2008). Taking care of business? Grateful processing of unpleasant memories. *Journal of Positive Psychology*, *3*, 87–99.

Watkins, P. C., Grimm, D. L., & Hailu, L. (1998, June). *Counting your blessings: Grateful individuals recall more positive memories*. Paper presented at the American Psychological Society Convention, Denver, CO.

Watson, D. (1988). The vicissitudes of mood measurement: Effects of varying descriptors, time frames, and response formats on measures of positive and negative affect. *Journal of Personality and Social Psychology*, *55*, 128–141.

Watson, D. (2000). *Mood and temperament*. Guilford.

Watson, D. (2002). Positive affectivity: The disposition to experience pleasurable emotional states. In C. R. Snyder & S. J. Lopez (Eds.), *The handbook of positive psychology* (pp. 106–119). Oxford University Press.

Watson, D., & Clark, L. A. (1994). *The PANAS-X: Manual for the Positive and Negative Affect Schedule–Expanded Form*. Unpublished manuscript, University of Iowa, Iowa City.

Watson, M., & Ecken, L. (200314says2019). *Learning to trust: Transforming difficult elementary classrooms through developmental discipline*. Jossey-Bass.

Watson, D., & Naragon-Gainey, K. (2014). Personality, emotions, and the emotional disorders. *Clinical Psychological Science*, *2*, 422–442.

Watson, M., & Ecken, L. (2019). *Learning to trust: Attachment theory and classroom management*. Oxford University Press.

Watson-Singleton, N. N., Hill, L. K., & Case, A. D. (2019). Past discrimination, race-related vigilance, and depressive symptoms: The moderating role of mindfulness. *Mindfulness*, *10*(9), 1768–1778.

Webb, J. R., Bumgarner, D. J., Conway-Williams, E., Dangel, T., & Hall, B. B. (2017). A consensus definition of self-forgiveness: Implications for assessment and treatment. *Spirituality in Clinical Practice*, *4(3)*, 216–227.

Webber, K. C., & Smokowski, P. R. (2018). Assessment of adolescent optimism: Measurement invariance across gender and race/ethnicity. *Journal of Adolescence*, *68*, 78–86.

Webster, G. D., Howell, J. L., Losee, J. E., Mahar, E. A., & Wongsomboon. V. (2021). Culture, COVID-19, and collectivism: A paradox of American exceptionalism? *Personality and Individual Differences, 178*, https://search.bvsalud.org/global-literature-on-novel-coronavirus-2019-ncov/resource/en/covidwho-1144889

Webster, J. D. (2010). Wisdom and positive psychological values in young adulthood. *Journal of Adult Development, 17*, 70–80.

Wei, M., Liao, K. Y.-H., Ku, T.-Y., & Shaffer, P. A. (2011). Attachment, self-compassion, empathy, and subjective well-being among college students and community adults. *Journal of Personality, 79*(1), 191–221.

Weinberg, M., Besser, A., Zeigler-Hill, V., & Neria, Y. (2016). Bidirectional associations between hope, optimism and social support, and trauma-related symptoms among survivors of terrorism and their spouses. *Journal of Research in Personality, 62*, 29–38.

Weir, K., & Duveen, G. (1981). Further development and validation of the Prosocial Behavior Questionnaire for use by teachers. *Journal of Child Psychology and Psychiatry, 22*, 357–374.

Weiss, A., Burgmer, P., & Lange, J. (2020). Surprise me! On the impact of unexpected benefits on other-praising gratitude expressions. *Cognition and Emotion, 34*, 1608–1620.

Weng, H. Y., Fox, A. S., Hessenthaler, H. C., Stodola, D. E., & Davidson, R. J. (2015). The role of compassion in altruistic helping and punishment behavior. *PLOS ONE 10*, 1–20.

Wenzel, M., & Okimoto, T. G. (2014). On the relationship between justice and forgiveness: Are all forms of justice made equal? *British Journal of Social Psychology, 53*, 463–483.

Werner, E. E., & Smith, R. S. (1982). *Vulnerable but invincible: A study of resilient children*. McGraw-Hill.

Werner, E. E., & Smith, R. S. (1992). *Overcoming the odds: High-risk children from birth to adulthood*. Cornell University Press.

Westburg, N. G. (2001). Hope in older women: The importance of past and current relationships. *Journal of Social and Clinical Psychology, 20*, 354–365.

Western Reform Taoism. (2003). *Our beliefs*. https://wrt.org

Weststrate, N. M., & Glück, J. (2017). Hard-earned wisdom: Exploratory processing of difficult life experience is positively associated with wisdom. *Developmental Psychology, 53*, 800–814.

Weststrate, N. M., Ferrari, M., & Ardelt, M. (2016). The many faces of wisdom: An investigation of cultural-historical wisdom exemplars reveals practical, philosophical, and benevolent prototypes. *Personality and Social Bulletin, 42*, 662–676.

Whalen, S. (1999). Challenging play and the cultivation of talent: Lessons from the Key School's flow activities room. In N. Colangelo & S. Assouline (Eds.), *Talent development III* (pp. 409–411). Gifted Psychology Press.

Whaley, A. L., & Davis, K. E. (2007). Cultural competence and evidence-based practice in mental health services: A complementary perspective. *American Psychologist, 62*, 563–574.

Whelan, R., & Garavan, H. (2013, June). When optimism hurts: Inflated predictions in psychiatric neuroimaging. *Biological Psychiatry, 75*(9), 746–748.

White, R. W. (1959). Motivation reconsidered: The concept of competence. *Psychological Review, 66*, 297–333.

Williams, D. R., Lawrence, J. A., & Davis, B. A. (2019). Racism and health: Evidence and needed research. *Annual Review of Public Health, 40*(1), 105–125.

Williams, J. L., & Deutsch, N. L. (2016). Beyond between-group differences: Considering race, ethnicity, and culture in research on positive youth development programs. *Applied Developmental Science, 20*, 203–213.

Williams, J. M. G., Russell, I., & Russell, D. (2008). Mindfulness-based cognitive therapy: Further issues in current evidence and future research. *Journal of Consulting and Clinical Psychology, 76*, 524–529.

Williams, O. F., & Houck, J. W. (1982). *The Judeo-Christian vision and the modern corporation*. University of Notre Dame Press.

Williams, V., & Wilson, D. (2016). White racial framing and its impact on African American male mental health. In W. Ross (Ed.), *Counseling African American males: Effective therapeutic interventions and approaches* (pp. 253–274). IAP Information Age.

Williamson, G. M., & Christie, J. (2009). Aging well in the 21st century: Challenges and opportunities. In S. J. Lopez & C. R. Snyder (Eds.), *Oxford handbook of positive psychology* (pp. 165–169). Oxford University Press.

Wills, T. A., & DePaulo, B. M. (1991). Interpersonal analyses of the help-seeking process. In C. R. Snyder & D. R. Forsyth (Eds.), *Handbook of social and clinical psychology: The health perspective* (pp. 350–375). Pergamon.

Wilson, T. K., & Gentzler, A. L. (2021). Emotion regulation and coping with racial stressors among African Americans across the lifespan. *Developmental Review, 61*.

Windsor, T. D., Anstey, K. J., & Rodgers, B. (2008). Volunteering and psychological well-being among young-old adults: How much is too much? *The Gerontologist, 48*, 59–70.

Winerman, L. (2005). Mirror neurons: The mind's mirror. *Monitor, 36*, 49–50.

Wink, P., & Staudinger, U. M. (2016). Wisdom and psychosocial functioning in later life. *Journal of Personality, 84*, 306–318.

Winston, A. S. (2020). Why mainstream research will not end scientific racism in psychology. *Theory & Psychology, 30*, 425–430.

Winter, E.L., Maykel, C., Bray, M., Levine-Schmitt, M., & Graves, M. (2022). Physical health as a foundation for well-being: Exploring the RICH theory of happiness. In S. Deb, & B. A. Gerrard (Eds.), *Handbook of health and well-being: Challenges, strategies and future trends* (pp. 3–33). Springer Nature Singapore.

Wohl, M. J. A., & Thompson, A. (2011). A dark side to self-forgiveness: Forgiving the self and its association with chronic unhealthy behaviour. *British Journal of Social Psychology, 50*, 354–364.

Wong, Y. J., & Liu, T. (2018). Dialecticism and mental health. In J. Spencer-Rodgers, & K. Peng (Eds.), *The psychological and cultural foundations of east Asian cognition: Contradiction, change, and holism*. Oxford University Press.

Wood, A. M., Brown, G. D. A., & Maltby, J. (2011). Thanks, but I'm used to better: A relative rank model of gratitude. *Emotion, 11*, 175–180.

Wood, J., De Santis, C., Desmarais, S., & Milhausen, R. (2021). Motivations for engaging in consensually non-monogamous relationships. *Archives of Sexual Behavior, 50*(4), 1253–1272.

Wood, M. D., Britt, T. W., Wright, K. M., Thomas, J. L., & Bliese, P. D. (2012). Benefit finding at war: A matter of time. *Journal of Traumatic Stress, 25*, 307–314.

Woodard, C. (2004). *Hardiness and the concept of courage*. Unpublished manuscript, The Groden Center, Providence, RI.

Woodard, C. R., & Pury, C. L. S. (2007). The construct of courage: Categorization and measurement. *Consulting Psychology Journal: Practice and Research 59*, 135–147.

Woodbridge, L. M., Um, B., & Duys, D. K. (2021). Women's experiences navigating paid work caregiving during the COVID-19 pandemic. *Career Development Quarterly, 69*, 284–298.

Woolfolk, R. L. (2002). The power of negative thinking: Truth, melancholia, and the tragic sense of life. *Journal of Theoretical & Philosophical Psychology, 22*, 19–27.

World Health Organization. (1986). *Health promotion*. https://www.who.int/teams/health-promotion/enhanced-wellbeing/first-global-conference

World Health Organization. (2019). *International statistical classification of diseases and related health problems (11th ed.)*. https://www.who.int/standards/classifications/classification-of-diseases

World Health Organization. (2023). *Health equity*. https://www.who.int/health-topics/health-equity#tab=tab_1

Worthington, E. L., Jr. (1998). An empathy-humility-commitment model of forgiveness applied within family dyads. *Journal of Family Therapy, 20*, 59–71.

Worthington, E. L., Jr. (Ed.). (2005). *Handbook of forgiveness*. Routledge.

Worthington, E. L., Jr., & Drinkard, D. T. (2000). Promoting reconciliation through psycho-educational and therapeutic interventions. *Journal of Marital and Family Therapy, 26*, 93–101.

Worthington, E. L., Jr., Hook, J. N., Utsey, S. O., Williams, J. K., & Neil, R. L. (2007,October). *Decisional and emotional forgiveness*. Paper presented at the International Positive

Psychology Summit. Washington, DC.

Wrzesniewski, A., McCauley, C. R., Rozin, P., & Schwartz, B. (1997). Jobs, careers, and callings: People's relations to their work. *Journal of Research in Personality, 31*, 21–33.

Wu, C. (2009). Factor analysis of the general self-efficacy scale and its relationship with individualism/collectivism among twenty-five countries: Application of multilevel confirmatory factor analysis. *Personality and Individual Differences. 46*, 699–703.

Wu, K., & Chang, E. C. (2019). Feeling good—and feeling bad—affect social problem solving: A test of the broaden-and-build model in Asian Americans. *Asian American Journal of Psychology, 10*, 13–121.

Xi, J., Lee, M., LeSuer, W., Barr, P., Newton, K., & Poloma, M. (2016). Altruism and existential well-being. *Applied Research Quality Life, 12*, 67–88.

Xie, W., & Zhang, W. (2016). The influence of emotion on face processing. *Cognitive and Emotion, 30*, 245–257.

Xing, C., & Sun, J.-M. (2013). The role of psychological resilience and positive affect in risky decision-making. *International Journal of Psychology, 48*, 935–943.

Xue, M., & Silk, J. B. (2012). The role of tracking and tolerance in relationship among friends. *Evolution and Human Behavior, 33*, 17–25.

Yadav, B. S., & Jhamb, S. (2015). Hope in palliative care: Cultural implications. *Journal of Palliative Care, 31*, 189–192.

Yamaguchi, M., Masuchi, A., Nakanishi, D., Suga, S., Konishi, N., Yu, Y.-Y., & Ohtsubo, Y. (2016). Experiential purchases and prosocial spending promote happiness by enhancing social relationships. *Journal of Positive Psychology, 11*, 480–488.

Yang, M.-J., & Chen, M.-H. (2011). Effect of altruism on the regulation of negative emotion. *Bulletin of Educational Psychology, 42*, 701–718.

Yang, Q., Ling, Y., Huebner, E. S., Zeng, Y., & Liu, C. (2021). Assessing the measurement invariance of the Children's Hope Scale in Chinese and American adolescents. *Journal of Personality Assessment, 103*(2), 195–203.

Yang, S. (2001). Conceptions of wisdom among Taiwanese Chinese. *Journal of Cross-Cultural Psychology, 32*, 662–680.

Yang, S. (2008). Real-life contextual manifestations of wisdom. *International Journal of Aging and Human Development, 67*, 273–303.

Yang, X. (2016). Self-compassion, relationship harmony, versus self-enhancement: Different ways of relating to well-being in Hong Kong Chinese. *Personality and Individual Differences, 89*, 24–27.

Yehene, E., Neeman, Y., Zaksh, Y., & Elyashiv, M. (2022). "Be realistic, hope for a miracle": On the coexistence of grief and optimism among caregivers of patients with prolonged disorders of consciousness. *Illness, Crisis, & Loss, 30*(2), 175–191.

Yeung, D. Y., Ho, S. M., & Mak, C. W. (2015). Brief report: Attention to positive information mediates the relationship between hope and psychosocial well-being of adolescents. *Journal of Adolescence, 42*, 98–102.

York, A. (22 July, 2023). *Gen Zers want to be in the office but their bosses are at home*. https://www.businessinsider.com/gen-z-wants-to-go-in-office-bosses-dont-2023-7#:~:text=Among%20Gen%20Z%2C%2057%25%20want,sentiment%20checks%20out%20for%20Farber.

Yosso, T. J. (2005). Whose culture has capital? A critical race theory discussion of community cultural wealth. *Race Ethnicity and Education, 8*, 69–91.

Young Kaelber, K. A., & Schwartz, R. C. (2014, January). Empathy and emotional intelligence among eastern and western counsellor trainees: A preliminary study. *International Journal for the Advancement of Counselling, 36*, 274–286.

Yu, E. A., & Chang, E. C. (2016). Optimism/pessimism and future orientation as predictors of suicidal ideation: Are there ethnic differences? *Cultural Diversity and Ethnic Minority Psychology, 22*, 572.

Yue, X-L, & Gao, Q-X. (2018). Contributions of natural systems and human activity to greenhouse gas emissions. *Advances in Climate Change Research, 9*, 243–252.

Yu, H., Cai, Q., Shen, B., Gao, X., & Zhou, X. (2017). Neural substrates and social consequences of interpersonal gratitude: Intention matters. *Emotion, 4*, 589–601.

Yu, H., Gao, X., Zhou, Y., & Zhou, X. (2018). Decomposing

gratitude: Representation and integration of cognitive antecedents of gratitude in the brain. *Journal of Neuroscience*, *23*, 4886–4898.

Yu, Y., Zhou, M.-J., Guo, X.-C., He, Q., & Zhang, J.-X. (2016). The effect of work-family balance on work engagement and job satisfaction: The moderating of personality. *Chinese Journal of Clinical Psychology*, *24*, 504–508.

Yue, X. D., Leung, C.-L., & Hiranandani, N. A. (2016). Adult playfulness, humor styles, and subjective happiness. *Psychological Reports*, *119*, 630–640.

Yule, K., Houston, J., & Grych, J. (2019). Resilience in children exposed to violence: A meta-analysis of protective factors across ecological contexts. *Clinical Child and Family Psychology Review*, *22*(3), 406–431.

Zaccoletti, S., Camacho, A., Correia, N., Aguiar, C., Mason, L., Alves, R. A., & Daniel, J. R. (2020). Parents' perceptions of student academic motivation during the COVID-19 lockdown: A cross-country comparison. *Frontiers in Psychology*, *11*, 1–13.

Zahn-Wexler, C., Robinson, J., & Emde, R. N. (1992). The development of empathy in twins. *Developmental Psychology*, *28*, 1038–1047.

Zamarro, G., Camp, A., Fuchsman, D., & McGee, J. B. (2022). Understanding how COVID-19 has changed teachers' chances of remaining in the classroom. *Sinquefield Center for Applied Economic Research Working Paper, No. 22-01*. https://ssrn.com/abstract=4047354

Zangri, R. M., Andreu, C. I., Nieto, I., González-Garzón, A. M., & Vázquez, C. (2022). Efficacy of mindfulness to regulate induced emotions in the laboratory: A systematic review and meta-analysis of self-report and biobehavioral measures. *Neuroscience & Biobehavioral Reviews*, *143*, 104957.

Zapolski, T. C. B., Faidley, M. T., & Beutlich, M. R. (2019). The experience of racism on behavioral health outcomes: The moderating impact of mindfulness. *Mindfulness*, *10*(1), 168–178.

Zeidner, M., & Hammer, A. L. (1992). Coping with missile attack: Resources, strategies, and outcomes. *Journal of Personality*, *60*, 184–199.

Zelazo, P., & Lyons, K. E. (2012). The potential benefits of mindfulness training in early childhood: A developmental social cognitive neuroscience perspective. *Child Development Perspectives*, *6*, 154–160.

Zheng, X., van Dijke, M., Leunissen, J. M., Giurge, L. M., & De Cremer, D. (2016). When saying sorry may not help: Transgender power moderates the effect of an apology on forgiveness in the workplace. *Human Relations*, *69*, 1387–1418.

Zhou, L., Lin, Y., Li, W., Du, J., & Xu, W. (2022). Mindfulness, attachment, and relationship satisfaction among heterosexual college student couples: An actor-partner interdependence model analysis. *Current Psychology: A Journal for Diverse Perspectives on Diverse Psychological Issues*, *41*(9), 5771–5780.

Zhu, W., Wang, C. D. C., Jin, L., & Lu, T. (2021). Adult attachment, sacrifice, and emotional wellbeing of couples: A cross-cultural comparison between the US and China. *Journal of Social and Personal Relationships*, *38*(2), 482–503.

Zimbardo, P. G. (2007). *The Lucifer effect: Understanding how good people turn evil*. Random House.

Zullig, K. J., Teoli, D. A., & Valois, R. F. (2011). Evaluating a brief measure of social self-efficacy among U.S. adolescents. *Psychological Reports*, *109*, 907–920.

GLOSSARY

Adaptive parental behaviors: Parents' appropriate responsiveness to a child's behavioral cues (e.g., smiling).

Affect: A person's instinctive response to a stimulus; characterized by a sense of arousal. Affect is considered the most basic element of feeling and often involves evaluation of a stimulus as good or bad.

Agape: The bestowal of love by the divine.

Agency thinking: The requisite motivations to use routes to desired goals. (Compare with *pathways thinking.*)

Altruism: Actions or behaviors that are intended to benefit another person.

Anishinaabe Teachings: Teachings that come from the Ojibwe tradition in American Indian culture emphasizing seven values (each represented by an animal) that should be followed.

Aspirational capital: refers to the "hopes and dreams" that students of color have as they enter higher education despite historical and current barriers that exist for members of their communities; part of Yosso's (2005) Cultural Wealth Model.

Assessment: An assessment is any tool, device, or other means by which researchers assess or gather data about study participants. Note, the following terms are all interchangeable in reference to an assessment: measure, test, instrument, and tool. In positive psychology, most assessments are self-report, questionnaire-based instruments.

Athenian tradition: Western philosophical tradition focused on the writings and teachings of Plato and Aristotle.

Attachment Anxiety (Brennan et al., 1998): A dimension of adult attachment insecurity marked by a belief that you are not worthy of love and that your partner is likely to abandon you.

Attachment Avoidance (Brennan et al., 1998): A dimension of adult attachment insecurity involving fear of dependence and interpersonal intimacy, an excessive need for self-reliance, and reluctance to self-disclose.

Attachment system: The sum of emotional and physical proximity-seeking behaviors toward the caregiver, developed by the child as a result of adaptive and maladaptive parent behaviors. Regulates the pattern of attachment characteristic of the child.

Authenticity: A dimension of courage in the Values in Action classification system. Authenticity involves acknowledging and representing one's true self, values, beliefs, and behaviors to oneself and others.

Autotelic personality: A cluster of traits exhibited by a person who enjoys life and who "generally does things for [their] own sake, rather than in order to achieve some later external goal" (Csikszentmihalyi, 1997, p. 117). From the Greek words *autos,* meaning "self," and *telos,* meaning "end."

Balance theory of wisdom: A theory developed by Sternberg (1998a) that specifies the processes used to balance personal interests with environmental context to achieve a common good. The processes involve using tacit knowledge and personal values to form a judgment of or resolution for competing interests.

Berlin wisdom paradigm: A theory developed by Baltes et al. suggesting that wisdom requires knowledge and insight into the self and others within a cultural context and is "the ways and means of planning, managing, and understanding a good life" (Baltes & Staudinger, 2000, p. 124). The paradigm addresses life-span contextualism, relativism of values, and managing uncertainty.

Black joy: a concept focusing on the Black community's enduring use of joy as a form of resistance in the face of suffering since times of slavery.

Broaden-and-build model of positive emotions: Model developed by Fredrickson (2000) that suggests positive emotions expand what an individual feels like doing at any given time. Fredrickson calls this expansion *broadening of an individual's momentary thought–action repertoire.* Positive emotions also allow people to build resources through the increasing of creative problem solving and recognition of personal resources.

Buddhism: A philosophical and religious system based on the teachings of Buddha: Life is dominated by suffering caused by desire, suffering ends when we end desire, and enlightenment obtained through right conduct, wisdom, and meditation releases one from desire, suffering, and rebirth.

Calling: A strong motivation in which a person repeatedly takes a course of action that is intrinsically satisfying. For example, a person who experiences a calling to teach teaches because the job is personally fulfilling, not just because of the paycheck.

Care-based altruism: Altruism thought to be motivated because of feelings of empathy (or care) for the recipient of the help offered.

Career consolidation: A life task that requires the development of a social identity and engagement in a career characterized by contentment, compensation, competence, and commitment.

Career decision-making self-efficacy (CDMSE): Personal confidence in one's capacity to handle career development and work-related activities.

Civil courage: Described by Greitemeyer et al. (2007) as "brave behavior accompanied by anger and indignation that intends to enforce societal and ethical norms without considering one's own social costs" (p. 115).

Collective efficacy: The degree to which a group of people believe they can work together to accomplish shared goals.

Collectivism: A cultural value that prizes the concepts of sharing, cooperation, interdependence, and duty to the group. A perspective in which the needs of the group are placed above the needs of the individual.

Commitment: The amount of psychological attachment a worker feels toward the organization for which they work.

Companionate love: A form of romantic love characterized by the soothing and steady warmth that sustains a relationship.

Compassion: An aspect of humanity that involves looking outside oneself and thinking about others as we care for and identify with them. In positive psychology, compassion requires (1) that the difficulty of the recipient be serious, (2) that the recipient's difficulties are not self-inflicted, and (3) that we, as observers, are able to identify with the recipient's suffering.

Complete state model: Model developed by Keyes and Lopez (2002) in which mental health is defined as high levels of emotional, psychological, and social well-being and the absence of mental illness symptoms; the model acknowledges that well-being and mental illness symptomatology change over time.

Conceptual equivalence: The extent to which a particular construct or concept has the same definition in two different cultures.

Confirmatory Factor Analysis: A multivariate statistical technique using structural equation modeling in which the researcher specifies which items load onto which factors and determines how well that model matches the actual data. In scale development, CFA helps assure researchers that the factor structure identified through an exploratory factor analysis in one sample can replicate and represents the true structure of an instrument in another sample.

Confucianism: A philosophical and religious system developed from the teachings of Confucius. Confucianism values love for humanity, duty, etiquette, and truthfulness. Devotion to family, including ancestors, is also emphasized.

Construct validity: The extent to which a scale measures the underlying attributes it intends to measure. Construct validity can be achieved by comparing your measure to other measures that assess a similar construct.

Consummate love: The most durable type of love, manifested when all three components (passion, intimacy, commitment) are present at high levels and in balance across both partners.

Cool Intelligence: According to Mayer et al. (2016), "Cool intelligences are those that deal with relatively impersonal knowledge such as verbal-propositional intelligence, math abilities, and visual-spatial intelligence" (p. 292).

Criterion validity: The extent to which scores on a scale can predict actual behavior or performance on another, related measure.

Culturally deficient perspective: A view that identifies a host of environmental, nutritional, linguistic, and interpersonal factors (namely, those factors that differ most from European American values) that supposedly explain the physical and psychological growth of members of selected groups.

Culturally pluralistic: Explanations that recognize distinct cultural entities and adopt some values of the majority group.

Culturally relativistic: Explanations that interpret behaviors within the context of cultures.

Culture: A common heritage or set of beliefs, norms, and values.

Developmental discipline: An attempt, based on attachment theory, at socialization that involves building caring and trusting relationships with students who have insecure attachments with their primary caregivers.

Dispositional optimism: The tendency of some to expect good things about the future in a general sense.

Egotism: The motive to pursue some sort of personal gain or benefit through targeted behavior.

Emotion: A feeling state resulting from the appraisal of an external object as salient to our own well-being. An emotion has a specific, "sharpened" quality, as it always has an object.

Emotional approach: Active movement toward, rather than away from, a stressful or emotional encounter.

Emotional avoidance: Active movement away from, rather than toward, a stressful or emotional encounter.

Emotional expression: Free and intentional display of feeling.

Emotional intelligence: According to Salovey and Mayer's four-branch ability model, the skills (1) to perceive and express feelings; (2) to use emotions and emotional understanding to facilitate thinking; (3) to understand complex emotions, relationships among emotions, and relationships between emotions and behavioral consequences; and (4) to manage emotions.

Emotional processing: The attempt to understand one's emotions.

Emotional storytelling: Written disclosure of emotional upheaval.

Empathy: An emotional response to the perceived plight of another person. Empathy may entail the ability to experience emotions similar to the other person's or a sense of tenderheartedness toward that person.

Empathy–altruism hypothesis: The view, borne out by Batson's (1991) findings, that empathy for another person leads to a greater likelihood of helping that person.

Empirically based: Developed using available research knowledge.

Engagement: An employee's involvement with their work. Engagement often depends on employees knowing what is expected of them, having what they need to do their work, having a chance to improve and develop, and having opportunities to develop relationships with coworkers.

Enlightenment: A human's capacity to transcend desire and suffering and to see things clearly for what they are.

Enthusiasm/zest: A dimension of courage in the Values in Action classification system. It involves thriving, or having motivation, in challenging situations or tasks.

Eros: Romantic love, including the search for and possession of the beautiful.

Etiology: The cause, origin, or a reason for something.

Eudaemonic primary enhancements: Enhancements that increase well-being through the setting and reaching of goals. These enhancements are the desirable result of the goal-pursuit process, which results in effective functioning and happiness.

Eudaimonia: Human flourishing, or happiness associated with living a life of virtue.

Eugenics: The study of methods of reducing "genetic inferiority" by selective breeding, especially as applied to human reproduction.

Experience sampling method: A research method used to study flow experiences and a variety of phenomena in psychology. Participants are signaled via watches, phones, or handheld computers and asked to answer questions about their experiences at various moments during the day.

Explicit theories: Explicit theories examine the externally visible aspects of a construct. For example, in the study of wisdom, explicit theories examine behaviors thought to demonstrate wisdom, such as problem-solving ability. These theories focus on the observable characteristics of a construct.

Exploratory Factor Analysis: A multivariate statistical technique used to reveal the underlying structure of a set of variables. In scale development, EFA is used to identify which latent factors may explain variation in groups of items. This determines how the instrument is scored by identifying which subset of items can be summed or averaged together to create a total or subscale score of a specific construct.

Familial capital: refers to the strength students of color in higher educational settings might obtain from being a part of rich family connections and support from extended as well as immediate families; part of Yosso's (2005) Cultural Wealth Model.

Flourishing relationships: Good relationships that continue to get better due to the concerted effort of both partners.

Flow: According to Csikszentmihalyi (1990), the pleasurable experience resulting from engagement in an interesting activity that properly matches or challenges a person's skills and abilities.

Forgiveness (as defined by Enright and colleagues): The willingness to give up resentment, negative judgment, and indifference toward the transgressor and to give undeserved compassion, generosity, and benevolence to him or her. Enright and colleagues also limit their definition of forgiveness to people and do not include situations.

Forgiveness (as defined by McCullough and colleagues): An increase in prosocial motivation such that there is less desire to avoid or seek revenge against the transgressor and an increased desire to act positively toward the transgressing person. This theory of forgiveness is applicable only when another person is the target of the transgression.

Forgiveness (as defined by Tangney and colleagues): A process involving "(1) [C]ognitive-affective transformation following a transgression in which (2) the victim makes a realistic assessment of the harm done and acknowledges the perpetrator's responsibility, but (3) freely chooses to "cancel the debt," giving up the need for revenge or deserved punishments and any quest for restitution. This "canceling of the debt" also involves (4) a "cancellation of negative emotions" directly related to the transgression. In particular, in forgiving, the victim overcomes his or her feelings of resentment and anger for the act. In short, by forgiving, the harmed individual (5) essentially removes himself or herself from the victim role" (Tangney et al., 1999, p. 2).

Forgiveness (as defined by Thompson and colleagues): A freeing from a negative attachment to the source of the transgression. This definition of forgiveness allows the target of forgiveness to be oneself, another person, or a situation.

Future orientations: Perspectives in which one emphasizes future events and the consequences of one's actions. Future-oriented people focus on planning for things to come.

Gainful employment: Work that contributes to a healthy life by providing variety, a safe working environment, sufficient income, a sense of purpose in work done, happiness and satisfaction, engagement and involvement, a sense of performing well and meeting goals, and companionship and loyalty to coworkers, bosses, and companies.

Generativity: A life task that requires one to "give the self away" and expand one's social circle. This may include mentoring the next generation of adults.

Genetic/personality predisposition theories: Theories of happiness suggesting that happiness may be a more stable personality trait or a characteristic that is genetically based.

Genetically deficient perspective: A view of human diversity that suggests that biological difference explains perceived gaps in intellectual capabilities among racial groups. Proponents of this perspective believe that those of inferior intelligence cannot benefit from growth opportunities and do not contribute to the advancement of society.

Gratitude: Being thankful for and appreciating the actions of another. Gratitude emerges upon recognizing that one has received a positive outcome from another person who behaved in a manner that was costly to him or her, valuable to the recipient, and intentionally rendered.

Harmony: A state of consensus or balance. Eastern traditions view harmony as essential to happiness.

Hedonic primary enhancements: Enhancements that increase well-being by maximizing pleasure. This often involves the satisfaction of appetites.

Hinduism: A diverse body of religion, philosophy, and cultural practice native to and predominant in India. Hinduism is characterized by a belief in the interconnectedness of all things and emphasizes personal improvement with the goal of transcending the cycle of reincarnation.

Hope: As defined by Snyder, goal-directed thinking in which a person has the perceived capacity to find routes to desired goals (pathway thinking) and the requisite motivations to use those routes (agency thinking). Snyder believes that hope is not genetically based but an entirely learned and deliberate way of thinking. (See Chapter 8.)

Hope: Goal-directed thinking in which the person uses *pathways thinking* (the perceived capacity to find routes to desired goals) and *agency thinking* (the requisite motivations to use those routes).

Hot Intelligence: According to Mayer et al. (2016), hot intelligence involves reasoning with information of significance to an individual . . . People use these hot intelligences to manage what matters most to them: their senses of social acceptance, identity coherence, and emotional well-being (p. 292).

Identity: A life task that requires one to develop one's own views, values, and interests instead of simply reflecting the beliefs of one's parents or others.

Implicit theories: Theories that examine the nature or essence of a construct, such as courage, that cannot be directly seen or revealed. Implicit theories or "folk theories" seek to explain through describing characteristics, qualities, and/or dimensions of the desired construct.

Individualism: A cultural value that emphasizes individual achievement, competition, personal freedom, and autonomy. A perspective in which the needs of the individual are placed above the needs of the group.

Industry/perseverance: A dimension of courage in the Values in Action classification system. It involves undertaking tasks or having initiative and determination to start and complete challenges.

Insecure-avoidant attachment: In the Strange Situation assessment, an attachment pattern characterized by a tension between the caregiver and child, resulting in the child's avoidance of the caregiver when reintroduced.

Insecure-resistant/ambivalent attachment: In the Strange Situation assessment, an attachment pattern characterized by a tension between the caregiver and child, resulting in the child's passive or active demonstration of hostility toward the caregiver while simultaneously wanting to be held and comforted.

Instrumental support: Support that involves giving assistance or help when needed.

Integrity: A life task that requires one to cultivate contentment with life and a sense of peace. Often accompanied by increased spirituality.

Internal Consistency: The most common measure of reliability for instruments with items that are summed or average to create total scores or subscale scores of a particular construct. An instrument demonstrates good internal consistency when scores from one item correlate highly with items on the same instrument with similar content. The most common internal consistency coefficient is Cronbach's alpha (an α greater than .70 are generally desirable, but most well-validated scales should have an α of .80 or greater for each total score or subscale score).

Intimacy: A life task that requires one to develop an interdependent, committed, and close relationship with another person.

Islam: A philosophical and religious tradition based on the teachings of Muhammad that emphasizes duty to one's fellow man. Followers believe in Allah as the creator and benefactor in all things.

Judeo-Christian tradition: Western religious tradition emphasizing Christianity and Judaism.

Keeper of meaning: A life task that engenders perspective on the workings of the world and of people and that is characterized by a willingness to share this wisdom with others. The keeper of meaning is seen as linking the present and the past by protecting traditions and rituals and passing them on to the next generation.

Kin-based altruism: Similar to care-based altruism in that a connection exists between helper and helpee, but this type of altruism is relegated only to altruism directed toward family.

Learned optimism: Characteristic use of a flexible explanatory style in which one has learned to make external (outside oneself), variable (not consistent), and specific (limited to a specific situation) attributions for one's failures. In contrast, pessimists have learned to view failures as due to internal (characteristics of the self), stable (consistent), and global (not limited to a specific situation) attributions.

Life-span contextualism: A component of the Berlin wisdom paradigm that requires understanding a problem in terms of its context. These contexts can be aspects of life, such as love, work, and play, as well as cultural and temporal contexts (time and place in society).

Linguistic capital: refers to the strengths in the type of communication styles common to communities of color and to the potential for bilingual and multilingual capabilities that may exist more often in students of color; part of Yosso's (2005) Cultural Wealth Model.

Linguistic equivalence: The extent to which a measure has been appropriately translated from its original language into another; items on the measure must have the same linguistic meaning in both languages, meaning that various idioms, vocabulary, and so on must be examined carefully.

Maladaptive parental behaviors: Parents' chaotic or unplanned attempts to meet a child's needs.

Meditation: A collection of techniques aimed at focusing the attention in a nonanalytic way that avoids ruminative, rambling, or digressive thought.

Mental illness: Within the pathology psychological approach, refers to a variety of problems that people may have. A catch-all term for someone having severe psychological problems, as in "they are suffering from mental illness."

Mindfulness: Openness to novelty and sensitivity to context and perspective. Mindfulness involves cultivating an awareness of everyday happenings and physiological and psychological sensations, overcoming the desire to reduce uncertainty in everyday life, overriding the tendency to engage in automatic behavior, and engaging less frequently in evaluating oneself, others, and situations.

Minding: A form of relationship maintenance that includes knowing and being known, making relationship-enhancing attributions for behaviors, accepting and respecting, and maintaining reciprocity and continuity.

Momentary Ecological Assessment: A research method where investigators study people's thoughts and behaviors in their daily lives by repeatedly collecting data in an individual's normal environment, at (or close to) the time they engage in those behaviors.

Momentary thought–action repertoire: Suggested by Fredrickson (2000), the broadening of a specific action tendency to include cognitive as well as physical responses to an emotion. Fredrickson suggests that specific action tendencies associated with negative emotions fail to consider responses to positive emotions, which often are more cognitive than physical. See also *specific action tendency.*

Mood: General, free-floating feelings that last longer than an emotion. Mood is thought to be tied to expectations of future positive or negative affect.

Moral courage: Part of O'Byrne et al.'s (2000) classification of courage; the authentic expression of one's beliefs or values in pursuit of justice or the common good despite power differentials, dissent, disapproval, or rejection.

Navigational capital: refers to the ability students of color have to navigate systems despite the many that were not set up for them originally; part of Yosso's (2005) Cultural Wealth Model.

Need for uniqueness: The pursuit of individualistic goals to produce a sense of specialness.

Need/goal satisfaction theories: Theories of happiness suggesting that happiness lies in the reduction of tension through the satisfaction of goals and needs.

Nirvana: A state in which the self is freed from desire. This is the final destination in the Buddhist philosophy.

Parochial altruism: Prosocial behavior that is shown toward members of an ingroup that preferences and values them over any outgroup members despite potential detriment to the self.

Passionate love: A form of romantic love characterized by the intense arousal that fuels a romantic union.

Pathways thinking: The perceived capacity to find routes to desired goals. (Compare with *agency thinking.*)

Pennebaker paradigm: Systematic written disclosure of emotional upheaval, often involving several timed sessions.

Person-centered research: Examining the characteristics of certain groups or groupings of people statistically.

Physical courage: Part of O'Byrne et al.'s (2000) classification of courage; an attempted physical behavior or action that seeks to uphold the values of a society or the common good.

Pleasure principle: Freud's idea that humans seek to reduce tension by gratifying instinctive needs. He believed that well-being was the result of satisfied biological and psychological needs and that humans will seek gratification regardless of the consequences.

Poignancy: Mixed emotions related to an ending or to losing something meaningful.

Positive psychology: The science and applications related to the study of psychological strengths and positive emotions.

Positive schooling: An approach to education that consists of a foundation of care, trust, and respect for diversity, where teachers develop tailored goals for each student to engender learning and then work with that student to develop the plans and motivation to reach their goals. Positive schooling includes the agendas of instilling hope in students and contributing to the larger society.

Positive youth development (PYD): Positive, healthy youth development is marked by the attainment of nine outcomes: (1) bonding; (2) social, emotional, cognitive, behavioral, and moral competencies; (3) self-determination; (4) spirituality; (5) clear and positive identity; (6) belief in the future; (7) positive behavior; (8) prosocial development; and (9) prosocial norms.

Positive youth developmentalists: Professionals who put the findings of resilience researchers and other positive psychologists into action and create opportunities for growth by developing and conducting programs that help youth capitalize on their personal assets and environmental resources.

Presenteeism: A state in which employees may be physically at work but, because of mental health problems resulting from aversive and repetitive work experiences, are unproductive and unhappy.

Primary enhancements: Enhancements made to establish optimal functioning and satisfaction.

Primary preventions: Actions intended to stop or lessen the likelihood of physical or psychological problems before they appear.

Principlism: Moral integrity; may be viewed as a potential contributor to some altruistic actions.

Process/activity theories: Theories of happiness suggesting that happiness is produced by engaging in certain activities or working toward a goal.

Psychological courage: Described by Putman (1997) as a form of vital courage that involves the strength to acknowledge and face personal weaknesses, destructive habits, or threats to one's own psychological stability.

Psychometric properties: The measurement characteristics of a scale that include its reliability, validity, and statistics on items of the measure.

Reciprocity-based altruism: Involves the type of helping behavior motivated by the likelihood that one might need future help from the person in need, who might feel the need to reciprocate in that circumstance (i.e., help the helper).

Relativism of values: A component of the Berlin wisdom paradigm; involves understanding that values and priorities are different across people, societies, and time. The value of any idea may vary depending on the context in which it is presented.

Reliability: The ability of a scale to produce consistent and reliable results over a number of administrations or over time.

Resilience: The ability to bounce back or positively adapt in the face of significant adversity or risk.

Resistance capital: described as the foundations that college students of color have as a result of the reality their communities had to face and fight (e.g., inequality, lack of rights, discrimination, etc.) and the benefit that this heritage plays in their navigation of higher education; part of Yosso's (2005) Cultural Wealth Model.

Restorative justice: A type of rehabilitation that focuses on the offender or transgressor repairing the harm done to their victim and/or the victim's community.

Savoring: Thoughts and actions aimed at appreciating and perhaps amplifying a positive experience.

Secondary enhancements: Enhancements that build upon already optimal functioning and satisfaction to achieve peak experiences.

Secondary preventions: Actions that lessen, eliminate, or contain problems after they appear.

Secure attachment: In the Strange Situation assessment, a form of attachment that involves a balance between exploration of the environment and contact with the caregiver.

Selective prevention: Primary prevention focused on a particular at-risk population.

Self-efficacy: Belief that one's skills and capabilities are enough to accomplish one's desired goals in a specific situation.

Self-expansion theory of romantic love: A theory developed by Arthur and Elaine Aron suggesting that humans have a basic motivation to expand the self. The Arons hypothesize that the emotions, cognitions, and behaviors of love fuel such self-expansion.

Situational perspective: A view of psychological concepts (such as self-efficacy) as situationally or context specific—that is, that the specific setting influences how a psychological phenomenon is manifested. As the situation varies, the concept varies in turn. (Compare with *trait perspective*.)

Social cognitive theory: A theory suggesting that people's self-efficacy (confidence in their abilities) influences their actions and thoughts in such a way that it shapes their environment. For example, a young girl who thinks she might be good at basketball tries out for the team. Trying out for the basketball team, in turn, gives the child opportunities to develop her skills and gain confidence in her abilities. Then the child thinks more positively about her ability to do a variety of sports. Therefore, the child's beliefs influenced the type of environment in which she pursued goals.

Social constructions: Perspectives or definitions that are agreed upon by many people to constitute reality (rather than some objectively defined "truth" that resides in objects, situations, and people).

Socioemotional selectivity theory: Carstensen's theory that, as compared to younger adults, older adults are more able to focus less on negative emotions, to engage more deeply with emotional content, and to savor the positive in life.

Socioemotional support: Support that involves providing friendship, kindness, and love for others.

Specific action tendency: Suggested by most models of emotion, the tendency to act in a specific manner that follows an emotion. The most famous specific action tendency is the "fight or flight" response, the theory of which suggests that, when confronted with a situation that elicits a negative emotion, humans and animals will act either by approaching (fight) or by retreating (flight) from the situation.

Sphere of influence: refers to the domain of social impact a particular individual may have

Spirituality: As commonly defined, the thoughts, feelings, and behaviors that fuel and arise from the search for the sacred.

State Measure: An assessment of a particular construct reflecting the exact moment of the assessment or a specific context/situation.

Strange Situation: An assessment strategy first used by Mary Ainsworth to study children's attachment styles. The Strange Situation exposes a child to a novel situation in the company of their caregiver; the caregiver is then removed and reintroduced to the situation twice while the researcher assesses the child participant's reactions.

Strength: A capacity for feeling, thinking, and behaving in a way that allows optimal functioning in the pursuit of valued outcomes (Linley & Harrington, 2006).

Strengths-based approach to gainful employment: The strengths-based approach to employment involves increasing an employee's awareness of their natural and learned talents, integration of these talents into the employee's self-image, and behavioral change in which the employee learns to attribute successes to their talents.

Stretch goals: Reasonably challenging goals in which the student seeks a slightly more difficult learning goal than attained previously.

Subjective well-being: A person's individual judgment about their current status in the world. Often used synonymously with happiness.

Successful aging: A lifestyle defined by avoiding disease, engaging in life, and maintaining high cognitive and physical functioning in one's later years.

Talent: Naturally recurring patterns of thought, feeling, or behavior that can be productively applied and manifested in life experiences characterized by yearnings, rapid learning, satisfaction, and timelessness.

Taoism: A philosophical and religious system developed by Lao-Tzu that advocates a simple, honest life and noninterference in the course of natural events.

Test Bias: The differential validity of test scores for groups (e.g., age, education, culture, race, sex, nationality). Bias is a systematic error in the measurement process that differentially influences scores for identified groups.

Trait Measure: An assessment that captures a stable or enduring quality or characteristic.

Trait perspective: An approach to understanding a psychological concept (such as self-efficacy) as part of the enduring characteristics of a person—a part of their disposition that is evident across situations. (Compare with *situational perspective.*)

Triangular theory of love: Robert Sternberg's theory that all types of love are made up of different combinations of passion, intimacy, and commitment.

Universal prevention: Primary prevention aimed at an entire community.

Valence: The direction of affect: positive (pleasant) or negative (unpleasant).

Validity: The ability of a scale to measure what it is intended to measure.

Valor: A dimension of courage in the Values in Action classification system. It involves taking a physical, emotional, or intellectual stance in the face of danger or fear.

Variable-focused research: Examining the characteristics and links between variables statistically.

Vital courage: Part of O'Byrne et al.'s (2000) classification of courage, formerly *health/change courage;* a person's persistence and perseverance through a disease, illness, or disability despite an uncertain outcome.

Worldview: "Ways of describing the universe and life within it, both in terms of what is and what ought to be" (Koltko-Rivera, 2004, p. 4).

INDEX